WORKSHOPS IN COMPUTING
Series edited by C. J. van Rijsbergen

Also in this series

continued on back page...

Malcolm Atkinson, David Maier and
Véronique Benzaken (Eds)

Persistent Object Systems

Proceedings of the Sixth International
Workshop on Persistent Object Systems,
Tarascon, Provence, France,
5–9 September 1994

Published in collaboration with the
British Computer Society

 Springer

London Berlin Heidelberg New York
Paris Tokyo Hong Kong
Barcelona Budapest

Malcolm Atkinson, BA, MA, PhD, Dip.Comp.Sci., FRSE
Department of Computing Science, University of Glasgow,
8–17 Lilybank Gardens, Glasgow, G12 8RZ, UK

David Maier, BA, PhD
Department of Computer Science and Engineering,
Oregon Graduate Institute, Portland, Oregon, 97291-1000, USA

Véronique Benzaken, PhD
Université de Paris I – Panthéon – Sorbonne,
12 Place du Panthéon, 75005 Paris, France

British Library Cataloguing in Publication Data
Persistent Object Systems. – 6th:
Proceedings of the Sixth International Workshop on Persistent Object Systems, Tarascon,
Provence, France, 5–9 September 1994. – (Workshops in Computing Series)
    I. Atkinson, Malcolm   II. Series
    005.11
ISBN-13: 978-3-540-19912-0   e-ISBN-13: 978-1-4471-2122-0
DOI: 10.1007/978-1-4471-2122-0
Library of Congress Cataloging-in-Publication Data
International Workshop on Persistent Object Systems (6th : 1994 : Tarascon
Bouches–du–Rhône, France)
    Persistent object systems : proceedings of the Sixth International Workshop on
Persistent Object Systems, Tarascon, Provence, France, 5–9 September 1994 / Malcolm
Atkinson, David Maier, and Véronique Benzaken, (eds.).
      p. cm. – (Workshops in computing)
    "Published in collaboration with the British Computer Society."
    Includes bibliographical references and index.
    ISBN-13: 978-3-540-19912-0
    1. Object-oriented databases–Congresses. 2. Object oriented programming
(Computer science)–Congresses. I. Atkinson, Malcolm, 1943–
II. Maier, David, 1953– . III. Benzaken, Véronique, 1960–
IV. British Computer Society. V. Title. VI. Series.
QA76.9.D3I59 1994   94-42659
005.75– dc20   CIP

Typesetting: Camera ready by contributors
Printed by Athenæum Press Ltd., Gateshead
34/3830-543210 Printed on acid-free paper

Preface

The Sixth International Workshop on Persistent Object Systems was held at Les Mazets des Roches near Tarascon, Provence in southern France from the fifth to the ninth of September 1994. The attractive context and autumn warmth greeted the 53 participants from 12 countries spread over five continents.

Persistent object systems continue to grow in importance. Almost all significant uses of computers to support human endeavours depend on long-lived and large-scale systems. As expectations and ambitions rise so the sophistication of the systems we attempt to build also rises. The quality and integrity of the systems and their feasibility for supporting large groups of co-operating people depends on their technical foundation. Persistent object systems are being developed which provide a more robust and yet simpler foundation for these persistent applications.

The workshop followed the tradition of the previous workshops in the series, focusing on the design, implementation and use of persistent object systems in particular and persistent systems in general. There were clear signs that this line of research is maturing, as engineering issues were discussed with the aid of evidence from operational systems. The work presented covered the complete range of database facilities: transactions, concurrency, distribution, integrity and schema modification. There were examples of very large scale use, one involving tens of terabytes of data. Language issues, particularly the provision of reflection, continued to be important.

The previous five workshops in the series were:

POS	Year	Venue	Organisers
1	1985	Appin, Scotland	Atkinson, Buneman & Morrison
2	1987	Appin, Scotland	Atkinson & Morrison
3	1989	Newcastle, Australia	Koch & Rosenberg
4	1990	Martha's Vineyard, USA	Dearle, Mitchell & Zdonik
5	1992	San Miniato (Pisa), Italy	Albano & Morrison

A related series of workshops is the international workshops on Database Programming Languages:

DBPL	Year	Venue	Organisers
1	1987	Roscoff, Brittany, France	Bancilhon & Buneman
2	1989	Salishan, Oregon, USA	Hull, Morrison & Stemple
3	1991	Nafplion, Greece	Kanellakis & Schmidt
4	1993	Manhattan, NY, USA	Beeri, Ohori & Shasha

This book consists of papers in the order in which they were presented at the workshop, revised in the light of the subsequent discussions. Each session is preceded by an introduction and evaluation by the session chair which includes the main questions addressed to each paper. There is also a report on one of the two panel discussions.

There were 54 papers submitted to the conference, and 29 of these were selected for presentation after being refereed by three or more members of the programme committee. Each presentation lasted about 20 minutes with 10 minutes for discussion. A further 15 minutes of discussion ensued after each group of papers. The discussion was lively and challenging, and is reported here for each session. For most papers, it has led to several improvements since the workshop concluded.

POS-6 was organised by Malcolm Atkinson, Véronique Benzaken and David Maier. They would like to thank Isabel Graham and Paul Philbrow for managing the processing of all the papers; ensuring copies reached referees, collecting the first revisions and assembling the workshop pre-prints, and finally collecting the second revisions and other material, ready for printing these proceedings. The workshop would not have been possible without the determined efforts of its treasurer, Ray Welland, assisted at a critical moment by Peter Dickman. Véronique Benzaken, Anne Doucet and Giuseppe Castagna found this most attractive location, where people could enjoy walking, running and bird watching in the local wooded hills, excursions to the Camargue, Arles, Nimes, Orange, etc. and were responsible for the local arrangements.

Malcolm Atkinson
December 1994

Editors

Malcolm Atkinson   University of Glasgow, Glasgow, Scotland
Véronique Benzaken   Université de Paris I, Paris, France
David Maier   Oregon Graduate Institute, Oregon, USA

Programme Committee

Antonio Albano   Università di Pisa, Pisa, Italy
Sonia Berman   University of Cape Town, Cape Town,
                          South Africa
Alfred Brown   University of Adelaide, Adelaide, Australia
Peter Buneman   University of Pennsylvania, Philadelphia, USA
Sophie Cluet   INRIA, Paris, France
Paul Cockshott   University of Strathclyde, Glasgow, Scotland
Richard Connor   University of St Andrews, St Andrews, Scotland
Richard Cooper   University of Glasgow, Glasgow, Scotland
Claude Delobel   O$_2$ Technology, Paris, France
Peter Gray   University of Aberdeen, Aberdeen, Scotland
Rick Hull   University of Colorado, Boulder, Colorado,
                          USA
Keith Jeffreys   EPSRC, Swindon, England
Barbara Liskov   Massachusetts Institute of Technology,
                          Mass., USA
Florian Matthes   University of Hamburg, Hamburg, Germany
Ken Moody   Computer Laboratory, University of
                          Cambridge, England
Ron Morrison   University of St Andrews, St Andrews, Scotland
Atsushi Ohori   Kyoto University, Kyoto, Japan
Tamer Özsu   University of Alberta, Edmonton, Canada
Paul Philbrow   University of Glasgow, Glasgow, Scotland
Fausto Rabitti   IEI-CNR, Pisa, Italy
John Rosenberg   University of Sydney, New South Wales,
                          Australia
Dave Stemple   University of Massachusetts, Amherst, USA
Fernando Velez   ObjectWare S.A., Santa Fe de Bogota, Colombia
Stan Zdonik   Brown University, Rhode Island, USA

Contents

Object Store Engineering 1

Malcolm Atkinson

Department of Computing Science, University of Glasgow
Glasgow, Scotland

This Session launched the workshop on the Monday afternoon with two papers on techniques for implementing improved Persistent Object Stores. Eliot Moss presented his paper with Antony Hosking on "*Expressing Object Residency Optimisations using Pointer Type Annotations*" and Dave Munro presented his paper with Richard Connor, Ron Morrison, Stephan Scheuerl and Dave Stemple on "*Concurrent Shadow Paging in the FLASK Architecture*". All the authors from both papers were present apart from Stephan Scheuerl, as the EC ESPRIT/ US NSF workshop had finished in the morning. It is amusing to note that both papers had at least one author from the University of Massachusetts at Amherst.

The first paper assumes that a strongly typed persistent language would perform better if redundant checks for data residency could be eliminated. For example, if whole objects are brought into active memory on an object fault[1] then code which inevitably follows code that would cause this object fault need not verify the object is resident. Such situations arise if the detection of object faults is by software inspection of the reference rather than by use of the protection mechanism.

The nub of the work in this paper is a notation for describing object references so that the circumstances under which they may fault is explicit. This has several advantages:

- the optimisers, which perform such tasks as data-flow analysis, may be separated from the code generation and execution system which generates different code or performs different actions depending on the annotation; and
- human-produced annotations can then be used with benchmark technology to assess the value of a putative optimisation.

Using typing technology to manipulate these annotations is reminiscent of an unimplemented proposal by Matthes and others [1]. The presented work, however, showed how this technique could be used practically in the implementation of persistent Modula-3 and how it could also be used to explore performance issues. The early stages of this usage were reported.

The second paper reported on a store implementation based on the opposing view that exploiting page protection to detect object faults and page mapping to construct a stable store via shadow paging will lead to efficiency. These techniques were reported to have been in use for several years supporting Napier88 and several other

---

[1] An object fault occurs when a program attempts to use a value that is still on backing store. Before the program can continue that value (e.g. an object) has to be made resident in active memory. Object faults may be detected by in-line code, as in the first paper, or by trapping memory access faults as protection violations, as in the second paper.

languages on the same store [2]. The novelty of this paper is a new scheme for making such shadow-paged implementations of a stable store concurrently usable. The motives for this work are experiments that explore an architecture that allows a variety of concurrency mechanisms to be implemented, from isolation typical of database technology to complex models of co-operation typical of programming language technology. Thus this is another step in the search for concepts that allow continuity between database requirements and programming language requirements.

The techniques necessary to achieve recoverability and stabilisation in concurrent shadow-paged systems are explained well. This depends on the architectural decision of separating the issue of synchronisation and access control from these stability mechanisms. Consistency is achievable because the store reports the read and write sets to the synchronisation layer. The trick is to do this efficiently, using the memory protection data and the results of logical combinations of the current and previous page images. The presenter indicated that experiments were underway to test the efficacy of re-combining these primitives in a variety of ways to obtain various concurrency models.

Discussion ranged over issues of what efficiency might be achieved in each case and what motivated the different assumptions. For example, the software object faulting in the former case was defended in not making use of features that differed between hardware architectures, in retaining any useful locality that existed in the data and in avoiding hardware protection faults which, at least in some cases had been measured to be slower than software faulting. The effect on code size in this approach was not known. The FLASK architecture could re-arrange pages to achieve temporal locality and could fault parts of very large objects. It was clear that discussions in the preceding workshop[2] had sensitised many of the store implementers present to ask hard questions about measurements. It was rewarding to find that, unlike earlier Persistent Object System workshops, each implementer had some measurements with which to join in the jousting. These two papers set the scene in that respect though everyone admitted that the measurements they had were not yet conclusive and that much more development and experiment was needed.

This was a welcome start as it established a workshop norm of increased awareness of engineering issues and the emergence of understanding about some of the crucial trade-offs. The papers, it was agreed, were reporting the beginnings of interesting and relevant experiments.

References

1. Matthes, F., Ohori, A. and Schmidt, J.W., Typing Schemes for Objects with Locality, In *Next Generation Information System Technology*. Proceedings of the First International East/West Database Workshop (Kiev, USSR, 9th--12th October 1990), Springer-Verlag, Lecture Notes in Computer Science No. 504 (1991), pp 106--123.
2. Brown, A.L., Mainetto, G., Matthes, F., Mueller, R. and McNally, D.J., An Open System Architecture for a Persistent Object Store, In *Proceedings of the Twenty-Fifth Hawaii International Conference on System Sciences, Volume II, Software Technology, Persistent Object Systems*, pp 766--776

---

[2] EC/US workshop mentioned earlier.

Expressing Object Residency Optimizations Using Pointer Type Annotations

J. Eliot B. Moss and Antony L. Hosking

Object Systems Laboratory, Department of Computer Science

University of Massachusetts; Amherst, MA 01003, USA

Sixth International Workshop on Persistent Object Systems

Tarascon, Provence, France, 5–9 September 1994

Abstract

We consider some issues in optimizing persistent programming languages. In particular, we show how to express optimizations of object residency checks in strongly typed persistent languages as "annotations" on pointer types. These annotations essentially extend and refine the type system of the language, and they have at least two significant uses. First, a programmer can use them to express desired residency properties to be enforced by the language implementation (compiler plus run time). Second, we can use them to separate a persistence optimizer, which adds annotations, from the remainder of the compiler, which simply obeys them. This gives rise to a nice separation of concerns in supporting high-performance persistence: the "intelligent" optimizer can be factored off from the rest of the compiler.

In addition to modularity benefits, the separation allows us to explore the value of various optimizations without actually implementing them in the optimizer. Rather, we can optimize programs by hand and compare optimized and unoptimized code to develop sound data to use when deciding whether to implement an optimization. While the approach is similar to source-to-source optimizers, which are by no means a new idea, in our case the target language is an extension of the source language, and one specifically designed to be *easier* to compile well. We are applying the approach in our ongoing implementation of Persistent Modula-3. We present the type annotation approach in the context of Modula-3, but it should be applicable to any strongly typed persistent programming language, as well as to a range of other kinds of optimizations.

1   Introduction and Motivation

We have been developing run time support and an optimizing compiler for Persistent Modula-3[1] for some time. In the process we have conceived of a number of optimizations one might consider to improve performance of persistent programs [HM90, HM91], and have compared several approaches to dealing with (among other things) *object faults* (attempts to use persistent objects that are not currently resident (i.e., not actually in the process's virtual address space)), in our Persistent Smalltalk implementation [HM93a, HM93b]. Most of the optimizations we have thought of require reasonably powerful data flow analysis and code transformations, such as hoisting or combining residency checks, or imposing special rules that complicate the compiler such as: "the first argument of

---

[1]For further information on Modula-3 see [CDG+88, CDG+89, CDG+91, Nel91, Har92]; for further information on our persistence work see [MS88, Mos89, Mos87, Mos90, HMB90, HM90, HM91, Hos91, Mos92, HM93a, HBM93, HM93b].

a method call (i.e., the target object) will (somehow) automatically be made resident throughout the execution of the method" (so that the method code need not contain checks on uses of the target object). Implementing these optimizations would require a lot of effort in the back end of a modern optimizing compiler (such as the GNU C compiler, whose back end we use in this work). We concluded that it would be best to explore the effectiveness of a variety of optimizations before trying to implement them.

We were willing to hand optimize a collection of benchmark programs, but we still needed a way to express the possible *results* of the optimizations. The point here is to be able to control the code emitted by the compiler. Since we were working in the context of a statically typed, compiled, object-oriented language (Modula-3 with persistence extensions), we decided to try expressing the results of optimizations in the type system, giving rise to the overall approach that is the point of this paper.

We organize the remainder of the presentation as follows. First we describe relevant aspects of Persistent (and non-persistent) Modula-3. Then we briefly review object faulting and object residency checking, and enumerate some ways of implementing them. Next, we argue for residency check optimization and present a list of residency related optimizations one might want to explore. We then explain how we use types and type conversions to express residency knowledge and residency checks, and show how the approach can express the desired optimizations in the various implementation approaches. We finish with a few concluding remarks.

2 Relevant Aspects of Persistent Modula-3

Modula-3 is a strongly typed object-oriented language in the tradition of Pascal and Modula-2. To Modula-2 it adds: object types (in a single inheritance hierarchy), automatic storage management (garbage collection), exception handling, threads (lightweight processes running in the same address space), and generic interfaces and modules (templates that are expanded syntactically as needed, to form members of a parameterized family of interfaces and modules). Here we are most concerned with types, procedure calls, and method calls in Modula-3, and assume the reader can grasp other constructs intuitively from a knowledge of Pascal or Modula-2.

Unlike some object oriented languages (e.g., Smalltalk [GR83] and Trellis/Owl [SCB+86]), Modula-3 is not *uniformly* object oriented: it has a full collection of non-object primitive types (INTEGER, REAL, range, enumeration, etc.) and type constructors (RECORD, ARRAY, REF, PROC, etc.) in addition to object types. Again we assume that our example code fragments can be grasped intuitively from knowledge of Pascal. A Modula-3 object type consists of a *supertype*, which must be another object type (possibly the built in type ROOT), zero or more (new) *fields*, declared and used analogously to record fields, zero or more (new) *methods*, which are names bound to procedures to be invoked when the named method is called, and zero or more *overrides* of supertype method bindings, with the following syntax:

[*super*] OBJECT *fields* [METHODS *methods*] [OVERRIDES *overrides*] END

This example shows a trivial point data type, giving only the methods for manipulating points, without implementations, and then giving representation and implementation details in a subtype.[2]

---

[2] In Modula-3 one would actually use *opaque types* to hide the representation type p_rep and yet have it be the actual type used for point. The type point here has no data and no method implementations; it is useful

```
TYPE
  point = ROOT OBJECT
                METHODS scale(by: REAL): point; ...
                END;
  p_rep = point OBJECT x, y: INTEGER;
                OVERRIDES scale := scale_point;
                END;
```

Modula-3 allows (appropriately constrained) self-reference, and use of names in a scope without respect to their order of declaration, so it is easy to define recursive types, such as this:

```
TYPE ilist = REF RECORD i: INTEGER; next: ilist; END;
```

It is worthwhile to note that Modula-3 object types are implicitly pointers to dynamically allocated memory containing the object fields (and a reference to the method suite of the object[3]), thus a more object oriented form of the integer list type would be:

```
TYPE olist = OBJECT i: INTEGER; next: olist; END;
```

Modula-3 procedure call is straightforward. There are three argument binding modes: by value, which is the default, by reference, indicated by VAR, and by reference but without rights to modify the argument, indicated by READONLY. Modula-3 exception handling is irrelevant here, so we will not describe it. A Modula-3 method call is in most respects like an ordinary procedure call. However, the target object is not explicitly listed in the method's call interface (being implied from the object type), as can be seen from scale in the point object type example. Note, though, that the procedure bound to scale *would* include the target object as its first argument, for example:

```
PROCEDURE scale_point (p: p_rep; by: REAL): p_rep = ...
```

The language's (sub)type checking rules allow scale_point as an implementation of scale in this case. Here is an example of a method call:

```
p: point := ...;
p.scale(2.5);
```

Thus far we have described non-persistent Modula-3. To add persistence to Modula-3, we changed very little [HM90]: we re-interpreted REF t to mean a reference to a (possibly) persistent instance of t, and likewise for object types. By "possibly persistent" we mean that newly created instances need not be created in the store (as opposed to existing only in main memory), unless they are reachable from a persistent root object at a designated time (checkpoint). As a side note, we observe that Modula-3 includes UNTRACED REF t in addition to REF t; untraced pointer types are managed with explicit allocation and deallocation and are not traced by the garbage collector. They are useful on occasion, e.g., for allocating fixed I/O buffers and the like. In [HM90] we added TRANSIENT REF t. By analogy with untraced types, transient pointer types refer to instances that can *never* become persistent. Again, they appear to have occasional uses, but from here on we will ignore untraced and transient pointer types since they are irrelevant here.

---

only to document the interface and as a foundation for implementations. Since opaque types are not relevant to this work, we discuss them no further.

[3] A Modula-3 method suite is a vector of pointers to code for methods; the C++ terminology is "virtual function table".

3   Object Faulting and Residency Checking

The whole idea of a persistent programming language is to provide transparent access to objects maintained in a persistent object store. Unlike simply reading and writing blocks of data using traditional file I/O, a persistent programming language and object store together preserve *object identity*: every object has a unique identifier (in essence, an address, possibly abstract, in the store), objects can refer to other objects, forming graph structures, and they can be modified, with such modifications being visible in future accesses using the same unique object identifier.

Given adequate address space, one could read in (or map into virtual memory) the entire object store, but, as many others do (and for good reasons we will not get into here), we assume that such an implementation strategy is not preferred. Thus, as a program runs, we will need to load objects on demand, from the persistent object store into main (or virtual) memory. An *object fault* is an attempt to use a non-resident object. Object faulting relies on *object residency checks*, which can be implemented explicitly in software, or performed implicitly in hardware and giving rise to some kind of hardware trap for non-resident objects. Object faulting also relies on mechanisms to load objects from the store into memory, and ultimately to write (at least the modified) objects back. In a complete environment one must also integrate support for concurrency control, recovery, and distribution, but we focus primarily on object residency aspects of persistent systems here.

A wide range of object faulting *schemes* have been devised ([ACC82, BC86, KK83, Kae86, CM84, RMS88, SMR89, BBB+88, Ric89, SCD90, WD92, HMB90, Hos91, HM93a, LLOW91, SKW92, WK92] are not exhaustive). Any scheme has some number of distinct *situations*, such as a reference to a resident object (which presumably can be used without causing an object fault), versus a reference to a non-resident object. We are concerned only with situations that require the compiler to generate *distinct code*; such distinct situations give rise to corresponding *representations*. For example, in schemes that drive all faulting with memory protection traps and make object faulting entirely transparent to compiled code (such as [SMR89, SCD90, LLOW91, SKW92]), there is only one representation: apparently resident objects. However, we have gathered evidence that such totally transparent schemes do not always offer the best performance [HM93a, HM93b, HBM93, HMS92]. Hence we will be most interested in schemes that have more than one representation.

We list below a range of possible representations. Any given scheme may combine a number of them, though not all subsets make a lot of sense. Also, at any given point in a program, an optimizer can develop an upper bound on the representations possible for each pointer, but in general multiple representations may be possible (e.g., it may not be able to establish whether a given object is resident or not, and the two situations may have different representations). We further observe that schemes differ in whether, when, and how they *swizzle* pointers, i.e., convert between (possibly) different formats used in the persistent store and in main memory.[4]

Direct pointer: a direct (virtual memory) pointer to an apparently resident object; either the object is actually resident, or hardware traps may be used to make it resident if the pointer is used; requires no check[5]

---

[4]For more background on swizzling, the reader may start with [Mos92, WD92, WK92].

[5]While the pointer manipulation code is the same, pointers to resident objects (arranged by prefetching, etc.), and pointers that will trap when used, have different performance characteristics, and ultimately we might care to distinguish between them.

Object Identifier: a unique object identifier, which requires some kind of table lookup to locate the corresponding object's data in memory; this is assumed complex enough to require a call, and the lookup routine will make the object resident if it is not yet so; avoids swizzling but may incur repeated lookup costs

Indirect pointer: a pointer to a cell containing a pointer to the object's contents; similar to the direct pointer scheme, but this is more flexible in that one need not allocate address space for object contents prior to loading the object (and hence need not know the object's true size in advance); requires no check

Fault block: a pointer to a fixed size block of memory that contains the object's unique identifier; causes a fault when used

Proxy object: a pointer to an object that stands in for a non-resident object; has a method suite, all of whose methods will load the true object; field access must load the object, but method call is transparent

Indirect object: a pointer to an object that stands in for a (now) resident object; has a method suite, all of whose methods forward calls to the true object; field access must forward explicitly, but method call is transparent.

A number of schemes can be developed by choosing appropriate subsets of these representations. Of course, when representations require different code, they must be distinguishable one from another, so that when a pointer has multiple possible representations at a given use, the compiler can generate tests to discriminate. Here are a few schemes, to give a sense of the possibilities:

- Direct pointer (only): completely transparent, requires either hardware traps or preloading all reachable objects

- Direct pointer + fault block: used in our Persistent Smalltalk implementation, requires explicit checks to discriminate (which, by system design, we localized primarily to method invocation)

- Direct pointer + object identifier: requires a tag bit in pointers; may result in excess object identifier lookups, which are partly avoided by faulting on load of a pointer ("swizzle on discovery") rather than on use of it

- Object identifier (only): useful if a pointer is not traversed very many times during a program's execution (avoids overhead of swizzling)

- Direct pointer + proxy object + indirect object: proxy, indirect, and ordinary objects must be distinguishable on field access, but method call is transparent; field access can be turned into method call to gain complete transparency (but possibly higher overhead)

- Direct pointer + proxy object: avoiding indirect objects speeds use of resident objects, but requires removal of indirections when objects are loaded, which can be costly

4 Some Residency Optimizations

We now consider residency checking optimizations one might want to use in trying to improve performance of programs written in a persistent programming language. Here is a list of some optimizations we have thought of in our work:

Local subsumption: If we dereference the same pointer multiple times in a piece of straight line code, the first use will force residency. If we additionally impose an appropriate rule *pinning* the object, i.e., preventing it from from being removed from the address space, at least until the last use in the straight line code, then remaining uses need not check residency. We note again that subsumption is similar to common subexpression elimination, but differs in that it has a side effect (but is idempotent).[6]

Global subsumption: Given appropriate data flow analysis, one can apply subsumption across basic blocks, intra- or inter-procedurally. The result is similar to *hoisting* common subexpressions.

Target object residency: Since invoking a method requires first making the target object resident, method code can assume target residency. This could yield great improvements in programs written in object-oriented style.[7]

Formal parameter assertions: It may be useful to require a procedure or method argument to be resident before making a call. If the caller knows the object is resident, no checks are needed in either the caller or the callee. If we only use hoisting, and perform residency checks near the beginning of a procedure, we cannot eliminate checks where the caller knows the object is resident. Formal parameter assertions are especially useful for "internal" methods (called only from public methods), some recursive calls, and non-object-oriented code.

Procedure result assertions: If a procedure returns a newly created object, or one guaranteed to be resident (either because the procedure caused it to be or because the object was guaranteed to be resident on entry to the procedure), then it can help the caller and other downstream code to know that.

Data type assertions: In the case of a data type with multiple levels of pointers, it might be convenient to fault in several levels of objects at once (they may arrive together anyway, with proper clustering[8]), and avoid checks when traversing the levels. This can be accomplished by associating residency assertions with pointers inside data structures. We observe that for *recursive* data structures, placing such assertions on the recursion pointers (such as the next field of our ilist type example) may require a large closure of objects to be made resident (but may be a good idea if the objects are likely to be used).

---

[6]The original implementation of the E programming language [Ric90, RC90, Ric89] included an optimization similar to subsumption. It operated in a more general model, where the unit of access was byte ranges of objects, and could unify overlapping ranges in both space and time. However, it was applied in a somewhat ad hoc manner in the *cfront* implementation of E, and abandoned in later versions of E (after Richardson's departure from the group).

[7]Actually, type inference and other techniques might enable the compiler to know the precise type and avoid an object oriented dispatch, in which case it might need to introduce an explicit check.

[8]Clustering is an important issue because it affects I/O performance, which can be more noticeable than incremental CPU overheads, but it is outside the scope of this paper. However, see the discussion of clustering towards the end of the paper.

A converse sort of assertion would be that a reference is rarely traversed, and would best be kept in object identifier form and looked up on each use.

Of these optimizations, subsumption is likely always to be profitable—its only negative effect is pinning objects longer (and requiring support for such pinning, which may in turn require compiler produced tables for the run time system to use in determining which objects are pinned (along the lines of compiler support for accurate garbage collection [DMH92, Diw91, HMDW91])). Similarly, target object residency is probably almost always a good idea: it would be rare for the target of a message not to be used *and* for the method to be statically known. Formal parameter assertions require more care to prevent objects from being loaded if they are not *always* used. Data type assertions run even more risks, but can have high payoff. They may require profile feedback in addition to static analysis for an optimizer to make good decisions.

5   Using Types in Residency Optimization

Now we describe in more detail the central idea of the paper, which is to express persistence representation assertions as qualifications on pointer types. It is convenient to choose a particular, fairly interesting, scheme as a basis for presentation; we trust the application to other schemes will then be obvious. Our example scheme's representations are proxy objects, direct pointers, and object identifiers. Now a scheme includes exactly the possible degrees of knowledge the implementation may have concerning object residency: each state of knowledge can be described as a non-empty subset of the set of allowed representations. In our scheme we allow precisely these subsets:

{ proxy, direct }, { direct }, { object identifier }

Why these? First, these groupings avoid the need to discriminate dynamically between pointers and object identifiers, which puts fewer constraints on the representation of object identifiers. That explains the absence of any other subsets containing "object identifier". Second, {proxy} just does not seem very useful, since it requires work in exactly the same cases as {proxy, direct pointer}. Note that one can certainly conceive of allowing more subsets, etc. Clearly there are many possible schemes in our approach!

We use REF t to indicate {proxy, direct pointer} knowledge, RES REF t (for *resident reference*) for {direct pointer}, and ID REF t for {object identifier}; we use similar annotations on object types.[9] In some sense these types do not all support the same operations: an ID REF requires lookup to dereference it or perform a method call, a REF requires discrimination and possible conversion on dereference (but not method call), a RES REF supports all operations directly. We can define a strict language, where field access is permitted only via a RES REF, and method call is allowed on REF or RES REF, and we supply conversion operators between all pairs of annotations. Note that all these kinds of pointers are equivalent at the level of language semantics—they differ only in their implementation properties. The situation is analogous to packed and unpacked data structures, which represent the same values in different ways. The strict language might be tiresome for humans. It is easy to extend the strict language to allow all operations on all pointer representations, with the necessary conversions being implied, into temporary variables that are used and then discarded. We will posit built-in functions TO_REF, TO_RES, and TO_ID that perform explicit conversions (again the syntax is

---

[9]The syntax really does not matter much for our purposes. In practice one might use pragmas rather than new keywords, so that annotated programs can still be processed by unextended compilers, etc.

not that important here). Let us now consider how the various optimizations can be represented using these annotations.

Local subsumption: We can introduce a new local variable that is a RES REF, and use it multiple times:

```
      Unoptimized                         Optimized
                              tmp: RES REF t := TO_RES(p);
... p^.x ...                  ... tmp^.x ...
... p^.y ...                  ... tmp^.y ...
```

Global subsumption: Again, we can introduce a new RES REF local variable, set it at the point where we want to hoist the residency check, and use it subsequently (no example needed).

Target object residency: The issue here is having a way to express, for each method of an object type, its target object residency assumptions, and to insure that the procedures bound to methods conform to those assumptions. One way to accomplish this is to associate annotations with method names in object types, e.g.,:

```
TYPE
  point = ROOT OBJECT
                 METHODS RES scale(by: REAL): point; ...
                 END;
```

Any procedure bound to scale must declare its first argument in a manner compatible with the method's RES annotation. In this case RES REF or plain REF would be all right, but ID REF would not be.

Formal parameter and result assertions: Similar to target object residency tags, we associate tags with procedure formals and results:

```
PROCEDURE scale_point (p: RES(p_rep); by: REAL):
                 RES(p_rep) = ...
```

This is more general than target object residency annotations because it can apply to any argument position for a procedure, and because it applies to ordinary procedure call in addition to method calls. Any necessary conversions are performed by the caller, either to arguments (before the call) or results (after the call, and only if the result is used). Note that here the RES built-in function is being applied to *types* rather than objects.

Data type assertion: It is easy to devise a form for these assertions: we allow residency annotations on the types used in record fields, object fields, arrays, etc., not unlike the parameter and result annotations. The meaning and the manipulation rules are a bit more subtle, however. Consider this recursive type declaration:

```
TYPE rolist = RES OBJECT i: INTEGER; next: rolist; END;
```

Here the entire list must be resident. If the entire list is not accessed, this may load more objects than necessary. (One can use hardware trap driven loading rather than software pre-loading to prevent this over-loading, but hardware traps come with their own fielding costs.) This only indicates that the assertions must be used with care. We have more of a problem if we wish to use different annotations with the same underlying type, in the same program. For example, suppose we have both the declaration above and this one:

```
TYPE idolist = ID OBJECT i: INTEGER; next: idolist; END;
```

At first glance one might think that we could convert between object references of type `rolist` and type `idolist`, though it might involve traversing the list and converting all the embedded references. Unfortunately, this does not work because the list could then be referred to via pointers of both types *simultaneously*, which gives rise to inconsistent assertions on the `next` field of the objects. This difficulty is not an artifact of our notation, but is inherent: a given program must represent a given object consistently.[10] Similar concerns precluded subtyping between record types (etc.) in Modula-3 (see the "How the Language Got Its Spots" discussions in [Nel91]). It is not yet clear whether the restriction to consistent annotations has significant performance impact.

As an additional note, we observe that one can "unroll" a recursive type any fixed number of times, and place different assertions at each place around the type "loop". However, since this appears to require similar unrolling of *all* related recursive procedures (as well as iterative loops), it is not obvious one would want to do it very often. (A similar optimization has been suggested for a Standard ML implementation [SRA94].)

6   Clustering

While we have focused on the problem of residency check optimization, the annotations we propose also bear some relation to clustering and prefetching of persistent data, especially in the case of data type assertions. In particular, if a data type annotation indicates that the target of a given pointer field should be resident, then we have two basic options in the implementation: force residency when the "root" of the data structure is made resident, or use a transparent (probably protection trapping) technique. Since the code generated is the same in each case, one can actually decide at run time what to do. For example, one can set up pointers for objects that are actually resident or that arrive in the same cluster as the root object, and use protection traps for excursions outside that region. A possibly interesting hybrid approach is to set protection traps while simultaneously requesting the non-resident clusters. When the clusters arrive, objects could be swizzled and page protections turned off (unless, of course the application has already hit the protection barrier, in which case it must wait anyway).

In any case, the annotations can be thought of either as expressing *existing* clustering (to the extent that such a static method can express it), or expressing *desired* clustering. Note, though, that clustering is a global decision affecting all applications using the same data, so if the different applications have different clustering preferences, we have to reach some compromise. (One might replicate data with different clustering, but this also induces tradeoffs if the data are updated often.)

The essential point is that while the clustering problem is *similar to* the residency check optimization problem, and while we might use similar annotation schemes for each, we probably need separate annotations for clustering and residency optimization. We also observe that while the annotations we have discussed are adequate to control the code produced, they are not adequate for more sophisticated control of prefetch. Prefetch is more closely related to residency, so we may prefer annotations that integrate residency and prefetch guidance to the compiler and run-time system, with clustering handled separately.

---

[10]Note, though, that residency annotations essentially do not exist in the object store, and different programs can use *different* annotations with no problems.

7 Conclusion

We have shown how one can control fairly precisely the placement of residency checks and conversions, and express a range of interesting residency optimizations, using pointer type annotations. The technique appears to be reasonably simple and should be effective in its goals of separating residency optimization decisions from their implementation. Of course the general idea is not new—source to source transformations are widely used in optimizing programs, especially for parallel machines. Even the type tagging approach was suggested by Modula-3's UNTRACED REF and REF types, and the notion of multiple representations of the same value is also fairly obvious (e.g., packed versus unpacked types). Similar annotation techniques have been used in distributed programming languages to distinguish local versus remote, and so forth [BHJ+87]. Perhaps we can take credit for a slightly new application of old ideas.

While we tentatively conclude that the approach is effective towards our goals, what are its limits? How else might the general technique be used? Since similar annotations have been used in distributed programming languages, the approach seems to extend to that situation. We also believe that pointer type annotations might be applied successfully in indicating compiler knowledge of concurrency control status. In a lock based system we might distinguish unlocked, share mode locked, and exclusive mode locked. Unlike the residency case, where we left unpinning an object as somewhat vague and unspecified, with concurrency control it is probably important to be clear about when an object becomes unlocked. The difference is that locking is semantically significant, whereas residency optimization affects only performance, not semantics. Another possible application of pointer type annotations is in reducing work in recording which objects are modified as a persistent program executes. Modification noting is analogous to residency checking in that it is idempotent (provided the object is not written back to the store in between the modifications). Thus similar techniques might apply. The problem is that modification is likely to be more dynamic, so the particularly static techniques we used might not work out as well.

More generally, the exact limits of applicability of pointer type annotations in optimization are not clear. Certainly source to source transformation is limited by the target language in its expressiveness. For example, address calculation such as that required for array subscripts cannot be expressed directly in Fortran, though it can be in C, etc. In any case, perhaps the point is that the technique works for us in this application.

References

[ACC82] Malcolm Atkinson, Ken Chisolm, and Paul Cockshott. PS-Algol: an Algol with a persistent heap. *ACM SIGPLAN Not.*, 17(7):24–31, July 1982.

[BBB+88] Francois Bancilhon, Gilles Barbedette, Véronique Benzaken, Claude Delobel, Sophie Gamerman, Cristophe Lécluse, Patrick Pfeffer, Philippe Richard, and Fernando Velez. The design and implementation of O_2, an object-oriented database system. In Dittrich [Dit88], pages 1–22.

[BC86] A. L. Brown and W. P. Cockshott. The CPOMS persistent object management system. Technical Report Persistent Programming Research Project 13, University of St. Andrews, Scotland, 1986.

[BHJ+87] A. Black, N. Hutchinson, E. Jul, H. Levy, and L. Carter. Distribution and abstract types in Emerald. *IEEE Transactions on Software Engineering*, 13(1):65–76, January 1987.

[CDG+88] Luca Cardelli, James Donahue, Lucille Glassman, Mick Jordan, Bill Kalsow, and Greg Nelson. Modula-3 report. Technical Report ORC-1, DEC Systems Research Center/Olivetti Research Center, Palo Alto/Menlo Park, CA, 1988.

[CDG+89] Luca Cardelli, James Donahue, Lucille Glassman, Mick Jordan, Bill Kalsow, and Greg Nelson. Modula-3 report (revised). Technical Report DEC SRC 52, DEC Systems Research Center/Olivetti Research Center, Palo Alto/Menlo Park, CA, November 1989.

[CDG+91] Luca Cardelli, James Donahue, Lucille Glassman, Mick Jordan, Bill Kalsow, and Greg Nelson. Modula-3 language definition. In Nelson [Nel91], chapter 2, pages 11–66.

[CM84] George Copeland and David Maier. Making Smalltalk a database system. In *Proceedings of the 1984 ACM SIGMOD International Conference on Management of Data*, pages 316–325, Boston, Massachusetts, June 1984. *ACM SIGMOD Rec. 14, 2* (1984).

[Dit88] K. R. Dittrich, editor. *Proceedings of the Second International Workshop on Object-Oriented Database Systems*, volume 334 of *Lecture Notes in Computer Science*, Bad Münster am Stein-Ebernburg, Federal Republic of Germany, September 1988. *Advances in Object-Oriented Database Systems*, Springer-Verlag, 1988.

[Diw91] Amer Diwan. Stack tracing in a statically typed language, October 1991. Position paper for OOPSLA '91 Workshop on Garbage Collection.

[DMH92] Amer Diwan, J. Eliot B. Moss, and Richard L. Hudson. Compiler support for garbage collection in a statically typed language. In *Conference on Programming Language Design and Implementation*, pages 273–282, San Francisco, California, June 1992. SIGPLAN, ACM Press.

[DSZ90] Alan Dearle, Gail M. Shaw, and Stanley B. Zdonik, editors. *Proceedings of the Fourth International Workshop on Persistent Object Systems*, Martha's Vineyard, Massachusetts, September 1990. Published as *Implementing Persistent Object Bases: Principles and Practice*, Morgan Kaufmann, 1990.

[GR83] Adele Goldberg and David Robson. *Smalltalk-80: The Language and its Implementation*. Addison-Wesley, 1983.

[Har92] S. P. Harbison. *Modula-3*. Prentice Hall, New Jersey, 1992.

[HBM93] Antony L. Hosking, Eric Brown, and J. Eliot B. Moss. Update logging for persistent programming languages: A comparative performance evaluation. In *Proceedings of the Nineteenth International Conference on Very Large Data Bases*, pages 429–440, Dublin, Ireland, August 1993. Morgan Kaufmann.

[HM90] Antony L. Hosking and J. Eliot B. Moss. Towards compile-time optimisations for persistence. In Dearle et al. [DSZ90], pages 17–27.

14

[HM91]   Antony L. Hosking and J. Eliot B. Moss. Compiler support for persistent programming. COINS Technical Report 91-25, University of Massachusetts, Amherst, MA 01003, March 1991.

[HM93a]   Antony L. Hosking and J. Eliot B. Moss. Object fault handling for persistent programming languages: A performance evaluation. In *Proceedings of the Conference on Object-Oriented Programming Systems, Languages, and Applications*, pages 288–303, Washington, DC, October 1993.

[HM93b]   Antony L. Hosking and J. Eliot B. Moss. Protection traps and alternatives for memory management of an object-oriented language. In *Proceedings of the Fourteenth ACM Symposium on Operating Systems Principles*, pages 106–119, Asheville, NC, December 1993.

[HMB90]   Antony L. Hosking, J. Eliot B. Moss, and Cynthia Bliss. Design of an object faulting persistent Smalltalk. COINS Technical Report 90-45, University of Massachusetts, Amherst, MA 01003, May 1990.

[HMDW91]   Richard L. Hudson, J. Eliot B. Moss, Amer Diwan, and Christopher F. Weight. A language-independent garbage collector toolkit. COINS Technical Report 91-47, University of Massachusetts, Amherst, September 1991.

[HMS92]   Antony L. Hosking, J. Eliot B. Moss, and Darko Stefanović. A comparative performance evaluation of write barrier implementations. In *Proceedings of the Conference on Object-Oriented Programming Systems, Languages, and Applications*, pages 92–109, Vancouver, Canada, October 1992. *ACM SIGPLAN Not.* 27, 10 (October 1992).

[Hos91]   Antony L. Hosking. Main memory management for persistence, October 1991. Position paper presented at the OOPSLA '91 Workshop on Garbage Collection.

[Kae86]   Ted Kaehler. Virtual memory on a narrow machine for an object-oriented language. In OOPSLA [OOP86], pages 87–106.

[KK83]   Ted Kaehler and Glenn Krasner. LOOM—large object-oriented memory for Smalltalk-80 systems. In Glenn Krasner, editor, *Smalltalk-80: Bits of History, Words of Advice*, chapter 14, pages 251–270. Addison-Wesley, 1983.

[LLOW91]   Charles Lamb, Gordon Landis, Jack Orenstein, and Dan Weinreb. The ObjectStore database system. *Communications of the ACM*, 34(10):50–63, October 1991.

[Mos87]   J. Eliot B. Moss. Implementing persistence for an object oriented language. COINS Technical Report 87-69, University of Massachusetts, Amherst, MA 01003, September 1987.

[Mos89]   J. Eliot B. Moss. Addressing large distributed collections of persistent objects: The Mneme project's approach. In Richard Hull, Ron Morrison, and David Stemple, editors, *Proceedings of the Second International Workshop on Database Programming Languages*, pages 269–285, Gleneden Beach, Oregon, June 1989. Morgan Kaufmann. Also available as COINS Technical Report 89-68, University of Massachusetts.

[Mos90]   J. Eliot B. Moss. Design of the Mneme persistent object store. *ACM Trans. Inf. Syst.*, 8(2):103–139, April 1990.

[Mos92]   J. Eliot B. Moss. Working with persistent objects: To swizzle or not to swizzle. *IEEE Transactions on Software Engineering*, 18(8):657–673, August 1992.

[MS88]   J. Eliot B. Moss and Steven Sinofsky. Managing persistent data with Mneme: Designing a reliable, shared object interface. In Dittrich [Dit88], pages 298–316.

[Nel91]   Greg Nelson, editor. *Systems Programming with Modula-3*. Prentice Hall, New Jersey, 1991.

[OOP86]   *Proceedings of the Conference on Object-Oriented Programming Systems, Languages, and Applications*, Portland, Oregon, September 1986. *ACM SIGPLAN Not. 21*, 11 (November 1986).

[RC90]   Joel E. Richardson and Michael J. Carey. Persistence in the E language: Issues and implementation. *Software: Practice and Experience*, 19(12):1115–1150, December 1990.

[Ric89]   Joel Edward Richardson. *E: A Persistent Systems Implementation Language*. PhD thesis, Computer Sciences Department, University of Wisconsin, Madison, WI, August 1989. Available as Computer Sciences Technical Report #868.

[Ric90]   Joel E. Richardson. Compiled item faulting: A new technique for managing I/O in a persistent language. In Dearle et al. [DSZ90], pages 3–16.

[RMS88]   Steve Riegel, Fred Mellender, and Andrew Straw. Integration of database management with an object-oriented programming language. In Dittrich [Dit88], pages 317–322.

[SCB+86]   Craig Schaffert, Topher Cooper, Bruce Bullis, Mike Kilian, and Carrie Wilpolt. An introduction to Trellis/Owl. In OOPSLA [OOP86], pages 9–16.

[SCD90]   D. Schuh, M. Carey, and D. DeWitt. Persistence in E revisited—implementation experiences. In Dearle et al. [DSZ90], pages 345–359.

[SKW92]   Vivek Singhal, Sheetal V. Kakkad, and Paul R. Wilson. Texas, an efficient, portable persistent store. In *Proceedings of the Fifth International Workshop on Persistent Object Systems*, pages 11–33, San Miniato, Italy, September 1992.

[SMR89]   Andrew Straw, Fred Mellender, and Steve Riegel. Object management in a persistent Smalltalk system. *Software: Practice and Experience*, 19(8):719–737, August 1989.

[SRA94]   Zhong Shao, John H. Reppy, and Andrew W. Appel. Unrolling lists. In *1994 ACM Conference on Lisp and Functional Programming*, Orlando, Florida, June 1994.

[WD92]   Seth J. White and David J. DeWitt. A performance study of alternative object faulting and pointer swizzling strategies. In *Proceedings of the Eighteenth International Conference on Very Large Data Bases*, pages 419–431, Vancouver, Canada, August 1992. Morgan Kaufmann.

[WK92]   Paul R. Wilson and Sheetal V. Kakkad. Pointer swizzling at page fault time: Efficiently and compatibly supporting huge address spaces on standard hardware. In *Proceedings of the 1992 International Workshop on Object Orientation in Operating Systems*, pages 364–377, Paris, France, September 1992. IEEE Press.

Concurrent Shadow Paging in the Flask Architecture

D.S. Munro[1], R.C.H. Connor[1], R. Morrison[1], S. Scheuerl[1] &
D.W. Stemple[2]

[1]Department of Mathematical and Computational Sciences, University of St
Andrews,
North Haugh, St Andrews, Fife, KY16 9SS, Scotland

[2]Department of Computer Science, University of Massachusetts,
Amherst, Massachusetts, MA 01003, U.S.A.

Abstract

The differing requirements for concurrency models in programming
languages and databases are widely diverse and often seemingly
incompatible. The rigid provision of a particular concurrency control
scheme in a persistent object system limits its usefulness to a particular
class of application, in contrast to the generality intended by the provision
of persistence. One solution is to provide a flexible system in which
concurrency control schemes may be specified according to the particular
task in hand, allowing the same data to be used in conjunction with different
concurrency control schemes according to the needs of the application.

A major difficulty in the engineering of such a system lies in the
building of generic mechanisms to provide the facilities of data visibility
restriction, stability, and atomicity, *independently* of the combination of
these employed by a particular concurrency control scheme. Flask is a
architecture which is designed to achieve this goal by defining a layering
whereby the memory management is not tied to any one concurrency control
scheme operating above. This paper outlines the Flask architecture and
focuses on an implementation based on concurrent shadow paging. The
architecture described is currently being used as the basis for
experimentation in generic concurrency specification.

1   Introduction

The notion of atomic transactions [Dav73, Dav78, EGL+76] can be identified as one
of the first forms of concurrency control in databases. Transactions provide users
with the so-called ACID properties, namely atomicity, consistency, isolation and
durability, with which to understand computations. For concurrent access,
transactions isolate the effects of one activity from another using a serializable

schedule. The transaction concept was extended to enable nesting [Ree78, Mos81] whilst Sagas [GS87] provided a non-serializable concurrency control model as a potential solution to certain classes of problems caused by long-lived transactions. More recently for many applications, especially those in design and interactive systems [Sut91, EG90, NZ92], it has been suggested that the serializability constraint of the atomic transaction model is too restrictive. Such systems need the global cohesiveness of the transaction model but also require the competing transactions to interact with each other in a structured way because of their inter-dependence.

With an increase in the number and diversity of such models, there is a growing need within database and persistent programming systems to support different styles of concurrency control scheme operating in conjunction over the same data. For example, an airline company may employ an atomic transaction system for flight-bookings whereas a tour operator or travel agent, operating on the same data, may utilise a saga-style scheme when booking connecting flights through different carriers.

Flask is a layered architecture which has the flexibility to support different models of concurrency over the same data. The architecture eschews any fixed notion of concurrency control. Instead it provides a framework in which models can be defined and supported. One of the major difficulties in engineering such a system lies in the building of generic mechanisms to provide the facilities of data visibility restriction, stability, and atomicity, independently of the combination of these employed by a particular concurrency control scheme.

One of the key features of the Flask architecture is that as little as possible is built-in to the lower layers providing increased functionality moving up the levels of abstraction. This provides the necessary flexibility but may also permit efficiency gains since many optimisations are achievable at a higher-level. The approach is comparable with that taken in RISC architecture where a simpler, more understandable hardware interface can be exploited more readily by software construction to forge efficiency gains. Promoting some of the complexity to the higher layers simplifies the memory management allowing a number of possible implementations.

The Flask architecture challenges the orthodoxy whereby most database systems, such as System/R [CAB+81], Ingres [Sto86], O2 [Deu90] and Oracle build in specific models of concurrency, usually at the store level. This design decision is taken for reasons of simplicity of implementation and arguably trades efficiency for flexibility. A drawback with the approach is that the specification of a particular concurrency control model is often described in terms of its implementation. For example, the conceptual simplicity of a transaction model can often become confused with particular locking tactics. Such situations can add to complexity of understanding the semantics of a concurrency control scheme.

This paper presents an overview of Flask but concentrates on the low-level memory management implementation that is structured to be independent of the concurrency control schemes operating above. One such implementation, based on shadow-paging, is described in detail.

2   Overview of Flask

The framework of the Flask architecture is shown in Figure 1 as a "V-shaped" layered architecture to signify the minimal functionality built-in at the lower layers. At the top layer the specifications of the model are independent of the algorithms used to enforce them and can take advantage of the semantics of these algorithms to exploit potential concurrency [Gar83]. For example a particular specification may translate into an optimistic algorithm or alternatively a pessimistic one while the information they operate over remains the same. More importantly such an approach can accommodate different models of concurrency control.

The Flask architecture is designed to work with processes or actions that maintain global cohesion under control of the concurrency control schemes. In general, changes to data do not overlap except where this happens co-operatively. In Flask, the significant events defined by a particular concurrency control scheme are generated from and reported to the higher layers enabling these schemes to undertake conflict detection. This assumption frees the lower layers from the onus of interference management.

Two systems which meet these requirements and which are major influences on the Flask approach are Stemple and Morrison's CACS system [SM92] and Krablin's CPS-algol system [Kra87]. The CACS system provides a framework in which concurrency control schemes can be specified. CACS is a generic utility for providing concurrency control for applications. The system does not actually manipulate any objects, but instead maintains information about their pattern of usage. In order for the system to collate this information, the attached applications must issue signals regarding their intended use of their objects. In return the CACS system replies indicating whether or not the operation would violate the concurrency rules. CPS-algol is an extension to the standard PS-algol system [PS87] that includes language constructs to support and manage concurrent processes. The concurrency model is essentially co-operative with procedures executing as separate threads and synchronising through conditional critical regions. Krablin showed that with these primitives and the higher-order functions of PS-algol, a range of concurrency abstractions could be constructed including atomic and nested transactions as well as more co-operative models.

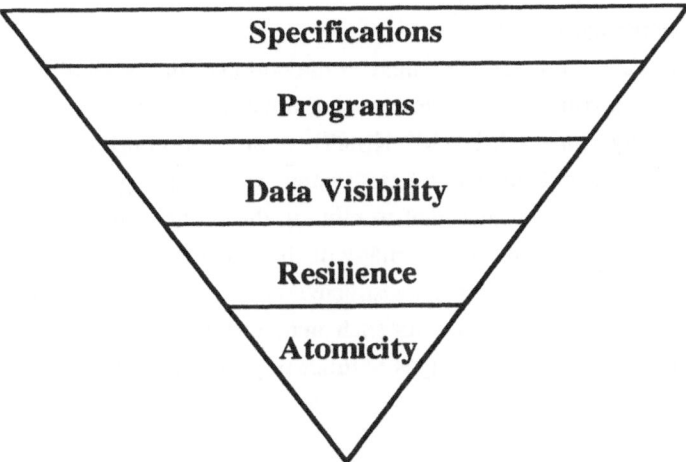

Figure 1: V-shaped layered architecture

This paper is not concerned with how the specifications are written or how the concurrency control algorithms initiate and receive events. Instead the main theme is concerned with low-level memory management implementations in the Flask architecture under the assumptions given above. The focus of interest then centres on the visibility of data from different actions. In Flask, the visibility is expressed in terms of the control of movement between a globally visible database and conceptual stores called access sets. Each action is associated with a local access set and may use other shared access sets. The interfaces to the data visibility are :-

- Start action

- End action

- Create and delete local access set

- Create and delete shared access set

- Copy from access set to access set

- remove object from access set

- Meld

At the lowest level the atomicity layer ensures consistent update to the access sets and the global database. The failure resilience layer utilises this atomicity to effect an action *meld*. The term *meld* is used to describe the action of making updates permanent rather than terms like *commit* or *stabilise* since they imply specific meanings in particular models.

One approach, presented here, marries the notion of data visibility as expressed by access sets to a concurrent shadow paging mechanism. Shadow paging [Lor77] has been seen by some [GMB+81, Kol87] as an inappropriate technology for concurrent systems and most database systems use logging techniques instead [OLS85, VDD+91]. It is argued that in moving the programming algebra and the concurrency control to higher layers many of the perceived difficulties concerning concurrent shadow paging have been abstracted out. Shadow paging is then seen as a mechanism worthy of consideration for such an architecture in essence because it can stabilise over arbitrary address ranges without requiring knowledge of objects and program behaviour.

3   Conceptual Concurrent Layered Architecture

The crux of the design of an architecture that can support different styles of concurrency is to define the global cohesion or understandability in terms of data visibility between concurrent activities. This is reflected in the design of a conceptual concurrent layered architecture in which visibility is defined and controlled by the movement of data between a hierarchy of conceptual address spaces. The architecture provides isolation by constraining data accessed by one activity to a separate address space from all others. Concurrency models using this architecture are defined in terms of data visibility through the sharing of address spaces and the control of movement between these spaces.

The conceptual concurrent architecture is layered in such a way that it separates the concurrency control mechanism, the atomicity and the persistence. These layers are described in terms of conceptual address spaces together with a protocol that controls the movement of data between these address spaces. By unbundling and distributing the concurrency intrinsics in this hierarchy, the architecture provides a generic layered store capable of supporting a number of different models of concurrency.

Figure 2 gives a diagram of the Flask architectural hierarchy shown as a layer of conceptual address spaces. Each layer implements a separate and independent property of concurrency. This permits any particular concurrency model the flexibility to choose a desired combination of intrinsics.

At the top level the concurrency control schemes contains a full definition of the concurrency control mechanism. No assumptions are made by the lower layers about the concurrency control and hence this leaves the implementor freedom to choose any desired scheme.

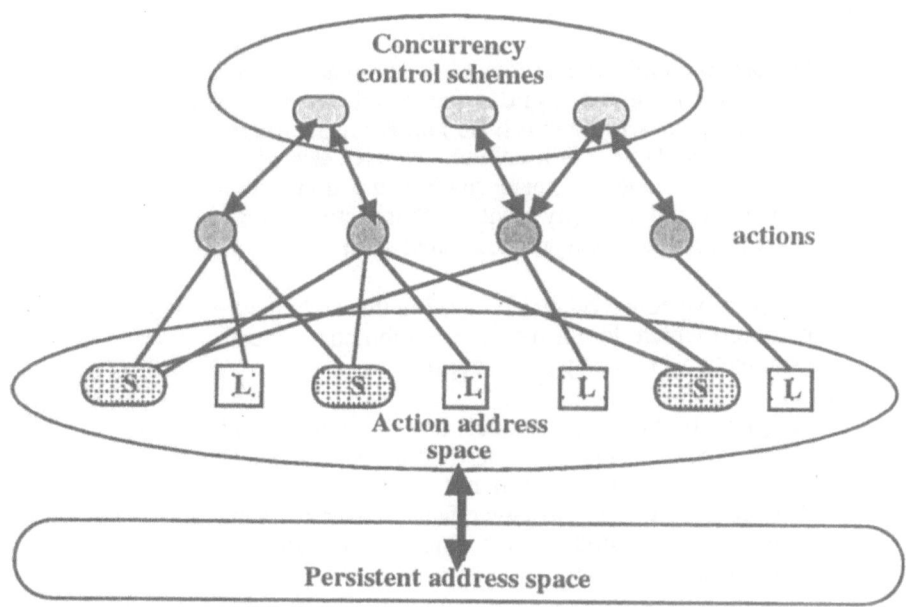

Figure 2: Flask Conceptual Concurrent Architecture

An action, in the Flask architecture, is an isolated thread of control that communicates with the concurrency control schemes and whose state is defined by the action address space. The action address space layer is a set of private and group address spaces. Each action has a private address space (marked "L" for local in Figure 2). In addition the action address space may house a number of group address spaces that are shared by a combination of actions (marked "S" for shared in Figure 2). The globally visible database is modelled by the persistent address space.

Schemes are defined in terms of action creation and abort along with the movement of data between address spaces. The different schemes control the visibility and interference among actions using them. The architecture ensures that all data movement is atomic. Movement of data from an action's private address space or a group of actions' group address space to the persistent address space is through a meld operation. The Flask architecture supports the atomic update of the persistent address space so that its data is permanent, recoverable and consistent. The meld operation is instantiated with different semantics dependent on the particular concurrency control scheme to ensure that data movement to the persistent address space becomes visible to all other actions. The effect of an action abort is to release the action's private address space. The relationship between action abort and group address space is determined by the concurrency control scheme.

The Flask architecture provides the versatility to support a range of concurrency models. For example:-

- Support for atomic transactions can be provided in this architecture through a concurrency control specification that constrains each action's updates to their private address space thereby isolating their effects. Transaction commit involves the atomic update of the persistent address space making the transaction's changes permanent and globally visible. Transaction abort is a trivial matter of discarding the private address space.

- Co-operative concurrency is viewed in this architecture as a group of actions which do not require isolation control and interact co-operatively over a group address space.

- Designer transactions model can be accommodated by a combination of private and group address spaces and a concurrency control specification that defines their creation, interaction and the movement of objects. Thus the effects of operations may be shared among actions without their objects being committed to the persistent address space.

4   Instantiating the Architecture

The discussion here of how an instance of the Flask architecture is achievable focuses on the provision of data visibility, resilience and atomicity. It is assumed that the concurrency control specifications and algorithms are handled by a mechanism such as CACS. One possible implementation strategy arises from the observation that each layer need only maintain copies of the portions of the underlying layer's address space that it has changed along with a table which provides a mapping between the original and the copy. Applying this strategy down the layers, the resulting architecture collapses into one flat address space with a hierarchy of mappings. One approach to providing such an address space is recoverable paged virtual memory.

There are a number of different mechanisms, such as write-ahead logging or shadow paging, which can provide the necessary resilience to support stable virtual memory. Many, if not most, databases and persistent systems, such as O2 [VDD+91], System/R [GMB+81] and Argus [Kol87], tend to favour a form of logging to provide failure recovery after crashes. The arguments against a shadow paging solution centre around efficiency issues and the mechanism's ability to handle concurrent access. In the instantiation of the Flask architecture described here an extended form of shadow paging has been developed. It is argued here that this concurrent shadow paging mechanism, under the assumptions described above, is not only a viable mechanism but also a potentially efficient solution.

4.1 Shadow Paging

A virtual memory system controls the movement of pages of the virtual memory on backing store to and from the page frames on main store and maintains a page table, the main memory page table, which records the allocation of page frames of main memory to pages of the virtual memory. The page table is transient since soft failure results in the loss of the main store. The operating system typically allocates the pages of the virtual memory to a contiguous range of disk blocks on backing store and records the disk address of the first disk block, the base address. Virtual memory addresses are usually relative offsets from the first page and hence the ith page can be found at the ith disk block from the base because the pages and disk blocks are always in one-to-one correspondence.

A shadow-paged virtual memory system is similar to virtual memory where the pages reside on backing store and a main-memory page table records the allocation of pages to physical memory page frames. The essential difference is that the system ensures that before a modified page is written back to non-volatile store that there is always a retrievable copy of the original page on non-volatile storage. This scheme then destroys the contiguous correspondence between the pages of the virtual memory and disk blocks and so shadow paged virtual memory requires another table, the *disk* page table, to record the mapping between pages of the virtual memory and disk blocks on backing store. There are two varieties of shadow paging :-

4.1.1 After-look Shadow Paging

With an after-look shadow paged scheme the mechanism makes sure that a modified page is never written back to non-volatile store to the same place it was read from. When a modified page is written back to non-volatile store an unused disk block is found and the disk page table updated to reflect the new mapping. This is analogous to deferred-write logging [Dav73, GMB+81]. Figure 3 illustrates the after-look scheme showing the modified pages being shadowed to a different disk page.

The system uses a root block which resides at a known disk address. The root block is stable by mirroring and from this the disk page table can be located. At system startup the disk page table is interrogated to re-establish the state of the address space. In fact two versions of the disk page table are maintained; the version held on disk which reflects the stable state and another in main memory which is updated by the shadowing mechanism. This *transient* disk page table reflects the current state of the address space. Figure 4 illustrates the mechanism. The stable disk page table records the mappings from the last consistent state whilst the transient disk page table in volatile store records the current mappings. The diagram shows that the third and fourth page have been shadowed to unused disk blocks. When the user melds all the modified pages are flushed to disk and then the in-memory version of the disk page table atomically replaces the disk version. The atomic update depends on the root block being written correctly. This can be performed using any mirroring technique such as Challis' algorithm [Cha78].

main store pages

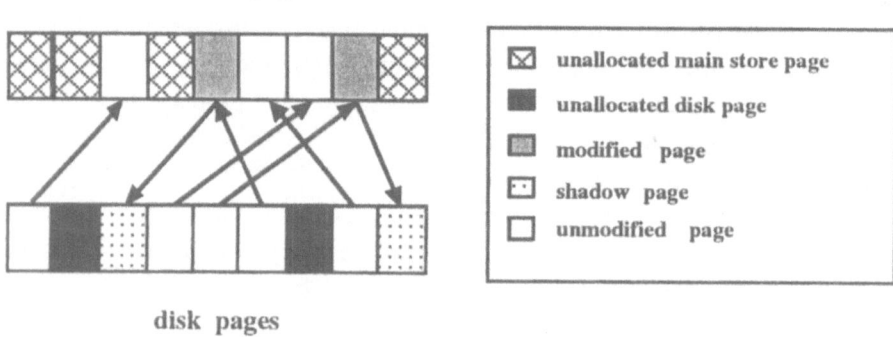

disk pages

Figure 3: After-look shadow paging

Challis' algorithm uses two fixed root blocks with known disk addresses. The root blocks contain information that allows the system to find the mapping table for a consistent state. From the root blocks then the two previous consistent states n-1 and n can be found. Each root block also contains a version number that enables the system to determine which contains the most recent state. This version number is written twice as the first and last word of the block. The atomic update operation entails overwriting the root block with oldest version number, in this case n-1, with a new version number, n+1, and a pointer to the new updated mapping table. The space occupied by the old consistent state n-1 may now be reused.

Challis' algorithm depends upon two critical points for safety. Firstly an error in an atomic update can only occur if the root block is written incorrectly. It is expected that if a disk write operation fails during the atomic update it will inform the system which can then take appropriate action immediately. If, however, the failure is more serious, the technique depends upon the version numbers at the start and end of the root block being different in order to detect failure.

On system startup the root blocks are inspected. If the version numbers are consistent within the root blocks, the most up-to-date version of the system can be found. If not, only one root block may have different version numbers at any one time unless a catastrophic failure has occurred, which in any case would have other implications for the integrity of the data. Thus, subject to the above proviso, the correct stable data can be identified.

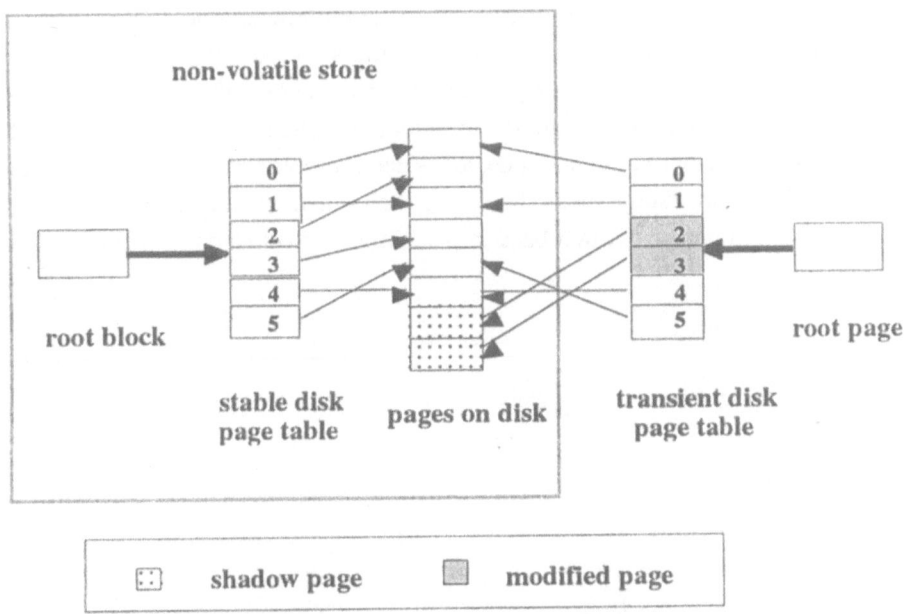

Figure 4: Layout of after-look shadow paging

For efficiency the transient disk page table is often kept in main store. The disk page table may, however, be too large and would in that case be stored in a transient area of disk. This causes difficulties in the disk mapping as there is now a transient disk area which has to be mapped in some manner and the disk area mapped by the disk page table. A solution to the above is to incorporate the disk page table in the virtual address space itself. This means that the page table is paged and that updates to it create shadow copies. The advantage of this is that there is only one paging mechanism and that changes to all data, including the page table, are incremental. The only requirement for such an organisation to work is that the address of the first page of the disk page table must be held at a fixed location, the root block, within the virtual address space.

On crash recovery the root block is read and the disk page table is recovered. This is used to re-establish the contents of the pages from their associated disk blocks. It will include the program state if it is considered part of the data. If this is the case then once the recovery manager has reconstructed the data the computation will automatically carry on from the last meld point. No changes to data in this mechanism get undone or rewritten and hence the after-look shadow paging recovery algorithm can be classified as a **no undo / no redo** algorithm.

4.1.2   Before-look Shadow Paging

With before-look shadow paging [BR91], the first modification to a page causes a copy to be written to a new block on non-volatile store, i.e., its shadow page. In contrast to after-look shadow paging modifications then take place in the original. The disk page table is used to record the location of the shadow pages and must itself be on non-volatile store before any updates reach non-volatile store. This is similar to logging with immediate writes. The before-look scheme is illustrated in Figure 5 where a modified page is written back in place after a shadow copy of the original has been taken.

main store pages

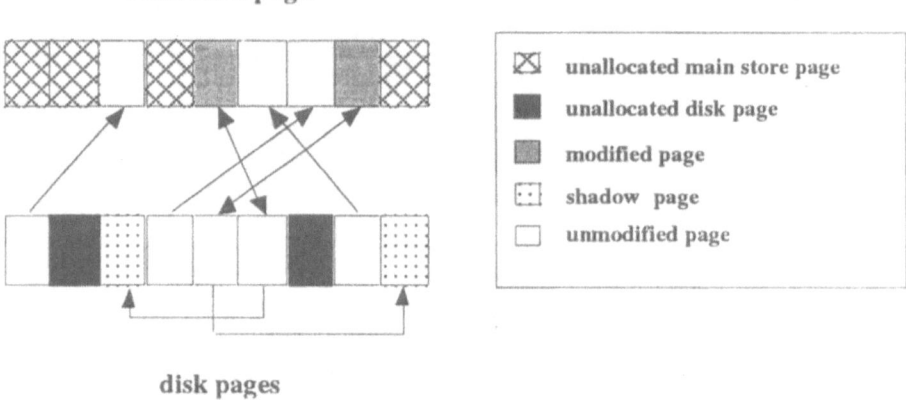

disk pages

Figure 5: Before-look shadow paging

These shadow pages must be locatable after a crash and effectively form a coarse-grain log of the previous values of the modified pages. On meld the modified pages are written to disk and a new consistent state is established. This log of previous values is then discarded.

Recovery from a system crash occurring before a meld involves using this "log" to overwrite the pages that have been modified since the last meld with their previous values. The system is thereby established to the same state as it was at the last meld. This undo of the pages is clearly idempotent. If the program state is considered part of the data then once the recovery manager has completed the undo operation the computation will automatically proceed from the last meld point. Before-look shadow paging can be classified as being **undo / no redo**.

5   The Flask Concurrent Shadow Paged Store

The main problem of concurrency and shadow paging is that transactions may make conflicting requests to modify the same page. When one of the transactions melds the modified page is written to its shadow page on non-volatile store. This of course will include the changes made by any unmelded transaction that modified objects on the same page.

One common solution is to use page-level locking whereby an atomic transaction obtains an exclusive lock on a page before shadowing the page [AD85b, Lor77]. Each transaction maintains its own page table of shadows and the locking guarantees that a page is never in more than one page table. The main drawbacks of this solution are firstly that it introduces phantom locking where two atomic actions are prevented from modifying different parts of the same page. Secondly it employs a built-in concurrency control mechanism at a low level. Problems of deadlock also have to be addressed.

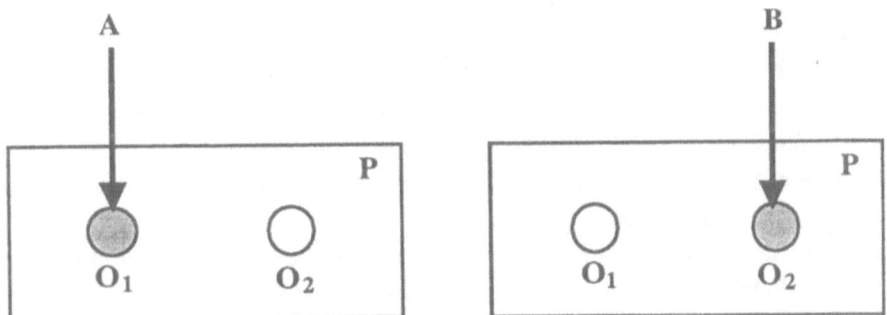

Figure 6: Flask shadow paging

The Flask solution involves not only keeping a disk page table of shadows for each process but to also maintain per-process shadow pages, i.e., an access set. Flask also maintains a global disk page table of pages which constitute the last meld point. When a process first modifies a page a shadow copy is made and its address is added to the process's shadow page table. To resolve a disk address on a page fault the process shadow page table is searched first and, if still unresolved, then the global disk page table. This mechanism ensures that the changes made by one process are completely isolated from other processes and the global state. Action abort is thus a trivial matter of discarding a process's shadow pages. Figure 6 illustrates the Flask shadow paging showing that both action A and action B can freely modify objects

O_1 and O_2 respectively from the same page P since each action has a shadow copy of page P.

When an action melds the changes it has made become globally visible to all other actions. There is therefore a requirement in the Flask architecture to ensure that the changes made to a page by the melding action are propagated to any other action holding a shadow copy of the same page.

5.1 Concurrency control and per-action melding

In the Flask architecture the access sets are implemented by paged address spaces. Because the meld resolution is at a page-level then the changes made by the melding action must be propagated to other actions' per-process shadows. Suppose that two actions A and B share a page but modify different objects on that page. Because of the isolation of the concurrent shadow paging mechanism A can meld without affecting B. For B to subsequently meld it must retain the changes that A made. And so a mechanism is required for B to ingest the changes made by A. The algorithm that meld uses to propagate changes is dependent on the particular concurrency model in operation. Under the assumption that the higher-layer concurrency control can detect object-level conflicts there a number of methods of achieving this.

In concurrency models that require isolation, where the concurrency control ensures that two transactions do not modify the same object, it is possible to use logical operations to propagate the changes. For example, in an atomic transaction model, suppose two actions A and B have changed different objects on the same page P and action A melds. The changes made by A to page P can be calculated by an xor of P onto the original page, i.e., as it was at the last meld. This derives a page of changes made by A to page P. These changes can now be xor'd onto action B's copy of page P. So the meld propagation formula can be written as :-

$$(P_A \text{ xor } P_O) \text{ xor } P_B$$

where P_A is the action A's shadow page P, P_O is the page P as it was at the last meld and P_B is action B's shadow page P. Thus B's version of page P now includes the changes made by A. This approach is not restricted to atomic transactions. In co-operative models where the actions agree to change an object to the same value using majority rules logical operations can also be used.

One other possible method of providing meld propagation is for an action to record the address ranges that it has modified for each page in its shadow page table as the changes are made. This could then be used to copy the modifications to other transactions holding a copy of the same page.

Whilst the cost of propagation may seem high it should be borne in mind that this is only necessary when an action melds. In the case of long-lived actions such a cost may be less burdensome. Furthermore, a meld propagation only affects actions that have accessed shared pages. On stock hardware logical operations are typically very fast machine instructions making this shadow page scheme not only viable but also potentially efficient.

5.2   The Flask Architecture

The concurrent shadow paging scheme works much as the single-user shadow paging described above whereby the virtual address space is mapped to non-volatile storage through a disk page table. Modified pages are shadowed and the transient disk page table reflects the current global state of the address space. In addition a separate disk page table is created for each private and group action address space used. Each action has its own private address space and so a disk-page table is created for each action. Similarly a disk page table is created for each group address space required by the model. Entries to the disk page tables are added for each page modified by the action. When an action first modifies a page a shadow copy is made and the action works on the copy. The concurrency control specification dictates whether the update is a private or group one. Hence the changes made by an action to its private address space are totally isolated from other actions' private address spaces. Also the group address spaces are isolated from each other and from the private address spaces.

The mechanism is illustrated in Figure 7 and shows that the transient disk page table and the action disk page tables are accessible from the root page. As in the single threaded case the transient disk page table and the stable disk page table maintain a page table entry for each page of the address space. When a page, modified by an action, is written out to non-volatile store it is written to its shadow and the mapping recorded in the per-action page table. The action page table only has entries for pages modified by that action and not the complete address space. The illustration in Figure 7 shows that there are five pages in the virtual address space and that there are currently two actions A and B. The disk page table for action A shows that A has modified pages 0 and 2 in its private address space and that action B has modified pages 0, 1 and 3 in its private address space. Note that page 0 has been modified by both actions but that the shadow page mechanism isolates their modifications. The third disk page table reflects a group address space that shows action A and B are working on a shared copy of page 2 and 4. A has a local object in page 2 and a shared object with B. The particular concurrency control scheme will disambiguate action A's access to page 2 since it knows which objects are shared and which are not.

The scheduler for this concurrent system must ensure that the correct mappings are established on a page fault. For example when action A accesses a page that results in a page fault, the system must search A's disk page table for the page (or a group that A is currently in). If there is no entry for the page in A's disk page table then the transient disk page table is searched.

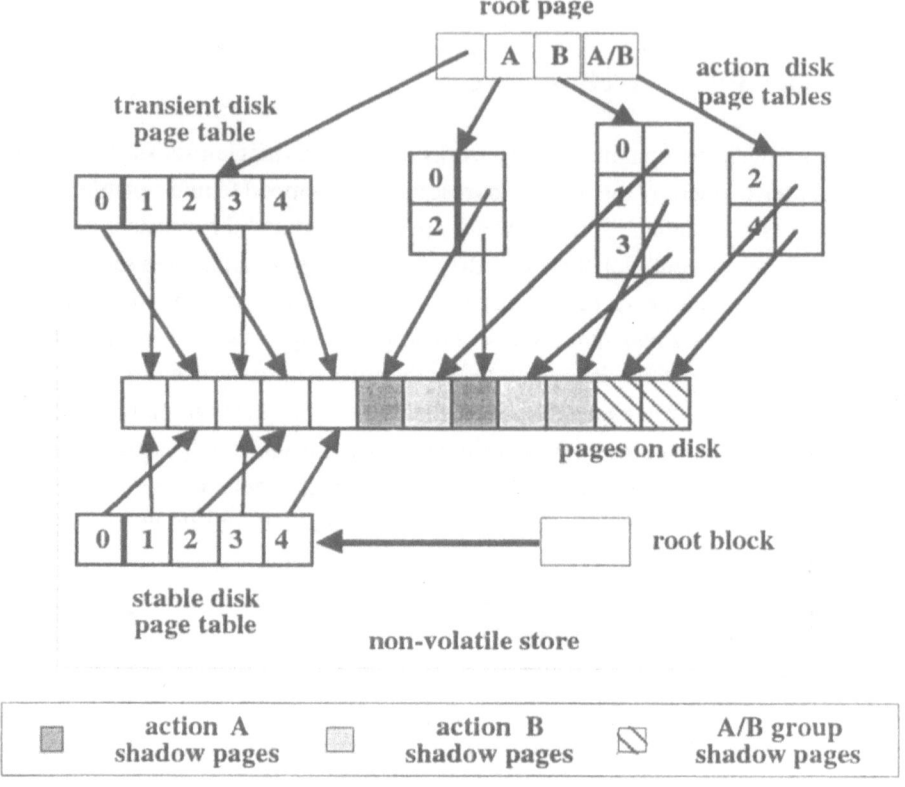

Figure 7: Concurrent shadow-paged architecture

A meld mechanism is provided on a per-action basis so that changes made by an action can become part of a new recoverable, consistent state and then these changes are made visible to other actions. It is possible for a number of actions to be working on shadow copies of the same page and the meld propagates the differences between the shadowed pages modified by the action and the originals through to any other action working on copies of the same original pages.

To establish a new consistent state all pages modified by the action are written to their shadows. Then the entries for these pages in the transient disk page table are updated to record the same mappings. For example, if a melding action had modified page P and its shadow page was disk block D then the transient disk page table entry for P must also record that it is mapped to D. To ensure atomicity of the meld the updating of the transient disk page table will involve shadowing of the page encompassing the transient disk page table entry. Once the transient disk page table reflects the new consistent state it atomically replaces the stable disk page table.

6   Evaluation

Two criticisms commonly associated with after-look shadow paging are its effects on the clustering of data and the cost of disk page table lookups. Two logically adjacent pages in the conceptual store may be allocated physically distributed shadow pages causing increased seek time. The effect of this can be reduced by using physical clustering techniques such as suggested by Lorie [Lor77] where shadow pages are allocated within a cylinder where possible. With after-looks, shadow pages need only be allocated disk blocks when the user melds or when main memory is exhausted and pages must be written back. Hence this provides an opportunity to use such a clustering scheme.

The cost of disk page table access can be reduced by maintaining the table in main store but where the disk page tables are themselves paged then extra disk hits are unavoidable. An evaluation of the worst case scenario of the Flask concurrent shadow paging mechanism is given below.

When a read request on page P by action A causes a page fault then the mechanism first searches action A's disk page table since action A may have already shadowed the page. This may result in a disk access to bring the table into memory. If page P is not in action A's disk page table then the transient disk page table is searched. This too may involve a disk hit to access the table entry. Finally there is a disk access for the original page fault for page P. In the worst case then a read request could result in three disk hits.

A write request on page P may also, in the worst case, require three accesses for the same reasons as a read request. In addition a first write to a page will require a shadow copy of the page and an update to the actions disk page table. However taking a shadow copy of P does not necessarily incur a disk write since it need only involve allocating a free disk block for the shadow.

On a meld, the propagation algorithm is dependent on the particular concurrency model being executed. However regardless of which scheme is in operation a meld requires that a new stable state is established before propagating the changes. This involves flushing each page of an action's disk page table to disk. Then the stable disk page table must be atomically updated to reflect the new global state.

As an example of the cost of meld propagation suppose that an atomic transaction model was implemented using the double xor meld propagation formula given above. Each page P that has been modified by the melding action A must propagate its changes to all other actions that have also been shadowed page P. For each such page P then P is xor'd onto the original O and this is then xor'd onto each of the actions that have shadow copies of P. Note that these propagations do not need to be written back to disk.

In the worst cases then this mechanism appears to require a heavy disk access cost. However, this cost is greatly reduced where the actions exhibit a high degree of locality of reference. In addition efficiency gains can be sought in implementations by using features such as memory mapping or tailoring an external pager. As an example, an instance of the Flask architecture has been implemented to support an atomic transaction package written in Napier88. This makes use of the SunOS memory-mapping facilities to enhanced performance since it uses the operating system's page-replacement mechanism and utilises the Sun memory management hardware to perform the address translations [Mun93].

7   Related Work

Attempts have been made at analysing and comparing the cost of different recovery schemes [AD85a, KGC85]. The results of these efforts do not produce a clear winner. Other research [GMB+81, Kol87, AD85b] would suggest that logging is a better technique especially when the system needs to support conflicting actions. Implementations of shadow paging are not widespread and it is believed by some to be an inappropriate technology for database applications. The implementors of System R used a complex combination of shadow paging and logging and claim that in hindsight they would have adopted a purely log-based recovery scheme. Furthermore they stated they were unable to conceive of an appropriate architecture based purely on shadows that could support transactions.

Agrawal and DeWitt produced a complex cost model used for comparing shadow paging with logging using a variety of concurrency control techniques. Their approach was purely analytical and their database simulations did not account for the costs of buffer management. The results for shadow paging in these simulations were poor when compared with logging. However closer inspection of their model reveals an unexplained assumption. In the logging case it is assumed that the size of the records that are written to the log for each page modified by a transaction is 10% of the page size. So if during a transaction's execution data is modified on 10 pages the assumption is that the size of the log records for that transaction amount to 1 page. This assumption may be valid in some models of computation. However if the transactions are generated from language systems that frequently update large objects, such as graphical objects, or higher order functions the assumption may not be sustainable.

In contrast the Predator project [KGC85] took an empirical approach to comparing the two methods. A realistic transaction-based database was constructed and logging and shadow paging recovery mechanisms implemented on stock hardware. A variety of transaction experiments were carried out using both recovery techniques and the results compared. The performance metrics were based on transaction throughput and mean response time. Their first observation is that there is no one best mechanism and that the choice of recovery method is application dependent. They concluded that shadow paging works best when there is locality of reference and where the page table cache is large. By using meld batching, shadow paging outperformed logging as the number of simultaneous transactions increased. Another interesting observation they made was that the shadow paging imposes a more evenly balanced I/O load than logging. Under load a noticeable performance drop was observed in the logging scheme as the system is divided between requests for sequential disk writes for the log and page reads and writes for the database.

Most of the objections to shadow paging performance are founded on a belief that the cost of writing a journal of updates to a log will almost always be more efficient than the maintenance of shadow pages. This may be true for a class of problems but may not be true in general. Many of the measurements that this notion was founded on were based on simulations or were taken from tests run on machine architectures and configurations that are now obsolete. It may be fair to suggest that the results of the comparisons related to the limitations of technology and systems available at the time. For example the overhead of page-table lookups in shadow paging was considered very costly. However the size and speed of memory in an average workstation have risen dramatically over the last few years so that the page table even for a large store could reside in main memory.

Computational models too have changed, not least with the rise in popularity of database programming languages and persistent systems. These systems make different demands on a database or stable store with different patterns of use from conventional database accesses. For example programs and data are not treated differently in orthogonal persistent systems. It is relatively straightforward to efficiently record program state in a shadow paged system by including the process state and stack frames in the address space that is shadowed since shadow paging requires no knowledge of objects or process behaviour. In contrast logging program state change would probably require a special case to handle stack frames. These arguments suggest that the decision on a superior model of recovery is not so clear cut. It may be that shadow paging is a better alternative. Certainly it is clear that shadow paging implementations can get significant performance improvements from an operating system that provides an external pager or memory-mapping support.

This support seems more forthcoming in stock systems than explicit support for fast logging [GMS87, ABB+86].

It has been argued [AD85b] that on a small scale, locality of reference would seem to favour a log-based solution since the amount of information that requires to be written to the log is small compared with the overhead of copying a whole page. Furthermore with logging there is no requirement to write back modified pages after a meld and hence a frequently modified page can reside in main store through a number of transactions. Kent's [KGC85] experimental observations suggest the exact opposite. As locality increases the page table overhead in shadow paging is soon amortised. With logging the amount of modified data that must be saved increases. There quickly comes a point where a lot of locality, especially within one page, along with frequent updates to objects on the page tips the balance in favour of a solution that makes a one-off copy of a page rather than maintains a journal of changes. Furthermore if the objects themselves are fairly big then frequent modifications to them will have an adverse effect on the log size but not on a shadow page. This kind of locality is exactly the type of behaviour that might be exhibited in persistent systems with higher-order functions.

8   Conclusions

The recent growth in the number and variety of concurrency control schemes in database and persistent systems has led to an increased need for such systems to support different schemes over the same data. The Flask architecture, described in this paper, presents one approach to providing a platform in which different concurrency control schemes can be supported.

The main feature of the Flask architecture is that as little as possible is built-in to the lower layers enabling the specification of a concurrency model to be separated from its implementation. This is very different from convention where traditional systems such as O2, Ingres and System/R use fixed models incorporated at the store level. Moving the concurrency control specifications and the programs that implement them to the higher layers relieves the constraints in handling data visibility, atomicity and resilience.

This approach has led to a re-examination of shadow paging as a viable mechanism to satisfy the requirements of the lower-levels of the Flask architecture. The advantage of shadow paging in this architecture over the more widespread logging mechanisms is that it can effect a stable state without requiring knowledge of the structure of the objects or program behaviour.

The shadow paging mechanism does not readily extend to accommodate concurrent operation. The problem of two actions wishing to modify parts of the same page has traditionally been addressed using page-level locking. This approach, however, introduces phantom locking. The mechanism presented here circumvents most of the common objections to concurrent shadow paging by creating shadow pages on a per-action basis together with a method of propagating the changes made by a melding action to other actions. The actual meld propagation function is dependent on the particular concurrency scheme in operation. In many concurrency models the meld propagation function can be implemented using logical operations increasing the potential efficiency of the mechanism.

Future work in this research includes using the Flask architecture to develop a suitable platform for measuring and comparing concurrent shadow paging with a log-based solution.

9   Initial Performance Evaluation

An initial evaluation of the performance of the FLASK store was carried out to determine the effects of different transaction workloads. A test suite of program simulations were written directly on top of the object store interface. Simulations at this low level enabled the experiments to have accurate control of: accesses and updates to the store; the size and number of objects being manipulated and the management of transaction creation, commitment, abortion and the interleaving of transactions.

The experiments were carried out on a Sun SPARCStation ELC with 40 MB main memory, 500MB SCSI disk and running SunOS 4.1.3. All blocks and pages are 8192 bytes. To suppress operating system cache interference the experiments were carried out on a cold single-user system. This involved flushing the memory of store pages and flushing the IO buffers before every experiment.

Experiment timings were obtained using the *getrusage()* system library function and the UNIX *time* command both of which gave the real time of process execution. The results include the execution time of relevant system processes on the machine, namely the swapper and pagedaemon.

The following experiments were carried out:

Experiment 1 - In the FLASK store, the meld propagation function for concurrent transactions uses the page-level double xor function to propagate changes to other transactions which use the same page. This experiment calculates the time to xor one memory resident page onto another memory resident page. The experiment chooses two pages and initially accesses both pages to make sure that they are resident in main memory in order to remove IO costs. An xor of one page onto another involves performing an xor on every pair of words in the pages. The experiment records the time to execute the page xor function 10000 times. **Result:** A single page xor = 2.3 milliseconds.

Experiment 2 - The FLASK implementation uses the memory mapping facilities of SunOS to control the mappings from pages to shadow disk blocks and is used by the FLASK store to re-map pages onto shadow disk blocks. This experiment gives the execution time of a SunOS *mmap()* system call. The experiment performs 20000 calls to *mmap()* using the same page and alternates between two different disk blocks to ensure the system updates its page mappings on every call. **Result:** A single *mmap()* call = 325 microseconds.

Experiment 3 - This experiment illustrates the effects of temporal and spatial locality of reference on the store. The experiment executes a transaction which performs 200 updates. On every execution, a different range of pages is updated with the range varying from 16 to 2048 pages. With a small range, the same pages are updated multiple times. With a large range (≥ 200 pages) 200 pages are updated.

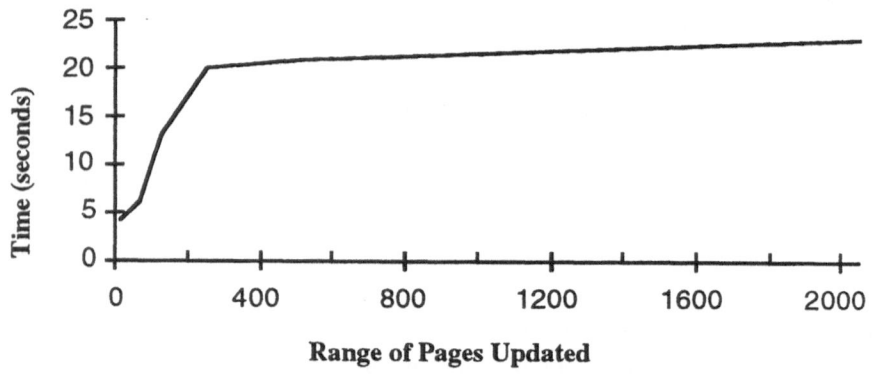

Range of Pages Updated

Figure 8: Effects of Locality

Figure 8 illustrates two results from the experiment. The first is shown by the increase in execution time as the range of updated pages expands to 200 pages. This is caused by the increased IO of updating increasing number of pages and highlights the sensitivity of the store to the locality of updates within pages.

The second result illustrates the increase in disk seek times. With page ranges greater than 200, the number of pages updated remains at a constant 200 but execution time slowly increases. As the range of pages increases, the cost of reading random pages over a larger area of disk increases, bearing in mind that pages are read before being updated.

This experiment is executed from a cold start. Experiment 4 gives the results of a hot experiment of multiple updates to the same pages.

Experiment 4 - This experiment illustrates the effect of performing multiple accesses to the same pages in memory. The experiment executes transactions which read 2000 pages and other transactions which read and update 2000 pages. The number of accesses performed on every page is varied.

	1 access per page	5 accesses per page	10 accesses per page	100 accesses per page
read only	23	23	23	25
read & write	148	148	148	151

Table 1: Experiment 4 (execution times in seconds)

Table 1 illustrates that the execution time of transactions does not increase greatly as the number of updates per page increases. The majority of the cost of updating a page is in shadowing the page on its first update, shown in column one. Subtracting the column one figures from the figures in the other columns gives the hot execution times of performing multiple updates on pages which have already been shadowed.

The difference in execution times between the rows is caused by the current FLASK implementation performing 2 page writes per updated page. The first write is required by the SunOS *mmap()* function to allocate a new shadow block onto which the updated page is mapped. The second is at commit time, when the updated page is written to the shadow block.

Experiment 5 - This experiment illustrates the effect of multi-programming on the store and highlights the cost of interleaving transactions. A range of concurrent transactions, from 1 to 100, are executed simultaneously. Every transaction performs a total of 40960 updates to the same 32 pages of the store. The degree of interleaving of the transactions is varied by adjusting the number of time slices per transaction. A time slice is the number of operations a transaction executes before context is switched to another transaction. Time slices per transaction vary from 1 (transactions are executed serially) to 10 (transactions are interleaved, with time slices of 4096 operations). Transactions commit at the end of their last time slice. This experiment, with more than one time slice per transaction, is a worst case example due the fact that all the pages are shared and shadowed by all transactions.

As Figure 9 illustrates, with a large number of transactions, there is a significant difference in execution time between serial and interleaved transactions. This is caused by two factors. The first is context switching. Due to the limited user control of the paging system in SunOS, the FLASK implementation requires all pages updated within a transaction's time slice to be written out to disk on a context

—switch. In a system with more flexible control over paging, these pages could be written back opportunistically [OS94], thus reducing context switch time.

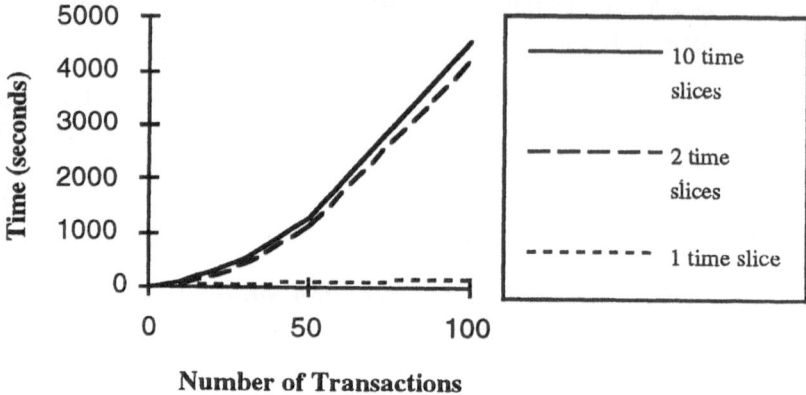

Figure 9: Worst case multi-programming

The second factor is the cost of installation reads and writes when propagating changes at commit time. In the current FLASK store, this involves reading from disk shadow pages onto which updates are being propagated. Once the changes have been made, the pages are written back to disk. Since all transactions shadow all the pages in this experiment, propagation adds a significant cost. Again, with greater control over the paging system, this cost could be reduced by keeping pages resident in memory and writing the pages opportunistically.

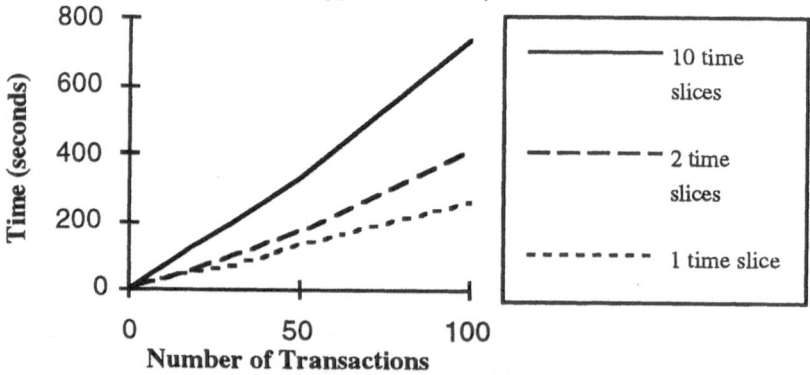

Figure 10: Less extreme multi-programming

Experiment 6 - This experiment illustrates the effects of multi-programming on the store using a less extreme transaction workload. The experiment is similar to Experiment 5 where transactions update 32 pages, performing 40960 updates. In this experiment, of the 32 pages updated, only one page is shared with one other transaction, while the other 31 pages are updated by that transaction alone. Context switching is varied as before.

This experiment reduces commit time, relative to Experiment 5, by having fewer pages shadowed by more than one transaction and therefore reduces the overall execution times. Execution times still increase from low to high interleaved transactions since context switch costs are still present.

9.1 Experiment Conclusions

The results illustrate that the cost of the xor propagation function in the FLASK model is relatively cheap compared to the other costs of transaction execution. With the present implementation, a large proportion of the execution time is spent performing IO in context switching and performing installation reads when propagating updates on commit. Therefore one method of increasing the performance of the FLASK store would be to reduce the amount of IO by keeping pages in memory, assuming that memory is large enough. This could be accomplished by building FLASK on an operating system which gives greater control over the paged memory system. With reduced IO for context switching and propagation, interleaved transaction execution times could be reduced and could be closer to the execution times of serial transactions.

The results also illustrate that the FLASK store performs better with high locality updates, since transactions performing multiple updates to the same pages do not produce more IO than transactions updating the pages once. FLASK is therefore well suited to persistent systems that perform a large number of updates which exhibit high temporal and spatial locality.

The major result of this experiment shows the effect of SunOS interference on the idealised FLASK model.

10 Acknowledgements

The authors wish to thank Chris Barter and Fred Brown for many helpful suggestions and comments on this work. The work was supported in part by SERC grant GR/G 17578 and ESPRIT III Basic Research Action 6309 - FIDE$_2$.

11 References

[ABB+86]   Acceta, M., Baron, R., Bolosky, W., Golub, D., Rashid, R., Tevanian, A. & Young, M. "Mach: A New Kernel Foundation for Unix Development". USENIX (1986) pp 93-112.

[AD85a]   Agrawal, R. & DeWitt, D. "Recovery Architectures for Multiprocessor Database Machines". In SIGMOD International Conference on Management of Data, (1985) pp 131-147.

[AD85b]   Agrawal, R. & DeWitt, D. "Integrated Concurrency Control and Recovery Mechanisms: Design and Performance Evaluation". ACM Transactions on Database Systems, 10,4 (1985) pp 529-564.

[BR91]   Brown, A.L. & Rosenberg, J. "Persistent Object Stores: An Implementation Technique". In Dearle, Shaw, Zdonik (eds.), Implementing Persistent Object Bases, Principles and Practice, Morgan Kaufmann, 1991 pp 199-212.

[CAB+81]   Chamberlin, D.D., Astrahan, M.M., Blasgen, M.W., Gray, J.N., King, W.F., Lindsay, B.G., Lorie, R.A., Mehl, J.W., Price, T.G., Selinger, P.G., Schkolnick, M., Slutz, D.R., Traiger, I.L., Wade, B.W. & Yost, R.A. "A History and Evaluation of System R". CACM 24,10 (1981) pp 632-646.

[Cha78]   Challis, M.P. "Data Consistency and Integrity in a Multi-User Environment". Databases: Improving Usability and Responsiveness, Academic Press, 1978.

[Dav73]   Davies, C.T. "Recovery semantics for a DB/DC System". In Proc. ACM Annual Conference, (1973) pp 136-141.

[Dav78]   Davies, C.T. "Data Processing Spheres of Control". IBM Systems Journal 17,2 (1978) pp 179-198.

[Deu90]   Deux, O. "The Story of O2". IEEE Transactions on data and knowledge engineering. March 1990.

[EG90]   Ellis, C.A. & Gibbs, S.J. "Concurrency Control in Groupware Systems". In Proc. SIGMOD International Conference on Management of Data. (1990) pp 399-407.

[EGL+76]   Eswaran, K.P., Gray, J.N., Lorie, R.A. & Traiger, I.L. "The Notions of Consistency and Predicate Locks in a Database System". CACM 19,11 (1976) pp 624-633.

[Gar83]   Garcia-Molina, H. "Using Semantic Knowledge for Transaction Processing in a Distributed Database". ACM Transactions on Database Systems, 8,2 (1983) pp 186-213.

[GMB+81]   Gray, J., McJones, P., Blasgen, M., Lindsay, B., Lorie, R., Price, T., Putzolu, F. & Traiger, I. "The Recovery Manager of the System R Database Manager". ACM Computing Surveys, vol. 13, no. 2, June 1981 pp 223-242.

[GMS87]   Gingell, R.A., Moran, J.P. & Shannon, W.A. "Virtual Memory Architecture in SunOS". USENIX Summer Conference Proceedings, Phoenix 1987.

[GS87]   Garcia-Molina, H. & Salem, K. "Sagas". In Proc. SIGMOD International Conference on Management of Data. (1987) pp 249-259.

[KGC85]   Kent, J., Garcia-Molina, H. & Chung, J. "An experimental evaluation of crash recovery mechanisms". In Proc. 4th ACM Symposium on Principles of Database Systems (1985) pp 113-122.

[Kol87]   Kolodner, E.K. "Recovery Using Virtual Memory". M.Sc. Thesis, MIT (1987).

[Kra87]   Krablin, G.L. "Building Flexible Multilevel Transactions in a Distributed Persistent Environment". 2nd International Workshop on Persistent Object Systems, Appin, (August 1987) pp 213-234.

[Lor77]   Lorie, A.L. Physical Integrity in a Large Segmented Database, ACM Transactions on Database Systems, 2,1 (1977) pp 91-104.

[Mos81]   Moss, J.E.B. "Nested Transactions: An Approach to Reliable Distributed Computing". Ph.D. Thesis, MIT (1981).

[Mun93]   Munro, D.S. "On the Integration of Concurrency, Distribution and Persistence". Ph.D. Thesis, University of St Andrews (1993).

[NZ92]   Nodine, M.H. & Zdonik, S. B. "Co-operative Transaction Hierarchies: Transaction Support for Design Applications". VLDB Journal 1,1 (1992) pp 41-80.

[OLS85]   Oki, B., Liskov, B. & Scheifler, R. "Reliable Object Storage to Support Atomic Actions". In Proc 10th Symposium on Operating Systems Principles, 1985 pp 147-159.

[OS94]   O'Toole, J. & Shrira, L. "Opportunistic Log: Efficient Installation Reads in a Reliable Object Server". Technical Report MIT/LCS-TM-506, March 1994. To appear in 1st International Symposium on Operating Systems Design and Implementation, Monterey, CA (1994).

[PS87]   "The PS-algol Reference Manual fourth edition". Technical Report PPRR-12 (1987), Universities of Glasgow and St Andrews.

[Ree78]   Reed, D.P. "Naming and Synchronisation in a Decentralised Computer". Ph.D. Thesis, M.I.T. (1978).

[SM92]   Stemple, D. & Morrison, R. "Specifying Flexible Concurrency Control Schemes: An Abstract Operational Approach". Australian Computer Science Conference 15, Tasmania (1992) pp 873-891.

[Sto86]   Stonebraker, M. (Editor) "The Ingres Papers". Addison-Wesley, Reading, MA (1986).

[Sut91]   Sutton, S. "A Flexible Consistency Model for Persistent Data in Software-Process Programming". In Dearle, Shaw, Zdonik (eds.), Implementing Persistent Object Bases, Principles and Practice, Morgan Kaufmann, 1991 pp 305-319.

[VDD+91]   Velez, F., Darnis, V., DeWitt, D., Futtersack, P., Harrus, G., Maier, D., and Raoux, M. "Implementing the O_2 object manager: some lessons". In Dearle, Shaw, Zdonik (eds.), Implementing Persistent Object Bases, Principles and Practice, Morgan Kaufmann, 1991 pp 131-138.

Object Store Engineering 2

Véronique Benzaken

Universite de Paris I, Paris, France

Three papers were presented during this session.

The first paper describes a database buffer-management scheme which is adapted to the management of long (multi-page) externally defined objects.

Externally defined object types (maps, spatial data, etc.) are usually imported in the database system together with their corresponding (manipulation) operations in order to address a domain-specific application.

A weakness of traditional database buffer managers resides in the fact that the page-based nature of buffering, prevents the externally defined operations to operate over long objects.

The paper presents a buffering policy based on memory mapping which reconstructs uniform address ability within client address space. This method has the advantage of conserving traditional database systems buffering policies while extending them to large objects. A first implementation is then described.

The second paper presents the Grasshopper protection mechanism. As persistent systems provide single storage abstraction in which the data may manipulated in a uniform manner, a protection mechanism is needed is order to guarantee that programs will not access objects they were not intended to.

The mechanism proposed is capability-based and treats in a uniform way both data and operating system functions. The main advantages of such a mechanism are the following: the mapping from relevant names to capabilities is managed outside the kernel allowing thus for the construction of arbitrary naming schemes; the creator of an entity as full control over the level of access provided to other users; restricted views of entities may be constructed; the need for garbage-collector across the entire store is avoided. This mechanism is implemented in a prototype version of Grasshopper.

The last paper presented a pointer swizzling method based on reservation and redundancy checking upon discovery in the P3L language. It differs from other approaches in the sense that LIDs (local identifiers) are assigned when a pointer is discovered rather than when a dereferencing occurs. After a survey of similar techniques, the paper details a performance analysis of the method. Although the method does not rely on hardware support adding reservation checks doesn't affect the efficiency. Indeed, navigation performance is maintained by reducing the frequency of such checks. In some test cases, the method outperforms an hardware based scheme. It is also shown that for pure in-memory navigation the method runs significantly better than other techniques.

Buffering Long Externally-Defined Objects

Stephen Blott
Helmut Kaufmann
Lukas Relly
Hans-Jörg Schek
Institute for Information Systems – Database Systems
ETH-Zentrum, 8092-Zurich, Switzerland
{blott,kaufmann,relly,schek}@inf.ethz.ch

Abstract

This paper describes a database buffer-management scheme which is adapted to the management of long, externally-defined objects. Multipage objects are fragmented by traditional buffer managers, and such fragmentation must be accommodated by higher-level software. However, externally-defined operations, which may be used to embed application-area specific object semantics within database systems, cannot accommodate such fragmentation. This paper describes a buffer manager combining traditional database techniques with a memory-mapping scheme which reconstructs uniform addressability within client address spaces.

This work is being pursued within our CONCERT prototype development effort. We describe our implementation considerations and report on our initial evaluation.

1 Introduction

This paper addresses a weakness of traditional database buffer managers which arises when existing, externally-defined types are embedded within database systems. Such types, and their corresponding externally-defined operations, may be used to embed application-area specific object semantics within database systems. However, the page-based nature of traditional database buffers prohibits the use of such operations over long (multi-page) objects. This introductory section first sketches the role a database buffer as a whole, and then discusses the problem of such a buffer with respect to externally-defined operations over long objects.

1.1 Database System Buffers

Traditional database-system buffers provide shared main-memory access to persistent data, and coordinate the migration of that data between main memory and disk with respect to the requirements of transaction and recovery management. Both these aspects are critical to performance. Such buffers are typically implemented in shared memory, consist of a fixed number of buffer frames, and these frames are all of some fixed size. We assume a recovery scheme based on the Write-Ahead Log principle throughout [14].

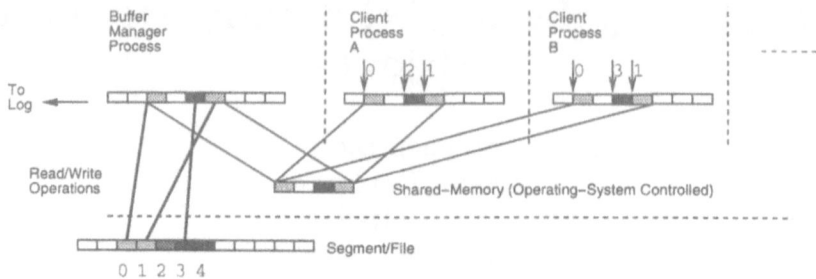

Figure 1: A Traditional Shared Database Buffer

An example of a traditional database buffer is shown in Figure 1. If client[1] A requires read-access to pages 0 and 1, and write-access to page 3, then those pages are read into the buffer (*fixed*), and pointers to the appropriate buffer frames in shared memory are returned. Subsequently, if client B also requests read-access to pages 0 and 1, then it too receives pointers to the buffer frames in shared memory in which those pages are already loaded. In particular, no further disk activity or copying need occur.

Assuming a page-based, two-phase locking scheme, if client B now also requests page 3, then it must wait until client A's transaction commits. When this happens, appropriate log records are generated and then written in a single, sequential disk operation. Client B may now be granted the lock on page 3, and no copying or further disk activity is required.

As fixes are relinquished, the buffer manager may autonomously (and asynchronously) write *dirty* and/or *updated* pages back into the database. However, it must do so in a manner which maintains the invariants required by the recovery manager. For dirty pages, undo-records must be generated and logged prior to writing the page itself. However, for updated pages no logging is required since persistency is guaranteed by the transaction manager at commit time.

In a scheme such as this, the database buffer is providing addressability of persistent objects, but it is also playing a central role with respect to correctness and performance. In particular, it is important that—to the greatest possible extent—synchronous disk activity, random-access disk activity, memory copying and data duplication are avoided.

1.2 Externally-Defined Objects

Outwith the context of database systems, there are many application areas in which highly-specialised techniques for the representation and processing of advanced classes of data have been developed: for example, spatial data, maps, images, continuous streams, time series, documents and scientific data. Such objects are frequently long—spanning many pages—and their representations and processing characteristics are tightly bound to one-another. Specialised

---

[1]Except where indicated otherwise, we use the term *client* to denote a process or thread running against the database (server); not in its client-server network sense.

representations are required to make certain classes of processing feasible, while efficient processing techniques are developed to accommodate limitations in reasonable object representations.

Our aim is to support the incorporation of such externally-defined objects within database systems.

One technique for this is based on Externally-Defined Types—or EDTs— and makes extensive use of externally-defined operations [25, 22, 31, 19, 12, 4]. We make the following assumptions about the characteristics of such operations:

- They operate in virtual memory against contiguous objects of some known or computable length, and such objects are identified by virtual-memory pointers to their first bytes.

- All subsequent navigation within objects is achieved through off-sets with respect to those starting addresses.

We assume that if objects ever change their sizes, then such occurs at their ends.

Returning to the buffer manager described above, a problem arises with respect to such externally-defined operations over long (multi-page) objects. For example, assume pages 0 and 1 contain a two-page object. While these pages are contiguous on segment, they are placed arbitrarily within the buffer. Any operation applying to such a two-page object must accommodate this fragmentation. Since this is counter to our assumptions about externally-defined operations, it prohibits their application against objects directly in the buffer.

This paper describes a buffer management scheme which overcomes this difficulty, while retaining the benefits of a traditional database buffer. Our solution is based on memory mapping, and is therefore closely related to the way the operating system interfaces to the MMU in supporting virtual memory.

1.3   From Object Buffers to the Database Buffer

In our earlier DASDBS System we also addressed the needs of advanced application areas [23]. A central aspect of the DASDBS approach is the management of page-sets, as opposed to single pages, and hence also the exploitation of set-oriented I/O [27]. DASDBS does not address the problem of uniform addressability, but manages instead two buffers: a traditional, shared, page-based buffer, and object buffers private to client address spaces. Entire complex objects in their disk-oriented representation are fixed in the page-based buffer, and only those parts required are then copied (and translated) into clients' object buffers. Since only the object translation routines operate on the page-based buffer, only they need accommodate fragmentation within that buffer. On evaluation, both the copying and translation proved to be expensive operations [23]. Similar solutions have been adopted by other systems such as Orion [15] and AIM [11].

In the current work we radically depart from this dual-buffered approach with a "hard-wired" storage-model; we envisage externally-defined objects of unknown structure to be operated upon directly in the buffer. As a consequence, we must accommodate externally-defined operations leading to the basic requirement of providing uniform addressability over long objects.

Document Structure

The remainder of this document is structured as follows: the following section surveys a number of existing approaches to related problems; Section 3 sketches our solution which is based on memory mapping; Section 4 discusses the details and pragmatics of our implementation; and Section 5 concludes.

2 Existing Solutions

The problem of uniform addressability arises in a number of contexts, and this section surveys several existing solutions.

Variable-Size Allocation. One solution is to assign contiguous buffer frames for long objects. However, long-lived, variable-size allocators are prone to fragmentation, even when based on variable-sized objects drawn from some "well-behaved" set of admissible sizes; for example, the Buddy System [16].

The Exodus Solution. For long objects, Exodus adopts a scheme which is tightly integrated to its shadow-based recovery strategy and its support for versions [9]. Exodus manages two buffers: a *page buffer* and a *chunk buffer*. When a part of a long object is requested, the necessary pages are retrieved into the page buffer, a chunk of the appropriate size is allocated in the chunk buffer, and the requested object parts are copied from the page buffer into that chunk. There are a number of disadvantages to this scheme: firstly, it requires two buffers and copying of data between these buffers, and secondly it results in fragmentation since chunks are variable-sized objects.

However, there is also a further difficulty. Under the Exodus scheme, overlapping parts of the same object may be copied into two or more separate chunks. This presents a problem when such object parts are to be updated. Exodus requires that all bar one of such chunks must first be relinquished before updates may take place.

Indirection. A further alternative is to avoid direct access to buffer frames, but rather pass all such accesses through some level of indirection. Typically *buffer handles*, rather than direct references to buffer frames themselves, are returned to clients. Lost contiguity of logical sequences of persistent pages can be masked by such a level of indirection. This is the approach adopted by the EOS storage manager [3] for long objects. However, this solution does not meet our requirement that long objects be uniformly addressable in virtual memory.

Indirection is also used within the main-memory heap of the Napier Store described in [8]. In that context, an indirection table allows fragmented and inaccessible space to be garbage collected. However, the garbage-collection algorithm described requires the quiescence of higher-level operation while it proceeds, and the explicit use of the indirection table on all accesses.

Single-level Stores. An approach of some history—pioneered by Multics [2] in the late sixties—which has gained popularity in recent years is that of a single-level store. Recent examples of such systems include ObjectStore [17], the Napier Store [7, 8], QuickStore [30], Bubba [5, 10] and Cricket [24].

QuickStore and ObjectStore exploit memory mapping to achieve a single-level store. However, both approaches are founded on the client-server paradigm where pages are shipped (copied) from a server to client sites (or private processes). Updated pages must first be shipped back to the server before they can be made available to other clients. That is, there is no shared buffer in the sense described in Section 1.1. Further, the pointer-swizzling schemes these systems adopt are similar to that described by Wilson [32]. Under this approach pointers are swizzled (updated) on the basis of local client-process tables, and therefore require that all threads/processes sharing the data in real memory operate within the same address space.

Cricket [24] and Bubba [5, 10] have more in common with the currently-proposed approach in that both are based on memory mapping to provide shared access. However, these systems map entire database areas into the virtual address space uniformly; they are therefore limited to databases which fit entirely into the available virtual address space. The problems of pointer-swizzling discussed above are overcome by having a fixed-binding of persistent to virtual address spaces. Both these systems differ also in that they exploit page-faulting techniques *exclusively* for implicitly obtaining locks and fixing data-pages. This is identified as a weakness in [5].

Cricket differs from the current approach in that it leaves all paging decisions to the MACH kernel [1]; this assumption then affects appropriate logging and recovery strategies (which are discussed but not determined in [24]). Bubba's recovery scheme is based on copy-on-write.

3   A Memory-Mapped Buffer

Most modern operating systems provide programmable interfaces to their virtual memory system. In Unix[2] this is referred to as *memory mapping*, and in MACH as *external pagers*. As for a number of the systems above, our solution exploits *memory mapping* these operating system features. Memory mapping allows pages of a file to be mapped into processes' virtual address spaces; thereby establishing addressability of the file's contents. If two or more processes on the same (shared-memory) machine map the same file pages, then the real-memory pages backing those mapped virtual addresses are shared. Thus, updates by one process become immediately visible to all other processes. Memory mapping is frequently the basis of operating systems' shared-memory mechanisms, and hence also the basis of traditional buffer managers.

While the shared-memory buffer described in Section 1.1 is based on an operating-system–assigned area of swap-space, we make this auxiliary file space explicit. This we term the *buffer-backing file*. In a traditional buffer, as illustrated in Figure 1, the whole buffer is shared between processes statically through shared memory. In our approach, as illustrated in Figure 2, only individual pages of the buffer are shared through memory mappings established dynamically. Our approach is therefore based on exploiting memory mapping at a finer granularity of sharing than described previously. Because the buffer-backing file is explicit, we are able to map individual buffer pages to relative positions in client address spaces, thereby achieving uniform addressability.

As in a traditional buffer, the basic operations are `bufferfix` to establish addressability, `bufferunfix` to relinquish addressability, and `emptyfix` to establish addressability to a newly-allocated area of persistent storage [14]. However, in the current context, these operations are extended to apply to *page ranges* rather than to only individual pages. For example, the call:

---

[2]Unix is a trademark of AT&T Bell.

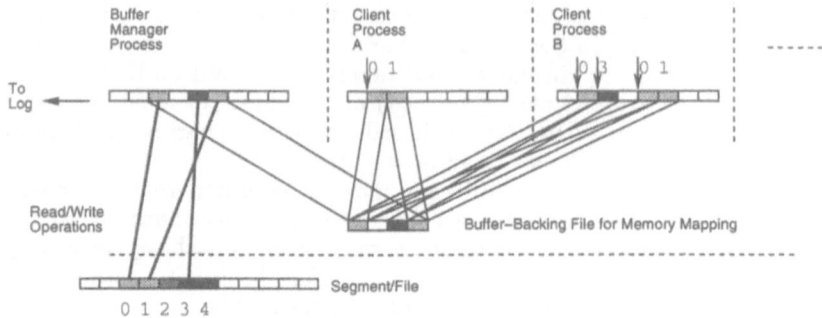

Figure 2: A Memory-Mapped Buffer

bufferfix(start-page, length)
requests addressability of the pages from **start-page** continuing for **length** pages.[3] We assume that access rights are granted by the transaction manager at a higher level.

Consider, for example, the situation illustrated in Figure 2; as previously, pages 0 and 1 contain a long object. Client A knows that the object is two-pages long and that it requires access to the whole object. It therefore requests:
bufferfix(0,2)
to establish addressability. If these pages are not already present, then they are loaded into the buffer and assigned arbitrary buffer frames, as previously. However, those frames are then memory mapped (through the auxiliary buffer-backing file) into the virtual address space of client A such that uniform addressability is reconstructed. Client A may now operate against pages 0 and 1 as if they are entirely and contiguously resident in its own address space. Our requirements for externally-defined objects are therefore achieved.

Client B, on the other hand, may not yet know whether access to the entire object is required, and may choose to access only the header page initially. In either case, however, we assume that client B chooses not to reserve address space for the entire object, and that addressability of page 3 has been established directly beside that of page 0. Therefore, when client B requests access to the entire object, a new mapping for the entire two-page object must be established elsewhere in its address space (to the right, in Figure 2).

Notice that, since the real memory backing mapped files is shared, updates through either of client B's mappings of page 0, or through client A's mapping, are immediately visible through each of the other mappings. This is the same property as that exhibited by the shared-memory buffer, and no copying or invalidation need occur. In fact, the considerations of concurrency control, logging and recovery in the memory-mapped scheme are exactly as they are in the case of the traditional buffer of Section 1.1.

---

[3]Additional parameters are required to flag the intended access class (read/write) and such variants.

4 Implementational Pragmatics

Storage-management within our CONCERT prototype is based on a uniform concrete (internally-defined) and abstract (externally-defined) type model [4]. Support for *abstract types* is central to the approach, as is, therefore, support for externally-defined operations through the buffer management scheme described previously. Our CONCERT implementation is influenced not only by the principles of the technique described above, but also by the need to optimise that basic technique, and by the pragmatics of the environment in which our prototype must operate.

4.1 A Write-Ahead Log

Most approaches to logging and recovery are based either on a Write-Ahead Log (WAL) [14] or on Shadow Paging [13]. For performance in large, high-concurrency systems, the WAL approach is to be preferred—System R [13] and POSTGRES [26] both identify their shadow-based techniques as weaknesses. The main reasons for this are the following. Firstly, the cost of maintaining the meta information necessary to identify current versions of pages on secondary storage is high. For large databases, this information cannot reside in real memory. This impacts random-access processing most strongly. Secondly, logically-contiguous pages may not be physically-contiguous on secondary storage; therefore additional seeks are required when retrieving contiguous pages. This impacts sequential processing most strongly, and hence also long-object processing. And thirdly, the amount of I/O necessary for check-pointing is high, while that for commit processing is not reduced. The major advantage of shadow paging is simplified and efficient recovery processing.

In CONCERT we aim to achieve high performance, and exploit sequential I/O for long objects. Because of the deficiencies of shadow-based approaches in these respects, we choose a WAL-based logging and recovery strategy.

4.2 Database-System Paging

We begin from the premise that: *all paging is explicitly controlled by the database system, and the buffer is always entirely resident in real memory.* The advantage of this assumption is that the database system controls all disk activity, and knows exactly that which is generated by database system paging and logging.

However, this assumption is too restrictive. Under it, we would be limited to objects which fit entirely into the real-memory buffer. *Very-long objects*—those larger than the real-memory buffer—would have to be accessed a-part-at-a-time, which is contrary to our assumptions about externally-defined operations.

We distinguish, therefore, between *addressability* and *buffer residency*. The bufferfix operation always establishes addressability. However, that addressability may be either *static* or *paged*. *Statically-fixed objects* are always resident in the real-memory buffer. *Paged-fixed objects* are addressable, but their pages may be paged out (back into the database) if insufficient space is available to satisfy other requests. The implementation of our paged approach is based on standard virtual-memory faulting techniques—as described in, say, [30].

4.3   A Hybrid Memory-Mapped Buffer

4.3.1   Single-Page Requests

While the focus of this work is on long objects, many of the objects we manage—
such as the nodes of a B-tree—remain oriented towards single pages. Therefore,
single-page operations must remain efficient. For this reason, we map the entire
buffer-backing file statically into each client's address space. This allows single-
page requests to be processed with no additional system-call overheads. We
assume that single-page requests are never paged (in the sense described above).

4.3.2   Operating-System Paging

There can be advantages to letting the operating system perform some limited
amount of paging of the database buffer [6, 18]. Under the memory-mapped
approach, this would imply allowing the operating system to page buffer frames
onto the buffer-backing file. For read-only data, such results in pages of the
database being effectively copied onto the buffer-backing file, and such copying
is clearly redundant.

   However, there is an alternative which we exploit in our CONCERT implementation. For multi-page read-only accesses, pages may be shared through
mappings directly into the database rather than via the buffer-backing file.
This has the advantage that corresponding memory pages are always clean
(from the point of view of the operating system), and therefore no disk-write
operation is generated by operating-system paging. Further, addressability for
such accesses can be established with a single memory-mapping system call.
We also use this directly-mapped approach for emptyfix-ed pages.

   Our implementation, therefore, is based on a hybrid approach combining
directly-mapped frames for multi-page read-only accesses, and *buffer-mapped*
frames for multi-page write-able accesses. For the read-only case, the hybrid
solution is illustrated in Figure 3 top. Pages 0 and 1 are read-only and so are
mapped directly from the segment. Figure 3 bottom illustrates the write-able
case. Pages 0 and 1 are allocated in the statically-mapped buffer, but are then
mapped to contiguous pages elsewhere to achieve uniform addressability.

   This hybrid solution, however, presents a problem when the lock for a page
is upgraded from read to write. Assuming a page is directly-mapped for read-
only access at address addr. Then the algorithm for re-buffering when a lock
is upgraded is as follows:

1. Obtain an unused buffer frame f.

2. Memory copy from addr to frame f.

3. Establish addressability of f at addr through an mmap system call.

Step 3 must be performed for every address at which the page is addressable
in the upgrading client's address space. Per-client tables are maintained to
simplify this procedure. In practise this operation is based on page ranges
rather than individual pages.

   We considered also using direct mappings for the sharing of write-able pages.
However, there would be a difficulty with such an approach. In particular, to
maintain the total number of dirty real-memory pages below some threshold,

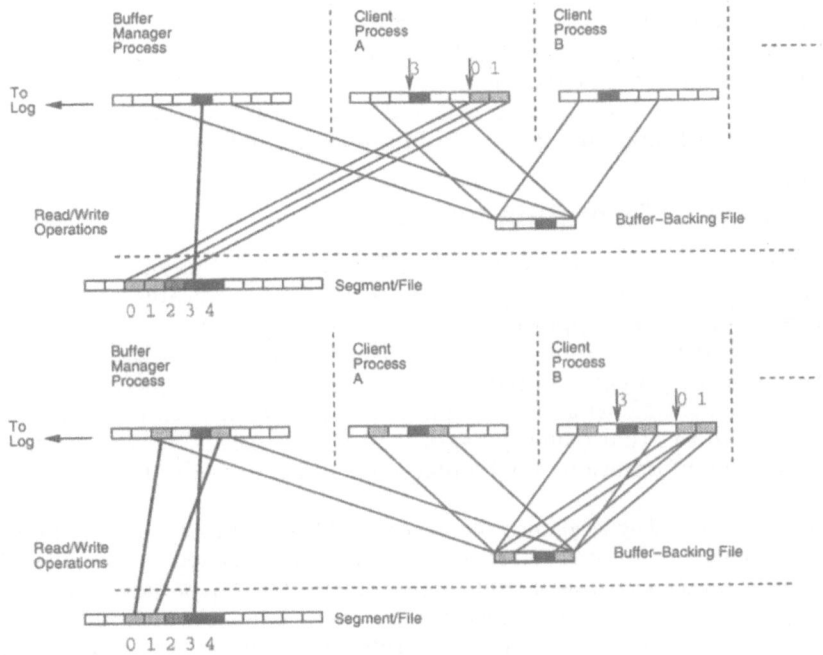

Figure 3: The CONCERT Hybrid Memory-Mapped Buffer

operating systems such as Unix may write dirty pages back into the database. Since this occurs without the knowledge of the buffer manager, the integrity of the database could be compromised. A pessimistic approach to logging (very early logging of whole-page undo information), or a shadow-based recovery scheme, would therefore be required. For this reason we chose not to use direct mappings for update-able pages.[4]

Further, precise control of real-memory residency is important for the efficiency of both database paging of, and logging of, dirty or updated pages.

4.3.3 System-Call Costs

Based on the optimised scheme above, we can calculate the maximum number of system calls required in various cases. For single-page requests no additional system calls are required, and the memory-mapped approach behaves exactly as a traditional database buffer. Overhead occurs only for multi-page accesses.

For multi-page read-access **bufferfix**-es, the total number of system calls depends on whether any of the pages are currently write-accessed. In particular, one **mmap** is required for each sub-range for which no write-mapping exists, and one for each currently write-accessed page. We anticipate that the most

---

[4]Our scheme could be implemented more elegantly under micro-kernels such as MACH [1], however we prefer CONCERT to run under standard Unix.

common case is that this amounts to only a single `mmap`. For multi-page write-access `bufferfix`-es, an `mmap` call is required for each page. For multi-page `emptyfix`-es, always exactly one `mmap` call is required.

For lock upgrades, an `mmap` call and a memory copy is required for each mapping of each upgraded page within the upgrading client's address space.

4.4   Meta-Information on Data Pages

We have stated above that our approach retains the characteristics of a traditional database buffer, and therefore techniques applicable to such remain applicable. However, appropriate techniques for logging and recovery are in fact influenced by our application-area assumptions, even if not by the particular solution we propose. In particular, we assume that long objects in virtual memory are contiguous and uniform. If a simple relationship between persistent pages and virtual-memory pages is to be retained, then this implies that no additional information may be placed on pages to facilitate the functioning of the database.

In particular, *Log Sequence Numbers* (or LSNs) cannot be placed on pages to help identify temporal versions during recovery. Based on the theory and practise of multi-level transaction management [29, 28], we are in the process of designing a concurrency-control and recovery scheme which retains the advantages of (in particular) logical undo recovery, while not requiring additional meta-data on pages.

4.5   Transaction Management

4.5.1   Light-weight Commit

CONCERT aims to achieve improved performance of higher-level operations through increased concurrency between their corresponding lower-level operations. That is, the exploitation of multi-level transactions [29]. Hence many lower-level transactions are generated whose individual persistency is of no concern, but whose collective persistency, atomicity and isolation is managed by a higher-level transaction manager. In particular, the updates of committed sub-transactions need only persist if their corresponding higher-level transaction commits [28].

At the lower-levels described in this paper, therefore, we are implementing a *light-weight commit* for which log records are generated and locks released, but no disk activity need occur. The writing of such log records is then effectively piggy-backed on the next log flush which is generated by other database activity.

Higher-level transaction managers maintain logs and perform recovery much in a similar fashion to those maintained at a lower level. There is, however, a temporal relationship (the WAL rule) between higher- and lower-level logs, and this relationship is important for correctness. This relationship is retained by allowing higher-level software to place records directly on the lower-level log. These are then guaranteed to "hit-the-disk" in such a way as to satisfy the WAL rules.

Such a light-weight commit mechanism also promises to be a useful primitive supporting efficient strategies for index-structure updates [21, 20], and other tasks for which standard two-phase locking is inadequate.

Concurrent Activities	1	10	Comments
`direct`	0.425	1.775	No uniform addressability
`copy-out-and-back-in`	1.1	8.5	Heavy on real memory
`copy-out`	0.9	6.374	Heavy on real memory
`concert`	0.75	4.88	
`concert-read`	0.425	1.75	
`unix-fs`	1.575	20.25	Heavy on real memory
`unix-mmap`	0.4	1.55	Implies costly recovery

Figure 4: A Preliminary Comparison with Other Approaches

4.5.2 Long Fixes

Real memory is a critical resource in traditional database systems. To give the buffer manager as much flexibility in managing that resource as possible, page-fixes are kept as short as possible. The `bufferfix` operation, therefore, must be as efficient as possible.

In CONCERT we have three reasons for relaxing this mode of operation: firstly, due to additional system calls the `bufferfix` operation over page-ranges is inherently more expensive; secondly, with increased real-memory sizes memory is less of a critical resource; and thirdly, the exploitation of multi-level transactions generates many lower-level transactions which operate upon the same data. We therefore allow clients to retain fixes over transaction boundaries. Such buffered data may only be accessed, however, when the appropriate locks have been re-obtained.

4.6 Practicability and Performance

We have implemented the buffer manager described above and have performed a number of preliminary experiments to "get a feel" for the costs and benefits of our approach. In order to understand our measurements, we implemented and compared a number of the simpler schemes for achieving uniform addressability. These were: through `copy-out` from the page-based buffer into clients' virtual memories, `copy-out-and-back-in` which is the same as the case above except that it accounts for updates, `concert` which is the approach described above, `concert-read` which is the CONCERT read-only approach described above, `unix-fs` which uses the Unix file-system buffer to provide sharing, and `unix-mmap` which exploits Unix memory mapping directly. Finally, for comparison we also measured the cost of applying operations directly in the buffer `direct`, an approach for which uniform addressability is *not* achieved.

The basic experiment was to apply an operation to a long object, and vary the number of concurrent threads and the size of the object. All experiments were performed against a warm buffer. Figure 4 contains a summary of two of the cases we measured, which are representative also of the others. All numbers are elapsed time in seconds, system and user times were also measured, though these provided little additional insight. The object size was 500 pages, and the machine (a SUN SPARCstation 10) had 96MB real memory.

56

The most important observations from these measurements are the following. Comparing `direct` against `concert` we see that the overhead of uniform addressability is approximately a factor of two or three. However, compared with all other approaches the CONCERT scheme performed well. With respect to `unix-mmap`, recall that that scheme would imply an approach to recovery which we find unacceptable. Comparing `unix-mmap` to `concert-read` we see that the overhead of our approach in the read-only case is in the region of around 10 percent. That is, this is the overhead of checking in the buffer before establishing the direct mapping. A final observation is that all the approaches involving copying data to clients' virtual memory (including `unix-fs`) degraded badly once the available real memory became scarce and swapping costs had to be incurred.

We should be careful to point out, however, that such "elapsed time" measurements provide us with little information as to relative resource consumption of the approaches. We are still working on a more detailed comparison of the approaches.

5 Summary

We have identified, within traditional systems, support for uniform addressability of long objects as a hindrance to the admission of externally-defined objects and their operations. We have described a buffer management scheme—based on memory mapping of individual buffer frames—which overcomes these inadequacies. Our approach has the advantage of maintaining the principle characteristics of a traditional database system's buffer, while extending such a buffer's functionality with respect to long objects. We achieve a solution which admits the direct application of externally-defined operations against the database buffer.

We then described our motivations in adopting a particular implementation strategy within our CONCERT prototype. While some of our argumentation is rather more pragmatic than fundamental, we achieve a scheme which incurs no overhead for traditional single-page operations, and incurs limited overhead for long objects.

Our initial implementation is operational (without transaction management), and this provides us both with an experimental platform for evaluation, and with an environment in which optimisations of our approach can be prototyped.

Acknowledgements

The following people have taken part in discussions concerning this work, and their contribution is gratefully acknowledged: Moira Norrie, Michael Rys, Gerhard Weikum and Andreas Wolf. We also acknowledge the help of Adriano Gabaglio for his development of our initial prototype system.

References

[1] M. Accetta, R. Baron, W. Bolosky, D. Golub, R. Rashid, A. Tevanian, and M. Young. Mach: A New Kernel Foundation for Unix. In *Proceedings of the Summer USENIX Conference*, 1986.

[2] A. Bensoussan, C. T. Clingen, and R. C. Daley. The Multics Virtual Memory. In *Proceedings of the Second Symposium on Operating Systems*, Princeton University, October 1969. ACM, New York.

[3] Alexandros Biliris and Euthimios Panagos. EOS User's Guide (Release 2.0.1). Technical Report BLO11356-930505-25TM, AT&T Bell Laboratories, 600 Mountain Avenue, Murray Hill, NJ, May 1993.

[4] Stephen Blott, Lukas Relly, and Hans-Jörg Schek. An Abstract-Object Storage Manager. Technical Report DBTN-94-5, Fachgruppe Datenbanken, Institut für Informationssysteme, ETH-Zentrum, 8092-Zürich, Switzerland, 1994.

[5] Boral, W. Alexander, L. Clay, G. Copelend, S. Danforth, M. Franklin, B. Hart, M. Smith, and P. Valduriez. Prototyping Bubba, A Highly Parallel Database System. *IEEE Transactions on Knowledge and Data Engineering*, 2(1):4–24, March 1990.

[6] Richard S. Brice and Stephen W. Sherman. An Extension of the Performance of a Database System in a Virtual Memory System Using Partially Locked Virtual Buffers. *ACM Transactions on Database Systems*, 2(2):196–207, June 1977.

[7] A. L. Brown and J. Rosenberg. Persistent Object Stores: An Implementation Technique. Technical Report CS/90/15, Division of Computer Science, Department of Mathematical and Computational Sciences, University of St. Andrews, North Haugh, St. Andrews, KY16 9SS, Scotland, 1990.

[8] Alfred Leonard Brown. *Persistent Object Stores*. Ph.d. thesis, Department of Computational Science, University of St. Andrews, North Haugh, St. Andrews, Scotland KY16 9SS, October 1989.

[9] Michael J. Carey, David J. DeWitt, Joel E. Richardson, and Eugene J. Shekita. Object and File Management in the Exodus Exstensible Database System. In *Proceedings of the 12th International Conference on Very Large Database Systems*, 1986.

[10] George Copeland, Michael Franklin, and Gerhard Weikum. Uniform Object Management. In *Proceedings of the International Conference on Extending Database Technology*, Venice, March 1990.

[11] P. Dadam, K. Kuspert, F. Anderson, H. Blankel, R. Erbe, J. Guenauer, V. Lum, P. Pistor, and G. Walch. A DBMS Prototype to Support Extended NF^2 Relations: An Integrated View on Flat Tables and Hierarchies. In *Procs. of the ACM SIGMOD Intl. Conf. on Management of Data*, pages 356–367, 1986.

[12] Gisbert Dröge, Hans-Jörg Schek, and Andreas Wolf. Erweiterbarkeit in DASDBS. *Informatik Forschung und Entwicklung*, 5:162–176, 1990 (in German).

[13] Jim Gray, Paul McJones, Mike Blasgen, Bruce Lindsay, Raymond Lorie, Tom Price, Franco Putzolu, and Irving Traiger. The Recovery Manager of the System R Database Manager. *ACM Computing Surveys*, 13(2):223–242, June 1981.

[14] Jim Gray and Andreas Reuter. *Transaction Processing: Concepts and Techniques*. Morgan Kaufmann Publishers, Inc., 1993.

58

[15] W. Kim, J.F. Garza, N. Ballou, and D. Woelk. Architecture of the ORION Next-Generation Database System. *IEEE Transactions on Knowledge and Data Engeneering*, 22(1):109–124, March 1990.

[16] Philip D. L. Koch. Disk File Allocation based on the Buddy System. *ACM Transactions on Computer Systems*, 5(4):352–370, November 1987.

[17] Charles Lamb, Gordon Lamdis, Jack Orenstein, and Dan Weinreb. The Object-Store Database System. *Communications of the ACM*, 34(10):50–63, October 1991.

[18] Tomas Lang, Christophen Wood, and Ieduardo B. Fernandez. Database Buffer Paging in Virtual Storage Systems. *ACM Transactions on Database Systems*, 2(4):339–351, December 1977.

[19] V. Linnemann, K. Küspert, P. Dadam, P. Pistor, R. Erbe, A. Kemper, N. Südkamp, G. Walch, and M. Wallrath. Design and Implementation of an Extensible Database Management System Supporting User-Defined Data Types and Functions. In *Proceedings of the 14th International Conference on Very-Large Databases*, pages 294–305, Los Angeles, California, USA, 1988.

[20] David Lomet. MLR: A Recovery Method for Multi-level Systems. In *Proceedings of the 1992 ACM SIGMOD Conference*, pages 183–194, 1992.

[21] David Lomet and Betty Salzberg. Access Method Concurrency with Recovery. In *Proceedings of the 1992 ACM SIGMOD Conference*, pages 351–360, 1992.

[22] Sylvia L. Osborn and T. E. Heaven. The Design of a Relational Database System with Abstract Types for Domains. *ACM Transactions on Database Systems*, 11(3):357–373, September 1986.

[23] Hans-Jörg Schek, Heinz-Bernhard Paul, Marc H. Scholl, and Gerhard Weikum. The DASDBS Project: Objectives, Experiences, and Future Prospects. *IEEE Transactions on Knowledge and Data Engineering*, 2(1):25–43, March 1990.

[24] Eugene Shekita and Michael Zwilling. Cricket: A Mapped, Persistent Object Store. In *Proceedings of the 4th International workshop on Persistent Object System Design, Implementation and Use*, Computer Science Department, University of Wisconsin, Madison, WI 53706., 1990.

[25] Michael Stonebraker. Inclusion of new types in relational database systems. In *Proceedings of the International Conference on Data Engineering*, Los Angeles, CA, February 1986.

[26] Michael Stonebreaker, Lawrance A. Rowe, and Michael Hirohama. The Implementation of POSTGRES. *IEEE Transactions on Knowledge and Data Engineering*, 2(1):125–142, March 1990.

[27] Gerhard Weikum. Set-oriented Access to Large Complex Objects. In *Proceedings of the 5th International Conference on Data Engineering*, pages 426–433, Los Angeles, February 1989.

[28] Gerhard Weikum and Christof Hasse. Multi-Level Transaction Management for Complex Objects: Implementation, Performance, Parallelism. *The VLDB Journal*, 2(4), 1993.

[29] Gerhard Weikum and Hans-J. Schek. Concepts and Applications of Multilevel Transactions and Open Nested Transactions. In *Database Transaction Models*, chapter 13. Morgan Kaufmann, 1992.

[30] Seth J. White and David J. DeWitt. QuickStore: A High-Performance Mapped Object Store. In *Proceedings of the ACM SIGMOD International Conference on Management of Data*, Minneapolis, Minnesota, USA, 1994.

[31] P.F. Wilms, P.M. Schwarz, H.-J. Schek, and L.M. Haas. Incorporating Data Types in an Extensible Database Architecture. In *Proceedings of the 3rd International Conference on Data and Knowledge Bases*, Jerusalem, June 1988.

[32] Paul R. Wilson. Pointer-Swizzling at Page-Fault Time: Efficiently Supporting Huge Address Spaces on Standard Hardware. *SIGARCH Computer Architecture News*, 19(4):6–13, 1991.

Protection in Grasshopper: A Persistent Operating System

[†]Alan Dearle, [*]Rex di Bona, [*]James Farrow, [*]Frans Henskens,
[†]David Hulse, [*]Anders Lindström, [*]Stephen Norris,
[*]John Rosenberg and [†]Francis Vaughan

[*]Department of Computer Science	[†]Department of Computer Science
University of Sydney	University of Adelaide
N.S.W., 2006, Australia	S.A., 5001, Australia
{rex,matty,frans,anders,srn,johnr}	(al,dave,francis}
@cs.su.oz.au	@cs.adelaide.edu.au

Abstract

Persistent systems support a single storage abstraction in which all data may be created and manipulated in a uniform manner, regardless of its longevity. In such systems a protection mechanism is required to ensure that programs can access precisely those objects they are supposed to access and no others. In a monolingual system this protection can be provided by the type system of the programming language; in systems which support multiple persistent languages a separate protection mechanism must be supported. This paper describes the capability-based protection mechanism employed in Grasshopper, a new operating system specifically designed to support persistent systems on a conventional workstation platform. We show that this mechanism provides sufficient power and flexibility to handle a wide variety of protection scenarios.

1. Introduction

In this paper we describe the protection mechanism in Grasshopper, an operating system designed to support orthogonal persistence. The two basic principles of orthogonal persistence are that any object may persist (exist) for as long, or as short, a period as the object is required, and that objects may be manipulated in the same manner regardless of their longevity [3]. Persistent systems provide a fundamentally different computation paradigm to conventional systems. In a conventional system different mechanisms are provided for creating and accessing temporary data and permanent data (e.g. virtual memory and a file system). A persistent system, on the other hand, supports a single storage abstraction in which all data may be created and manipulated in a uniform manner, regardless of its longevity. Thus, programs may create data structures which outlive their execution and there is no need to write code to "flatten" data structures in order to store them in files.

A number of persistent systems have been constructed, most of which have been built above conventional operating systems, usually Unix [1,4,25,26,32]. Although these systems have been successful in terms of demonstrating the feasibility of persistence as a programming paradigm, efficiency has been a major problem. This is not surprising since they are being constructed above operating systems with a model that is fundamentally different from the persistence model. Other groups have developed specialised hardware in order to provide a more appropriate environment [9,17,33]. These groups have encountered difficulties because of the cost of building hardware using the latest technology and the problems associated with making the results of the research available to other research groups.

In Grasshopper [12,13] we have adopted a third approach which is to develop a new operating system on a conventional workstation platform. Some other research groups have also taken this route [5,6,10]. We see the advantages of this approach as:

- workstations are cheap and readily available,

- their performance is improving rapidly, and

- most research groups have access to these machines and so the results of our work can be easily made available.

Unfortunately, the use of workstations designed to support Unix does place some constraints on our design, particularly related to addressing issues. These problems have been discussed elsewhere [13]. Despite these difficulties we believe that it is possible to provide an efficient environment for persistent systems on conventional hardware.

An important issue in the design of a persistent system is the protection mechanism. Some form of protection is necessary for two reasons:

1. to ensure that programs can access precisely those objects they are supposed to access and no others, and

2. to restrict access to certain operating system functions.

In a monolingual persistent system built using a type-safe language the first category of protection can be provided by the programming language and type system [27]. However, Grasshopper is intended to be language independent. It is expected that persistent application systems employing different languages will run concurrently above the kernel. We therefore cannot rely on a single type system.

In most conventional operating systems access to operating system functions is controlled by a separate mechanism from that used to control access to data. Each user is given an access level and this determines the operations which may be performed. In Unix there are effectively only two such access levels, normal user and super-user. Just as we have argued that there should be a single data creation and manipulation mechanism for all data, it is sensible to have a single protection mechanism which provides all access controls. Such a uniform approach has been adopted on some object-based operating systems (e.g. Monads [22]) and is employed in Grasshopper, which has a single protection mechanism controlling access to both data and operating system functions.

This paper concentrates on the issue of protection in the Grasshopper operating system. We begin with a description of the basic abstractions over storage and execution in Grasshopper and the protection requirements for these abstractions. We then provide some background on capabilities as a protection mechanism for persistent systems in general. This is followed by a description of the structure of capabilities in Grasshopper and a discussion of access rights and revocation. Finally we describe the operations supported for the manipulation of capabilities in Grasshopper.

2. Grasshopper Basic Abstractions

In this section we describe the two basic abstractions in Grasshopper. The abstraction over storage is the *container* and the abstraction over execution is the *locus*. Conceptually, each locus executes within a single container, its *host container*. Containers are not virtual address spaces. They may be of any size, including larger than the virtual address range supported by the hardware. The data stored in a container is supplied by a *manager*. Managers are responsible for maintaining a consistent and recoverable stable copy of the data represented by the container. The use of managers, which is vital to the removal of the distinction between persistent and volatile storage, is beyond the scope of this paper and is discussed in [12].

2.1 Containers

Containers are the only storage abstraction provided by Grasshopper; they are persistent entities which replace both address spaces and file systems. In most operating systems, the notion of a virtual address space is associated with an ephemeral entity, a process, which accesses data within that address space. In contrast, containers and loci are orthogonal concepts. A Grasshopper system consists of a number of containers which may have loci executing within them. At any moment in time, a locus can only address the data visible in the container in which it is executing. Of course, there must be facilities which allow the transfer of data between containers. The mechanisms provided in Grasshopper are *mapping* and *invocation*.

The purpose of container mapping is to allow data to be shared between containers. This is achieved by allowing data in a region of one container to appear (either as read-only or read-write) in another container. In its simplest form, this mechanism provides shared memory and shared libraries similar to that provided by conventional operating systems. However, conventional operating systems restrict the mapping of memory to a single level. Both VMS [24] and variants of Unix (such as SunOS) provide the ability to share memory segments between process address spaces, and a separate ability to map from disk storage into a process address space. Several other systems [7, 8, 28, 31] provide the notion of a *memory object*, which provides an abstraction over data. In these systems, memory objects can be mapped into a process address space, however memory objects and processes are separate abstractions. It is therefore impossible to directly address a memory object, or to compose a memory object from other memory objects.

By contrast, the single abstraction over data provided by Grasshopper may be arbitrarily (possibly recursively) composed. Since any container can have another mapped onto it, it is possible to construct a hierarchy of container mappings as shown in Figure 1. The hierarchy of container mappings forms a directed acyclic graph. The restriction that mappings cannot contain circular dependencies is imposed to ensure that one container is always ultimately responsible for data. In Figure 1, container $C2$ is mapped onto container $C1$ at location $a1$. In turn, $C2$ has regions of containers $C3$ and $C4$ mapped onto it. The data from $C3$ is visible in $C1$ at address $a3$, which is equal to $a1 + a2$.

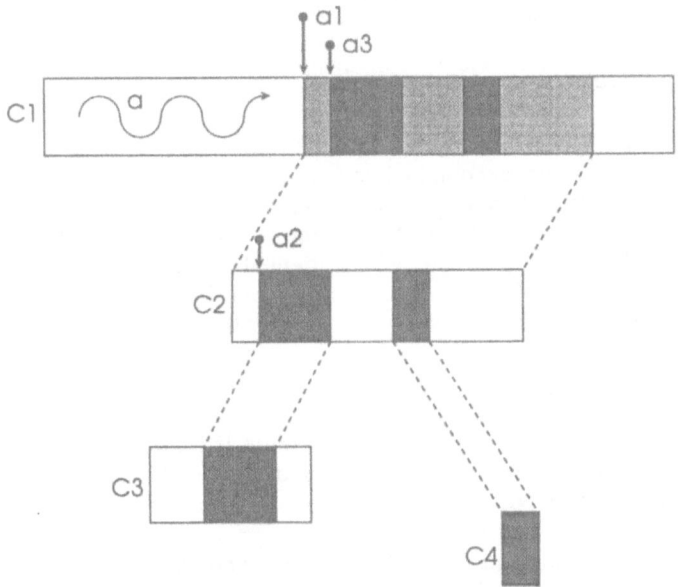

Figure 1: A container mapping hierarchy

Loci perceive the address space of their host container. Therefore, all loci executing within a container share the same address space. However, a locus may require private data, which is visible to it, yet invisible to other loci that inhabit the same container. To satisfy this need, Grasshopper provides the notion of a *locus private mapping*.

Locus private mappings are visible only to the locus which created them and take precedence over host container mappings. This allows, for example, each locus to have its own stack space with the stacks of all loci occupying the same address range within the host container. This technique both simplifies multi-threaded programming and provides a useful security mechanism that is unavailable with conventional addressing mechanisms.

2.2 Loci

In its simplest form, a locus is simply the contents of the registers of the machine on which it is executing. Like containers, loci are maintained by the Grasshopper kernel and are inherently persistent. Making loci persistent is a departure from other operating system designs and frees the programmer from much complexity [22].

A locus is associated with a container, its host container. The locus perceives the host container's contents plus any containers mapped by locus private mappings within its own address space. Virtual addresses generated by the locus map directly onto addresses within the host container and the locus private mapped containers. A container comprising program code, mutable data and a locus forms a basic running program. Loci are an orthogonal abstraction to containers. Any number of loci may execute within a given container; this allows Grasshopper to support multi-threaded programming paradigms.

2.3   Inter-Container Communication

An operating system is largely responsible for the control and management of two entities: objects, which contain data (containers); and processes (loci), the active elements which manipulate these objects. One of the most important considerations in the design of an operating system is the model of interaction between these entities. Grasshopper uses the procedure-oriented model in which communication is achieved via procedure calls and processes move between entities [23]. Thus a locus may *invoke* a container thereby changing its host container.

Any container may include, as one of its attributes, a single entry point known as an *invocation point*. When a locus invokes a container, it begins executing code at the invocation point. The single invocation point is important for security; it is the invoked container that controls the execution of the invoking locus by providing the code that will be executed.

A locus may invoke and return through many containers in a manner similar to conventional procedure calls. The Grasshopper kernel maintains a call chain of invocations between containers. Implicitly each locus appears to be rooted in the container representing the kernel: when a locus returns to this point it is deleted. However some loci may never need to return to the container from which they were invoked; such a locus may meander from container to container. In such circumstances, a parameter to the invoke system call allows the locus to inform the kernel that no call chain need be maintained.

Access to operating system functions is also achieved by invocation. This provides a uniform interface for applications and blurs the distinction between system and user functions.

2.4   Protection Requirements

In the previous sections we have described the basic abstractions in Grasshopper and the operations over these abstractions. Given that containers are the *only* abstraction over storage, some access control mechanisms are required. These include control over:

- which containers may be invoked

- the setting of an invocation point

- which containers may be mapped and the type of access one has to the mapped region, e.g. read/write

- the creation and destruction of containers

Similarly, it is desirable to have control over loci. The control required includes:

- control over the creation of locus private mappings

- the ability to block and unblock loci

- management of locus exceptions

- control over the creation and destruction of loci.

In a conventional operating system many of these controls are provided by the file system, which maintains access lists, usually on a hierarchical basis. This is not appropriate in Grasshopper since there is no file system. Some persistent systems use the type system to provide control over access, however, as we have stated earlier, we propose to support multiple languages with different type systems, and so this is not an alternative. For these reasons we believe that it is essential for Grasshopper to support a third abstraction: a protection mechanism. That abstraction is capabilities and in the following section we provide some background and justification for this choice.

3. Capabilities as a Protection Mechanism

Capabilities were first proposed by Dennis and Van Horn [14] as a technique for describing the semantics of controlled access to data. The idea was extended by Fabry who proposed a computer system based on capabilities [15]. There have been several capability-based systems constructed. Some of these enlisted hardware support [30,33,35], others were purely software implementations [29,36]. Although these systems differ greatly, the fundamental principles of capability-based access control are the same.

The basic idea is that access to objects is controlled by the ownership and presentation of capabilities. That is, in order for a program to access an object it must produce a capability for that object. In this sense capabilities may be viewed as keys which unlock the object to which they refer. Since the possession of a capability gives an undeniable right to access an object it is important that programs are unable to access data for which no authorisation is held. A capability for an object can only be obtained by creating a new object or by being passed a capability by another program holding that capability.

There are three well-known techniques for achieving this requirement:

tagging: in which extra bits are provided by the hardware to indicate memory regions representing capabilities and to restrict access to them,

66

passwords:	in which a key, embedded in a sparse address space, is stored with the entity and a matching key must be presented to gain access to that entity, and
segregation:	in which capabilities are stored in a protected area of memory.

In all of the above methods, capabilities have three components: a unique name identifying some entity, a set of access rights related to that entity, and rights pertaining to the capability itself, for example, whether the capability can be copied. Capability systems use entity names which are unique for the life of the system, that is, the name given to an entity will never be re-used, even if the entity is deleted. This avoids aliasing problems and provides a means of trapping dangling references. Such unique names may be generated by using a structured naming technique where each machine is given a unique name and each entity created on that machine has a unique name [18,19].

Although the ownership of a capability guarantees the right to access the corresponding entity, the access rights field may restrict the level of access allowed. The facilities provided by access rights vary greatly between different capability systems. They may be as simple as read, write and execute, or they may be based on the semantics of the different objects, for example a list of procedures for accessing an abstract data type. When a capability is presented in order to access an object, the system checks that the type of access does not conflict with that allowed in the capability. There is usually an operation which allows a new capability to be created from an existing one with a subset of the access rights. This allows for the construction of restricted views.

The third component of a capability contains status bits which indicate which operations can be performed on the capability itself. Again, these vary greatly. The minimum usually provided is a *no copy* bit which restricts the copying of the capability, perhaps on a per user basis. This may be used to stop some user from passing a capability on to other users, i.e. to limit propagation. Other status bits may include a *delete* bit which allows the holder of the capability to delete the object.

A further facility provided on some capability systems is the ability to revoke access. That is, after giving a program a capability it may be desirable at a later time to revoke this capability. Implementation of revocation is not easy. The simplest technique is to change the unique name of the object. This will effectively invalidate all existing capabilities. Selective revocation may be supported by using indirection through an owner-controlled table of access rights or by providing multiple names for the object which can be individually invalidated.

Capabilities provide a uniform model for controlling access of data. However, entry to the system itself, by logging on, must in the end be based on some form of password. An advantage of capability-based systems is that, even if the password system is broken, there need not be any single password which provides access to all data of the system. That is, there need not be a super-user.

In summary we see the major advantages of capabilities as a protection mechanism as being:

- unique naming of entities, avoiding aliasing problems

- flexibility, in that a number of different protection paradigms may be implemented

- restricted access to entities may be supported

- revocation allows lifetime control over access

- avoidance of the need for a super-user

For all of these reasons capabilities are supported as the basic protection abstraction in Grasshopper.

4. Capabilities in Grasshopper

The basic access and protection mechanism in Grasshopper is the capability. In order to perform any operation on a container or locus an appropriate capability must be presented. From an abstract point of view, capabilities in Grasshopper have five fields as shown in Figure 2. The unique name identifies the entity to which this capability grants access. The category defines the kind of the entity represented. The categories supported include containers, loci and devices. However, it is anticipated that there will be additional categories supported in the final system.

Figure 2: The logical structure of a capability in Grasshopper

The next three fields define the access granted by the capability. The capability rights indicate rights relating to the capability itself while the category rights relate to operations on a particular entity category. The capability and category rights are described in section 4.4.

The entity rights are uninterpreted by the system and are meaningful only to the particular entity referenced by the capability. They are stored in a secure manner by the kernel with the other access rights and are passed as an implicit parameter on invocation. They may be used for a variety of purposes; for example, they could be used as tags to represent a primitive type system allowing a container to implement a domain specific protection mechanism. Alternatively, they may be used as an identifier; a device manager may represent different physical devices using capabilities that differ only in their entity rights field. In this case the entity rights field represents the physical device. They may also be used to describe the level of service available from an invoked container using this capability. This could be implemented as a bit list, with one bit for each operation provided by the container. Such an arrangement would allow the construction of capabilities with different views of a container. Alternatively, the entity rights could be used as a tag to identify the capability used to effect an invoke. This would allow some form of accounting for the service provided. In both of these case the kernel does not interpret the meaning of the entity rights; it simply stores them and makes them available as part of the invoke mechanism.

The two major issues in the design of a capability system are the naming scheme and the method used to protect the capabilities themselves. The allocation of unique names to entities and the method used to locate these entities is beyond the scope of this paper. However, as will be shown in the following sections, these unique entity names are not directly visible to users of the system and so we have considerable flexibility in the design of the low-level naming scheme.

As we have described in Section 3 there are three basic techniques for protecting capabilities, namely tagging, passwords and segregation. The merits of each of these have been well discussed in the literature [2,16,21,34]. Given that Grasshopper is to be implemented on conventional hardware, tagging is not an option. Password capabilities have the advantage that they may be embedded within applications and require no special software to protect them. However, it is precisely this feature which makes them less appealing. Since the kernel cannot know how many (if any) capabilities for an entity exist at any point in time, it cannot perform garbage collection and must rely on explicit destruction of entities or some form of aging [2].

In a segregated system the kernel always knows how many capabilities exist for an entity. Using segregated capabilities allows garbage collection to be performed in association with explicit destruction of entities by loci. Reference counts may be maintained and, when the reference count on a capability falls to zero (i.e., there are no more extant references to the corresponding entity) the entity may be deleted. For these reasons segregated capabilities are used in Grasshopper.

4.1 Association of Capabilities with Entities

In Grasshopper, capabilities provide access to entities and also control the level of access to those entities. Since the Grasshopper system uses a segregated capability system, capabilities are protected from direct manipulation by programs. Associated with each entity, but protected from user access, are two tables known as the *permission group table* and the *capability table*. Capabilities owned by an entity reside in its capability table whilst control over access to an entity is effected by entries within its permission group table. Capability table entries are indexed by fixed length keys and refer to permission group entries which contain sets of permissions; together these tables implement the Grasshopper capability regime.

Loci may only use capabilities owned by themselves or their host container; these capabilities are accessed via the presentation of a *capability reference* or *capref*. Caprefs are the way in which capabilities appear to the application programmer. A capref comprises a pair consisting of a flag and a key. The flag specifies whether the key should be interpreted with respect to the locus or its host container. The key refers to an entry in the selected entity's capability table. Caprefs are not protected by the system and may be constructed arbitrarily. This does not constitute a security risk since a useful capref can only refer to those capabilities legitimately held by the host container or locus.

On presentation of a capref, the key is looked up in the selected capability table. Assuming a match is found, the permission group field of the selected capability table entry is used to identify the entity being referenced and the permission group containing the permissions associated with that capability.

In Figure 3 the container *C1* is the host container of locus *L1*. Two caprefs, *CR1* and *CR2* are stored within Container *C1* and are therefore addressable by locus *L1*. When presented by *L1*, capref *CR1* refers to a capability in *L1*'s capability table whereas *CR2* refers to the capability in the *L1*'s host container, *C1*. In both cases the capabilities refer to the entity C2. However, since they refer to different permission group entries, they may have different protections associated with them.

On creation of an entity, a single permission group called the *master permission group*, granting all access, is also created and a capability referring to it is returned. Appropriate operations are provided for creating new permission groups with reduced access; these are discussed later in the paper. Such groups are called *derived permission groups* and capabilities referring to these are called *derived capabilities*.

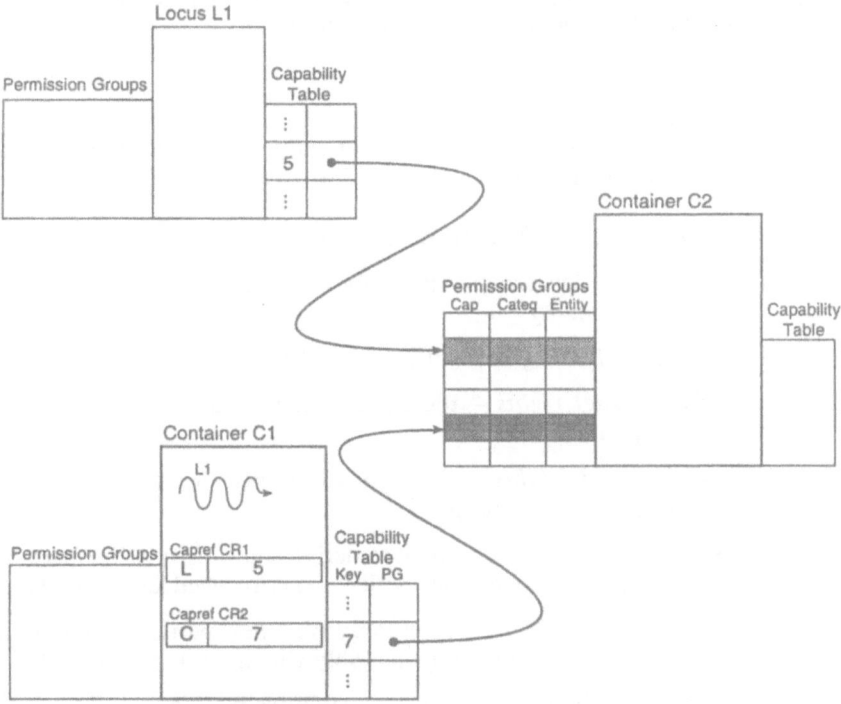

Figure 3: Permission groups, capability tables and caprefs

There are two distinct advantages of this structure. First, it makes no assumptions about the relationships between capabilities. The kernel simply maintains the capabilities in a table in a secure manner. Arbitrary naming schemes and structures can be constructed above the kernel. For example, it would be possible to build a hierarchical naming scheme similar to that provided by Unix. Alternatively, more flexible naming schemes such as those described in [11, 20] could be implemented. Indeed, alternative naming schemes may coexist within a running Grasshopper system. Second, the separation of the capabilities from the permission groups provides considerable flexibility, particularly in relation to revocation of access. This is discussed in Section 4.3.

4.2 Access Rights

In this section we summarise the access rights supported by the Grasshopper capability system. These access rights are stored in permission groups and define the operations that may be performed using a corresponding capability. All system functions (i.e. mapping, invocation, etc.) are controlled by capabilities and require the presentation of capabilities with appropriate access permissions.

As we have indicated above, there are three sets of rights: capability rights, category rights and entity rights. The first two groups of rights, capability and category rights, are defined by the Grasshopper kernel and are collectively referred to as kernel rights. The last group, entity rights, are not interpreted by the kernel, but are held in a secure manner in the permission groups.

4.2.1 Capability Rights

The capability rights apply to all categories of entities and control the operations on the capability tables and permission groups. The capability rights are:

- *destroy* – the right to destroy the corresponding entity

- *copy permission group* – the right to create a copy of a permission group for an entity

- *delete permission group* – the right to delete a permission group

- *reduce kernel rights* – the right to reduce the kernel rights in an existing permission group

- *modify entity rights* – the right to modify the entity rights in an existing permission group

- *derive kernel rights* – the right to derive a new permission group from an existing permission group with equal or reduced kernel rights

- *derive entity rights* – the right to derive a new permission group from an existing permission group, possibly with modified entity rights

- *inject* – the right to insert new capabilities into an entity's capability table

The first right allows the destruction of an entity. This is effectively achieved by deleting all of the permission groups for the entity. The next two rights control copying and deletion of permission groups. The following four rights permit the modification of the rights in a permission group and the creation of new permission groups with modified access rights. The separation of control over manipulation of kernel rights and entity rights reflects the fact that entity rights are uninterpreted by the kernel. The meaning of kernel rights is universally known. On the other hand, only programs which understand the format of the entity rights for a particular entity can sensibly modify these. It is thus necessary to be able to separately restrict the ability to manipulate entity rights to appropriate programs.

There are no rights which control the manipulation of capability tables. Loci can always refer to their own capability table and the capability table of their current host container. The *inject* right controls access to other entity's capability tables. This is further discussed in Section 4.4.

4.2.2 Category Rights

The category rights apply to specific categories of entities. However, there are some common category rights which apply to both containers and loci. These are:

- *alter read-only mappings* – the right to define and remove read-only mappings of containers into this entity

- *alter read-write mappings* – the right to define and remove read-write mappings of containers into this entity

- *alter exception handler* – the right to define and remove an exception handler for this entity

The container category rights are:

- *map read-only* - the right to map this container into another entity with read-only access

- *map read-write* - the right to map this container into another entity with read-write access

- *invoke* - the right to invoke this container

- *set invocation point* - the right to modify the invocation point for this container

The locus category rights are:

- *raise exception* - the right to raise an exception for this locus

- *block/unblock* - the right to control the scheduling of this locus

There are two sets of mapping rights. The first set, alter read-only/read-write mappings, defines whether the holder of the capability is allowed to map containers into the corresponding entity. The second set applies to containers and indicate whether the holder of the capability is permitted to map the specified container into other containers and loci. For example, in order to map container A into container B with read-write access, a locus must have a capability for A with at least *map read-write* rights and a capability for container B with at least *alter read-write mappings* right.

Grasshopper supports a concept of exception handlers. There are several rights associated with these, however they are beyond the scope of this paper. They are included here for completeness.

As described earlier, Grasshopper provides an invocation mechanism which permits loci executing in different host containers to communicate. A capability with the *invoke* right is required in order to invoke another container. Invocation causes the locus to begin execution at the invocation point of the invoked container. The invocation point may be changed by the holder of a capability with the *set invocation point* right.

Finally, the *block/unblock* right allows the holder of such a capability to control the execution of a locus. This may be used to implement higher level synchronisation and scheduling mechanisms in a controlled manner.

4.3 Permission Groups and Revocation

One of the most powerful features of Grasshopper protection system is support for revocation. It is possible to grant access to some entity by the provision of a capability and then to revoke this access at a later stage. Revocation is achieved in Grasshopper via the permission group mechanism.

Recall that a capability effectively consists of the name of an entity and the identification of one of the permission groups associated with that entity. Access may be revoked by deleting the permission group with which the capability is associated. Any future use of the capability will result in an exception because the permission group no longer exists. Such draconian measures are not always required; Grasshopper therefore also supports the ability to reduce the access rights for the permission group, thereby reducing the operations allowed.

The mechanism described above, combined with the ability to copy permission groups and to derive new permission groups, provides a powerful and flexible protection paradigm. The set of permissions groups associated with an entity form a tree. Copying a permission group creates a new sibling, whilst derivation creates a new child. This is similar to a scheme for password capabilities described by Anderson [2].

The properties of permission group trees are simple:

- The access rights available in any permission group are always greater than or equal to those available from any descendant of that permission group.

- If any permission group is deleted then all of its descendants are also deleted.

- If the access rights in a permission group are reduced then all its descendants are similarly reduced.

Consider as an example a class of students to whom we wish to give access to some entity required for an assignment in such a way that it is possible to revoke access for any individual student, or for all students, e.g. when the assignment is due. This can be achieved by creating a new permission group and then deriving a permission group below this for each student. Providing a capability for each permission group is held by the person in charge, then an individual student's access

may be revoked by deleting that student's permission group and access for all
students may be revoked by deleting the permission group from which they were
derived.

4.4   Operations on Capabilities

In the previous sections we have referred to various operations for manipulating
and copying capabilities and permission groups. In this section we provide type
definitions for the various data structures along with a description of each of the
operations.   The structure of the types *entity_rights_type* and *cap_key_type* is
implementation dependent and is not important to the discussion which follows.
The notation *capability*(*x*) is used to refer to the capability found in the capability
table indicated by *x.cr_flag* in the location indicated by *x.cr_key*.

Types

permissions **is structure** (capability_rights_type *capability_rights*;
category_rights_type *category_rights*;
entity_rights_type *entity_rights*)

permission_group **is structure** (permissions *pg_permissions*)

capability **is structure** (cap_key_type *cap_key*;
permission_group *cap_pg*)

caplist_selector **is enum** (locus, host_container)

capref **is structure** (caplist_selector *cr_flag*;
cap_key_type *cr_key*)

Operations

copy_cap (capref *source, destination*)
delete_cap (capref *target*)
copy_pg (capref *source, destination*)
reduce_pg (capref *target*; permissions *new_permissions*)
delete_pg (capref *target*)
derive_pg (capref *source, destination*; permissions *new_permissions*)
delete_entity (capref *target*)
inject_cap (capref *source, destination*; cap_key_type *new_cap_key*)

The **copy_cap** operation allows capabilities to be copied between and within the
currently accessible capability tables (i.e. current locus table and current host
container table). The capability referred to by *source* is copied to the capability
table indicated by *destination.cr_flag* in the location indicated by *destination.cr_key*.
Note that this operation does not affect the permission groups. After a **copy_cap**
operation, both *source* and *destination* refer to the same permission group.

The **delete_cap** operation removes the entry referred to by *target.cr_key* in the table indicated by *target.cr_flag*. Again, permission groups are not affected by this operation.

The **copy_pg** operation creates a new permission group for the entity indicated by *capability(source)*. The new permission group has the same permissions as the source. A new capability is created and is stored in *capability(destination)* . This capability refers to the new permission group. The new permission group is a sibling to *capability(source).cap_pg*, in the permission group tree; revocation of *capability(source)* does not revoke *capability(destination)*. Similarly, revocation of *capability(destination)* does not revoke *capability(source).cap_pg*. *Capability(source).cap_pg.pg_permissions* must include *copy permission group* for this operation to take place.

The capability copy operations are used for two main purposes. First, they allow the re-organisation of the capabilities in a capability table. Second, they may be used to pass and return capability parameters on invocations, i.e. capabilities to be passed to a container on an invocation are copied to the locus' capability table prior to the invocation. These capabilities may then be accessed by the locus in the invoked container. Capabilities may be returned by the same mechanism. Notice that the allocation and management of keys is the responsibility of the code executing in the container. Appropriate library routines are provided for this purpose.

The **reduce_pg** operation replaces *capability(target).cap_pg.pg_permissions*, with *new_permissions*. All permission groups below *capability(target).cap_pg* in the permission group tree are reduced in the same way. *Capability(target).cap_pg.pg_permissions* must include appropriate permissions (*reduce kernel rights* and/or *modify entity rights*) for this operation to take place.

Delete_pg deletes the permission group *capability(target).cap_pg*, and any permission groups below this one in the permission group tree. Any capability referring to any of the deleted permission groups will be invalid following this operation. *Capability(target).cap_pg.permissions* must include *delete permission group* for this operation to take place.

The **derive_pg** operation is similar to **copy_pg**, but creates the new permission group as a child in the permission group tree, possibly with reduced permissions. The new permission group is created below *capability(source).cap_pg* in the permission tree, and with permissions *new_permissions*. A new capability is created as *capability(destination)* and this capability points at the new permission group. Since the new permission group is a child of *capability(source).cap_pg*, revocation of *capability(source)* will cause revocation of *capability(destination)*. *Capability(source).cap_pg.pg_permissions* must include *derive kernel rights* and *derive entity rights* (assuming both are modified) for this operation to take place.

The permission group operations provide control over the construction of the permission group tree in order to allow revocation as discussed in Section 4.3. They also allow for the construction of restricted views of an entity by appropriate use of the entity permissions.

Delete_entity deletes all permission groups relating to the entity referred to by *capability(target)*. As a result, all capabilities referring to the entity are invalidated, making the entity inaccessible and effectively deleting it. *Capability(target).cap_pg.permissions* must include *destroy* for this operation to take place.

The final operation, **inject_cap**, is the only operation which can access a capability table other than the current locus and current host container tables. *Capability(source)* is copied to the capability table of the entity referenced by *capability(destination)* in the location indicated by *new_cap_key*. This operation does not affect the permission groups; both source and the new capability point at the same permission group. *Capability(destination)cap_pg.permissions* must include *inject* for this operation to take place.

The inject operation is particular useful for populating a new entity with some initial capabilities. For example, a new locus may be created and given some capabilities for basic system functions such as input-output.

5.   Conclusions

In this paper we have described the protection mechanism for the Grasshopper operating system. The fact that this mechanism is based on capabilities results in a number of advantages:

1.   The system does not enforce any particular naming or protection paradigm. The mapping from meaningful names to capabilities is managed outside the kernel. Thus it is possible to construct arbitrary naming schemes.

2.   The creator of an entity has full control over the level of access provided to other users.

3.   Arbitrarily restricted views of entities may be constructed using the entity rights field of permission groups.

4.   Access to entities may be selectively revoked.

5.   By the use of unique names and explicit deletion the need for garbage collection across the entire store is avoided.

A secondary advantage of our approach to capabilities relates to the scheme used to provide unique names for capabilities. This naming scheme is not visible outside the kernel; applications always use caprefs to refer to entities. This leaves considerable flexibility in the design of the kernel entity naming scheme and also permits distribution to be completely transparent.

Although it has been argued in the past that capabilities are an expensive mechanism, this has been in an environment where capabilities are used for all addressing. It will be noted that in Grasshopper, capabilities are only used for validating course-grain operations such as invocation and mapping. Normal memory accesses are directly handled by the conventional virtual memory hardware. It is therefore expected that the proposed scheme will be no more expensive than protection mechanisms provided by existing operating systems and may well be more efficient.

The scheme described in this paper has been implemented in a prototype version of Grasshopper on DEC Alpha machines. This prototype system is already capable of executing simple user programs and it is expected that a fully usable version of the system will be available later this year.

Acknowledgments

The work described in this paper is supported by Australian Research Council grant A49130439 and by an equipment grant under the Alpha Innovators Program from Digital Equipment Corporation.

References

1.   Albano, A., Cardelli, L. and Orsini, R. "Galileo: A Strongly Typed, Interactive Conceptual Language", ACM Transactions on Database Systems, 10(2), pp. 230-260, 1985.

2.   Anderson, M., Pose, R. and Wallace, C. S. "A Password-Capability System", *The Computer Journal*, vol 29, 1, pp. 1-8, 1986.

3.   Atkinson, M. P., Bailey, P., Chisholm, K. J., Cockshott, W. P. and Morrison, R. "An Approach to Persistent Programming", *The Computer Journal*, 26(4), pp. 360-365, 1983.

4.   Atkinson, M. P., Chisholm, K. J. and Cockshott, W. P. "PS-algol: An Algol with a Persistent Heap", *ACM SIGPLAN Notices*, 17(7), pp. 24-31, 1981.

5.   Campbell, R. H., Johnston, G. M. and Russo, V. F. "Choices (Class Hierarchical Open Interface for Custom Embedded Systems", *ACM Operating Systems Review*, 21(3), pp. 9-17, 1987.

6.   Chase, J. S., Levy, H. M., Baker-Harvey, M. and Lazowska, E. D. "Opal: A Single Address Space System for 64-Bit Architectures", *Third IEEE Workshop on Workstation Operating Systems*, IEEE, 1992.

7.   Cheriton, D. R. "The V Kernel: A Software Base for Distributed Systems", *Software*, 1(2), pp. 9-42, 1984.

8.   Chorus Systems "Overview of the CHORUS Distributed Operating Systems", *Computer Systems - The Journal of the Usenix Association*, 1(4), 1990.

9.   Cockshott, W. P. "Design of POMP - a Persistent Object Management Processor", *Proceedings of the Third International Workshop on Persistent Object Systems*, (ed J. Rosenberg and D. M. Koch), Springer-Verlag, pp. 367-376, 1989.

10.   Dasgupta, P., LeBlanc, R. J. and Appelbe, W. F. "The Clouds Distributed Operating System", *Proceedings, 8th International Conference on Distributed Computing Systems*, 1988.

11. Dearle, A. "Environments: A Flexible Binding Mechanism to Support System Evolution", *Proc. 22nd Hawaii International Conference on System Sciences*, vol II, pp. 46-55, 1989.

12. Dearle, A., di Bona, R., Farrow, J. M., Henskens, F. A., Lindström, A., Rosenberg, J. and Vaughan, F. "Grasshopper: An Orthogonally Persistent Operating System", *Computer Systems (to appear)*, 1994.

13. Dearle, A., Rosenberg, J., Henskens, F. A., Vaughan, F. and Maciunas, K. "An Examination of Operating System Support for Persistent Object Systems", *Proceedings of the 25th Hawaii International Conference on System Sciences*, vol 1, (ed V. Milutinovic and B. D. Shriver), IEEE Computer Society Press, Hawaii, U. S. A., pp. 779-789, 1992.

14. Dennis, J. B. and Van Horn, E. C. "Programming Semantics for Multiprogrammed Computations", *Communications of the A.C.M.*, 9(3), pp. 143-145, 1966.

15. Fabry, R. S. "Capability-Based Addressing", *Communications of the A.C.M.*, 17(7), pp. 403-412, 1974.

16. Gehringer, E. F. and Keedy, J. L. "Tagged Architecture: How Compelling are its Advantages?", *Twelth International Symposium on Computer Architecture*, pp. 162-170, 1985.

17. Harland, D. M. "REKURSIV: Object-oriented Computer Architecture", Ellis-Horwood Limited, 1988.

18. Henskens, F. A. "A Capability-based Persistent Distributed Shared Memory", PhD Thesis, University of Newcastle, N.S.W., Australia, ISBN 0 86758 668 0, 1991.

19. Henskens, F. A. "Addressing Moved Modules in a Capability-based Distributed Shared Memory", *Proceedings of the 25th Hawaii International Conference on System Sciences*, vol 1, (ed V. Milutinovic and B. D. Shriver), IEEE Computer Society Press, Hawaii, U. S. A., pp. 769-778, 1992.

20. Hitchens, M. and Rosenberg, J. "Binding between Names and Objects in a Persistent System", *Proceedings of 2nd International Workshop on Object Orientation in Operating Systems*, IEEE, Dourdan, France, pp. 26-37, 1992.

21. Keedy, J. L. "An Implementation of Capabilities without a Central Mapping Table", *Proc. 17th Hawaii International Conference on System Sciences*, pp. 180-185, 1984.

22. Keedy, J. L. and Vosseberg, K. "Persistent Protected Modules and Persistent Processes as the Basis for a More Secure Operating System", *Proceedings of the 25th Hawaii International Conference on Systems Sciences*, vol 1, IEEE, Hawaii, USA, pp. 747-756, 1992.

23. Lauer, H. C. and Needham, R. M. "On the Duality of Operating System Structures", *Operating Systems Review*, 13(2), pp. 3-19, 1979.

24. Levy, H. M. and Lipman, P. H. "Virtual Memory Management in the VAX/VMS Operating System", *Computer*, 15(3), pp. 35-41, 1982.

25. Matthes, F. and Schmidt, J. W. "The Type System of DBPL", *Proceedings of the Second International Workshop on Database Programming Languages*, Morgan Kaufmann, pp. 219-225, 1989.

26.   Morrison, R., Brown, A. L., Conner, R. C. H. and Dearle, A. "Napier88 Reference Manual", Universities of Glasgow and St. Andrews, Persistent Programming Research Report PPRR-77-89, 1989.

27.   Morrison, R., Brown, A. L., Connor, R. C. H., Cutts, Q. I., Dearle, A., Kirby, G., Rosenberg, J. and Stemple, D. "Protection in Persistent Object Systems", *Proceedings of the International Workshop on Computer Architectures to Support Security and Persistence of Information*, Springer-Verlag, Bremen, Germany, pp. 48-66, 1990.

28   Moss, J. E. B. "Addressing Large Distributed Collections of Persistent Objects: The Mneme Project's Approach", *Proceedings of the Second International Workshop on Database Programming Languages*, Gleneden Beach, Oregon, Morgan Kaufmann, pp. 358-374, 1989.

29.   Mullender, S. J., van Rossum, G., Tanenbaum, A. S., van Renesse, R. and van Staveren, H. "Amoeba: A Distributed Operating System for the 1990s", *Computer*, 23(5), pp. 44-53, 1990.

30.   Pose, R. D. "Capability Based, Tightly Coupled Multiprocessor Hardware to Support a Persistent Global Virtual Memory", *Proceedings of the 22nd Annual Hawaii International Conference on System Sciences*, (ed B. D. Shriver), pp. 36-45, 1989.

31.   Rashid, R., Tevanian, A., Young, M., Golub, D., Baron, R., Black, D., Bolosky, W. and Chew, J. "Machine-Independent Virtual Memory Management for Paged Uniprocessor and Multiprocessor Architectures", *Proceedings of the Second International Conference on Architectural Support for Programming Languages and Operating Systems (ASPLOS II)*, ACM Order Number 556870, pp. 31-39, 1987.

32.   Richardson, J. E. and Carey, M. J. "Implementing Persistence in E", *Proceedings of the Third International Workshop on Persistent Object Systems*, (ed J. Rosenberg and D. M. Koch), Springer-Verlag, pp. 175-199, 1989.

33.   Rosenberg, J. and Abramson, D. A. "MONADS-PC: A Capability Based Workstation to Support Software Engineering", *Proc, 18th Hawaii International Conference on System Sciences*, pp. 515-522, 1985.

34.   Tanenbaum, A. S. "Experiences with the Amoeba Distributed System", *Communications of the ACM*, 33(12), pp. 46-63, 1990.

35.   Wilkes, M. V. and Needham, R. M. "The Cambridge CAP Computer and its Operating System", North Holland, Oxford, 1979.

36.   Wulf, W. A., Levin, R. and Harbison, S. P. "HYDRA/C.mmp: An Experimental Computer System", McGraw-Hill, New York, 1981.

An Efficient Pointer Swizzling Method for Navigation Intensive Applications

Shinji Suzuki, Masaru Kitsuregawa, Mikio Takagi

Institute of Industrial Science, The University of Tokyo

3rd Dept. 7-22-1 Roppongi Tokyo 106, Japan

suzuki@tkl.iis.u-tokyo.ac.jp

Abstract

In this paper we introduce the notion of *reservation* and *residency* in the context of *object faulting* and describe the *pointer swizzling* method employed in our implementation of a persistent C language *P3L*. Although the method does not assume any special hardware support, our experiments indicate that the reservation checking method is efficient enough that the addition of reservation checks does not severely compromise the performance in navigation intensive applications. Navigation performance is maintained by reducing the frequency of reservation checks and by replacing each persistent reference with a surrogate upon object fault. The replacement condenses a long persistent identifier down to the size of a virtual memory pointer. The virtual memory requirement of our scheme is modest compared to *pointer swizzling at page fault time*[1]. In one of the test cases, our software based scheme outperformed the hardware based scheme. Compared to *pointer swizzling upon discovery* as is implemented in [2], our implementation runs about 4 to 10 times faster in terms of pure in-memory navigation.

1 Introduction

The cost of memory chips continues to decline steadily with increasing package density. Research on main-memory databases and log structured file systems rely upon this trend.

Generally speaking, objects touched during a session of engineering and design applications are relatively limited in number and size. And most frequent operations performed on them is read operations from main memory. These applications are often navigation intensive, i.e. repeatedly performs pointer chasing. For example, a connection of cells in a programmable logic-cell-array (LCA) is most likely represented by an object reference. Calculating the delay for signals arriving at an I/O pad to propagate to a cell through the interconnect channel would involve a number of navigation, which is proportional to the number of cells on the path. Thus simulating the state of entire LCA for extended time period would results in significant amount of navigation.

Many papers on swizzling methods have focused on reducing the cost of actually performing swizzling and unswizzling, i.e. the cost of translation between OID and LID[1], along with the cost of accompanying I/O operations.

---

[1] Please refer to section 2 for definitions of OID and LID

And little consideration has been given to in-memory navigation performance when all nodes visited are cached in virtual memory.

Under the assumption that memory is plentiful and the applications' working set is relatively limited, most of reservation checks and residency checks succeed[2]. However, these checks should not be totally omitted in order to incrementally fault-in objects during a program run. Thus when dealing with navigation intensive applications, which have rather limited working set size, attention should be directed towards reducing the cost of the reservation and residency checks.

P3L is a persistent C compiler based on the Gnu C compiler [3], which implements an efficient reservation checking by furnishing memory access instructions of a certain kind with additional machine instructions. In addition, P3L emits type descriptions and ancillary functions for each data type defined, which are to be consulted and called at fault time or when structures are copied and evicted, etc. These are free standing funtions instead of being member functions (methods) inherited from a persistent root class. Thus the orthogonality of type system is not compromised.

In the next section, we explain the notion of reservation and residency checking in the context of persistent object faulting, looking at two different implementations, LOOM[3] and Texas[1].

In section 3, four persistent object systems are presented, whose performance were studied in the performance evaluation sections of this paper. Before proceeding to the presentation of the results of the evaluation, we compare our work with those published in related salient papers. Then last three sections present the results. The results obtained back up our claim that the method employed in P3L is very efficient in terms of pure in-memory navigation. Then our final comments conclude the paper.

2 Object Faulting and Swizzling

When persistent objects are dealt with, an identifier by which an object is referred to in the persistent store likely differs from an identifier by which the same object is referred to on the *physical storage*. By physical storage we refer to the combination of RAM and backing store, which appears to be a single indistinguishable area for storage from an application's point of view. An identifier used in the persistent store is often called OID or PID. On the other hand, we call a temporary and process specific identifier, LID (local identifier) hereafter. LID may take any form though it is usually a direct virtual memory pointer or an indirect pointer. OID is usually very long compared to LID due to such reasons as:

- need to assign world-wide unique names
- need to avoid reuse of names
- need to manage versioned objects
- need to deal with huge objects
- need to hold huge number of objects

Under the scenario outlined above, a LID must be assigned to an object in order to access the contents of the object. By *reservation* we refer to this

---

[2]Explanation on these checks will be given in the next section.
[3]We are in the process of putting the same modification into the Gnu G++ 2.4.8.

allocation of LID to an object. Reserving LID is not enough to make the contents of an object available to a running program. The contents itself must be transferred from the persistent store to the physical storage. By *residency* we refer to the state of an object, where the contents have already been transferred to the physical storage. *Object faulting* is this transfer of object contents, which is triggered as a result of a use, or anticipation of a use of, a reference. Through this transfer, residency of the target object is established.

Based on the above observation and definition, we propose that the act of object faulting be considered to consist of two distinct stages. One is the reservation of LID and the other is the transfer of the contents. The transfer may be triggered when a LID is reserved or it can be deferred until the contents are actually needed.

In a persistent object system in which objects are always accessed via a lookup in the resident object table [4], checking the reservation status of objects is subsumed by the OID-to-LID translation. A failed lookup means that a reservation is required. The transfer of the actual contents can be delayed in this case as well.

By embedding the result of an OID-to-LID translation in a reference, the number of translation can be reduced and the reservation checking can be made more light weight. That is, if a reference contains the result of an OID-to-LID translation, i.e. a LID, completion of the reservation is guaranteed thus no probing of resident object table is needed [5]. By *reservation check* we specifically refer to this check required to determine whether a reference has been already translated to LID or not, which is followed by the *swizzling* of the reference. And by *pointer swizzling* we refer to the overwriting of a reference with a valid LID, which is performed on the physical storage.

When swizzling is employed, an important issue is how to distinguish a swizzled reference from a unswizzled reference. If a reference consists of both the OID part and the LID part, as seen in E implementation, the distinction can be easily made and having OID readily available makes the logic of swizzling less complicated. However, a longer reference means more CPU cycles for copying and more pressure on register allocation. For the application scenario we assume, making a reference as short as possible is crucial for improving navigation performance. Thus we wanted to squeeze an OID into 32 bit word [6]. As will be shown shortly, this issue is irrelevant to *pointer swizzling at page fault time* because all references are swizzled to LIDs at fault time in the scheme.

There are a few methods conceivable for encoding an OID in a 32 bit quantity. Of course, every such method requires actual OIDs be stored separately from the reference. One is to tag a reference using lower bits of a pointer, assuming that those bits for a valid LID are all zeros. The benefit of this method is that bits not used for the tag can be exploited to contain certain information which accelerates retrieval of the OID. Another is to tag a reference using a special LID value as seen in LOOM [3] and P3L implementation. Depending on the CPU architecture and compiler code generation, this scheme may allow

---

[4] A runtime data structure which records the correspondence between OIDs of faulted in objects and assigned LIDs. Abbreviated as ROT.

[5] The reverse is not always true though. A reference may contain OID while the target object has been already assigned with a LID.

[6] 64bit on 64bit address machines

faster check compared with a tagged reference. The last one is to mark a reference not by its value but by the property of the virtual memory region it points to. A region of this kind is called *fault block* in [4]. If properly used, memory protection through MMU can be taken advantage of, eliminating additional instructions for explicit checks against tagged pointers [7].

As stated, making a reference short improves navigation performance under the application scenario we assume. It gives another advantage that compatibility with existing libraries may be maintained without re-compilation via a persistence-aware compiler. Near full compatibility can be achieved only through the use of *pointer swizzling at page fault time*, though. In case of P3L, a binary library compiled with genuine C compiler should not access a unswizzled pointer. Most unix system calls satisfy this condition. Finally reassigning names in virtual memory space increases spacial locality. Of course, the benefits of pointer swizzling do not come for free. [1] and [5] detail trade-offs in pointer swizzling.

Along with the two checks mentioned, other dimensions of swizzling methods are listed below. We do not include dimensions which are discussed elsewhere such as copy vs. in-place swizzling, object at a time or page at a time swizzling, etc and the list is not exhaustive.

1. When the first attempt to swizzle is made.

2. When the reservation check is made.

3. When and how the residency check is implemented.

4. How the physical storage and local identifiers are reclaimed.

5. Whether narrowing is employed.

(1)(2) Fewer translations are likely to be performed, the earlier an OID is replaced. Allowing un-swizzled pointers to be copied tends to increase the number of translations performed. Certain attempts to swizzle are allowed to fail provided that the reference will be reservation checked later. Compilers and/or runtime systems assume that a reference contains a valid LID after the reservation check is performed. Thus a reservation check must ensure that a reference is swizzled. This property affects frequency of performing reservation checks. The frequency can be reduced in two ways. One is through static analysis of program flow. The other way is to force the assumption, that a reference is already swizzled, to hold for longer periods of time by anticipating the use of the pointer well before the pointer is dereferenced.

(3) Many persistent object systems make an object resident when a LID is assigned to it thus eliminating the residency checks. On the other hand, Texas takes advantage of access protection via MMU in order to implement the hardware-based residency check.

(4) The size of the physical storage is usually limited by the size of the backing store, which is very small compared to persistent address space. Therefore reclaiming the physical storage from the least recently accessed resident objects is essential. The physical storage can be reclaimed by detaching it from

---

[7] An implementation would not be trivial because, unlike paging, the pointer itself needs to be updated. In case of paging, only state of the target page must be manipulated. See [12] for a possible implementation.

selected resident objects while keeping all LIDs assigned to them intact. By keeping LIDs intact, no need to unswizzle references arises. For this to be possible, a mechanism of residency checking must be present. In [6] a proposal was made for a swizzling method that use indirect pointer as LIDs. A LID is a pointer to a descriptor which in turn points to the target object. Eviction can be performed by simply marking descriptors corresponding to victim objects as not-present. However, as pointed out in [1] [7] [8], LID reclamation becomes inevitable as objects keeps faulted-in. In this case, reclamation of descriptors must be considered, otherwise, excessive amount of the physical storage will become occupied by descriptors.

Reference counting was proposed in [6] as a means of handling the above problem. However, decades of research on garbage collection techniques indicate that reference counting is the most problem laden automatic memory management technique. Structures containing cycles can not be reclaimed, counters may overflow, and finally and most importantly it is very inefficient. Another solution is to discard all associations between OID and LID at some point, e.g. transaction commit, and start rebuilding [1] [8]. Care must be taken that no dangling pointers are left and used after that point. We are looking into using tracing collector like mechanism to recycle LIDs. A conservative collector seems to fit our needs best.

(5) We will describe about narrowing in the next section.

2.1 LOOM

Now we look at the LOOM implementation paying attention to dimensions mentioned in the previous subsection. LOOM was developed as an enhancement to Smalltalk-80 which was using 16bit *Oops* [8] at that time. An Oop points to an entry in the object table [9] which indirects to the content of the object in the physical RAM (*heap*). Due to the shortness of an identifier, the number of objects manageable was very limited. The heap was not plentiful either. LOOM was needed in order to expand the number of objects manageable as well as to increase the size of the heap.

In LOOM , when an objects is faulted in, each references in the object gets translated to a LID if so chosen. A LID is an index to an OTE, which is called a *short Oop* in LOOM parlance. In case the target object has not yet given a LID, a new entry (i.e. a new LID) is allocated from the object table and the OID of the targe is remembered in the block of memory which is linked to the OTE. This proxy for a non-resident object is called a *leaf*. Since a LID is assigned at fault time, no reservation check is needed as long as only leaves are involved.

The OID contained in the attached memory block makes it easy to locate the real contents of the object in a persistent store when it is needed. A message sent to a leaf is detected by the message dispatcher built into Smalltalk Virtual Machine and the target object gets transferred at this point. That is , LOOM carries out residency checks by software at message send. The process of object faulting using leaves is depicted in the left part of Fig.1.

LOOM has another mechanism for representing non-resident objects. With

---

[8] Object Oriented Pointer

[9] OTE,Object Table Entry. The table also serves as the ROT.

the use of leaves, LID assignment is carried out very eagerly. This makes the mechanism prone to exhaustion of OTEs. To alleviate this problem, a special short oop value named *lambda* was introduced. Lambda stands for a reference which has not yet been swizzled. When the VM fetches lambda from memory, it goes over to the image of the containing object in the persistent store to fetch the OID from the relevant field. Then it creates a leaf or a normal object. Reducing the consumption of OTE through lambda incurs the cost of extra I/Os and extra check (reservation check) required in the virtual machine. Use of lambda is illustrated in the right of Fig. 1

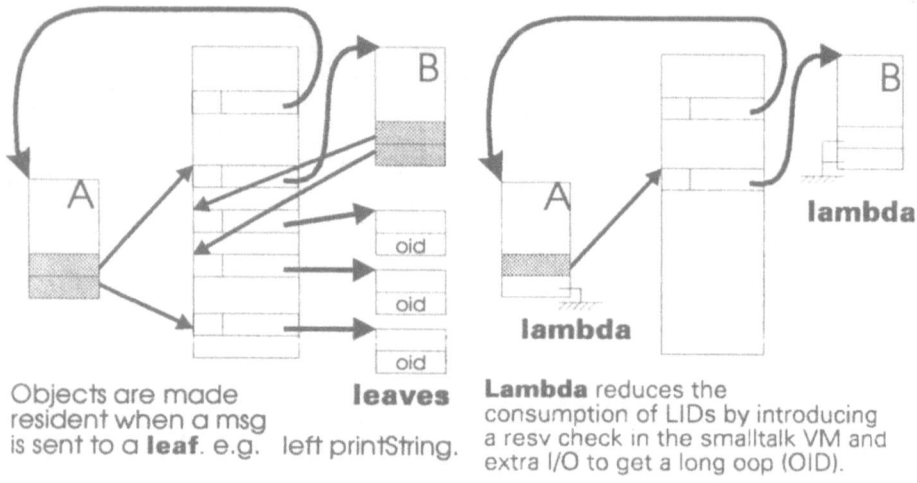

Objects are made resident when a msg is sent to a **leaf**. e.g. left printString. **leaves**

Lambda reduces the consumption of LIDs by introducing a resv check in the smalltalk VM and extra I/O to get a long oop (OID).

Figure 1: Leaf and Lambda in LOOM

Physical memory can be reclaimed by contracting a regular object into a leaf object without scanning all the resident objects. In this case, only update of OTEs is required. For reclaiming LIDs, each OTE is reference counted. Note that contracting resident objects into leaves will free some OTEs.

In summary LOOM tries to swizzle upon object fault and optionally narrows references through the use of lambda. Residency checks are carried out when a message is sent. Reservation checking is performed by software as well.

2.2 Texas Persistent Store

Texas implements pointer swizzling and object faulting method similar to the leaf scheme in LOOM. However, unlike LOOM, Texas uses a virtual memory pointer as a LID and exploits memory protection via MMU in order to implement residency checking. Shown in the left of Fig.2 (in the next section) is what happens at page fault time in Texas. The longer box on the left represents allocateion of objects in the persistent store and on the right is the allocation in virtual memory space.

When a page is faulted in, all references in the page are swizzled to a virtual memory pointer. If the target of a reference is already assigned with a LID (virtual memory address), the reference is simply swizzled with the address. Otherwise, a new LID is assigned to the object and the virtual memory pages corresponding to the LID is access protected. When an object is accessed for the first time, the protection causes an exception to be generated and the handler will transfer the contents of the page into the physical storage. Because this residency check is implemented utilizing MMU, no extra instruction is needed for implementing either checks.

3 Implementations studied in the Evaluation

In this section we describe the implementations of object faulting and pointer swizzling methods used in the systems evaluated.

3.1 E (EPVM2)

E is a persistent C++ designed and implemented in Exodus project [9]. The implementation of EPVM2 (E Persistent Virtual Machine Ver.2) is described in [2], where the swizzling method is termed *pointer swizzling upon discovery*. In the implementation, a LID takes the form of a virtual memory pointer which points to a 16 byte structure called DBREF. DBREF consists of a virtual memory pointer (*offset*) to the target object and an OID. The completion status and the result of reservation checking is recorded in the *offset* field. Unlike OTEs of LOOM implementation, each DBREF stands for only one reference. Thus copying a reference consists of a copy of both a DBREF and the pointer to the DBREF.

Swizzling is attempted when a reference is fetched from memory, i.e. when it is discovered. However, in order to avoid unnecessary faulting, the swizzling is performed only when the target object has been already made resident. Because of this decision, made in favor of reduced faulting, reservation checks still have to be performed upon every use (dereference) of a pointer. The frequent checks adversely affect the performance of applications with a lot of dereference operations.

The source of deterioration in navigation performance are:

1. Reservation checks are frequent and each check costs one extra memory access to the DBREF.

2. The dereference operation costs one extra memory access to DBREF, which is hidden by the extra access for the reservation check.

3. The cost of copying pointer increases due to the length of the pointer and the indirection present.

4. Because DBREFs are passed in a special stack dedicated to pointers, manipulating the software maintained stack further increase the cost of function calls.

It should be noted that these costs are paid for benefits. E does not assume a limited working set size in comparison with the amount of the physical storage available while P3L does. Because of the indirection in the format of the LID, evicting object is relatively easy. Recycling DBREF entries mandates neither

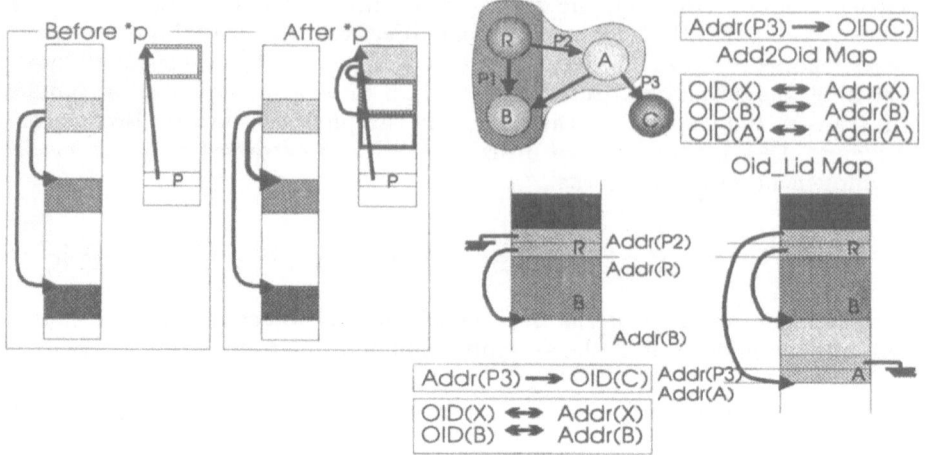

Figure 2: Object Faulting in Wilson's scheme and the one in P3L

tracing of references nor reference counting, because a DBREF entry can be disposed of when the pointer to it is destroyed.

3.2 Texas Persistent Store

The Texas Persistent Store employs *Pointer swizzling at page fault time*, which makes use of virtual memory protection for residency checking [1] as described in the previous section. Object Store by Object Design Inc is rumored to use a similar technique [10]. The proposal [1] was made for 'page at a time' swizzling so that ordinary memory management hardware can be utilized. Details are described in the previous section.

This method is likely the fastest in terms of in-memory navigation speed because residency checking is taken care of by hardware and reservation checks are not needed[10]. And it has the added advantage that a compiler as well as runtime libraries do not need to be modified for handling residency checking.

In fact, though this scheme may have portability problems over operating systems due to its reliance on a rather special operating system primitive[11], this scheme has the highest level of inter-operability with existing software tools such as compilers and third vendor libraries. The problem in inter-operability may arise with: debuggers which captures access protection faults before Texas does and garbage collectors which may pull-in all objects from the persistent store if not appropriately modified.

---

[10] As stated in the abstract, we found a counter example to this intuition which is presented in section 6.

[11] At the time of writing this final manuscript, Microsoft has added virtual memory management capability to Microsoft Windows 3.1(16bit) through extension DLL, in addition to Windows NT which had the facility from the beginning. Also a free unix clone Linux has added mprotect() system call recently. Therefore memory protection is not such an exotic feature anymore in terms of the number of installations.

3.3 P3L

In the implementation of P3L, *reservation checking upon Discovery* is employed. It is similar to *pointer swizzling upon discovery* [2]. The difference is that with this scheme the assignment of LID is always performed upon discovery of a pointer, not by a dereference unlike the latter. Thus no reservation checks have to be performed at dereference time. Unlike *pointer swizzling at fault time* for which residency checking is mandatory, the check needs to be performed only if faulting is to be delayed until after reservation. Deferring the load of target objects, for example by using MMU, eliminates unnecessary I/O which the E implementation avoided by not performing residency checking upon discovery. In the current implementation of P3L, an object gets loaded when a LID is assigned to it. A LID is a virtual memory pointer.

Persistent references get swizzled or narrowed when the containing object is faulted in. Narrowing is the process which is performed at fault time, where an OID is replaced with a marker value. We call a LID which contains the marker value a *surrogate*. When a surrogate is created, the correspondence between the address where the surrogate is placed and the OID of the target is remembered in a table (Addr2OID) so that the OID the surrogate represents can be looked up later. Remembering the OID is optional since the OID corresponding to a surrogate can be obtained by going over to the containing object in the persistent store. There is a tradeoff between the physical storage requirement and the number I/O (thus latency).

A surrogate is a 32 bit entity, that is a special LID value. Therefore, in P3L, all references get shrunk down to the size of a virtual memory pointer at fault time. Some are replaced with surrogates and others are swizzled to virtual memory pointers.

The reservation check is made by comparing the value of a pointer with the marker value. When a reservation check fails, i.e. when a surrogate is detected, the following procedures take place:

1. The original OID is retrieved from the Addr2OID table, using the address of the surrogate as a key, and the relevant entry is removed from the table.

2. Search the ROT using the OID as a key. If an entry is found, retrieve the LID in the entry and proceed to step 5.

3. Virtual memory space (LID) is allocated for the target and the object gets loaded in there. References within the loaded object are either swizzled or narrowed. Narrowed references populates the Addr2OID table.

4. A new entry is added to the ROT which records the association between the OID and the LID.

5. The marker value is replaced with the LID.

The use of a surrogate in the narrowing scheme is equivalent to the use of a *lambda* in the LOOM implementation.

Now we look at how marker values get discovered. Execution of a program starts with the loading of persistent roots as is done in Texas. But unlike Texas, target objects need to be loaded at this point due to the lack of residency checking in the current implementation. A persistent root is an objects which can be bound to a pointer at program startup by specifying its name.

Because each pointer to a persistent root is initialized in the way described above and persistent objects are loaded in the heap only, the sole possibility of a surrogate being discovered by a running program is through a memory fetch from the heap. Thus by screening surrogates upon those memory access and performing swizzling if needed, the invariant can be maintained that every pointer read from memory to be fed into a register or stack frame is all reservation checked. The screening is performed by having the compiler add extra instructions to those for an expression which involves a pointer dereferencing and yields a pointer or a pointer-containing aggregate value. This strategy may pose problems with memory-indirect addressing modes in some CISC machines. However, it is not a problem with GCC because inserted checking prevents the compiler from combining two memory access instructions into a single machine instruction, which could have been performed at rather late stage of code generation.

The modification made to GCC for the generation of reservation checking code is very little. The addition consists of a few dozen lines to existing files (mainly in 'c-typeck.c') and about 500 lines in two new files. Following optimizations are included.

- If a single member of an aggregate is extracted by .-operator, swizzling all pointers in the aggregate is avoided.

- Pointers to functions are not reservation checked.

- A pointer,whose value is compared with 0 and immediately discarded, is not reservation checked.

For the storage layer, Exodus Storage Manager is used. We plan to add support for more. One of our goals is to provide a set of storage manager independent interface functions so that varieties of persistent storage systems and file systems can be plugged and played. As a summary the swizzling schemes, The right of Fig.2 illustrates what happens when an object (A) gets faulted in due to the discovery of pointer P2.

3.4 A Commercial ODBMS

We have included a commercial ODBMS as a representative of a non-swizzling object faulting method with references whose size matches virtual memory pointer. The database system implements a reference to be placed in virtual memory using 32bit value. The length of an OID is unknown as well as whether the system rewrites references upon object fault. For brevity, in the following we use the term LID to refer to a reference which exists in the physical storage. The LID is contained in an instance of a class, which includes a method for translating the LID into a virtual memory pointer. Because the method of LID reservation is exposed to an application program, implementation of reservation checking depends on each application program. Though we expect the system does not use pointer swizzling nor a hardware based residency checking method, as a commercial system, the details are not clear.

4   Related Papers

[5] presented detailed description of the dimensions of pointer swizzling techniques and the results of performance experiments. The paper also introduced the notion of edge-marking and node-marking. This paper concentrates primary on the cost of translation between OID and virtual memory pointer instead of the cost of reservation/residency checks. The node-marking and edge-marking scheme proposed are samples in the design space made of the two checks proposed in this paper. Roughly speaking, edge-marking is the case where only reservation checks are performed while node-marking is the case where only residency checks are performed.

[2] presented a *pointer swizzling upon discovery* method. Their interest was in reducing the number of OID translations and in fact there was no improvement over a more naive approach (*pointer swizzling upon dereference*) in terms of the frequency of reservation checks. Relevant to our paper is the fact revealed in this paper that their approach is 5 times slower than an implementation using *pointer swizzling at page fault time*.

[4] picks up the issue of reservation checking in the context of the Persistent Smalltalk implementation and reports excellent results about the effectiveness of their residency checking method. The differences are that in general Smalltalk takes more cycles to do the same number of navigation than C/C++ does because of the messaging paradigm and dispatching mechanism, thus diluting the overhead of reservation checks. Because it so happens that Smalltalk has richer semantics in a pointer dereferencing that each access to class object, literals, contexts, etc. can be distinguished from others. This is utilized for improving the efficiency of the scheme. Therefore the result is interesting and relevant to our research, the method and the results are not directly applicable to the environment we target.

Most relevant to our research are [1] and [11], considering the similarity of the target applications our systems seek to support. However, their approach is different from ours and provides a good contrast to ours. [12] also is as relevant. The authors have the same goal of reducing virtual memory requirement and overhead for reservation checking as we do. The differences from ours are that virtual memory space is further conserved by performing reservation checking upon dereference of a pointer and reservation checking instructions are eliminated by exploiting MMU.

In summary, the primary contribution of this paper is that it shows a software swizzling method can be competitive with hardware based schemes such as Texas even in terms of pure in-memory navigation, i.e. without updates or time consuming calculation intermingled with traversals. Another is that we have obtained results by performance an evaluation using a real application as a test case.

5   Small Benchmarks

We modified the Gnu G++ compiler in two ways to make it generate residency checking instructions. In one way, residency checking instructions are added when a parse tree is converted into RTL, the Register Transfer Language. This results in the generation of a compare and a branch instructions for each discovered pointer. As the common subexpression elimination phase of the compiler does not try to optimize beyond a basic block, redundant residency checking code is not eliminated. The other way, a RTL instruction for a relevant memory access is just marked as 'need-to-reservation-check' during the conversion phase. Then after finishing the CSE and jump optimizations, an extra RTL sequence is inserted in front of the marked RTLs. In the discussion below, the former is referred to as P3L(tree) and the latter as P3L(RTL).

We have run three micro tests and one toy, but real, program by compiling them with the Gnu G++ 2.3.3, P3L(tree), P3L(RTL) and EG++. Both P3L and EG++ are derived from version 2.3.3 of the Gnu G++ Compiler. EG++ is the compiler for the E programming language. We made the structure of the nodes to be manipulated *dbtype* in the programs written in E. All compilations are done using -O flag. These micro tests examine the overhead of the reservation checking code. The times reported are user CPU time, which was gathered through two *getrusage* system calls placed before and after the measured region of code. The programs were executed on a Sun4/330 with 32MB of memory. For each benchmark, measurements were performed 10 times and the two fastest and slowest results were eliminated and the remaining 6 were averaged.

The first micro test is a pathological one.

```
LXstruct foo {              | int main(int ac, char **av) {
   struct foo * next; |        int i, sum=0;
   int                v; |     struct foo * p = &a;
};                          |     a.next = &b; a.v = 1;
struct foo a, b;            |     b.next = &a; b.v = 2;
                            |     for(i=0;i<1000*1000*10;++i)
                            |         { /* sum += p->v; */ p = p->next; }
                            |     /* return sum; */
                            |     return (int)p;
                            | }
```

This program does pointer chasing only. Both structures are supposed to reside entirely within the processor cache.

compiler	G++	P3L(RTL)	P3L(tree)	EG++
time(msec)	2040	3276	4493	17380
ratio	1.00	1.61	2.20	8.52

In the case of P3L(RTL), the compiler succeeds in placing the instruction for fetching the 'next' field into the delay-slot of the branch for the loop. This reduces the pipeline stall. And the instruction for loading p and the compare instruction for residency checking are separated by several instructions. This reduces or eliminates the stall time due to data dependencies. These seem to be the reasons why P3L(RTL) does much better than P3L(tree).

The next program adds a small work to the navigation loop. The program is the same one except that the commented out statements are now executed.

compiler	G++	P3L(RTL)	P3L(tree)	EG++
time(msec)	4088	4506	6135	23131
ratio	1.00	1.10	1.50	5.65

The overhead of the three reservation checks has decreased considerably. This agrees with the results presented in [2] that effectively says that the cost of residency checks becomes rather insignificant when a small amount of work is added. However, the relative value of the overhead is still high.

The last micro test examines the performance of navigation when pointers are not in the processor cache. A linked list of 500K nodes is created then traversed 10 times calculating the sum. The time for creating the list is not included. The overhead falls to less than 10% for P3L(RTL).

compiler	G++	P3L(RTL)	P3L(tree)	EG++
time(msec)	5721	6228	6948	22676
ratio	1.00	1.09	1.21	3.96

The last test is with a small program which inserts 4096 nodes into an AVL-tree. The type of the nodes is defined below.

```
struct node {
    struct node * left, *right;
    int             balance;
    char            key[32];
};
```

The code to handle the insertion is taken from [13]. The values of the key arc generated at random. The time for generating nodes before insertion into the tree is not included in the results.

compiler	G++	P3L(RTL)	P3L(tree)	EG++
time(msec)	14511	15463	15821	150066
ratio	1.00	1.07	1.09	10.34

Because P3L(RTL) makes it possible for the compiler to take better advantage of the CSE optimization, two successive dereferences of a pointer result in only one pair of load and check instructions. The benefit is not small if time saved is compared to the total overhead. However, the relative value of the difference is so small that it is not tangible. Eliminating redundant translation instructions or check instructions is surely more crucial for faulting methods without swizzling and *swizzling upon dereference*, though. The reason why E does so poorly seems to be that this test contains many function calls and many accesses to chars through db pointers.

6 OO1 Benchmark

We have measured the performance of the selected persistent object systems using traversal potion of the Sun Engineering Database Benchmark. The experiment has only been done using small databases. The machine used for the test was a SparcStation 10 Model 40 with 64MB of memory and a Fujitsu 2624SA hard disk drive dedicated for the benchmark. The P3L compiler used is based on the Gnu C 2.4.8 (not the Gnu G++ 2.4.8). For the insertion of reservation checking codes, P3L(tree) method was used. EG++ used is based on the Gnu G++ 2.4.8 and, for Texas, plain Gnu G++ 2.4.8 was used. The result of the cold-warm traversal is shown in Fig 3. The elapsed time from 5 consecutive iterations are combined to derive a single mean value, resulting in 100 points to be plotted.

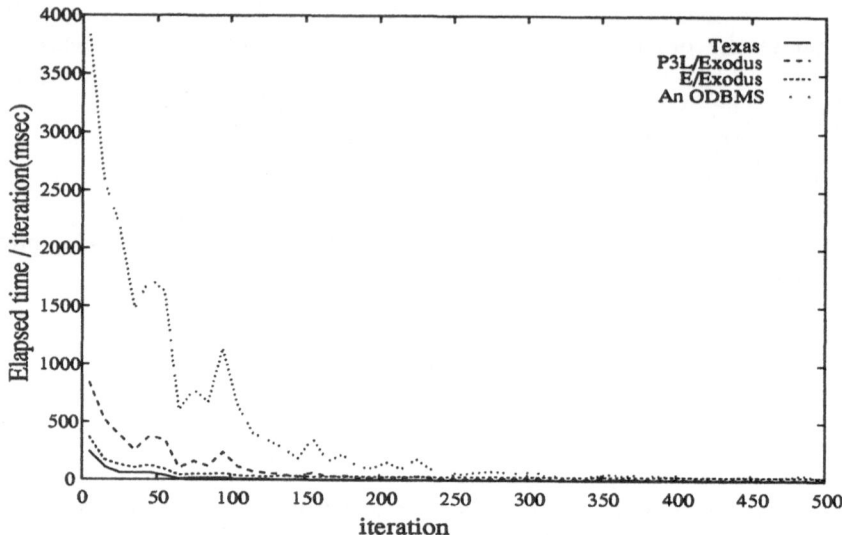

Figure 3: Traversal: cold⇒hot (with locality in connection)

Since our interest is in the traversal speed when all visited nodes are cached in the physical storage, we run the same iteration of traversals after finishing 1000 iterations, i.e. the same 1000 staring points were selected again in the second run with all the nodes so far visited in the first run cached in memory. The results are shown in Fig 4.

Finally we ran a non-standard benchmark by removing the locality in the connection of parts in the OO1 benchmark database. This change most significantly affects Texas. Because of its eagerness to reserve virtual memory space, the use of virtual memory pages get fragmented. P3L is affected less.

Parts in the database are connected randomly with no locality. And the first batch of traversals is performed in the same way as the previous test was. For the second run, however, only the part which was selected as the starting node in the first iteration of the first batch was used as the starting point. And exactly the same traversal was repeated 1000 times. The results are shown in Fig 5.

Interestingly, our implementation outperforms the hardware based mechanism by about 10%. Unfortunately we have not yet identified the exact reason why it does. We ran the same benchmark on an old SPARC based machine which has a page size of 8192 bytes [12] and this phenomenon was not observed. Contrarily, a MicroSPARC based machine (SparcStation/) reproduced the result mentioned here. From this we speculate the effect of TLB misses but no hard data have yet been acquired.

---

[12] Others mentioned here have 4096 byte page.

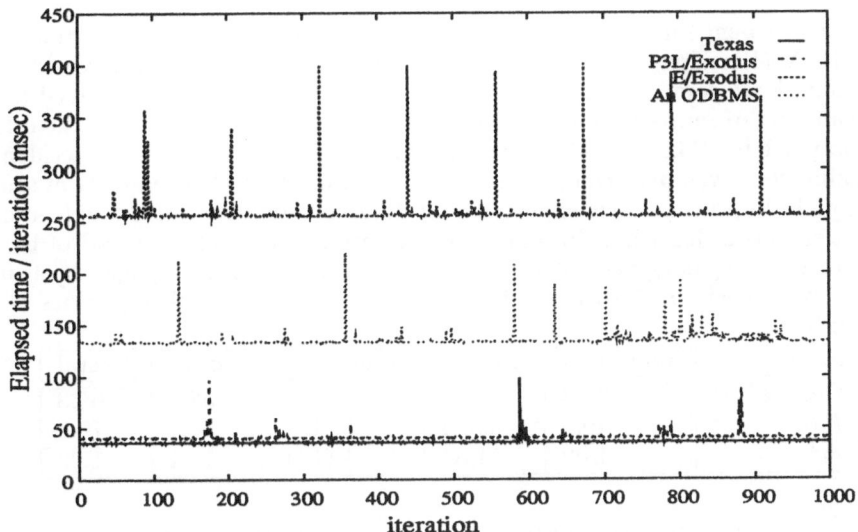

Figure 4: Traversal: hot (with locality in connection)

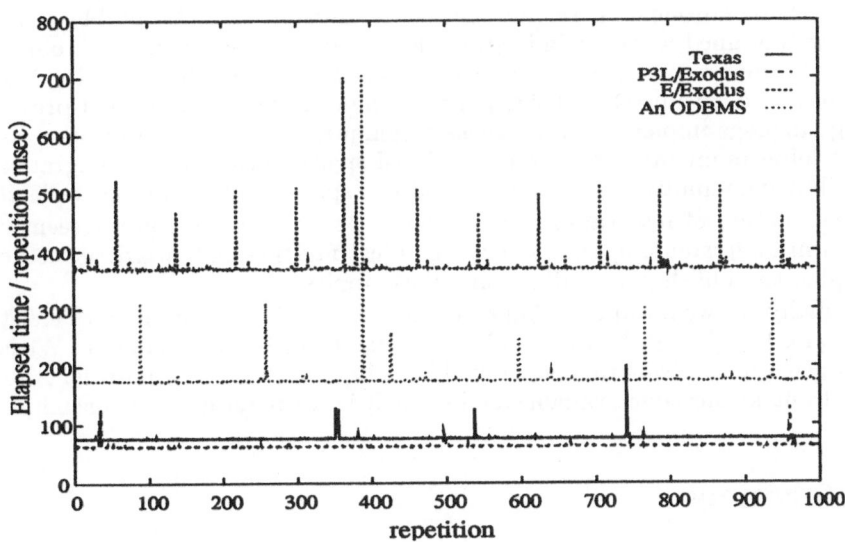

Figure 5: Traversal: hot (w/o locality in connection)

7 An Evaluation using a real Application

For the last benchmark, we picked up a freely distributed ray-tracing program, POVRAY (Persistence Of Vision RAYtracer), which is written in C. In this benchmark we compared the execution speed of two executables derived from the same set of sources. One is compiled using plain Gnu-C 2.4.8 and the other is compiled by P3L compiler based on Gnu-C 2.4.8. Insertion of residency checking code was performed by using the *tree* method. Five models of scene were picked up because we expected that difference models would result in different traversal densities. Produced images are saved in files instead of being sent to the output device. The results are shown in the next page. Measurements were performed 10 times for each scene and the resulting values were averaged.

Scene	polywood	skyvase	stonewal	magglass	crystal
Plain GCC	37.3	94.2	36.0	32.8	69.3
P3L	40.9	98.4	39.0	36.4	70.5
ratio	1.09	1.04	1.08	1.11	1.02

Time for rendering POV images (in seconds).

8 Conclusion

We have presented the pointer swizzling method used in our implementation of the P3L compiler, contrasting it with other swizzling methods. We also reported the result of our evaluations which verify effectiveness of the method under the conditions where the method is targeted for. A notable result is that we obtained a strong indication that, under certain situations, our software scheme can outperform a hardware based swizzling method using MMU. Although we have presented this paper in the context of a persistent programming language implementation, these techniques are applicable to other areas where objects migrate between two isolated spaces such as object migration in distributed computing environments and two space copying garbage collection.

The notion of reservation and residency proposed in this paper seem very useful in understanding and classifying object faulting and swizzling methods. We plan to publish papers discussing these topics.

Finally we would like to thank the authors of E/Exodus, Texas Persistent Store, POVRAY and the Gnu C/C++ for making their code available. Without their generous decision this paper could not have been made what it is. And we plan to make our code available as soon as it is ready for general consumption.

References

[1] Paul R.Wilson and Sheetal V.Kakkad,'Pointer Swizzling at Page Fault Time: Efficiently Supporting Huge Address Space on Standard Hardware', Proc. Int'l Workshop on Object Orientation in Operating Systems, Paris, Sept 92,pp. 364-377

[2] Seth J. White and David J.Dewitt, 'A Performance Study of Alternative Object Faulting and Pointer Swizzling Strategies', Proc. of Conference on Very Large Data Bases 1992

[3] Ted Kaehler and Glenn Krasner, 'LOOM - Large Object Oriented Memory for Smalltalk-80 Systems', Smalltalk-80 Bis of History, Words of Advice, Addison Wesley

[4] Antony L. Hosking, J.Eliot B. Moss, 'Object Fault Handling for Persistent Programming Lanugages: A Performance Evaluation', Proceedings ACM Conference on Object Oriented Programming Systems, Languages and Applications, Washington DC, Sep. 1993, pp.288-303

[5] J. Eliot B. Moss, 'Working with Persistent Objects: To Swizzle or Not ot Swizzle', Trans. on Software Engineering Vol 18, Aug 1992

[6] Alfons Kemper and Donald Kossmann,'Adaptable Pointer Swizzling Strategies in Object Bases', Int'l Conf. on Data Engineering, 1993, pp.155-162

[7] Gordon Russel and Paul Cockshott, 'A Survey of Architectures for Memory Resident Database', Research Report ARCH-10-93, University of Strathclyde 1993

[8] W.P. Cockshot, M.P. Atkinson and K.J. Chisholm, 'Persistent Object Management System', Software Practice and Experience Vol.14 1984

[9] Carey, M., et. al.,'The EXODUS Extensible DBMS Project: An Overview' in Readings in Object Oriented Databases., S. Zdonik and D.Maier,eds.,Morgan-Kaufman,1989

[10] Charles Lamb, Gordon Landis, Jack Orenstein and Dan Weinreb:"THE OBJECTSTORE DATABASE SYSTEM" Vol.34 No.10 CACM91

[11] Vivek Singhal, Sheetal V. Kakkad, and Paul R. Wilson, 'Texas: An Efficient, Portable Persistent Store', Proc. Fith Int'l Workshop on Persistent Object Systems, San Miniato, Italy, Sept 1992.

[12] Francis Vaughan, Alan Dearle, 'Supporting large persistent stores using conventional hardware', 5th intl. workshop on Persistent Object Systems

[13] Aaron M.Tenenbaum, Yedidyah Langsam and Moshe J. Augenstein, 'DATA STRUCTURES USING C' Prentice Hall ISBN 0-13-199746-7

Object Caching

Alan Dearle
al@cs.adelaide.edu.au
Department of Computer Science
University of Adelaide
Adelaide 5005
Australia

The subject of the second session held on Tuesday 6th of September was caching technology. Two papers were presented: one by Liuba Shrira on a hybrid page/object based client cache, the other by Carsten Gerlhof on page based prefetching.

The thesis of the first paper is that hybrid caches have the potential to be more efficient than either purely page or object based approaches. When page based systems are employed to support object based systems, many unreferenced objects may be stored on pages in the client which are not part of the computation's working set. This is wasteful of client memory and may prevent the working set from fitting in memory even if the total size of the objects being manipulated is smaller than the size of the client cache. Object caches do not suffer from this potential problem since the cache is managed purely in terms of objects. However, object based systems do suffer from the problem that in order to install a modified object in the object store, the disk block on which the object is stored needs to be re-read, modified and installed. In a page based system, the reads known as installation reads are not required. Liuba and Jim propose a hybrid caching policy based on objects and pages that aims to derive the benefits of both approaches without the disadvantages.

The subject of the second paper in the session was prefetching pages into the client cache. If prefetching is accurate this can considerably reduce latency and hence increase response time. Carsten described the predictor based and code based approaches currently used for calculating which pages to prefetch. The first technique has a low overhead but can have low accuracy, the second has excellent accuracy but can have a high overhead. In contrast, Prefetch Support Relations (PSRs), a new technique described in this paper, exhibit high accuracy and low overhead. They also have the important property of being able to cope with assignments which invalidate predicates upon which prefetches are based.

Half an hour of discussion was scheduled following the paper presentations; this proved to be a lively half hour. True to form, Eliot Moss started the ball rolling with an observation and a question. The observation was that the measurement in the first paper focused on total throughput whereas the measurements in the second paper refer to response time by client programs. The question was what was being hidden by ignoring the other? Liuba said that for the simulations described in her paper, measuring either throughput or response time is equivalent since you can deduce one from the other. This is due to the fact that the simulations modelled a closed system in which in a steady state throughput is an inverse of response time. Some members of the audience misunderstood what Liuba was saying at this point and believed that she meant that the inverse relationship was true in all cases which, of course, it is not.

Carsten said that prefetching can increase throughput, especially if the time between page faults is large when compared with server response time. This is due to the fact that computation can overlap I/O and that all resources in the system are more uniformly utilised. However, this statement proved to be highly contentious.

Jim O'Toole, a co-author of the first paper, was of the opinion that pre-fetching could only increase throughput when the server was not loaded to capacity. He argued that if the server was loaded to capacity, prefetching could only help throughput if the prediction accuracy was 100% correct. If it were 99% accurate, the prefetched data would never be referenced 1% of the time. Therefore if the server was running at 100% capacity, throughput would drop. Although the logic of this statement seems clear, this statement fuelled rather than dowsed discussion. Carsten later pointed out that PSRs have the property of being 100% accurate on the first prefetch.

Olivier Gruber stated that a server that is running at 100% capacity is not necessarily incapable of delivering more capacity. To support this argument he pointed out that a disk that is busy may be spending much of its time seeking rather than delivering data, especially if the server is supporting multiple clients. Often disk requests may be serviced more efficiently if there are outstanding requests in the queue. This will help throughout at the expense of response time. Carsten agreed with this but stated that the small increase in response time is masked by the client computation possible due to the fact that clients are no longer blocked waiting on I/O. Eliot stated that clearly there exists a trade-off between throughput prefetch versus server load versus disk scheduling. Nobody said much to this.

Never exhausted by such discussions, Malcolm Atkinson asked if the server could distinguish between prefetches and real fetches. Clearly the client knows which are which and if the server knew, it could solve the problem by scheduling prefetches at a lesser priority than real fetches. Bob Grossman suggested that the system could be tuned further by only prefetching if the program was accessing pages sequentially.

Malcolm asked Liuba why there was such a big difference in performance between the hybrid and object based systems described in her paper. Liuba explained that this was predominantly due to the cost of installation reads. By now things were calming down which gave Liuba the opportunity to ask the following question of the audience: "the hybrid system ignores the CPU cost of swizzling and unswizzling and is primarily concerned with I/O cost – is this a good idea and can you build a cache that knows which objects are hot or cold?"

Paul Wilson (who the next day was to have a nasty run in with a Camargue bull) said that the CPU cost was not a problem for two reasons: firstly, usage could be tracked by a couple of instructions and a bit in the object header. Secondly, fast machines that are I/O bound may not notice the extra code anyhow. Fred Brown suggested that you could do better than this using a second chance object discard algorithm which synthesises the same behaviour. Eliot Moss expressed concern that these schemes were difficult to implement and there was no evidence for them helping in practice. He suggested that those studying object caches needed real implementation and measurement on real systems since this had proved valuable in the area of object storage. Malcolm asked how accurate the information gathered has to be since low grade information was easy to collect. Liuba stated that accuracy may not matter if optimisation was possible and that static rather than dynamic analysis may prove promising.

Until this point David Koch had been sitting quietly at the back of the room. However, when invited to voice an opinion as a hardware person he stated that he thought that not enough consideration was being given to working sets. All the discussion about page and object discard assumes that there is not enough space in the client to support the working set of the computation. The space aspects of the computation needed to be given the same attention as the time complexity. To this, Liuba responded that RAM could be added to both the client and the server with potentially quite different behaviours.

In order to get the final word, Malcolm suggested that perhaps the whole client-server architecture was the wrong model and that we were looking at symptoms of bad architectural decisions. This hurt everybody's head so much that we all went out to the garden for coffee and some of those nice French cakes:)

Hybrid Caching for Large-Scale Object Systems
(Think Globally, Act Locally)

James O'Toole

Massachusetts Institute of Technology

Cambridge, Massachusetts, USA

Liuba Shrira

Massachusetts Institute of Technology

Cambridge, Massachusetts, USA

Abstract

Object-based client caching allows clients to keep more frequently accessed objects while discarding colder objects that reside on the same page. However, when these objects are modified and sent to the server, it may need to read the corresponding page from disk to install the update. These *installation reads* are not required with a page-based cache because whole pages are sent to the server.

We describe a hybrid system that permits clients to cache objects and pages. The system uses a simple cache design that combines the best of object caching and page caching. The client increases its cache hit ratio as in object-based caching. The client avoids some installation reads by sending pages to the server when possible. Using simulated workloads we explore the performance of our design and show that it can offer a significant performance improvement over both pure object caching and pure page caching on a range of workloads.

1 Introduction

In a client/server persistent object system, objects are fetched from the server over the network into the client cache, manipulated locally, and the modifications are sent to be committed at the server. In a scalable system many clients will be competing for server resources. Given current hardware trends, we assume that the server will be disk I/O bound. Therefore it is important to design the client/server caching system to reduce the disk I/O bandwidth consumed at the server.

Previous studies have shown that when hot data is densely packed on pages, page-based caching performs well. When the hot objects are sparsely packed,

This research was supported in part by the Advanced Research Projects Agency of the Department of Defense, monitored by the Office of Naval Research under contract N00014-91-J-4136, in part by the National Science Foundation under Grant CCR-8822158, and in part by the Department of the Army under Contract DABT63-92-C-0012.

object-based caching works better because it is able to hold more hot objects in the cache. However, there is an additional cost associated with object caching: On commit, an object cache sends to the server the modified object, but it does not send the page. To install the modified object onto its containing page, the server may need to read the page from the disk if it is not present in the server cache. In a previous study [13] we have shown that the cost of these installation reads can be significant.

In this paper we present a design of a hybrid cache that manages at the client both pages and objects. We suggest a hybrid cache management policy that uses a simple eviction rule to avoid some installation reads. The modified eviction rule protects some objects from eviction in order to help keep pages intact. By keeping a page intact, the client can send the whole page to the server when it modifys an object on that page. This enables the server to avoid an installation read.

To study the performance of the hybrid cache we construct a simple performance model that focuses on the I/O costs in object and page caching. Using simulation we compare the throughput of a system with object-based caching, page-based caching and hybrid caching over a range of workloads. We consider the workloads where page caching is advantageous (densely packed hot objects) workloads where object caching is advantageous (sparsely packed hot objects) and workloads that represent a combination of both. Our results show that when disk I/O is the performance bottleneck, the hybrid system can outperform both pure object caching and pure page caching.

In the following sections, we introduce the basic scalable persistent object system design (Section 2) and describe the hybrid cache and its policy (Section 3). We then introduce our simulation model (Section 4), present the experimental system configurations (Section 5), and present simulation results that illustrate the value of our techniques (Section 6). Finally, we discuss related research (Section 7) and our conclusions (Section 8).

2   Persistent Object Systems

This section introduces our baseline persistent object system and describes the context of our work. The system supports atomic modifications to persistent objects. We briefly discuss our assumptions about the system architecture. The persistent objects are stored on disk at the server. We assume that objects are grouped into *pages* and updated in place. Pages are the unit of disk transfer and caching at the server. Objects are small and a page can contain many objects. Client cache performance is the dominant factor that we consider because our focus is on reducing the disk load at the server.

Client Caching

In a persistent object system, clients fetch data from a server and operate on it in a local cache. In an object-based architecture, clients fetch objects, update them, and send back updated objects in a commit request to the server. In a page-based architecture, the client and server exchange whole pages, as shown in Figure 1.

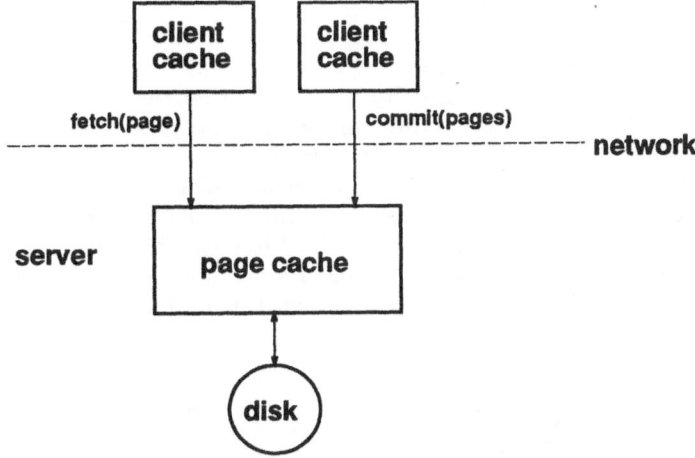

Figure 1: Clients using a Page Server

Previous work shows that each approach may be superior to the other depending on how the objects (on pages) are accessed by application programs [6]. When the clustering of objects on pages corresponds to the client access pattern, the page-based architecture should work well. On the other hand, object-based systems may pack frequently accessed objects more densely into the client cache. There are also other issues that complicate matters: swizzling, object prefetching, object clustering strategies, etc. Our focus is on disk performance, so we are ignoring these issues here.

Transaction Validation

We assume a server architecture similar to that of the Thor persistent object system [11]. The features that we assume are optimistic concurrency control with in-memory commit [2]. If the client and server are using a page-based architecture, then we assume that the page server also uses optimistic concurrency control and in-memory commit.

We use an optimistic concurrency control scheme, so a transaction that reads stale objects is aborted when the server rejects its commit request. The server uses a concurrency control protocol to ensure that all committing transactions are serialized. Committing transactions are validated by the server using a method that does not require disk access; see Adya [2] for the details. The server notifies clients when cached objects are modified, so that client caches are "almost" up-to-date.

When considering the choice between page and object servers we ignore the question of whether the server uses page level or object level concurrency control. Though this choice of granularity is important to the semantics and performance of transaction validation, it is orthogonal to the I/O costs that concern us here.

Installing Modifications

When a transaction commits in a page-based architecture, the entire page is returned to the server. For simplicity, we assume that the server is implemented using a non-volatile memory so that committing a transaction does not require an immediate disk write. Without non-volatile memory, the server would record committed modifications in a log on a dedicated disk.

When a transaction commits in an object-based architecture, the client sends modified objects back to the server. After validation, the server records the modified objects in a non-volatile log. Later, modifications from the log are applied to their corresponding pages; we call this update process *installation*.

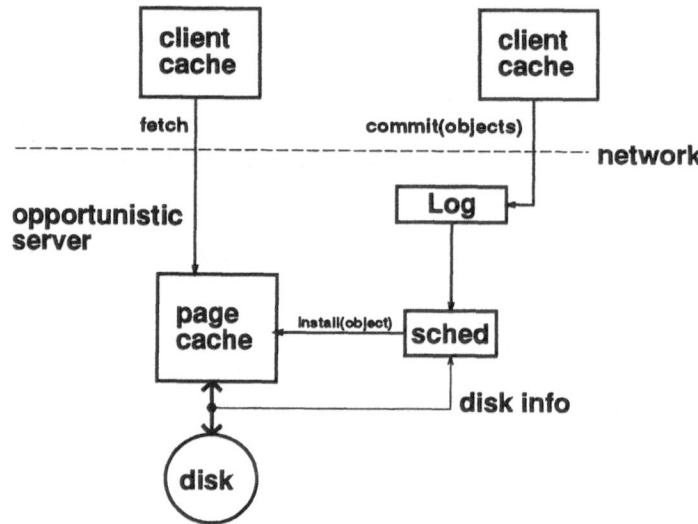

Figure 2: Object Server with Opportunistic Log

Note that installing an object modification may require a disk read if the corresponding page is not in the server cache. In recent work, we found that these *installation reads* can have a large impact on the performance of large-scale object servers [13]. We showed that the transaction log provides a large pool of pending installation reads that can be processed opportunistically, as shown in Figure 2. In particular, we showed that using well-known disk scheduling techniques allows the cost of installation reads to be reduced to a fraction of the normal random-access cost.

3 Hybrid Caching

In practice, we expect the objects that are frequently used by a client to be sometimes packed densely into pages and sometimes not. Therefore, we are motivated to design a hybrid system that permits clients to cache both objects and pages. This allows clients to selectively retain some objects from a page and discard the others, or to keep a page intact. In a hybrid system, clients may be able to take advantage of increased cache memory utilization while also avoiding some installation reads.

3.1 Hybrid Server

To enable the client to cache pages, the server must provide whole pages to the client when responding to fetch requests. Then the client will be able to return whole pages to the server, at least when it has retained the whole page in its cache. Previous work tells us that object servers can help avoid fetches by sending groups of related objects in response to fetch requests. We would expect a hybrid system to do this just as well, but we note that sending objects instead of pages may produce more installation reads.

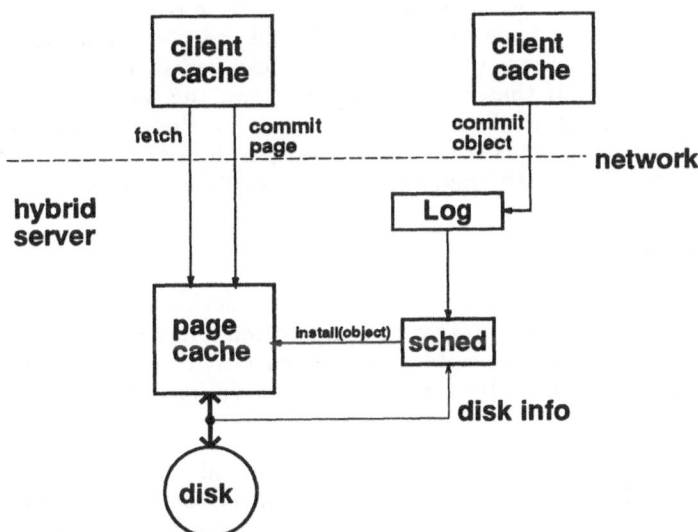

Figure 3: Hybrid Server accept Page and Object Commits

So the hybrid server provides whole pages to the client. The server accepts commit requests from the client for either whole pages or individual objects, as shown in Figure 3. When the server receives a commit request that provides a page, it validates the transaction according to the individual object that was modified (i.e. the hybrid server uses object-based concurrency control). If the transaction is valid, then the server can consider whether to use the containing page to avoid an installation read. This is possible if the other objects on the page are not stale. Otherwise, it is still possible that the valid objects on the page can be combined with pending installations to produce the whole page. But in any case, we should at least expect the hybrid server to be able to avoid an installation read whenever a page-based system would avoid concurrency control conflicts within the page.

3.2 Cache Tradeoffs

When the client receives a page from the server after a cache miss, it may already have information about how hot the objects on the page are. This kind of information could be used to guide promotion or eviction policies in any kind of cache. In a hybrid design, this information could be especially useful.

If the page contains just a few hot objects, it might be best to keep these objects but discard their cold companions. Discarding the rest of the page will prevent a later page-commit, and may very likely mean that more installation reads are required at the server. However, the memory occupied by these cold companions might be better used to hold yet more hot objects. This is what makes object-based caching work. Also, an opportunistic log [13] can make installation reads much less expensive than disk reads produced by fetch operations, because installation reads can be deferred and scheduled, unlike fetch reads which are blocking the progress of clients and must be performed immediately. Therefore the tradeoff generally favors increasing the client cache utilitization at the expense of additional installation reads.

In contrast, when a page contains mostly hot objects, it may be worth keeping a few cold companions in the cache to avoid generating more installation reads at the server. If the cache is very effective, the memory occupied by a few cold objects may not be so valuable. Keeping the cold objects that help eliminate installation reads is then beneficial (to the server). In some sense we intend that the client cache manager think globally and act locally.

3.3 Cache Policy

We do not know how to make perfect caching decisions in a hybrid system. In the discussion here, we present the motivation and intuition for the hybrid cache design rules. The concrete cache design that results from these rules is presented in Section 5.2. Here are some basic design rules for how a hybrid cache should work:

- When objects arrive in the cache they should be treated fairly, because they may be either hot or cold. If the cache is working well, then incoming objects will usually be cold. Otherwise, they will usually be hot.

- When an object in the cache is accessed, it should be promoted individually, because we infer that it may be hot, but we are not so sure about its page-companions.

These two ideas reflect basic facts about object caching, but promoting based on page relationships will be sometimes useful. We've chosen to ignore this issue to simplify our work. If page-relationships can be used in object promotion, the hybrid cache should do what the best object cache does.

The goal of our hybrid cache policy is to avoid installation reads when possible. This new motivation should affect the caching policy primarily in the area of eviction because eviction (hopefully) relates to cold objects. Here is a simple rule that captures the essential idea:

- When an object is about to be evicted, and it is the first object of its page to be evicted, give it another chance if its page-companions appear to be hot.

This policy expresses the basic motivation behind hybrid caching and completes our hybrid cache design. It seems likely to protect a cold object when doing so is likely to eliminate installation reads. It will not protect cold objects that are from mostly-cold pages.

Ideally, we would also like to base our eviction decisions on how likely the hot objects are to be *written*. There is less reason to protect a cold object whose hot page-companions are rarely modified. So predictive information about the frequency of update of objects would also be useful.

In practice, it seems entirely likely that the best sources of predictive information about object access patterns will depend on the application. Object types or historical information might be useful and could be collected by the server or the client. However, we do not aspire here to solve this part of the cache design problem. Our goal here is simply to explore the interaction between caching policy in a hybrid design and the cost of installation reads.

We know from previous work that installation reads can be optimized to be less costly than fetch reads. Therefore, we want the hybrid cache to behave mostly like an object cache and obtain the maximum possible benefit from packing hot objects into the client cache. When the pressure to evict cold objects is reduced, the hybrid cache should keep the cold objects that will eliminate the most installation reads.

4   Simulation Model

To examine cache performance tradeoffs, we built a simulator for a system of clients and a reliable server. The simulator emphasizes the disk I/O requirements of the server because we expect client cache performance to affect aggregate system throughput by loading the disk. The simulation model is described by the parameters shown in Table 1. We discuss simplifications and assumptions in the sections that follow.

4.1   Network

The network provides unlimited bandwidth and a fixed message delivery latency. Each message transmission also incurs a small cpu overhead. We ignore contention because we assume that network bandwidth will not significantly affect the performance of reliable servers. If network bandwidth were a limiting factor, then we would expect object caching to benefit because objects are smaller than pages, so commit messages for objects are smaller. In general we use low message costs to reflect our expectation that network performance will be improving much faster than disk performance in the foreseeable future.

4.2   Disk

The disk services requests issued by the server in FIFO order. The disk geometry and other performance characteristics are taken from the HP97560 drive described by Wilkes [14]. We chose this disk because it is simple, accurate, and available.

Network	
Message latency	1 msec
Per-message cpu overhead	100 μsecs
Disk	
Rotational speed	4002 rpm
Sector size	512 bytes
Sectors per track	72
Tracks per cylinder	19
Cylinders	1962
Head switch time	1.6 msec
Seek time ($\leq$ 383 cylinders)	$3.24 + 0.4\sqrt{d}$ ms
Seek time ($>$ 383 cylinders)	$8.00 + 0.008d$ ms
Server	
Database size (full disk)	335,500 pages
Page size	4 Kbytes
Log-size	100 pages
Log-entries-per-page	5
Server memory (1% of database)	3,355 pages
ValidationTime	5 μsecs
InstallationTime	1 msec
WriteTrigger	$>$ 2000 dirty pages
IReadTrigger	$<$ 50 empty log entries

Table 1: System Parameters

4.3   Server

The server processes fetch and commit requests from clients by reading and writing relevant database pages that are stored on an attached disk. The server has a non-volatile primary memory that holds cached pages. When a fetch request is received from a client, the page corresponding to the requested object is read from the disk into the server cache if necessary. The entire page is then sent to the client.

The non-volatile primary memory is also used as a transaction log. *Log-size* pages of the primary memory are statically allocated to hold log entries. The *Log-entries-per-page* parameter defines the number of log entries that can be stored per page of log memory. The log entries represent the collection of modified objects that have not yet been installed.

Concurrency control at the server is described by the *ValidationTime* parameter, which defines the cpu time required to validate a transaction. Aborted transactions are indistinguishable from read-only transactions for our purposes. If the client has provided an entire page containing a modified object in the commit request, then the server stores the page into its cache memory and marks it dirty. The server then sends a confirming message to the client. When the number of dirty pages in the cache exceeds the *WriteTrigger* threshold, the server writes one dirty page to the disk. The page is selected using the shortest positioning time algorithm [15].

If the client provides only the modified object in the transaction commit request, then the server adds the object to the log and sends a confirming message to the client. If the page containing the object is in the cache, then the object is installed immediately. However, if the page is not in the cache, then the installation is postponed. When the number of empty log entries decreases below the *IReadTrigger* threshold the server issues an installation read to obtain the page needed for a pending log entry. The server selects the pending installation from the log opportunistically, as described in previous work [13]. An installation read is initiated for the page that has the shortest positioning time, which can be determined fairly quickly using a branch and bound implementation.

Whenever a page enters the cache, whether due to a disk read or from the client, all modified objects that belong to that page are installed onto it. Every installation consumes *InstallationTime* cpu time at the server.

5   Experimental Setup

For our simulations we chose a workload setup that provides skewed accesses both among pages and within individual pages. We also implemented several cache designs for comparison in our simulations. The workload setup and cache designs are described separately below.

5.1   Client Workload

Each simulated client contains a cpu and a local memory for caching objects. The client executes a sequence of transactions, each operating on a single object in the database. If necessary, the client sends a fetch request for the object to the server and waits for the server to respond with a full page containing the object. The client then computes for *ClientThinkTime* and possibly modifies the object (*WriteRatio*). Finally the client ends the transaction by sending a commit request to the server. After the commit is confirmed by the server, the client immediately starts its next transaction. Table 2 lists the parameters that control the workload generated by the clients.

We expect scalable object systems to have many clients that compete for the server memory. However, we found it impractical to simulate more than 50 clients because our simulator uses too much memory. Therefore, we artificially chose a very small server memory (1% of the database).

We expect each client in real systems to operate mostly on private data and to cache most or all of this data locally. Each simulated client directs 90% of its operations at some set of hot pages within the database. These hot pages do not overlap with the hot pages of other clients. The other 10% of the transactions use the rest of the database, including the hot pages belonging to other clients.

In order to experiment with hot pages that have hot objects more densely or more sparsely packed upon them, we designate some of the objects on each page to be hotter than the others. Each page contains 10 objects, and 99% of the transactions that access the page choose one of the hot objects on that page. The number of hot pages and hot objects within pages varies by actual workload and is described with the experimental results in Section 6.

Client Workload Parameters	
Number of clients	50
Client cache size	1000 pages
ClientThinkTime	100 msec
Page Access Pattern	90% Hot, 10% Cold
HotWriteRatio	20%
ColdWriteRatio	0%
Objects-per-page	10
Object Access Pattern	99% to hot (per page)
Number of hot pages	(various, see section 6)
Hot objects per page	(see section 6)

Table 2: Workload Parameters

We chose this access pattern so that the page-based cache will be unaware of the number of hot objects per page, because changing the number of hot objects on a page does not change the frequency of access for the page. However, this means that the hot objects on a sparsely-hot page will be much hotter than on a densely-hot page. We don't know whether this aspect hot object distribution is realistic. Section 6.3 discusses the relevance of the hot object distribution to the relative performance of hybrid and non-hybrid cache designs.

5.2   Cache Designs

The cache designs treat the client memory as a chain of objects. This "usage chain" is nearly an LRU chain. We implemented three client cache designs for use with the simulation model. The cache designs differ in how objects are promoted and how they are selected for eviction. Figure 4 depicts how each cache design moves data into, within, and back out of the cache.

Page Cache

In the page cache design, a page that is fetched from the server is entered into the middle of the usage chain. If a later transaction references the page, then it is promoted to the top of the usage chain. Whenever a page enters the cache, the page at the bottom of the chain is evicted to make room. The client always sends whole pages to the server when committing a modified object.

Object Cache

In the client object cache, as in the page cache, the page received from the server in response to a fetch request is placed in the middle of the usage chain. However, when an object that is cached is referenced, only that object is promoted to the top of the chain. When a page enters the cache, some objects at the bottom of the chain are evicted to make room. The client sends only the modified object to the server in a transaction commit message.

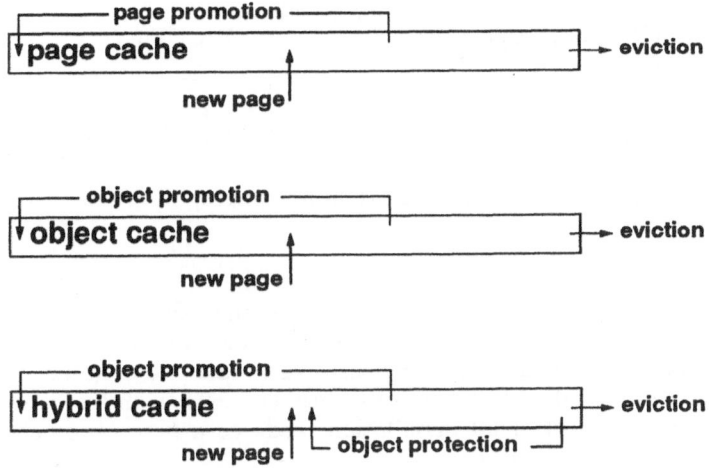

Figure 4: Movement of Data in the Cache Designs

Hybrid Cache

In the hybrid cache, the client enters and promotes objects in the usage chain exactly as in the object cache. However, the eviction rule is biased against evicting an object that belongs to a well-used page. When space is required, the object at the bottom of the chain is examined. If all of its page-companions are in the cache, and if more than half of them are currently in the upper-half of the usage chain, then this object is not evicted. Instead, this object is moved to the middle of the chain. When the client is committing a transaction, the whole page containing the modified object is sent to the server if all of the objects on that page are available in the client cache. Otherwise, only the modified object is supplied to the server.

6   Experiments

In the sections that follow, we focus on aggregate system throughput when the disk drive is fully utilized. We use one workload to illustrate the importance of installation reads. We use another to show the importance of object caching in increasing the client cache hit ratio. Finally, we examine a more realistic workload and show that hybrid caching performs much better than the other methods.

6.1   Dense Hot Workload

To illustrate how installation reads can hurt the performance of an object cache, we chose a workload in which each client directs its hot accesses to 600 hot pages. In this workload, 9 of the 10 objects on each page are hot objects. There are thus 5,400 hot objects packed very densely onto the hot pages.

The table in Figure 5 shows the throughput (tx/sec) of all three designs

Metrics for 50 clients

Cache Design	%hit	tx/sec	I-Cost	I-Disk
Pages	90%	375	—	0%
Objects	85%	228	6.0 ms	21%
Hybrid	90%	373	5.8 ms	<1%

Figure 5: Dense Workload (600 hot pages, all are dense)

when the system is fully loaded. We can see that the page cache performs much better than the object cache. The table also provides the client cache hit ratio (%hit) and installation read costs. The last two columns of the table provide the individual installation read cost (I-Cost) in milliseconds and the aggregate cost (I-Disk) of all installation reads as a percentage of total disk bandwidth.

Of course, the page cache produces only page-commit requests at the server, so there are no installation reads. In contrast, in the pure object system, every writing transaction can potentially cause an installation read. Installation reads consume 21% of the available disk bandwidth in this simulation. The hybrid design converted almost all object commits into page commits, eliminating essentially all installation reads.

Yet, in this example the biggest improvement still comes from the client cache hit ratio. The page and hybrid systems get a 90% hit ratio, but the object system only achieves 85%. The page system is keeping all hot pages in the cache because when a hot access takes place that hits in the cache, the entire page is promoted. The hybrid design also performs well, but because of its eviction rule. The modified eviction rule is making it less likely that hot data will be removed from the cache. Eliminating installation reads freed up 21% of the disk bandwidth, but the increase in the cache hit ratio decreased the disk load due to fetch operations by an even greater amount (about 33%). The result is that the hybrid design nearly equals the page server in throughput. However, the lesson is that for the hybrid design to compete with a page server on a dense hot workload, changes to the promotion rule might be needed.

6.2   Sparse Hot Workload

As another extreme case, we examine a workload where the hot objects are scattered across many pages, one per page. Each client directs its hot accesses to 1,000 hot pages. On each hot page, only a single one of the 10 objects are designated as hot. In this workload, there are one thousand hot objects scattered very sparsely one per page. Object caching should now perform much better than page caching because page caching will not be able to keep the hot pages entirely within the client cache.

The table in Figure 6 contains the performance metrics for 50 clients using the sparse hot workload. The object cache achieves a much higher hit ratio and also higher system throughput. The improvement in throughput is obtained in spite of the installation reads, which now consume 28% of the disk bandwidth.

Note that each installation read consumes only 6 milliseconds of disk time,

Metrics for 50 clients

Cache Design	%hit	tx/sec	I-Cost	I-Disk
Pages	77%	198	—	0%
Objects	89%	262	6.3 ms	28%
Hybrid	89%	296	5.8 ms	18%

Figure 6: Sparse Workload (1000 hot pages, all are sparse)

although the average seek time for this disk is approximately 19 milliseconds. This is due to the effect of the opportunistic log [13]. Without this improvement, the object system would have had much worse performance than the page system.

In the simulation shown here, the hybrid design converted about one third of the object commits to page commits, presumably because many of the colder objects on the hot pages are resident in the cache. It appears that some hot pages are being kept whole. Since the hottest objects fit easily into the object cache, it makes sense that the hybrid eviction rule helps.

6.3 Mixed Workload

Finally, we examine a somewhat more realistic workload where some of the hot pages are densely packed with hot objects and some are not. We now set the total number of hot pages to 1,200, of which 600 pages have 9 hot objects per page and the other 600 pages each have only one hot object.

Metrics for 50 clients

Cache Design	%hit	tx/sec	I-Cost	I-Disk
Pages	67%	142	—	0%
Objects	82%	197	6.0 ms	18%
Hybrid	85%	251	6.0 ms	11%

Figure 7: Mixed Density Workload (1200 hot pages, 600 are dense)

Figure 7 shows the results for the mixed workload. The hybrid cache now performs significantly better than the other designs. It has a much higher hit ratio than the page cache because there are sparsely-hot pages in the workload. It also causes fewer installation reads than the object cache because it keeps densely-hot pages intact in the cache and uses page commits when updating them.

As in the densely hot workload, some of the improvement of the hybrid system relative to the object system is due to an increase in cache hit ratio. However, the important feature of the hybrid cache design is that it biases eviction policy against removing a cold object that has hot page-companions. This policy helps eliminate installation reads for all the modifications that go to densely-hot pages.

It is important to note that the hot objects in this workload are not equally hot. The sparsely-hot pages get just as many total accesses as the densely-hot pages, even though there are 5,400 densely packed hot objects and only 600 sparsely-hot objects. We should consider whether this reflects plausible assumptions about how objects might be clustered onto pages.

We imagine it to be more likely that the hottest objects would be better packed. We plan to simulate such a workload soon, but we can already guess what results we will see. Because most operations will then involve densely packed objects, the hybrid system will save a much larger fraction of the installation reads as compared to a pure object system. Yet, as long as there are some hot objects that are sparse within their pages, the increase in cache hit ratio due to squeezing them into the cache will ensure that the hybrid system performs better than the page system. So, the relative advantage offered by a hybrid cache design on real workloads may be larger than for the mixed workload shown here.

7   Related Work

To put our work in perspective we consider studies addressing the overall architecture choice for persistent object systems, and studies comparing object and page-based client cache designs.

Many persistent object systems use the more traditional page-based architecture where all interaction between clients and servers takes place at the granularity of individual pages [1, 7, 12, 9]. Other systems [5, 10] use object server architectures but do not specifically address the problem of installation reads.

Dewitt et. al. [6] is one of the first studies that investigated the design choices for a persistent object system architecture. The study focused on the question of distributing the functionality of the persistent object system between the client and the server. It measured and compared a page based system and an object system that fetched a single object at a time. Though the functionality of their object server is different from ours, and single object fetching affects the comparison, our work capitalizes on Dewitt's basic findings that the relative performance of page and object caches are very sensitive to how well hot objects are packed on pages and the relative sizes of the client cache and the client working set.

Similarly, Cheng and Hurson [3] demonstrated how an object server architecture can enable more efficient client cache utilization.

Numerous studies [4, 8, 16, 17] have addressed issues related to comparing object- and page-based client cache designs, emphasizing the importance of pointer swizzling costs to the client. Some of these studies considered using hybrid approaches. The important contrast with our work is that our focus is on the impact of client caching decisions on the critical shared resource: the server disk.

We are not aware of any other work that explores a hybrid object and page based client cache design in light of the cost imposed by installation reads on the server disk.

8 Conclusion

Previous studies considered the tradeoffs in the performance of an object and page-based client cache in terms of the cost of in memory data structure manipulation [4, 8, 16, 17] and in terms of recovery cost [16]. In a scalable object system, client cache design has important effects on the disk load at the server [13].

We explored a cache design that takes into account a previously overlooked aspect of the server disk load: installation reads. We proposed that after first optimizing the client cache to reduce the disk load due to fetches, it is then important to concentrate on avoiding unnecessary installation reads.

We designed a hybrid system that permits clients to cache both objects and pages. The cache uses a simple eviction policy to reduce unnecessary installation reads. To investigate the performance of the hybrid system, we built a simulator and compared the throughput of I/O bound systems with object-based caching, page-based caching and hybrid caching. Our results show that when disk I/O is the system performance bottleneck, the hybrid system can outperform both pure object caching and pure page caching.

References

[1] Using the EXODUS Storage Manager V2.0.0. Technical report, Department of Computer Sciences, University of Wisconsin-Madison, January 1982. Technical documentation.

[2] Atul Adya. A distributed commit protocol for optimistic concurrency control. Master's thesis, Massachusetts Institute of Technology, February 1994.

[3] Jia bing R. Cheng and A. R. Hurson. On the performance issues of object-based buffering. In *Proceedings of the Conference on Parallel and Distributed Information Systems*, pages 30–37, 1991.

[4] M. Day. *Managing a Cache of Swizzled Objects and Surrogates*. PhD thesis, miteecs, In preparation.

[5] O. Deux et al. The story of O_2. *IEEE Trans. on Knowledge and Data Engineering*, 2(1):91–108, March 1990.

[6] David J. DeWitt, Philippe Futtersack, David Maier, and Fernando Velez. A study of three alternative workstation-server architectures for object oriented database systems. In *Proceedings of the 16th Conference on Very Large Data Bases*, pages 107–121, Brisbane, Australia, 1990.

[7] M. Hornick and S. Zdonik. *A Shared, Segmented Memory System for an Object-Oriented Database*, pages 273–285. Morgan Kaufmann, 1990.

[8] Antony L. Hosking and J. Eliot B. Moss. Object fault handling for persistent programming languages: A performance evaluation. In *Proceedings of the ACM Conference on Object-Oriented Programming Systems, Languages, and Applications (OOPSLA)*, pages 288–303, 1993.

[9] Object Design Inc. An Introduction to Object Store, Release 1.0. 1989.

[10] W. Kim et al. Architecture of the orion next-generation database system. *IEEE Trans. on Knowledge and Data Engineering*, 2(1):109–124, June 1989.

[11] B. Liskov, M. Day, and L. Shrira. Distributed object management in Thor. In M. Tamer Özsu, Umesh Dayal, and Patrick Valduriez, editors, *Distributed Object Management*. Morgan Kaufmann, San Mateo, California, 1993.

[12] D. Maier and J. Stein. Development and implementation of an object-oriented dbms. In B. Shriver and P. Wegner, editors, *Research Directions in Object-Oriented Programming*. MIT Press, 1987.

[13] James O'Toole and Liuba Shrira. Opportunistic Log: Efficient Reads in a Reliable Object Server. In *Proceedings of the First Conference on Operating Systems Design and Implementation*, 1994.

[14] Chris Ruemmler and John Wilkes. Modelling disks. Technical Report HPL-93-68rev1, Hewlett-Packard Laboratories, December 1993.

[15] M. Seltzer, P. Chen., and J. Ousterhout. Disk scheduling revisited. In *Proceedings of Winter USENIX*, 1990.

[16] Seth J. White and David J. DeWitt. A performance study of alternative object faulting and pointer swizzling strategies. In *Proceedings of the 18th VLDB Conference*, pages 419–431, 1992.

[17] Paul R. Wilson and Sheetal V. Kakkad. Pointer swizzling at page fault time: Efficiently supporting huge address spaces on standard hardware. In *Proceedings of the International Workshop on Object-Orientation in Operating Systems*, pages 364–377, Paris, France, September 1992.

Prefetch Support Relations in Object Bases

Carsten A. Gerlhof   Alfons Kemper

Universität Passau, Fakultät für Mathematik und Informatik,
D-94030 Passau, Germany
[*gerlhof* | *kemper*]@db.fmi.uni-passau.de

Abstract

In this paper we devise and assess a method for optimizing the execution of encapsulated operations (possibly with side-effects) based on the precomputation of the *page answer* (i.e., the set of referenced pages). For (important) parameter combinations, (1) the page answer, (2) the *reference frequency* of pages, (3) and the ordering of the page answer according to the first reference of a page during the execution of an operation are stored in a so-called *Prefetch Support Relation* (PSR). The PSR is used for two purposes: determining "good" candidates for prefetching and for replacement decisions. We devise the algorithms for maintaining the PSR in a consistent state and demonstrate selected benchmark results to assess the viability of the approach.

1   Introduction

In a recent paper [7], we investigated prefetching techniques in a client/server architecture. We concluded that prefetching yields a significant performance gain in situations of a highly utilized (page-)server; a reduction in running-time of 50% is not unrealistic. However, prefetching techniques crucially depend on the quality of their predictors [15, 4]. In [7] we investigated a page-oriented predictor as well as an object-oriented predictor and observed that page-oriented predictors exhibit a moderate prediction overhead but prediction quality often fails in case of poor clustering. In contrast, object-oriented predictors facilitate an excellent prediction quality but the overhead induced by an object-oriented predictor, especially in the case of good clustering, cannot be tolerated.

In this paper, we propose a new page-oriented predictor—called *Prefetch Support Relation* (PSR)—which combines the advantages of both techniques mentioned above. PSRs are very similar to the *Generalized Materialization Relations* (GMRs) introduced in [11, 12] which are used to store materialized (i.e., precomputed) function results. GMRs store the precomputed function result and are, therefore, only applicable for side-effect-free functions. On the other hand, PSRs facilitate support even for operations which do cause side effects, i.e., operations which modify the database. Instead of function results PSRs store the precomputed *page answer* of an operation, i.e., all pages which are referenced by a particular operation invocation.

The Prefetch Support Relation maintains a "compressed" list of pages for certain operation invocations with (particularly important) parameter combinations. This list is divided into (1) the raw page answer (i.e., the set of

```
type Vertex is                          type Cuboid is
  public translate                        public volume, translate
  body [X, Y, Z: float;]                  body [V1,···,V8: Vertex;
  operations                                    Material: string, Weight: int]
    declare translate: Vertex → void:     operations
  implementation                            declare volume: → float;
    define translate(v) is                  declare translate: Vertex → void;
      begin                               implementation
        self.X := self.X + v.X;             define translate(v) is
        self.Y := self.Y + v.Y;               begin
        self.Z := self.Z + v.Z;                 self.V1.translate(v);
      end define translate;                     ...
end type Vertex;                                self.V8.translate(v);
                                              end define translate;
                                            ...
                                        end type Cuboid;
```

Figure 1: Skeleton of the Type Definitions *Vertex* and *Cuboid*

referenced pages), (2) the frequency counts of pages, and (3) the ordering of the page answer according to the first reference of a page during the execution of an operation. The latter information is primarily utilized for prefetching. In addition, the frequency count associated with every page in the page answer can be exploited for making page replacement decisions. For this purpose, the buffer manager maintains actual usage statistics during the operation execution and compares them with the information stored in the PSR.

The paper is organized as follows. Section 2 gives the motivation and the definition of PSRs. In Section 3 we introduce our probability-based paging policy. Section 4 addresses the algorithms to maintain a PSR in a consistent state. In Section 5 we present some results of our quantitative analysis. Section 6 concludes the paper.

2   Static Aspects of Prefetch Support Relations

Figure 1 shows the definitions of the types *Cuboid* and *Vertex* in GOM [13] which serves as the running example throughout the remainder of this paper. A sample database and its corresponding (rather poor) mapping to pages is shown in Figure 2. The object identifiers are denoted by id_1, id_2, etc.

Now, assume that the following two program fragments are to be executed:

```
w : integer = 0;                        extern persistent var v : Vertex:
foreach c in ext(Cuboid) begin          foreach c in ext(Cuboid) begin
  w := w + c.volume;                       c.translate(v);
end foreach;                             end foreach;
```

During execution of either program all cuboids have to be visited and the function *volume* and the operation *translate* is invoked, respectively. For our sample database up to seven pages must be read from secondary storage. To expedite the evaluation of the first query the results of *volume* can be precomputed:

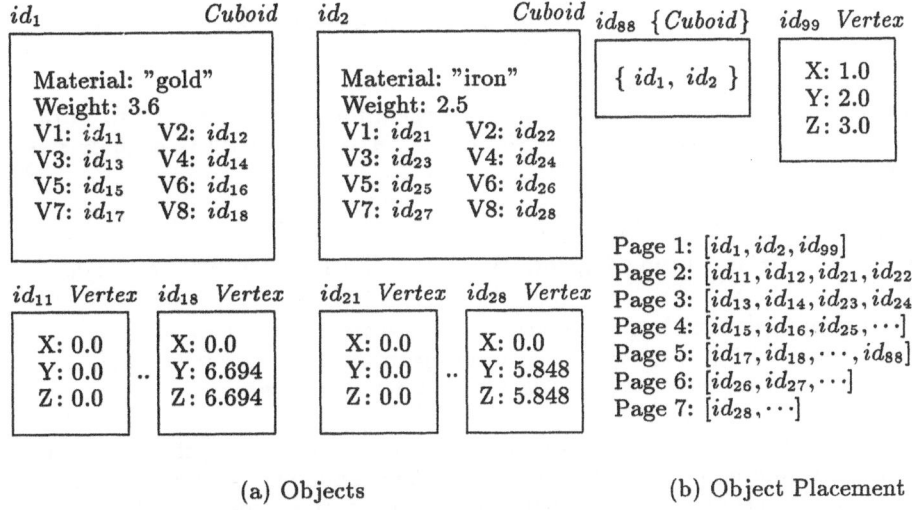

(a) Objects   (b) Object Placement

Figure 2: Sample Database with Storage Structure

we call this the *materialization* of the function *volume* [11]. All function results are stored in a separate index structure called GMR. In this case we only need to read one page, namely the page containing the materialized results of function *volume*. However, materialization is only applicable for side-effect free functions.

Now, consider the second program fragment. In this case there is (a) no function result for *translate* and (b) the operation *translate* produces side-effects, i.e., it updates the attributes X, Y, and Z of all referenced vertices. Consequently, function materialization cannot be applied to support the second program fragment. Nevertheless, the operation result in terms of referenced pages (the so-called *page answer* of an operation) can easily be precomputed and stored in a separate index structure. Before invoking operation *translate* all pages containing the entire cuboid could then be requested within a single prefetch statement, thus, saving the (expensive) stepwise request for the subobjects of each cuboid:

```
foreach c in ext(Cuboid) begin
    prefetch(⟪translate⟫, c, v);
    c.translate(v);
end foreach;
```

Clearly, because of the poor clustering, the above example is not very realistic—it is only chosen for its simplicity. A realistic application of PSRs would be in one of the following cases:

- Retrieval of large composite objects which cover many pages (as is the case in the OO7 benchmark [2]).

- Sequential scans over the extension of a specific type and its subtypes.

- Extensive traversals on a database with a high degree of sharing for which finding a good clustering is known to be very difficult [6].

Now let us define the Prefetch Support Relations as follows:

Definition 2.1 (Prefetch Support Relation)
Let $t_1, \cdots, t_{n+1}$ be types and let op be an operation with $op : t_1, \cdots, t_n \to t_{n+1}$. The prefetch support relation (PSR) $\langle\!\langle op \rangle\!\rangle$ for operation op is of arity $n+3$ and has the following form:

$$\langle\!\langle op \rangle\!\rangle : \{ \, [\; O_1{:}t_1, \; \cdots, \; O_n{:}t_n, \\ PA{:}\; \langle \, [\, pid : PageId, \; W_{pid} : int, \; L : Lock \,] \, \rangle, \; N{:}int, \; V{:}float \,] \, \}$$

The list of tuples in the page answer PA is ordered according to the first reference of page pid during the execution of operation op—the angle brackets $\langle \cdots \rangle$ denote a list and the square brackets $[\cdots]$ a tuple structure. □

The attributes $O_1, \ldots, O_n$ store the arguments, i.e., values if the argument type is atomic or references to objects if the argument type is complex; the attribute PA stores the entire page answer of an operation, i.e., the identifier of all pages that were accessed during the execution of that operation. The page answer is a list of tuples of the form $[pid, W_{pid}, L]$ where pid is the page identifier of a page, W_{pid} is the associated frequency count (see Definition 3.1), and L is the strongest lock on that page needed by operation op. This allows the server to set the appropriate lock upon the first request. If a page is already resident at the client, the server only sends an upgrade note to the client if the PSR tuple indicates a stronger lock for that page. Since clients have to piggyback information about dropped pages on other messages to the server due to the *Callback-Read* algorithm [5], this information is available to the PSR manager. The frequency count is used for paging, see Section 3 for details. The attribute V (standing for *validity*) indicates whether the stored results are currently valid,[1] the attribute N stores the cardinality of the page answer PA. In Section 3 it will become clear why we maintain an ordering of the page answer list. Operations that invalidate a precomputed operation are addressed in Section 4.

Example: The extension of the PSR $\langle\!\langle translate \rangle\!\rangle$ for the sample database in Figure 1 is depicted below. In this paper frequency counts are determined by precomputing operations in absence of pointer swizzling, thus every dot operation (.) in Fig. 1 generates a page reference.

$\langle\!\langle translate \rangle\!\rangle$				
$O_1{:}Cuboid$	$O_2{:}Vertex$	PA	$N{:}int$	$V{:}float$
id_1	id_{99}	$\langle (P_1, 32, S), (P_2, 12, X), (P_3, 12, X),$ $(P_4, 12, X), (P_5, 12, X) \rangle$	5	1.0
id_2	id_{99}	$\langle (P_1, 32, S), (P_2, 12, X), (P_3, 12, X),$ $(P_4, 6, X), (P_6, 12, X), (P_7, 6, X) \rangle$	6	1.0

◇

---

[1]Using a float value in the range of [0,1] instead of a boolean value allows us to express the validity as a probability.

3   Operation-Specific Probability-Based Paging

If the precomputed page answer of an operation is too large to fit entirely into the currently unoccupied buffer portion, we have to replace a page from the buffer when fetching the next page from the precomputed page answer. By exploiting PSRs we are able to devise a better page replacement policy than, for example, conventional LRU. Thus, we are able to set up a replacement policy which works for each operation separately, more precisely, for every parameter combination of an operation. Before we describe our probability-based paging policy in more detail, we briefly describe other paging information which could alternatively be stored in our PSRs (instead of the frequency counts):

- One could maintain the entire page reference string to compute the optimal replacement policy, but the costs for computing and storing this information in a PSR appear to be unacceptable for practical purposes.

- One could use a Markov-based paging policy [10] where the reference string of pages constitutes a Markov chain. All pages which are unreachable from the current state are candidates for replacement since these pages will never be accessed again.

- One could use Rete-like networks to cache selected subsets of entire page answers in order to support caching for multiple queries [9].

- One could use the page reference string to compute (and store) good values for the *Correlated Reference Period* and the *Retained Information Period* needed by the LRU-K algorithm [14].

In this section we outline a paging policy that is based on *frequency counts* for pages. Similarly to Markov paging we definitely know when a page is not used any more during an operation's execution. In fact, our buffering policy is a synthesis of prereleasing and prepaging. The implementation thereof is quite easy and is based on an efficient table lookup. Frequency-based page replacement has also been used successfully in [16].

Definition 3.1 (Weighted Page Answer)
Let $\langle pid_1, \cdots, pid_n \rangle$ be a reference string of page identifiers and let W_{pid} denote the number of occurrences of a page pid in the page reference string. The weighted page answer (WPA) is a list of tuples of the form (pid, W_{pid}) sorted by descending W_{pid}.   □

The weighted page answer is a distribution of page access frequencies; the linear ordering is often called *probability ranking*. Based on the weighted page answer we can now define a probability-based paging policy which is derived from the IR model [3]. This will work well in practice if the ratio of the length of WPA to the number of buffer frames is not too large.

Definition 3.2 (WPA paging policy)
Let wpa be the weighted page answer of operation $op(o_1, \cdots, o_n)$ and let k be the number of buffer frames. Further, we define $\mathcal{P}_{max}(t)$ as the set of non-resident pages having the greatest W_{pid} value at time t. Then, the WPA paging policy for an operation $op(o_1, \cdots, o_n)$ whose precomputed page answer in a PSR is still valid is defined as follows:

- *On invocation of $op(o_1, \cdots, o_n)$ prefetch the first k non-resident pages according to the page answer stored in the PSR. The prefetch quantity k is determined at run-time and denotes the client's total number of available (i.e., free or unpinned) buffer frames at the time of the prefetch request.*

- *On a reference to page pid at time t do*

  1. *if $W_{pid} \geq 1$ update $W_{pid} := W_{pid} - 1$ in wpa.*
  2. *if $W_{pid} = 0$ then (pre-)release page pid by marking the corresponding page frame as free and prefetch a page from $\mathcal{P}_{max}(t)$.*
  3. *make page pid recently used.*

- *On a page fault at time t replace the least recently used page by the fault page and, optionally, replace up to $k-1$ resident pages pid_i which satisfy the condition $W_{pid_i} \neq 0 \wedge \exists pid \in \mathcal{P}_{max}(t) : W_{pid} > W_{pid_i}, \quad 1 \leq i < k$ by pages from $\mathcal{P}_{max}(t)$.* □

Example: Let $\langle P_1, P_1, P_2, P_1, P_2, P_3, P_4 \rangle$ be the page reference string and let $k = 2$. Thus, wpa $= \langle (P_1, 3), (P_2, 2), (P_3, 1), (P_4, 1) \rangle$. The replacement policy will become clear from the table below. Note that pages P_1 and P_2 are prefetched according to the ordering in the PSR, whereas pages P_3 and P_4 are prefetched according to the WPA.

buffer contents	——	$(P_1,3)$ $(P_2,2)$	$(P_1,2)$ $(P_2,2)$	$(P_1,1)$ $(P_2,2)$	$(P_2,1)$ $(P_1,1)$	$(P_3,1)$ $(P_2,1)$	$(P_4,1)$ $(P_3,1)$	$(P_4,1)$ ——
reference		P_1	P_1	P_2	P_1	P_2	P_3	P_4
prefetch	P_1, P_2				P_3	P_4		

◇

Paging Deficiencies. In general the IR model cannot compete with the more expressive Markov model because serial dependencies cannot be captured by the independent and identically distributed random variables of the IR model. Thus, we expect that there are cases for which the paging decisions made according to the WPA are not advantageous. For example, consider the reference string $\langle (P_1, \cdots, P_{k+1})^n, (P_x, P_y)^m \rangle$, $n \geq m$. If we have only k buffer frames, pages P_x and P_y will be unnecessarily fetched as soon as n drops below m. However, we expect that such "obscure" access patterns as sketched above are not very likely to happen in well-structured (mostly encapsulated) operations. If no such dependencies occur the prefetching policy can easily be proven to be optimal under the IR model [3]. Nevertheless, prefetching according to the IR model is optional in our paging policy and can be turned off at run-time.

4 Dynamic Aspects of Prefetch Support Relations

The main disadvantage of all predictors that are based on monitoring is that they generally provide no mechanism to check the validity of the collected information after a sequence of object updates. However, massively prefetching the wrong pages according to an "outdated" predictor dramatically degrades system performance. For this purpose, we investigate in this section the algorithms that are needed to check the validity of PSRs and to maintain them in a consistent state upon object base modifications.

In this section we describe the basic invalidation techniques which reduce the overhead significantly. For maintenance purposes, the PSR manager maintains so-called reverse references—in contrast to the Reverse Reference Relation proposed in [11] for precomputed function results—based on pages, therefore called *Reverse Page Reference Relation* (or RPRR in short). The RPRR contains tuples of the form $[pid, a, op, \langle o_1, \ldots, o_n \rangle]$. Here, *pid* is an identifier of a *page* which is utilized during the computation of the page answer of $op(o_1, \ldots, o_n)$ *and* this page contains an object with attribute a whose value has had some influence on the program flow of that operation. An attribute value can influence the program flow if that value is used inside a conditional statement during the execution of an operation (let us call this attribute *conditional attribute*) or because the attribute contains an object reference (a so-called *reference attribute*). An update of either type of attribute can change the navigation through the object base. The union of both sets of attributes constitutes the set of *relevant attributes*:

Definition 4.1 (Relevant Attributes) *Let* $op : t_1, \ldots, t_n \to t_{n+1}$ *be a precomputed operation and let A be an attribute identifier—for simplicity we assume that all attribute names are unique. Then, the set of relevant attributes is the union of the sets CondAttr(op) and RefAttr(op) which are defined as:*

$CondAttr(op) = \{A \mid$ *there exist objects* $o_1, \ldots, o_n$ *and an object o with attribute A such that o.A has had some influence in an expression inside a conditional statement during execution of* $op(o_1, \ldots, o_n)\}$

$RefAttr(op) = \{A \mid$ *there exist objects* $o_1, \ldots, o_n$ *and an object o with attribute A such that o.A contains an object reference and it is used during execution of* $op(o_1, \ldots, o_n)\}$ □

Thus, during precomputation we only need to insert pages into the RPRR containing objects that have relevant attributes. The RPRR is defined as follows:

Definition 4.2 (Reverse Page Reference Relation) *The Reverse Page Reference Relation RPRR is a set of tuples of the form*

$$[P: PageId, A: AttributeId, OP: OperationId, L: \langle OID \rangle].$$

For each tuple $r \in RPRR$ *the following condition holds: The page (with the identifier) r.P has been accessed during the execution of operation r.OP with the argument list r.L and page r.P contains an object such that for one of its attributes* $r.A \in CondAttr(r.OP)$ *or* $r.A \in RefAttr(r.OP)$ *holds.* □

The data-flow equations for computing the set of relevant attributes are given in the full paper [8]. Based on the RPRR we can now describe the algorithm for invalidating a page answer, i.e., the computations that have to be performed by

$\langle\!\langle\,Scale\,Gold\,Ingots\,\rangle\!\rangle$			
O:{ $Cuboid$ }	PA	N:int	V:$float$
id_{88}	$\langle (P_1, 10, S), (P_2, 12, X), (P_3, 12, X),$ $(P_4, 12, X), (P_5, 14, X) \rangle$	5	1.0

```
define ScaleGoldIngots(CuboidSet) is
var v : Vertex = (1.2, 1.2, 1.2);
begin
   foreach c in CuboidSet begin
      if c.Material = "gold" then
         c.scale(v);
      end if;
   end foreach;
end define ScaleGoldIngots;
```

```
define DetectGoldPlate(GoldIngot) is
begin
```
$\quad$ **if** ($\frac{\text{GoldIngot.Weight}}{\text{GoldIngot.Volume}} \neq 19.3 \pm \epsilon$) **then**
```
      GoldIngot.Material := "iron";
   end if;
end define DetectGoldPlate;
```

Figure 3: PSR $\langle\!\langle\,Scale\,Gold\,Ingots\,\rangle\!\rangle$ can be invalidated by $Detect\,Gold\,Plate$

the PSR manager when an object o has been updated. Because the RPRR contains only pages—remember the Reverse Reference Relation of GMRs contains objects—we are able to substantially reduce the overhead (otherwise associated with GMRs), i.e., we do *not* immediately invalidate a PSR at the time when an object becomes updated. We only record the identifiers of all updated attributes into the header of the buffer frame of the updated page. When a modified page has to be sent back to the server, the set of attribute identifiers is also sent along with the page in the attachment of the message. Then, the server invalidates all page answers which match a tuple in the RPRR containing that page and any of the updated attributes.

Example: Consider the PSR for the operation $Scale\,Gold\,Ingots$ in Fig. 3. The vertices that will be referenced during the execution of $Scale\,Gold\,Ingots$ depend only on the value of the attribute $Material$, hence $CondAttr\,(Scale\,Gold\,Ingots\,) = \{Material\}$. Note that $id_1.translate(v)$ does not affect the page answer of $Scale$-$Gold\,Ingots$ in any way. However, $Detect\,Gold\,Plate(id_1)$ would directly invalidate the page answer of $Scale\,Gold\,Ingots(id_{88})$ if cuboid id_1 were detected as painted gold, i.e., "degraded" from gold to iron. $\diamond$

The main advantages of this invalidation algorithm are that we (1) pay no additional I/O costs at the time of an update and (2) concerning the PSR all modifications of objects which reside on the same page are considered only once—in a bulk. In conclusion, the overall overhead for updates is reduced to a tolerable extent—as is also verified by the quantitative analysis of Section 5. The disadvantage is that we increase the granularity by giving up the object level. However, the precision of determining the exact set of operations whose page answers are invalid depends only on the page cardinality (in objects). Note that a page answer will only be invalidated erroneously when a modified page contains an object of the *same* type whose attribute is relevant and becomes updated.

Object Moving. When an object is moved from page p to page p' and page p is in the page answer of some operation op we generally do not know whether the correct page answer now contains p, p', or both. For this reason we don't want to replace each occurrence of p by p' in the PSR. Instead, we just add page p' to all page answers which include page p—the same has to be done for the corresponding entries in the RPRR. The new frequency count $W_{p'}$ is copied from that of page p, the old frequency count W_p is decreased by one. Additionally, we *weaken* the validity for all page answers containing page p by setting $V := V - 1/N$ where N is the cardinality of the original set of pages. However, if the probability for the validity reaches a low "water mark", the page answer will be finally invalidated.

Initial Setup. PSRs can be created for all operations which do not immediately invalidate themselves. The buffer manager of the client's run-time system monitors all page accesses, maintains the WPA statistics, and finally sends all WPA information (including page answer and statistics) to the server. This can be done either on-line or—to initially support operations with database updates—this can be done off-line using slightly modified operations in which all statements with side-effects are "neutralized".

5 Quantitative Analysis

In this section we present some typical benchmark results for PSR retrieval (Section 5.1) and for PSR update (Section 5.2).

We implemented the PSR manager in our multi-threaded server engine introduced in [7]. The PSRs are implemented by a hash table using *Filtered Hashing* [1] since in practice the keys, i.e., the combination of parameter values, are highly correlated. The default PSR bucket size is configured to 1KB, the initial size of both hash tables is 10 000 buckets. There is full support for concurrency and R1–R3 recovery[2] on PSRs.

5.1 PSR Retrieval

We generated a database segment with 10 000 pages of 4KB size. The PSR contained up to 10 000 entries with varying sizes of the page answer. The client fetched the entire database segment into it's buffer and referenced each page one time. As reported in [7] a highly utilized server is the overall bottleneck, thus we again conducted multi-client experiments to emphasize the need for prefetching in a client/server-environment. Fig. 4 shows the results for a varying number of additional heavy I/O-weighted clients (plotted on the x-axis) which operated on a segment which is different from the segment we prefetched, and varying prefetch cardinalities (indicated by curves labeled with *pref #*). All experiments were started "cold", i.e., with empty buffer caches (both the client and the server caches).

The most important result of Fig. 4(a) is that the break-even point in case of no additional clients can be found at a page answer of at least 6 pages. For smaller page answers the use of PSRs is counterproductive. However, this

---

[2] Only a page-oriented recovery technique is currently implemented in our system.

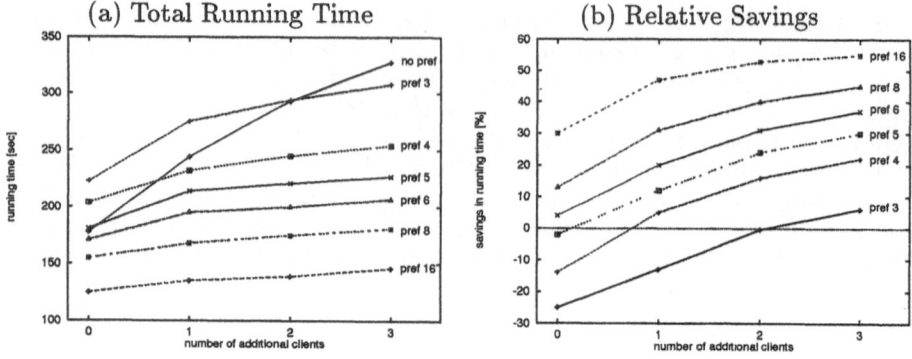

Figure 4: Performance of PSR Retrieval

changes as more clients join the server (witness curves *pref 3*, *pref 4*, and *pref 5*). Fig. 4(b) exhibits that the relative savings in total running-time compared to no prefetching can easily reach more than 50% when prefetching 16 pages.

5.2 PSR Update

In this experiment we designed a typical CAD-transaction where we fetched approximately 1 000 pages from the server (with and without prefetching) into the client's buffer and then updated one relevant attribute on a varying number of pages—this relative number is plotted (in %) on the x-axis. The relative savings to no prefetching are plotted on the y-axis. The RPRR recorded 1 000 pages with one relevant attribute each. We assume a lazy rematerialization for PSRs. Fig. 5 shows the results for a page answer of 6 and 16 pages.

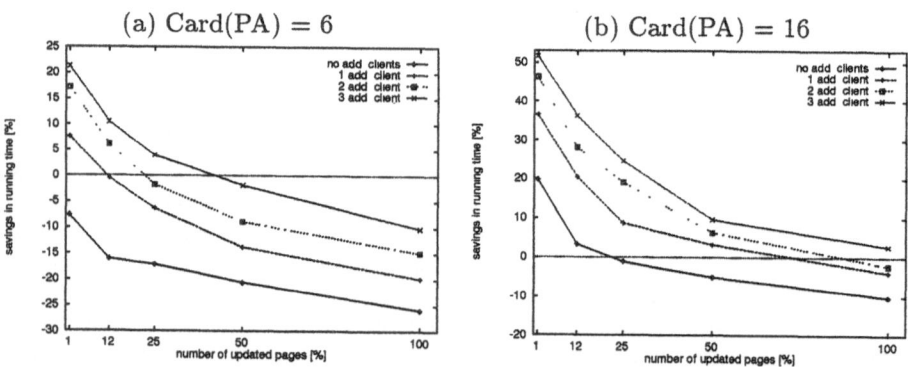

Figure 5: Performance of PSR Update

Both diagrams show that if we increase the number of updated pages the performance gain by prefetching smoothly decreases. This is because (1) the buffer hit rate for both, PSR pages and RPRR pages, is very high when performing a bulk update, and (2) due to the sequential access pattern many updated pages are already asynchronously written to disk at commit time. We also see that the break-even point significantly depends on the server utilization. In Fig. 5(a) server utilization must be very high to remedy the additional penalties induced by PSR update. However, Fig. 5(b) exhibits that 25% updates in case of low server utilization and 100% updates in case of high server utilization can be tolerated when prefetching 16 pages.

6 Conclusion

In this paper we devised a method for optimizing the execution of encapsulated operations based on the precomputation of the *page answer* (i.e., the set of referenced pages). For (important) parameter combinations, (1) the page answer, (2) the *reference frequency* of pages, (3) and the ordering of the page answer according to the first reference of a page during the execution of an operation are stored in a so-called *Prefetch Support Relation* (PSR). The PSRs were used for two purposes: determining "good" candidates for prefetching and for replacement decisions. We also devised and benchmarked the algorithms for the consistency of the PSRs under database modifications.

Our quantitative analysis indicates that in case of low server utilization one can expect a clear gain in running time if the page answer contains at least 6 pages. Operations which modify the database are not significantly penalized by the additional overhead incurred by maintaining the PSRs if relevant information on only a few pages becomes updated. Note that all techniques in [12] which are developed to reduce the invalidation overhead for materialized functions can be adapted to PSRs.

So far we have only considered (completely) consistent page answers in the PSRs. However, even (partially) invalid page answers are very useful for prefetching decisions—as long as the validity of the page answer does not drop below a certain threshold. In the future, we want to apply fuzzy logic to model the uncertainty of page answer consistency after database updates. Further, we will spend more work on static code analysis to facilitate finer grained control over the invalidation of PSRs. We will also investigate alternative paging policies which can make better use of the access patterns stored in a PSR.

Acknowledgement This work was supported by the German Research Council DFG under contract Ke 401/6-1. We thank Florian Waas for the prototypical implementation and the extensive benchmarking of various paging policies.

References

[1] I. Ahn. Filtered hashing. In *Proc. of the Intl. Conf. on Foundations of Data Organization and Algorithms (FODO)*, volume 730 of *Lecture Notes in Computer Science (LNCS)*, pages 85–100, Chicago, IL, October 1993. Springer-Verlag.

[2] M. J. Carey, D. J. DeWitt, and J. F. Naughton. The OO7 benchmark. In *Proc. of the ACM SIGMOD Conf. on Management of Data*, pages 12–21, Washington, DC, USA, May 1993.

[3] E. G. Coffman and P. J. Denning. *Operating Systems Theory*. Prentice Hall, Englewood Cliffs, NJ, USA, 1973.

[4] K. M. Curewitz, P. Krishnan, and J. S. Vitter. Practical prefetching via data compression. In *Proc. of the ACM SIGMOD Conf. on Management of Data*, pages 43–53, Washington, DC, USA, May 1993.

[5] M. J. Franklin, M. J. Carey, and M. Livny. Local disk caching for client-server database systems. In *Proc. of the Conf. on Very Large Data Bases (VLDB)*, pages 543–554, Dublin, Ireland, August 1993.

[6] C. Gerlhof, A. Kemper, C. Kilger, and G. Moerkotte. Partition-based clustering in object bases: From theory to practice. In *Proc. of the Intl. Conf. on Foundations of Data Organization and Algorithms (FODO)*, volume 730 of *Lecture Notes in Computer Science (LNCS)*, pages 301–316, Chicago, IL, October 1993. Springer-Verlag.

[7] C. A. Gerlhof and A. Kemper. A multi-threaded architecture for prefetching in object bases. In *Proc. of the Intl. Conf. Extending Database Technology (EDBT)*, volume 779 of *Lecture Notes in Computer Science (LNCS)*, pages 351–364, Cambridge, England, March 1994. Springer-Verlag.

[8] C. A. Gerlhof and A. Kemper. Prefetch Support Relations in Object Bases: Design, Implementation and Assessment. Technical report, Universität Passau, 94030 Passau, Germany, 1994. (forthcoming).

[9] N. Kamel and R. King. Intelligent database caching through the use of page-answers and page-traces. *ACM Trans. on Database Systems*, 17(4):601–646, December 1992.

[10] K. R. Karlin, S. J. Phillips, and P. Raghavan. Markov paging. In *Proc. IEEE Symp. on Foundations of Computer Science*, pages 208–217, October 1992.

[11] A. Kemper, C. Kilger, and G. Moerkotte. Function materialization in object bases. In *Proc. of the ACM SIGMOD Conf. on Management of Data*, pages 258–268, Denver, USA, May 1991.

[12] A. Kemper, C. Kilger, and G. Moerkotte. Function Materialization in Object Bases: Design, Implementation and Assessment. *IEEE Trans. Knowledge and Data Engineering*, 6(4), August 1994.

[13] A. Kemper and G. Moerkotte. *Object-Oriented Database Management: Applications in Engineering and Computer Science*. Prentice Hall, Englewood Cliffs, NJ, USA, 1994.

[14] E. J. O'Neil, P. E. O'Neil, and G. Weikum. The LRU-K page replacement algorithm for database disk buffering. In *Proc. of the ACM SIGMOD Conf. on Management of Data*, pages 297–306, Washington, DC, USA, May 1993.

[15] M. L. Palmer and S. B. Zdonik. FIDO: A cache that learns to fetch. In *Proc. of the Conf. on Very Large Data Bases (VLDB)*, pages 255–264, Barcelona, September 1991.

[16] J. T. Robinson and M. V. Devarakonda. Data cache management using frequency-based replacement. In *Proc. of the ACM SIGMETRICS*, pages 134–142, 1990.

Concurrency

Ken Moody
Department of Computing Science
University of Newcastle upon Tyne
Newcastle upon Tyne
NE1 7RU

Both papers in this session were about enhancing pessimistic R/W schemes for concurrency control. In the first Andrea Skarra described extensions to a 2PL scheme to take advantage of the semantics of operations on index sets. Use of an extra locking mode offers potentially greater concurrency. The system had been implemented, but as yet there were no hard figures on the performance. In discussion a number of detailed suggestions were made: path expressions could be used to control the invocation order of operations (not considered); an optimistic strategy might be better suited to handling operation semantics (not practicable with the current server architecture, but certainly worth bearing in mind). Ron Morrison thought that most production systems handle indexes specially anyway, and that solid experimental evidence was needed before additional lock modes could be justified.

Laurent Daynes presented work with Olivier Gruber at INRIA to manage locks on 'capabilities', groups of objects that share access status. Capability locks can be manipulated with a single call to the lock manager, so offering reduced overheads and therefore improved performance. Locks can be delegated between capabilities, a principal motivation being to handle locks on groups of objects participating in nested transactions. Detailed measurements were presented to show that the new method of lock management gave significantly better performance on benchmarks than some currently in use, including certain ones recoded from standard products. Why do the systems in the market place perform so badly? In discussion the point was made that some of the costs might be associated with extra services that a research prototype can ignore, but even so the disparity in performance is marked. Eliot Moss suggested that a more cunning data representation might further reduce the overheads of the capability locking scheme, but Olivier Gruber was doubtful.

General Discussion

David Blakeman warned of a potential snare with semantic concurrency control in object-oriented systems. Conflict depends on the detail of methods: overriding a method can introduce conflict at subclass level where none existed within the super class. So to take advantage of semantics safely requires good software engineering practice.

But discussion soon returned to the INRIA experiments on methods of implementing nested transactions. Malcolm Atkinson was concerned that it would seem partial to quote performance figures that depended on a reimplementation of others' algorithms, which were unlikely to be coded with the same care and insight as the new methods with which they were in competition. Both authors protested that justice had been done; in any case it is difficult to make comparisons when the commercial systems restrict information, and when in addition they have no representatives at the conference to make their case.

This is a major problem. Paul Wilson cited an instance of a product which includes in its licence agreement a condition of no bench marking. Inevitably there are problems with any comprehensive system, and these come to light only with experience: subsequent releases may correct the deficiency, and a benchmark against an obsolete version would be misleading, even possibly damaging. Algorithms in commercial systems must support the whole functionality of the product, and it is not necessarily fair to abstract them for the purposes of comparison in a restricted context.

The absence of delegates from industry is a worry in itself. Times are hard at present, and it would be difficult for any business under pressure to do without key employees for as long as a week. But it is bad for the POS community, which must keep in touch with those nearer to the market place in order to ascertain which research areas are of greatest concern to the wider community.

Semantic Synchronization in a Persistent Object System Library

Andrea H. Skarra
Naser S. Barghouti
Software and Systems Research Laboratory, AT&T Bell Laboratories
Murray Hill, NJ 07974 USA

Alexander L. Wolf
Department of Computer Science, University of Colorado
Boulder, CO 80309 USA

Abstract

The paper describes a synchronization scheme that exploits the semantics of collections and indexes to improve concurrency in a persistent object system library. The library implements a common execution model in which data (rather than operations or queries) are shipped between a transaction and the database at a granularity no smaller than an object. The paper describes the impact of the execution model on the extent to which semantics can be used in synchronization, and it develops several techniques that yield higher concurrency levels in this common though restrictive model. Finally, it examines the process and tradeoffs involved in designing a semantic synchronization protocol.

1 Introduction

Applications typically interact with a database in the context of transactions to maintain consistency. In particular, a transaction is a sequence of operations that satisfies all consistency constraints on a database, and the database management system (DBMS) synchronizes concurrent transactions to produce an interleaved history that is *serializable* (i.e., equivalent to some serial execution of the transactions). A database remains consistent across repeated and concurrent access when an application uses transactions.

Most commonly, a DBMS uses a two-phase locking protocol to enforce serializability. Each transaction requests locks according to the protocol, and the DBMS evaluates each request for conflict with the locks held by other transactions. It grants requests that do not conflict, it delays requests that do conflict, and it denies requests whose delay would result in deadlock. A traditional protocol uses just the two lock types Read (Share) and Write (Exclusive) with the usual conflict semantics [1, 7]. It associates every data access with one or the other of the locks automatically, regardless of the kind of data or the context. If a DBMS instead uses a synchronization protocol that exploits the semantics of the data and the application, however, the number of transactions that can execute concurrently increases [14].

A semantic protocol and its lock types may be "hardwired" into the DBMS synchronization algorithm. For example, the multigranularity locking protocol employs a fixed set of five lock types that capture the access semantics of physically nested objects such as records within files [8]. A DBMS that supports the protocol may implement just those lock types and no others.

Alternatively, the DBMS may support semantic protocols with an *extensible* synchronization algorithm, namely one whose behavior is modified by semantic specifications that it takes as input from the database administrator. The form of the specification is typically a compatibility matrix over a set of transaction types [5, 17] or a set of synchronization primitives such as events, semantic lock types, or abstract type operations [9, 13, 29]. The synchronization algorithm uses the specifications to decide conflict among concurrent transactions in much the same way that a traditional algorithm uses the conflict relation over Read and Write locks.

The correctness criterion in semantic protocols that corresponds to serializability is *semantic serializability*. A concurrent transaction history satisfies the criterion when its effect is equivalent to that produced by some serial execution of the transactions *as discernible through the data's functional interface*.

For example, a data type Collection_of_Autos (collection of automobiles) defines the following operations:

Add(a:Auto):OK inserts a and returns OK.

Del(a:Auto):OK removes a if present and returns OK, else returns NoOP.

List():Sorted_Auto_List returns the automobile identifiers in numerical order.

Member(a:Auto):Boolean returns true if a is a member; otherwise false.

Under semantic serializability, transactions that add automobiles to a Collection_of_Autos object can be arbitrarily interleaved. The physical representation of the resulting collection may be different from any produced by a serial execution of the transactions, but the difference is not visible through the interface. List() returns a sorted list that hides the insertion order.

We designed and implemented a synchronization protocol that guarantees semantic serializability in Persi [31], a persistent object system library that supports a transaction execution model commonly used in object-oriented database systems (OODBMSs). The objective of the protocol is to maintain consistency across the database while maximizing concurrency among transactions, whether they navigate to objects or use associative retrieval. The contribution of the work is that it develops semantics-based techniques that improve concurrency in a common though restrictive transaction execution model. In addition, it highlights the dependence of a semantic protocol on the underlying execution model.

We first describe the transaction execution model in Persi and other OODBMSs, and we compare it to those that are required by the currently proposed semantic synchronization schemes. We explain why the model restricts the extent to which a synchronization algorithm can use semantics to improve concurrency. We then develop several synchronization techniques that exploit the semantics of collections and indexes to an extent, and in a manner, that is compatible with the execution model. We describe the relevant portions of Persi, and we detail the synchronization protocol within a standard library interface. We then illustrate our approach with an example. Finally, we conclude with a discussion about the process of designing a semantic scheme and the tradeoffs that are involved.

2 Execution Models

Persi implements a common execution model: a transaction's operations execute within the private address space of the process that contains the transaction. That is, a transaction does not ship operations or queries to a database execution engine and await the result. Rather, it acquires a copy of the data from the database system and performs the computations itself. Moreover, the unit of data transfer between a transaction and the database is at least the size of an object; a transaction does not read or write individual attributes alone. The commercial object-oriented DBMSs [4, 15, 21, 23, 27] support the same model, and henceforth we call it the *OO execution model.*

In contrast, the currently proposed models of semantic concurrency control (*cf.* Section 7) imply one of the following two execution models:

- *Finely-grained Read/Write access*

  The DBMS supports Read and Write access to small portions of the database. As a result, transactions can lock smaller regions and execute with greater concurrency.

  In the multigranularity protocol, for example, a transaction can read and write individual tuples in a relation. It does not have to write an entire relation in order to insert a single tuple. Thus, concurrent transactions can lock slots in disjoint segments of the same relation and insert tuples without risk of overwriting each other.

- *Encapsulated shared memory (ESM)*

  The DBMS supports a single shared copy of each object, and it allows transactions to access an object only through the abstract interface. A transaction does not cache objects in its private address space; operations on an object execute only on the shared copy. ESM may be viewed as a generalization of finely-grained Read/Write access. An operation typically touches only part of an object, and it does so with well-defined semantics that a synchronization scheme can use to improve concurrency.

  In a client-server setting, the DBMS implements ESM with an object server that executes operations on behalf of transactions. Transactions send operations to the server, and the server returns the results. All the operations on an object execute in the server on the same physical object. In other settings, a DBMS can implement ESM using the shared memory primitives provided by the operating system. Transactions load the interface operations for each object they access, and they execute the operations on the objects in shared memory under a suitable access protocol (e.g., one that preserves operation atomicity).

To illustrate, consider an object c of type Collection_of_Autos and transactions T_1 and T_2 that insert automobiles into c. Suppose c contains (auto1) initially, T_1 adds auto2 and auto3, and T_2 adds auto3 and auto4. In a serial execution, c contains (auto1,auto2,auto3,auto3,auto4) after T_1 and T_2 commit (in either order).

In a concurrent execution, T_1 and T_2 can be arbitrarily interleaved under semantic serializability. If the execution model supports finely-grained Read/Write access to the slots in c, the insertions can proceed independently at different slots, and regardless of the interleaving, c is correct after the transactions commit. Alternatively, if c resides in ESM and each Add() operation is atomic, c also ends up with the correct membership for any interleaving.

In contrast, transactions cannot add automobiles to the same Collection_of_Autos object concurrently under the OO execution model. Transactions execute with private copies of an object, and thus, an arbitrary interleaving of T_1 and T_2 may yield an incorrect result. Specifically, if T_1 and T_2 begin execution and fetch c at the same time, each receives the initial version of c in its entirety. Each then does its computation in isolation, and if the DBMS allows both to commit, c contains either (auto1,auto2,auto3) or (auto1,auto3,auto4) instead of the correct value. One transaction overwrites the other.

We conclude that this common execution model restricts the extent to which semantic synchronization can be implemented. In particular, it restricts the data access semantics available to the synchronization algorithm to simply Read and Write on the finest-grained access unit, where the unit is no smaller than an object. Transactions cannot invoke abstract type operations on fragments of an object. Thus, a multigranularity locking protocol cannot be used to improve concurrency at a coarse-grained object (unlike using the protocol on a relation and its tuples), since a change to any part of an object requires writing the whole object back to the database with a Write lock. Semantic serializability reduces to standard Read/Write serializability in the OO execution model.

3 A Semantic Approach

We propose a synchronization scheme that uses two techniques to improve concurrency within the OO execution model: *delay* and *re-fetch*.

Intuitively, an operation's execution can be delayed (along with the acquisition of the associated locks) when its return value does not depend on the object's initial state. The operation simply returns the value immediately, and the transaction's execution continues on other objects. A delayed operation executes when its effect is required for a subsequent operation in the transaction or for commit. The delay shortens the interval during which the transaction holds a lock on the object, and thus it improves concurrency; other transactions can commit changes during the delay interval.

For example, the Collection_of_Autos operation Add() can be delayed, because it always returns the value OK to the invoking transaction. When the transaction commits or invokes another operation on the object that cannot be delayed, such as List() or Member(), any and all the delayed Add()s execute before the transaction proceeds. Using the delay technique, T_1 and T_2 delay their Add()s until commit, when each in turn fetches c with a Write lock, performs the insertions, and writes the resulting c to the database.

In the other technique, a transaction (re)fetches an object o before every nondelayable operation on o to incorporate (nonconflicting) changes that other transactions have committed. It also fetches o before commit if it modifies o. The re-fetch technique simulates encapsulated shared memory for committed results, improving concurrency while preventing the occurrence of overwrites that are due to the object-level access granularity. To use re-fetch on an object o, a transaction maintains a queue of its modifying actions on o, and each time it fetches o, it applies the actions locally before proceeding. A transaction's intermediate changes remain local to the transaction to simplify abort/undo.

For example, transaction T_3 with the following operations on Collection_of_Autos object c uses delay and re-fetch and executes concurrently with T_1 and T_2:

Add(auto5) Member(auto2) Member(auto4)

At Add(auto5), T_3 delays the operation and adds it to the queue for c. At Member(auto2), T_3 executes the queued Add() (i.e., it fetches c and inserts auto5), and it invokes Member().[1] If T_1 has committed but not T_2, Member() returns true, and c does not contain auto4. At Member(auto4), T_3 again fetches c and inserts auto5 before it invokes Member(). If T_2 has committed by then, Member() again returns true, because c now contains auto4. When T_3 commits, it fetches c with a Write lock, inserts auto5, and writes c to the database.

The final version of c reflects the actions of all three transactions, even though T_3 initially fetches c before T_2, and it commits afterward. It does not overwrite T_2. If T_3 does not use re-fetch, however, it avoids overwriting T_2 only by getting a lock when it first fetches c. The lock forestalls T_2's commit until after T_3 terminates and reduces concurrency.

The technique chosen to synchronize transactions at a particular object depends on the object and the anticipated access patterns. Re-fetching supports more concurrency and may be preferred for frequently accessed objects. For large objects, however, re-fetching may be prohibitively expensive. The synchronization scheme we developed in Persi uses delay for both collections and indexes. It uses re-fetch for indexes alone, however, due to the frequency of index use and the anticipated size of collections.

Importantly, both delay and re-fetch can be used in conjunction with a multigranularity protocol that propagates intention locks from one object to another object such as a container, even though we do not describe such a protocol for Persi.

4 An Overview of Persi

Persi is a persistent object system library providing high-level abstractions for typed persistent objects, for stable-storage repositories of objects, and for (concurrent) access to repositories. In addition, Persi provides abstractions for defining and maintaining collections of objects, iterators over collections, and indexes on collections. The type model used by Persi is that of C++.

Persi is designed with two kinds of developers in mind: class developers and application developers. Class developers act as database administrators (DBAs), defining the object, collection, and iterator classes used in applications, as well as establishing the indexes. Application developers write programs that make use of the classes defined by class developers. They (and their programs) are shielded from the details of object management by the functional interfaces defined by the class developers.

Persi provides two basic methods of accessing objects, namely object navigation and collection scan. Object navigation is a directed traversal from one object to another along paths defined by object pointers and is often referred

---

[1]For simplicity, we omit the locking for Member(), since none is required for correctness in the example.

to as "pointer chasing". Collection scan is an iterative retrieval of the members of a collection that satisfy some predicate.

The store for persistent objects in Persi is called a repository. Persi provides a transaction mechanism to logically group together the operations performed by a process on the objects in a repository. A transaction is atomic—that is, either all or none of its operations take effect. An application process can perform a sequence of one or more non-overlapping transactions on a given repository; transactions on the same repository by different processes can, of course, be concurrent. During a transaction, an application process can see its own updates to objects, including any effect those updates have on indexes.

Below, we briefly describe the features of Persi required to understand the work presented in this paper. We do this by detailing the class developer interface to Persi's features for persistence, collections, and automatic index maintenance. A more complete description of Persi can be found in [32].

4.1 Persistent Objects

A persistent object is an instance of a class that is a subclass of the Persi class Object.[2] Class Object serves to define the operations used in a special, hidden protocol between Persi and persistent objects. The protocol allows Persi to automatically manage the persistence of, and access to, the objects. It is hidden in the sense that applications using subclasses of Object are not involved in the protocol. There are two protocol operations of relevance to the work described here. Both are operations on instances of class Object.

Touch() This function is used to guarantee that an object is resident in the primary memory space of an application. It is needed because Persi uses (logical) object faulting to move objects from secondary memory into primary memory.

ValueChange() This function is used to indicate the fact that a data component of a persistent object has changed value. It is needed because Persi, being a library, has no way to automatically detect when changes are made to values.

Both functions are typically invoked from within the operations of a class and are not invoked directly by applications themselves.

Object persistence is defined dynamically by reachability from a designated root (persistent) object of a repository. Therefore, not every instance of a subclass of Object necessarily persists.

4.2 Collections and Iterators

Class Collection is an abstract class, derived from Object, for homogeneous collections[3] of objects, where a common superclass of the objects is itself a subclass of Object. Collection defines a special, hidden protocol between Persi and objects that are collections. This protocol allows Persi to help coordinate

---

[2] All identifiers defined by the Persi library actually begin with the prefix Persi_. For brevity, we do not use the prefix in this paper.

[3] A collection is homogeneous only in the sense that members of that collection must have a common superclass.

index maintenance invisibly and automatically for applications. Because it is an abstract class, Collection does not in and of itself collect any objects. Instead, developers of subclasses of Collection determine what objects are to be collected and the semantics of those collections (e.g., sets versus sequences). There are three protocol operations of relevance to the work described here. All are operations on instances of class Collection.

CollectionInsert(Object) is used to insert an object into a collection.

CollectionRemove(Object) is used to remove an object from a collection.

IsMemberOf(Object) returns the value true for collection members.

The first two functions must be specialized for each kind of collection class (i.e., subclass of Collection).

Along with collections, Persi provides an abstraction for iterating over collections. The abstraction, called a *collection accessor*, captures the notion of a state of an iteration (i.e., a "cursor"). Typically, each subclass of Collection would have a corresponding collection accessor, tailored to the kind of collection defined by that subclass of Collection. The iteration is modeled as an "initiate-next-terminate" loop and any number of such iterations may be simultaneously active. Persi provides loop steps implementing both unique and non-unique index-key predicate scans.

Persi provides a large degree of flexibility in its concept of collection. In particular, objects can be in more than one collection at the same time, and there can be multiple access paths to an object, not all of which are through some collection (i.e., they may involve object navigation). This latter property means that an object's value can be changed independently of its membership in a collection, yet any indexes on that collection must be updated. Persi handles this by keeping with each object a list of the collections in which that object is a member; when an object's value is changed, then the list, called the *collection set*, is consulted to determine if any indexes need updating.

4.3   Indexes

A collection can have any number of indexes on values of its members. An index contains an entry for every object in its associated collection. Indexes in Persi use standard ordered keys and are currently implemented using B-trees. The interface to indexes is provided by the Persi library class Index, which is completely hidden from applications. There are three operations of relevance to the work described here.

Insert(Object, KeyVal) is used to insert an index key-value for an object.

Remove(Object, KeyVal) is used to remove an index key-value for an object.

InitiateQuery(KeyVal) initiates an iteration over an index for a key-value.

Persi updates the indexes on a collection (if necessary) when it is notified that the value of an object has changed (i.e., through ValueChange()) or when it is notified that membership in the collection has changed.

5 A Semantic Synchronization Protocol

The synchronization protocol in Persi consists of the following key components, which we discuss more fully later in the section.

- The scheme defines a set of semantic lock types for collections and indexes and a protocol for requesting the locks. It uses standard Read/Write locking for instances of user-defined classes (i.e., *data objects*).

- The scheme uses delay for collection operations.

- The scheme combines delay, re-fetch, and versioning for index synchronization. It uses only latches on indexes: it locks objects that an index references rather than the index itself.

- The scheme uses the operating system (OS) as a storage manager and lock server.

The protocol is implemented entirely within Persi's interface operations. Details of the protocol, such as lock requests, delaying operations, or fetching objects from disk upon access, are hidden from the application.

5.1 Operations

When a transaction invokes CollectionInsert() or CollectionRemove() on a collection c and an object o, Persi must update c, o, and every index i defined on c. It must add/remove o to/from c's list of members, add/remove c to/from o's collection set, and add/remove o's key-value to/from i.

For each object c and o, Persi performs the insert or remove action immediately if the object is *resident* in the transaction's primary memory space. Otherwise, Persi queues the action as part of the delay technique. For each index i, Persi simply queues the action as part of re-fetch.

When a transaction changes one or more attributes in a data object o, it invokes ValueChange() on o, and Persi must update the indexes on collections containing o that are affected by the change. Specifically, for each index i where o's old key-value is different from its new key-value, Persi must remove i's old key-value and add its new one. As part of re-fetch, it simply queues the actions.

5.2 Queues

Persi maintains a queue of Insert and Remove operations for each index that a transaction modifies. For each collection, Persi maintains a queue of insert and remove actions that add or delete members (i.e., the collection's *member queue*). For each object, Persi also maintains a queue of insert and remove actions that add or delete collections to or from the object's collection set (i.e., the object's *collection queue*). Thus, a collection object potentially has two queues: a member queue for adding or deleting its members, and a collection queue for adding or deleting collections to or from its collection set. Data objects and indexes have at most one queue apiece.

The queues for different objects are managed and used independently. Thus, the insert and remove actions on collection c and member object o are decoupled: depending on which of the objects are resident, both actions can be queued (delayed), both can execute immediately, or only one may be queued (delayed). Further, the actions on indexes are decoupled from each other and from the actions on c and o. The decoupling improves concurrency.

5.3 Collections and Data Objects

The protocol uses object-level locking with three modes for both collections and data objects: Read, Update, and Write. The following table illustrates the lock semantics, where an entry of x signifies conflict between the lock modes:

LOCK	Read	Update	Write
Read			x
Update		x	x
Write	x	x	x

The use of Update locks reduces the occurrence of deadlock among transactions that read and then write the same object (as compared to those that upgrade from Read to Write at commit), while not blocking transactions that merely read the object. The protocol extends prior use of Update locks on flat objects [13] to its use on collections. The conflict table is symmetric, however, because we implement the lock types with standard Read and Write locks (cf. Section 5.5).

When Persi fetches a collection or a data object o from disk, it obtains a Read lock on o for the transaction. If there is a collection queue of insert or remove actions pending for o and/or a member queue (if o is a collection), Persi upgrades the Read lock on o to Update, and executes the queued actions. The actions in the collection queue add or remove collections to or from o's collection set. Those in the member queue add or remove o's members. Finally, Persi removes the queue(s). Subsequent operations on the object execute immediately. If there are no queues pending upon fetch, but the transaction later invokes CollectionInsert() or CollectionRemove() on o, Persi upgrades the Read lock at that time.

If a transaction invokes ValueChange() on a data object o, Persi upgrades o's lock to a Write lock, keeping track of the upgrade so as not to inadvertently downgrade the lock to Update mode. At commit, Persi upgrades any Update locks to Write locks, and it saves all Write-locked objects to disk.

5.4 Indexes

Persi synchronizes access to an index by means of locks on the objects that the index references, rather than locks on the index itself. The scheme derives from Aries/IM [18]. For each key-value kv for which an index i has at least one entry, there is some nonempty set of objects in the associated collection, whose attributes have the values in kv. For each such set KV, the synchronization scheme designates a member of the set to be the *canonical object for* kv. A lock on this object stands for a lock on the entire set KV.

We define a distinct set of lock types for canonical objects (i.e., the *canonical lock types*). Unlike the object-level locks, Read, Update, and Write, which govern access to an object's contents, a canonical lock on an object governs access to the contents of a set that contains the object. Thus, canonical locks do not conflict with object-level locks, and we define a separate conflict table as follows:

LOCK	QS	MS	QP	MP	CC
QuerySet (QS)		x			x
ModifySet (MS)	x				x
QueryPrev (QP)				x	x
ModifyPrev (MP)			x	x	x
ChgCanon (CC)	x	x	x	x	x

When a transaction invokes InitiateQuery(kv) on an index, Persi gets a QuerySet lock on the canonical object for kv before it executes the query. When a transaction invokes Insert(obj,kv) or Remove(obj,kv) on an index, Persi gets a ModifySet lock on the canonical for kv. If the set KV is empty, Persi gets a QueryPrev lock on the canonical object for the lexically next key-value instead of a QuerySet lock on the canonical for kv. By analogy, it gets a ModifyPrev lock instead of a ModifySet in the same way. Persi gets a ChgCanon lock when it designates a new canonical object for a set (e.g., when the current canonical object for a set is removed from the collection).

A QuerySet lock on the canonical object for kv must prevent insertions by other transaction into the set KV, a possible violation of serializability.[4] Consequently, QuerySet conflicts with ModifySet (and QueryPrev conflicts with ModifyPrev). If transactions T_1 and T_2 invoke InitiateQuery() and Insert() respectively on the same index with the same key-value, the conflicting locks associated with the operations will force one transaction to wait for the other, and the execution will be serializable.

In contrast, ModifySet does not conflict with itself: transactions can insert (or delete) objects with the same key-value into (or from) an index concurrently until commit. ModifyPrev does conflict with itself, however, because the insertion of a key-value into an empty set creates the canonical for the set.

The Insert() and Remove() operations that a transaction invokes on an index i are added to i's queue. The operations do not execute until the transaction reads from i or commits. To guarantee the atomicity of operations on i, the scheme uses *latches* (i.e., short-term locks that a transaction releases before commit or its unlock phase). Each time a transaction invokes InitiateQuery(kv) on an index i, Persi gets a Read latch on i, fetches the latest version of i from disk, and locally applies the Insert() and Remove() operations in i's queue. Persi then locates and locks the canonical object for kv, and it unlatches the index. When a transaction invokes Insert(obj,kv) or Remove(obj,kv), Persi gets the ModifySet lock in the same way.

When a transaction commits with changes to index i, Persi gets a Write latch on i, fetches the latest version of i, executes the queued Insert() and Remove() operations, writes the result out to disk, releases the latch, and removes the queue. It releases the canonical locks associated with the index only when all updates to the database have completed.

The index package implements a B-tree that is versioned upon transaction commit. In addition, it keeps track of the last version of an index i that a transaction T read, and it continues to return subnodes of the same version to T until T rereads i's root. Consequently, Persi latches index i only for the time required to locate and lock the canonical for the kv of interest. The canonical lock prevents conflicting operations on the set KV, and the index package guarantees a consistent view of i.

---

[4]Object-level locks are sufficient to prevent deletions from KV.

The advantage of this approach is that predicate locks on sets of objects are dissociated from physical locks on the index itself. In particular, transactions that access different sets of objects are free to use the index concurrently; a transaction can commit its changes even before another terminates. Our solution is similar to key range locking [16], a mechanism developed independently at approximately the same time. For brevity, we refer the reader to [25] for a more complete description of the locking algorithm.

5.5 OS Services

Persi uses the OS as a storage manager (i.e., SunOS or UNIX System V together with NFS[5]). It does not implement an object server; transactions read and write data directly from and to files in the OS. In addition, Persi uses the OS locking services to synchronize transactions instead of a dedicated lock server. The OS supports Read and Write locks at the byte-level with the usual conflict semantics, and it detects conflict and deadlock among processes on the same or different machines. The semantic locks in the synchronization scheme are implemented as functions that request Read or Write locks from the OS in a way that simulates the concurrency behavior defined by the scheme. A tool SLEVE [25] generates the functions automatically from concurrency specifications in the form of conflict tables.

6 Example

Consider an instance, Hondas, of the data type Collection_of_Autos that was defined in Section 1. The Hondas object groups instances of the class Auto whose make is Honda. There is one index defined on color (e.g., all red Hondas).

Consider a concurrent schedule of three transactions, in which all operations are on the Hondas collection. The schedule is shown in Figure 1, where the operation parameters have been abbreviated for space considerations. The operation Add(Black) stands for "insert the object Black Honda into the collection object Hondas." The operation Count() scans the collection Hondas and returns the number of its members. Finally, Member(Red) returns true if the object Red Honda is a member of the collection Hondas.

The schedule would not be allowed under a scheme that uses only Read and Write locks on collections and indexes because the three transactions read and/or write the same collection concurrently. Under our scheme, however, the schedule is allowed.

Both T_2 and T_3 update the collection Hondas by inserting auto objects into it. Each of these two transactions maintains a member queue for the Hondas collection, in which they push the insert operations, as shown in Figure 2. Since T_1 is a read-only transaction, it does not create any queues. We show three snapshots of the queues, corresponding to steps 1, 2, and 4 in the schedule.

T_2 delays the execution of Add(Black) (step 1) and instead pushes it on the queue. Similarly, T_3 pushes Add(Red) (step 2) on its own queue. In step 3, T_3 commits by popping the operation Add(Red) from its queue, acquiring a Write lock on the collection Hondas, executing the add operation and writing the

---

[5]SunOS and NFS are trademarks of Sun Microsystems, Inc. UNIX is a registered trademark of UNIX System Laboratories.

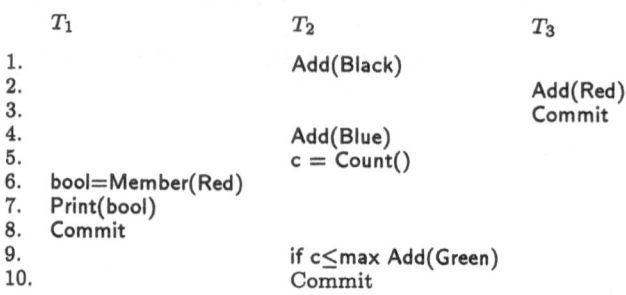

Figure 1: Concurrent schedule of three transactions that invoke operations on the collection object Hondas

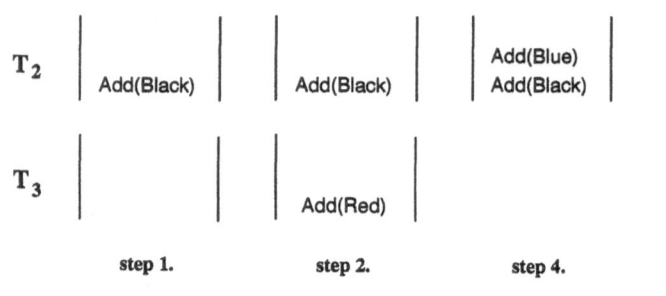

Figure 2: Snapshots of the member queue of Hondas during the execution of transactions T_1, T_2, and T_3

modified collection to disk. Note that this does not conflict with T_2 because T_2 has not yet acquired any locks on Hondas. In step 4, T_2 again pushes Add(Blue) on its queue.

In step 5, T_2 counts the number of members of Hondas at this point; it first pops the operations from the queue, acquires an Update lock on Hondas, reads in the object Hondas from the repository, executes the two add operations on Hondas, and deletes the queue. From that point on, T_2 immediately executes any operation involving Hondas (step 9) directly on the collection object resident in its memory.

T_1 (steps 6-8) is a read-only transaction, which acquires a Read lock on the collection Hondas. This lock does not conflict with the Update lock that T_2 holds on Hondas. Therefore, T_1 will proceed and commit without any delays.

Finally, when T_2 is ready to commit, it acquires a Write lock on Hondas, which does not cause conflicts because no other transaction holds a lock on the collection at this point, and writes out its changes.

7 The Work in Perspective

There has been a great deal of research in the area of concurrency control for advanced applications. Three main approaches have been proposed to improve concurrency: (1) extended transaction models [6, 10, 17, 19], (2) new correctness criteria [2, 5, 26, 28], and (3) semantics-based concurrency control schemes [9, 20, 22, 24, 30]. Our scheme follows the third approach.

Schemes that follow the third approach maintain the atomicity of transactions, but use application semantics to allow more concurrency than traditional Read/Write serializability. The semantic information used is either information about transactions, such as the access pattern of a transaction (e.g., [24]), or information about operations, such as whether or not two operations commute (e.g., [9]). Some models exploit commutativity of operations at multiple levels of abstraction (e.g., [20, 30]). The semantic information is used to allow executions that would be disallowed under traditional Read/Write serializability. Unlike our scheme, however, most of the semantics-based schemes assume either finely-grained data access or encapsulated shared memory.

The execution model we assume is similar to those of most commercial OODBMSs, including O_2 [4], ObjectStore [15], Objectivity/DB [21], ONTOS [23], and Versant [27]. In these OODBMSs, as in Persi, objects are cached in the client process memory, and the client is responsible for computations on these objects. O_2 supports only traditional transactions with Read/Write semantics; O_2 also provides "read-only transactions" that do not require any locks (are not guaranteed consistent values). ObjectStore supports only Read and Write locks with page-level granularity. Versant provides *update* locks that are similar to Persi's Update locks. Unlike Persi, however, it does not support delaying of operations or the re-fetch technique on collection objects or index structures.

Both ObjectStore and Versant support "semantic sharing" of objects across long transactions. However, this is done only through versioning, whereby concurrent long transactions can read and update different versions of the same object. These versions can either co-exist indefinitely or can be merged into a single consistent version, if needed. In that respect, they are similar to data sharing models based on *read-only versions* [3, 11, 12]. Versioning schemes, however, fail to provide correctness criteria for concurrent access. Moreover, unrestrained proliferation of versions requires complex, human intervention to reconcile coexistent, parallel versions. Finally, the schemes that enforce linear version histories commonly place the burden of reconciliation on the later-committing transactions. This raises fairness issues: while transaction T is reconciling its changes with one set of committed versions, another transaction can commit other versions with which T must reconcile its changes.

8 Discussion

The paper describes a semantic synchronization scheme for a persistent object system library. The library implements an execution model commonly used in commercial OODBMSs in which operations execute within the address space of a transaction, and the granularity of data access is at least the size of an object. The model restricts the application of semantic synchronization mechanisms, most of which imply either fine-grained data access or an encapsulated shared memory execution model. In designing our synchronization scheme, we developed semantics-based techniques that improve concurrency within this restrictive execution model.

We conclude with a discussion of three important issues: (1) the generality of the techniques, (2) the expected overhead of our scheme, and (3) the tradeoffs we considered in designing the scheme.

8.1   Generality

The delay technique is a dynamic form of code optimization for reducing the duration of locks. A delayed operation O effectively moves past operations in the transaction code to a later position. The resulting execution of the transaction must achieve the same effect as an execution with no delays, where the effect includes the actions on the database as well as those on any external systems such as a monitor screen. Thus, O can be delayed until the transaction commits or executes some other operation whose effect depends on O.

Clearly, an operation's context (i.e., the transaction code that contains the operation) determines whether it can be delayed and for how long. One transaction may ignore the return value of operation O and contain no other operations that depend on O, while another transaction may contain such operations or use O's return value to branch in a conditional statement.

In general, however, a synchronization mechanism controlled by context- or program-specific information has disadvantages over one controlled by type-specific information alone. The control specification is more complex (i.e., each operation O must be compared to every other operation that could possibly follow O in the program execution), and it is harder to maintain in a changing world (i.e., if the program changes, the specification for each operation must be reevaluated and possibly changed).

Consequently, we choose to define operation O's *delayability* (i.e., whether O can be delayed or not) and its *delay endpoint* (i.e., how long O can be delayed) only in terms of other operations that are defined on the same type as O. We arrive, however, at a very strict definition: operation O(obj) is *delayable iff* (1) its return value does not depend on obj's initial state, and (2) O does not read or write any objects other than obj; O's delay endpoint is the next operation on the same object in the transaction that is not delayable.

The condition regarding other objects is due to the following: if O invokes an operation on another object obj', the control specification must include all the operations defined on obj' and indicate which of them commute with O (i.e., which of them are delayable beyond O and vice versa).

We can relax the requirement that an operation's specification consists only of operations defined on the same type if we define the following: for each operation O on type T, we define a *Read-* and a *Write-set* of objects that O accesses at run-time. O is *delayable iff* (1) its return value does not depend on any object in its *Read-set*, and (2) there is no object in either set that is also in the *Read-* or *Write-set* of an operation on a different type T' that some transaction in the application invokes. That is, the only way an application accesses objects in O's *Read-* and *Write-sets* is by invoking operations defined by T.

The approach is more conservative than a purely context-sensitive mechanism, but the advantages in reduced complexity and maintenance outweigh the slight reduction in concurrency. However, if experience should indicate their usefulness, mechanisms that handle context-sensitive delay could be applied to the problem using well-known data- and control-flow techniques.

8.2 Overhead

The techniques used in our scheme involve more overhead than does a simple two-phase locking scheme. There are two main sources of the overhead: (1) queue maintenance and (2) index re-fetch.

The scheme minimizes the first overhead on collections and data objects by removing the object's queue when the object becomes resident. While index queues have to be maintained until transaction commit, the scheme avoids locks on the indexes themselves by re-fetching indexes upon each read and by maintaining the queues. This avoids the overhead associated with locking indexes and the complexity of a B-tree locking algorithm. Finally, read-only transactions require no queues for any of the objects.

The re-fetch technique is essentially a cache-update strategy, where the cache is updated during transactions rather than just between them. An implementation for re-fetch could use a standard cache-maintenance algorithm to reduce the actual number of fetches. Moreover, the implementation could optimize performance by characterizing the operations in an object's queue, such that when it fetches the object for execution of an operation O, it applies only those queued operations that affect O's result. For example, when Persi fetches an index i for a query on key-value kv, it applies only those operations in i's queue that insert or delete kv.

8.3 Tradeoffs

The first tradeoff we considered in the design of the scheme is between the complexity of an application-defined synchronization specification and the level of concurrency provided by the synchronization scheme. The more elaborate the specification, the more opportunities the scheme has for allowing more concurrency. It is often unrealistic, however, to expect users to provide very elaborate specifications. In our scheme, we have not exploited the semantics of user-defined operations on objects (i.e., we use Read/Write semantics for non-collection objects) in order to avoid having the application builder provide a conflict table for user-defined operations.

The second tradeoff we considered is between the amount of semantics used in the scheme and the complexity of the implementation in terms of bookkeeping and overhead. Although an elaborate specification may allow more concurrency, the overhead incurred in implementing a scheme based on the specification might actually reduce its viability.

Consider the semantics of inserting and removing objects from collections. Each object in Persi maintains a membership list of all the collections that contain the object. The list is used to update indexes when the object is modified. Inserting an object into a collection or removing it does not semantically conflict with modifying the object. To use these semantics within the OO execution model, an object's membership list must be maintained separately from the data part of the object. Two transactions can then write these two separate parts of the object concurrently without conflicting. This however requires two disk accesses every time the object is modified (one to write the object and another to read its membership list in order to update indexes). As a result, a complete use of the conflict semantics of operations in this case might actually decrease performance.

The third complication concerns the access patterns of transactions. We considered an alternative scheme that reduces the possibility of deadlock at the expense of read-only transactions. We decided to use the scheme based on Update locks, however, because we anticipate that most transactions in Persi will be read-only transactions. The protocol we described improves concurrency for such transactions.

Acknowledgments

We wish to thank Rick Greer for the many discussions on the index synchronization scheme and Alvaro Monge for his implementation of the protocol.

References

[1] P. A. Bernstein, V. Hadzilacos, and N. Goodman. *Concurrency Control and Recovery in Database Systems*. Addison-Wesley, Reading, MA, 1987.

[2] W. Du and A. K. Elmagarmid. Quasi Serializability: a Correctness Criterion for Global Concurrency Control in Interbase. In *Proceedings of 15th International Conference on Very Large Data Bases*, 1989.

[3] D. J. Ecklund, E. F. Ecklund, R. O. Eifrig, and F. M. Tonge. DVSS: A Distributed Version Storage Server for CAD Applications. In *Proceedings of 13th International Conference on Very Large Data Bases*, 1987.

[4] O. Deux et al. The O_2 System. *Communications of the ACM*, 34(10), October 1991.

[5] H. Garcia-Molina. Using Semantic Knowledge for Transaction Processing in a Distributed Database. *ACM Transactions on Database Systems*, 8(2), June 1983.

[6] H. Garcia-Molina and K. Salem. SAGAS. In *Proceedings of ACM SIGMOD Annual Conference*, 1987.

[7] J. Gray and A. Reuter. *Transaction Processing: Concepts and Techniques*. Morgan Kaufmann Publishers, Inc., San Mateo, CA, 1993.

[8] J. N. Gray, R. A. Lorie, G. R. Putzolu, and I. L. Traiger. Granularity of Locks and Degrees of Consistency in a Shared Data Base. Technical Report RJ 1654, IBM Research Laboratory, September 1975.

[9] M. P. Herlihy and W. E. Weihl. Hybrid Concurrency Control for Abstract Data Types. *Journal of Computer and System Sciences*, 43:25–61, 1991.

[10] G. E. Kaiser and C. Pu. Dynamic Restructuring of Transactions. In A. K. Elmagarmid, editor, *Database Transaction Models for Advanced Applications*. Morgan Kaufmann Publishers, Inc., San Mateo, CA, 1992.

[11] R. H. Katz and E. Chang. Managing Change in a Computer-Aided Design Database. In *Proceedings of 13th International Conference on Very Large Data Bases*, 1987.

[12] R. H. Katz and S. Weiss. Design Transaction Management. In *Proceedings of 21st ACM/IEEE Design Automation Conference*, 1984.

[13] H. F. Korth. Locking Primitives in a Database System. *Journal of the Association for Computing Machinery*, 30(1), January 1983.

[14] H. T. Kung and C. H. Papadimitriou. An Optimality Theory of Concurrency Control for Databases. In *Proceedings of ACM SIGMOD Annual Conference*, 1979.

[15] C. Lamb, C. Landis, J. Orenstein, and D. Weinreb. The ObjectStore Database System. *Communications of the ACM*, 34(10), October 1991.

[16] D. B. Lomet. Key Range Locking Strategies for Improved Concurrency. In *Proceedings of 19th International Conference on Very Large Data Bases*, 1993.

[17] N. A. Lynch. Multilevel Atomicity—A new Correctness Criterion for Database Concurrency Control. *ACM Transactions on Database Systems*, 8(4), December 1983.

[18] C. Mohan and F. Levine. ARIES/IM: An Efficient and High Concurrency Index Management Method Using Write-Ahead Logging. In *Proceedings of ACM SIGMOD International Conference on Management of Data*, 1992.

[19] J. E. B. Moss. *Nested Transactions: An Approach to Reliable Distributed Computing*. The MIT Press, Cambridge, MA, 1985.

[20] J. E. B. Moss, N. D. Griffeth, and Marc H. Graham. Abstraction in Recovery Management. In *Proceedings of ACM SIGMOD International Conference on Management of Data*, 1986.

[21] Objectivity, Inc., Menlo Park, CA. *Objectivity Database Reference Manual*, 1990.

[22] P. E. O'Neil. The Escrow Transactional Method. *ACM Transactions on Database Systems*, 11(4), December 1986.

[23] Ontologic, Inc., Billerica, MA. *ONTOS Reference Manual*, 1989.

[24] K. Salem and H. Garcia-Molina. Altruistic Locking. Technical Report UMIACS-TR-90-104 CS-TR-2512, Institute for Advanced Computer Studies, Department of Computer Science, University of Maryland, July 1990.

[25] A. H. Skarra. SLEVE: Semantic Locking for EVEnt synchronization. In *Proceedings of Ninth International Conference on Data Engineering*. IEEE Computer Society Press, 1993. An expanded version is Technical Memorandum 59113-920303-03TM, AT&T Bell Laboratories, March, 1992.

[26] D. Stemple and R. Morrison. Specifying Flexible Concurrency Control Schemes: An Abstract Operational Approach. In *Proceedings of 15th Australian Computer Science Conference*, 1992.

[27] Versant Object Technology, Menlo Park, CA. *VERSANT ODBMS: A Technical Overview for Software Developers*, 1992.

[28] H. Wächter and A. Reuter. The ConTract Model. In A. K. Elmagarmid, editor, *Database Transaction Models for Advanced Applications*. Morgan Kaufmann Publishers, Inc., San Mateo, CA, 1992.

[29] W. E. Weihl. Commutativity-Based Concurrency Control for Abstract Data Types. In *IEEE Proceedings of 21st Annual Hawaii International Conference on System Sciences*, 1988.

[30] G. Weikum and H.-J. Schek. Concepts and Applications of Multilevel Transactions and Open Nested Transactions. In A. K. Elmagarmid, editor, *Database Transaction Models for Advanced Applications*. Morgan Kaufmann Publishers, Inc., San Mateo, CA, 1992.

[31] A. L. Wolf. An Initial Look at Abstraction Mechanisms and Persistence. In A. Dearle, G. M. Shaw, and S. B. Zdonik, editors, *Implementing Persistent Object Bases: Principles and Practice. The Fourth International Workshop on Persistent Object Systems*. Morgan Kaufmann Publishers, Inc., San Mateo, CA, 1991.

[32] A. L. Wolf. The Persi Persistent Object System Library. Available from the author, June 1993.

Customizing Concurrency Controls using Graph of Locking Capabilities

Laurent Daynès*

Computing Sciences Department, Glasgow University, Scotland[†]

laurent@dcs.gla.ac.uk

Olivier Gruber

Projet Rodin, INRIA Rocquencourt, France

Olivier.Gruber@inria.fr

Abstract

As persistent object store technology reaches a mature state with respect to orthogonal persistence support, the lack of efficient and flexible concurrency control that could make them an attractive alternative to database systems is cruelly felt. In the search for more flexibility, an increasing trend towards independent control over the basic transaction properties of atomicity, permanence and serializability has emerged [11, 13].

Following this approach, this paper propose a new mechanism, called *locking capability graph*, which allows quick prototyping of concurrency control independently of other transaction properties. This mechanism allows (1) generic conflict detection based on a *no conflict with* relationship between lock owners, (2) arbitrary delegation of locks, and (3), automated tracking of dependencies between lock owners. The mechanism is flexible enough to support a variety of popular transaction models' concurrency control. Our measurements using a first prototype show that a nested transactions' locking protocol, built with locking capability graph, outperforms significantly other known implementations of a lock manager dedicated to this protocol.

1 Introduction

As persistent object store (POS) technology reaches a mature state with respect to orthogonal persistence, the lack of concurrency control and fault-tolerant support that could make them competitive with database systems is cruelly felt. The problem is exacerbated by the aim of POS at replacing both conventional operating and database systems in their platform's role to the development and execution of persistent applications.

Therefore, the challenge for POS designers is to provide the flexibility of an operating system mechanism and to fulfill database system's performance requirements, while promoting easy writing of robust persistent multi-user applications.

---

*This work has been funded by ESPRIT BRA project FIDE2.

[†]The author is currently seconded to the computing sciences department of the University of Glasgow by the RODIN project, INRIA Rocquencourt, France.

In the search for more flexibility, an increasing trend towards independent control over the basic transaction properties of atomicity, permanence and serializability has emerged [11, 13]. This leads to a layered system architecture where the common needs for fault-tolerant mechanisms such as failure atomicity and permanence of effects are provided at the bottom layer. Thus, functionalities such as concurrency control and distribution can benefit from the clean failure semantics of this layer, making their implementation easier.

In this paper we subscribe to this approach, and tackle more specifically concurrency control. We address the challenge of flexibility by identifying the commonalities of the concurrency control mechanisms used in popular transaction models. Practicality, efficiency and simplicity are favored over absolute generality. The first implication of this guideline was to rule out all non locking based alternatives. Locking is a well-understood and relatively simple mechanism to deal with concurrency control [5]. Moreover, locking has been shown to exhibit the most stable behavior with respect to other mechanisms when used under varying workloads.

The solution proposed in this paper is an original locking mechanism called *locking capability graph* (LCG for short). LCG supports efficiently generic conflict detection based on a *no-conflict with* relationship between lock owners, arbitrary delegation of locks, automated tracking of dependencies between lock owners, and re-organization of isolation spheres to eliminate such dependencies. Our measurements using a first prototype show that LCG competes with state-of-the-art lock management techniques under light workloads, and significantly outperforms them as soon as complex workloads are experienced.

The rest of this paper begins with an overview of LCG. The next two sections discuss LCG's flexibility and performance. It is first shown how a broad set of concurrency control techniques can be easily built using LCG. Then we show that this flexibility does not sacrifice performance. To this goal, we compare the performance of three implementations of a lock manager supporting nested transactions' locking protocol. One lock manager is built using LCG, the two others follow traditional lock management techniques. We conclude with a summary of LCG's benefits and how we envision its integration with a persistent object store.

2   Locking Capabilities Graph

Locking capabilities graph is an attempt to group together, in a simple and efficient locking mechanism, the commonalities of concurrency control used in most transaction models.

To synchronize themselves by mean of locks, computations must first create one or several locking capabilities and request locks on behalf of their capabilities.

A locking capability (or capability for short) holds five informations : An unique capability identifier, the name of the unique holder of the capability, a callback to an abort handler for the capability's holder, the set of locks that has been granted to the capability, and the relationships with other capabilities in the LCG. Typical capability's holders are transactions, but any entity requiring an protected execution in a concurrent environment can use capabilities (e.g. a group of transactions, a user).

A lock is requested on behalf of a capability, and is granted to this capability if the request is compatible with the current state of the lock. Once granted to a capability, a lock[1] cannot be managed separately: the capability's interface allows only changes which are applied to all the locks owned by a capability (e.g. it releases or delegates all locks of the set).

If a locking protocol requires to hold locks with different behavior, then several capability must be created. For instance, each transaction in an RDBMS would use one capability per class of locks used with different regimes: one for long-term locks on tuples, one for short-term locks on pages of tuples, and so on.

There are three ways to release the locks held by a capability. (1) Deleting a capability releases all the locks that the capability owns. (2) Aborting a capability releases all its locks and call the abort handler specified by the capability holder. (3) Delegating a capability C_1 delegate all its locks to another capability C_2, which means that every C_1's locks becomes C_2's.

Conflicts are determined by two means: a compatibility matrix defining conflict relationships between locking modes (in this paper, we will consider only the classical read/write modes), and a *directed graph* defining *no conflict with* relationships between capabilities (the LCG itself).

The vertices of this graph are capabilities, and each directed edge from a vertex C_a to a vertex C_b means that C_b does not conflict with C_a, *whatever the compatibility of C_b's lock requests with C_a's granted locks.*

This relation is transitive, which means that a vertex C does not conflict with any of its transitive predecessors in the graph[2].

Based on these two informations, the locking mechanism uses the following rule to decide whether there is a conflict:

A capability C may acquire a lock in a mode M if all capabilities owning the lock in a mode incompatible with M are transitive predecessors of C in the LCG.

This locking rule allows incompatible lock request to be granted because of *no conflict with* relationships. In that case, a dependency $C_r \to C_p$ is created between the requester C_r and each C_p such that C_p owns the lock in a mode incompatible with C_r's request, and C_p is a transitive predecessor of C_r in the LCG. These dependencies are tracked across delegation. That is, if there is a dependency $C_2 \to C_1$ and C_2 delegates its locks to C_3, then the dependency is updated to $C_3 \to C_1$.

The LCG uses these dependencies to forbid both the abort and the deletion of any capability C_p such that it exists at least one dependency on C_p.

For instance, in the abort case, the concurrency control upon the LCG must specify whether granted incompatible lock requests will raise the abort of the holder of the dependent capabilities (then it corresponds to the classical notion of abort dependencies) or not. In the latter case, the concurrency control must change the ownership of the locks so that the dependent capabilities look like they have always been independent. Similarly, if a deleted capability has

---

[1] Each lock is a list (or set) of lock requests. We use, according to the context, the term lock for a granted request of one capability for this lock.

[2] Cycles can be created in the LCG. A cycle disables any concurrency control between the capabilities belonging to the cycle, while normal conflict detection is applied with respect to any other capabilities which are not part of the cycle.

allowed some incompatible lock requests and has created dependencies, the concurrency control must specify whether the deleted capability drives the fate of the dependent capability (typically, because of a commit dependency) or not.

Thus, managing dependencies and forbidding the deletion or the abort of any capability they involve forces a concurrency control built on top of the LCG to (1) acknowledge the existence of these dependencies, and (2) specify a way of eliminating them.

There are three ways to discard a dependency $C \rightarrow C_p$: abort C, delegate the locks of one capability to the other, or re-structure C_p so that all incompatible locks between C_p and C become C's exclusive property, making C_p and C independent.

Aborting a dependent capability releases the dependent capability's incompatible lock requests and so the dependency they implied. The abortion of a capability is equivalent in effect to a deletion, except that it raises the abort of its holder.

Delegating one of the capability of the dependency to the other makes the incompatible lock requests belonging to the same owner, thus eliminating the dependency[3].

The re-organization of capabilities is done by means of *split filters*. Split filters are associated to LCG's edges, which we call thereafter filtering edges. The capability starting (respectively, ending) a filtering edge is called the input (output) of the split filter. A split filter automatically changes the ownership of locks in order to eliminate all dependencies from the input side of the filter to its output side. Two kinds of filter are available: *X-split* and *S-split*[4]. The kind of a filter defines which locks is filtered. A *X-split* filters only locks which participate in dependencies and are requested from any capability in the filter's output side. A *S-split* filters all locks which are requested in read mode from the output side, in addition to the locks a *X-split* would have filtered. Whatever the used filter, both parts of the filter are independent once the filter's output is either delegated or deleted. Figure 1 shows a *X-split* operating on a given lock. *Rowner* (respectively, *Wowner*), hold the identities of all capabilities owning the lock in read (write) mode.

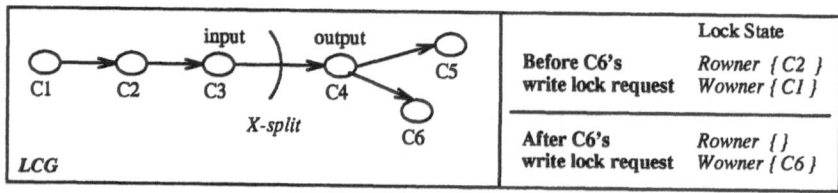

Figure 1: *A simple example of a filter*

The effect of a filter is atomic, which means that it takes effect only when the filter's output is either delegated or deleted, or not at all if the filter's

---

[3] It is expected that the concurrency control built on top of the LCG takes a consistent behavior with respect to other aspects of transaction management, such as recovery and atomicity, upon delegation (e.g., delegating log records for instance).

[4] As well, the more complex the compatibility matrix, the more important the number of filter's kinds.

output is aborted.

In this latter case, all filtered locks are recovered to the state they had before the filter was set. Note, that in both cases, the filter stops as its edge in the LCG ceases to exist.

The next section will illustrate how, using an LCG, one can implement the underlying concurrency control of various transaction models. It will be shown how to support simple flat transactions, nested transactions allowing both sibling and parent/child parallelisms [8], coloured actions [12], and split-join transactions [10].

3 Implementing Concurrency Control Techniques

To describe the implementation of concurrency control, we use a graphical representation which is easy to read. Figure 2 shows the meaning of each graphical symbol, and lists the related set of primitives to manage a capability.

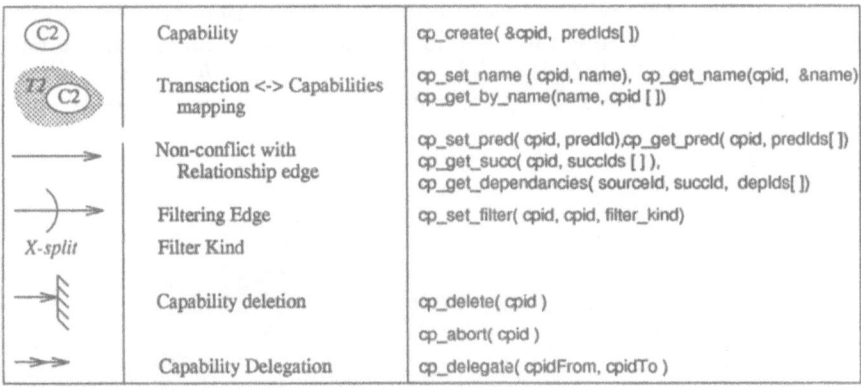

Figure 2: *LCG's paradigms and the interface to manage them*

We use two graphs to describe each of the concurrency control studied hereafter. One graph is the LCG representing the *no conflict with* relationship between capabilities. The other graph, called the completion graph, is used to describe how each capability ends. We number the edges of each graph when we need to show the order on which operations are executed.

For instance, the pictorial representation of flat transactions' concurrency control is depicted in Figure 3. Flat transactions run in strict isolation and release their locks at the end of their computations. Strict isolation means that a transaction does not tolerate incompatible locks during its execution, and therefore does not use *no conflict with* relationship. Therefore the resulting LCG has no edges.

• *Nested transactions* with parent/child parallelism usually require distinguishing lock requests granted to a transaction (held locks), from locks delegated to that transaction from its committed child transactions (retained locks) [8]. The rationale for this distinction is that a parent transaction T_p could not

152

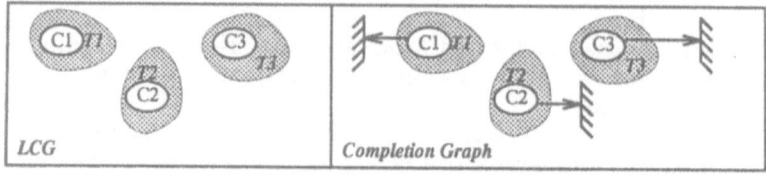

Figure 3: *Flat Transactions*

allow its parallel sub-transactions to access its own objects without endangering the correctness of its computation. However, the locks of T_p's committed descendants must be grantable to the other running descendants of T_p. That is, the work of any committed inferiors of a transaction T must be visible to T (upward inheritance of locks) and T's running inferiors (downward inheritance of locks).

These different lock ownerships can be implemented using two capabilities per transaction: One for their retained locks, the other for their held locks. Retaining capabilities are used by sub-transactions to delegate their locks. Figure 4 exemplifies this protocol. For instance, transaction T_4 holds two capabilities: Cr_4 for its retained locks, and Ch_4 for its held locks. Notice how T_4 downwardly inherits only T_2's and T_1's retained locks: Ch_4 has Cr_4 as unique predecessor, which makes Ch_4 non conflicting with Cr_4 and transitively with Cr_2 and Cr_1.

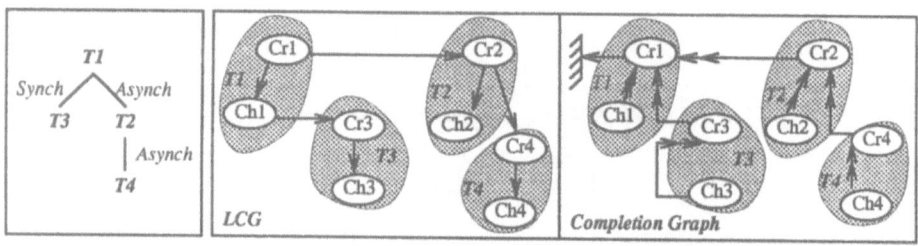

Figure 4: *Nested Transactions allowing both sibling and parent/child parallelism*

In practice, strict isolation between a parent and its child transactions is not desirable when sub-transactions are called synchronously, typically to provide a inner sphere of rollback. In this case, making a synchronous sub-transaction conflicting with its caller would forbid the sub-transaction to update its caller's working set, which is in contradiction with the effect one looked for with this sub-transaction.

Most implementations of nested transactions simplified the locking protocol by allowing only synchronous invocation and so, sibling parallelism only. That way, the parent transaction is always blocked until all invoked child transactions have completed, and all locks of the parent transaction can safely be granted to all inferiors of that transaction. Thus, *automated downward inheritance* of locks is done upon sub-transaction invocations. Notice that this does not affect nested transactions' atomicity property since the parent transaction does not become dependent of the outcome of its inferiors transactions, i.e., if a child fails, its updates are rolled back.

Automated downward inheritance of locks can be applied also to asynchronously invoked sub-transactions. An asynchronous invocation is a two-step process [14]: a calling step which triggers the execution of the invoked code, and a claiming step which yields the result of the call. The calling step returns immediately, without waiting for the completion of the invoked code, and provides the caller with a handle for the invocation. This handle can be used at any time later to reclaim the results of the invocation. The claiming of results is a synchronous process: the claimer has to wait until the desired invocation is completed and the corresponding result is available. Thus, the parent transaction can add its holding capability in the predecessor list of the claimed sub-transaction's capability. Remark that a synchronous invocation is just a special case of asynchronous invocation, where the callee is claimed immediately after the call. In our example, transaction T_3 is such a claimed transaction (Cr_3 has Ch_1 as predecessor instead of Cr_1, which makes Ch_3 non conflicting with Cr_3, Ch_1 and Cr_1.)

In all cases, when a sub-transaction completes, it always delegates its locks to its parent's retaining capability in order to make its work visible to all its parent's inferiors (For instance, when Cr_4 delegates its locks to Cr_2, they become grantable to Ch_2 because of the LCG's structure).

• *Chained transactions* were introduced for implementing some kind of durable savepoint while retaining the privacy of the work. Chaining a transaction commits this transaction while denying the access to its objects to any transactions but the next one in the chain. Achieving this behavior just consists of delegating the committed transaction's locks to the next transaction in the chain (step 1 on the left-hand side of Figure 5) until the end of the chain, where the last transaction will commit and release all locks the chain kept (step 2). Alternatively, one could have written this operation using a special capability representing the chain, and specifying this chain capability as the predecessor of the next transaction in the chain (right-hand side of Figure 5).

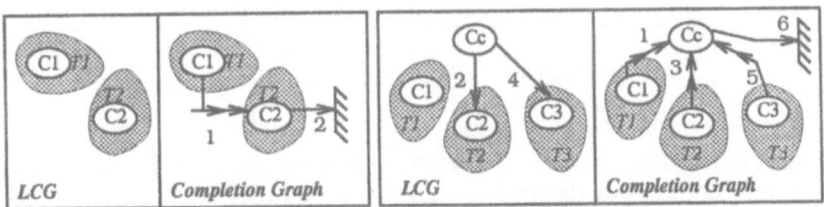

Figure 5: *Chained Transactions and Serializing Actions*

This latter form is much more general and has more in common with *coloured actions* system [12] than with chained transactions. Indeed, from this example, one can note that supporting coloured action is obvious: one has just to create a capability for each colour used in a coloured actions system. For instance, the chain capability stands for the colour of the chain. Supporting coloured actions means supporting a wide variety of transaction semantics,

154

such as serializing actions, glued actions or n-level independent top-actions, which where proved to be very useful for building complex robust multi-user applications.

• Open-ended activities are characterized by uncertain duration (from hours to months) and uncertain developments (actions un-foreseeable at the beginning). Therefore, a major requirement of open-ended activities is the ability to dynamically re-structure the shape of the initial transaction implementing an activity. This semantics is best supported by the *split* and *join* transaction primitives [10].

A transaction joins another one by delegating its locks to this transaction, which is simply done by delegating its capabilities. The split operation is a straightforward use of a *split filter* (see Figure 6). The decision to split one transaction into two or more transactions is taken at any time during the transaction lifetime. In practice, users have to select the objects to split from the re-structured transaction. Here follows one way to implement such a split operation using capability locking. Upon a split event, the program is diverted to a routine that displays to users each object they have worked on, and asks which should be freed. Based on the user's decisions, the routine builds a list of the objects to split. To split a transaction, a capability must first be created and set as the output of a split filter whose input is the transaction's capability. The list of selected objects is then scanned, requesting a read[5] lock on each object using the new capability to migrate the ownerships of the object's lock. The new capability can then be delegated to another transaction which decides the fate of the delegated objects.

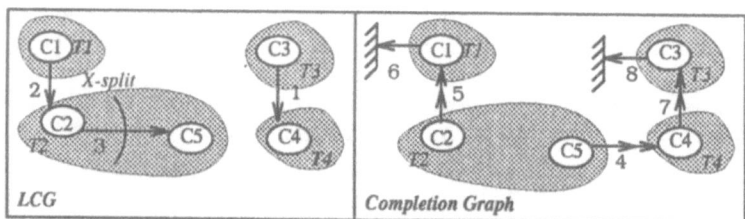

Figure 6:   *Split-join Transaction*

The kind of filter mostly depends on what users intend to do. Typically, a *X-split* is enough for delegating updates to another transaction, while early release of read locks is only possible using a *S-split*. An example of split-join transaction used for update delegation is depicted Figure 6. A sub-transaction $T2$ of a transaction $T1$ is split so that the selected objects' locks are owned by $C5$ (step 3 on the LCG). These objects are then joined to a sub-transaction $T4$ of transaction T3 (step 4).

---

[5]The filter always keeps the stronger mode between its input and output side. Thus, acquiring the lock in read mode is enough.

4 Performance

A first version of a lock manager supporting LCG has been achieved and already used to implement a nested transactions' concurrency control. This version fully supports arbitrary delegation and *no conflict with* relationships as described above, but not yet *split-filters*. Dependencies are also tracked, but interfaces to exploit them have not yet been implemented.

The purpose of this section is twofold: First, to give insight on the techniques we use to implement efficiently the LCG, and second, to show that a given concurrency control implemented using LCG competes easily with dedicated state-of-the-art techniques. We choose to compare nested transactions' locking protocol to evaluate the performance of LCG. Since, nested transactions are the basis of most extended transaction models advocated for design process and collaborative work, it is natural to evaluate how well LCG could support them.

For the sake of comparison, we have prototyped and measured two other lock managers built using classical techniques. For simplicity, we limited our implementation of these two lock managers to sibling only parallelism.

Our experiments are set in a client/server framework, where each client runs an arbitrary number of transactions at a time against its cache of objects. Concurrent accesses to this cache are synchronized using the service of a local lock manager. At a lower level, a cache coherency protocol synchronizes, transparently to the upper layers, the accesses to the server's master copy of data. In this context, we are interrested in evaluating the performance degradation when pointer chasing workloads are best supported. That is, when the client's cache is warmed with a working set which fits in main memory, any preprocessing such as those needed for swizzling pointers are already done, and the client already holds consistency locks in a mode strong enough to protect subsequent accesses to its cache. In this case, most client/server POSs exhibit performance equivalent to those of a non-persistent program running in virtual memory [1]. Reproducing this best case is simply done by integrating each of the three lock managers with a very simple virtual memory of objects.

Due to lack of space, we only outline the salient features of the three lock managers we implemented, and report the main conclusions of our experiments. Details on design choices, implementation issues, and performance analysis of the various techniques we used to implement these lock managers, are available in [3].

Our first lock manager follows the specification of a lock manager for *non-standard database systems* described in [7]. Briefly, it organizes locks in a hash table of lock header chains, each lock header being the head of a list of transactions' lock requests. In this alternative, called *NDBS* thereafter, the lock and the cache managers work independently.

The second alternative, we call *OODB*, implements what we suspect to be the implementation of object locking in most OODBMS and POS using pointer-swizzling. Basically, when an object is brought in the cache, an *handle* describing the object is created, a lock header similar to those used in our *NDBS* alternative is created, and both the object's and lock header's pointers are stored in the handle. The cache maintains a hash table which maps object identifiers to handles, and uses the service of the lock manager to store lock headers. Indeed, this lock manager is similar to the *NDBS* one, except that it allows the cache manager to use direct pointers to lock headers. That way, the client's transactions only pay the cost of a pointer dereference to look up locks.

Both *NDBS* and *OODB* alternatives implement the locking protocol designed by Moss [9]. Each transaction keeps track of the identity of its ancestors, and uses them in a conflict detection rule to downwardly inherit their ancestors' locks. At commit-time, a sub-transaction delegates its locks to its parent transaction. This delegation is implemented by changing the requester identity to those of the sub-transaction's parent in every lock request held by this sub-transaction. The combination of the conflict detection rule and the delegation of locks forms the lock inheritance mechanism. In this approach, the cost of delegating locks is proportional to the number of owned locks. This may rapidly exhibit poor performance if delegation of locks occurs often, that is, if the hierarchies of nested transactions are deep or large.

The third alternative, called *LCG*, implements the nested transactions' locking protocol using LCG, as explained earlier in the paper. The main problems of implementing the LCG itself are to support efficiently (1) arbitrary delegations of potentially large sets of locks, (2) conflict detection based on an arbitrary *no conflict with* relationship, and (3), dynamic tracking of dependencies. Our solution to these problems relies on the management of capability identity sets and their efficient implementation.

Each lock is implemented as two sets of capability identities and a waiting queue. Each *owner* set is assigned a locking mode (read or write) and holds the identities of capabilities owning the lock in that mode.

Each capability C manages several sets of identities: A set denoted $Pred(C)$ holds the identities of all C's transitive predecessors in the LCG. A *Delegated Identities Set*, noted $DIS(C)$, holds the identity of all capabilities which have been delegated to C. An *Active Predecessor Identities Set*, noted $APIS(C)$, holds the identities of all capability C_p such that $C_p \in (\ Pred(C) \cup DIS(C)\ )$ and $\exists\ C \to C_p$. A *Passive Predecessor Identities Set*, noted $PPIS(C)$, holds the identities of all C_p such that $C_p \in (\ Pred(C) \cup DIS(C)\ )$ and $\nexists\ C \to C_p$.

Delegation is done by adding the delegated capability's identity to the set of non conflicting capabilities used for conflict detection, instead of changing the requester identity in every delegated locks. Thus, the conflict detection rule uses the identities of both the requester's transitive predecessors $(Pred())$ and delegated capabilities $(DIS())$. In order to maintain the transitivity of the *no conflict with* relationships, any identity inserted in $DIS(C)$ is inserted also in any $PPIS(C_s)$, where C_s are transitive successors of C.

The conflict detection rule is performed in three stages. The first stage checks if the capability can own the lock without augmenting its number of dependencies. In other words, the conflict detection rule first checks if all incompatible owners of the lock are **active** predecessors of C. If it is the case, the lock is granted and the requester's identity is inserted in the lock's owner set corresponding to the requested locking mode.

Otherwise, the second stage does the same check but using **both passive and active** predecessors of the requester, instead of only its active one. If the checks is false, the requester is inserted in the lock's waiting queue[6]. Otherwise, a dependency is created between the requester and each of its incompatible

---

[6] If the set of passive predecessor identities is empty, the requester is immediately inserted in the lock's waiting queue without passing the other stages.

passive predecessors, and the identity of these passive predecessors are moved
to the set of active predecessors. These updates make the third stage of the
conflict detection rule.

Notice that delegation updates only $DISs$ and $PPISs$ which are used only
at the second stage of the conflict detection rule. In other words, synchronization is needed only between delegation and the last two stages of the conflict
detection. These stages are rarely applied because they happen only if there
is a conflict, and they are bounded by the number of delegated identities and
predecessors of the requester. Similarly, updates to the LCG impact only the
$PPIS$ of some capabilities and therefore need synchronization only with the
last two stages of the conflict detection. Finally, the $APIS(C)$ corresponds
exactly to the set of capability whose C depends on. Thus, tracking dependencies is done as a side effect of an efficient way of synchronizing delegation and
conflict detection.

Within the lock manager, all sets of capability identities are implemented as
bitmaps. Each capability is uniquely identified and assigned a bit number. This
choice sounded obvious as bitmaps represent the ideal marriage of low space
and time overheads to implement small scale set of simple data elements such
as identities. A background collection of delegated capability identities is used
to maintain bitmaps as small as possible. Identities which are referenced from
any DIS of a capability C can be regularly changed to C's identity wherever
they appear, and assigned to incoming capabilities.

Finally, as in the $OODB$ alternative, locks are allocated upon object-faults
and their reference are stored in object handles to provide fast access for subsequent lock requests.

The three lock managers and the cache manager were written in C++. All
measurements have been made on a 486 PC at 33 MHz running the OSF/MK
operating system. We set the size of bitmaps to 64 bits for the measurement of
LCG. Furthermore, we did not put the collection of bit numbers in background,
so that the time overhead of collections appears in the response times of the
transactions we have measured. A bit number collection is raised whenever all
bit numbers are consumed.

Recall also that all measurements have been made on a warm cache. An
important side effect of warming the cache is to pre-allocate lock headers in both
$OODB$ and LCG alternatives. In contrast, if the lock manager is decoupled from
the client's cache manager, as in the $NDBS$ alternative, lock's headers can be
created and deleted by each transaction. The impact of this design aspect is
already visible in the cost of taking a single free lock, summarized in table 1.

Lock Request	$NDBS$	$OODB$	LCG	Starburst
Read Mode	$42.5\mu s$	$22.5\mu s$	$9.1\mu s$	$25\mu s$
Write Mode	$42.2\mu s$	$23.2\mu s$	$10\mu s$	$25\mu s$

Table 1:   Times for acquiring a Free Lock.

The performance gap between $OODB$'s and $NDBS$'s lock operations illustrates the cost of both allocating the lock header and looking up the lock in the
hash table. LCG further eliminates the cost of allocating a lock request control
block as taking a lock for the first time just consists in setting a bit in one of

the lock's bitmaps.

We also report in a fourth column the times given in [4] for the lock manager of the Disk-Oriented version of Starburst. This lock manager has a design very close to the *NDBS* one. Starburst's measurements were made on a RS/6000 model 350 running AIX 3.1, which is roughly twice faster than our 486 PC[7]. These numbers make us confident in the quality of our implementations of traditional lock managers.

To better estimate the overhead each lock manager introduces, we used the OO7 benchmark [1]. The OO7 benchmark synthesizes the data organization and access patterns of applications with complex structures such as CAD/CAM or CASE systems. However, it does not include any specification of the use of nested transactions to perform data access. Therefore we slightly modified OO7 so that each OO7's traversal is implemented as a hierarchy of nested transactions, and locks are set on each object of the OO7 database.

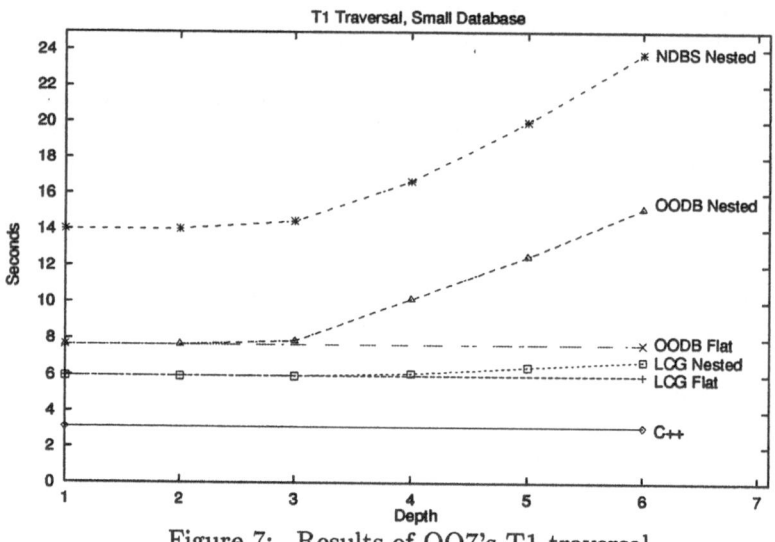

Figure 7: Results of OO7's T1 traversal.

Figures 7 and 8 report the measurements OO7 yields for, respectively, T1 and T2b traversals[8]. Both traversals were run against the small database, set with the lowest number of interconnections between objects (3 inter-object connections per object). The measurements are the average of three executions, as specified in OO7. The three alternatives differ only by the way they implement locking: they all use the same cache manager, locking granule, and OO7's implementations. In addition to the times of each alternative, we add to each figures the times of C++ traversals, i.e., traversals using the cache manager only.

---

[7]The numbers we got from the SPECNewsletter establishe the performance of a RS6000 model 350 running AIX 3.2 to 35 SPECint (72 SPECfpt), whereas our measurements indicate 16 SPECint (35 SPECfpt) for our platform.

[8]T1 implements a read-only traversal while T2b implements a read-write one. Traversals simulate well-identified CAD-CAM database operations which navigate through the object database. Please, refers to [1] for a detailed specification of traversals.

We map transaction invocation to the OO7's hierarchy of complex objects and measure the elapsed time for different depths of transaction hierarchies. At depth 6, this results in a tree of 364 transactions for traversing the database. Using object locking, each T2b traversal issues 353,201 lock requests against 40895 locks.

The curves clearly state that the implementation based on LCG outperforms the two other alternatives: At depth 1, which corresponds to flat transaction, *NDBS* does 14 seconds, whereas *OODB* lock manager does 7.6 seconds. Both are outperformed by *LCG* which takes 6 seconds, that is 25% better than *OODB* and about 2 times better than *NDBS*.

When nesting of transactions is introduced, the locking overhead becomes even worse due to the additional overhead of lock inheritance. However, LCG is significantly less sensitive to the depth of hierarchies than the two other alternatives: While the *OODB* (respectively *NDBS*) lock manager's performance varies from 7.6 to 15.5 seconds (13.5 to 23 seconds), *LCG* manages to stay under 7.5 seconds in spite of several collections of bit numbers (up to 5 collections at depth 6).

Indeed, both *NDBS* and *OODB* lock managers suffer the hindering effects of Moss's lock inheritance algorithm, which uses a scan of transaction's locks and changing of transaction's identities in each lock. These repetitive scans hurt performance. For a better understanding of these numbers, the reader is reported to the detailed analysis discussed in [3].

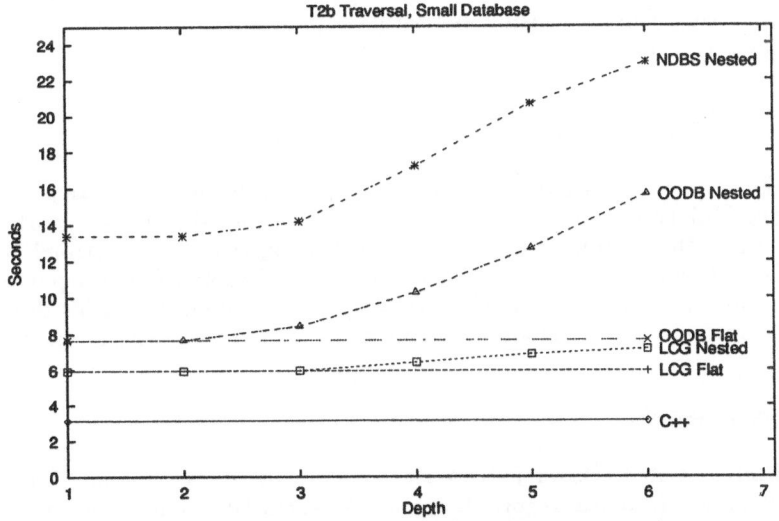

Figure 8: Results of OO7's T2b traversal.

The full set of measurements OO7 yeld have shown that LCG achieves a performance improvement of at least 25% with respect to the two other alternatives [3].

5 Conclusion

In the search for more flexibility with respect to robust concurrent computing, an increasing trend towards independent control over the basic transaction properties of atomicity, permanence and serializability can be seen [11, 13]. This calls for a layered system architecture where failure atomicity and permanence of effects are provided at the bottom layer. Upper layers can then count on the clean failure semantics of this layer to build components implementing distribution or concurrency.

In this paper, we have addressed the latter kind of component and proposed a new technique, called *Locking Capabilities Graph* (LCG). LCG allows quick prototyping of concurrency controls independently of other transaction properties. Measurements of a first prototype have shown that a locking protocol built with LCG outperforms significantly two state-of-the-art implementations of a lock manager dedicated to this protocol. Such performance includes the cost of rich functionalities not found in the two other lock managers. In particular, LCG keeps track of dependencies which may have been created as a result of arbitrary delegation or *no conflict with* relationships. To assert the flexibility of LCG, we have shown how the underlying concurrency control of different transaction models can be supported. Though this cannot prove an absolute flexibility, it demonstrates that a satisfying marriage of flexibility and competitive performance can be achieved.

Our future work includes the integration of LCG into Eos [6], an experimental persistent object store currently being implemented at INRIA. More specifically, we plan to change the current nested transactions implementation of Eos [2] to a more flexible and easily customizable repository. The combination of LCG with the recoverable persistent virtual memory implementing the bottom layer of Eos will be the key components of this repository.

Acknowledgements

We thank the people of the FIDE group at the Computing Science department of Glasgow University who kindly host the first author during this work, and provide him with the equipments needed for the experiments described in this paper. Huw Ewans and Susan Spence, from the aforementioned department, deserve a special thank for the time they spent commenting earlier drafts of this paper and clarifying on some curious aspects of the english language.

References

[1] Michael J. Carey, David J. DeWitt, and Jeffrey F. Naughton. The OO7 Benchmark. Technical report, Computer Sciences Departement, University of Wisconsin-Madison, April 1993.

[2] Laurent Daynès and Olivier Gruber. Nested actions in Eos. In *5th Proc. of International Workshop on Persistent Object Systems*, pages 115–138. Springer-Verlag, 1992.

[3] Laurent Daynès, Olivier Gruber, and Patrick Valduriez. Object locking in OODBMS clients supporting multiple nested transactions. To appear in "Pro-

ceedings of the 11th International Conference on Data Engineering, Tai-pei (Taiwan)", March 1995.

[4] Vibby Gottemukkala and Tobin J. Lehman. Locking and latching in a memory-resident database system. *Proc. of International Conference on Very Large Database*, pages 533–544, 1992.

[5] Jim Gray and Andreas Reuter. *Transaction Processing : Concept and Techniques*. Morgan Kaufmann, 1993.

[6] Olivier Gruber and Patrick Valduriez. An object-oriented foundation for desktop computing. In *Second International Conference on Cooperative Information Systems*, 1994.

[7] T. Härder, M. Profit, and H. Schöning. Supporting parallelism in engineering databases by nested transactions. Technical Report 34/92, Kaiserslautern University, December 1992.

[8] T. Härder and K. Rothermel. Concurrency control issues in nested transactions. *VLDB Journal*, 2(1):39–74, 1993.

[9] J. Eliot B. Moss. *Nested Transactions : An Approach to Reliable Distributed Computing*. PhD thesis, Massachussets Institute of Technology, April 1981.

[10] Calton Pu, Gail E. Kaiser, and Norman Hutchinson. Split-transactions for open-ended activities. In *Proc. of ACM SIGMOD International Conference on Management of Data*, pages 26–37, Los Angeles, California, August 1988.

[11] M. Satyanarayanan, Henry H. Mashburn, Puneet Kumar, David C. Steere, and James J. Kistler. Lightweight recoverable virtual memory. In *Proceedings of the Fourteenth ACM Symposium on Operating System Principles*, pages 146–160, Asheville, NC, December 1993.

[12] Santosh K. Shrivastava and Stuart M. Wheater. Implementing fault-tolerant distributed applications using objects and multi-coloured actions. In *Proc. of International Conference on Distributed Computing System*, pages 203–210, Paris, France, May 1990.

[13] David Stemple and Ron Morrison. Specifying flexible concurrency control schemes: an abstract operational approach. Technical Report FIDE/92/35, ESPRIT BRA project n 3070, FIDE, 1992.

[14] Edward F. Walker, Richard Floyd, and Paul Neves. Asynchronous remote operation execution in distributed systems. In *Proc. of International Conference on Distributed Computing System*, pages 253–259, Paris, France, May 1990.

Object Store Engineering 3

Ron Morrison

School of Mathematical and Computational Sciences,

University of St Andrews
St Andrews, Scotland

This third session on the engineering of object stores concentrated on the generation of code for higher order persistent languages and the garbage collection of persistent objects in distributed shared memory. The link between the two papers in this session is indeed garbage collection since the generation of code for higher order persistent languages is complicated by the problems of garbage collection. An essential part of both papers is that the work has been implemented, experience of its utility gained, and some measurement undertaken.

Al Dearle delivered the first paper of the session by Bushell, Brown, Dearle and Vaughan entitled "Native Code Generation in Persistent Systems". He outlined the area of interest which was that of higher order persistent languages that supported persistent code as well as data, dynamic compilation to support reflection, garbage collection for automatic storage reclamation and the ability to recover from system failures. Al asserted that this combination of requirements possibly produced the worst of all cases for generating efficient code. Of course, one such persistent programming language, Napier88, exists and has all of these problems.

The paper reviews the history of code generation in the Napier88 context which used direct generation of native code from the compiler and the register transfer language RTL and concludes that the most portable method is that of generating C. This is perhaps the most efficient in terms of generated code since there are a number of well tried C optimisers.

The technique proposed in this paper is illustrated by showing how code is mapped onto persistent objects, the linkage mechanisms for linking code to code and code to data, and how to manage garbage collection or stabilisation together with some optimisations. This is backed up with some implementation measurements.

Mapping code on to persistent objects is performed by the Napier88 compiler producing a source C function for every Napier88 procedure. This C function is then compiled and executed. Its execution calculates the compiled code that is equivalent to the Napier88 procedure and this is then placed in the persistent store by the Napier88 compiler. In order to perform the calculation the C program utilises the GNU C facilities for label arithmetic.

The linking mechanism used to bind the code to the run time environment is that of using a global register to point at the environment by convention. This is essentially the same mechanism as the Global Vector used in BCPL. Linking code to code is done through the closure mechanism.

Managing garbage collection and stabilisation is the essence of the paper and requires the ability to identify Napier88 pointers in the C code, and restartable functions.

The paper concludes with some measurement figures which show a useful level of performance for compute related activities. In the discussions, questions were asked on the performance of programs with space allocation in them to exercise garbage collection, with string manipulation and programs with nested functions or function producing functions which require explicit stack frames. A further question was asked in a lively debate on how the technique would integrate with an incremental garbage collector. Al assured the audience that it would and well.

The second paper of the session by Ferreira and Shapiro entitled "Garbage Collection for Persistent Objects in Distributed Shared Memory" was delivered by Paulo Ferreira. The essence of this paper is a garbage collector for persistent objects accessed via distributed shared memory, in a loosely coupled network. Objects are allocated in bunches which are supported by recoverable non-overlapping segments. There is a single 64 bit address space that addresses the whole network including disk storage. The objects are kept weakly consistent by an entry consistency protocol.

The garbage collector comprises of three sub-systems that run independently. They are: the bunch garbage collector (BGC), the scion cleaner and the inter-bunch cycle reclaimer (GGC). It is claimed that the mechanism is scalable, allows parallel collection of the bunches, collects cyclic garbage, keeps the number of messages for garbage collection to a minimum and does not require synchronisation nor causality support.

A lively debate followed this presentation and centred around the questions of how objects are allocated to bunches automatically and how large a cycle could be.

Using C as a Compiler Target Language for Native Code Generation in Persistent Systems

S.J. Bushell, A. Dearle, A.L. Brown & F.A. Vaughan
Department of Computer Science
University of Adelaide
South Australia, 5005
Australia.
email: jsam, al, fred, francis@cs.adelaide.edu.au

Abstract

Persistent programming languages exhibit several requirements that affect the generation of native code, namely: garbage collection; arbitrary persistence of code, data and processes; dynamic binding; and the introduction of new code into a running system. The problems of garbage collection are not unique to persistent systems and are well understood: both code and data may move during a computation if a compacting collector is employed. However, the problems of garbage collection are exacerbated in persistent systems which must support garbage collection of both RAM resident and disk resident data. Some persistent systems support a single integrated environment in which the compiled code and data is manipulated in a uniform manner, necessitating that compiled code be stored in the object store. Furthermore, some systems assume that the entire state of a running program is resident in a persistent store; in these systems it may be necessary to preserve the state of a program at an arbitrary point in its execution and resume it later. Persistent systems must support some dynamic binding in order to accommodate change. Thus code must be capable of binding to arbitrary data at a variety of times. This introduces the additional complexity that code must be able to call code contained in the persistent store produced by another compilation. In this paper native code generation techniques using C as a target language for persistent languages are presented. The techniques described solve all of the problems described above. They may therefore be applied to any language with these or a subset of these features.

1 Introduction

When orthogonal persistence is introduced to a programming language, several requirements emerge which affect code generation:

    a. data in the system may persist,

    b. code in the system may persist, and

    c. the dynamic state of the system may persist.

Since all data may potentially persist, it must be held in a suitable form. Typically, a persistent object store will support one or more object formats onto which all data must be mapped. For example, objects must be self-describing to support automatic garbage collection and persistent object management. In particular, it must be possible to discover the location of all inter-object pointers contained in an arbitrary object. As a consequence, the code generation techniques employed must ensure that the objects constructed by the code conform to the appropriate object formats.

In languages that support first class functions and procedures, a further consequence of persistence is that these values may also persist. This implies that executable code must be mapped onto persistent objects. This requirement would defeat most traditional code generation techniques since the traditional link phase links together all the procedural values contained in a single compilation unit using relative addresses. If all code resides in relocatable persistent objects then the compiler/linker cannot determine the relative positions of code segments at run-time. Furthermore, facilities such as garbage collection and persistent object management may result in code segments moving during execution.

Persistent systems support potentially long-lived applications whose functionality may evolve over time. To accommodate this, many persistent systems provide facilities to dynamically generate new source code which is compiled and linked into the running system. This facility may be provided by making the compiler a persistent procedure [6,7].

In order to provide resilience to failure, many persistent systems periodically take snapshots. A system snapshot contains at least the passive data within the system but may also include the dynamic state of all executing programs. If a failure should occur, the data is restored from the last snapshot and if the dynamic state was saved, the system resumes execution. To support this, it is necessary to automatically preserve the state of a program at some arbitrary point in its execution and resume it later. This can give rise to problems in determining what constitutes the dynamic state of a program. For example, a traditional code generation technique includes a run-time stack containing return addresses, saved register values and expression temporaries. The task of saving state must establish what information on the stack should be saved and how it should be saved in order to support rebuilding the stack when the system is restarted.

In summary, code generation for a persistent programming language must address the following issues:

    •   mapping generated code onto relocatable persistent objects,

    •   linking generated code to the necessary run-time support,

    •   linking generated code to other generated code,

- preserving pointer values, including code linkage, over garbage collections,
- run-time compilation and execution of dynamically generated source, and
- preserving the dynamic state over checkpoint operations.

In this paper, the techniques employed to generate native code for the persistent programming language Napier88 [11] are presented. Napier88 is a persistent programming language which supports first class procedures, parametric polymorphism and abstract data types. The Napier88 system provides an orthogonally persistent integrated mono-lingual programming environment. The techniques described may be applied to any language with the features described above or a subset of these features.

2   Choosing A Compiler Target Language

Perhaps the most obvious method of code generation is to generate native code directly. This has the advantage that the writer of the code generator has complete control over:

- the mapping of code onto objects,
- linkage to the run-time support, and
- the location of pointers in data structures and registers.

Generating native code directly is also extremely costly since the compiler produced is architecture-dependent. An alternative to generating native code directly is to utilize existing code generation tools. Some advantages of this approach include:

- reuse of existing code generation technology,
- sophisticated optimisers are available, and
- the compilers can abstract over architecture-specific features.

The ability to reuse existing code generation technology is a significant advantage. For example, even low level tools such as assemblers include optimisers which relieve the compiler of the complexities of generating and backpatching instruction sequences. Higher level tools, such as compilers, incorporate more sophisticated optimisers which have been the subject of considerable research and development effort. Thus, this approach is a potentially cost-effective method of generating high quality code.

The range of tools investigated included assembly language, RTL and C [9]. Register Transfer Language, RTL, is an intermediate form used by the GNU C compiler [14]. RTL provides a rich set of abstract operators to describe a computation in terms of data flow between an arbitrary number of virtual registers. The GNU C compiler parses C source to produce a parse tree decorated with RTL. A range of optimisation techniques are applied to the parse tree which include the allocation of virtual registers to physical registers.

It was originally thought that a Napier88 compiler could generate an RTL representation of a program and have the GNU C code generator produce architecture-specific native code. However, RTL proved to be a poor choice since it does not completely define the program semantics without a parse tree, and it depends on machine specific descriptions. The developers of the GNU C compiler suggested generating of C code and passing it to the full GNU C compiler [16]. C is an excellent target language since it is:

- low level,
- easy to generate,
- can be written in an architecture-independent manner,
- highly available, and
- has good optimisers.

The C system chosen was GNU C, since it provides two very useful extensions over ANSI C. Firstly, it allows arithmetic on goto labels. This feature may be used to support saving and restoring state over checkpoints and garbage collections. Secondly, it is possible to explicitly map global variables onto fixed registers. This feature may be used to efficiently link generated code with the run-time support. A further advantage is that GNU C is freely available for most architectures, thus the use of GNU specific C extensions need not limit portability.

3   Seven Tricks for Compiling Persistent Languages

In this section, seven tricks are described which may be employed to efficiently solve the problems described in Section 1. They are:

1. the introduction of native code into a running system,
2. the ability to call other native code,
3. linking to persistent data and environment support code,
4. linking to the static environment,
5. reducing memory accesses,
6. the ability to run programs that cope with garbage collection and snapshot, and
7. reducing memory allocation overhead by allocating frames lazily.

3.1   The Introduction of Native Code Into a Running System

In order to support both integrated programming environments and run-time reflection, the Napier88 system contains a compiler that is callable at run-time. Various compiler interfaces exist and are described elsewhere [5]. All the interfaces take a description of the source text and environment information as parameters and produce an executable procedure injected into an infinite union type.

This functionality requires that the code generation technology be capable of supporting the dynamic generation of native code and its introduction into the persistent system. This may be achieved in four steps:

1. the compiler generates a C program,
2. the resulting C program is compiled in the normal manner to produce an object or executable file,
3. the executable native code is extracted from the object or executable file, and
4. the compiler creates one persistent object per compiled procedure and copies the instruction sequence for each procedure into the object.

Two techniques may be used to extract native code from the executable file produced by the C compiler: writing a utility based on the C linker or by generating self extracting code.

Object files generated by the C compiler contain linkage information that is used by the C linker. This information could be extracted by other programs capable of reading the object code format. However, the format of object files is operating system and/or architecture-dependent and therefore a separate utility needs to be written for each host environment. A viable alternative is to generate *self extracting* code, i.e. a program which, when run, will output all or some of its executable code.

The use of self-extracting code makes the compiler independent of the architecture-dependent structure of executable programs. Using this approach, the C compiler is directed to produce an executable program which is immediately executed. This program copies the executable code for each function into a temporary file in a known format, independent of the host architecture. Function pointers are used to find the start of each instruction sequence. It is assumed that all memory between function pointers is code. This may result in extra data being copied, but guarantees that all the instructions of each function are copied.

This technique relies on specific assumptions about the C compiler. In particular, each compiled C function is assumed to contain no non-local references and all the local references are relative. That is, the compiled code is individual *pure* code sequences.

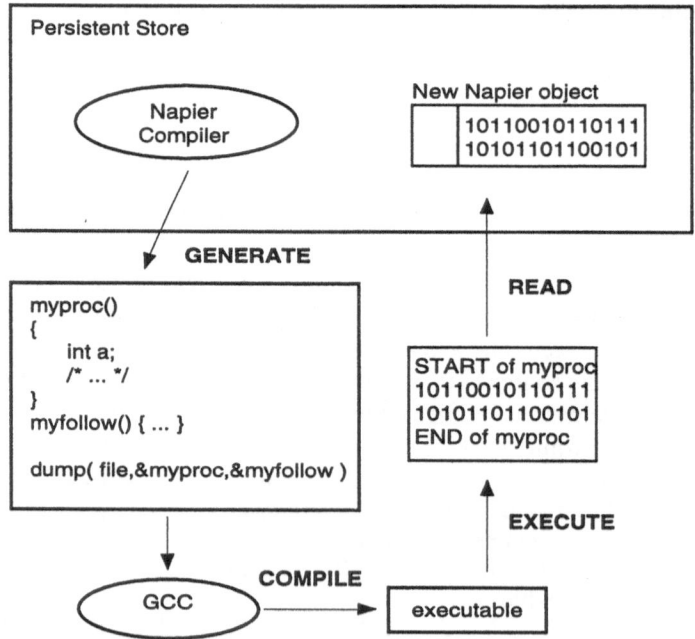

Figure 1: Introducing code into the persistent store

3.2 The Ability to Call Other Native Code

Since Napier88 supports first class procedures, a piece of native code must be able to call arbitrary compiled Napier88 procedures. These procedures may either be in the static environment of the caller, extracted from a data structure in the store, or passed as a parameter. When C is used as a target language, procedure call conventions may be based on jumps (gotos) or C function calls.

A major reason for using C as an intermediate form is to obtain access to the considerable optimisation technology already in existence. This optimisation technology is given more scope when Napier88 procedures are encoded as C functions with all invocation performed using C function calls. This presents the C compiler with independent compilation units over which its optimisers may operate. However, due to the presence of first class procedures, many global optimisations such as in-line expansions are not possible. For example, the C compiler is unable to trace execution between functions. Indeed, some functions may not exist at the time of compilation.

Utilising C functions has the advantage that calls to and from the run-time support can pass parameters, get results and save return addresses automatically. On some processors such as the SPARC [17], this is optimised by the use of windowed register sets. Native code-generated procedures can also use this mechanism to call each other.

C function calls have one major disadvantage: the C stack contains compiler and architecture-dependent data such as return addresses and saved register values. These addresses include object pointers that may be modified by the garbage collector and addresses which must be rebound over a snapshot and system restart. In both cases, some mechanism is required that allows both pointers and dynamic state information to be accessed and relinked to the appropriate addresses following a garbage collection or system restart. Ideally this mechanism should be architecture independent. This problem is addressed in Section 3.6.

An alternative is made possible by a GNU C extension called *computed gotos*. GNU CC lets you obtain the address of a goto label using the prefix operator "&&". Such an address may be stored in a C variable and later used as the target for a jump instruction with a statement of the form "goto *(expression)".

The Napier88 run-time system can call arbitrary generated code by computing an address within the code object and jumping to it. When generated code requires some support code to be executed, it jumps to an address within the run-time system. (How this address is calculated is discussed in Section 3.3.) Before jumping, it saves the address at which its execution should continue in a global variable.

Implementing source level procedure calls using jumps requires the provision of a mechanism to enable parameter passing. This may make procedure calling inefficient since any hardware support for procedure calling cannot be employed. This technique does have two advantages: it is extremely easy to implement and the location of all data is entirely under the control of the code generator.

A final point is that the decision to use jumps or C procedure calls affects the form of the generated code. If jumps are to be used, the code is structured as a collection of blocks, with each block corresponding to a source level procedure. If C function calls are employed, the generated code consists of a collection of C function definitions.

3.3 Linking to Persistent Data and Environment Support Code

By definition, programs written in persistent programming languages access persistent data held in some persistent object store. Programs may be statically bound to persistent data, as is the case in languages such as Galileo [1] or DBPL [10]. However, the exclusive use of static binding precludes system evolution. For this reason, many persistent languages, including Napier88, permit dynamic binding to persistent data. This requirement necessitates that native code be capable of dynamically binding to data in the persistent object store. In addition to user level code, compiled code must be capable of invoking the run-time support system. The support system contains functions such as the persistent object management code and garbage collector that would be extremely space inefficient to include in every piece of compiled code. The linking mechanism employed to link to persistent data naturally influences the mechanism used to invoke the run-time support.

Dynamic linking may be achieved in one of three ways:
1.   by performing a linkage edit on compiled code,
2.   through register indirection, and
3.   through parameter passing.

The requirements of dynamic linking may be met by performing a linkage edit on generated code whenever the addresses it contains may have changed. This approach requires that code objects be modified dynamically and that all code objects include symbolic information which are architecture/operating system dependent.

```
/* declare a structure containing */
/* the address of an object creation function */
struct global_data {
     int (*create_object)(int) ;
} the_globals ;
/* declare a  fixed register */
/* %g7 is a sparc global register */
register struct global_data *fixed_register asm( "%g7" ) ;

void init_table(void)
{
     /* the store's object creation function */
     extern int SH_create_object( int ) ;

     fixed_register = &the_globals ;
     fixed_register->create_object = &SH_create_object ;
}
```

Figure 2: Register indirection.

An alternative strategy is to note that many systems address global data by indexing through a fixed global register. BCPL employed this technique by providing a data structure called the *global vector*. Dynamic linking by register indirection can be easily encoded in GNU C since specific registers can be treated as C variables. The implementation of this technique requires that, upon initialisation, the support code construct a data structure containing the addresses of persistent data and support code. A pointer to this data structure is placed in some register. Whenever generated code wishes to address global data or the run-time support, it simply dereferences the allocated register variable. Figure 2 illustrates the initialisation of a fixed register and a global table with the address of an object creation function. Figure 3 illustrates how a C function could use dynamic linking via the fixed register to create an object of size 7.

```
struct global_data {
        int ( *create_object )(int) ;
} ;
register struct global_data *fixed_register asm( "%g7" ) ;

void Cfunction(void)
{
        int object_id ;

        /* create an object of size 7 */
        object_id = fixed_register->create_object( 7 ) ;
}
```

Figure 3: Dynamic linking.

The advantage of this technique is that it allows the persistent store and run-time support to be freely re-implemented as long as they retain their specified interfaces. The disadvantages are that it permanently reserves a register for this purpose and cannot be implemented on some architectures.

An alternative to the fixed register approach is available if generated code is structured as C functions as describe in Section 3.2. A pointer to the global data structure may be passed as parameter. The invoked procedure passes this pointer to any procedures it calls and so on. The advantage of this technique is that it is architecture independent. The disadvantage is that a pointer must be passed as a parameter on every procedure call; although this overhead is not onerous on architectures such as SPARC that support register windows.

3.4 Linking to the Static Environment

Napier88 is a block structured Algol-like language with nested scope. Although C is block structured, it does not support nested functions and therefore some mechanism must be provided in the generated code to support scope. The interpreted version of Napier88 executes on a machine known as the Persistent Abstract Machine (PAM) [2]. In this implementation, procedure values or *closures* are implemented as a pair of pointers: one to an object containing code, the *code vector*, the other to the activation record of the defining procedure, the *static link*. Since procedures are first class values, they may escape the scope in which they were declared, therefore an activation record may be retained beyond the execution of the procedure which created it. Consequently, some stack activation records may not be deleted on procedure return and may only be reclaimed by garbage collection.

Consequently activation records must be allocated on a heap rather than a conventional stack.

This run-time architecture may be reused in a system that generates native code by implementing each closure in the same manner as PAM and presenting each procedure call with a pointer to a heap object containing the activation of the lexicographically enclosing procedure. This pointer is placed in the activation record of the invoked procedure so that it may be dereferenced by the native code in order to access variables that are in scope.

A disadvantage of this technique is that, if C functions are generated, two stacks need to be maintained: a heap based Napier88 stack and the C stack. However, it has the advantage that object pointers are automatically rebound if the objects they address are moved by garbage collection since the pointers to them all reside in the heap.

3.5   Reducing Memory Accesses

As described in Section 3.4, in order to support block structure, all Napier88 variables may be placed in an activation record contained in a heap object. In the interpreted system, in order to perform a computation such as "a := a + b", the PAM pushes the values of a and b onto the stack, incrementing a stack pointer each time. Then the plus instruction pops both values, adds them and pushes the result. Finally, the result is removed from the stack, the stack pointer decremented and the result written to its destination. Such computation is expensive because it dynamically maintains stack pointers and operates on memory rather than in registers. This expense can be reduced in three complementary ways: the elimination of stack pointers, the transformation of source expressions into C expressions and the use of local C variables.

In an interpretative system, many memory accesses are due to stack top relative addressing. In practice, there are very few cases where the stack top cannot be statically determined by the compiler's internal stack simulation.

In a system that generates C code, many simple sequences of stack-based PAM instructions may be directly replaced by C expressions. In order to implement "a := a + b", a C sequence may be generated such as:

```
local_frame[ a_index ] =
    local_frame[ a_index ] + local_frame[ b_index ]
```

Such optimisations must be applied with care if the semantics of the high level programming language are to be preserved. In general, C does not guarantee the order of evaluation whereas Napier88 specifies left to right evaluation order. For this reason, expressions which cannot be guaranteed to be free from side-effects (including function calls) are not permitted in the generated C expressions. Nevertheless, this class of optimisation has a dramatic effect on the speed of generated code, largely due to optimisation possibilities.

In Section 3.4 we describe why a heap based Napier88 stack is required in addition to the C stack if Napier88 procedures are mapped onto C functions. Whilst many Napier88 expressions may be translated into C expressions, they still contain a performance bottleneck: all the data is referenced relative to the current Napier88 activation frame base.

A solution to this problem is to declare C variables, local to each generated function, which corresponded to locations in the PAM activation record. However, it is not always possible to represent source-level variables as C variables. For example, local procedures must be able to access variables in outer scope levels. Thus these variables must be stored in PAM objects if accessed by other procedures. On the other hand, leaf procedures (those that do not contain any other procedures) can keep their local variables in C variables with impunity, provided that they are still able to save their data into PAM frames when it is necessary to checkpoint the store or perform garbage collection.

This problem was solved by dividing generated code for procedures into two groups: the easy cases and the harder cases. The easy procedures, like leaf procedures, use C variables and are prepared to copy their values into PAM stack frames when necessary. The harder cases always keep their data in PAM stack frames. Since simple leaf procedures are a common case (akin to class methods in object-oriented languages) this yields a significant performance improvement.

3.6 Surviving Garbage Collection and System Snapshots

As described in Section 3.2, some mechanism is required that allows both pointers and dynamic state information to be accessed and relinked to the appropriate addresses following a garbage collection or system restart. The mechanism described in this section explicitly encodes source-level procedures as restartable C functions which are parameterised with a *restart point* and return a scalar *status value*. The restart point is used to indicate where in the procedure the code should start executing. The first call to a Napier88 procedure is performed by a C function call with a 0 restart point. The status value indicates if the procedure executed to completion or encountered some hindrance such as a request to make a system snapshot to invoke a garbage collection.

The PAM stack of persistent activation records, described in Section 3.4, is utilised by the restartable C functions. When a Napier88 procedure is called, a persistent object is created to represent its activation record. This object provides a repository in which data may be saved over garbage collections and checkpoints.

3.6.1 Garbage Collection and Checkpointing

In the Napier88 system, all garbage collection is performed synchronously with the computation: that is the computation stops when the garbage collector is running. Napier88 procedures recognise the need for garbage collection when heap space is exhausted.

```
struct global_data{
      int (*create_object)(int);
      int *local_frame;
};
register struct global_data *fixed_register asm( "%g7" ) ;

int Nproc(int restart_point)
{
      int x ;              /* the variable x */
      int *S ;             /* object id for structure S */

                           /* restart using label arithmetic */
      goto *(&&start + restart_point);

start:
      x = 7 ;
create:
      S = fixed_register->create_object( SIZE_OF_S ) ;
      if ( S == NULL )/* did the create fail */
      {                    /* YES, garbage collect */

                           /* save x in current stack frame */
          fixed_register->local_frame[ x_offset ] = x ;
                           /* save restart point in stack frame */
          fixed_register->local_frame[ ResumeAddress ]
            = &&restart-&&start ;
                           /* return garbage collect request*/
          return unwind_and_continue ;

restart:                   /* restore x */
          x = fixed_register->local_frame[ x_offset ] ;
          goto create ;/* repeat attempt to create S */
      }
      S[ 2 ] = x ;    /* initialise S */
      .....
                           /* update local_frame */
                           /* to point at caller */
      fixed_register->local_frame
        = fixed_register->local_frame[ DLink ] ;
      return OK ;     /* normal completion*/
}
```

Figure 4: The C function implementing the
Napier88 procedure shown in Figure 5.

When they start executing, all Napier88 procedures register the address of the heap object containing the activation record in a global data structure. This ensures that the activation record can be located following a garbage collection. Before a garbage collection or checkpoint is executed, the generated code must ensure that their entire dynamic call chain is stored in PAM heap objects over which the garbage collector can operate. This is achieved by each procedure saving its entire state in the corresponding PAM stack frame. The saved state includes a resume address which may be passed to the function when it is restarted to indicate where it should continue computation. After saving its state, each procedure returns a status value to its caller indicating that it too should save its state and return the same status value to its caller.

Eventually, the flow of control returns to the run-time support which services the request by reading the global data structure and applying the appropriate function. Since each executing C function has saved its state in a heap object and returned, there is no data on the C stack. The mechanism is therefore architecture independent. Figure 4 shows a restartable C function for the Napier88 procedure shown in Figure 5.

```
proc()
begin
    let x := 7                  ! declare an integer x
    let S := struct( a := x )   ! declare a structure S
        !intialised using x
    .....
end
```

Figure 5: Napier88 procedure.

In the code generation system which we constructed, the status value is an enumeration containing three labels:

OK: which indicates that the procedure ran to completion,

unwind_and_reapply: which indicates that something abnormal occurred in the procedure so the caller should save state and unwind and that the procedure should be *reapplied* when computation re-commences, and

unwind_and_continue: which indicates that something abnormal occurred in the procedure so the caller should save state and unwind, but that the procedure has completed therefore the caller's next instruction should be executed when computation of the caller re-commences.

3.6.2 Restarting a Napier88 Program

Restarting a saved Napier88 program execution is performed in 3 steps. The first step is to find the PAM stack frame for the currently executing procedure; the address of this frame is held in the global data structure. Secondly, a pointer to the code object for the currently executing procedure is read from the stack frame. Finally, the C function in the code object is called and passed the restart point saved in the stack frame.

When a restarted procedure returns, it returns to the run-time support rather than its original caller. It will also have copied its Napier88 result, if any, into the caller's stack frame. This frame is found by following the dynamic link information stored in the stack frame. Since the caller's state has been stored in its stack frame together with an appropriate resume address, it can also be restarted.

3.7   Lazy Frame Allocation

The final trick employed was to avoid allocating stack frames for procedure unless absolutely necessary. As described in Section 3.5, many procedures are leaf procedures and as such only require their state to be saved in a heap object if a garbage collection or system snapshot is required. A considerable performance increase in performance may be obtained by only creating heap objects for stack frames when required to do so. This trick needs to be applied with care. Garbage collections are usually only invoked when the system has run out of space. The creation of objects at such times can be counter-productive!

In our system, when a Napier88 procedure call is made, space is reserved in the heap for the frame that may be required. When the procedure returns the reserved space is released. This ensures that there is always space available for dumping procedure state even when a garbage collection is required.

4   History

The techniques described above were not all conceived or implemented at once, but at different stages in continuous development. The compiler and run-time system to support native code were built from a working compiler that generated PAM code and PAM code interpreter written in C. The run-time system still contains the interpreter code; interpretative and native code may coexist and call one another in our implementation.

4.1   Threaded Code

The first step was to utilise the PAM abstract machine architecture by generating C code which replaced PAM instructions with explicit calls to the C functions that interpret them. This kept the changes to the compiler and interpreter manageable. Where the compiler previously generated PAM instruction n, it would now generate an instance of a C macro called "Pam_n"; this macro expanded into a call to the C function that implemented instruction n.

The structure of the code generation mechanism and the communication between generated code and the run-time system was established and tested prior to the development of efficient code generation patterns.

4.2   Simple Macros

The second step was to replace calls to the simpler interpreted instructions with equivalent in-lined C code. This was accomplished by rewriting the C macros for these instructions.

The net effect of this step was to produce a working Napier88 system where most of the interpretative decoding overhead had been removed. However, the generated code still followed the PAM stack model, explicitly manipulating a persistent activation record through stack pointers. Since the C compiler cannot determine the global effects of assignments to the frame, it will ensure they are all performed. This effectively defeats an optimiser since it cannot elide superfluous frame assignments.

4.3 C Expressions

The first attempt to diverge from the PAM stack model was to translate simple Napier88 expressions like "(a + b * c) > 5" into isomorphic C expressions. This optimisation was only performed where the semantics were guaranteed to be faithful to the defined Napier88 semantics; no side-effects were permitted except for those in assignment statements, and neither were Napier88 procedure calls.

Where appropriate this allowed the C compiler to perform constant folding and avoided unnecessary memory references. This resulted in excellent optimisation of this class of Napier88 expressions.

4.4 Removing Run-time Stack Pointers

The next stage was to take advantage of the fact that the locations of the stack tops are statically known. Stack-based operations were rewritten so that they read and wrote directly to known offsets into stack frames rather than incrementing and decrementing stack pointers and performing stack loads. Run-time stack pointers are still needed to handle polymorphism [12], but only during short and well-defined windows of uncertainty. Extra parameters were supplied to the C macros to indicate the relative stack locations.

Although this technique simplified the C code produced, it still encoded calculations as manipulations of stack locations in main memory and so inhibited effective use of an optimiser.

4.5 Local Variables

The next major stage was to declare C variables, local to the generated function, which corresponded to locations on the PAM stack. The word at location n, previously accessed as Frame[n], was now treated as the variable F_n. As described earlier, this optimisation is only applied to leaf procedures. Code was also generated to save and restore the variables, where necessary.

4.6 Lazy Frame Allocation

Having decided to keep local data in C variables, we realised that many leaf procedures do not actually need to have PAM frame objects allocated at all, and that we could reduce the time overhead of function call by omitting this allocation. However, as described above, it is sometimes necessary to have a frame later in the execution of the procedure – for example, if a garbage collection is imminent. We therefore implemented lazy frame allocation for non-polymorphic leaf procedures. This required that the native code calling mechanism be modified so that the callee allocated the activation record. Arguments to Napier88 procedure calls were passed as C arguments.

5 Performance

To indicate the relative merits of some of the above code generation techniques, timing results for the following simple benchmarks are provided:
- nfib – a recursive, function call intensive program, listed in appendix 1.
- dhrystone – an Ada benchmark [19].
- quicksort – sorting a 10,000 element array of integers, listed in appendix 1.

Measurements were made on a Sun Sparcstation 2 with 64 megabytes of main memory. The native code generation experiments were conducted using a Napier88 system based on a single user, page based (CASPER [18]) object store held on a local disk. Computation-intensive benchmarks are used for two reasons. Firstly, the performance characteristics of the persistent object store cannot significantly affect the results. Secondly, a C implementation of the benchmarks can be used to give an upper bound on our performance expectations.

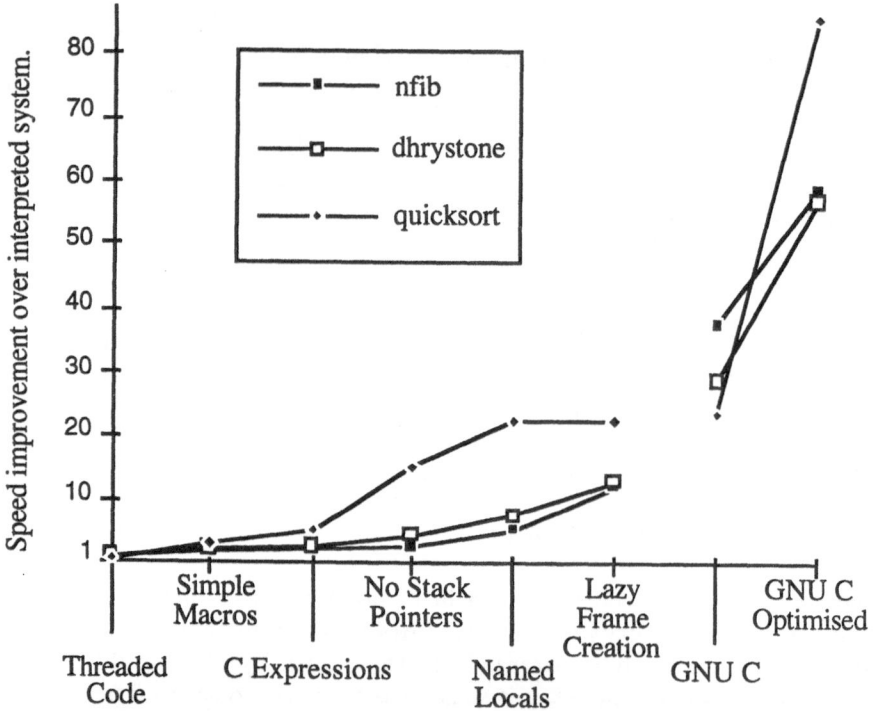

Figure 6: Performance increase relative to interpreted system.

The graph in Figure 6 shows the speedup relative to the CASPER PAM achieved by the incremental application of the code generation techniques. For comparison the graph includes the performance of the benchmarks written in GNU C when optimised and un-optimised. Note that procedure calls are relatively infrequent in the quicksort algorithm; hence the flat spot on the quicksort curve.

One drawback of the generated code is its size. It is only fair to expect that native code be significantly larger than PAM code, since PAM instructions can describe complex operations in a single byte, while the smallest machine instruction available on the SPARC architecture occupies four bytes.

Code files containing native code can exceed the size of their PAM code counterparts by a factor of ten, or more. As the graph in Figure 7 illustrates, code file sizes have varied significantly during our experiments with code generation techniques.

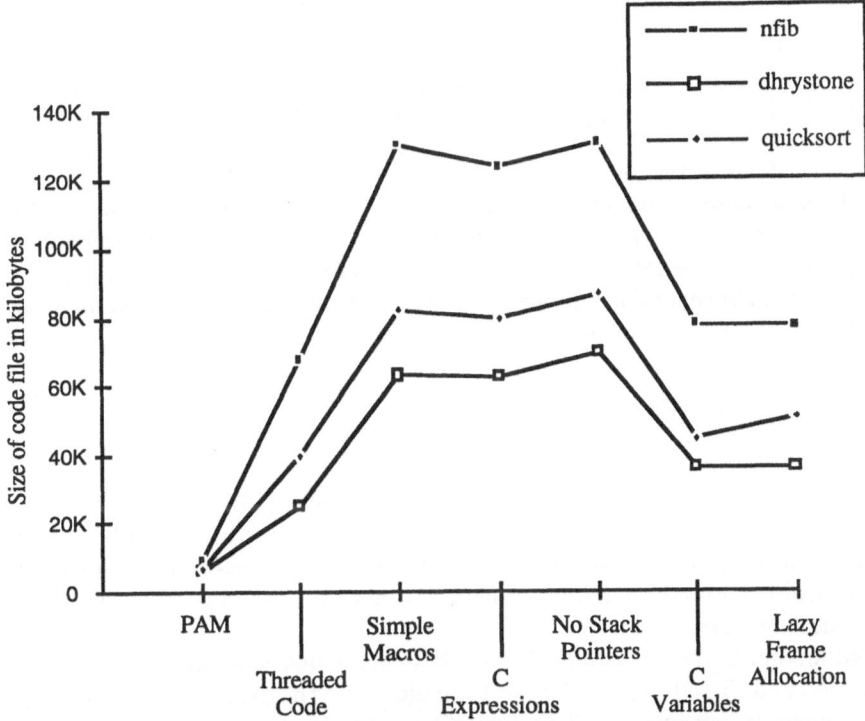

Figure 7: Sizes of the code files for the benchmark programs (kb).

The other drawback is that compilation to native code is relatively slow. The native code compiler takes between three and fifteen times as long as the PAM-code generating compiler on which it is based. For instance, compiling the Dhrystone benchmark into PAM code takes about 10 seconds; compiling it with the native code compiler takes about 35 seconds, or 105 seconds with GNU C optimisation level 2.

The extra time is spent almost entirely in GNU CC. This is not surprising, since large amounts of C code are generated. Compiling Dhrystone produces 100K of macros which are expanded into 480K of C source by the pre-processor.

We have endeavoured to reduce code size and compilation time by making the code generation patterns as simple as possible, factoring out common segments of code into new run-time support calls.

6   Conclusions

This paper presents techniques for generating native code for persistent programming languages. C is used as a compiler target language resulting in a portable and efficient code generation technique whose performance approaches that of equivalent C programs. The full functionality of a strongly typed persistent object store is freely available without the undesirable aspects of programming in C. The code generation techniques presented permit:

- the co-existence of interpreted and native code,
- code to be mapped onto relocatable persistent objects,
- linked to the necessary run-time support and other generated code,
- the use of compacting garbage collectors,
- the run-time compilation and execution of dynamically generated source, and
- the preservation of dynamic state over system snapshots.

We have recently re-implemented the code generator's C macros to abstract over address sizes. This enhanced portability permits the code generation technology to be employed on the latest 64 bit RISC architectures such as the DEC Alpha [15]. We expect to have a robust native code generator running on an Alpha platform by the time this paper is published.

7   Future Work

We are currently investigating the use of boxed values [13] as implemented in the interpreted Napier88/Octopus system [8]. We believe that the use of boxed values will permit lazy code, as described in Section 3.7, to be generated in many more cases than is currently possible. Whether or not this proves to be an optimisation remains to be seen.

We are currently assembling Napier88 systems that will permit us to compare swizzled and directly mapped store technologies. The system under construction will support independent configuration of the following options:

- whether the store is directly mapped with page granularity, or swizzled with object granularity;
- whether the code in the store is native code or interpreted PAM code;
- whether the code in the store uses the Octopus model [8] or the original PAM frame model [4] ; and
- whether the system will run on the Sun SPARC architecture or the DEC Alpha AXP architecture.

We plan to measure the performance of the OO7 benchmark [3] under all combinations of the above options, comparing object-swizzled and page-mapped stores.

Acknowledgments

We would like thank the POS VI referees for their anonymous comments on this paper. We would particularly like to thank Ron Morrison for his un-anonymous and very helpful comments. Thanks must also go to Karen 'the comma' Wyrwas for her stylistic suggestions; any t$_y$pos are her fault!

References

1. Albano, A., Cardelli, L. and Orsini, R. "Galileo: a Strongly Typed, Interactive Conceptual Language", *Association for Computing Machinery Transactions on Database Systems*, vol 10, 2, pp. 230-260, 1985.
2. Brown, A. L., Carrick, R., Connor, R. C. H., Dearle, A. and Morrison, R. "The Persistent Abstract Machine", Universities of Glasgow and St Andrews, Technical Report PPRR-59-88, 1988.
3. Carey, M., DeWitt, D. and McNaughton, J. "The 007 Benchmark", *SIGMOD*, vol 5, 3, 1993.
4. Connor, R., Brown, A., Carrick, R., Dearle, A. and Morrison, R. "The Persistent Abstract Machine", *Proceedings of the Third International Workshop on Persistent Object Systems*, Newcastle, Australia, Springer-Verlag, pp. 353-366, 1989.
5. Cutts, Q. "Deviering the Benefits of Persistence to System Construction and Execution", Ph.D. thesis, Computational Science, St Andrews, 1994.
6. Dearle, A. "Constructing Compilers in a Persistent Environment", Universities of Glasgow and St Andrews, Technical Report PPRR-51-87, 1987.
7. Dearle, A. and Brown, A. L. "Safe Browsing in a Strongly Typed Persistent Environment", *The Computer Journal*, vol 31, 6, pp. 540-545, 1988.
8. Farkas, A. and Dearle, A. "The Octopus Model and its Implementation", *17th Australian Computer Science Conferenc, Australian Computer Science Communications*, vol 16, pp. 581-590, 1994.
9. Kernighan, B. W. and Ritchie, D. M. "The C programming language", Prentice-Hall, 1978.
10. Matthes, F. and Schmidt, J. W. "The Type System of DBPL", *Proceedings of the Second International Workshop on Database Programming Languages*, Portland, Oregan, Morgan Kaufmann, pp. 219-225, 1989.
11. Morrison, R., Brown, A. L., Connor, R. C. H. and Dearle, A. "The Napier88 Reference Manual", University of St Andrews, Technical Report PPRR-77-89, 1989.
12. Morrison, R., Dearle, A., Connor, R. C. H. and Brown, A. L. "An Ad-Hoc Approach to the Implementation of Polymorphism", *Transactions on Programming Languages and Systems*, vol 13, 3, pp. 342 - 371, 1991.
13. Peyton-Jones, S. "The implementation of functional languages", Prentice-Hall, 1987.

14. R. Stallman, R. "Using and Porting GNU CC", Free Software Foundation, Technical Report 1991.
15. Sites, R. L. "Alpha Architecture Reference Manual", Digital Press, 1992.
16. Stallman, R. 1993.
17. Sun Microsystems Inc. "The SPARC Architecture Manual, Version 7", 1987.
18. Vaughan, F., Schunke, T., Koch, B., Dearle, A., Marlin, C. and Barter, C. "Casper: A Cached Architecture Supporting Persistence", *Computing Systems*, vol 5, 3, California, 1992.
19. Weicker, R. P. "Dhrystone: A Synthetic Systems Programming Benchmark.", vol 27, 10, Communications of the ACM, pp. 1013-1030, 1984.

Appendix 1 Benchmark Sources

A1.1   Nfib Napier88 Source

```
rec let nfib = proc( n:int -> int )
if n < 2 then 1 else 1 + nfib( n-1 ) + nfib( n-2 )
```

A1.2   Quicksort Napier88 Source

```
let partition = proc( A : *int; l,r : int -> int )
begin
      let k = ( l + r ) div 2
      let al = A( l ) ; let ar = A( r ) ; let ak = A( k )
      let t = case true of
              al < ar :if ak < al then al else
                      if ak < ar then { A( k ) := al ; ak }
                      else { A( r ) := al ; ar }
              ak < ar :{ A( r ) := al ; ar }
              ak < al : { A( k ) := al ; ak }
              default : al
      let v := l ; r := r + 1
      let notdone := true
      while notdone do
      begin
              repeat l := l + 1 while l < r and A( l ) < t
              if l = r then notdone := false else
              begin
                      repeat r := r - 1
                      while l < r and t < A( r )
                      if l = r then notdone := false else
                      begin
                              A( v ) := A( r ) ; A( r ) := A( l )
                              v := l
                      end
              end
      end
      l := l - 1
      A( v ) := A( l ) ; A( l ) := t
      l
end

rec let quicksort = proc( A : *int ; l,r : int )
while l < r do
begin
      let k = partition( A,l,r )
      if k - l > r - k
      then {quicksort( A,k + 1,r ) ; r := k - 1}
      else {quicksort( A,l,k - 1 ) ; l := k + 1}
end
```

Garbage Collection of Persistent Objects in Distributed Shared Memory*

Paulo Ferreira[†]

INRIA - Projet SOR

Rocquencourt - France

Marc Shapiro

INRIA - Projet SOR

Rocquencourt - France

Abstract

This paper describes a garbage collection algorithm for distributed persistent objects in a loosely coupled network of workstations. Objects are accessed via a weakly consistent shared distributed virtual memory with recoverable properties. We address the specific problem of garbage collecting a large amount of distributed persistent objects, cached on several nodes for efficient sharing.

For clustering purposes, objects are allocated within segments, and segments are logically grouped into *bunches*. The garbage collection subsystem combines three sub-algorithms: the *bunch garbage collector* that cleans one bunch (possibly multiply-cached) independently of any other, the *scion cleaner* that propagates accessibility information across bunches, and the *group garbage collector* aimed at reclaiming inter-bunch cycles of dead objects.

These three sub-algorithms are highly independent. Thus, the garbage collection subsystem has a high degree of scalability and parallelism. On top of this, it reclaims cycles of garbage, it does not require any particular communication support such as causality or atomicity, and is well suited to large scale networks.

1 Introduction

Garbage collection (GC) is a fundamental component of a platform supporting distributed persistent objects. As a matter of fact, applications are becoming more and more complex, and their object graphs extremely intricate. Thus, manual storage management is increasingly difficult and error-prone. Even in 64-bit address spaces, memory reorganization and address recycling are necessary [12]. Otherwise, garbage ends up filling the secondary storage, and the address space becomes fragmented.

Our GC design is integrated in a platform, called BMX (Bunch Manager Executive) [6], supporting distributed persistent objects, not only via a weakly consistent distributed shared memory (DSM), but also via remote procedure calls (RPC). The garbage collection design is language independent and can be used in other systems supporting distributed persistent objects.

---

*This work has been done within the framework of the ESPRIT Basic Research Action Broadcast 6360, and was partially supported by Digital Equipment Corporation.
Author's address: Paulo.Ferreira@inria.fr, INRIA, Rocquencourt, B.P. 105, 78153 Le Chesnay Cedex, FRANCE, Tel: +33 (1) 39 63 52 08, Fax: +33 (1) 39 63 53 30.
[†]Supported by a JNICT Fellowship of Program Ciência (Portugal). Also affiliated with Université Pierre et Marie Curie (Paris VI).

In this paper, we focus our attention on garbage collecting a single address space (implemented with a DSM mechanism) spanning several machines on a network, including secondary storage (see Plainfossé[17] for GC of objects accessed via RPC). There are two fundamental problems related to GC in such a DSM platform: (i) how to garbage collect the large amount of objects cached on several nodes without stopping the system, and (ii) how to perform a GC without interfering with the consistency protocol. Due to space limitations, in this paper we address only the first issue. The second one is addressed by Ferreira[7].

This paper is organized as follows. The next section presents the most important aspects of the BMX platform. In Section 3 we describe the GC design. Sections 4, 5, and 6 describe the GC sub-algorithms, and Section 7 presents the implementation. The paper ends with sections on related work and conclusion.

2   The BMX Platform

This section describes the most important aspects of the BMX platform that are relevant for the GC design (see Ferreira[6] for more detail). BMX offers a 64-bit single address space spanning all the nodes of a network, including secondary storage.

2.1   Objects, Segments, and Bunches

An object is a contiguous sequence of bytes. The granularity of identification and invocation is the object. An object is identified by its address. We assume that objects are passive and generally small, i.e., the size of most objects is much smaller than a virtual memory page.

For clustering purpose objects are allocated within segments. A *segment* is a set of contiguous virtual pages. The size of a segment is defined at creation time and remains constant. BMX ensures that segments have non-overlapping addresses.

Segments are logically grouped into *bunches* because a single segment is not flexible enough for holding an application's data (for instance, segment overflow could occur). Each bunch has an associated owner and protection attributes (the usual Unix read, write and execute permissions), and a set of manager methods that provide a specific management policy of the enclosed objects.

2.2   Programming Model

The user program (usually called the *mutator* in the GC literature [5]) sees a huge graph of objects allocated within a large number of bunches. The bunch where an object is to be allocated is chosen by the programmer taking into account its protection attributes and the management policy provided by the bunch's set of manager methods.

Bunches are potentially persistent: a bunch enclosing a persistent object becomes a persistent bunch; an object becomes persistent by reachability, i.e., when it becomes reachable from the persistent root.

Bunches are mapped in shared memory, and can be simultaneously cached on several nodes of the network. For consistency purposes, the system supports a weakly consistent DSM with the entry consistency protocol [2]. This protocol supports the traditional model of multiple readers and a single writer. There can be either several read tokens, or (exclusively) a single write token associated with each object. Nodes holding a read token are ensured to be reading a consistent version of the object. The possession of the write token ensures that there is no other consistent copy of the object in any other node of the network. Otherwise, i.e., if a process does not possesses a token, the observed object's state is undefined.

There is a notion of object owner, which is either the node holding the corresponding write token, or the node that last held it. A write token can only be obtained from the owner, and a read token can be obtained from any node already holding a read token. Thus, the copy-set of an object (set of nodes with a read token) is not centralized by its owner; rather, it is distributed among the owner and those nodes holding a read token that have given a read token to other nodes. The token management is done with an algorithm similar to Li's dynamic distributed manager with distributed copy sets [15]. Thus, for each object, there is a forwarding pointer mechanism indicating which node is the current object's owner. We call such a pointer, `ownerPtr`.

In order to support persistent objects capable of surviving workstation crashes, bunches are supported by a recoverable virtual memory mechanism [18]. When there is an object fault (the application is trying to invoke an object not locally mapped) the BMX gets the enclosing bunch and maps it. This mapping automatically initiates a logging mechanism for the range of addresses that will be modified by the application. Thus, every modification performed on that range of addresses has an associated log, and can be recovered in case of a crash, using a mechanism of recoverable virtual memory. Before un-mapping a bunch, the system automatically flushes the associated log (intermediate flushes can be also made).

3 Garbage Collection Design

In this section we describe the main problems the GC design has to deal with, and the guidelines of the corresponding solutions, i.e., the three sub-algorithms that are utilized.

3.1 Main Issues

The specific problems the GC is faced with can be summarized as follows:

- *Amount of objects.* The graph of objects is enormous and widely distributed, therefore it is not feasible to collect them all at the same time.

  The solution is to reclaim groups of related objects independently: each bunch is collected by its own garbage collector, called the *bunch garbage collector* (BGC), independently of other bunches and of other copies of the same bunch on other nodes.

- *Accessibility propagation.* Grouping objects into bunches raises the problem of propagating accessibility information concerning inter-bunch references.

  The *scion cleaner* is the sub-algorithm that is responsible for propagating accessibility information, and discovering which objects are no longer reachable from other bunches or from other copies of the same bunch.

- *Cycles of garbage.* Independent GC of bunches (BGC) with accessibility propagation (scion cleaner) fails to collect inter-bunch cycles of dead objects.

  The *group garbage collector* (GGC) collects groups of bunches in order to reclaim inter-bunch cycles of dead objects.

- *Performance.* The mutator must not be subjected to long pauses due to the GC.

  Therefore, we use an incremental copying algorithm (for the BGC and GGC), and the GC of different bunches (or of different copies of the same bunch) is done in parallel with no synchronization constraints.

3.2   Outline of the Algorithms

To keep the isolation of a bunch for the purpose of GC, and in addition to the set of outgoing and entering `ownerPtrs`, each cached copy of a bunch has two associated tables (see Figure 1). The *scion table* contains information about which objects are referenced from which other bunches. The *stub table* contains information about which referenced objects are allocated in which other bunches. Thus, for each stub there is a corresponding scion: these two entities form a stub-scion pair (SSP)[1].

There are two kinds of slightly different SSPs: an *inter-bunch* SSP describes inter-bunch references; an *intra-bunch* SSP records relevant dependencies between replicas of a given bunch.

Inter-bunch SSPs have the same direction of the inter-bunch reference they represent (e.g., 07→05 in Fig. 1). Intra-bunch SSPs have the opposite direction of the corresponding `ownerPtr`, i.e., they start at the owner node. This is due to the purpose they serve: to preserve an object's replica at a node that stores inter-bunch stubs created when the node was previously the owner of the object, but is no longer so. For example, in spite of being unreachable by the mutators at N1, object 03 must be kept alive because it is reachable by a mutator in N2, and there is an inter-bunch reference starting from 03, for which the corresponding stub is allocated in N1.

Each execution of the local BGC reconstructs a new version of the stub table in which each entry points to remote scions still reachable after the collection, and a new list of outgoing `ownerPtrs` (non-owned objects still alive locally). When the local BGC terminates, the new stub table and the new list of `ownerPtrs` are sent to other nodes on which the scion cleaner (based on

---

[1]Our stub-scion pairs are much simpler than the ones used in RPC-based distributed systems [19] because they are not used for indirections, that is, they are just auxiliary data structures that describe relevant references, and do not perform any kind of marshaling/unmarshaling.

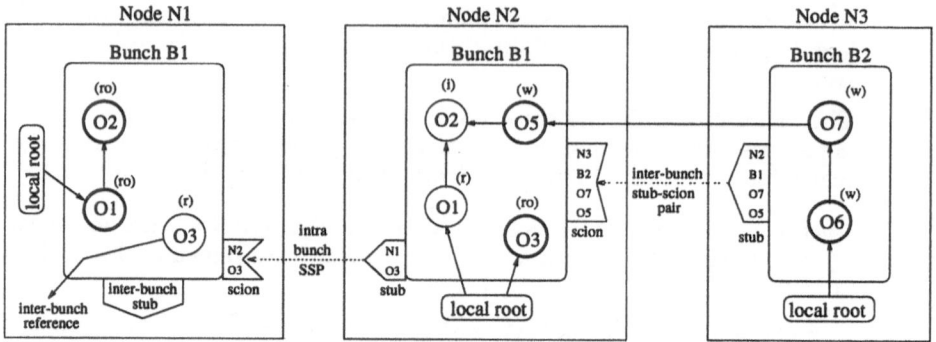

Figure 1: Stub and scion tables contain inter-bunch and intra-bunch SSPs. For each object the state of its token is indicated as follows: letters r and w indicate that the node has a read or a write token respectively; o means that the node is the object's owner (ownerPtrs are not represented); i is used for inconsistent copies. The local root includes the mutators stacks.

the received information), will delete the unreachable scions and unnecessary entering ownerPtrs. Later, those objects that were reachable only from the just deleted scions or entering ownerPtrs, will be reclaimed by the local BGC.

When the scion cleaner looks at a scion in order to find if it is still reachable (e.g., (N3,B2,O7,O5) in Fig. 1), it scans the stub table of the source bunch indicated by the scion (B2 in this case). Note that the scion cleaner does not have to scan the stub tables of all cached copies of the source bunch. For example, even if B2 was cached on nodes N3 and N4, the scion cleaner only has to scan the stub table of the cached copy indicated by the scion being considered (see Section 5.2).

The BGC and scion cleaner do not reclaim cycles of dead objects spanning more than one bunch. To collect them involves scanning every bunch containing an object of such a cycle. For this purpose, the GGC groups bunches in a dynamic way. The heuristic used for grouping bunches does not disrupt the applications working set because it takes into account their locality behavior, as described in Section 6.

The three sub-algorithms above outlined perform complementary tasks: local collection of a bunch (BGC), find which objects are no longer reachable from other bunches (scion cleaner), and reclaim inter-bunch cycles of garbage. Together, these sub-algorithms support an integral GC solution for DSM.

4   Bunch Garbage Collector

In order to maintain the bunch isolation for the purpose of GC, the system must keep track of exported and imported references (with respect to each bunch), without reducing applications performance. This reference tracking is similar to the inter-generation pointer tracking performed in generational garbage collectors [20]. Thus, we use the same kind of write-barrier [8]: every pointer assignment is tested (by code generated by the compiler) to see if the new pointer crosses a bunch boundary (from a source bunch to a target bunch).

If so, then: (i) create a stub in the source bunch's stub table, and (ii) create the corresponding scion in the target bunch's scion table (see inter-bunch reference 07→05 in Fig. 1). Section 5.2 describes the creation of such an SSP in detail.

For the local BGC, every object referenced (either directly or indirectly) from the root is considered live. The root of a local BGC is the union of: local mutators stacks, intra-bunch and inter-bunch scions, and those objects for which there is at least one entering ownerPtr. The set of entering ownerPtrs ensure that a shared object locally owned and no longer reachable by local mutators, is kept alive as long as there are ownerPtrs coming from other nodes. As described in Section 5.1, a shared object is detected as being dead by the local BGC executed at its owner node. A necessary condition for such death is the unexistence of entering ownerPtrs for that object.

Each bunch is cleaned by its own garbage collector: the BGC incrementally copies live objects from from-space to to-space within the same bunch. When a bunch has several copies, the BGC is composed of a garbage collector per copy (local BGC). The local collection of a bunch can proceed independently (i.e. asynchronously, with no synchronization) from the collection of other bunches, and from the collection of copies of the same bunch at other nodes.

The BGC is an incremental copying collector. We use a copying algorithm because this solution seems to be more efficient than others [20, 21]; in particular, it improves locality. However, any other algorithm could be used as well. Currently, the BGC is based on Nettles's algorithm [16]. We use this technique because it is is well suited to systems in which there is already a log (for making objects tolerant to crashes), as is the case of BMX (see Section 2.2).

It would seem that copying live objects would interfere with consistency because copying a live object invalidates all its cached copies. However, our solution avoids such a negative effect. The main idea consists of: (i) a live object is copied by the local BGC only at its owner node, and (ii) the scanning of a live object can be done on an inconsistent copy (this results in a more conservative approach w.r.t. scanning a consistent copy). This solution is based on the observation that GC needs in terms of consistency, are less strict than applications'. See Ferreira[7] for more detail.

When the BGC copies a live object from from-space to to-space (in the same bunch), a forwarding pointer is written in the object's header (left in place of the copied object). Other references to that same object will be updated accordingly. In particular, remote references (from objects in other bunches) must be updated because inter-bunch references are direct (i.e., SSPs do not provide any indirection). Such an update is done lazily, and does not imply sending extra messages. In fact, such information (object's new address in to-space segment) is piggy-backed on messages either used by the consistency protocol, or containing new stub tables. Thus, applications are not disrupted.

5 Scion Cleaner

The scion cleaner propagates accessibility information, and discovers which scions are no longer reachable from any stub and which entering ownerPtrs are no longer necessary. In this section we first describe how intra-bunch SSPs are created and deleted. Then, inter-bunch SSPs are considered.

5.1   Intra-bunch SSPs

Intra-bunch scions are created when the ownership of an object moves from one node to another and the old owner holds an inter-bunch stub for this object. Thus, the intra-bunch SSP takes care of creating a forwarding link between the new owner and the inter-bunch stub at the old owner. For example, in Figure 1, when the ownership of O3 goes from N1 (where the inter-bunch reference was created) to N2, the corresponding intra-bunch SSP from N2 to N1 is created.

For each shared object there is a forwarding pointer used for the purpose of token management, i.e., an `ownerPtr` pointing to the object's owner node. As long as such an object is alive, there is an intra-bunch SSP going from the object's owner to every node sharing that object (opposite direction of `ownerPtrs`) in which there is an associated inter-bunch stub. Now, suppose that a shared object is no longer reachable by any mutator in any node. Thus, this object is in fact dead. The GC subsystem will detect such death as explained now.

A local BGC starts scanning those objects that are referenced from: local mutator stacks, inter-bunch scions, and entering `ownerPtrs` (objects locally owned still alive on other nodes). While the local BGC is executing, not only a new stub table is created (containing inter-bunch and intra-bunch stubs), but also a new set of exiting `ownerPtrs` (indicating the owner node of each not locally owned live object). An object not locally owned that is not locally reachable, is not found by the local BGC. Therefore, the corresponding `ownerPtr` will not be part of the new set of outgoing `ownerPtrs`.

Then, the local BGC scans those objects that are reachable from intra-bunch scions. Contrary to the previous scanning (done from the other elements of the root), the resulting outgoing `ownerPtrs` are not created. As a matter of fact, such objects are alive only because they are reachable from some mutator at some other node and there is at least an associated inter-bunch stub in the local node. Only the resulting stubs are inserted in the new stub table being created by the local BGC (see O3 at N1 in Fig. 1).

Finally, the new intra-bunch stubs constructed by the local BGC (due to locally owned live objects), are sent to other nodes sharing the corresponding objects, and the new set of exiting `ownerPtrs` (not locally owned live objects) is sent to the nodes they point to. Once received by the destination nodes, the intra-bunch stubs are scanned by the scion cleaner for the purpose of finding the unreachable intra-bunch scions. The same reasoning applies to entering `ownerPtrs`. Both unreachable scions and unused entering `ownerPtrs` are deleted.

Hence, a shared object no longer reachable by any mutator at any node, will end up not being referenced by any entering `ownerPtr` in its owner node. Thus, when the local BGC at the owner node is executed, the mentioned object will not be *seen*, and the corresponding intra-bunch stub(s) will not be part of the new stub table. The scion cleaner running at other nodes, after receiving the new intra-bunch stubs from the owner, will delete the unreachable intra-bunch scion(s), and the referenced object will be reclaimed by the next local BGC.

Figure 2 illustrates how a shared object is reclaimed: O1 is no longer reachable by any mutator at any node, and the local BGC has not started yet in any node. Now, suppose that the local BGC in N2 is executed. The new set of exiting `ownerPtrs` from N2 will no longer contain the `ownerPtr` correspond-

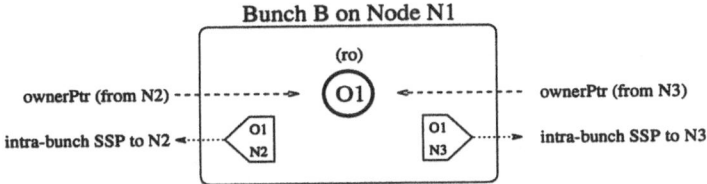

Figure 2: Reclamation of a shared object: O1 is cached on nodes N1, N2, and N3. In nodes N2 and N3 there is an inter-bunch stub due to O1 (that is why there is an intra-bunch SSP from N1 to each one of those nodes).

ing to O1. This fact will be communicated to N1, and the local scion cleaner will delete the entering ownerPtr from N2. Because there is still an entering ownerPtr from N3, O1 will be kept alive by the local BGC in N1, and the intra-bunch SSPs ensure that O1 remains alive in N2 and N3. After the local BGC in N3 has executed and the new set of exiting ownerPtrs has been communicated to N1, there will be no entering ownerPtrs in N1, and the local BGC will consider O1 to be dead. Thus, the intra-bunch stubs in the figure will no longer exist in the new stub table, and this information is communicated to N2 and N3. The scion cleaner and the local BGC in these two nodes will delete the unreachable intra-bunch scions and reclaim object O1, respectively.

Finally, note that a new stub table and/or a new set of exiting ownerPtrs, can be piggy-backed in messages used by the consistency protocol, or exchanged in the background. Thus, they do not disrupt applications functioning.

5.2 Inter-bunch SSPs

In DSM there is only one way for creating an inter-bunch reference (see Fig. 3): assignment operation that reads a reference from an object cached on several nodes (e.g., O1), and writes it into another object (O2). Thus, for instance, the reference to O3 has been passed to node N2, through O1 that is cached on N1 and N2 (references only travel between nodes inside objects).

When creating an inter-bunch reference, either both source and target bunches are already mapped on the local node, or only the target bunch is not yet locally mapped. In the first case, the corresponding SSP is created locally. The second case, requires sending a message to the node where the target bunch is mapped. This message is called *scion-message* and is used to inform the target bunch about the new (inter-node) inter-bunch reference that has been created, and the necessity of creating the corresponding scion. Figure 3 illustrates both cases: locally created SSP corresponding to O1→O4 on N1, and inter-bunch SSP due to O2→O3 (from N2 to N3).

When an object becomes cached on multiple nodes, the inter-bunch stubs that are due to its references do no have to be replicated. In fact, inter-bunch stubs and scions are not exactly the same in every copy of the same bunch. This is not problematic because a single SSP is enough to keep the target object alive. Instead of replicating inter-bunch SSPs, we use intra-bunch SSPs because no scion message is necessary and the amount of memory consumed for GC purposes is smaller. Figure 3 illustrates such a situation: in spite of the

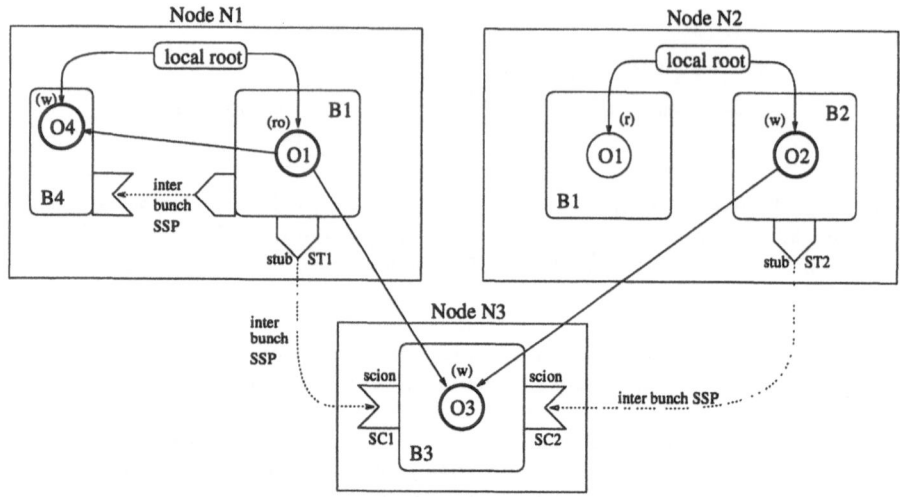

Figure 3: Bunch B1 is cached on nodes N1, and N2. Bunch B3 is mapped only on N3. Object O1 was initially mapped only on N1. Then, as the result of an acquireRead, it becomes mapped also on N2. Object O3 is not reachable from the mutators in N3 (no references from the local root).

fact that O1 is cached on N1 and N2, there is only one inter-bunch stub due to O1→O3 that is kept at N1 (node where the inter-bunch reference was created). If O1 becomes reachable only from the local root at N2, O1 will be kept alive at N1 by the corresponding entering ownerPtr that comes from N2.

As already mentioned, each time a local BGC is executed, a new version of the bunch's stub table is constructed. A bunch only receives new versions of stub tables from other bunches that are mapped either on the same node, or on a node from which a scion-message has already been received. Thus, B3 must receive a scion-message from N1 when the inter-bunch reference O1→O3 is created. Otherwise, the scion cleaner in N3 is not aware of such inter-bunch reference. The same reasoning applies to the reference O2→O3.

The main advantage of sending stub table messages over sending increment/decrement messages [3] is that the former are idempotent. In case of lose they can be retried, and is not necessary a reliable communication protocol. However, scion messages and stub tables must be received in FIFO order. Otherwise, the scion cleaner may use an old stub table that is not consistent with the scions being considered. Such inconsistency could result in the erroneous deletion of a scion. For example (see Figure 4), if a scion message is sent after a stub table message, and they are received in the opposite order, the scion cleaner in the receiving node will not find the stub corresponding to the scion just created (SC1), in the new stub table. Since these messages are exchanged between a pair of nodes (point-to-point communication), FIFO ordering is easily guaranteed by numbering them.

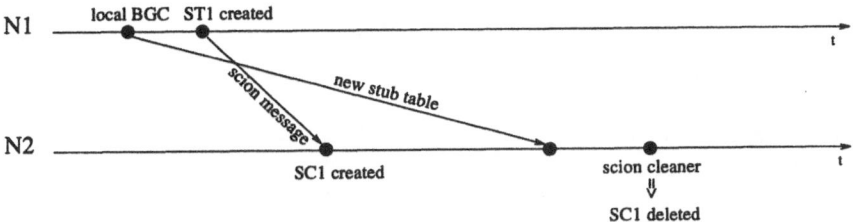

Figure 4: A new inter-bunch reference is created between nodes N1 and N2: situation in which the scion-message and a stub table message are received in the opposite order w.r.t. their sending.

5.3 Race Conditions

A fundamental issue that arises in the context of distributed GC is that of races. A race situation occurs when, due to the different amount of time taken by related messages sent from different nodes to reach the same target node, one or more objects might become erroneously unreachable from the point of view of the GC algorithm. In this section, with the help of a few examples, we describe how such race problems are solved in our GC subsystem. Neither extra messages, nor causal communication support is necessary.

Consider Figure 3 at the moment when the inter-bunch reference O2→O3 has not been created yet. Now the system evolves as follows (see Figure 5):

1. The mutator in N2 reads the pointer to O3 from O1, and stores it into O2. This assignment creates an (inter-node) inter-bunch reference. Thus, stub ST2 is locally created, and a scion-message is sent to B3 on N3, in order to create the corresponding scion SC2.

2. A mutator in N1 acquires the write token of O1 and deletes the reference to O3.

3. The local BGC of B1 is executed at N1 which results in the creation of a new stub table that does not contain stub ST1.

4. Bunch B3 receives B1's new stub table from N1, and the scion cleaner finds out that scion SC1 is no longer reachable. Thus, this scion is deleted.

5. The local BGC of B3 is executed and O3 is (erroneously) collected.

6. The scion-message sent in the first step arrives at node N3 but it is too late.

This race problem is solved by ensuring that the scion-message sent from N2 is received by N3 and the corresponding scion SC2 created in B3, before the new B1's stub table. This can be done without any extra communication overhead by taking advantage of consistency protocol dedicated messages. As the acquisition of the write token of O1 by node N1 implies the invalidation of every copy of O1 (copy-set is in N1), the scion-message is piggy-backed in the reply (to the invalidation message) sent from N2 to N1. When the new B1's stub table is sent to N3, it will carry along the scion-message. Thus, the scion

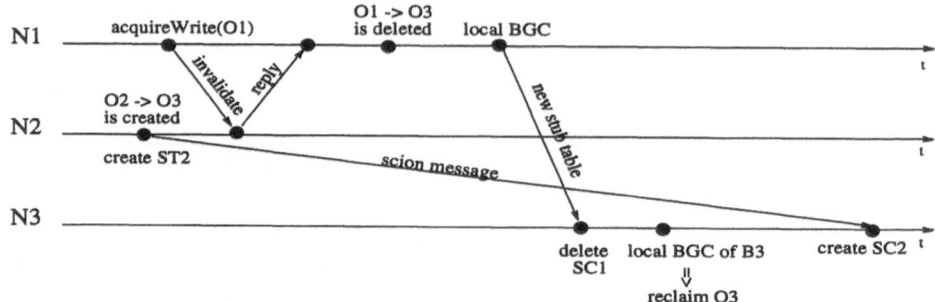

Figure 5: Time diagram showing a race problem.

cleaner in N3 will first create scion SC2, and only then deletes scion SC1. Hence, the local BGC of B3 will not reclaim O3.

Another race situation in which O3 could be erroneously collected is the following (consider the same initial condition of the previous example and its first step already done):

1. The mutators on nodes N1 and N2 delete their references from the local root to O1.

2. One or more local BGCs are executed at nodes N1 and N2, collecting bunch B1. Because O1 is dead, the local BGC of B1 at N1 will create a stub table without stub ST1. This stub table is then propagated to N3 and results in the deletion of scion SC1 by the scion cleaner.

3. The local BGC of B3 is executed and O3 is (erroneously) collected.

4. The scion-message sent in the first step arrives at node N3 but it is too late.

In this case, as opposed to the previous one, there is no communication between nodes N1 and N2 on behalf of the consistency protocol. Thus, we can not piggy-back the scion-message as in the previous solution. To solve this race problem we must ensure that object O1 is kept alive until the scion-message is received by N3, and the corresponding scion SC2 created. Obviously, we maintain the requirement of generating a minimum number of extra messages. Hence, when a reference to O3 is stored into O2, to ensure that O1 is kept alive, it is conservatively created a special SSP on node N2 from B2 to B1. When the reply to the scion-message is received at N2, the special SSP is deleted. Clearly, mutators in N2 do not have to wait for the reply to the scion-message, i.e., they may continue to execute freely as if no (inter-node) inter-bunch reference has been created.

Note that, in the two examples presented above, a scion-message is sent to N3 because bunch B3 is not cached on N2. If B3 was also cached on N2, the scion-messages would not be necessary because every inter-bunch SSP would be locally created (in N2).

A possible optimization concerning the accessibility propagation, consists of avoiding to send a scion-message per each new (inter-node) inter-bunch reference created. Thus, only the first scion-message must be sent. Such message informs the destination node that there are some inter-bunch references for which the corresponding scions may not have been created yet. Since such scions are only necessary for the purpose of the local BGC on the destination node, the *missing* scion-messages can be postponed until explicitly asked (before starting a local BGC).

6 Group Garbage Collector

The GGC has the goal of reclaiming inter-bunch cycles of garbage. The algorithm is basically the same used by the BGC, only that it operates on a group of bunches, rather than on a single bunch. The root of the GGC includes: mutators stacks, intra-bunch scions, entering `ownerPtrs`, and those inter-bunch scions identifying source bunches that are *not* members of the group being collected. The inter-bunch scions corresponding to SSPs that originate within the group that is being collected are not part of the root. Therefore, objects in the group, which are not reachable from any sources other than these SSPs, will be collected. In particular, objects that form an inter-bunch cycle, but are non-reachable from bunches outside the group or the mutator's stack, will be collected, because they are not artificially held over by SSPs from within the group.

For grouping bunches, the GGC uses a very simple heuristic: a group is constituted by bunches that are already mapped on the local node. We expect this heuristic to be effective on collecting cycles of garbage because bunches will be traveling through the network from node to node. Thus, this heuristic relies on applications locality.

This locality-based heuristic does not collect cycles of garbage that partially reside on disk, i.e., cycles with objects in bunches not currently mapped in memory. Collecting such a cycle involves input-output costs that need to be balanced against the expected gain. In addition, if an application does not move bunches around the nodes there is a possibility that some dead cycles may not ever be collected at all. We believe that some of these cycles can be removed by improving the heuristic. However, we intend to do that only after having experimented with the locality-based heuristic. If experimental results mandate it, we will explore more complex heuristics.

Grouping was first proposed by Lang[13]. However, our solution is much simpler because a group collection occurs at a single site. Therefore, we expect our solution to be more scalable.

7 Implementation

The BMX prototype is being implemented on a local network comprising DEC Alpha workstations running OSF/1.

Our implementation results from a straightforward transposition of the three sub-algorithms of the GC subsystem (BGC, scion cleaner, and GGC) to a loosely coupled network of Unix based workstations. Each application is supported by one or more processes (each one possibly multi-threaded) executing at several nodes of the network. A local BGC is supported by a thread inside a process accessing the bunch being collected. The scion cleaner and the GGC are each one supported by a privileged process that can access any bunch, on each node of the network.

Bunches are mapped in shared memory. There is no more than one cached copy of a bunch per node. Every bunch can be freely accessed by any process that does not violate the bunch protection attributes.

On each node, a single *BMX-server* process provides basic system services such as allocating non-overlapping segments. Executing this server in a separate process protects it from misbehaving or malfunctioning applications. A library called *BMX-client* is linked with each application process. This library acts as a proxy that interacts with the system internals (the BMX-server in particular). Some sites on the network manage the secondary storage for persistent bunches. Each one of these nodes executes an Object Repository (OBR) process that performs such managing task.

For persistence support we use the RVM (Recoverable Virtual Memory) subsystem [18]. There is a log where segment modifications are registered (a segment is implemented as a file). Segment modifications are done in *flush mode* in order to guarantee that the log reflects such modifications accurately. However, at this stage, the segment on disk does not contain yet the changes done since it was mapped in memory. Only after the *truncation* of the log is the segment on disk guaranteed to reflect the modifications done.

In BMX, the node where a segment is first mapped (i.e., the one that initiated the current set of modifications) behaves as a coordinator for other nodes where the segment is also cached. For example, suppose that segment S1 is first mapped on node N1 (a log is automatically created). In order to map S1, node N1 asked the segment to the OBR responsible for managing the secondary storage where S1 is stored. This server ensures that, later when another node (say, N2) tries to map S1, it will receive a reply from OBR with the identification of N1. From this point on, node N2 becomes a subordinate of N1, i.e., S1 modifications done on node N2 are stored in a log kept on N2, and when the truncation is made, the log that has to be considered is the union of each local log on every node where the segment has been cached (N1 and N2).

8 Related Work

To our knowledge little work has been done on garbage collecting objects in a large DSM. On the contrary, a large amount of work has been done in the domain of GC of objects either in multiprocessors [1, 4], or in RPC-based distributed systems (see Plainfossé[17] for a survey).

For the purpose of GC, the fundamental difference between our system and a multiprocessor, is that of scale and synchronization overhead. This difference implies that, if we apply a GC algorithm designed for multiprocessors to our case (for instance, Appel[1]), the overhead will be unacceptable due to communication and synchronization costs. These costs are due to the fact that current multiprocessor GC algorithms implicitly assume the existence of strongly consistent objects. In fact, communication and synchronization overhead arises because of the necessity of providing strongly consistent objects and the interference with applications' consistency needs.

Furthermore, our GC problem is more difficult than in distributed RPC-based systems (e.g., [9]); in such systems there is only one copy of each object, which is remotely invoked by those nodes that are sharing it. Thus, objects are modified by explicit messages that can be easily intercepted for the purpose of reference control by the GC algorithm. Additionally, since there is no memory sharing, there is no such problem as interference with the consistency protocol.

A GC system for DSM that we are aware of is due to Le Sergent[14]. His garbage collector was first developed for a multiprocessor machine, then extended to a loosely coupled network with DSM. The algorithm is of the copying type, is incremental, and uses virtual memory protection traps to synchronize the mutator and the garbage collector, as suggested by Appel[1]. The heap is seen as a contiguous set of pages, and the shared memory is strongly consistent. With respect to our design, the main differences are the following: (i) we divide the virtual heap into bunches, in order to deal with the huge amount of objects, and allow parallel collection of bunches (we flip each bunch separately, not the whole memory as in Le Sergent's design), (ii) our GC subsystem is composed of three sub-algorithms with complementary functionality, (iii) we use a write-barrier rather than virtual memory protection for synchronization purposes, and (iv) our shared memory is weakly consistent. All these differences contribute to make our design much more scalable and efficient.

Another collector for DSM was developed by Kordale[11]. His design is very complex and relies on a large amount of auxiliary information in the form of tables. These tables are used basically to control inter-node references and the algorithm is a variation of mark-and-sweep.

Casper [10] is a system that supports a single persistent address space shared by several clients in a network. Objects are cached by clients that are served by a central server where persistent objects are stored. Each client creates its objects within a separate area of the persistent address space, called local heap. A local heap can be garbage collected independently from the rest of the heap by maintaining the information of which objects inside a local heap (not yet persistent) are referenced from the persistent store. This pointer tracking is done just like in generational based garbage collectors [20], i.e., with a write barrier. With respect to our GC design, we may see the local heap as a bunch. Both systems use the same kind of reference tracking; however, in BMX every inter-bunch reference is tracked, i.e., not only the ones that point from the persistent store to objects inside a mapped bunch, but also the references between mapped bunches not yet stored on disk.

Our GC design borrows some ideas from current distributed GC techniques: (i) stubs and scions describing inter-bunch references are based on the SSP Chain mechanism developed by Shapiro[19]; however, our stubs and scions neither introduce any indirection, nor perform marshaling/un-marshaling, (ii) we collect inter-bunch cycles of garbage similarly to Lang[13] but his groups are distributed, which is much more complex and less scalable.

Our original contributions are: (i) independent GC (i.e. asynchronously, with no synchronization) of different groups of objects (done by the BGC), (ii) the set of local group collections done by the GGC approximates a global collection without the synchronization costs of the latter, (iii) use of locality-based heuristics for group collection by the GGC, and (iv) taking advantage of consistency protocol messages to reduce the number and ensure the causality of messages used for the purpose of distributed GC (done by the scion cleaner).

9 Conclusion

We have presented a GC design for persistent objects accessed via DSM, in a loosely coupled network. Objects are allocated in bunches supported by recoverable non-overlapping segments in a single 64-bit address space spanning the whole network, including secondary storage. Objects are kept weakly consistent by the entry consistency protocol.

The GC subsystem combines three sub-algorithms with complementary functionality that run without synchronization constraints: GC of a bunch (BGC), accessibility propagation (scion cleaner), and reclamation of inter-bunch cycles of garbage (GGC). This solution is scalable, allows parallel collection of different bunches, collects cyclic garbage, and does not need special communication support such as atomicity or causality. Furthermore, messages for the purpose of distributed GC are reduced to a minimum, and are exchanged in the background. Thus, applications are never disrupted.

Acknowledgments: We thank the anonymous referees for their comments on an initial version of this paper.

References

[1] Andrew W. Appel, John R. Ellis, and Kai Li. Real-time concurrent collection on stock multiprocessors. In *SIGPLAN'88 - Conference on Programming Language Design and Implementation*, pages 11–20, Atlanta (USA), June 1988.

[2] Brian N. Bershad and Matthew J. Zekauskas. The Midway distributed shared memory system. In *Proceedings of the COMPCON'93 Conference*, pages 528–537, February 1993.

[3] D. I. Bevan. Distributed garbage collection using reference counting. In *PARLE'87—Parallel Architectures and Languages Europe*, number 259 in Lecture Notes in Computer Science, pages 117–187, Eindhoven (the Netherlands), June 1987. Springer-Verlag.

[4] Hans-J. Boehm, Alan J. Demers, and Scott Shenker. Mostly parallel garbage collection. In *Proc. of the SIGPLAN'91 Conf. on Programming Language Design and Implementation*, pages 157–164, Toronto (Canada), June 1991. ACM.

[5] E. Dijkstra, L. Lamport, A. J. Martin, C. S. Scholten, and E. F. M. Steffens. On-the-fly garbage collection: an exercise in cooperation. *Comm. of the ACM*, 21(11):966–975, November 1978.

[6] Paulo Ferreira and Marc Shapiro. Distribution and persistence in multiple and heterogeneous address spaces. In *Proc. of the International Workshop on Object Orientation in Operating Systems*, Ashville, North Carolina, (USA), December 1993. IEEE Comp. Society Press.

[7] Paulo Ferreira and Marc Shapiro. Garbage collection and DSM consistency. In *Proc. of the First Symposium on Operating Systems Design and Implementation (OSDI)*, Monterey, California (USA), November 1994. ACM.

[8] Antony L. Hosking, J. Eliot B. Moss, and Darko Stefanovič. A comparative performance evaluation of write barrier implementations. In *Conf. on Object-Oriented Programming Systems, Languages, and Applications*, volume 27 of *SIGPLAN Notices*, pages 92–109, Vancouver (Canada), October 1992. ACM Press.

[9] Niels C. Juul. *Comprehensive, Concurrent, and Robust Garbage Collection in the Distributed, Object-Based System Emerald.* PhD thesis, Dept. of Computer Science, Univ. of Copenhagen, Denmark, February 1993.

[10] Bett Koch, Tracy Schunke, Alan Dearle, Francis Vaughan, Chris Marlin, Ruth Fazakerley, and Chris Barter. Cache coherency and storage management in a persistent object system. In *Proceedings of the Fourth International Workshop on Persistent Object Systems*, pages 99–109, Martha's Vineyard, MA (USA), September 1990.

[11] R. Kordale, M. Ahamad, and J. Shilling. Distributed/concurrent garbage collection in distributed shared memory systems. In *Proc. of the International Workshop on Object Orientation and Operating Systems*, Ashville, North Carolina (USA), December 1993. IEEE Comp. Society Press.

[12] David Kotz and Preston Crow. The expected lifetime of single-address-space operating systems. In *Proceedings of SIGMETRICS'94*, Nashville, Tennessee, (USA), May 1994. ACM Press.

[13] Bernard Lang, Christian Queinnec, and José Piquer. Garbage collecting the world. In *Proc. of the 19th Annual ACM SIGPLAN-SIGACT Symp. on Principles of Programming Lang.*, Albuquerque, New Mexico (USA), January 1992.

[14] T. Le Sergent and B. Berthomieu. Incremental multi-threaded garbage collection on virtually shared memory architectures. In *Proc. Int. Workshop on Memory Management*, number 637 in Lecture Notes in Computer Science, pages 179–199, Saint-Malo (France), September 1992. Springer-Verlag.

[15] Kai Li and Paul Hudak. Memory coherence in shared virtual memory systems. *ACM Transactions on Computer Systems*, 7(4):321–359, November 1989.

[16] Scott Nettles and James O'Toole. Real-time replication garbage collection. In *Proceedings of the Conference on Programming Language Design and Implementation*, pages 217–226, Albuquerque, N. Mexico, June 1993. ACM-SIGPLAN.

[17] David Plainfossé. *Distributed Garbage Collection and Reference Management in the Soul Object Support System.* PhD thesis, Université Paris-6, Pierre-et-Marie-Curie, Paris (France), June 1994. Available from INRIA as TU-281, ISBN-2-7261-0849-0.

[18] M. Satyanarayanan, Henry H. Mashburn, Puneet Kumar, David C. Steere, and James J. Kistler. Lightweight recoverable virtual memory. In *Proceedings of the 14th ACM Symposium on Operating Systems Principles*, pages 146–160, Asheville, NC (USA), December 1993.

[19] Marc Shapiro, Peter Dickman, and David Plainfossé. SSP chains: Robust, distributed references supporting acyclic garbage collection. Rapport de Recherche 1799, Institut National de la Recherche en Informatique et Automatique, Rocquencourt (France), nov 1992. Also available as Broadcast Technical Report #1.

[20] David Ungar. Generation scavenging: A non-disruptive high performance storage reclamation algorithm. *Proceedings of the ACM SIGSOFT/SIGPLAN Software Engineering Symposium on Practical Software Development Environments, SIGPLAN Notices*, 19(5):157–167, 1984.

[21] B. Zorn. Comparing mark-and-sweep and stop-and-copy garbage collection. In *Proc. 1990 ACM Conf. on Lisp and Functional Programming*, pages 87–98, Nice, France, June 1990.

Applications of Persistent Object Systems I

David Maier

Oregon Graduate Institute, Portland, USA

In the past few years, persistent object systems have reached a level of maturity where significant applications can be built and studied. The first two presentations in this session each concentrated on a single application of a persistent system; the third dealt with an analysis of multiple applications implemented in the same persistent language.

In "Making Real Data Persistent: Initial Experiences with SMRC," Berthold Reinwald described the SMRC system for providing persistence for C++ objects on top of a relational store. He presented his group's experience with moving an existing C++ application for viewing relational query plans onto SMRC to give it persistence. (Thus, they have part of a relational database system implemented in C++ supported on top of a relational database!)

Robert Grossman discussed the distribution of the ptool persistent object system across multiple processing nodes and across a storage hierarchy in "Managing Physical Folios of Objects Between Nodes." Ptool is being used to support experiment data from a particle accelerator, where parts of that data, by it size, must currently reside in tertiary storage.

The final presentation, "Analysing Persistent Language Applications," reported on a static analysis of applications written in the Napier-88 persistent programming language. Dag Sjøberg showed how certain program characteristics correlated with experience of the application author and familiarity with a particular programming methodology. The plan is to embody certain of these characteristics in automatic tools to help support the methodology.

DISCUSSION

Most of the discussion of the first presentation dealt with the features and implementation of the SMRC system, rather than the query-viewer application per se. SMRC stores C++ objects in long fields of relational tuples, and several questions dealt with the interaction between SQL queries and functions on the C++ object. While the connection is somewhat loose at the typing level, C++ methods can execute as part of SQL query processing. In one mode, SMRC stores "heaps" of C++ objects in a single field of a tuple, and there was a question about what happens if one tries to store a heap into a field of insufficient size. While such a field cannot have its size changed dynamically, it can be declared of a very large size (2GB), where physical storage is only allocated to it as needed. Another group of questions concerned the handling of method (member function) code. Executable C++ code does not get stored persistently with the object state, but rather is held in the application that manipulates the object. If a heap is to be moved to another machine, the code must be available on that machine. As for how binding of code to object state works, the answer is that the SMRC runtime makes use of default objects. Default objects are created in the current invocation of an application, and SMRC routines copy function pointers from them into persistent objects that are being moved back into memory.

Many issues raised on the ptool talk dealt with the data sizes involved and the need for a storage hierarchy and data movement within it. While it was desirable to present the data logically as residing in a single-level store, there is simply too much data to manage in that manner. The data in question comes in terabytes, while rotating storage is denominated in hundreds of gigabytes. In the current system, when data is moved between tape and disk storage, it is also converted from a data interchange format to objects. Also, derived objects can be computed and stored at that point. Another topic for discussion was the OQL-like query interface to objects that ptool currently provides. Existing programs have to be modified to take advantage of this interface---there is no attempt to automatically translate existing FORTRAN or C++ code into OQL queries. Also, there is no sophisticated optimization of OQL queries currently taking place. As to whether different management policies can exist for different segments, the answer is that there can be a different policy per store, but there is not currently a systematic approach for defining those policies. Asked if there was a message from the research for OODB vendors, Grossman replied that it is that there is a role for lightweight object managers.

The discussion after Sjøberg's presentation focused on the constraints that the SPASM methodology embodies. Many of the measurements of this study were of the degree to which programs satisfy those constraints. Some of the research questions are whether programs from different classes of programmers show any variation in how well constraints are observed and if there are other constraints that should be considered to add to the methodology. Reasons to enlarge the set of constraints include better supporting software evolution and get better automation of the methodology with tools. It was suggested that a good follow-up study would be to try to correlate different constraints with ability to evolve software. When asked if programmers find the constraints irksome, Sjoberg reported that in general all four classes of programmers in the study found them acceptable. It was pointed out that there are sometimes good reasons to violate constraints or other kinds of design rules, and there should be some way to document or control enforcement on such exceptions. Other suggested follow-up work included examining dynamic aspects of programs and seeking explanation of why programmers violated particular constraints in given situations.

In the open discussion at the end of the session, the only question addressed to multiple presenters was how schema evolution is handled. SMRC does not handle evolution automatically. Schema evolution with ptool is a problem, because it requires repopulation of the database, which could take days. However, for the physics application presented, the schema has been voted on by the physicists involved, and should be stable for many years.

Making Real Data Persistent: Initial Experiences with SMRC

B. Reinwald,* S. Dessloch, M. Carey,
T. Lehman, H. Pirahesh
IBM Almaden Research Center
San Jose, CA, USA

V. Srinivasan
IBM Santa Teresa Laboratory
San Teresa, CA, USA

Abstract

The Shared Memory-Resident Cache (SMRC) facility under development at IBM Almaden enables persistent C++ data structures to reside in a relational database by utilizing its binary large object (BLOB) facilities. Through SMRC, persistent C++ data then can be accessed both programmatically and through relational queries. Testing and refinement of the SMRC persistence facility has been driven by the early adoption of a challenging application, "graphical explain," which provides support for the storage and visualization of optimized relational query plans. The purpose of this paper is to report on our early experiences with this application, as it has been enlightening with respect to the sorts of C++ data structures and programming practices that must be dealt with in order to make "real" C++ data persistent.

1 Introduction

For the past 5-10 years, a number of researchers and developers have been working towards the goal of providing support for programmers who need to store and manipulate pointer-based persistent data structures. In addition to various research prototypes, this work has led to the appearance of a number of commercial object-oriented database system (OODBMS) products. Most of these products, including ObjectStore, Objectivity, Versant, and Ontos, have focused on providing support for persistent C++ data [2]. Moreover, a significant C++ oriented standards effort is currently underway in the OODBMS vendor community [3]. Based on these activities, one can conclude that a significant demand exists for C++ persistence.

Like the C++ OODBMSs mentioned above, the goal of the SMRC project at IBM Almaden Research Center is to support persistence for C++ applications. Unlike those systems, however, SMRC application data resides in a relational DBMS. Specifically, in SMRC, persistent C++ data is stored in binary large object (BLOB) fields of relational tables [1]. To support application programming requirements, high-performance navigational access is provided

---

*On assignment from the University of Erlangen-Nuernberg, Germany.

via the transparent swizzling of C++ pointers. To support declarative and/or exploratory access to the same C++ data, it can also be viewed through relational queries that invoke table functions [6] that have been written in C++ to provide access to the contents of these BLOB fields. It is our belief that SMRC will enable a new class of applications, those which need to mix relational data with moderately-sized persistent C++ data structures, which are not well-supported by existing OODBMS products and prototypes.

To stress-test the SMRC C++ persistence facilities, the development of the first actual SMRC application has been taking place in parallel with the implementation of SMRC itself. This application, referred to informally as "graphical explain," supports the storage, retrieval, and visualization of SQL query plans for queries that have been optimized and compiled in IBM's Starburst extended relational DBMS prototype [6]. Most relational DBMSs have a simple "explain" facility that enables users to see (usually in an ASCII form) what sort of query plan the optimizer has selected for executing a given query. In Starburst, these query plans can be displayed and explored graphically, and they can also be saved and retrieved for later use. Developing graphical explain as a SMRC application involved taking a number of existing C++ classes, defined in the Starburst query optimizer, and making their data persistent. Doing so raised several interesting challenges and issues that are likely to arise in other settings where such C++ "legacy" data structures need to be made persistent.

The remainder of this paper reports on our graphical explain experience and its impact on the current design of SMRC. In Section 2, we provide a brief overview of the SMRC facility and illustrate its use by showing pieces of a very simple binary tree application. Section 3 describes the graphical explain application in enough detail to convey an appreciation of its data structure challenges. Following this description, Section 4 explains the SMRC facilities that now exist to meet such challenges. Finally, the status of SMRC and our plans for future work are discussed in Section 5.

2 SMRC

2.1 Overview

As described in the Introduction, SMRC supports the storage of persistent C++ data structures in BLOB fields of a relational database, thus enabling C++ data to coexist with relational data in the same database.[1] Figure 1 depicts such a database, showing a relation (*Projects*) that has several regular attributes (*name* and *budget*, with the obvious semantics) as well as a BLOB attribute containing persistent C++ data (*schedule*, which holds a PERT chart of the steps and deadlines involved in completing the project). Application programs are provided with two distinct interfaces to the same C++ data — a high-performance C++ interface and a relational query interface — and can choose between these interfaces as appropriate. When using the C++ interface, application programmers see instances of BLOB fields as individual C++ heaps,

---

[1] The original SMRC design supports several other mappings of C++ data into relational tables as well, but the current SMRC implementation supports only the BLOB mapping. The BLOB mapping will thus be our sole focus here.

and C++ pointers are swizzled between their on-disk representation and their in-memory representation upon retrieval by SMRC.

To create and populate a relation like the *Project* relation of Figure 1, the application programmer first creates the relation; "BLOB" is given as the field type for all fields that will contain persistent C++ data structures. To make SMRC aware of the C++ classes whose instances are required to persist, the SMRC schema compiler is invoked on the files containing the relevant C++ class definitions together with a (separate) schema source description that flags the persistent classes and provides certain other auxiliary information (which Section 4 will discuss). To store C++ data in the database, the application programmer then creates an instance of a SMRC heap; in doing so, the name of the application schema created by the schema compiler is passed to the SMRC heap constructor and the schema becomes associated with the heap. This schema enables SMRC to discover the layout (size, pointer offsets, and so on) of instances of the potentially persistent classes for use in saving them and swizzling their pointers at runtime. Once the programmer has created a SMRC heap, C++ objects of classes that were flagged as persistent can be allocated in the heap using an overloading of the C++ *new* operator (or by asking SMRC to copy objects from an existing in-memory C++ data structure). Each SMRC heap has a "root object" that provides access to its contents, which in turn must be reachable from this root object.

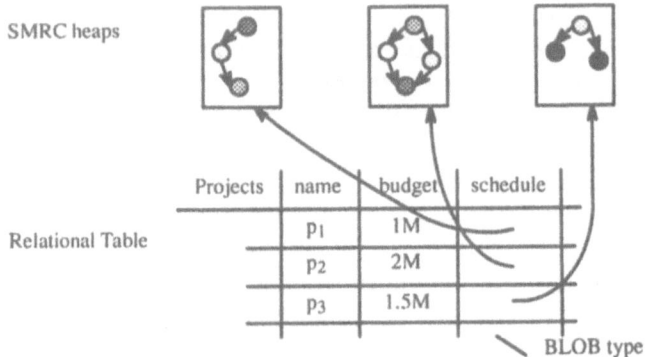

Figure 1: Coexistence of C++ and Relational Data

The SMRC runtime system provides support for allocating and deleting objects in heaps. In addition, SMRC provides methods that store a SMRC heap in a specified BLOB field in the database and that activate the objects in a heap after it has been retrieved from the database. As in ObjectStore [5], the C++ pointers in a heap are actually written to disk in swizzled (i.e., virtual memory address) form and are relocated by SMRC when the heap is reactivated in a new memory location following its retrieval. Currently, SMRC stores, retrieves, and reactivates heaps with regular (intra-heap) C++ pointers in their entirety. Only inter-heap pointers, which are typed differently, are swizzled in a more incremental fashion via an overloaded dereference operator. We believe that this "heap-at-a-time" approach will prove to be a reasonable fit for the kinds of applications being targeted by SMRC.

2.2 Writing A Simple SMRC Application

To illustrate the use of SMRC, we will now describe the steps involved in storing and retrieving persistent instances of a simple binary tree class. For concreteness, we will assume that we wish to maintain an *Employee* relation that has attributes *name, salary*, and *family_tree* (with the last attribute being a C++ data structure). For simplicity (and a touch of silliness), we will assume that family trees are always binary.

2.2.1 The Binary Tree Application

Figure 2 shows relevant portions of the C++ code that would reside in the files *tree.h* and *tree.C*. Basically, this class definition looks just as it would without the involvement of SMRC.

```
class node {                           #include <stdio.h>
    public:                            #include "tree.h"
        char   name[50];
        node *left, *right;            void node::print_node ( ) {
    node (char *n) {                       printf ("%s;", name);
        strcpy (name[0], n, strlen(n));    if (left)   left->print_node;
        left   =   NULL;                   if (right) right->print_node;
        right  =   NULL;               };
    };
    ~node ( ) { };
    void print_node ( );
};
```

Figure 2: Binary Tree Example (files tree.h and tree.C)

```
#include <smrc/smrc.h>                 #include <smrc/smrc.h>
#include "tree.h"                      #include "tree.h"
...                                    ...
main ( ) {                             main ( ) {
    exec sql begin declare section;        exec sql begin declare section;
        sql type is BLOB (1M) family;          char name[50];
    exec sql end declare section;              sql type is BLOB (1M) family;
                                           exec sql end declare section;
    smrc_heap *hp;
    node      *fam_root;               smrc_heap *hp;
    char      name1[50], name2[50];    node      *fam_root;

    hp = new smrc_heap ("tree");
    fam_root  = new(hp, "node") node ("Public");   exec sql  select name, family_tree
    fam_root->left  = new(hp, "node") node (name1);          into :name, :family
    fam_root->right = new(hp, "node") node (name2);          from employee
    hp->set_root(fam_root);                                  where name = "Public";
    hp->pack(&family);
                                       hp = swizzle (&family);
    exec sql insert into employee      fam_root = (node *) hp->get_root();
      (name, salary, family_tree)
      values ("Public", "100K", :family);   fam_root->print_node;
};                                     };

(a) appl1.sqc: Creating and Storing a Tree    (b) appl2.sqc: Retrieving a Tree
```

Figure 3: Application Code using SMRC (file appl*.sqc)

206

Figure 3a shows application code fragments from a program that creates a heap containing a binary tree, storing it in the *family_tree* field of the employee "Public," and Figure 3b shows code from a program that retrieves this heap and reactivates it for further use. The *pack()* function in the store program moves the allocated objects in the heap into the BLOB host variable. Reactivation of a heap in the retrieve program is accomplished via the *swizzle()* function that is applied to the heap in Figure 3b, and the data objects themselves are then accessed by traversing from the root object of the restored heap.

2.2.2 The SMRC Compilation Process

Figure 4 shows the steps involved in compiling the schema and programs for the family tree example. The file *tree.h* is included in a file called *tree_ss.C* (application schema source file) that flags the persistent classes (all of them, in this case) for processing by the SMRC schema compiler. Persistent classes are flagged inside a function body with calls to SMRC macros, which work quite similar to Objectstore's schema source macros [8]. The output of the schema compiler is a file *tree_cnt.C* which contains SMRC type information (e.g., pointer offsets) that is compiled together with the SQL precompiled *tree.sqc* file to produce object files that can be linked with the SMRC runtime library to yield executable persistent programs.

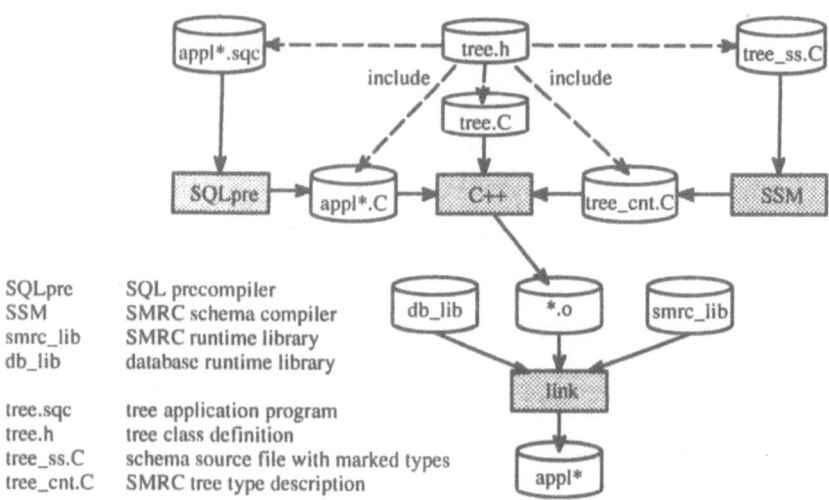

SQLpre	SQL precompiler
SSM	SMRC schema compiler
smrc_lib	SMRC runtime library
db_lib	database runtime library
tree.sqc	tree application program
tree.h	tree class definition
tree_ss.C	schema source file with marked types
tree_cnt.C	SMRC tree type description

Figure 4: Compilation Steps for Binary Tree Example

2.3 Heap Implementation

C++ objects that are allocated in a SMRC heap are stored in their native main memory representation. Thus, when a SMRC heap is reloaded into memory, pointer swizzling must be performed in order to make the pointers useable once again by the application program. For pointer swizzling to be possible, of course, it is necessary for SMRC to be able to find and modify all of the pointers in the objects in the heap. To facilitate this, SMRC associates two data structures with each heap – a *type table* and an *object table* – as shown in Figure 5. The type table contains enough information to enable SMRC to find all of the pointers in an instance of a given type. The object tables, which can be addressed via the type entries, record the locations of all allocated objects of each type in the heap, thereby providing addressability of the objects by type. Given the pointer information in the type table and the address information in the object table, the SMRC *swizzle* operator is thus able to find each object in the heap and each pointer in the objects. Since SMRC heaps are relocated in memory as a whole, the swizzle operator simply adds the *load difference* of the heap to each pointer, i.e., it adds to each pointer the difference between the heap's current memory address and its address from the last time it was loaded.

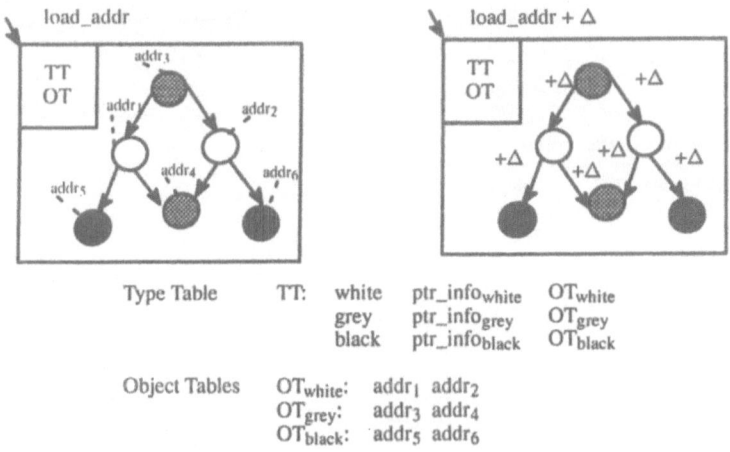

		white	ptr_info$_{white}$	OT$_{white}$
Type Table	TT:	grey	ptr_info$_{grey}$	OT$_{grey}$
		black	ptr_info$_{black}$	OT$_{black}$

Object Tables	OT$_{white}$:	addr$_1$ addr$_2$
	OT$_{grey}$:	addr$_3$ addr$_4$
	OT$_{black}$:	addr$_5$ addr$_6$

Figure 5: Relocating and swizzling heaps of objects

3 The "Graphical Explain" Application

To help drive the SMRC development and testing effort forward, we decided to develop the first application in parallel with SMRC itself. As discussed earlier, the application that we decided to use is "graphical explain," which allows users of a relational DBMS to save, retrieve, and visualize query plans[2] for their application's SQL queries. For our purposes here, it suffices to say that query plans are built up from plan operators and that the plans are represented as (very) complex C++ data structures that describe the sequence of relational operations (e.g., scan, sort, union, join) that should be executed to compute

---

[2]The query plans manipulated by the graphical explain facility might better be referred to as query *optimizer* plans; they are the direct output of the optimizer, and include information about cost estimates and so on. A subsequent query processing step translates query optimizer plans into actual query *execution* plan structures for execution by the Starburst runtime system.

the answer to a given SQL query. These data structures pose a number of interesting challenges from the standpoint of successfully making them persistent. We will point out the challenges here, drawing on some fragments of actual optimizer data structure definitions [7], while deferring the issue of how SMRC addresses the challenges to Section 4.

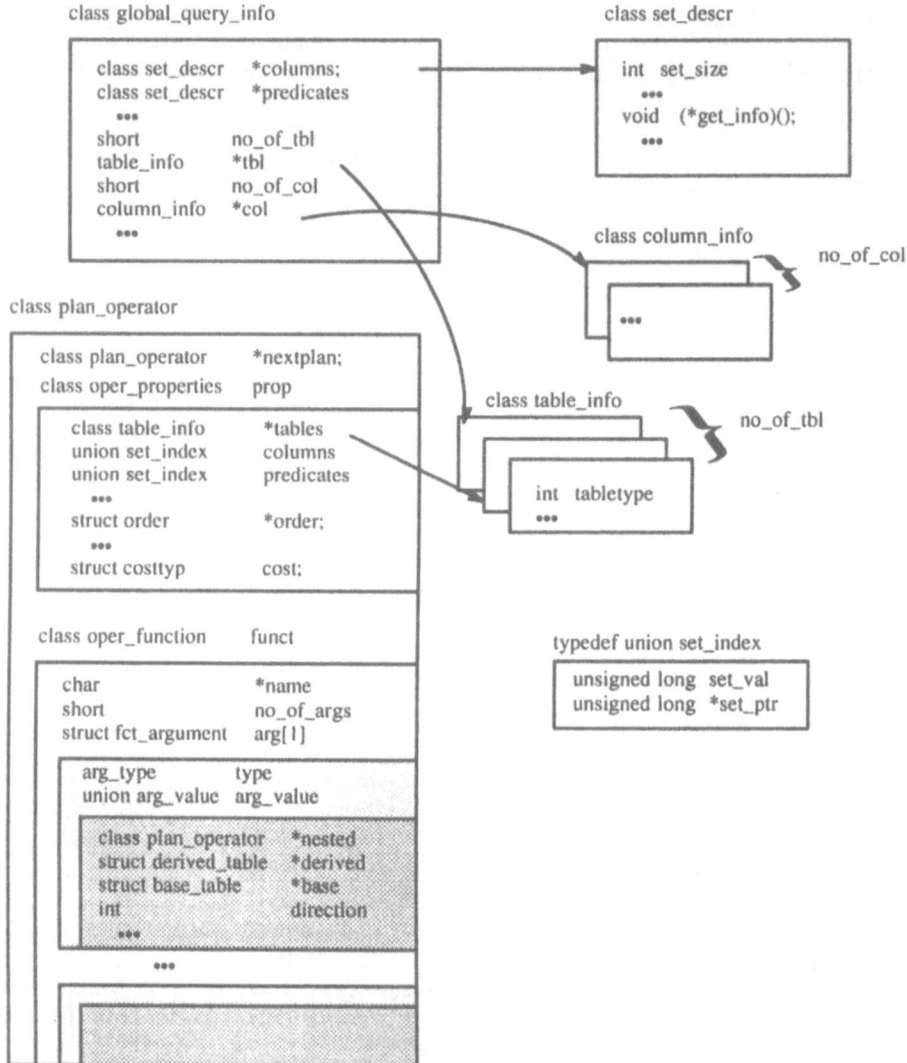

Figure 6: Some "Graphical Explain" Data Structures

In order to illustrate many of the problems encountered in making the graphical explain application persistent, Figure 6 shows several of its data structure declarations. Among the challenges present in these declarations are: untagged unions (unions with no discriminators), repeating groups (i.e., variable-length arrays) of two different flavors, pointers to functions, and pointers to transient data. In what follows, we briefly elaborate on each of these challenges. Before we do so, however, we need to answer the obvious questions: No, the people who wrote this code aren't crazy, and yes, they're still working for IBM. These structures were designed with one objective in mind – to save space in memory. Despite the fact that today's workstations and larger machines have ample main memories, good query optimization algorithms are inherently exponential in their space (and time) requirements. Every byte counts when implementing a query optimizer: The less space a query plan requires, the more plans the optimizer can explore, and the more complex the queries are that the optimizer can handle without exhausting its resource limits.

Unions can be seen in a number of places in the definition of the *plan_operator* class in Figure 6. The *plan_operator* class is primarily made up of two nested class instances, one of type *oper_properties* and one of type *oper_function*. The class *oper_properties* contains several untagged union attributes, called *columns* and *predicates*, that are defined as containing either a long integer or a pointer to a long integer (actually several long integers). These are used to represent bit sets; if there are 32 or fewer bits, then the bit set is stored inline, and otherwise it is stored elsewhere with a pointer inline. Unfortunately for SMRC, the number of bits is not obtainable using local information within the data structure that is being swizzled – the number of columns and predicates present in a given query is constant over the entire query, and is thus held in a separate object of type *global_query_info*. (An actual query plan is a recursive structure containing many *plan_operator* instances, so it would be wasteful to repeatedly store this information throughout the plan_operator data structure.)

Repeating groups, or variable-length arrays, can also be found in several places in Figure 6. One example is in the class *global_query_info*, which contains two repeating groups of types *table_info* and *column_info*. These are represented in the C++ data structure by a pointer to the first instance of the appropriate type and a count of the number of instances that are actually being pointed to; the instances themselves are allocated as one contiguous memory block. An example of a different representation of a repeating group can be found in the nested *oper_function* class of the *plan_operator* class. An instance of this class, which physically resides at the end of the *plan_operator* class, contains a variable number of instances of the structure type *fct_argument* (which in turn has quite a complicated internal structure, i.e., all of these difficulties can even appear in a combined manner). That is, before a *plan_operator* node is allocated, its actual number of *fct_argument* instances is decided upon, and the actual space allocation is set to accommodate the desired repeating group size *in line* in this case. Note that for both kinds of repeating groups (these are explained in 4.2), the count of the number of elements in the group may not be stored next to the group itself (though it was in the two examples discussed here).

The last two problems, function pointers and pointers to transient data, can be found in the classes *set_descr* and *plan_operator*, respectively. Pointed-to functions are used in some cases to make certain context-dependent information available about the query plan; this is the case for the *get_info* field of the *set_descr* class in Figure 6. Finally, during query optimization, potentially millions of plans are generated and linked to each other. At the end of optimization, all the plans are scanned and the most cost-effective plan will be selected. Only this plan should be made persistent; all of the other plans are irrelevant and transient. The field *nextplan* in class *plan_operator* in Figure 6 is an excellent example of a transient pointer; it is a pointer which should not be followed when making the chosen query plan instance persistent.

4 User-Provided Information for C++ Class Definitions

Currently SMRC is a relatively simple system, as its basic purpose is to provide persistence for C++ objects. Although this sounds like a relatively simple task, it underwent several modifications to its initial (naive) design in order to support graphical explain. This section describes the SMRC facilities that were added to support the challenges presented by the graphical explain application.

An application programmer using SMRC can use two different modes to make objects persistent. In the first mode, called the *new mode*, an application creates objects using the SMRC overloaded *new* operator. This option allocates and initializes a new instance of the type in a SMRC heap and updates the object table information (Figure 5). The new mode is useful for applications that are written or modified to work specifically with SMRC. However, for applications that already exist and for which such modifications are undesirable, SMRC provides an alternative called the *copy mode*. Using the copy mode, an application creates objects using standard C++ new operators. Then, when the application is ready to store a graph of objects, it calls the SMRC "store" function with a pointer to a root of the object graph. SMRC performs a "deep-copy" of the object graph into its own SMRC heap, recursively copying each object instance of the graph into the heap and registering it in the heap's object table.

The *heap* is the structure that SMRC writes to disk and later retrieves back into memory. To be able to restore (*swizzle*) all of the pointers in the heap, SMRC must have a complete blueprint of each object type and instance in the heap. In fact, it must support more than the standard language constructs (e.g. unions, virtual functions, pointers to functions, etc.). As illustrated by Figure 6 in Section 3, it must also support constructs that are "outside" the language, specifically, dynamic arrays and transient pointers. For some of these constructs, SMRC cannot determine what to do without help from the application programmer. Therefore, when dealing with these constructs, SMRC requires user input. These constructs are: unions containing pointers, dynamic arrays, function pointers, and transient pointers. The remainder of this section describes the forms that this input takes.

4.1 Union Types

If there are embedded objects or pointers in one or more members of a union type, then SMRC must be able to determine which member is "active" during object relocation. Unfortunately, there are no C++ language constructs for denoting this information at compile-time or run-time, so SMRC requires input from the application (in the form of *discriminant functions*) to specify which member of a union is active.

Discriminant functions are called, as part of the pointer swizzling process, when an object containing a union-typed member is brought from persistent storage into virtual memory. The value returned by a discriminant function indicates the active union member. In general, the active member could be specified by member *number*, as in ObjectStore [8], or by member *name*, as in SMRC. We chose to use the member name because it is symbolic and less error-prone for the discriminant functions in the event of adding new members.

Typically, user-provided functions are treated as un-trustworthy by database engines, as these functions could, through intentional or unintentional maliciousness, damage data or structures in the engine. In addition, other problems could plague the swizzling mechanism if the discriminant function gets into trouble. For example, when a union-type object is faulted in and, as part of swizzling, the union discriminant function is called, the system cannot guarantee that other member pointers or global data have already been swizzled. Consequently, any references to this data could either fail or trigger other object faults, which could in turn result in "swizzle deadlock."

ObjectStore avoided the "swizzle deadlock" problem by imposing restrictions on the use of discriminant functions: computations are restricted to the data members of a particular class (i.e., they must not rely on any global program state); operations on pointers are restricted to comparisons with NULL; and, function calls are restricted to regular (and not virtual) functions. It is no surprise then, that ObjectStore requires discriminant functions to be member functions of the class.

```
char *fct_argument_discriminant (void *object, char *mem,
                                 void *env_object) {

  struct fct_argument  *obj     = (struct function_arg *) object;
  plan_operator        *env_obj = (plan_operator *) env_object;

  switch (obj->Type) {
  case SUBPLAN :
    return ("nested");       /* fct. argument is a nested plan */
    break;
  case TABLE    :
    if (env_obj->oper_properties.tables->tabletype == 0)
      return ("derived"); /* fct. argument is a derived table */
    else
      return ("base");       /* fct. argument is a base table */
    break;
  case GLOBAL_PREDICATE :  /* use of global var. global_query_info_var */
    if (global_query_info_var->predicates->set_size == 0)
      return ("direction");
    else
      ...
    break;
  };
  return 0;
};
```

Figure 7: Discriminant function for object *"fct_argument"*

Despite the excellent reasons for restricting the scope of union discriminant functions, SMRC did not have the luxury of placing such restrictions since it

212

is SMRC's motto to make *any* old "legacy" C++ data persistent without requiring major changes to the code. Placing such severe restrictions would have essentially made SMRC unable to make the graphical explain data persistent since the designers of graphical explain used these sophisticated data structures in order to achieve major performance gains.

In SMRC, discriminant functions need to be provided for types which contain union-typed members which are pointers themselves or contain pointers in their structure. Discriminant functions return the name of the currently active member. Figure 7 shows the discriminant function for the shaded *fct_argument* structure defined in Figure 6. The sample discriminant function returns the active member of the *arg_value* union. Depending on *arg_type*, *fct_argument*'s union value may need to be decided using local object information alone, table-specific information (via pointer *tables* in class *oper_properties*), or global information (via pointer *tbl* in class *global_query_info*). To provide addressability to the table-specific information in the discriminant function, SMRC supports passing the "environment object" of the current object[3] as an input to the discriminant function. Although it might appear risky to base decisions on global information, in this case the global information is attached to the entry point of the SMRC heap, so it is guaranteed to be swizzled first and will thus be present for all subsequent object swizzling operations.

4.2 Dynamic Arrays

In C++, an array is a sequence of contiguously allocated elements of the same type and is declared by giving the type of the array elements and the type modifier "[ ]" specifying the number of elements in the array. For statically allocated arrays, compilers allocate enough memory to hold all of the elements in the array, which are then addressed using the "[ ]" notation.

Unfortunately, it is not always this easy. In reality, many (if not most) arrays in complex programs are allocated dynamically, not statically. C++ programmers commonly exploit the fact that most C++ compilers do not perform runtime bounds checking on array accesses by dynamically allocating and using storage that is much larger than the language definition of the array. In this way, a dynamic array can be modeled using one of two programming techniques:

Array pointer: Using this approach, the programmer declares a pointer to a given type. For example, in Figure 6 we see:

```
table_info *tbl;
```

The programmer attaches a dynamically allocated section of memory to this pointer at runtime, and can then reference it using the same syntax that might be used for a statically allocated array, such as:
```
tbl[no_of_tbl - 1].
```

Minimal array: Using this alternative approach, the programmer declares an array of size 1, either by itself or embedded in a structure (as the last

---

[3]The "environment object" is the object through which an object gets its context. Thus, in Figure 6, for an object of type fct_argument, the context is provided by an environment object of type plan_operator.

structure member), but then allocates an amount of memory that is much greater than "sizeof" the object. For example, in Figure 6 we see:

```
struct fct_argument arg[1];
```

In either case, it is not possible for SMRC to recognize the size of the array, and in the case of an *array pointer* it is not possible for SMRC to know that an array is even present. Thus, in the application schema source file that is fed into the schema compiler, SMRC requires the application programmer to use a SMRC macro to mark specific class members as being dynamic arrays. Furthermore, the programmer also needs to supply a function (similar to a union discriminant function) known as a *repeating function*—so named because it returns the length of a repeating group or dynamic array.

The following code fragment shows a repeating function for the embedded minimal array *fct_argument* of class *oper_function* in Figure 6.

```
int oper_function_repeat (void *object, char *member) { struct
  oper_function *obj = (struct oper_function *) object;
  return obj->no_of_args; /* number of arguments of the operator fct. */
};
```

Figure 8: Repeating function for object *"oper_function"*

Repeating functions are always supplied, via the object parameter, with a pointer to the object containing the declaration of the dynamic array. In the case of the *minimal array* this is the object containing the array itself, whereas in the case of the *array pointer* this is the object containing the pointer to the array. In our example, the object parameter contains an object of class *oper_function*. The size of the embedded array is readily accessible from another member of this class. For purposes of generality, the second parameter of the repeating function identifies the current member in cases where more than one dynamic array is used (e.g., see class *global_query_info* in Figure 6).

4.3 Object Initialization and Function Pointers

When loading an object into memory from disk, SMRC must correctly restore not only the object's *data* pointers, but it must also restore the object's *function* pointers (for both regular and virtual functions). The interesting twist in swizzling function pointers is that the information for function pointers lies not with the data but with the current instantiation of the code. SMRC gets the valid function pointer values from default objects created in the current instance of the code, storing them in the class members that were marked by the user. The user marks such class members with a SMRC macro call in the schema source file.

To accomplish function pointer restoration, an application communicates with SMRC via an *initialization function* which is called by SMRC during pointer swizzling. The initialization function takes as input a pointer to the object to be initialized, and it returns a pointer to an appropriate default object. The initialization function can be either user-supplied (to improve flexibility) or SMRC-supplied (to lessen programmer burden). The more general method is *user-supplied*, since this provides a mechanism where object initialization can be arbitrarily complex or context-sensitive.

As an example, the initialization function for the class *set_descr* in Figure 6 might look as follows. The default objects in this case exist in the application environment as global variables.

```
void* set_descr_init (void* obj) {
  struct set_descr *object = (struct set_descr *)obj;

  /* Depending on the set size value */
  if ( ((struct set_descr *)object)->set_size == 1 )
    return (&default_set_descr_1);  /* use default obj. of "short" set */
  else                              /* or of "long" set.               */
    return (&default_set_descr_N);  /* Both have the same structure,   */
};                                  /* but have different values in it.*/
```

Figure 9: Initialization function for object "*set_descr*"

In the event that an appropriate default object does not already exist in the application, the initialization function could simply create (and delete) a default object "on the fly." This approach is also employed in the case where the user marks class members to be initialized but does not provide an initialization function. Such a function, which uses the default constructor of the class, will then be automatically created by SMRC. (Since the creation of objects "on the fly" is not wise from a performance standpoint, we plan to improve the approach by having SMRC manage an array of default objects for all of the registered types. This particular piece of work has not yet been completed however.)

4.4   Transient Pointers

Most legacy applications, and specifically graphical explain, cannot use the overloaded SMRC new operator to create objects directly in SMRC heaps. Instead, these applications first create their objects in regular memory and then later specify that the objects are to be made persistent. As mentioned earlier, SMRC provides a "deep copy" routine to move objects from regular memory into a SMRC heap. The arguments of this copy routine are a pointer to a "root" object and the type of the root object. SMRC copies the root object and then recursively follows all of the pointers in all of the objects until the entire graph of objects has been copied.

In the case of graphical explain, many objects in the graph are needed only for temporary or intermediate values, and hence do not need to be made persistent. However, it would impose undue hardship on the graphical explain application to require that it first remove all of the transient objects from the graph before making it persistent. Instead, SMRC allows application programmers to mark specific object members (pointers) in a class as being *transient*. During the copy, these pointers are set to NULL and the objects that they point to are not copied. In fact, the SMRC schema compiler provides two transient pointer marking modes. Instead of marking transient pointers, a programmer can instead elect to mark pointers as *permanent* (and SMRC will "follow" only those pointers) if this is more convenient for a given application.

Our limited experience has shown the labelling of transient pointers to be a valuable feature. In the case of graphical explain, typical SMRC heap sizes initially ranged between 300 and 400 kilobytes. By marking unneeded object pointers as transient pointers, the size of these SMRC heaps was reduced by 60 to 80 percent, down to just 50 to 80 kilobytes.

5   Lessons and On-going Work

We started the SMRC project with many goals, one of which was to build a simple persistence mechanism that would collaborate with a relational database system to store C++ objects. Our initial naive view of objects was that they were usually of a known size and shape. We also assumed that every pointer in an object should be swizzled (i.e., why was it there if it shouldn't be made persistent?). Finally, although we were aware of the C++ virtual function table swizzling problem, we had overlooked the regular function pointer problem.

Both from our experience with graphical explain, which was our first "real" application, and from looking at other persistent object systems, we've learned a few things, gained a few insights and, as a result, modified our system accordingly. We now understand that objects will rarely be regular; instead, they will be as complex and obscure as the clever programmer(s) who invented them. Furthermore, an object's user-supplied discriminant function may require information from outside the object to determine its size or shape. We also understand that objects being loaded from disk storage must be initialized with the current runtime environment so that regular and virtual function pointers are restored. Finally, we understand that not all objects in a graph must be made persistent and subsequently restored. In fact, by avoiding the storage and retrieval of "unnecessary" objects in the graphical explain application, we were able to reduce the storage overhead (and probably the performance overhead as well) by 60 to 80 percent.

As we dive into the next set of tasks we will no doubt encounter a whole new set of educational problems. For example, we have not yet put in a mechanism to ensure that the object type definitions of the data stored in the database match the type definitions used to compile the associated methods in the code. Obviously, we must be able to detect and address such code and data "version mismatches."

Secondly, SMRC currently manages one *schema* (the set of types that exist in a particular SMRC heap) per application. To be truly useful, SMRC must manage multiple schemas and multiple heaps simultaneously. The issues of type name collisions between schemas and of "external" references between objects in different heaps remain to be resolved.

Finally, one of the most important aspects of SMRC is (or will be) its ability to offer SQL processing on C++ data. When a SMRC heap is stored in the relational database engine in the form of a BLOB, the SMRC swizzling functions can be imported into the engine to load the C++ data into a heap in the database engine process itself. Then, using an SQL construct known as a *table function*, which returns a table (just as a *scalar function* returns a scalar value), an SQL query can use as input the data that was extracted from the SMRC heap. We view this as a very important feature of SMRC, as the ability to query C++ structures from SQL could very well open up a whole new set of applications.

Acknowledgment   We wish to thank Guy Lohman for explaining the challenging optimizer data structures to us.

References

[1] R. Ananthanarayanan, V. Gottemukkala, W. Kaefer, T. Lehman, H. Pirahesh, Using the Co-existence Approach to Achieve Combined Functionality of Object-Oriented and Relational Systems, **Proc. of the ACM SIGMOD Conf.** (Washington DC), pp. 109-118, ACM Press, 1993.

[2] R. Cattell, **Object Data Management: Object-oriented and Extended Relational Database Systems**, Addison-Wesley, Reading, Mass., 1991.

[3] R. Cattell, **The Object Database Standard: ODMG—93**, Morgan Kaufmann Publishers, San Mateo, 1994.

[4] O. Deux, et al., The O2 System, **CACM** 34 (1991) 10, pp. 34-48.

[5] C. Lamb, G. Landis, J. Orenstein, D. Weinreb, The ObjectStore Database System, **CACM** 34 (1991) 10, pp. 50-63.

[6] G. Lohman, B. Lindsay, H. Pirahesh, B. Schiefer, Extensions to Starburst: Objects, types, Functions, and Rules, **CACM** 34 (1991) 10, pp. 94-109.

[7] G. Lohman, Grammar-Like Functional Rules for Representing Query Optimization Alternatives, **Proc. of ACM SIGMOD Conf.** (Chicago), pp. 18-27, ACM Press, 1988.

[8] Object Design Inc.: **Objectstore Reference Manual**, Release 2.1, 1993.

Managing Physical Folios of Objects Between Nodes*

R. L. Grossman, N. Araujo X. Qin, and W. Xu
Laboratory for Advanced Computing
University of Illinois at Chicago

Abstract

With modern operating systems, it is becoming easier to implement single level stores using memory management techniques to manage memory pages or slot segments between virtual memory and local disk. In this paper, we describe the ptool management system, which, in addition, gathers physical collections of segments into UNIX files we call *folios*. Ptool can cache and migrate folios from a hierarchical storage system, between nodes in a high performance cluster, or between nodes in a wide area network. We describe our experience to date using ptool for the analysis of high energy physics data, aeronautics data, and financial data.

1   Introduction

Improvements in operating systems and file systems are making it easier to implement a simple single level object store by using memory management techniques to manage memory pages or physical segments throughout a local area network [30] and [24]. We are interested in how to modify this basic architecture when a single node is attached to a hierarchical storage device [7], when multiple nodes are used as the basis for a high performance computer [11], and when widely separated nodes are used with protocols such as WWW [31]. The goal is to keep the design and architecture of the system simple and "light weight", and yet provide the flexibility to work with hierarchical storage and local and wide area clusters.

This paper describes our experience using a system we developed called the ptool management system for scientific computing. Ptool gathers physical collections of segments into UNIX files which we call *folios*. Our basic idea is to divide the system into two parts: objects and physical segments are managed as usual by the ptool Persistent Object Manager. In addition, we have developed several Persistent Folio Managers for ptool which interfaces to ptool's Persistent Object Manager in order to provide a single level store which can

---

*This research was supported in part by NASA grant NAG2-513, DOE grant DE–FG02-92ER25133, and NSF grants IRI 9224605 and CDA-9303433. For more information, contact Robert Grossman, Laboratory for Advanced Computing, m/c 249, University of Illinois at Chicago, 851 South Morgan Street, Chicago, IL 60607, grossman@uic.edu.

transparently access hierarchical storage, pass folios between nodes in high performance computing environments, or pass folios between nodes in wide area networks. By using different Persistent Folio Managers, a given application can exploit an architecture appropriate policy for folio management.

The ptool management system consists of several software tools. Ptool itself can be thought of as a "light weight" object manager: it is a C++ library which provides persistence through an overloaded "new" operator and consists of a Persistent Object Manager and one or more Persistent Folio Managers. The different applications we describe require different policies for managing folios: these policies are provided by using the correct Persistent Folio Manager. Qtool is a companion tool which accepts Object Query Language queries and requests the appropriate objects from the ptool Persistent Object Manager.

The problems we are interested in require that we manage, analyze, and provide wide area access to large amounts of data, especially numerical, statistical or scientific data which is infrequently updated. We describe our experience to date using ptool for the analysis of high energy physics data, aeronautics data, and financial data. Part of the contribution of the work described here is to demonstrate the utility of using light weight object managers for projects requiring numerically intensive computing in these three different application domains. Each of these applications makes use of a different folio management policy which we describe.

Our work is novel, as far as we are aware, in interfacing a persistent object manager to a hierarchical storage system. In addition, by supporting different policies for folio management, the system provides the flexibility to either move the query close to the data as is standard for distributed database systems, or to move the data close to the query as is standard in distributed and hierarchical file systems.

To summarize, the ptool management system manages objects as is usual for a single level persistent object store using memory management techniques. In addition, it can respond to queries from remote nodes in one of several ways: it can locate the relevant node containing the data, execute the query, and return the corresponding objects as is usual in a distributed database management system. It can also locate the relevant data, and return the folios containing the data, so that the query can be executed locally, as is usual in a distributed file system. Also, folios on any given node can be retrieved from a hierarchical storage system so that large amounts of data can be managed by the ptool management system. We describe how our three applications exploits this functionality.

The rest of the paper is organized as follows: Section 2 covers related work; Section 3 describes the design of ptool; Section 4 describes the implementation of ptool; the following three sections describe applications of ptool; and the last two sections contain some discussion and conclusions.

2   Related Work

Ptool is a software tool which provides persistence for instances of C++ classes through an application program interface (API) and class libraries. The API is essentially that proposed by ODMG-93 [6]. Persistent objects are grouped together into persistent container classes provided by the class libraries. This is one of the standard approaches to provide persistence in C++. Other approaches include using a data manipulation language and using inheritance to provide persistence. These approaches are summarized in Atwood [2].

Our interest in this paper is adapting this approach to work with hierarchical storage systems, high performance clusters, and wide area clusters, especially for the needs of scientific computing.

The necessity of coupling hierarchical storage systems to scientific computing environments has been recognized for some time driven by applications including high energy physics, computational fluid dynamics, seismic analysis, and climate modeling. For example, the IEEE has held a series of symposiums on mass storage systems which have addressed these issues. The twelfth symposium was held in 1993.

More recently, there has been growing interest in coupling databases to hierarchical storage systems. Implementations which interface a hierarchical storage system to a relational database are described in [10] and [23], for example. A proposal for extending POSTGRES to provide support for accessing tertiary storage was made by Stonebraker [27]. A proposal for extending object stores to provide support for accessing tertiary storage for the needs of high energy physics was made by Baden and Grossman [3]. Access to data provided by NASA's proposed Earth Observing System also requires that databases be interfaced to hierarchical storage systems [8]. The challenges to the database community provided by trying to access tuples on tape was nicely summarized by Carey, Haas and Livny [5].

Our approach is analogous to caching algorithms used for distributed file systems such as Sprite [26] and Andrew [29]. There have been a variety of caching algorithms for client server database systems which utilize a page-server architecture; see [24] and [9], for example. In these systems, a number of clients make requests for pages to a server. Our caching algorithm can be viewed as a multi-level analogy to these types of systems.

3 Design of Ptool

Ptool is a scalable persistent object manager developed by the Laboratory for Advanced Computing at the University of Illinois at Chicago. It is designed to provide low overhead, high performance access to large amounts of data, to interface to hierarchical storage systems, and to operate in local and wide area clusters. The current version is 0.6.

Ptool provides persistence for instances of C++ classes through an application program interface (API) and class libraries. The API is essentially that proposed by ODMG-93 [6]. Persistent objects are grouped together into persistent container classes provided by the class libraries.

The physical design of version 0.6 of ptool is based upon three concepts: segments, folios and stores. A *segment* is a continuous range of virtual memory that is managed by ptool. A segment may contain one or more objects. A *folio* is a physical collection of segments. Both segments and folios are managed by ptool as files. A *store* is a physical collection of folios.

Version 0.4 of ptool managed folios to provide a single level caching algorithm between the (hierarchical) storage system and the object manager. This algorithm is described in [13]. Ptool with this caching algorithm has been used in high energy physics [4] and aeronautics [20]. On the basis of this experience, a multi-level caching algorithm involving segments and folios was designed and implemented in Version 0.6 of ptool. This version of ptool has been used for applications in high energy physics [16], aeronautics [12], decision support [17], and multi-media applications.

The ptool management system consists of several components. The *Persistent Object Manager* uses the virtual memory system and mapping to manage persistent objects. It handles the creation and accessing of persistent objects and creates, opens, and closes stores.

The *Segment Cache Manager* uses the virtual memory system to map segments from a local disk to a slot in virtual memory. If the segment containing a referenced persistent object is not currently available in virtual memory, the Persistent Object Manager generates a fault to the Segment Cache Manager. If the segment is available in the local disk cache, it is returned to the Persistent Object Manager to be mapped into virtual memory. A client-server version of the Segment Cache Manager been used for some applications.

The *Folio Cache Manager* manages segments and folios from network and hierarchical storage to local disk. If the segment required by the Segment Cache Manager is not available in the local disk cache, then the Segment Cache Manager generates a fault to the Folio Cache Manager. The Folio Cache Manager then determines the location of the folio containing the required segment, retrieves the folio, extracts the segment, and returns the segment to the Segment Cache Manager. The Folio Cache Manager interfaces to the hierarchical storage system. One or more Segment Cache Managers are clients of the Folio Cache Manager.

The cache manager of a scalable object store in a high performance computing environment necessarily interacts with the caches managed by other component systems in the environment, including the virtual memory system, the (distributed) file system, and the hierarchical storage system. Our philosophy in the design of ptool was to rely on operating and file system services as much as possible, despite the performance penalties this entails. This decision was motivated by the fact that scalable operating and file systems are now being designed and prototyped.

Specifically, ptool relies on the virtual memory system for caching objects between memory and local disk. Also, by storing segments as UNIX files, ptool can rely on distributed and hierarchical storage systems to handle large numbers of segments.

4   Implementation

We have designed and developed a working prototype of ptool using C++. Version 0.6 Release 2 of ptool runs on several UNIX systems, including SunOS, RS6000/AIX, SGI/IRIX, PC/Linux, and the IBM SP-1. It should run under other UNIX systems which provide virtual memory and file mapping facilities. As will be described below, several different variants of some of the components of Version 0.6 of ptool were developed.

The ptool management system consists of ptool, together with a number of related tools, including a query tool called qtool, which support a subset of OQL, tools for distributing queries in local area clusters, tools for data mining,

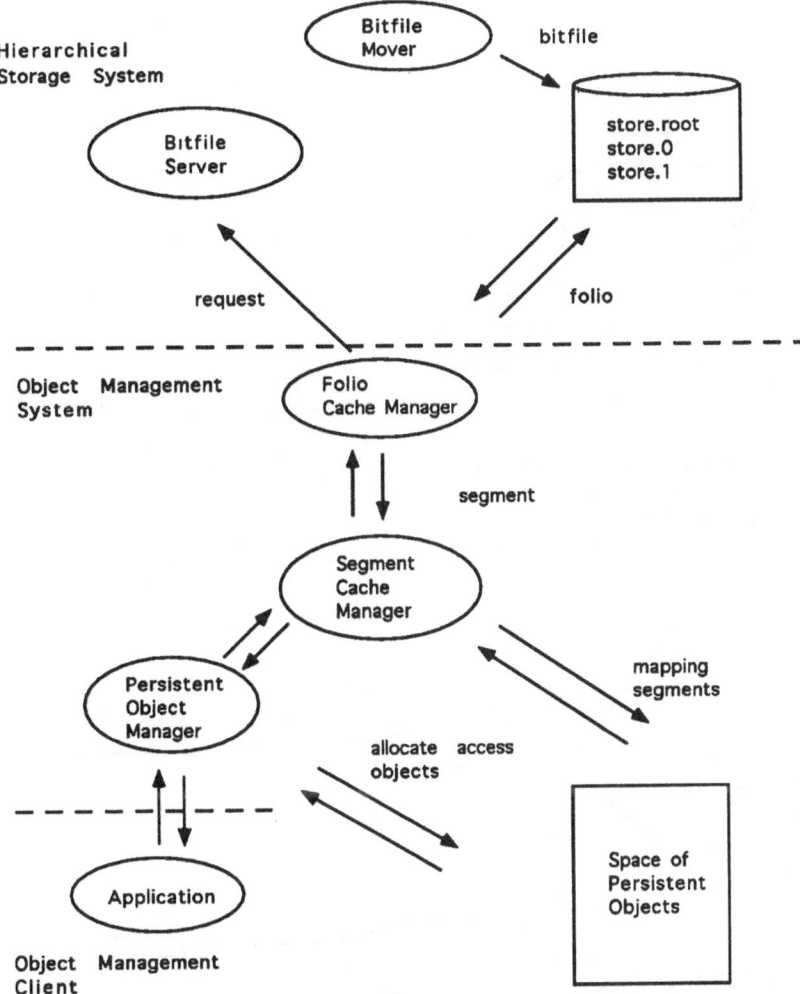

Figure 1: This diagram illustrates how ptool interfaces to a hierarchical storage system. Ptool provides uniform, scalable access to a persistent space of objects. The Persistent Object Manager provides persistence by slotting segments of objects into virtual memory. When a segment that is not currently mapped is needed, the Persistent Object Manager generates a fault to the Segment Cache Manager. If the segment is available in the local segment cache, it is mapped into virtual memory. Otherwise a fault is generated and passed to the Folio Cache Manager. The segment may be available in the Folio Cache Manager's segment cache; if not, a fault is generated to a hierarchical storage system to retrieve the corresponding physical collection of segments called a folio which contains the needed segment. Pre-emptive prefetching is used to improve performance.

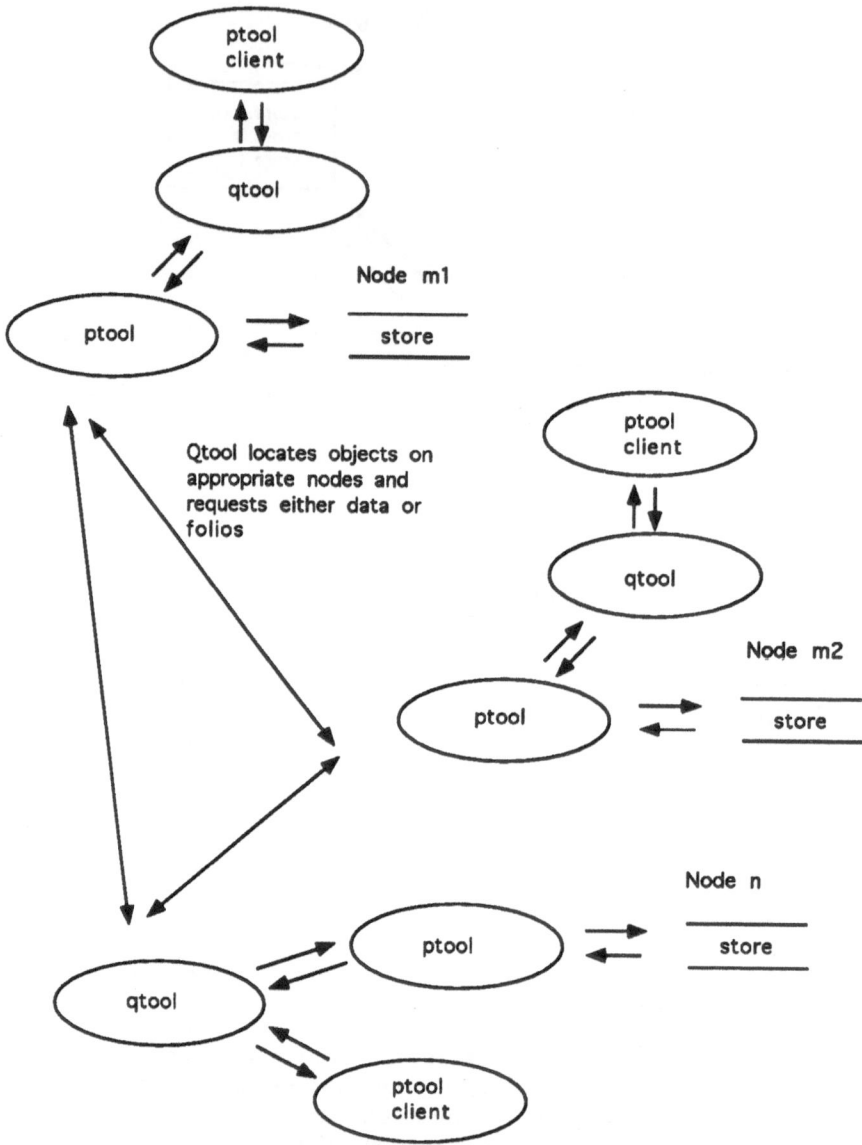

Figure 2: This diagram illustrates how ptool is used in local and wide area clusters. In a local cluster, a master node can divide a query up among several client nodes. The client nodes can then return objects to the master node by embedding them in folios. In a wide area cluster, remote nodes can query nodes containing data. The data can be returned as a sequence of folios so that subsequent queries can be executed locally. This is especially important if the subsequent queries involve extensive computation or visualization.

and tools for visualization.

Addresses in ptool are 64 bits long and consist of a store number, folio number, segment number and offset. The store number, folio number, and segment number together constitute a single 32-bit machine word, which is the identifier for a segment in the persistent space. Putting the segment identifier in single word saves space and improves speed when invoking and executing memory manager functions.

Since ptool is designed to manage very large stores, a conventional page table would be too large and too slow. In order to provide adequate performance, ptool uses both multilevel paging and inverted page table techniques to speed up address translation.

PTool maintains store and folio tables, but does not maintain segment tables, because they would be too large and inefficient. Rather, it finds segments directly from the object identifiers, in one of two ways: When segments are physically contiguous in a folio, the segment numbers serve as an offset into the folio. When segments are stored as individual files in disk, their names can be constructed from the object identifiers.

4.1 High performance clusters

In this section, we follow [22] and [1]. We developed a version of ptool for tightly coupled high performance clusters, such as the IBM SP-1. The IBM SP-1 we used for our implementation consisted of input-output nodes, which contained tens of Gigabytes of disk, and compute nodes, which contained only a small amount of disk. The nodes were connected via a high performance switch and communicated via a message passing protocol.

For this implementation, the Persistent Segment Manager was split into a Persistent Segment Manager Client and Persistent Segment Manager Server to mirror the split of the nodes into input-output nodes and compute nodes. Queries from local and wide area clusters are sent to compute nodes, where the queries are executed. On each compute node, a Persistent Object Manager and a Persistent Segment Manager Client are resident. Object faults are generated by the Persistent Object Manager and, if necessary, passed to the Persistent Segment Manager Client in order to obtain the necessary segment. In turn, the Persistent Segment Manager Client determines the appropriate input-output node which manages the segment and sends a request to a Persistent Segment Manager Server on the appropriate node. The Persistent Segment Manager Server obtains the segment, perhaps by generating a fault to the Persistent Folio Manager, which, in turn, obtains it from the hierarchical storage system. The Persistent Segment Manager Server then maps the segment into the virtual memory of the compute node.

To summarize, in this implementation, most of the object management consisted of moving physical segments between input-output nodes and compute nodes within a tightly coupled local cluster, and when necessary moving folios from the hierarchical storage system to the appropriate input-output node.

4.2 Wide area clusters

In this section, we follow [17]. We have also developed a variant of the Persistent Segment Manager and Persistent Folio Manager for loosely coupled wide area clusters. The decision support application we developed uses the Forms Package in Mosaic to send OQL messages in http [31] to a WWW server, which, in turn, calls qtool, which processes the query.

The query can return results in one of two different forms. The data itself which satisfies the query can be returned. Alternatively, the folios containing the objects which satisfy the query can be returned. In the latter case, a ptool application running on the originating node is used for the subsequent queries, analysis, and visualization of the returned folios.

Although we have experimented with different heuristics, we know of no good way at this time of deciding whether to return the data or the folios containing the objects. This is currently an area of research. In practice, different ptool applications exploit different defaults. The applications we have developed can switch between formats with a mouse click.

A limitation of this current implementation is that for folios to be passed between nodes in a local or wide area cluster, all of the nodes in the cluster must run the same operating system. We are investigating for future releases maintaining a base format for the folios and translating them when formats for other platforms are needed.

To summarize, with this implementation, applications have the option of moving the query to the data and returning the results of the query, or moving the objects to the query in the form of folios. The latter is particularly appropriate when intensive further analysis or visualization is required. This is not done automatically, but rather the ptool application or the user must explicitly request one form or the other.

5   EventStore

As part of the PASS Project, we have used the ptool management system to analyze approximately 10 Gigabytes of data on particle collisions from the CDF experiment at Fermi National Laboratory [18] and [22]. In this experiment counter-rotating proton beams produce particle collisions or "events". Each event can be described by approximately 10K bytes of data organized into attributes which the physicists call "banks". We have put enough of these banks into our store to complete some simple physics analysis in order to gain a preliminary understanding of how the entire database (consisting of approximately 1.5 Terabytes of data stored on several thousand 8mm tapes) may be analyzed. A typical query consists of several hundred lines of C++ code. Our implementation is about an order of magnitude faster than the production code currently used.

In our experiments [19] and [22], we have used 16 Megabytes folios and used the ptool Persistent Folio Manager to manage folios from a hierarchical storage system consisting of 8mm tape, D2 tape, and local and networked disk.

Finally, we have recently introduced two variants of ptool for this application. In one [22] and [1], described briefly in the section above, a client server version of the Persistent Segment Manager requests segments from an appropriate input-output node in a tightly coupled cluster. In another, also described briefly in the section above, a client ptool process allows remote physicists in a wide area cluster to use OQL to request an interesting sample of events to be returned to their workstation for subsequent analysis with ptool. Since a

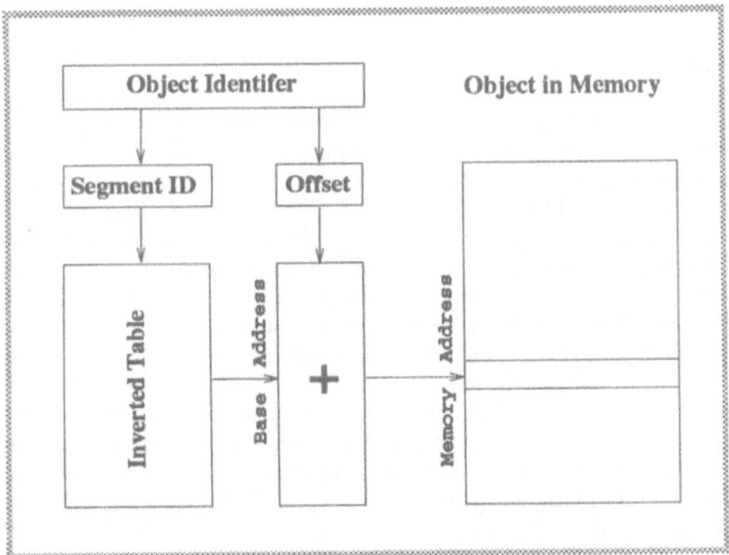

Figure 3: Object IDs in ptool are 64 bits long and consist of a store number, folio number, segment number and offset. The store number, folio number, and segment number together constitute a single 32-bit machine word, which is called the segment ID and identifies a unique segment in the persistent space. The base address of a segment is found using an inverted table. The memory address of the object to be accessed is determined by adding the offset to the segment base address.

typical analysis may consist of a large number of individual queries stretching over a period of hours, it is clearly advantageous to provide the ability to return replicated historical data for subsequent local analysis instead of paying for the overhead for the remote analysis of the original data.

To summarize, for this application three different variants of the ptool Persistent Segment and Persistent Folio were developed, each exploiting different folio management policies: one adapted to a single node with attached hierarchical storage system, one for a tightly coupled local area cluster, and one for a loosely coupled wide area cluster.

6 TrajectoryStore

We have created stores consisting of short duration trajectory segments from models describing robotic and aeronautic systems [20] and [12]. The goal is to develop a real time path planning system. The input to the system would be the desired long duration flight path. In general, such a path is not physically feasible, but rather must be approximated by trajectory segments which are physically feasible. For example, the desired flight path may involve maneuvers which the aircraft cannot sustain. These would be approximated by close-by trajectories which would in fact describe physically reasonable trajectories.

Our approach was to populate a store containing a large number of trajectory segments. Given a desired flight path of long duration, a query retrieves a list of short duration trajectory segments with the property that when these are laid end to end they approximate the original query path. Each short duration trajectory segment contains the controls and other parameters necessary to actually fly the aircraft along the trajectory segment. In this way, the result of the query contains all the information necessary to actually fly the aircraft along the approximating path.

A "light weight" persistent object manager proved essential for this application. The goal was to obtain as close to real time performance as possible. Two strategies were used: functionality was traded for performance, and a variant of ptool which provided little more than persistence was used. In addition, data centered parallelism was used. The space of persistent trajectory segments was divided into separate physical regions and each stored on a separate node in a tightly coupled cluster. The query was then divided up, shipped to each node, the query run locally, the results returned, and the final approximating trajectory path assembled from the local results.

To summarize, for this application, the ptool management system was used as a traditional distributed database management system in which the queries were split apart, moved to the data, executed locally, with the results returned to a central site and assembled. It was essential for our application that ptool provide very high performance and minimum overhead.

7 BudgetStore

We have used the ptool management system to develop a digital library to provide wide area access to the U.S. Government Budget for FY 93 and FY 94. FY 95 data will be available shortly. The budget for each fiscal year contains

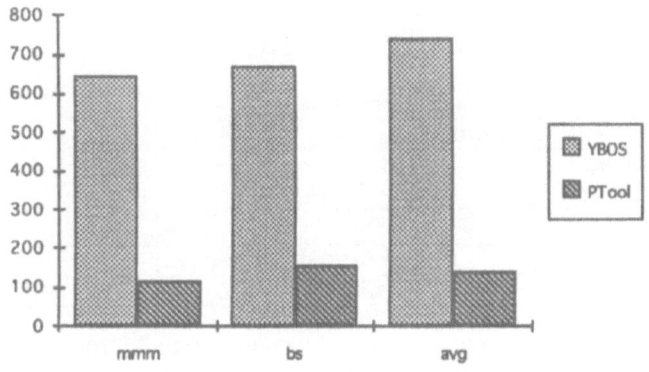

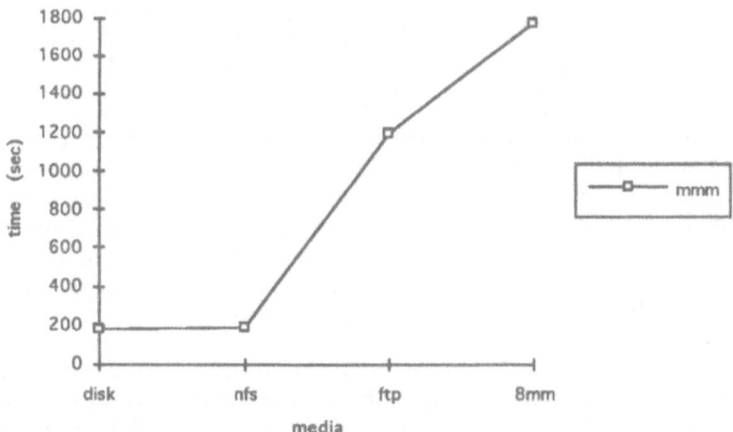

Figure 4: Currently events at FNAL are analyzed using a Fortran based data management (YBOS) and data analysis system. The goals of the project described here were to provide scalable access to event data, in a manner which is independent of the storage media on which the data is stored. The top chart illustrates that ptool is significantly faster than the current system for three application specific benchmarks (mmm, bs, and avg) developed by the PASS Project [22]. The bottom chart illustrates that ptool can access data at approximately the speed of the input-output channel in a media independent fashion.

Data Sample	Number of of Events	ptool file size	Number of 16MB folios
psi-1	1309	0.805 GB	48
psi-1-3	3072	1.845 GB	110
psi-1-5	13469	6.556 GB	391

YBOS			Elapsed Time (secs)		
machine	data	media	mmm	bs	avg
SS 2	psi-1	disk	737	773	844
SS 670	psi-1	disk	646	669	741

Ptool			Elapsed Time (secs)				
machine	data	media	mmm	mmm2	bs	avg	vfit
SS 2	psi-1	disk	181	176	241	247	177
SS 2	psi-1	nfs	189	197	228	228	199
SS 2	psi-1	ftp	1192	1104	1165	1118	1206
SS 2	psi-1	8mm	1775	1744	1774	1795	5340
SS 2	psi-1-3	8mm	4013	3987	4079	4097	20012
SS 670	psi-1	disk	115	114	157	140	123
SS 670	psi-1	dd2	1092	1080	1093	1109	1464
SS 670	psi-1-3	dd2	2522	2508	2554	2588	3418
SS 670	psi-1-5	dd2	8945	8904	9046	9160	9936

Notes: SS 2 denotes a Sun SparcStation 2 running Sun OS 4.1.3 with 32 Megabytes of RAM. SS 670 denotes a four processor Sun SparcStation 670MP running Sun OS 4.1.3 with 128 Megabytes of RAM. Disk refers to a local attached SCSI disk. NFS refers to data accessed via a remote disk using nfs and ethernet. FTP refers to data accessed via a remote disk using ftp and ethernet. 8mm refers to a Exebyte 8500 8mm tape drive attached locally. DD2 refers to a Ampex DD2 tape drive on IPI 3 I/F attached locally.

Table 1: The tables above from [21] summarize the performance of the ptool management system analyzing high energy physics data distributed over a variety of media, including 8mm and DD2 tape. Currently, the data is stored on several thousand 8mm tapes. Ptool provides a means to analyze the data independently of its physical location.

Five benchmarks—mmm,mmm2,bs,avg, and vfit—were developed by the PASS Project. The mmm benchmark, for example, iterates over the set of events to locate all events which contain two muons, extracts the energy, momentum, and charge from the muons, and calculates the effective two particle mass and transverse momentum from the combined two particle state. The benchmark requires several hundred lines of C++ code to implement. The other benchmarks are similar, but more complicated.

The top table details the data sizes used. The middle table details the results of the benchmarks using the current production system data management system called YBOS. The bottom table details the results of the benchmarks using ptool.

Central Site Stores				
System	Dim.	Trajectories	Size[a]	Time[b]
robot	3	121,500	68.6	8.19/1.74
car	4	198,000	138.3	12.29/2.92
harrier	6	705,600	356.1	19.40/3.40
Distributed Stores (two client sites)				
System	Dim.	Trajectories	Size	Time
robot	3	60,750	34.3	4.45/0.98
car	4	99,000	69.15	7.12/2.01
harrier	6	352,800	178.05	10.18/2.11

[a]The "size" is in MBytes.

[b]Times are given in minutes in the form *(user time) / (CPU time)*, where *user time* is the CPU time used while executing instructions in the user space of the calling process and *CPU time* is the CPU time used by the system on behalf of the calling process.

Central Site Stores			
System	Grouping[c]	Approximating[d]	Accuracy
robot	5.00/10.38	71.16/12.41	0.05713
car	9.97/19.87	65.4/30.01	0.09022
harrier	15.34/27.65	80.75/44.59	0.12357
Distributed Stores (two client sites)			
System	Grouping	Approximating	Accuracy
robot	3.10/6.12	37.13/7.48	0.05839
car	5.92/11.01	33.46/16.46	0.09142
harrier	8.41/15.47	41.89/23.18	0.12358

[c]Times for "grouping" are given in seconds, according to the form *(user time) / (CPU time)*.

[d]Times for "approximating" are given in the form *(user time) / (CPU time)*, where the user time is in seconds and the CPU time in ticks.

Table 2: These performance results are from [12]. The point of view in [12] is to interpret path planning as a query to a persistent object store of trajectory segments. The algorithm consists of two phases: in the first phase, geometric hashing is used to retrieve and *group* trajectory segments which are nearby the desired path; in the second phase, the trajectory segment which best *approximates* the desired path is selected. The times for these two phases are reported separately. Times are reported for a distributed query in which the query is moved to data at a fixed location and the results returned to a central site. We are currently experimenting on a 128 node IBM SP-1, which we will report on in the next version of this report.

approximately 5000 tables and 50,000 line items, as well as a modest amount of accompanying text. The challenge was to provide distributed access and analysis tools for tabular data of this type. Digital libraries of textural data supporting full text searches are common. On the other hand, it is still a challenge to provide similar access for tabular, scientific, or statistical data.

For example, a typical query in a textural database can easily retrieve all references to the keyword "research". On the other hand, a typical query to a statistical database should be able to retrieve all line objects containing the keyword "research" in which the attribute "fiscal year 94 outlays" is greater than $100 million.

The analysis pattern is similar to the eventstore. Some queries are most efficiently shipped to the data and the results returned to the client node. On the other hand, some analyses require sequential statistical analysis and visualization of the data. These turn out to be most efficiently handled by using an initial query to select a moderate size store consisting of a number of folios to return to the requesting node. Subsequent analysis is then handled locally.

Our initial prototype currently asks the user to make the determination of whether to return numerical data or folios as the result of a query. We plan with the next prototype to use a simple rule system to automate this decision.

To provide wide area access to the data, we used the Forms Package in NCSA's Mosaic to send OQL queries to one of several data servers, which then returned the desired data in the requested format.

8 Discussion and Conclusions

One of the contributions of the work summarized here is that light weight object managers such as ptool have a role in numerically intensive computing applications. Evidence for this is provided by the results of the five application specific high energy physics benchmarks and the one aeronautic benchmark described above.

The purpose of this paper was not to advocate a specific design for a light weight object manager. In this case, it would have been more appropriate to have compared several different object managers using one of the more commonly accepted object oriented benchmarks which have arisen recently. Rather, it was to show that light weight object managers have a role in numerically intensive high performance computing and to clarify some of the different policies appropriate for the physical management of folios for these applications. For this reason, application specific benchmarks were used that were developed in collaboration with the appropriate domain scientists.

To summarize, in this paper, we have briefly described the design of the ptool management system. Ptool was designed to support long duration, numerically intensive queries on large amounts of data distributed in hierarchical storage systems and clusters. For this reason, not only does it manage segments which are mapped from local disk to virtual memory, but also physical collections of segments called folios, which can be cached, migrated, and replicated between nodes in local and wide area clusters and retrieved from hierarchical storage systems.

Ptool was designed to have very low overhead and high performance, especially when working with large amounts of data or large numbers of objects. This is obtained by using a multi-level caching algorithm to manage physical collections of objects of different granularity. At one end of the physical hierarchy, ptool exploits standard memory mapping techniques; at the other end of the physical hierarchy, ptool interfaces to hierarchical storage systems and can pass physical collections of objects (folios) from node to node in local and wide area clusters.

Ptool was primarily designed for high performance computing, especially with historical data. For this reason, it was designed to have very low overhead, and does not support any functionality beyond persistence. We have illustrated its performance on applications from high energy physics, aeronautics, and finance.

References

[1] N. Araujo, K. Denisenko, M. Fischler, M. Galli, R. Grossman, D. Hanley, D. Malon, E. May, and W. Xu, "Data Mining High Energy Physics Data Using a Persistent Object Manager: A Case Study," *Laboratory for Advanced Computing Technical Report Number 95-R1*, University of Illinois at Chicago, 1994, submitted for publication.

[2] T. Atwood, "Two Approaches to Adding Persistence to C++," in *Implementing Persistent Object Bases: Principles and Practice*, A. Dearle, G. M. Shaw, and S. B. Zdonik, editors, Morgan-Kauffmann Publishers, San Mateo, California, 1991.

[3] A. Baden and R. Grossman, "Database computing and high energy physics," *Computing in High-Energy Physics 1991*, edited by Y. Watase and F. Abe, Universal Academy Press, Inc., Tokyo, 1991, pp. 59–66.

[4] C. T. Day, S. Loken, J. F. MacFarlane, E. May, D. Lifka, E. Lusk, L. E.Price, A. Baden, R. Grossman, X. Qin, L. Cormell, P. Leibold, D. Liu, U. Nixdorf, B. Scipioni, T. Song, "Database Computing in HEP — Progress Report," *Proceedings of the International Conference on Computing in High Energy Physics '92*, C. Verkerk and W. Wojcik, editors, CERN-Service d'Information Scientifique, 1992, ISSN 0007-8328, pp. 557-560.

[5] M. J. Carey, L. M. Haas, and M. Livny, "Tapes Hold Data Too: Challenges of Tuples on Tertiary Storage," in *Proceedings of the 1993 ACM SIGMOD, SIGMOD Record*, Volume 22, ACM, New York, 1993, pp. 413-417.

[6] R. G. G. Cattell, *The Object Database Standard: ODMG-93* Morgan Kaufmann Publishers, 1993.

[7] S. S. Coleman, editor, *Proceedings of the Twelfth IEEE Symposium on Mass Storage Systems*, IEEE Press, Los Alamites, 1993.

[8] J. Dozier, "Access to Data in NASA's Earth Observing System," in *Proceedings of the 1992 ACM SIGMOD, SIGMOD Record*, Volume 21, ACM, New York, 1992, page 1.

[9] EXODUS Project Group, "EXODUS Storage Manager Architectural Overview," EXODUS Project Document, University of Wisconsin, Madison, 1991.

[10] W. E. Farrell and Jean Anderson, "Very Large Databases and Mass Storage Technology," *Digest of Papers: Eleventh IEEE Symposium on Mass Storage Systems*, IEEE Press, Los Alamites, 1991, pp. 61-62.

[11] W. Gropp, "Early experiences with the IBM SP-1 and the High-Performance Switch," *Argonne National Laboratory Technical Report*, ANL-93/41, 1993.

[12] R. L. Grossman, D. Valsamis and X. Qin, "Persistent stores and Hybrid Systems," *Proceedings of the 32st IEEE Conference on Decision and Control*, IEEE Press, 1993, pp. 2298-2302.

[13] R. L. Grossman, D. Likfa, and X. Qin, "An object manager utilizing hierarchical storage," *Twelfth IEEE Symposium on Mass Storage Systems,* IEEE Press, Los Alamites, 1993, pp. 209–214.

[14] R. L. Grossman and X. Qin, "Ptool: a scalable persistent object manager," *Proceedings of SIGMOD 94,* ACM, 1994, page 510.

[15] R. L. Grossman, X. Qin, D. Valsamis, W. Xu, C. T. Day, S. Loken, J. F. MacFarlane, D. Quarrie, E. May, D. Lifka, D. Malon, L. Price, "Analyzing High Energy Physics Data Using A Persistent Object Manager," *Proceedings of the Seventh International Working Conference on Scientific and Statistical Database Management,* IEEE Press, 1994, to appear.

[16] R. L. Grossman, "Working With Object Stores of Events Using ptool," in *Proceedings of the Cern Summer School in Computing,* C. Verkerk, editor, CERN-Service d'Information Scientifique, 1994, to appear.

[17] R. L. Grossman, A. Sundaram, H. Ramamoorthy, M. Wu, S. Hogan, J. Shuler and O. Wolfson, "Viewing the U.S. Government Budget as a Digital Library," *Proceedings of Digital Libraries 1994: Conference on the Theory and Practice of Digital Libraries,* ACM, 1994, to appear.

[18] D. Malon, D. Lifka, E. May R. Grossman, X. Qin, W. Xu "Parallel Query Processing for Event Store Data," *Proceedings of Computing in High Energy Physics 1994,* to appear.

[19] E. N. May, D. Lifka, D. Malon, L. E. Price L. Cormell, A. Gauthier, J. Marsteller, S. Mestad, U. Nixdorf R. Grossman, X. Qin, D. Valsamis, M. Wu, W. Xu "A Demonstration of a Multi-level Object Store and its Application to the Analysis of High Energy Physics Data," *Proceedings of Computing in High Energy Physics 1994,* to appear.

[20] R. L. Grossman, S. Mehta, X. Qin, "Path planning by querying persistent stores of trajectory segments," *Laboratory for Advanced Computing Technical Report Number 93-R3,* University of Illinois at Chicago, 1993, to appear.

[21] R. L. Grossman, X. Qin, and D. Valsamis, and D. Lifka, E. May, and D. Malon, and L. Price, "The Architecture of a Multi-level Object Store and its Application to the Analysis of High Energy Physics Data," *Laboratory for Advanced Computing Technical Report,* Number LAC 94-R8, University of Illinois at Chicago. December, 1993.

[22] R. L. Grossman, D. Lifka, D. Malon, E. May, X. Qin, D. Valsamis, W. Xu, "High performance object stores," *Laboratory for Advanced Computing Technical Report,* Number LAC 94-R12, University of Illinois at Chicago. January, 1994.

[23] D. Isaac, "Hierarchical Storage Management for Relational Databases," *Twelfth IEEE Symposium on Mass Storage Systems,* IEEE Press, Los Alamites, 1993, pp. 139–144.

[24] C. Lamb, G. Landis, J. Orenstein, and D. Weinreb, "The ObjectStore Database System," *Communications of the ACM,* Volume 34, 1991.

[25] "Mass Storage System Reference Model, Version 4" edited by Sam Coleman and Steve Miller, IEEE. to appear.

[26] M. N. Nelson, B. B. Welch, and J. K. Ousterhout, "Caching in the Sprite Network File System," *ACM Transactions on Computer Systems*, Volume 6, 1988, pp. 134–154.

[27] M. Stonebraker, "Managing persistent objects in a multi-level store," in *Proceedings of the 1991 ACM SIGMOD, SIGMOD Record*, Volume 20, ACM, New York, 1991, pp. 2–11.

[28] Object Management Group, *The Common Object Request Broker: Architecture and Specification, Revision 1.1*, OMG TC Document 92.12.1, 1991.

[29] M. Satyanarayanan, J. H. Howard, D. A. Nichols, R. N. Sidebotham, A. Z. Spector, and M. J. West, "The ITC Distributed File System: Principles and Design," in *Proceedings of the 10th Symposium on Operating Systems Principles*, ACM Press, New York, 1985, pp. 35–50.

[30] E. Shekita and M. Zwilling, "Cricket: A Mappled, Persistent Object Store," in *Implementing Persistent Object Bases: Principles and Practice*, A. Dearle, G. M. Shaw, and S. B. Zdonik, editors, Morgan-Kauffmann Publishers, San Mateo, California, 1991.

[31] http://info.cern.ch/hypertext/www/LineMode/Defaults/Default.html

Analysing Persistent Language Applications

Dag I.K. Sjøberg
Department of Informatics, University of Oslo
Oslo, Norway. dagsj@ifi.uio.no

Quintin Cutts
Department of Mathematical and Computational Sciences, University of St Andrews
St Andrews, Scotland. quintin@dcs.st-andrews.ac.uk

Ray Welland, Malcolm P. Atkinson
Department of Computing Science, University of Glasgow
Glasgow, Scotland. {ray, mpa}@dcs.glasgow.ac.uk

Abstract

Most research into persistent programming has been directed towards the design and implementation of languages and object stores. There are few reports on the characteristics of systems exploiting such technology. This paper reports on a study of the source code of 20 applications consisting of more than 108,000 lines of persistent language code. The authors of the applications range from students to experienced programmers. The programs have been categorised and examined with respect to a persistent application model and the extent of inconsistencies relative to this model is presented. The results confirm the need for and give input to the design of programming methodologies and tools for persistent software engineering. Measurements also include the use of names, types, (polymorphic) procedures and persistent bindings. It is hoped that analysis of the measurements will be used as input to the next generation of languages and programming environments. As part of this new generation, a measurements system is outlined operating entirely within the persistent environment, thus simplifying access to and measurement of both static and dynamic information.

1 Introduction

This paper reports on an analysis of applications written within a persistent programming environment. Whilst much persistence research has been directed towards the design and implementation of persistent languages and object stores [1-3], there are few reports on the characteristics of application systems exploiting such technology. As the programming effort using persistent languages expands from the current core system building domain to the wider application building domain, results of this nature are required to ensure that the expected wide-ranging benefits of persistent systems are realised. The analysis of persistent language applications presented in this paper aims to inform research in the areas of persistent programming methodology design, the design and implementation of persistent programming environments and associated tools and the design and implementation of persistent programming languages.

The analysed software was written in Napier88 [4], a strongly typed, higher-order persistent programming language. The applications derive from a number of sources, from the Napier88 programming environment software, to student programs to the first major non-system applications written using the Napier88 system. The measured software comes from three separate sites: University of St Andrews, University of Glasgow and Napier University in Edinburgh.

These programs have been written over a number of years during which time different application construction styles have evolved. Each style is termed a programming methodology, and the adherence to and design of these methodologies are of particular interest here. The designer of a programming methodology takes the features of a programming language and its associated environment and generates guidelines and constraints to aid construction of applications according to a clear, widely used and coherent framework. Such a standardisation is intended to improve the quality of software engineering and is particularly important in a fledgling programming style such as persistent programming since there are few, if any, well-founded and proven methodologies available.

The measurements collected in this study are assessed against one of the first well-defined persistent programming methodologies, first to see to what degree the applications adhere to the methodology and second to determine how the methodology should best evolve to meet the requirements of application builders. Statistics on the dependencies among the various parts of an application system indicate the consequences of change, including the extent of necessary change propagation [5].

As a supplement to anecdotal description of user experiences, attempts should be made to quantify the potential benefits of new and enhanced methodologies and tools [6, 7]. This may be achieved by measuring software before and after the methodologies have been adhered to and the supporting tools applied. A strictly controlled experiment was not conducted, but groups of different kinds of programmers were compared.

The measurements are also used to indicate areas of concern in current persistent programming languages and environments. In Napier88, for example, some application construction styles are not efficiently supported by the current programming environment because it is outside the persistent environment. An integrated persistent programming environment is required to make the most of the benefits offered by persistence.

The measurements presented here are taken from a static analysis of source code only. Studies based on static analysis have been reported for other languages, e.g. FORTRAN [8, 9], PL/1 [10] and APL [11], but these studies focused on other issues than those reported in this paper. Also programs written in persistent programming languages have been analysed by others, but only some dynamic aspects relating to performance have been measured [12-14]. The analysis reported in this paper is restricted to static analysis and to a particular language environment but represents a first attempt at analysing the characteristics of persistent language applications. The emergence of integrated persistent programming environments, e.g. [15], will allow measurement of both static and dynamic application characteristics within a fully persistent system. Such measurements should give a more complete analysis of persistent applications. Although measurements from such systems are not yet available, this paper outlines measurement techniques that exploit the power of the new technology and will be used in the next stage of persistent language analysis. As the size and complexity of persistent applications increase, these features will be required to ensure that effective and enhanced measurement and analysis can be performed.

The paper is organised as follows. Section 2 describes the apparatus used to gather the measurements. Sections 3 reports the main results, which are analysed in Section 4. Section 5 outlines new measurement technology. Section 6 concludes.

2 Measurement Apparatus – Methodology, Tools and Applications

The methodologies, tools and measurements presented here are drawn from experience using the first release of the Napier88 system. In this version, the programming environment in which source programs are constructed and compiled into executable programs is the Unix™ system [16] (Figure 1). Compiled programs are executed against a persistent store. The internal structure of the store is not defined by the language or the store and may consist of an arbitrary graph of Napier88 values, both data and first-class procedures. The graph is reachable from a single point known as the root of persistence. By convention, the graph is structured using a Napier88 type constructor known as an environment [17], which is a collection of name-type-value-constancy bindings [18]. A binding in an environment is to a location containing a value of the given type that may be overwritten with another according to the binding's constancy. Nesting of environments allows a typed hierarchical structure analogous to the directory structure of a file system. A value persists beyond the invocation of the program that created it if it is within the transitive closure of the persistent root.

Libraries of values may be constructed within the store by executing compiled programs that create the new values and bind them to the environment structure where they may be accessed by other programs. Bindings between values and environments are just one example of the bindings between values that may be created during program execution. Applications are typically made up of a number of independently constructed values bound together in such a way that the required task may be performed. In addition, some or all of these values may be bound to the environment structure to allow, for example, an entry point for execution of the application or application components to be examined and possibly updated.

The programming environment embedded within the Unix system allows source program files to be constructed and compiled into executable program files. Where complex type descriptions are shared by many programs, a single version of the type descriptions may be created in a file and compiled into a type library against which source programs may subsequently be compiled.

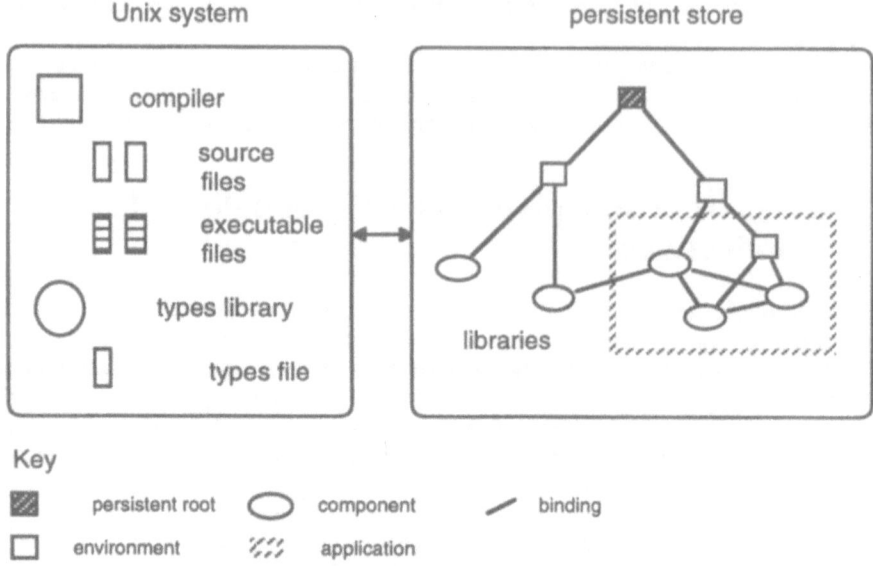

Figure 1: The programming environment

Using a persistent system of this kind, the starting point for the work described here is defined by the following components:

- the persistent programming methodology known as the Structured Persistent Application System Model (SPASM)
- the Thesaurus-based Software Information Tool (TSIT), used to gather information from the source programs
- EnvMake, used to assess this information against SPASM, and
- a collection of persistent applications

2.1   The SPASM Methodology

SPASM defines a programming methodology as a set of constraints to which each suite of application software should adhere in order to help ensure correctness and maintainability [19, 20]. Well-structured software is a requirement for easy maintenance in the future [21, 22]. The SPASM constraints apply to the static software characteristics determined during source code analysis. Some of the constraints are explicit formulations of rules and conventions in a programming culture already adhered to by experienced Napier88 programmers. Other constraints have been defined as a result of the inconsistencies detected in this study.

As a means to improve the way applications are organised around the persistent store, SPASM restricts each program to perform only one kind of operation on the store. Any program should belong to exactly one of the following categories:

- *Insert-program* – inserts at least one binding into an environment in the persistent store but neither updates a persistent location nor deletes any binding.

- *Update-program* – updates at least one persistent location but neither inserts nor deletes any binding.
- *Drop-program* – deletes at least one binding but neither updates a persistent location nor inserts any binding.[1]
- *Startup-program* – uses at least one binding but neither changes the binding to a persistent location, nor inserts or deletes any binding. A startup-program's distinguishing feature is that it does not change any of the bindings in any persistent environment; it typically invokes an interactive menu or any persistent procedure.
- *Type-program* – its contents are exclusively type definitions.

Several constraints help ensure adherence to an incremental construction methodology based on updatable persistent locations [23]. Using the methodology, insert-programs create stub locations in environments, one for each component of the application. For each component, an update-program finds bindings to locations of components required by the component under construction. The update-program creates the new component with bindings to these locations, and updates the component's location with the newly constructed version.

The following are examples of another category of SPASM constraints:

- all type definitions should be used within the application
- a binding inserted into the store, not intended for export, should be used somewhere within the application
- programs and data in the persistent store should be used in at least one application program

2.2 The TSIT and EnvMake Tools

The measurements were provided by TSIT which integrates the notions of data dictionary in the database area and cross-referencer in the programming language area [20, 24]. The TSIT analyser is based on the Napier88-in-Napier88 compiler [25] and extracts a variety of information during source code analysis and inserts it into the thesaurus, which is a fine-grained, cross-reference database containing information about all user-introduced names occurring in the source programs of an application and the names of the bindings to code and other data in the associated persistent stores. A thesaurus entry holds information relevant to our study such as: *name, type, constancy* of an identifier and *usage* and *context* of identifier occurrences. Usage indicates how the identifier is being used, e.g. declaration or use of a type identifier, or declaration, left context or right context of a value identifier. Context indicates whether the identifier occurs in an environment operation or as a declaration of a type parameter, procedure parameter, structure field, variant tag, etc. or as a dereferenced structure field, projected variant, etc.

Another thesaurus-based tool, EnvMake, verifies programs against the constraints of SPASM, using the thesaurus built up by TSIT. EnvMake gives warnings when violations are detected and can be compared with modern grammar

---

[1] "Delete" is called "drop" in Napier88 terminology. These terms are used synonymously in this paper.

checkers; they check the text against some internal rules and give a warning if the text is not compliant with those rules. EnvMake does not invalidate the program if violations are detected; it informs the programmer about the kind and source of violation and then checks the next constraint. EnvMake features optional selection of the constraints; programmers may "switch off" the check of individual constraints. For example, a programmer may know that certain constraints will not be adhered to during periods of development (typically during initial construction) and may wish to avoid the noise of unnecessary inconsistency messages.

2.3 The Applications

An application is a collection of related programs expected to support a task. Source code information collected from 20 Napier88 applications developed by students and experienced persistent programmers forms the basis for this analysis. The application collection consists in total of 1544 programs, 108,000 lines of code and 180,000 name occurrences (which may be a better measure for the size than the traditional lines of code). A *program* in this context is a unit of compilation, typically contained in a single file.[2] The analysis focuses on the use of names and identifiers. The same name can denote different identifiers if they appear in different scopes. In those cases there are more identifiers than names.[3] In the following program example there are one name, two identifiers and three name (or identifier) occurrences:

```
let counter := 0
begin
   let counter := 1
end
counter := 1
```

In order to investigate the potential benefits of recent innovations in programming methodologies, the applications were divided into four groups: OLD applications developed before the latest methodologies were developed, applications of the STUDENTS who were taught the latest methodologies, new applications of experienced programmers who were AWARE of those methodologies, without fully committing to them, and finally, applications with authors who were explicitly COMMITTED.

3 Results

Table 1 lists a sample of the measurements and summarises immediate findings. Following the table, the measurements are described in more detail. The reader is reminded that these are static measurements of source code.

---

[2] In principle, a program may be represented by several files (e.g. assembled first by a pre-processor, held in a source code control system like RCS, etc.) or may be extracted from one file. The term *module* is often used in the literature synonymously with our definition of program.
[3] In the analysed applications 13% of the names denote more than one identifier.

241

Table 1: Summary of measurements

Measurement	Immediate findings
Program categories	• old programs do not adhere to the categories, the newest ones do
Inconsistencies	• a relatively large proportion of the SPASM constraints are violated
Use of names	• a name is used between 1 and 7124 times, 13 on average, 90% less than 25 • significant correlation (Spearman [26] 0.88) between number of different names and size of application; no correlation (0.14) between application size and the number of times a name is used • average name length 8 characters, ranging from 4 to 10 in the respective applications; maximum 29
Use of types	• identifiers: structure 21%; monomorphic procedures 18%; ADT only 0.2% • 52 type definitions are used on average 34 times in the applications; average use varies significantly: from 2 to 313 • no significant correlation between the three pairs of number of type definitions, type uses and application size
Use of procedures	• procedures are the most common kind of persistent binding • procedures are used 5 times on average; range of application average: $3-9$ • one quarter of all procedures are polymorphic
Constancy	• 76% variables, 24% constants
Variable usage	• 15 times more read than update
Store operations	• 73% use, 12% insert, 8% contains check and 7% delete

3.1 Adherence to SPASM

The measurements reported in this section are intended to stimulate persistent methodology designers and tool builders. The large number of inconsistencies and violations of constraints drawn from the measurements justify the implementation of the SPASM verification tool, EnvMake.

3.1.1 Program Categories

Table 2 shows the percentage of the programs belonging to the categories defined in Section 2.3 and illustrates SPASM's effect on the program organisation of the applications under study. The "insert/drop" and "ins/drop/update" columns show the percentage of programs (discouraged by SPASM) containing both insert and drop (and update) statements. It appears that 34% of the programs in the old applications violate the constraint that a program should belong to exactly one of the program categories, as opposed to 6%, 10% and 0% in the other groups. The reason for the large proportion of combined "insert/drop" and "insert/drop/update" programs in the old applications is that many of them adhered to a pre-SPASM methodology in which operations on the same binding were collected in one program. Note also the extremely low proportion (4%) of pure update-programs in the old applications.

242

Table 2: Distribution of program categories, expressed in percentages

Application group	insert	update	drop	start-up	type	insert/ drop	ins/drop /update	Total
OLD	19	4	3	25	15	22	12	100
STUDENT	34	22	1	29	8	6	0	100
AWARE	11	63	2	8	6	9	1	100
COMMITTED	25	28	25	21	1	0	0	100
MEAN	22	29	8	21	7	10	3	100

One of the two committed applications has one type-program and for each of the persistent components exactly one insert, update, drop and startup program. (The startup programs are test programs in this case.) The average program length is 35 lines in the committed group as opposed to 137 in the other groups. Keeping programs small is in compliance with good software engineering, as maintenance costs have been measured to be significantly affected by program size [27]. On the other hand, there are indications that too small programs should also be avoided [27]. However, if programs have simple semantics and are as well-structured as in this case, they may be the subject of (semi) automatic creation and maintenance [19].

3.1.2   Inconsistencies

SPASM and EnvMake were developed to support software builders in creating more consistent and maintainable application systems. The inconsistencies enumerated in Tables 3 and 4 are examples of inconsistencies the SPASM constraints aim to prevent. Some constraints operate within programs only (Table 3); other operate between programs, i.e. at the application level (Table 4). The applications were operational at the time of the analysis. One would expect an even larger number of inconsistencies during periods of development. A violation of a constraint could be a logical error or could just indicate a situation that might eventually cause problems. For example, redundant type and value declarations do not affect the functionality of a program, but should be avoided since they may cause confusion when someone tries to understand the program, and the programs become unnecessarily large and complex, which in turn may impair performance and maintainability. In a study of FORTRAN programs a correlation was found between the proportion of unused variables and fault rate [9].

Table 3: Measurements of inconsistencies within a program

Inconsistency within a program	Percentage	Percentage of
Variables not updated	35	all variables
Unused value identifiers	8	all declared identifiers
Variables updated but not read	4	all updated variables

Table 4: Measurements of inconsistencies within an application

Inconsistency within an application	Percentage	Percentage of
Repeated type declarations	29	all type identifiers
Unused type identifiers	24	all type identifiers
Repeated drop statements	10	all drop statements
Inserted procedure variables not updated	9	all inserted procedures
Inserted bindings not used	8	all inserted bindings
Repeatedly inserted bindings	7	all inserted bindings
Inserted procedure variables updated more than once	5	all updated procedures

More than one third of all variables are never updated and could therefore have been declared constants (Table 3, row 1). Store managers might exploit this information, which also indicates possible improvement in programming precision. There are large individual variations among the applications (from 0% to 83%, the student applications in the upper range). In addition to being updated, the value of a local (i.e., transient) variable should also be read within the program (row 3 shows 4% violations). A *persistent* variable should be assigned but not necessarily read within the program since its value may be read in other programs.

The majority (72%) of unused value identifiers (8%, row 2) are declared in the constructs used to access bindings in the persistent environment. There are several reasons for why this kind of redundancy occurs: large specifications are copied indiscriminately from other programs; too many identifiers are declared in the belief that they would be needed later; and code using identifiers is removed without the programmer remembering to remove the corresponding declarations. One application has a very low value (0.6%) due to the use of EnvMake, which detects and invites the programmers to eliminate such anomalies.

In a language allowing definition of types in different scopes, two or more types may be defined with the same name and type (expression). In that case, according to the model of SPASM, they should be replaced by exactly one definition in the innermost scope covering the scope of the replaced type definitions. Also, type definitions may have the same name, but denote different types. To avoid confusion they should then be renamed to acquire unique names. Multiple declarations of type names are confusing, require unnecessary compilation and are a potential problem concerning change. Maintaining consistency requires that all declarations describing the same concept (e.g. *Person*) must be changed if the intention is to modify the implementation of the concept (e.g. add a new attribute). It is difficult to arrange that when several programmers (responsible for several components) who require use of a common type, each writes out equivalent type definitions (particularly if they are complex). It is even harder to ensure that when the type is amended, the same amendments are applied in every usage context. One concept should therefore be represented by only one type definition. In our sample 29% of the type declarations are re-declarations (Table 4, row 1). In the most extreme application all types are declared within the program in which they are used. In that application there are 5.6 declarations per name. A requirement for type management is identified here.

The second row of Table 4 shows that 24% of the type identifiers are unused. Some applications use all the type identifiers declared within the application; other applications use only one third. In the latter extreme cases the reason is that when libraries are used, all the types associated with the library are copied even though only a small part of the library is actually used in the application. This indiscriminate copying of types is indicative of a requirement for a tool to collect required items (types or values).

Bindings inserted into a persistent store by one program should be used in some other program (row 5). Even library components intended for export should be used in at least one program testing the component. More than one declaration of insert for the same binding may cause confusion and are unnecessary. Row 6 shows that 7% of all insert declarations are re-declarations. Several drop statements for the same binding should also be avoided (row 3). Attempts to re-insert a binding already present in a persistent store or drop a binding not present will cause run-time errors.

The fourth and seventh rows of Table 4 relate to the methodology where code resides in updatable persistent locations in the form of procedures. Each such procedure should have exactly one corresponding program updating it. The measurements show that 9% of the procedures are not updated at all; 5% are updated twice or more. Not all the applications have explicitly committed to the methodology at the time of development. This is reflected in great individual variations. Generally, the extent of inconsistencies is clearly smallest in the COMMITTED group, but still not ignorable – automatic detection tools would be useful for all the applications.

3.2 Use of Names

Names are central to system builders' thinking and thus influence the way software is organised. Meaningful names are important for problem solving, understanding of semantic structure and memorisation [28-30]. Within an application people should use names with a consistent intended meaning. The choice of names for identifiers is crucial for the readability of programs and is particularly important when trying to administer and manage change.

A property of a name is its length. There may be different guidelines for the optimal length: the names should generally be long since long names can convey more information than short ones; the less frequently an identifier is used the longer it should be; the greater the distance between the declaration and use of an identifier the longer it should be; etc.[4] Another view is that the important thing is that the name is carefully chosen – which is independent of the name length (e.g. abbreviations can be very meaningful). The appropriateness of these guidelines, which are not mutually exclusive, is not an issue of this paper. The point is, however, that the thesaurus provides a means for testing the software against such guidelines.

3.3 Use of Types

The language under study (Napier88) supports a rich type system, including labelled Cartesian products (structures), labelled disjoint sums (variants), polymorphic procedures [31] and abstract data types [32]. Knowledge of the distribution of base types and type constructors (*kinds*) may be useful for language designers. The most

---

[4] However, longer names are harder to type correctly. There is therefore a case for completers and information retrieval tools that operate using the thesaurus.

frequently used kinds in all the applications are structures (records) and monomorphic procedures. Some kinds vary significantly, such as polymorphic procedures (from 0.1% to 10%). (The use of polymorphic procedures is discussed further in Section 3.4.) The abstract data type construct is hardly used (see Section 4.3).

Studies have confirmed that type definitions undergo considerable change in large application systems [33, 34]. Measurements on the use of type definitions are interesting when studying the consequences of type evolution. A change to a type definition in the applications under study would require 34 individual edits on average. In the best (but useless) case only the definition itself needs to be changed (no uses), while 3211 places in the worst case.

The argument above should be modified slightly. A renaming of a type definition would require all the places where the type identifier is used to be edited. If the expression of a type definition is changed, the places of use must be changed depending on the context and whether the type is parameterised. If a type identifier is used to create instances of the type denoted (16% of all uses), a change must be propagated to all places where the identifier is used to create new instances (five places on average in the applications). If a type identifier is used in the declaration of another type, in the signature of a procedure parameter declaration or in the construct used to access persistent bindings from a program (these three cases constitute 84% of all uses), a change does not affect the code if the type is not parameterised; only recompilation is necessary. (For the 18% of type definitions that are parameterised, the place of use must be edited if the number of parameters is changed.) However, in addition to the required edits on the places where a type is used, cascades of consequential change might be necessary (e.g. the places where instances of the types are used).

The number of programs affected by a type change may be a measure for how modular the code is. On average a type definition is used in respectively 38%, 13%, 12% and 5% of all programs in the OLD, STUDENTS, AWARE and COMMITTED groups, indicating that the "committed" programmers produce the most modular code. In any case, the measurements presented above confirm that software builders and maintainers need sophisticated change management tools and that SPASM will make this kind of change easier to manage.

The type equivalence model of the language must be taken into account when attempting to manage types. In a language with structural type equivalence, such as Napier88 [35], determining the consequences of type change can be difficult. The thesaurus information about the use of types, on which our measurements are based, may be incomplete. Instead of the name of a type definition, anonymous types may be used in value instantiations and other declarations. A problem occurs when an anonymous type is semantically the same as another explicitly defined type. This illustrates that programmers should be encouraged to use named types in order to facilitate efficient change propagation. However, sometimes using names only may impair readability. Change management tools could in those cases pass back information to the programmer on an interactive basis when an anonymous type is found that is equivalent to a changed named type. The programmer could then specify the desired course of action.

From the point of view of language implementors, information about the types involved in type checking would be useful to collect in a future study (Section 5). Choosing an efficient strategy for managing representations of types depends on the proportions of time spent on, for example, constructing the representations,

246

examining components of representations and testing for type equivalence over representations. In conjunction with dynamically gathered information of this kind, static information about the structure and use of types will help indicate the appropriate implementation strategy.

3.4 Use of Procedures

In an orthogonally persistent language providing first-class procedures, executable code can be contained in persistent stores in the form of procedures. Our study shows that this feature is heavily exploited: 58% of all bindings inserted into a persistent store are monomorphic or polymorphic procedures (as opposed to only 16% of the transient identifiers). The large proportion of procedures is primarily caused by the kinds of the analysed applications. The infancy of our programming environment has resulted in more tools and libraries than application systems with huge amounts of data.

The name, type or value of a procedure may change. A change to the value (body) will normally not require any propagation to other parts of the application. Renaming or changing the type implies in general that all places of use must be changed accordingly. In the analysed applications an average of five places was measured.

Language designers should note that polymorphic procedures, a relatively new construct, are becoming more widely used. Table 5 shows the use of polymorphic and monomorphic procedures in proportion of all identifier occurrences.

Table 5: Use of polymorphic and monomorphic procedures

Application group	Polymorphic procedures %	Monomorphic procedures %
OLD	1.4	18.1
STUDENT	4.7	21.8
AWARE	5.0	17.9
COMMITTED	7.6	20.4
MEAN	4.7	19.6

Useful information for language implementors is that 86% of the polymorphic procedures have only one quantifier, 13% have two and 1% have three. Moreover, the most efficient implementation strategy for polymorphic procedures will depend on the number of specialisations [25]. Procedures are specialised without call in only four of the 20 applications, in contrast to the belief that specialisation without call is the expected method of using polymorphic procedures [36]. This may affect the chosen implementation of polymorphism. In the four applications, 43% of the polymorphic procedures are involved in specialisations without calls, each procedure being specialised, but not called, on average 4.4 times, with 2.7 different type combinations. However, dynamic measurements of specialisations and calls are also important to get a complete picture of what is going on (Section 5).

3.5 Constancy and Name Usage

A value identifier is declared to be either constant or variable. The proportion of constants is between 2% and 47% in the applications and is significantly lower in the applications of the undergraduate students than in the other applications.[5] Section 3.1.2 reported measurements showing that in many cases programmers use variables where they should have used constants.

Name usage has been divided into type declarations, type uses, value declarations, left contexts and right contexts. Among the value identifiers respectively 33%, 5% and 62% occur in declarations, left and right contexts, indicating that identifiers are rarely updated compared with how often their values are read.

3.6   Persistent Store Operations

In the applications under study, it appears that in total about 20% of all name occurrences pertain to the access and manipulation of bindings within the persistent store. Figure 2 shows the distribution of the operations in terms of used, inserted and dropped bindings and a check to determine if an environment contains a certain binding. Introducing persistent bindings in the scope of a program is the dominant operation (73%). This is a tedious task that may impair programming efficiency – particularly for large applications with complex type expressions and many bindings. Furthermore, 10% of the identifiers declared in such binding specifications are unused (see also Section 3.1.2). This may result in confusing, verbose and inefficient programs. A binding construct represents a view of an environment (a partial specification of the environment's contents), but the precision in the view identification is lost if the view contains unused bindings as well. Hence, the measurements confirm the need for tools that (partly) automate the process of specifying bindings. Such tools are under development.

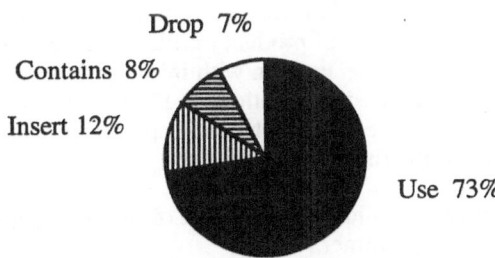

Figure 2: Operations over the persistent environment

The 20% proportion concerning operations over the persistent environment may be compared with corresponding measurements in other programming environments. One example is the classical figure in the persistent literature that typically 30% of all code in conventional languages is concerned with transferring data to and from secondary storage [37]. Comparing those figures requires a closer analysis, however. First, the current language system under test is not a complete self-contained persistent programming environment. Source and executable exist outside the environment, and on execution many bindings to data within the persistent

---

[5] Probably because the languages the students used previously did not offer initialising declarations.

environment must be made. As Figure 2 reveals, most of the 20% will be concerned with these bindings. Once the complete programming exercise may be carried out within the persistent environment, new technologies such as hyper-programming [38] may be used to remove almost all of this code. Second, even in the integrated persistent environment, such code may still be required when constructing programs in isolation from the data over which they will operate, for example constructing code in one store to be executed against another store [39]. However, note that finding bindings in the store requires relatively simple specifications, which might be (semi) automated. The literature's 30% contains complex data translation algorithms in addition to any binding constructs.

4 Analysis

Some of the results were discussed in the previous section. This section shows how a deeper analysis of the results gives input to further research in persistent methodology design, language design and programming environments.

4.1 SPASM

In the existing programming environment, where source programs are represented as Unix files, adherence to SPASM gives more well-structured (each program performs only one kind of operation on the persistent store, for example) and more maintainable programs (unused identifiers and bindings are an obvious source of confusion, for example). The results also show that there are fewer inconsistencies in the applications that have explicitly committed to the methodology. However, the study reveals many suggestions for improvement of SPASM.

In our study 8% of all value identifiers were unused, which is in contrast to, for example, 28% reported in a study of production PL/1 programs [10]. As opposed to Napier88, PL/1 does not allow declaration with initialisation, which is surely a cause for the large proportion of unused declarations in PL/1. Three quarters of the unused identifiers in our study were declared in binding specifications. This finding of the paper may suggest one of the following:

i) Binding specifications should be the subject of automation, possibly with some interaction with the programmer [19].

ii) In conjunction with new programming environments (Section 4.3), SPASM could evolve to actively support improved ways of binding values and type representations to programs.

Many inconsistencies relative to a methodology like SPASM might be due to poor software development or insufficient detection tools. On the other hand, programmers might deliberately violate the constraints due to new ways of constructing applications. For example, in the current version of SPASM a component should have only one update-program, but one could envisage programming styles where one would wish several update-programs for each component, e.g. a compiler could be implemented with different versions for different machine architectures. Each update-program may configure the application in a slightly different way, by inserting a component of the right type but with differing internals. The point is that the programming methodology and supporting tools should be easy to modify in compliance with changed working practices, which can be detected by measurements such as those reported in this study.

4.2 Suggestions for the Language Designers

Abstract data types are hardly used in the applications under study. (It should be noted though that many of the applications measured are system programs which would not be expected to depend heavily on the use of abstract data types of this kind.) Little use of a construct could indicate that it is useless, but in this case discussion with the language designers and with programmers indicates that the low usage is through lack of understanding of how to use them and of the extra power they give over first-order information hiding. Better tuition is required – a programmer's tutorial manual in particular.

The large proportion of variables not updated (35%) might suggest that identifiers in binding specifications, procedure headers, etc. should be declared constant by default, instead of variable which is the default at present. This is a borderline case, however, since given a reduction of 35% in the number of variables there would still be as many variables as constants.

4.3 Suggestions for Programming Environments

The results show that there are two areas requiring examination in the measured programming environment. The first involves the binding mechanism between components. The underlying binding architecture, where a component links to the typed *locations* of other components that it uses, and performs a dereference on each access, gives the advantage of type-safe incremental linking. However, the programming environment does not support a simple mechanism for setting up an application in this style; indeed, the dependence on dynamic binding constructs during application construction has been detected here as a major cause of programming inconsistency.

The second area for examination is the management of type information. In a persistent system, use of the type system plays a major rôle in any application for both data modelling and protection. The measured programming environment has very limited support for controlling type information causing essential processes such as type evolution to be hard to support. Even with a tool such as TSIT it is difficult to detect the manner in which types are used and related to one another.

The next generation programming environments [40] aim to overcome the problems detected here. The principal change is that the entire application construction process is supported within a single persistent environment. The separate processes of program construction, compilation, linking and execution may all be performed within the environment. The advantages of such a construction environment are described in [25].

Of interest here is the hyper-programming concept [38], where links to values and locations already existing in the persistent store may be included directly in source programs under construction. By analogy with hyper-text, a hyper-program is a structured version of the traditional flat source code representation that contains both flat code and links to language values. Using hyper-programming, linking between components and locations may take place during code construction, avoiding the requirement for the error-prone dynamic binding clauses required in the generator/update programs of the current programming environment.

Hyper-links may be used to represent the values of free variables in a source-code representation of a procedure closure. This style of source code, known as hyper-code, may be used to construct a source representation for any language value [41]. Using hyper-code, the two separate entities of source and executable exist as alternative views of a single value. A value may be analysed by directly examining its state via the bindings contained in its hyper-code source representation.

In addition, hyper-links to type representations may be included in programs. These may be used to form the basis of a type management system. Programs are linked only to the types they use directly. So the spread of type information, viewed as a problem here, is minimised.[6] Engineering reverse links from types to the programs that use them might optimise some aspects of the difficult task of type evolution [34, 42]. In general, the features supported by hyper-programming [43] will play a major part in the formulation of new programming methodologies in addition to the direct knowledge gained from use of current methodologies and the measurement results as described here.

5   The Next Generation Measurement Tools

TSIT gathers information based on a purely static analysis of the source code of the programs making up an application. A drawback of this approach is the inability to collect measurements on the dynamic behaviour of programs. Examples of dynamic measurements that have been requested by the language implementors and that cannot currently be determined using TSIT include:

- The proportions of type equivalence checks that fail and succeed. The efficiency of type equivalence checking is significant in persistent systems [44], and a measurement such as this would inform decisions on the appropriate implementation for the checking algorithm.

- Specialisations of polymorphic procedures. Information about the range and frequency of types used to specialise particular polymorphic procedures can be used to provide optimised implementations for those procedures. *Ad hoc* measurement techniques to gather this information have been used in an optimisation of polymorphic procedures described in [25].

In addition, TSIT is not well integrated with the operation of current persistent programming environments. Programs making up an application are passed to TSIT in isolation from the processes of compilation and linking. Unless use of such a tool can be simply incorporated into the programming process, it is unlikely to be used regularly. Solutions to these two problems will be addressed separately.

5.1   Integrating TSIT into a Persistent Programming Environment

TSIT may be integrated into a persistent programming environment by making it an optional part of the compilation process. It has many of the features of a parser anyway in its ability to examine code. Such features may be shared between both

---

[6] However, this approach does not help when we consider types as descriptive meta-data to aid program understanding. In that context identifiers are vital.

TSIT and the parser. For each application, a database of information may be built up as the separate components are compiled.[7] The TSIT part of the compiler may be parameterised by this database before compilation begins, enabling access to meta-data during compilation.

5.2 Measuring Dynamic Behaviour

In an integrated persistent programming environment, the compilation process may augment programs with extra code to gather information during subsequent execution of the compiled code. This information is cheaply retained in the persistent environment where it can be accessed by analysis programs at a later time. Whilst such a process is possible to achieve in a non-persistent programming environment, it will generally be more expensive as the compilation, execution and analysis phases are less well integrated. A full discussion of this style of measurement, used as part of a general optimisation scheme, is described in [45].[8]

In this context, the new version of TSIT has access to application source code and may add measurement code during the compilation process. The data gathered during execution may be made available to an analysis program making up part of the measurements suite. Linking the static and dynamic analyses is important and not yet done.

6 Conclusions

As a means to acquire more knowledge about persistent software engineering, relevant measurements should be obtained. Claimed problems and proposed solutions should be quantified. The explorative study of 108,000 lines of persistent language code in 20 applications reported in this paper is one step in that direction. Some of the results are applicable to any programming environment, for example:

- The extent of unused types, repeatedly declared types, unused variables, variables not updated, etc. confirm the need for automatic prevention or detection tools.
- Statistics on the use of type definitions and procedures illustrate the consequences of change and the need for change management tools.

Other results are specific to persistent programming:

- The effect of persistent design principles applied in some applications was measurable in terms of improved program structure and consistency.
- The study detected inconsistencies relative to a certain methodology such as bindings inserted into a persistent store but not used, repeatedly inserted bindings, bindings dropped more than once, etc. Automatic prevention or detection tools are needed.

---

[7] The disadvantage of this approach is that it slows compilation and collects "noise". It is a pertinent move to the design of the compiler but less to the design of the language. The registration model with user activated and periodic scans also has advantages and can be easier to use.

[8] Also Jackson's monitor at Glasgow allows relevant instrumentation [14].

In the current programming environment, in which source code is contained in Unix files, measurements show a relatively large proportion of code containing specifications of persistent bindings to be used in a program and a high inconsistency rate in this code. This indicates the usefulness of tools for (semi) automatic generation of such specifications when building applications in the current environment. In a fully integrated persistent programming environment [40], however, the proportion is expected to be significantly reduced.

The measurements were collected by first extracting information about all the identifier occurrences in all the software of the applications. The information was stored in a meta-database that was then the subject of statistical analysis. This measurement technique can be applied to any programming language. One example is an earlier study we conducted in an industrial (C, C++, X Window System and relational database) environment [34]. However, studying the pattern of how programs operate on persistent data, the consequences of change, etc. are simpler in a persistent programming environment in which only one language is used and the application programs, database schema (set of type definitions) and extensional data are integrated in the same store.

The results of this experiment enable us to design controlled experiments that could, for example, test the real effect of persistent programming methodologies and tools such as SPASM and EnvMake [19, 20]. Knowledge of the use of language constructs (little use of abstract data types, increased use of polymorphic procedures, etc.) is useful for language designers. The results also form a basis for further experiments on optimisation, consequences of change, etc. by combining static and dynamic analysis.

Acknowledgements

The St Andrews persistent programming team provided the underlying language technology and made several useful comments on the analysis and on this paper. We also thank the anonymous referees for their helpful suggestions for improvement. We are grateful to Paul Philbrow and others who helped providing the software that was analysed. Dag Sjøberg was supported by the Research Council of Norway. Some of the reported work was also supported by a European Community ESPRIT Basic Research Action, FIDE$_2$, number 6309.

References

1.   Dearle A, Shaw GM, Zdonik SB. Proceedings of the Fourth International Workshop on Persistent Object Systems, Their Design, Implementation and Use. Martha's Vineyard, USA, 23rd–27th September: Morgan Kaufmann, 1990

2.   Albano A, Morrison R. Proceedings of the Fifth International Workshop on Persistent Object Systems: Design, Implementation and Use. San Miniato, Italy, 1st–4th September: Springer-Verlag and British Computer Society, 1992

3.   Beeri C, Ohori A, Shasha DE. Proceedings of the Fourth International Workshop on Database Programming Languages – Object Models and Languages. Manhattan, New

York City, USA, 30th August – 1st September: Springer-Verlag and British Computer Society, 1993

4. Morrison R, Brown F, Connor R, Dearle A. The Napier88 Reference Manual. Technical Report PPRR-77-89, Universities of Glasgow and St Andrews, 1989

5. Atkinson MP, Sjøberg DIK, Morrison R. Managing Change in Persistent Object Systems. In: Nishio S, Yonezawa A, ed. First JSSST International Symposium on Object Technologies for Advanced Software. Kanazawa, Japan, 4th—6th November: Lecture Notes in Computer Science 742, Springer-Verlag, 1993, pp 315–338

6. Basili VR, Reiter RW. A Controlled Experiment Quantitatively Comparing Software Development Approaches. IEEE Transactions on Software Engineering 1981; SE-7(3):299–320

7. Law D, Naeem T. DESMET – Determining an Evaluation Methodology for Software Methods and Tools. In: Spurr K, Layzell P, ed. CASE, Current Practice, Future Prospects. J. Wiley & Sons, Chichester, England, 1992, pp 167–181

8. Knuth DE. An Empirical Study of FORTRAN Programs. Software – Practice and Experience 1971; 1(2):105–133

9. Card DN, Church VE, Agresti WW. An Empirical Study of Software Design Practices. IEEE Transactions on Software Engineering 1986; SE-12(2):264–270

10. Elshoff JL. An Analysis of some Commercial PL/1 Programs. IEEE Transactions on Software Engineering 1976; SE-2(2):113–120

11. Saal HJ, Weiss Z. An Empirical Study of APL Programs. Computer Languages 1977; 2(3):47–59

12. Bailey PJ. Performance Evaluation in a Persistent Object System. In: Rosenberg J, Koch D, ed. Third International Workshop on Persistent Object Stores. 10th–13th January 1989, Newcastle, New South Wales, Australia: Springer-Verlag and British Computer Society, 1989, pp 289–299

13. Loboz Z. Monitoring Execution of PS-algol Programs. In: Rosenberg J, Koch D, ed. Third International Workshop on Persistent Object Stores. 10th–13th January 1989, Newcastle, New South Wales, Australia: Springer-Verlag and British Computer Society, 1989, pp 279–288

14. Atkinson MP, Birnie A, Jackson N, Philbrow PC. Measuring Persistent Object Systems. In: [2], pp 63–85

15. Morrison R, Brown AL, Connor RCH, Dearle A, Kirby GNC, Cutts QI. The Napier88 Reference Manual (release 2.0). Technical Report CS/93/15, Department of Mathematical and Computational Sciences, University of St Andrews, 1993

16. Ritchie DM, Thompson K. The UNIX Time-Sharing System. The Bell System Technical Journal 1978; 63(6):1905–1930

17. Dearle A. Environments: A Flexible Binding Mechanism to Support System Evolution. In: 22nd International Conference on Systems Sciences. Hawaii, January 1989, pp 46–55

254

18. Morrison R, Brown AL, Dearle A, Atkinson MP. On the Classification of Binding Mechanisms. Information Processing Letters 1990; 34(1):51–55

19. Sjøberg DIK. Thesaurus-Based Methodologies and Tools for Maintaining Persistent Application Systems. Ph.D. thesis, Department of Computing Science, University of Glasgow, 1993

20. Sjøberg DIK, Atkinson MP, Welland R. Thesaurus-Based Software Environments. Workshop on Software Engineering and Databases in conjunction with the 16th International Conference on Software Engineering. Sorrento, Italy, 16th–17th May 1994

21. Lehman MM, Belady L. Program Evolution, Processes of Software Change. A.P.I.C. Studies in Data Processing No. 27. London: Academic Press, 1985

22. Gibson VR, Senn JA. System Structure and Software Maintenance Performance. Communications of the ACM 1989; 32(3):347–358

23. Dearle A, Cutts Q, Connor R. Using Persistence to Support Incremental System Construction. Microprocessors and Microsystems 1993; 17(3):161–171

24. Sjøberg DIK, Atkinson MP, Lopes J, Trinder P. Building an Integrated Persistent Application. In: [3], pp 359–375

25. Cutts QI. Delivering the Benefits of Persistence to System Construction and Execution. Ph.D. thesis, Department of Mathematical and Computational Sciences, University of St Andrews, 1993

26. Kendall MG. Rank Correlation Methods. (Second ed.) London: Charles Griffin, 1955

27. Banker RD, Datar SM, Kemerer CF, Zweig D. Software Complexity and Maintenance Costs. Communications of the ACM 1993; 36(11):81–94

28. Barnard P, Hammond NV, MacLean A, Morton J. Learning and Remembering Interactive Commands in a Text-Editing Task. Behaviour and Information Technology 1982; 1:347–358

29. Weiser M, Shneiderman B. Human Factors of Computer Programming. In: Salvendy G, ed. Handbook of Human Factors. John Wiley & Sons, 1987, pp 1398–1415

30. Anand N. Clarify Function! ACM SIGPLAN Notices 1988; 23(6):69–79

31. Cardelli L, Wegner P. On Understanding Types, Data Abstraction, and Polymorphism. ACM Computing Surveys 1985; 17(4):471–522

32. Mitchell JC, Plotkin GD. Abstract Types Have Existential Types. Twelfth ACM Symposium on Principles of Programming Languages. New Orleans, 1985, pp 37–51

33. Marche S. Measuring the Stability of Data Models. European Journal on Information Systems 1993; 2(1):37–47

34. Sjøberg DIK. Quantifying Schema Evolution. Information and Software Technology 1993; 35(1):35–44

35. Connor RCH. Types and Polymorphism in Persistent Programming Systems. Ph.D. thesis, Department of Mathematical and Computational Sciences, University of St Andrews, 1991

36. Morrison R, Dearle A, Connor RCH, Brown AL. An Ad Hoc Approach to the Implementation of Polymorphism. ACM Transactions on Programming Languages and Systems 1991; 13(3):342–371

37. Internal Report on the Contents of a Sample of Programs Surveyed. IBM Research Centre San Jose, California, 1978

38. Kirby G, Connor R, Cutts Q, Dearle A, Farkas A, Morrison R. Persistent Hyper-Programs. In: [2], pp 86–106

39. Atkinson MP, Buneman OP, Morrison R. Binding and Type Checking in Database Programming Languages. The Computer Journal 1988; 31(2):99–109

40. Morrison R, Connor RCH, Cutts QI, Kirby GNC. Persistent Possibilities for Software Environments. Workshop on Software Engineering and Databases in conjunction with the 16th International Conference on Software Engineering. Sorrento, Italy, 16th–17th May 1994

41. Connor RCH, Cutts QI, Kirby GNC, Moore VS, Morrison R. Unifying Interaction with Persistent Data and Program. Second International Workshop on User Interfaces to Databases, 1994

42. Connor RCH, Cutts QI, Kirby GNC, Morrison R. Using Persistence Technology to Control Schema Evolution. In: Deaton E, Oppenheim D, Urban J, Berghel H, ed. Ninth ACM Symposium on Applied Computing. Phoenix, Arizona: ACM Press, 1994, pp 441–446

43. Morrison R, Baker C, Connor RCH, Cutts QI, Kirby GNC. Approaching Integration in Software Environments. Accepted subject to revision, Computer Journal 10/93 1993

44. Connor RCH, Brown AB, Cutts QI, Dearle A, Morrison R, Rosenberg J. Type Equivalence Checking in Persistent Object Systems. In: Dearle A, Shaw GM, Zdonik SB, ed. Implementing Persistent Object Bases. Morgan Kaufmann, 1990, pp 151–164

45. Cutts QI, Connor RCH, Kirby GNC, Morrison R. An Execution Driven Approach to Code Optimisation. 17th Australasian Computer Science Conference. Christchurch, New Zealand, 1994, pp 83–92

System Evolution

Andrea Skarra

Software & Systems Research Laboratory
AT&T Bell Laboratories
Room 2B-101 600 Mountain Avenue
Murray Hill NJ 07974 USA

The last session on Thursday dealt with heterogeneity issues in building large persistent object system applications. Two papers were presented, one by David Blakeman on the inter-application communication mechanism in the Feinman system, the other by Jean-Claude Franchitti on the Amalgalme interoperability toolkit.

The first paper described a type-safe communication mechanism for interconnecting applications that need to share and communicate objects without sharing a common object type system. This addresses a common problem that arises in long lived industrial strength systems.

The Feinman communication mechanism is based on the interconnecting applications establishing an identity based type equivalence relation for the shared message types, and type checking at runtime that only messages of the expected type or its subtype are received. When the relationship between the message types can not be captured by simple subtype relationship, the Feinman system provides a mechanism called user-guided transformer, supported by tools, that allow the application integrator to introduce more complex mappings between the message types.

The second paper presented the Amalgame interoperability toolkit that supports integration mechanisms for combining and evolving existing persistent object systems. A designer interacts with the toolkit by submitting scripts written in Amalgame specification language. The two main toolkit components are the Amalgame framework, providing a repository of software components and application schemas, and the Amalgame toolset, providing an extensible set of services that operate on the framework by interpreting the Amalgame scripts. The toolkit was used in a concrete experiment to extend the Chimera hypertext link manager application from originally accessing a single persistent object base to accessing multiple persistent object bases.

Lively discussions followed both presentations and a joint discussion session went into gear when a discrete note from Malcolm was forwarded to Liuba pointing out that there was no joint discussion time planned in the program...

The discussion following David's presentation started out by Malcolm asking to clarify David's statement about large applications being boring, contrary to Malcolm's experience that large applications are the most interesting. Turns out, what David considers as boring is writing the large Cobol applications that he used to handle in the past. Instead of rewriting these Cobol applications anew to accommodate changes in other parts of the system, David prefers to build an infrastructure that allows him to reuse the old code by gluing together old and new application pieces. This is in fact the main motivation for his current work.

Peter Dickman asked what experiments could be used to evaluate the Feinman approach. David suggested that migrating an existing application to a new system and looking at the required modifications would be a good potential stress test for the Feinman framework.

Richard Cooper expressed a doubt, shared also by Malcolm, whether identity based type equivalence is at all practical in a very large system. David suggested that in real world applications shared types are "semantically co-ordinated" so even though there is no common type system, the interconnecting applications have a common model which is used to establish the type equivalence.

Peter Dickman wondered how the unique type names actually be achieved. David answered that uniqueness is obtained by a combination of a context and a unique identity within a context.

Malcolm wondered whether an application composition without a common type system is possible at all. David agreed that indeed it is a very hard problem and therefore the glue (transformers) is necessary.

Liuba questioned the scalability of the Feinman approach that requires pairwise connections and so n square mappings. David answered that in real applications only few types are widely used and shared while the rest are not. Moreover, in practice, one does not interconnect all application to each other which further reduces the total number of required pairwise mappings.

The discussion following the second presentation started out with David Grossman asking Jean-Claude how the Amalgame approach relates to the CORBA effort.
Jean-Claude explained that Amalgame supports CORBA OMG object service as one of the communication mechanism. The main focus of Amalgame is to address and explore complex interoperability issues that arise in providing additional OMG-compliant services like persistence, language translation, and activeness modules. Amalgame provides extensions to IDL and programming language bindings for supporting these various services.

Malcolm wanted to know what are the guidelines that an engineer could use in putting components together with the Amalgame toolkit. Jean-Claude explained that Amalgame uses active database technology to guide selection of the candidate components, infer about validity of their interconnections, and supply the partial mappings. This partially automates the process and therefore the engineer would need to resolve the limited amount of heterogeneity issues that cannot be resolved by the underlying rule base.

Peter Dickman was confused and asked for clarification of what is done where is this system. Jean-Claude explained that the main part of the work is done in the Amalgame services within the toolset.

Eliot wondered if the main complexity of the Amalgame approach resides in writing the wrappers. Jean-Claude answered that it all depends on how much of the required wrapper functionality is available initially.

Stephen Blott commented that hiding complexity in the wrappers is a practical approach but it can easily get out of hands and become too complicated. Jean-Claude replied that some of the services allow to generate wrappers automatically instead of writing everything by hand.

At this point, the above mentioned discrete message from Malcolm arrived..

Storage Class Extensibility in the Brown Object Storage System

David E. Langworthy
Stanley B. Zdonik

Department of Computer Science
Brown University
(del,sbz)@cs.brown.edu

Abstract

The Brown Object Storage System (BOSS) provides extensible support for persistence in a distributed multi-client, multi-server environment. BOSS is built on a loosely coupled, asynchronous computation model. One of the artifacts of asynchrony is increased extensiblity. This paper presents the storage class, the means by which the BOSS client interface is extended.

The BOSS prototype is completed and operated in a network of Sparc10s running SunOS 4.1. Currently the untuned prototype operates at 6 short transactions (20 reads, 4 writes) per second.

New applications such as CAD, hyper-media, and programming environments stress existing database technology to the limit [2]. Object Oriented Databases (OODBs) were developed to meet the demands of these new domains. OODBs support new application domains with extensible type systems that allow new abstractions to be added easily. All OODBs use some distinct service that provides stable storage for objects or pages, referred to as object servers and page servers respectively [11, 5, 19, 13, 1]. Whenever an OODB attempts to model a domain for which specialized secondary storage structures exist, the object store causes a problem. Concurrency control, recovery and other modules need to be changed in order to accommodate the new storage structure. An extensible object store would accommodate new interfaces without causing major disruptions to the existing system.

The Brown Object Storage System (BOSS) achieves extensibility by providing well defined interfaces to the designers of specialized storage structures. Through these interfaces the designer augments the structure with correct concurrent operation, fault tolerance and client-server distribution. BOSS aims to minimally constrain storage structure designers. To this end, BOSS is constructed from loosely coupled entities that cooperate asynchronously through well defined interfaces that communicate by message passing.

This work was partially supported by the United States Advanced Research Projects Agency order number 8220 under the Office of Naval Research contract number N00014-91-J-4085.

1   Architecture

Figure 1 illustrates BOSS as it fits into a distributed environment. It shows three end user applications: a VLSI tool, a CAD tool, and a Hyper-Media application. Each of these is implemented using a client OODB, which in turn is implemented on top of BOSS. Clients communicate with BOSS via a client stub. The client stub takes advantage of local resources and communicates over the network to take advantage of BOSS servers.

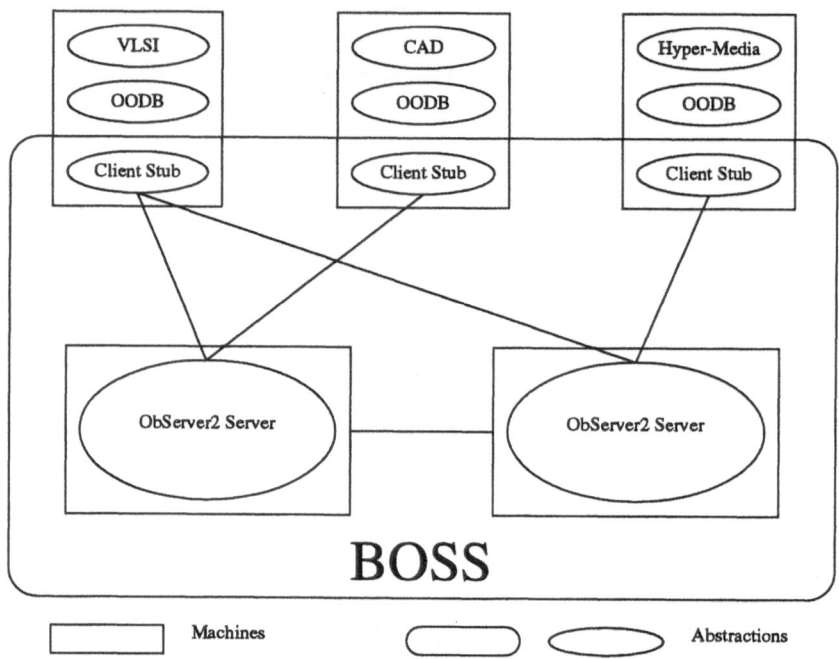

Figure 1: An overview of the BOSS system architecture.

BOSS's client stub runs in the address space of the client OODB. The protection boundary between the database and the application must be implemented by the OODB. Application-level operations can result in computation at the client or communication with the server. Not all operations will result in communication with the server. For example, if an object is cached at the client, no communication is needed at the time of either a read or a write. These operations are buffered and can be sent to the server at commit.

Servers are safe, relatively passive repositories for persistent information. Clients pull what ever information they need to accomplish their tasks from the servers. BOSS's computation model does not hide distribution. The client explicitly contacts each of the required servers. A server never forwards a method or object request to another server. The servers communicate with each other only to synchronize for distributed commit.

1.1 Vertical Partitions

Figure 2 takes a closer look showing an abstract view of BOSS system internals. The rounded rectangles are abstract data types (ADTs) that span the client and server. The rounded rectangle contains the operations which the ADT provides to the client OODB.

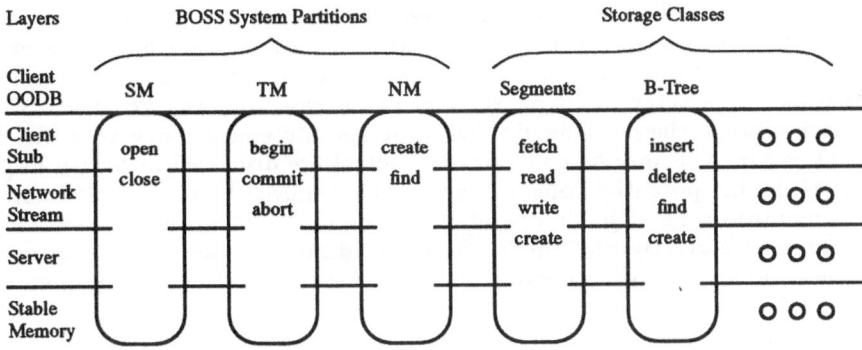

Figure 2: Layers & Vertical Partitions

BOSS allows new storage structures to be added to the system as a **storage class**. A storage class is a vertical slice through the layers in the memory hierarchy. Each piece of this slice has a well defined internal interface. The external interface it presents to the client OODB depends on the semantics of the storage class. Figure 2 shows BOSS configured with two storage classes: Segment and B-Tree. Segments are comprised of any number of variable sized byte streams which support **fetch, read, write**, and **create**. B-Trees contain associations between values and objects and provide **insert, delete, find**, and **create** operations.

Figure 2 also shows how BOSS vertically divides basic system services. There is a Session Manager (SM) which is responsible for maintaining connections to active clients and other servers. The transaction manger (TM) synchronizes the operations on all objects in all the different classes. The Name Manger (NM) allocates names that the classes use to identify objects. The basic system services are the same in all configurations of BOSS, only the storage classes change. The remainder of this paper describes exactly how the storage class fits into the vertical partitioning.

1.2 The Storage Class

The base implementation of BOSS includes one storage class that implements simple objects that consist of a byte stream and an Object Identifier (OID). These simple objects provide adequate support for many applications. A new storage class could be implemented if an application needed to take advantage of a specialized secondary storage structure.

One of the major advantages of a storage class is that it gives the implementor control over how and where the state of an object is implemented. As an example we can consider the B-Tree mentioned in Section 1. One way to implement a B-Tree would be to send its pages up to the client on demand

and perform the **insert**, **delete**, and **lookup** operations at the client. Alternatively, these operations could be sent to the server and performed there. The result would then be sent back to the client. Each option performs best under different workloads. BOSS allows both implementations to coexist.

Although the storage class has few constraints, all BOSS objects are addressed by a unique OID which encodes the class of an object and are stamped with a version number. An OID and a version number together identify a copy of an object. All copies of an object with the same version number and the same OID have the same state. BOSS uses an optimistic concurrency control algorithm which allows multiple versions of the same object to coexist.

Each storage class defines its own type specific concurrency control. The advantages of type specific concurrency control are discussed at length in [21]. In short, higher potential concurrency can be achieved by taking advantage of the semantics of an object's operations. The class determines if each object was accessed correctly and the Transaction Manager determines if the entire transaction can commit. Recovery is also based on an object's semantics.

2 Designing a Storage Class

The intended client of BOSS is an OODB or some advanced application with special storage requirements. The basic functionality that BOSS provides is enough to implement any such application. However, new application domains such as Geographic Information Systems or the Human Genome Project, occasionally require new storage structures, such as multi-dimensional search trees or structures for approximate string matching. Traditionally, such applications have to make a choice between using an OODB or taking advantage of their own specialized storage structures. Usually, the performance of a standard OODB is too poor and the application is built from scratch.

BOSS allows the addition of new storage structures. Adding new storage structures will not be a common activity, but the option is available to allow developers of new applications to integrate their specialized storage structures into BOSS.

2.1 Criteria for a Good Storage Class

The BOSS storage class designer requires special skills and an understanding of BOSS system internals. The first question the designer must answer is, "Should the abstract data type (ADT) under consideration be implemented as an abstraction in the application running above the object store or in the object store itself, as a storage class?" Nothing beats experience, but the designer can use this checklist as a guide.

A. Will significant performance advantages be gained by implementing the ADT as a storage class?

The primary reason for considering a storage class is to significantly improve performance. The BOSS storage class facility was designed to allow applications to use an OODB without losing the performance advantages of their specialized storage structures. BOSS gives the designer control of memory management so the performance of a storage class can rival that of a fully custom implementation built directly on the operating system. An added advantage of implementing an ADT as a storage class rather than on the OS is consistent transaction semantics across not only the one new ADT but all other ADTs incorporated into the object store.

This criterion is difficult to test without knowing the specific qualities that a storage class can exploit. The next several points expound on this theme.

B. Can the ADT exploit the storage media?

A storage class has direct access to both the server's disk for persistent storage and the client's disk for local disk caching. Significant performance improvements are attainable by exploiting the disk geometry. Sequential storage of B-Tree pages is one example, and sequential storage of large segments containing objects is another.

Another facility that BOSS provides in this area is the mapping of object identifiers to objects. OIDs are 32 bits long, but BOSS uses only the first 10 of these bits. The remaining 22 are left to the storage class to implement whatever sort of OID-to-storage mapping best suits its needs. A storage class that provides pages might use direct mapping, whereas a storage class that provides mobile objects would require more sophisticated OID-to-object mapping.

C. Is the access behavior predictable or exploitable?

If data access can be predicted, it can be exploited A storage class can have more knowledge about how its own data is accessed. It knows both the semantics of the operations it provides and the history of the objects it manages. Using this information, a storage class can make predictions about future access behavior. It can exploit this knowledge by moving an object to the appropriate place in the memory hierarchy. An object that will be accessed in the near future can be moved closer to the client, and an object which will not be used for some time can be moved further from the client to free limited resources.

D. Does the ADT offer new functionality that cannot be constructed using existing storage classes?

The base configuration of BOSS includes the fixed segments storage class, which provides generic objects that are no more than unique OIDs associated with byte streams. There is little that cannot be constructed with this class of objects, but occasionally there is a need for different functionality. Active objects require the setting of triggers and therefore require more functionality than any passive storage class can deliver.

E. Does the ADT offer enough general utility to warrant the effort of constructing a new storage class?

This last criterion is just good software engineering practice. A storage class should serve as wide an audience as possible, and if it will not be generally used, don't build it. To improve the utility of a storage class, reduce the functionality to the absolute minimum. Often a specific functionality is needed in a particular application domain, such as gene-sequence matching in the Human Genome Project. The BOSS approach is to include only the core functionality in a storage class and build the rest of the functionality as an application.

To demonstrate the use of this checklist we consider three different abstractions– the B-Tree, the employee, and the condition variable (CV)– and their implementations as storage classes. Almost every database implements a B-Tree for associative access, so *a priori* it is a likely candidate. Another common element in business databases is the employee object. The implementation of the employee as a storage class is more questionable because this abstraction is usually included as an application-level object, not built in to the database. However, an objective of BOSS is to help capture and exploit the semantics of objects, so we will consider the employee as a storage class to see how well if fares. The condition variable is on the other end of the commonality spectrum from the B-Tree. A CV is common in multi-threaded operating systems but does not exist in any database implementation. However, a CV is a very desirable tool in modern database implementations. Triggers and cooperative transactions, neither of which are implemented within BOSS, could be implemented as a layer above the database using the CV as a fundamental building block. Table 1 shows the results of applying the to each ADT.

Table 1: The Criteria Evaluated for Three Potential Storage Classes

	B-Tree	Employee	CV
A.	√	X	√
B.	√	X	X
C.	√	X	X
D.	√	X	√
E.	√	√	√

Not surprisingly, the B-Tree turns out to be a highly desirable candidate for implementation as a storage class. Its pages can be laid out sequentially, its nodes are always accessed from the root downward, and its operations provide opportunities for more concurrent interleavings.

The Employee as a storage class does fare as well. This abstraction can be handled effectively in an existing record oriented database. The one operation that could be optimized is iterating through all employees, but a B-Tree could be used for this operation.

The CV is an interesting case. It does not have specialized storage structures or predictable access behavior. It is, however, an active object and cannot be constructed using any passive storage class. Also, there is a broad class of applications that can take advantage of a CV. For these last two reasons, the CV would make an excellent storage class, and it will be used as an example later in the paper.

3   Recovery & Persistence

A key design decision that makes the storage class notion feasible is our approach to recovery. This approach is based on operation logging and asynchronous update of copies. Thus, a storage class does not have to constantly return cached object versions whenever a transaction commits.

BOSS relies on the service of a persistence layer (i.e. the stable store) to achieve stability for data and transactions. This layer consists of two fundamental components. One is a memory-mapped log and the other compontent is a database partition that contain the base versions of the data. Durability of modifications made by transactions is achieved by entering an intentions record in the log. The coordination of the log and the heap of base versions that provides full persistence.

A new recovery algorithm, no-redo write ahead logging (NR-WAL), reduces the overhead of recovery. Intentions lists are used to eliminate the undo phase of recovery [3]. There is no redo phase because NR-WAL does not require and up-to-date copy of an object to exist, so it does not need to be recreated immediately after a crash.

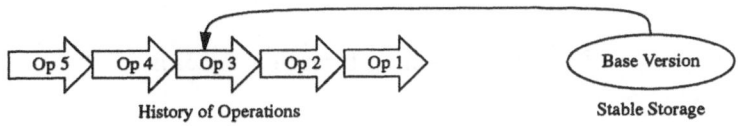

Figure 3: Components of the Current State of an Object.

The stable state of an object is composed of a base version and a sequence of operations called a history. Operations could be as simple as read and write or more sophisticated semantic operations such as insert, delete, and lookup. Operations are either modifications or observations. An observation does not change the state of the object.

Figure 3 shows the history of a series of modifications on an object. The modifications are stored in a list with the most recent operation at the head of the list. The base version contains a pointer to the last operation that was applied to the base version. During normal operation the base version can fall behind the current state. The object is brought up-to-date by applying the appropriate operations from the history. In the figure, the base version is two operations out-of-date. Applying **Op 4** then **Op 5** brings the object up-to-date.

3.1   Implementation

A further explanation of NR-WAL requires a discussion of our concurrency control algorithm. BOSS uses a timestamp based, optimistic concurrency control algorithm [10]. A transaction stores its operations in operation records. These records are collected in an intention list [3]. During the transaction the intention list is incrementally sent to the server then written to a sequential log in stable storage. Figure 4 shows the transaction table and two intention records in the log.

A record in the log is addressed by its log sequence number (LSN). As records are added to the log, their LSNs strictly increase. Since the LSN of an

266

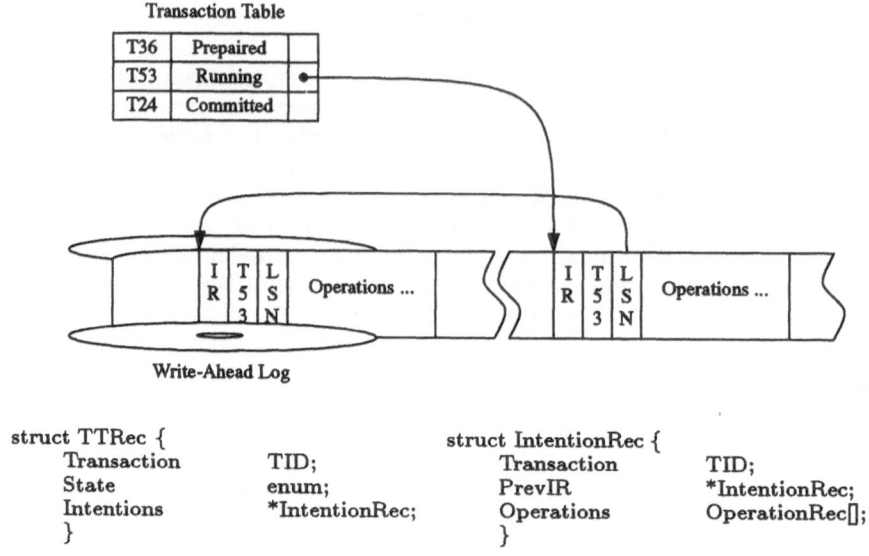

Transaction Table

T36	Prepaired	
T53	Running	•
T24	Committed	

Write-Ahead Log

```
struct TTRec {                          struct IntentionRec {
    Transaction      TID;                   Transaction      TID;
    State            enum;                  PrevIR           *IntentionRec;
    Intentions       *IntentionRec;         Operations       OperationRec[];
}                                       }
```

Figure 4: Chaining Intention Records

operation is a strictly increasing value, it can be used as a timestamp for the purpose of concurrency control. To check for correctness, every operation in the intentions list contains the version of the object it should be applied to. The version "points" directly to the previous operation on the object. These links implement the history of operations shown in Figure 3.

The operation record stores the OID and the LSN of the copy that was read. An modification operation changes the state of the object. So, in addition to the OID and the LSN of the object its operation record needs some indication of how to transform the old state in to the new state. It can take the form of an operation, a new value, or a delta. The choice of how to derive the new value from the old value and what to log is made on a class by class, operation by operation basis.

Applying the appropriate operation to a copy of an object brings that copy up-to-date, but it does not actually modify the base version. It only modifies the copy in volatile memory. The base version is finally modified when the buffer manager at the server needs more space. The buffer manager keeps track of which objects have been modified and sends them to stable storage before it discards a volatile copy.

4   The Fixed-Segment Storage Class

The storage class in the base configuration of BOSS is the fixed segment storage class (also known as Fixed). It provides objects clustered into segments. Neither the objects nor the segments can change size after creation, thus the name Fixed. The functionality and implementation of these segments are similar to those provided by the original ObServer system [11].

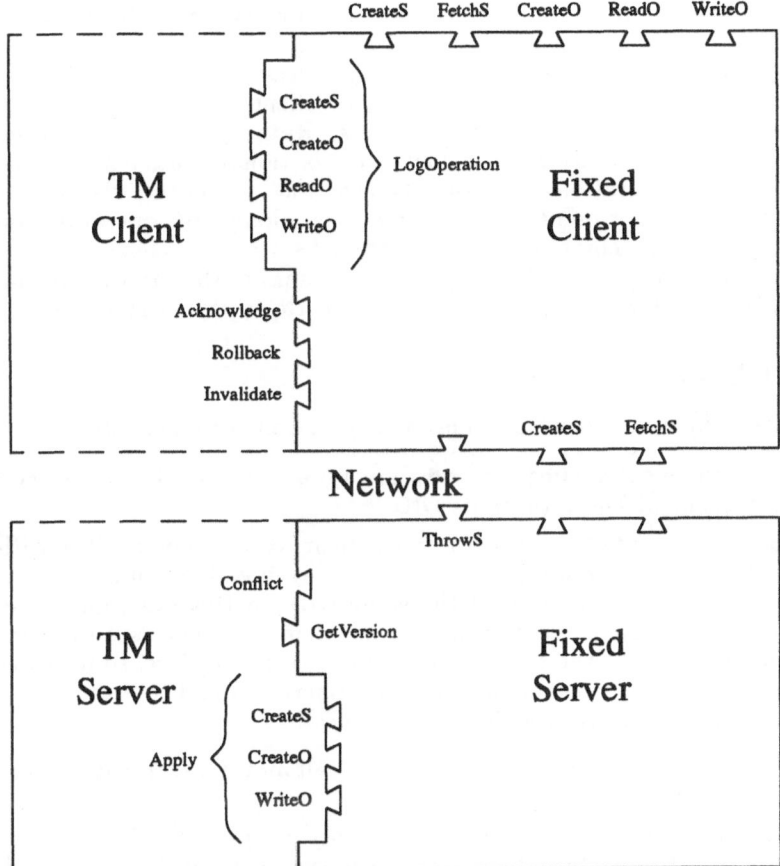

Figure 5: The Fixed Storage class module interface.

A segment is a collection of variable length byte streams. A byte stream is what is typically meant by an object in an object store, although in BOSS the meaning of object is more general. To be explicit, the segments are called fixed segments and the byte streams are called fixed objects. The fixed segment and each fixed object have a unique identity. Identifiers are structured so that the class of an object can be determined by the identifier. The implementation of the Fixed storage class encodes the identity of the segment in the identity of each object it contains.

Figure 5 zooms in on the interaction between the storage class and the transaction manager and the distribution of the storage class across the client and server. The interface has four main components: Fixed to client, Fixed to TM client, Fixed to TM server, and Fixed client to Fixed server.

The API that Fixed provides to BOSS clients runs along the top of the diagram. This interface is completely determined by the storage class. BOSS places no restrictions on the client interface that a storage class provides.

The interface between the client and server portions of Fixed runs along the middle of the diagram. This interface is also unrestricted. Notice that it is a peer-to-peer interface not strictly client-server.

A standard interface seperates the storage class and the transaction manager on both the client and server. Storage class clients do not directly call transactional operations on storage class servers. Rather, the transaction manager moderates these operations to achieve transactional consistency. The Fixed client passes operations to the transaction manager via the generic **LogOperation** entry point. These operations, along with operations on other storage classes are combined into intention lists by the client portion of the transaction manager. If these operations commit, the transaction manager applies them to the base versions via the generic **Apply** entry point.

4.1   Client Interface

The Fixed client interface[1] provides five operations to its clients.

FixedStatus CreateS(ObjID& oid, unsigned size); This call creates a new segment and returns its OID.

> Because **CreateS** creates a new segment, it does not conflict with operations on any existing objects. The only possible conflict occurs when two segments are assigned the same OID. In this case, one transaction must be aborted. To prevent this problem, the client stub makes a synchronous rpc to the server portion of the storage class, so it can assign a unique OID. The client then logs this operation and the resulting OID for persistence and transactional correctness.

FixedStatus FetchS(ObjID& oid); This call moves a segment into the client machine.

> **FetchS** makes no modifications and does not give the client access to any objects. It merely indicates that the segment will be used in the near future and that it should be resident. Because it has no impact on transactional correctness and makes no changes to the persistent state, this operation does not need to be logged. It simply makes an asynchronous call to the server requesting the segment.

FixedStatus CreateO(ObjID& oid, unsigned size); This call creates a new object and returns its OID.

> Like **CreateS**, **CreateO** does not conflict with operations on existing objects. The only possible conflict occurs if two objects are assigned the same OID. The client specifies the segment where the object should reside and this location is encoded in the OID to differentiate objects created in different segments. This encoding makes concurrent creation of conflicting OIDs unlikely. The operation generates the OID locally at the client without contacting the server. The operation and the resulting OID are logged for persistence and transactional correctness.

FixedStatus ReadO(ObjID& oid, FixedObject *&obj); This call notifies the system that the object is to be read and returns a handle to the object.

---

[1] The interfaces here are taken directly from the BOSS implementation.

The handle returned by this call is implemented as a virtual memory pointer which requires that the object be resident. If the object is not resident, its segment will be synchronously fetched from the server. Once this operation is complete, the segment is pinned in virtual memory (see Section 6). The segment is pinned so the handle will be valid until the end of the current transaction. ReadO can cause a transaction to abort if it returns old data, so before the call returns, the operation is logged for transactional correctness.

FixedStatus WriteO(ObjID& oid); This call notifies the system that the object has been modified.

Clients have virtual memory pointers to objects they have read. These pointers allow the clients to make modifications directly on the cached copies. However, these modifications will not become permanent unless the WriteO operation is called. This operation takes the modifications from the object and logs them for persistence and transactional correctness.

4.2   TM Client Interface

The storage class client and the transaction manager client have a peer-to-peer relationship. The storage class client informs the transaction manager of the operations it performs during a transaction. In return, the transaction manager informs the storage class client of global events that could affect the correctness of future operations.

4.2.1   Transactional Operations

The transactional operations performed at the storage class client in the client interface are not passed directly to the server portion of the storage class. Rather, they are mediated by the transaction manager to ensure that no out-of-date objects are observed and that only committed operations take effect. A client gathers an operation's relevant information into a record and gives the record to the transaction manager at the client via the generic LogOperation entry point. LogOperation constructs an intentions list that eventually is sent to the server.

OperationRecord, in Figure 6, contains a tag defined in Figure 8 that indicates what sort of operation is being performed. Next, it stores the LSN of the copy that the operation observed. Then the OID of the object the operation affects appears. The final entry that all operation records contain is the size of the entire record. Individual storage classes add entries to the operation record's structure to contain whatever information they need to check the operation for correctness and propagate its effects.

The FixedOpRecord is passed as data after an OperationRecord. All Fixed's operations record the size of the object. CreateO records the offset at which the object is allocated in the segment header. For a WriteO operation, this same location is the beginning of the new value of the object.

```
class OperationRecord {
public:
    OperationType        type;
    Lsn                  object_lsn;
    ObjID                oid;
    unsigned long        record_size;     // length of entire record

    // There will be more data here following these fields. The record_size
    // field contains the length of the header plus this extra data.
    };

class FixedOpRecord : public StorageOpRecord{
public:
    unsigned  osize;     // size of the object
    unsigned  offset;    // offset is the begining of the data field
    char *data()         {return (char *) &offset;}
    };
```

Figure 6: The definition of the operation record

4.2.2 Callbacks

The TM client informs Fixed of the state of objects through three calls:
Invalidate, Acknowledge, and Rollback.

```
class ClientStorageClass : public StorageClass {
public:
    virtual int  Invalidate(VerList&);
    virtual void Acknowledge(VerList&);
    virtual void Rollback(VerList&);
    };
```

Figure 7: The interface all storage classes clients present to the TM

The server calls Invalidate to notify clients of objects that have been
updated. Invalidate passes all updates performed at the server since a certain
point in time and then selects from the notification those objects that are
cached locally and either discards them or requests the most recent version.
Acknowledge is called after a transaction commits. It contains the new LSNs of
all the objects the transaction modified. It places those new LSNs in the objects
at the client, thereby completing the transaction, so the dirty copies of old
versions become clean copies of the new versions. When a transaction aborts,
Rollback discards all of the modified objects in the clients cache. Invalidate
takes care of the out-of-date copies that caused the abort.

4.3 TM Server Interface

All classes register their transactional operations in the class OperationType
(see Figure 8).   Each operation is assigned a numonic operation code
(FIX_OP_WRITE_O and so on). Transactional operations support isModifier and
all operations that are modifiers support Apply. The TM determines whether
a committed operation is a modifier and, if so calls Apply which dispatches
the appropriate storage class operation (AppFixedWriteO etc.) based on the

operation code. The storage class operation is given raw data which it casts to the appropriate type so that a method may be called.

```
class OperationType {
  public:
    enum   StorageOpType {
        STORAGE_OP_NULL,
        FIX_OP_CREATE_S,
        FIX_OP_CREATE_O,
        FIX_OP_READ_O,
        FIX_OP_WRITE_O,
        STORAGE_NUM_OPS
    };

    int    isModifier()const;

    int    Apply(StorageClass *, const ObjID&, const Lsn&,  StorageOpRecord *);

  private:

    int    AppFixedCreateS(FixedServer *, const ObjID&, const Lsn&,
                           FixedOpRecord *);
    int    AppFixedCreateO(FixedServer *, const ObjID&, const Lsn&,
                           FixedOpRecord *);
    int    AppFixedWriteO(FixedServer *, const ObjID&, const Lsn&,
                          FixedOpRecord *);
};
```

Figure 8: Definition of `OperationType`

The TM has no knowledge of the operations clients perform. Therefore, it cannot determine or moderate their concurrent semantics. This is handled generically by `Conflict`. Each storage class implements its own conflict predicate, which returns true if a conflict occurs and false otherwise. To provide a consistent interface to the rest of the system, the common functionality of all the server portions of storage classes is bundled together in the `ServerStorageClass` shown in Figure 9. The name manager and the server storage class cooperate to determine which conflict predicate to use. The transaction manager calls `ServerStorageClass::Conflict` with the LSN of an operation record. Using the OID in the operation record, the name manager determines the class to which the operation belongs. `ServerStorageClass` then calls a method on the appropriate storage class.

```
class ServerStorageClass : public StorageClass {
 public:
    static bool Conflict(const Lsn&);

 private:
    virtual bool LocalConflict(const Lsn&) = 0;
};
```

Figure 9: Definition of `ServerStorageClass`

`Conflict` determines if any previously committed operation conflicts with the operation currently under consideration. Each storage class determines exactly the semantics that it wants its operations to have and encodes those in the conflict operation. The concurrent semantics of the fixed segment storage class operations are described at their introduction. The pseudo-code in Figure 10 shows the implementation of the semantics.

```
bool
FixedServer::LocalConflict(const Lsn& lsn) {
    // Cast the LSN to an OperationRecord
    OperationRecord *or = (OperationRecord *) lsn;

    if (or->object_lsn.isNull()) {
        // The operation is a creator
        if (_tm->GetVersion(or->oid) == NULL)
        // No one else has already created it.
            return FALSE;
        else
            // The OID has already been used
            return TRUE;
    }
    else {
        // Get the previous operation from the version table
        Lsn *prev = _tm->GetVersion(or->oid);

        if (*prev == or->object_lsn) {
            // Read the most up-to-date version
            return FALSE;
            }
        else {
            // Read an out of date object, Abort
            return TRUE;
            }
    }
}
```

Figure 10: Pseudo-code for the fixed segment conflict operation

Storage classes must implement the **Conflict** operation to provide consistent transaction semantics for its operations. Sorting through the C++ code in Figure 10 reveals a simple binary decision tree with four leaves. The first condition tests whether the operation is a creator or not. If the operation is a creator, **CreateS** or **CreateO**, the only possible conflict is the previous existence of another object with the same identifier. If the operation is not a creator it is either **ReadO** or **WriteO**. In either case the operation succedes if the most resent version of the object was observed and fails otherwise. Falure occurs when another transaction performs an wrte after the current transaction's read but before the commit.

4.4   Internal Client Server Interface

The client stub is built on a network services layer that connects it to the server portion of the storage class. It implements its services using the API presented in Figure 11. The two calls from the client to the server are **CreateS** and **FetchS**. **CreateS** takes an OID and a size parameter. **FetchS** takes an OID as an argument and returns a pointer to a memory object (see Section 6) containing the desired segment unless an error occurs then it returns some error status indicating why it could not complete the operation. The one call from the server to the client, **ThrowS**, passes the client a segment asynchronously.

```
class ClientRPCDisp : public MTCP_RPCDisp {
public:
    // Generate a unique id and reserve space at the server.
    FixedStatus RPCFixCreateS(ObjID&, unsigned);

    // Synchronously move a segment to the client
    FixedStatus RPCFixFetchS(const ObjID &, Mo *&);
};

class ServerRPCDisp : public MTCP_RPCDisp {
public:
    // Asynchronously move a segment to the client
    FixedStatus RPCFixThrowS(const Fixed & , const SesID & );
    };
```

Figure 11: The API for fixed segment network services

Notable by their absence are **ReadO**, **WriteO**, and **CreateO**. None of these operations requires any resources from the server during a transaction because they all operate on segments cached in memory or on local disk. If the segment is resident, the client stub logs the operations and the transaction manager takes care of the rest as described in Section 4.3. If the target segment is not cached, this call generates a **FetchS** and waits for it to complete before proceeding.

CreateS does not actually have to contact the server. A client stub could be implemented that generated the OID locally. The problem with this approach is the uniqueness of the OIDSemantically, creating two segments at the same time does not cause a conflict. However, if the implementation assigns them both the same OID a conflict occurs at the physical level.

5   Adding a Condition Variable Storage Class

Once the designer has an ADT that is a good candidate for implementation as a BOSS storage class, the interface of the ADT must be refined and integrated into the BOSS framework. The process begins by determining the ideal semantics of the ADT and gradually refining the interface to maintain the necessary invariants for correct concurrent, fault-tolerant operation. To illustrate the refinement process, we use the condition variable. A standard CV provided by an operating system has the following operators:

Create This operator creates a new condition variable

Wait This operator suspends the calling thread.

Signal This operator signals the condition and wakes one blocked thread.

Broadcast This operator signals the condition and wakes all blocked threads.

The CV needs several semantic refinements to be used in a transactional context. A transaction contains a thread of control, but there is no formal concept of thread in BOSS. Signal and Broadcast are somewhat redundant. The semantics of Signal can actually be implemented using Broadcast and another simple read/write object in a transactional context.

Further, in the proceding description a well defined notion of time is taken for granted. Such a notion does not exist in BOSS and must be constructed using the facilitates that BOSS provides. Unlike threads, transactions have a well defined ordering.

CV semantics must prevent a transaction from waking up <u>before</u> it is signaled. For example, transaction S signals the variable and then does some work before it commits. Transaction W wakes up and commits immediately. W is likely to be serialized before S, a clear violation of CV semantics.

Another problem, that a transaction can be awakened by a transaction that aborts, creating the appearance that the transaction was awakened by nothing at all. For example, transaction S signals the variable, then transaction W wakes up, and then transaction S aborts. A transaction that aborts must appear to have never run, so W appears to have been awakened by nothing at all.

Both of the previous problems arise from a transaction which is signaled and commits before the transaction that signaled it. We correct the problems by enforcing an ordering on the condition variable's operation. A transaction which signals a condition variable must commmit before a transaction that is awoken by the signal. This constraint creates a well defined, but artifical, notion of time for the condition variable.

The constraint is implemented using timestamps. Wait keeps track of the timestamp of the condition when it was called. Notify increments the timestamp when it commits. Wait cannot commit successfully if the timestamp is the same as when the condition was first observed. The first column in table shows the time stamp of the condition variable. All operations are tagged with the timestamp of the version that was observed.

Table 2 consists of three possible interleavings of two transactions. The first two interleavings have a semantic error that causes an abort. The last interleaving does not have and error, so both transactions commit successfully.

The first interleaving has the problem that transaction W tries to commit before transaction S. This sequence is forbidden because the timestamp on the base object is equal to that of the version observed.

The second interleaving has the problem that transaction W apparently wakes up for no reason, though it is actually awakened by transaction S's notify and abort. Again transaction W cannot commit because the timestamp on the base object is equal to that of the version observed.

In the final interleaving, Transaction S notifies and commits before Transaction W thereby incrementing the timestamp and allowing Transaction W to commit.

Table 2 does not explicitly show the log, but its contents can be inferred. Location 73 in the log stores an operation record containing "notify@57." Location 98 stores an operation record containing "notify@73." The actual records contain more information, but it is clear that modifiers for the CV storage class also form a linked list.

Determining the concurrent semantics of the candidate storage class is the first step in integrating a new storage class into BOSS. The next step is determining how the semantics can be implemented using the facilities that BOSS

Table 2: Condition Varable Semantics

Condition	Transaction S		Transaction W	
@57	begin	ok	begin	ok
	wait@57	(delay)		
			notify@57	ok
	(resume)	ok		
	commit	fail		
@73			commit	ok
	begin	ok	begin	ok
	wait@73	(delay)		
			notify@73	ok
	(resume)	ok		
			commit	fail
	commit	fail		
	begin	ok	begin	ok
	wait@73	(delay)		
			notify@73	ok
	(resume)	ok		
@98			commit	ok
	commit	ok		

provides. Now the storage class designer is ready to begin integrating the storage class into BOSS.

5.1 Storage Class Integration

This section presents the integration of the CV storage class (Cond) into the existing BOSS system.

5.1.1 CV Client Interface

Cond is different from Fixed in many ways, but integrating Cond requires a similar description of the operations. One difference is that clients never requires access to the representation of a Cond object. Another difference is in the size of a Cond object. Buffering these objects is not much of an issue, so there is no explicit fetch operation for the Cond storage class.

CondStatus Create(ObjID& oid); Create a new CV and return its OID.

Like the create operators for Fixed, Create does not conflict with any existing object. The only possible conflict is the return of an OID that was already allocated. To avoid this possibility, Create makes a synchronous call to the server.

CondStatus Notify(ObjID& oid); Wake up all transactions waiting on this CV.

As the transaction examples illustrate, waking up another transaction before the notifier commits is likely to cause aborts, so the implementation of Notify actually does nothing except log the operation. After the transaction commits, the cache coherency policy informs other clients that the object is out-of-date.

`CondStatus Wait(ObjID& oid);` Block until the condition variable is notified.

Wait simply logs the operation and blocks until the cache coherency policy notifies the client that the object is out-of-date. At that time, the Wait call returns, and the transaction can continue processing.

5.1.2 CV TM Server Interface

The three operations that Cond registers with OperationType are COND_OP_CREATE, COND_OP_WAIT and COND_OP_NOTIFY. Figure 8 illustrates the requirements for Fixed; the additions necessary for Cond are trivial. A more significant difference exists in the Conflict operator because it has very different semantics.

```
bool
CondServer::LocalConflict(const Lsn& lsn) {
    // Cast the LSN to an Operation Record
    OperationRecord *or = (OperationRecord *) lsn;

    // Get the previous operation from the version table
    Lsn *prev = _tm->GetVersion(or->oid);

    if (or->type == COND_OP_CREATE) {
        if (prev == NULL)
            // No one else has already created it.
            return FALSE;
        else
            // The OID has already been used
            return TRUE;
    }
    else if (or->type == COND_OP_NOTIFY) {
        if (*prev == or->object_lsn)
            // Read the most up-to-date version
            return FALSE;
        else
            // Read an out of date object, Abort
            return TRUE;
    }
    else if (or->type == COND_OP_WAIT) {
        if (*prev == or->object_lsn)
            // No one has called Notify, Abort
            return TRUE;
        else
            // Notify has been called
            return FALSE;
    }
    else
        // There is an error.
        return TRUE;
}
```

Figure 12: C++ code for the CV Conflict operation

Again, in Figure 12 we have a decision tree. The first two cases are analogous to those in Fixed. The creator succeeds so long as the OID has not already been allocated and Notify succeeds so long as it observed the most recent state of the object, which raises the question of why Notify should ever fail.

The examples in Section 5 do not show an invocation of **Notify** ever failing, because the only semantic constraint on the CV is that a transaction cannot be awakened before another transaction notifies it. There is no semantic constraint on when notify can be called. There is, however, a physical conflict. A physical conflict in the absence of a semantic conflict is called a false conflict.

Simple read/write objects such as pages or the variable length objects in Fixed naturally link modifiers in a linear order because the write operation both observes and modifies the state of the object. A modifier that does not observe the state of the underlying object is said to be a blind operator [21]. **Notify** is such an operator. Blind operators never cause semantic conflicts, but can cause physical conflicts.

BOSS recovery has a physical requirement that modifiers be linearly linked. In Weihl's terminology, modifiers cannot commute. For Cond, this means that **Notify** can cause an abort. This constraint is not as bad as it might at first seem. First, any physical conflict that occurs in BOSS would occur in a system that offered only physical concurrency control; thus, BOSS is strictly better than a physical system with respect to false conflicts. Second, observers can commute over modifiers, and modifications tend to be less frequent than observations, which implies modifier/modifier conflicts are far less frequent than modifier/observer conflicts.

The final operator, **Wait**, does cause semantic conflict. The semantics of **Wait** are that it cannot commit before the transaction that notified it, which means that a modification must occur between the time the transaction waits and the time the transaction commits. Thus, **Wait** causes a conflict if the object is in the same state as when it was first observed, in direct contrast to almost every other possible operator.

5.1.3 CV TM Client and Internal Interface

The Cond server is trivial. All it needs to do is keep track of the most recent version of every CV and give clients access to this information. The operations that it provides to the client are correspondingly simple.

Create generates a unique identifier, as explained in Section 4.1. **Fetch** is needed because the client needs to know the most recent version of the CV when **Wait** is called. Note that no state is returned. Since, no state is required for Cond there is no **CondOpRecord**. Cond uses the default operation record because this record contains all the information on what operation was invoked on which object and when the invocation occurred, and that is all that Cond requires.

6 Memory Object Management

The storage class allows new ADTs to be added safely. Memory Object Management (MOM) makes the addition of a storage class easier. MOM hides much of the complexity of dealing with the operating system and mediates between conflicting demands of storage classes. We considered many architectures for this service and experimented with several. The one we have settled on places one MOM on each BOSS host, client or server. This provides the storage class

```
class ClientRPCDisp : public MTCP_RPCDisp {
public:
    // Stuff for Fixed deleted . . .

    // Generate a unique id
    CondStatus RPCCondCreate(ObjID&, unsigned);

    // Synchronously give the client the most recent version number
    CondStatus RPCCondFetch(const ObjID &, Lsn &);
};
```

Figure 13: RPC Stub for the Cond internal interface.

implementer with a consistent interface, reuses the MOM source code, and gives BOSS intelligent client disk caching.

The unit of memory that MOM manages is the Memory Object (MO). A MO is a variable length, continuous piece of memory. All MOs have a piece of non-volatile memory allocated to them. When the storage class needs to use the MO, it pins the MO into virtual memory. This does not guarantee that the page will be loaded into RAM, but it does allocate a virtual memory handle that the storage class can use to access the contents of the MO.

6.1 Storage Class Interface

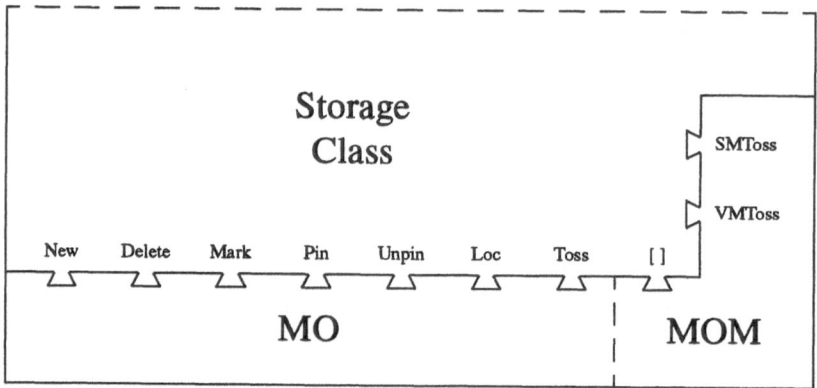

Figure 14: The Storage Class interface to the Mom module.

The interface that MOM presents is the same at both the client and the server. Most interactions are with Memory Objects themselves. Actually, MOM presents only one operation to the storage class which will be discussed later. The MO interface is fairly straight forward. There are seven calls:

new (int size) (ObjID oid) New creates a new memory object of the requested size, pins it into virtual memory, and returns a handle to that memory. The MO is associated with the OID passed to the constructor.

delete *Mo Delete frees the non-volatile memory and any virtual memory associated with the MO.

`int mark()` Marks the object read for the purposes of the default replacement algorithm. Mark returns 1 on success.

`void *pin()` Pin allocates a portion of virtual memory to the MO and returns a pointer to that memory if successful.

`int unpin()` Unpin does not deallocate memory, it only gives MOM the option to do so.

`void *loc()` If a MO has virtual memory allocated to it, Loc will return its address without pinning the object or allocating virtual memory. Storage classes use this call to determine whether or not an MO is already cached.

`int toss()` Toss indicates that the storage class will not be using the MO for some time and that it should be discarded.

Just as important as the calls in the MO interface are the calls that are not. There are no calls to mark a MO dirty or to write its contents out to disk. MOM handles these tasks, but notifies the storage class when it takes an action via the two callbacks:

`int VMToss(Mo *mo)` MOM notifies the storage class that it intends to discard an object via this call. The storage class does have the option of refusing the request. The storage class should only do so if the MO will be used in the immediate future. Consistently refusing to discard MOs will quickly cause the entire system to deadlock.

`int SMToss(Mo *mo)` SMToss serves the save function that VMToss but in the domain of non-volatile memory. This call is only made at the client where non-volatile memory is used as a cache. The server non-volatile memory is used only for persistent MOsso if it fills up new simply fails.

The last operator we have to discuss is the association operator, [ ]. There was a great deal of debate about whether to include this operator. Its function is simple, given an OID return a MO, but it has major implications on the sort of storage classes that can be constructed. It does not restrict the interface of the storage class, but it does have some performance implications.

A performance critical operation in an OODB is the mapping of logical OIDs to physical data locations and there are many ways this mapping can occur [16, 6, 4]. Previous MOM designs did not include this mapping. The rationale was that storage classes should implement what ever logical to physical mapping that best suits its semantics. For instance this would allow a storage class that implemented pages to compute the physical location from the logical identifier and save a table lookup. However, MOM does not allow a class to choose a MO's physical location, so this is not of much use. A storage class which required this sort of mapping could be built with out using MOM, but this would require a greater implementation effort.

The design decision for this iteration was that MOM should also perform the physical to logical mapping since MOM determined the physical location of MO sThis decision did not significantly complicate the implementation of MOM and greatly simplified the implementation of the existing storage classes. A future design may allow specialization of the association operator which would allow storage classes to choose its implementation. Static binding in C++ makes this sort of specialization difficult to accomplish.

6.2   Example B-Tree Memory Management Policy

B-Tree page replacement is an example of how a storage class can use MOM to achieve good overall resource utilization. MOM implements a global LRU policy. LRU performs well for general purpose computing but fails for special applications. To correct this in BOSS the B-Tree augments the global policy to exploit the semantics of its application. B-Trees are always accessed from the root downwards, so there is no point to keeping a child of a node that is being discarded. This augmentation occurs within the VMToss and SMToss calls. Whenever a node is discarded, the storage class recursively descends the tree using loc and tosses all resident child nodes.

6.3   Related Work

The topic of object servers has been well explored in the literature. Here we draw comparisons with this work. Further, as an extensible system, BOSS must be compared to efforts to create extensible databases in the relational community. Finally, BOSS draws from novel distributed file system technology so the similarities and differences are noted.

6.4   Object & Page Servers

ObServer [11], the precursor to BOSS, introduced several features: semantic clustering of related objects, a novel lock set for cooperative work, and a notification system which also supports cooperative work. BOSS improves on ObServer in the areas of distribution, extensibility, and performance. ObServer offered only multi-client, single-server distribution. There was some work done to tie together multiple servers, but it lacked correctness guarantees. Much of the functionality that ObServer offered is encapsulated in the segment storage class within ObServer 2. The ability to add new storage structures allows BOSS to be specialized for high performance on specific applications.

The Exodus Storage Manager (ESM) [5], a page server developed at Wisconsin, provides support for values and indices. It generalizes the Aries Transaction Recovery System [15] to operate in the client-server model. Aries uses the concept of a Log Sequence Number to reduce the time that a lock must be held and facilitate recovery in a pessimistic system. The Aries implementation of a Log Sequence Number is different from that presented here, but the concept is basically the same. The LSN is a strictly increasing address into the log. The BOSS implementation allows faster access to a record in the log by using memory mapping.

The Mneme Persistent Object Store [16] explores the integration of an object store with a persistent programming language. It provides a persistent heap of objects that are available in a distributed system. The object model for Mneme is fixed, but it does offer some support for specialized buffering policies. A general policy is called a strategy and an instantiation of a strategy is called a pool. For example, a strategy might be LRU paging and a specific pool might be an LRU cache with 2000 elements. Every object belongs to a pool and this pool can change. Planned improvments to Mneme will allow it to provide resiliant storage in a fully distributed environment.

Camelot [8] is another system that could be classified as a page server, but with a slightly different computation model. Camelot provides the abstraction of persistent virtual memory to data servers that run on the same node as the persistent data is stored. A Camelot server node must perform all disk I/O and computation associated with a transaction. The BOSS model allows clients to operate on remote machines and lets a specialized server can handle all disk operations, so client workstations with large main memories and fast CPUs cache their data and perform computation locally instead of using an RPC call to a remote server for every computation.

The Avalon [8] language uses Camelot to provide a persistent C++. Because Camelot provides only persistent virtual memory, the semantics of the objects implemented in Avalon are lost at the persistence layer. BOSS captures semantics within the persistence layer to allow for special memory management policies or type specific concurrency control.

Arjuna [7] offers functionality similar to Avalon, but the internal architecture is completely different. There is no seperate persistence layer. Persistence is implemented within Arjuna using replication and atomicity is provided based on read/write locking.

6.5 Extended Relational

Starburst [18] extends relational databases in five areas, external data storage, storage management, access methods, abstract types, and complex objects. Many of the issues that Starburst addresses are at the data model level and should be compared to an OODB, not to an object store. Abstract types, complex objects, and most of the access methods fall into this category. The one category of access method that is comparable within BOSS are what Starburst calls "exogenous" access methods. Starburst adds new functionality with specialized components "on the side" of a conventional database system. These components will be "called as they are needed directly from within components of the primary system." "An 'exogenous' access method is one for which the data structure used to store access information is not managed by the primary database system."

This differs from the BOSS architecture which is designed to add new functionality in a new storage class. In BOSS the storage class can define its own storage layout and access methods as Starburst allows. In addition, a BOSS storage class can define its concurrency control semantics at the level of the operations it supports rather than at the level of physical storage. We exploit the concurrency semantics of these operations. A new BOSS storage class actually extends the BOSS interface with a new ADT. The storage class implementor has exact control over whether parts of the abstraction are built up at the client or the server.

The goals of the Postgres Storage Manager are instantaneous recovery, historical access, and utilization of new technology [20]. Postgres provides a linear history and allows more than one version of an object to be viewed in a transaction. Since Postgres keeps the entire history of all its data, the recovery system differs from conventional systems. It provides instantaneous recovery without using conventional write ahead logging (WAL) or disk shadowing. Their algorithm requires large amounts of Non-volatile main memory to perform as well as WAL for normal processing. BOSS's NR-WAL performs as well as WAL during normal processing and offers instantaneous recovery without the requirement of large amounts of non-volatile memory.

6.6 File Systems

A page server is very close to a file system with added support for transactions. Two interesting developments in file systems that influence BOSS, the Sprite Log Structured File System (LFS) and the Andrew File System (AFS).

LFS is interesting because it shows the feasibility of reading from a log given a reasonable cache. BOSS uses this facility to accelerate recovery and simplify transaction management data structures. LFS [17] keeps all data in a log, significantly reducing the cost of a write. The disadvantage of a log is that it does not support random access. The file location information must be kept stable resulting in a major overhead cost because it is constantly changing. In an object store the problem would be even worse because of the finer granularity of naming. Also, garbage collection in a distributed persistent heap is much more complex than segment compaction [14].

AFS is interesting for its distribution properties. AFS 3.x [12] is a distributed file system that serves a similar purpose to Sun's NFS. However, the scale of the distributed system that AFS can operate within is much larger than Sun's NFS. NFS was meant to operate within a single organization, while AFS can handle global distribution. One interesting feature of AFS that BOSS shares is non-volatile client caching. Data can be cached on a client's local disk for extended periods of time. Cache coherency becomes a problem when caching data for long periods of time. AFS introduced call back locking which caches locks as well as data at clients. Franklin [9] shows that this is a desirable protocol for database systems as well. Failures cause problems with consistency when locks are cached. AFS solves this problem by using locks that expire after a well known period of time. BOSS does not require that the cache be kept perfectly coherent. The version number associated with each object will indicate whether the object is up-to-date, so BOSS can tolerate failures without any special means.

References

[1] M. Atkinson et al. The persistent object management system. Technical Report PRRR-1, The Universities of Glasgow and St. Andrews, 1983.

[2] F. Bancilhon, C. Delobel, and P. Kanellakis, editors. *Building an Object-Oriented Database System: The Story of O_2*, chapter 1. Morgan Kaufmann, 1992.

[3] P. Bernstein, V. Hadzilacos, and N. Goodman. *Concurreny Control and Recovery in Database Systems.* Addison Westley, 1987.

[4] A. Brown and J. Rosenberg. Persistent object stores: An implementation technique. In *The Fourth International Workshop on Persistent Object Systems*, 1990.

[5] M. Carey et al. Object and file management in the EXODUS extensible database system. In *Proceedings of the Twelfth International Conference on Very Large Data Bases*, pages 91–100, Kyoto, Japan, August 1986.

[6] G. Delott. Performance improvements in the observer object server. Masters thesis, Department of Computer Science, Brown University, 1989.

[7] G. Dixon, G. Parrington, S. Shrivastava, and S. Wheater. The treatment of persistent objects in arjuna. In *Proceedings of the Third European Conference on Object-Oriented Programming*, July 1989.

[8] J. Eppinger, L. Mummert, and A. Spector, editors. *Camelot and Avalon.* Morgan Kaufmann, 1991.

[9] M. Franklin and M. Carey. Client-server caching revisited. In *Int'l Workshop on Distributed Object Management*, Edmonton, Canada, 1992.

[10] M. Herlihy. Apologising versus asking permission: Optimistic concurrency control for abstract datatypes. *ACM Trans. on Database Systems*, 15(1):96–124, March 1990.

[11] M. Hornick and S. Zdonik. A shared, segmented memory system for and object-oriented database. *ACM Transactions on Office Information Systems*, 5(1):70–85, January 1987.

[12] J. H. Howard et al. Scale and performance in a distributed file system. *ACM TOCS*, 6, 1988.

[13] B. Koch et al. Cache coherency and storage management in a persistent object system. In *The Fourth International Workshop on Persistent Object Systems*, 1990.

[14] E. Kolodner, B. Liskov, and W. Weihl. Atomic garbage collection: Managing a stable heap. In *ACM SIGMOD Proceedings*, 1989.

[15] C. Mohan et al. Aries: A transaction recovery method supporting fine-granularity locking and partial rollbacks using write-ahead logging. *ACM TODS*, 17(1), 1992.

[16] J. Eliot B. Moss. Design of the Mneme persistent object store. *ACM Trans. Inf. Syst.*, 8(2):103–139, April 1990.

[17] M. Rosenblum and J. K. Ousterhout. The design and implementation of a log-structured file system. In *13th SOSP*, 1991.

[18] P. Schawarz et al. Extensibility in the starburst datbase system. In *Intl. Workshop on Object-Oriented Database Systems*, 1986.

[19] E. Shekita and M. Zwilling. Cricket: A mapped, persistent object store. In *The Fourth International Workshop on Persistent Object Systems*, 1990.

[20] M. Stonebraker. The design of the postgres storage system. In *Proc. 13th VLDB*, 1987.

[21] W. Weihl and B. Liskov. Implementation of resilient atomic data types. In *ACM Transactions on Programing Languages and Systems*, April 1985.

Correctness of Lazy Database Updates for Object Database Systems

Fabrizio Ferrandina
Thorsten Meyer
Roberto Zicari

J. W. Goethe-Universität
Fachbereich Informatik
Frankfurt am Main, Germany

Abstract

Current object database management systems support user–defined conversion functions to update the database once the schema has been modified. Two main strategies are possible when implementing such database conversion functions: immediate or lazy database updates. In this paper, we propose a correctness criteria for implementing conversion functions as lazy database updates. We also show that the algorithms defined in [1] are correct.

1 Introduction

Schema evolution in an object database system (ODBS) refers to the ability to change both the schema and consequently the database [2], [3], [4]. Every time the schema is modified the database has to be updated to be brought up to a consistent state with respect to the new schema.

Normally a schema can be changed using special primitives, see for example [2]. As a consequence of a schema change, in some database systems the database is modified automatically by executing so called user-defined *conversion functions* [1], [4], [5], [6], [7]. A conversion function takes as input parameters the old and new schema class definitions and when executed transforms the objects of the database to conform to the new schema.

The designer has to define a conversion function for each modified class in the new schema. Default conversion functions are applied in case no explicit conversion functions are given by the designer [5], [6], [8], [9].

From an implementation point of view, conversion functions are updates to the database. There are mainly two strategies for implementing database conversion functions:

1. Conversion Functions as Immediate Database Updates: with this approach the database system executes the conversion functions on *all* objects of the modified classes as soon as the schema modification is performed. All objects of the database are transformed, both *logically* and *physically*, to be consistent with the new schema definition *before* any further program can use again the database.

The advantage of this solution is that after execution of the conversion functions the entire database is in a consistent state wrt the new schema.

The problems with this approach are:

- All running programs have to be suspended until the application which updates the database is finished. The database remains locked until the database update is finished. The time when the database is locked can be very long depending on specific parameters, e.g. size of the database, type of update performed, object retrieving strategy, etc..

- All objects of the modified classes have to be updated at once. This could be expensive, especially if the system does not internally keep class extents.

2. Conversion Functions as Lazy Database Updates: with this approach objects are expected to *logically* conform to the new schema after the change to the schema has been performed, but, they are *physically* restructured and transformed by conversion functions only when they are *effectively* used. If and only if an object is accessed and it is in an old format (and value), then it is transformed to the new definition (and value) consistent with the current definition of the schema. Note that the schema may undergo in the meanwhile several changes before an object is really used.

The advantage of this solution is that we do not have to lock the entire database to execute a conversion function. Only objects that are effectively used are transformed.

The problems with this approach are:

- There is the need to store and "remember" the *history* of all schema updates that have been performed in the system.

- Every time an object is accessed by an application, a test has to be done in order to check whether the object is already in the new format/value or not, i.e. if the object has to be updated or not.

We believe it is important that whatever strategy is chosen to implement conversion functions, the result of execution of conversion functions must be the same [10].

This paper analyses the algorithms for performing deferred updates presented in [1] and proves some useful properties such as "correctness".

The rest of the paper is organized as follows: in Section 2 we first present by means of an example how conversion functions are defined and associated to one or more schema transformations. We then give the formal definition of a conversion function execution.

In Section 3 we point out that, when implementing conversion functions as database updates using a lazy approach, special care has to be paid to conversion functions which use objects of different classes. We call such conversion functions complex. In Section 4 we give the formal definition of correctness of a lazy database transformation. In Section 5 we prove some properties of lazy updates algorithms. In 6 we present the conclusions and future work.

2 User-defined Conversion Functions

We show in this section how conversion functions are normally defined and associated to a modified class. For more details the reader is referred to the user manuals of database systems such as ObjectStore [6], GemStone [5].

Changing the schema in an ODBS implies changing the database, i.e. the changes to the schema have to be "propagated" to all objects in the database. We will refer to this activity as database transformation. The database system should perform the database transformation after a schema modification has been made. Transforming an object in the database means changing its internal structure and its value. Changing the objects internal format is task of the database system and it is done automatically.

Changing the objects value is a typical application-dependent task. The most common applied solution is to allow the schema designer or application builder to define a conversion function which "instructs" the database systems how to change the value of the objects. A conversion function is associated to the class that has been changed.

If no conversion function is provided for a modified class, the system uses a default conversion function for the transformation.

We show the use of conversion functions with a simple example. We use throughout the paper the notation of the O_2 Object Database System [11], [12]. However, the results presented here are general and applicable to a broader class of ODBSs.

2.1 An Example

Example 1: Consider that at time t_0 we have defined the following schema, called *Test_schema*:

```
time t0:    class X type tuple ( a : Y,
                                  b : real )
            end;

            class Y type tuple ( j : integer,
                                 k : X )
            end;
```

If the designer wants to change this schema, say at time t_1, adding an attribute c of type *real* to class X, he/she will have to write a conversion function that tells the system how to compute the value of the new attribute c for objects of class X already stored in the database.

In the example this is done by the compute_c conversion function associated to the updated class X defined as follows:

```
time t1:        modify class X type tuple ( a : Y,
                                            b : real,
                                            c : real )
                with conversion compute_c {
                    new->c = 2 * old->b; }
                end;
```

In the conversion function, "->" returns the attribute value of an object. Old refers to an object conforming to the structure of class X before the modification has been performed, whereby new refers to the same object after its modification. In the conversion function the transformation is not defined for all the attributes of class X but only for the attribute c.

We assume default conversion functions are *always executed on objects before a user–defined conversion function is executed*. This simplifies the writing of user–defined conversion functions. In fact, in the example, there is no need to write trivial transformations such as:

```
new->a = old->a; new->b = old->b;
```

These transformations are taken into account by default conversions[1].

2.2 Conversion Function Execution

We consider a conversion function as a program updating objects in the database as a consequence of a schema change. We represent the general execution of a conversion function $cf_i[x]$, where x is an object of class X, as a sequence of read, write, and delete operations as follows:

$$rcf_i[x] \rightarrow \Big[dcf_i[x]\Big] \rightarrow \Big\{rcf_i[y_j]\Big\}_n \rightarrow wcf_i[x]$$

where: $[\ldots]$ denotes an optional operation, and $\{\ldots\}_n$ a sequence of n operations. $rcf_i[x]$ denotes that object x is read by the conversion function cf_i, $dcf_i[x]$ denotes that part of object x is deleted by the conversion function (due, for instance, to a *delete attribute* operation), $rcf_i[y_1], \ldots, rcf_i[y_n]$ denote that objects other than x are read in the database, and finally $wcf_i[x]$ is the write operation on x. Adding information to x (due, for instance, to an *add attribute* operation) is represented by means of $wcf_i[x]$. The arrow $\rightarrow$ indicates the order of execution of the operations.

The subscript identifies the particular conversion function and distinguish it from other conversion functions that happen to access the same object. We assume that no conversion function reads or writes an object more than once.

The formal definition of an execution of a conversion function is the following:

Definition 1 (Conversion function execution) *A conversion function execution $cf_i(x)$ transforming an object x of class X (denoted as $x \in ext(X)$) is a partial order with ordering relation $<_{cf_i}$ where:*

1. $cf_i(x) \subseteq \{rcf_i[y], dcf_i[x], wcf_i[x] \mid x \in ext(X),$
   y is an object in the database$\}$;

2. $rcf_i[x] \in cf_i(x)$;

---

[1]For reasons of brevity, we do not mention here the transformation rules used in the default conversion. Default transformations are automatically executed by the database system for all modified classes and are defined by considering each kind of class change and determining how to transform existing objects to conform to the new class definition while retaining the maximum amount of information.

3. *for any operation* $p = rcf_i[y] \in cf_i(x)$ *with* $y \neq x$
$$rcf_i[x] <_{cf_i} dcf_i[x] <_{cf_i} p <_{cf_i} wcf_i[x].$$

Condition (1) defines the kind of operations allowed in a conversion function. Condition (2) says that this set contains at least the operation $rcf_i[x]$ (when a conversion function is executed on an object, the object has to be read). Condition (3) is a restriction on the partial order representing the order of execution.

We will usually represent the execution of conversion functions as directed acyclic graphs with the arrow indicating the ordering defined by $<_{cf_i}$.

In our example, the conversion function compute_c can be represented as follows:

$$compute\_c[x] = rcf_{compute\_c}[x] \rightarrow wcf_{compute\_c}[x]$$

where $rcf_{compute\_c}[x]$ denotes that x is read in the database, and $wcf_{compute\_c}[x]$ denotes that an attribute has been added to x and has been appropriately initialized. The operations $dcf_{compute\_c}[x]$ and $rcf_{compute\_c}[y]$ with $y \neq x$ do not occur because no attribute is deleted from x and no objects other than x are read.

In order to differentiate conversion functions from application programs, we give hereafter the formal definition of an application execution. As for conversion functions, we assume that no application reads or writes an object more than once. We denote application reads and writes by $r[x]$ and $w[x]$, to distinguish them from reads and writes of conversion functions.

Definition 2 (Application execution) *An application execution a_j is a partial order with ordering relation $<_{a_j}$ where:*

1. $a_j \subseteq \{r_j[x], w_j[x] \mid x$ *is an object in the database*$\}$;

2. *if* $r_j[x], w_j[x] \in a_j$, *then either* $r_j[x] <_{a_j} w_j[x]$ *or* $w_j[x] <_{a_j} r_j[x]$.

When conversion functions and applications are executed, their operations may be interleaved depending on whether the lazy or the immediate database transformation is implemented. In both cases, operations performed by applications are mixed with conversion function operations. In the next section we will present concrete examples showing that, in the lazy database transformation, the result of mixing conversion functions and applications operations can lead to an undesired database transformation. In section 4 we give the formal definition of a "correct" execution of a conversion function.

3 Implementation Problems of Lazy Database Updates

Special care must be taken when implementing user-defined conversion functions with lazy database updates.

In this section we show two important problems that have to be taken into account when implementing conversion functions under the above assumption.

3.1 Complex Conversion Functions

Reconsider the definition of the schema *Test_schema* after its last modification at time t_1 (see Section 2). Suppose at a later time, say t_2, we have modified the attribute j of class Y to be of type *real*. The value of j is computed by the following expression: $j = k \rightarrow b * j$. This is expressed by the conversion function **compute_j** associated to the class Y as follows:

```
time t2:    modify class Y type tuple ( j : real,
                                         k : X )
            with conversion compute_j {
                    new->j= old->k->b * old->j ;
            }
            end;
```

Assume later, at time t_3, we modify the type of the attribute a of class X to be of type *real* instead of a reference to class Y. The class modification along with the conversion function are presented below:

```
time t3:    modify class X type tuple ( a : real,
                                         b : real,
                                         c : real )
            with conversion deref_a {
                new->a = old->a->j;
            }
            end;
```

Let us now assume we make a final modification at time t_4 deleting the attribute j from the class Y. The new definition of class Y is:

```
time t4:    modify class Y type tuple ( k : X )
            end;
```

The modification performed at time t_4 does not have any conversion function associated to it. This means that the default conversion is used for the transformation of the objects.

Using the notation presented in Section 2, an execution of the three conversion functions can be represented as:

$$compute\_j[y] = rcf_{compute\_j}[y] \rightarrow rcf_{compute\_j}[x] \rightarrow wcf_{compute\_j}[y];$$
$$deref\_a[x] = rcf_{deref\_a}[x] \rightarrow rcf_{deref\_a}[y] \rightarrow wcf_{deref\_a}[x];$$
$$default[y] = rcf_{default}[y] \rightarrow dcf_{default}[y] \rightarrow wcf_{default}[y].$$

In Figure 1 we show a graphical representation of the schema modifications performed on the two classes. Classes connected by a solid arrow mean a modification has been performed on them, the label on the arrow indicate the user-defined conversion functions.

We should also note in the example the difference between the conversion function **compute_c** associated to X at time t_1 and the conversion function

290

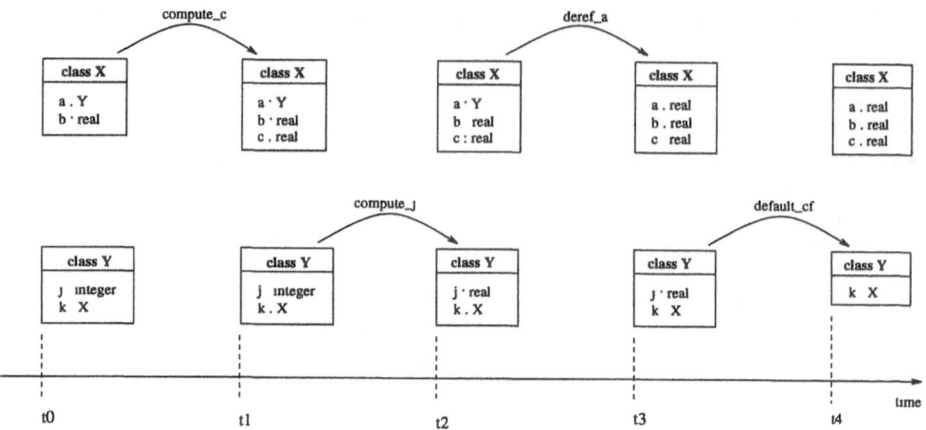

Figure 1: Schema evolution until time t_4.

deref_a defined at time t_3 . For the first one the value of a "restructured" object of class X is computed using the objects local value only. The second one uses the value of an object belonging to another class in the schema, i.e. class Y.

This is an important distinction when implementing conversion functions, as we will see in the rest of this section. We therefore classify conversion functions as follows:

- *Simple conversion functions*, where the transformation of the object is done using only the local information of the object being accessed (for example the conversion function defined at time t_1).

  A general execution of a simple conversion function is represented as follows:

  $$rcf_i[x] \rightarrow \left[dcf_i[x] \right] \rightarrow wcf_i[x],$$

  no $rcf_i[y]$ operations appear between $rcf_i[x]$ and $wcf_i[x]$.

- *Complex conversion functions*, where the object transformation is done using the local value of the object **and** other objects of the database other than the current object being accessed (see the conversion functions defined at time t_2 and t_3).

  A general execution of a complex conversion functions is represented as follows:

  $$rcf_i[x] \rightarrow \left[dcf_i[x] \right] \rightarrow \left\{ rcf_i[y_j] \right\}_n \rightarrow wcf_i[x]$$

  with $n \geq 1$.

3.2 Conversion function execution: Correctness

Complex conversion functions implemented as lazy database updates pose some problems. We show the problems by means of examples.

Let objects x and y of class X and Y respectively, be conformant to their class definitions in the schema as defined at time t_2 (see Figure 2).

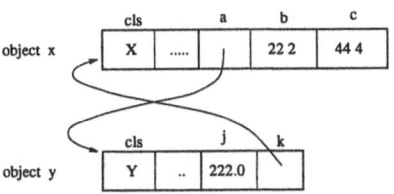

Figure 2: Objects x and y conforming to their class definitions at time t_2.

Our assumption is that, no matter what strategy is used for implementing conversion functions, the expected result of a lazy transformation of x and y should be "equivalent" to the result obtained with the execution of the same transformation in an immediate way.

In the example, if the immediate transformation were used, this would require that at time t_2 all objects of class Y must be transformed before the modification on X at time t_3 can take place. The same is true at time t_3: all objects of class X must conform to the new definition of the class before the update on Y at time t_4 can be performed[2]. In Figure 3 the modifications to objects x and y respectively at time t_3 and t_4 are shown in the immediate database transformation approach.

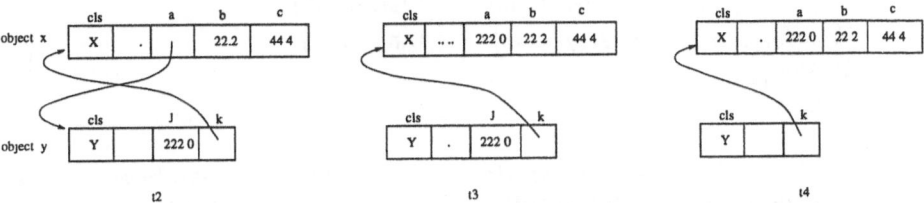

Figure 3: Evolution of objects y and x using the immediate database transformation.

Consider now that the same update is performed using the lazy database transformation. Suppose that at time t_4 objects x and y have not been accessed by an application since time t_2. Since we use lazy updates, the structure of x and y is not changed from the one they had at time t_2. If at time t_a, with $t_4 < t_a$, an application accesses the object y, then y is restructured automatically by the system and its new value is computed applying the default transformation. In Figure 4 the restructured object y is shown at time t_a.

If, at time t_b, with $t_a < t_b$, the application uses object x, then x has to be restructured and its new value has to be computed applying the conversion function deref_a defined at time t_3.

---

[2]To keep the exposition simpler, we suppose that an immediate database update is launched every time a modification on a class has been performed. I.e. at time t_i, all objects of the updated class are transformed before the modification at time t_{i+1} is considered. The results we present can be easily generalized to the case of an immediate transformation launched after more than one class transformation is performed.

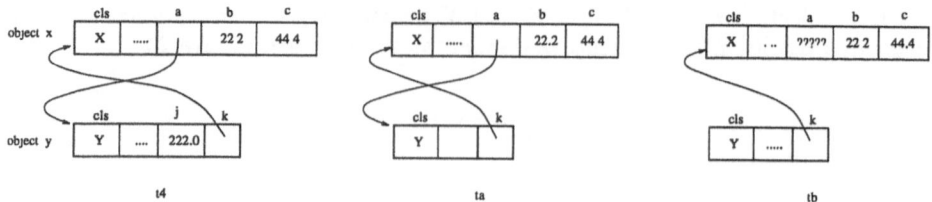

Figure 4: Evolution of objects y and x using the lazy database transformation.

The bad news is that the function deref_a accesses object y via the attribute j. But object y now does not have anymore all the information required for the transformation of x because it has lost the attribute j when it was transformed at time t_a. In this special case, execution of deref_a would result in a run-time type error.

In general, using default values for the restructured object x does not solve the problem, as it could result in an incorrect database transformation.

The problem can be seen as well using the conversion function notation presented in Section 2. In the immediate database transformation the execution of conversion functions and application operations (i.e. the read operations $r[y]$ and $r[x]$) would result in executing the following operations at times t_3, t_4, t_a and t_b:

$$
\begin{aligned}
&\xrightarrow{t_3} rcf_{deref\_a}[x] \rightarrow rcf_{deref\_a}[y] \rightarrow wcf_{deref\_a}[x] \\
&\xrightarrow{t_4} rcf_{default}[y] \rightarrow dcf_{default}[y] \rightarrow wcf_{default}[y] \\
&\xrightarrow{t_a} r[y] \\
&\xrightarrow{t_b} r[x]
\end{aligned}
\tag{1}
$$

whereby the same conversion functions executed as a lazy database transformation would trigger the following operations at time t_a and t_b:

$$
\begin{aligned}
&\xrightarrow{t_a} rcf_{default}[y] \rightarrow dcf_{default}[y] \rightarrow wcf_{default}[y] \rightarrow r[y] \\
&\xrightarrow{t_b} rcf_{deref\_a}[x] \rightarrow rcf_{deref\_a}[y] \rightarrow wcf_{deref\_a}[x] \rightarrow r[x]
\end{aligned}
\tag{2}
$$

If we look at the lazy database transformation (2), the order of execution of the two conversion functions deref_a and default differs with respect to the immediate database transformation (1). In particular, being the operation $dcf_{default}[y]$ (i.e. the deletion of an attribute in y) before $rcf_{deref\_a}[y]$ in the lazy database transformation causes the occurrence of a run-time type error.

An additional case when the immediate and lazy database transformations do not give the same results arises in the example if attribute j is not deleted from class Y, but its value in object y is changed at time t_a before object x is transformed at time t_b. The two executions would change as follows:

$$
\begin{aligned}
&\xrightarrow{t_3} rcf_{deref\_a}[x] \rightarrow rcf_{deref\_a}[y] \rightarrow wcf_{deref\_a}[x] \\
&\xrightarrow{t_a} w[y] \\
&\xrightarrow{t_b} r[x]
\end{aligned}
$$

whereby in the lazy database transformation the execution results in:

$$\overset{t_a}{\rightarrow} w[y]$$
$$\overset{t_4}{\rightarrow} rcf_{deref\_a}[x] \rightarrow rcf_{deref\_a}[y] \rightarrow wcf_{deref\_a}[x] \rightarrow r[x]$$

In the immediate database transformation the value read from object y in the conversion function deref_a (represented by $rcf_{deref\_a}[y]$) would have been the one of y at time t_3 and not the one at time t_a. Looking at the two executions, this is represented by the fact that the order of the two operations $rcf_{deref\_a}[y]$ and $w[y]$ differ. In this case we say that the lazy and the immediate database transformations are not "time equivalent".

The formal definition of correctness and time equivalence between the lazy and immediate database transformations will be presented further in the paper in Section 4.

3.3 Cycles

The second problem that need be solved in the implementation of conversion function with lazy database updates is that of *cycles* .

Let us reconsider the schema modifications performed at time t_2 and t_3 (see Figure 1).

Both the class modifications are associated to a complex conversion function. Note that compute_j defined at time t_2 (associated to class Y) "uses" information belonging to objects of class X, and deref_a defined at time t_3 (associated to class X) "uses" information belonging to objects of class Y. This situation leads to a *cycle* in the history of conversion functions and to some problems during objects update.

Suppose, in fact, at time $t_c > t_4$ an application accesses an object y of class Y which is in a format conforming to the definition of the class at time t_1 (see Figure 5). The conversion function compute_j is applied in order to convert the object to the subsequent definition along the class history. Suppose now that the function accesses the object x of class X which is in a format conforming to the definition of X at time t_1 (see Figure 5). The object x has to be transformed as well according to deref_a. Unfortunately, deref_a accesses the same y under transformation. This means that, if no contra-measures are taken into account, the system would try to transform y again because its format does not conform to the most recent class definition.

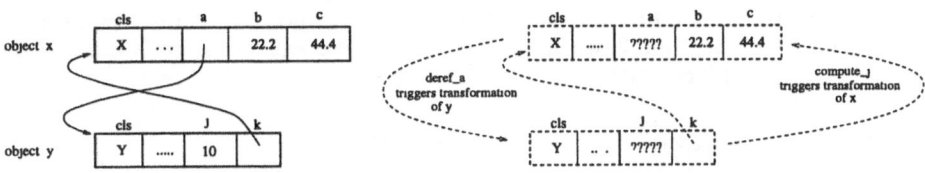

Figure 5: Cycle during objects' transformation.

Using the notation presented in Section 2, the immediate execution of conversion functions would result in:

$$\overset{t_3}{\to} rcf_{compute\_j}[y] \to rcf_{compute\_j}[x] \to wcf_{compute\_j}[y]$$
$$\overset{t_3}{\to} rcf_{deref\_a}[x] \to rcf_{deref\_a}[y] \to wcf_{deref\_a}[x]$$
$$\overset{t_4}{\to} rcf_{default}[y] \to dcf_{default}[y] \to wcf_{default}[y]$$
$$\overset{t_5}{\to} r[y]$$

in contrast, the lazy database transformation execution of the example results in the following infinite loop:

$$\overset{t_5}{\to} rcf_{compute\_j}[y] \to rcf_{deref\_a}[x] \to rcf_{compute\_j}[y]$$
$$\to rcf_{deref\_a}[x] \to rcf_{compute\_j}[y] \to \cdots$$

In order to avoid such infinite loops, the cycle has to be detected and the system should not try to transform y a second time.

After detection of the cycle, the transformation of x should continue. The conversion function deref_a could use the information present in the old y. This is equivalent to the following lazy execution:

$$\overset{t_5}{\to} rcf_{compute\_j}[y] \to rcf_{deref\_a}[x] \to rcf_{deref\_a}[y]$$
$$\to wcf_{deref\_a}[x] \to rcf_{compute\_j}[x] \to wcf_{compute\_j}[y]$$
$$\to rcf_{default}[y] \to dcf_{default}[y] \to wcf_{default}[y]$$
$$\to r[y]$$

This solution does *not* always work properly. In fact, in the example, deref_a needs the field j of object y in the format and value written by compute_j, but the conversion of y has been blocked before the system were able to update the field j. Therefore the cycle cannot be solved using the old information of y. In the rest of the paper we call these cycles *"critical"*.

In the lazy conversion function execution approach this can be recognized by looking at the order of execution of $wcf_{compute\_j}[y]$ and $rcf_{deref\_a}[y]$ which is different than in immediate execution of the same conversion function.

4 Correctness and Time Equivalence of the Lazy Database Transformation

In this section we give the formal definition of the execution of conversion functions embedded in an application program. In particular, we will define two notions: *correctness* and *time equivalence* of a lazy database transformation.

We recall in Section 2 we have introduced the execution of a conversion function on an object x as:

$$rcf_i[x] \to \left[dcf_i[x] \right] \to \left\{ rcf_i[y_j] \right\}_n \to wcf_i[x]$$

We will be using an adapted version of the concept of a *history*, defined in [13], to model the execution of conversion functions embedded in an application program. In our context a *history* indicates the order in which the operations of conversion functions and applications are executed with respect to each other.

Informally, if a conversion function execution cf_i, or an application execution a_j, specifies the order of its operations, then these operations must appear in the same order in any history that includes cf_i or a_j. In addition, we require that a history specifies the order of all conflicting operations that appear in it.

Definition 3 *Two operations op_i and op_j, with $op_i <_H op_j$ in a history H (see def. 5) conflict if they both operate on the same object and a "N" is present in the corresponding entry of a so called* compatibility matrix. *The compatibility matrix for the operations rcf, wcf, dcf, r, and w is shown in Table 1.*

Table 1: The compatibility matrix used for the definition of *conflicting* operations.

$<$	rcf_j	wcf_j	dcf_j	r_j	w_j
rcf_i	Y	N	N	Y	Y
wcf_i	N	N	N	Y	Y
dcf_i	N	N	N	N	N
r_i	Y	Y	N	Y	N
w_i	Y	Y	N	N	N

Definition 4 *Two operations op_i and op_j, with $op_i <_H op_j$ strong conflict if they both operate on the same object and a "N" is present in the corresponding entry of a so called* strong compatibility matrix. *The strong compatibility matrix for the operations rcf, wcf, dcf, r, and w is shown in Table 2.*

Table 2: The strong compatibility matrix used for the definition of *strong conflicting* operations.

$<$	rcf_j	wcf_j	dcf_j	r_j	w_j
rcf_i	Y	N	N	Y	N
wcf_i	N	N	N	N	N
dcf_i	N	N	N	N	N
r_i	Y	N	N	Y	N
w_i	N	N	N	N	N

Definition 5 (History) *Let $cf = \{cf_1, ..., cf_n\}$ be a set of conversion function executions and $a = \{a_1, ..., a_m\}$ be a set of application program executions. A history H over cf and a is a partial order with ordering relation $<_H$ where:*

1. $H = (\cup_{i=1}^n cf_i) \cup (\cup_{j=1}^m a_j)$;

2. $<_H \supseteq (\cup_{i=1}^n <_{cf_i}) \cup (\cup_{j=1}^m <_{a_j})$;

3. *if $\{rcf_i[x], wcf_i[x]\} \subseteq H$, for any other operation $p \in \{r_j[y], w_j[y]\} \wedge$*
   $$p \in H \quad p <_H rcf_i[x] \text{ or } wcf_i[x] <_H p;$$

4. *if $\{rcf_i[x], dcf_i[x]\} \subseteq H$, for any other operation $p \in \{r_j[y], w_j[y]\} \wedge$*
$$p \in H \qquad p <_H rcf_i[x] \ or \ dcf_i[x] <_H p;$$

5. *for any two possible strong conflicting operations p, $q \in H$,*
$$either \ p <_H q \ or \ q <_H p.$$

Condition (1) states that the execution represented by H involves precisely the operations submitted by $cf_1, ..., cf_n$ and $a_1, ..., a_m$. Condition (2) says that the execution respects all operation orderings specified within each conversion function or application execution. Conditions (3) and (4) denote that no read or write operation of an application appears respectively within read and write or read and delete operations of a conversion function. Finally, condition (5) says that the ordering of every pair of conflicting operations is determined by $<_H$.

In order to be able to state when a lazy database transformation is correct, we give hereafter two definitions of equivalence between two histories.

Definition 6 (Equivalence) *We define two histories* H *and* H' *to be* equivalent *if*

1. H *and* H' *are defined over the same set of conversion function and application executions;*

2. H *and* H' *order conflicting operations in the same way; thus, for any conflicting operations p_i and q_j in* H*, where $p_i <_H q_j$, then $p_i <_{H'} q_j$.*

A similar definition holds for histories which are *strong equivalent* to each other.

Definition 7 (Strong equivalence) *We define two histories* H *and* H' *to be* strong equivalent *if*

1. H *and* H' *are defined over the same set of conversion function and application executions;*

2. H *and* H' *order strong conflicting operations in the same way; thus, for any strong conflicting operations p_i and q_j in* H*, where $p_i <_H q_j$, then $p_i <_{H'} q_j$.*

The idea underlying these definitions is that the result of an interleaved execution of applications and conversion functions depends on the relative order of conflicting operations. In the immediate database transformation, when the designer associates a conversion function to a class, he/she is implicitly defining the order of execution of that conversion function with respect to application operations (i.e. the order $<_{H_{imm}}$). We call this order of execution the *immediate history*.

If the lazy database transformation is used, the correspondent *lazy history* with ordering relation $<_{H_{lz}}$ depends on the moment when objects are accessed by applications and is related to the immediate history as shown in the following lemma:

Lemma 1 *For any two distinct operations op_1, op_2, where $op_i \in \{r_i[x], w_i[x], cf_i[x]\}$, $i=1,2$, if $op_1 <_{H_{imm}} op_2$ then $op_1 <_{H_{lz}} op_2$.*

Lemma 1 states that in the lazy history, the order of execution of the operations $r_i[x]$, $w_j[x]$, and $cf_k[x]$ on the same object x must be the same as in the immediate history.

The proof of the lemma is done considering the following 4 cases:

1. $op_1 \in \{r_1[x], w_1[x]\}$ and $op_2 \in \{r_2[x], w_2[x]\}$ Since the time when application operations are executed does not differ in the immediate and the lazy database transformations, the order between op_1 and op_2 is the same in both transformations.

2. $op_1 = cf_1[x]$ and $op_2 = cf_2[x]$ This condition is always true because the order of execution of conversion functions transforming an object x, instance of a class X, is stored in an appropriate *type_history_list* which is associated to the class X itself.

3. $op_1 \in \{r_1[x], w_1[x]\}$ and $op_2 = cf_2[x]$ In a lazy history a conversion function cf_i is delayed only, i.e. no read or write operation of an application which happened to be before cf_i in the immediate history can appear after cf_i in the lazy history.

4. $op_1 = cf_1[x]$ and $op_2 \in \{r_2[x], w_2[x]\}$ This is given by the definition of lazy updates, because in the lazy database transformation the execution of a conversion function $cf_i[x]$ is delayed and executed before the first $r[x]$ or $w[x]$ operation in the lazy history.

Now we can give the definitions of *correct* lazy execution of conversion functions:

Definition 8 (Correctness) *A lazy database transformation is* correct *if for* any *immediate history* given by the designer, the correspondent *lazy history is* equivalent *with respect to the* immediate history.

A stronger correctness criteria is given by what we called *Time Equivalence*:

Definition 9 (Time equivalence) *A lazy database transformation is* correct and time equivalent *with the immediate database transformation if for any* immediate history *given by the designer, the correspondent* lazy history *is* strong equivalent *with respect to the* immediate history.

5   Ensuring Correctness

In [1] we defined three possible algorithms for solving the problems described in Section 3. In this section we will briefly describe how the algorithms presented in [1] work and show their correctness or time equivalence with respect to an immediate database transformation.

A first important result dealing with the execution of *simple* conversion functions is expressed by the following Theorem:

Theorem 1 *The result of the execution of* simple *conversion functions implemented as a lazy database transformation is always* correct and time equivalent.

Proof Sketch Assume an *immediate history* with ordering relation $<_{H_{imm}}$ has been given by the designer. In a correspondent *lazy history* (with ordering relation $<_{H_{lz}}$), the execution of a simple conversion function $cf_i[x] = rcf_i[x] \rightarrow [dcf_i[x]] \rightarrow wcf_i[x]$ on an object x is delayed up to the first $r_j[x]$, or $w_j[x]$ operation following $cf_i[x]$ in the immediate history. Since in $cf_i[x]$ no operation $r_j[y]$ on other objects in the database other than x occurs, the order of *strong conflicting* operations does not change with respect to the immediate history. □

As a direct consequence of **Theorem 1**, a simple solution for ensuring a correct and time equivalent lazy execution of conversion functions is to allow only simple conversion functions. With this limitation, the problem encountered with the implementation of the conversion functions described in Section 3 does not apply. This approach is used by some commercial systems, such as Itasca [8] and Versant [9].

We believe this solution is too restrictive to be used in practice.

If we want to preserve the possibility to define *complex* conversion functions and implement them as lazy database updates, we can think of three possible alternative implementation strategies [1]:

1) Using a *pessimistic mix-in* modality for updating the database.

This strategy works as follows: after a *complex* conversion function is associated to an updated class, an immediate transformation is always launched on the specified class to implement the database transformation. On the contrary, for database objects for which a simple conversion function has to be executed, the transformation is deferred until they are effectively used. We can assume the system to perform automatically the "switch" from lazy to immediate and back to lazy when necessary. The switch process should be transparent for the schema designer.

This approach avoids storing a complex conversion function in a class history. In this way, by **Theorem 1**, the correctness and time equivalence of the lazy database transformation is obtained. In fact, in the pessimistic mix-in database transformation, simple conversion functions only can be delayed with respect to the immediate history, and this is exactly what is allowed by **Theorem 1**. Furthermore, since no complex conversion functions are present in the history of classes, no cycle will ever occur during the update of the objects.

The drawback of this approach is that an immediate transformation of objects is launched even when not needed.

2) Using a *optimistic mix-in* modality for updating the database.

The basic idea behind this approach is to avoid as much as possible the use of the immediate database transformation. In contrast to the pessimistic mix-in approach, the system does not start an immediate update every time a complex conversion function is associated to a class, but it starts an immediate update only before executing those schema modifications which might compromise the equivalence with the immediate database transformation (i.e. those schema modifications which lead to run-time type errors when conversion functions are executed). Cycles are detected at run-time by the system by associating a *mark* every time an object which is not up to date is accessed. *Critical cycles* are solved by *stopping* the transformation of an object to conform to a specific format in the history of a class. Objects accessed by applications are converted to conform to the most recent definition of the class whereas objects accessed by a conversion function are converted to conform to the format "visible" by the conversion function at the time it was defined by the designer.

Theorem 2 *The* optimistic mix-in *database transformation is correct but not time equivalent.*

Proof Sketch Assume an *immediate history* with ordering relation $<_{H_{imm}}$ has been given by the designer. In a correspondent *lazy history* (with ordering relation $<_{H_{lx}}$), the execution of a conversion function $cf_i[x] = rcf_i[x] \rightarrow [dcf_i[x]] \rightarrow rcf_i[y_1] \rightarrow \ldots \rightarrow rcf_i[y_n] \rightarrow wcf_i[x]$ on an object x is delayed up to the first $r_j[x]$, $w_j[x]$, $rcf_j[x]$ and certainly not after a $dcf_j[y_1]$, ..., $dcf_j[y_n]$ operation following $cf_i[x]$ in the lazy history.

In this way there is no possibility to have *conflicting* operations in the immediate and the lazy history, but there is still the possibility to have *strong conflicting* operations because in the lazy history the conversion function $cf_i[x]$ might appear in a different order with respect to the operations $w_j[y_k]$ with $k = 1, \ldots, n$. □

3) Using a *screening* modality for updating the database.

Screening resembles the pure lazy approach, i.e. no immediate transformation has to be launched for updating the database. Basically, when some information is deleted from the schema, it is only logically filtered out, but not physically deleted in the database. When, for instance, a deletion of an attribute (or a change in the type which would correspond to a deletion and an addition of the same attribute) is performed, the update is not physically executed on the object structure but simply a different representation of the object is presented to the user. With this approach, the Schema Manager is in charge of managing the different representations of the objects (one representation visible to applications and one representation visible to conversion functions). **Theorem 3** shows that the database transformation using *screening* is *correct* but not *time equivalent*.

Theorem 3 *The database transformation using* screening *is correct but not time equivalent.*

Proof Sketch Assume an *immediate history* with ordering relation $<_{H_{imm}}$ has been given by the designer. In a correspondent *lazy history* (with ordering relation $<_{H_{lx}}$), the execution of a conversion function $cf_i[x] = rcf_i[x] \rightarrow rcf_i[y_1] \rightarrow \ldots \rightarrow rcf_i[y_n] \rightarrow wcf_i[x]$ on an object x is delayed up to the first $r_j[x]$, $w_j[x]$, $rcf_j[x]$ operation following $cf_i[x]$ in the immediate history.

Note that, because of screening, no $dcf_i[x]$ operation is present neither in the immediate nor in the lazy history. Therefore, the delay of conversion functions in the lazy history does not cause any conflicting operations with respect to the immediate history. Nevertheless, since in the lazy history $cf_i[x]$ might appear in a different order with respect to the operations $w_j[y_k]$ with $k = 1, \ldots, n$, the order of *strong conflicting* operations is not preserved. □

The reader is referred to [1] for a detailed presentation of the three algorithms mentioned in this section.

300

6 Conclusions

The main contribution of this paper is the definition of a correctness criteria for conversion functions updating an object database system. We focused our attention to implementation strategies using a lazy database transformation approach and we presented implementation problems related to it. We formally introduced the notion of conversion functions, their execution, and showed that when complex conversion function are used, problems due to deletion of information and the presence of critical cycles can compromise the result of having a lazy database transformation which is equivalent to an immediate transformation.

We have proven some properties of the algorithms presented in [1], which are summarized by the following table:

Table 3: Algorithms and Compatibility

	Correct	Time equivalent
Pessimistic mix-in	Y	Y
Optimistic mix-in	Y	N
Screening	Y	N

The decision which of the three algorithms has to be used does not have a simple answer. A decision has to be taken based on how important the property of *time equivalence* is for the designer. Moreover, the decision must also take into account implementation issues based on the object persistence model associated to the particular ODBS. In fact, whether class extension are maintained by the system or not has a major performance impact when the algorithms are implemented.

We are currently evaluating the suitability of the algorithms for different ODBSs, concentrating our analysis on performance evaluations [14] extending the work of [15].

Acknowledgments

The work presented in this paper is part of the broader Goodstep project funded by the Commission of the European Communities under the ESPRIT III programme.

We would like to thank Guy Ferran, and Joëlle Madec at O_2 Technology for the interesting and stimulating discussions which helped us to better understand the problems.

References

[1] F.Ferrandina, T.Meyer, and R.Zicari. Implementing Lazy Database Updates for an Object Database System. In *Proceedings of the 20th International Conference on Very Large Databases*. Morgan Kaufmann, September 1994.

[2] R. Zicari. A Framework for Schema Updates in an Object–Oriented Database System. In *Building an Object Oriented Database System - The Story of O_2*. Morgan Kaufmann Publishers, San Mateo, CA, 1992.

[3] J. Banerjee, W. Kim, H.J. Kim, and H.F. Korth. Semantics and Implementation of Schema Evolution in Object–Oriented Databases. In *Proc. of ACM SIGMOD Conf. on Management of Data*, San Francisco, CA, May 1987.

[4] Andrea H. Skarra and Stanley B. Zdonik. Type Evolution in an Object–Oriented Database. In Shriver and Wegner, editors, *Research Directions in Object-Oriented Programming*.

[5] Robert Bretl, David Maier, Allan Otis, Jason Penney, Bruce Schuchardt, Jacob Stein, E. Harold Williams, and Monty Williams. The GemStone Data Management System. In Won Kim and Frederick H. Lockovsky, editors, *Object-Oriented Concepts, Databases and Applications*, chapter 12. ACM Press, 1989.

[6] Object Design Inc. *ObjectStore User Guide, chapter 9*, 1993.

[7] Barbara Staudt Lerner and A. Nico Habermann. Beyond schema evolution to database reorganization. In *Proceedings of the Joint ACM OOPSLA/ECOOP '90 Conference on Object-Oriented Programming: Systems, Languages, and Applications*, pages 67–76, Ottawa, Canada, October 1990.

[8] Itasca Systems, Inc. *Itasca Systems Technical Report Number TM-92-001. OODBMS Feature Checklist. Rev 1.1*, Dec 1993.

[9] Versant Object Technology, 4500 Bohannon Drive Menlo Park, CA 94025. *Versant User Manual*, 1992.

[10] F. Ferrandina and R. Zicari. Object Database Schema Evolution: are Lazy Updates always Equivalent to Immediate Updates? *Presented at the OOPSLA Workshop on Supporting the Evolution of Class Definitions*, Washington, September 1993.

[11] F. Bancilhon, C. Delobel, and P. Kanellakis eds. *Building an Object–Oriented Database System - The Story of O_2*. Morgan Kaufmann Publishers, San Mateo, CA, 1992.

[12] C. Lécluse and P. Richard. The O_2 Database Programming Language. In *Proceedings of the 15th International Conference on Very Large Databases*, Amsterdam, Aug 1989.

[13] P.A. Bernstein, V. Hadzilacos, and N. Goodman. *Concurrency Control and Recovery in Database Systems*. Addison-Wesley, 1987.

[14] F.Ferrandina, T.Meyer, and R.Zicari. Lazy Database Updates Algorithms: a Performance Analysis. Technical report, J.W. Goethe Universität, 1994. In preparation.

[15] G. Harrus, F. Vélez, and R. Zicari. Implementing Schema Updates in an Object-Oriented Database System: a Cost Analysis. Technical report, GIP Altaïr, 1990.

Changing Persistent Applications

Alex Farkas and Alan Dearle

{alex,al}@cs.adelaide.edu.au
Department of Computer Science, University of Adelaide
Adelaide, Australia

Abstract

During the lifetime of an application, the objects and bindings in a persistent store may require modification in order to fix bugs or incorporate changes. Two mechanisms, Octopus and Nodules, supporting the evolution of persistent applications are presented. The first, Octopus permits code and data values to be evolved, even if they are encapsulated. Type evolution is addressed by the separation of type information from the executable code. In many cases type evolution is possible, without the expense of total or partial system recompilation. Nodules are a complementary mechanism to Octopus in that they allow generic templates to be defined independently of any referencing environment. Nodules may be specialised in order to yield instances by binding them to values and types. When combined into a single system, Nodules and Octopus enable a rich collection of information about the structure and state of applications to be maintained and made available to programmers not only during the construction phase, but during the entire lifetime of applications.

1 Introduction

Persistent applications consist of graphs in which the nodes are data objects and the arcs are bindings between them. In a persistent programming language which supports first class procedures[1], such as Napier88 [10], the objects in the store include procedures with bindings to data, and data with bindings to procedures. Persistent systems support incremental construction [4] and component reuse [9] by allowing components to be created, stored in the persistent object store and bindings between them established. Bindings may be established at different times: during program construction, at program compile time and when the program is executing [7].

---

[1] Throughout this paper, the terms program, procedure and functions are used synonymously.

```
type Part is structure( name : string ; id,quantity : int )

!** The database is encapsulated within the partsDatabase procedure whose
!** parameters are a command, a part name and a quantity.
let partsDatabase =
begin
        let database = !** generate a b-tree for storing Parts.

        !** Declare three procedures which are bound to and manipulate
        !** the database.
        let create = proc( partName : string ; amount : int )
        begin
            let newId = ... !** generate a new unique identifier.
            let newPart = Part( partName,newId,amount )
            database( enter )( newPart )
        end

        let update = proc( partName : string ; amount : int )
        begin
            let apart = database( lookup )( partName )
            !** Next line is an error, rhs should be apart( quantity ) + amount
            apart( quantity ) := apart( id ) + amount
        end

        let display = proc( partName : string )
        use PS() with IO in
        use IO with writeInt : proc( int ) ; writeString : proc( string ) in
        begin
            let apart = database( lookup )( partName )
            !** call a procedure to display the number of parts.
            writeString( apart( name ) )
            writeInt( apart( id ) )
            writeInt( apart( quantity ) )
        end

        !** Define the partsDatabase procedure which is bound to the utility
        !** procedures.  This procedure is returned as the result of the
        !** computation between the outermost begin and end.
        proc( command,partName : string ; amount : int )
        begin
            case command of
            "CREATE"    :   create( partName,amount )
            "BUY"       :   update( partName,amount )
            "SELL"      :   update( partName,-amount )
            "PRINT"     :   display( partName )
            default     :   !** error ...
        end
end
```

Figure 1: A simple program creating a database of *Parts*.

During the lifetime of an application, the objects and bindings in the object store may require modification in order to fix bugs or incorporate changes. In general, evolution involves traversal of the object graph in order to modify, create and delete objects and bindings. This may be achieved through the use of a persistent store browser [3]: a general purpose tool which traverses object graphs applying a function to the objects it encounters. This is analogous to providing a generic *map* operation over an object graph. For example, a browser may be used to find and update all the instances of a given type in a database. The use of browsers to aid evolution has been proven in the context of Napier88 persistent object stores. However, a number of limitations have been encountered, namely:

1. Encapsulated values in the object graph cannot be reached using a browser, since it is impossible to browse through functional interfaces.
2. Evolved code cannot be bound to existing data and evolved data cannot be bound to existing code since the existing code and data cannot be named or referenced.
3. The lack of support for type evolution.

Encapsulation plays an important role in the construction of many applications. Abstract Data Types (ADTs) [8] and the Object-oriented design methodology [1] rely heavily on encapsulation in order to hide the underlying data structures of an application. Such information hiding is often cited as an aid to system evolution since the implementation of an abstract type can be changed without affecting the programs that make use of that abstract type. However, abstract types can cause difficulties when used as a mechanism to encapsulate persistent objects – when the source of an abstract type is recompiled and a new abstract type installed, the persistent state will be lost. If the interface to the abstract type is complete, it may be possible to extract all the encapsulated data from the old instance and place it in the new instance with no loss of information. However, this is not always the case, as in the *partsDatabase* example shown in Figure 1 in which the data is encapsulated but cannot be accessed through the (degenerate) functional interface.

System evolution consists of three activities: evolving data, evolving code and evolving types. Evolution of data is perhaps the simplest activity: provided that the data structure is not encapsulated and therefore reachable, a browser can traverse it and create a new isomorphic data structure. However, in order to ensure referential integrity, all the references to the old data structure must be found and consistently updated. This is also possible using a browser (if a little time consuming). However, bindings to data structures encapsulated within the closures of functions, present a problem; for example, the binding to *database* from *create* in Figure 1. There is no method of finding these bindings using existing browser technology. A similar problem exists with evolved code – if referential integrity is to be preserved, the evolved version of the code should contain the same bindings as the old. Clearly some general purpose mechanism is required that is capable of reaching all data regardless of whether it is bound or encapsulated.

Applications generally make use of an arbitrary set of types. As an application evolves, these types may undergo changes which effect the application in two primary ways: firstly, programs which manipulate values of the evolved types may also need to be evolved to reflect the change in type. Secondly, programs which perform dynamic type checking and create instances of the types must be updated.

In the remainder of this paper, we present evolutionary techniques which address the problems discussed above. The mechanisms are based on the principle that all mutable information should be removed from the code and stored separately. The technique also provides a way in which generic executable code may be obtained and reused with different values and types. A mechanism called a *Nodule* is presented that allows such unbound code to be specified and bound at a later time.

This paper is structured as follows. Section 2 describes Octopus, a mechanism for interrogating and manipulating bindings, Section 3 describes a mechanism for propagating type changes through existing programs, Section 4 describes Nodules and section 5 describes how these mechanisms form a part of the programming environment.

2   Octopus

A mechanism called Octopus is described in [5] and [6] which allows all bindings in an arbitrary graph of objects to be examined and manipulated. In essence, Octopus provides a uniform viewing mechanism with which values and bindings of any type may be viewed and manipulated using the same set of operations. The mechanism allows values to be hoisted up to a meta level and manipulated in ways which the programming language would not otherwise permit. When manipulation is complete, values may be dropped back into the value space provided they still conform to the language's type system.

An Octopus is a set of three operations which allow the bindings within a value to be examined and manipulated. The corresponding type declaration for an Octopus is shown in Figure 2. The *getType* operation returns a representation of the type of the value encapsulated in the Octopus. This representation is a value in the programming language space and may not be used as a denotation for a type. A complete set of selector, constructor, equivalence and iterator functions that operate on this representation are provided by the Napier88 system [2]. Using these functions, the programmer can obtain any information about the type.

```
type Octopus is structure(    getType      :  proc( → TypeRep );
                              getSource    :  proc( → Source ) ;
                              getBinding   :  proc( string → Binding ) ;
                              scan         :  proc( proc( Binding ) ) )
```

Figure 2: The structure of an Octopus.

The *getSource* operation returns a representation of the source code for the value. If the value is a procedure, this source code is similar to the hyper-program model of source code described in [7]. If the value encapsulated in an Octopus is not a procedure, then *getSource* returns a representation of the value which is suitable for use in hyper-programs. The *getBinding* operation returns the binding associated with the given name if one exists. A *scan* procedure is provided to iterate over the bindings contained in an Octopus. *scan* takes as its single parameter a programmer specified procedure which is iteratively applied to each binding in the Octopus. The specified procedure may perform an arbitrary computation on a binding; for example, the procedure may be used to display a binding's value.

The Octopus model provides the ability to *cut* and *rewire* the bindings within hoisted values. When a value from the value space is hoisted up to the meta level, all of its bindings are treated as hooks from the hoisted value to the bound values. A

306

binding is cut by detaching the hook from the bound value, and is rewired by attaching the hook to another value of the same type; it is not possible to rewire values of an incompatible type. Neither is it possible to drop the hoisted value back into the value space until all bindings are correctly rewired.

```
type Binding is structure(    cut       :  proc( → bool );
                              add       :  proc( Value → bool );
                              get       :  proc( → Value );
                              resolved  :  proc( → bool );
                              getType   :  proc( → TypeRep );
                              getName   :  proc( → string ) )
```

Figure 3: The representation of a binding.

A binding is represented as a package of six operations, as shown in Figure 3. The operations on bindings behave as follows:

cut   causes the associated binding to be dissolved; the process of cutting a binding is simply a meta level indication that the binding is no longer resolved. Cut bindings may still be accessed via direct bindings to the naked value.

add   permits an unresolved binding to be rewired, or resolved, using the given value. The operation fails if the binding is already resolved or if the supplied value is of the wrong type.

get   returns the current value of the binding. If the binding is unresolved, a fail value is returned.

resolved   returns *true* if the binding is in a resolved state and *false* otherwise.

getType   returns a representation of the type of the corresponding bound value.

getName   returns the name of the bound value.

2.1   Implementation of Octopus

Octopus has the ability to traverse and manipulate arbitrary object graphs, including encapsulated values. The ability of Octopus to access encapsulated bindings requires special attention in the implementation architecture. To illustrate this, we will describe how the *partsDatabase* application is represented and how Octopus manipulates this representation. Readers are referred to [5] for a more detailed description of the Octopus architecture.

In systems supporting Octopus, all bindings encapsulated in procedures are stored separately from executable code. All procedural values are represented by two entities: a structure containing only executable code, known as a *code vector*, and a structure containing the encapsulated bindings, known as an *environment vector*. Together, a code vector and environment vector form the *closure* of a procedure. The *partsDatabase* procedure is represented as shown in Figure 4.

On the left hand side of the figure, the closure for the *partsDatabase* procedure is shown. The environment vector contains bindings to each of the three operations *create*, *update* and *display*. Similarly, the environment vector of each operation contains a binding to the database.

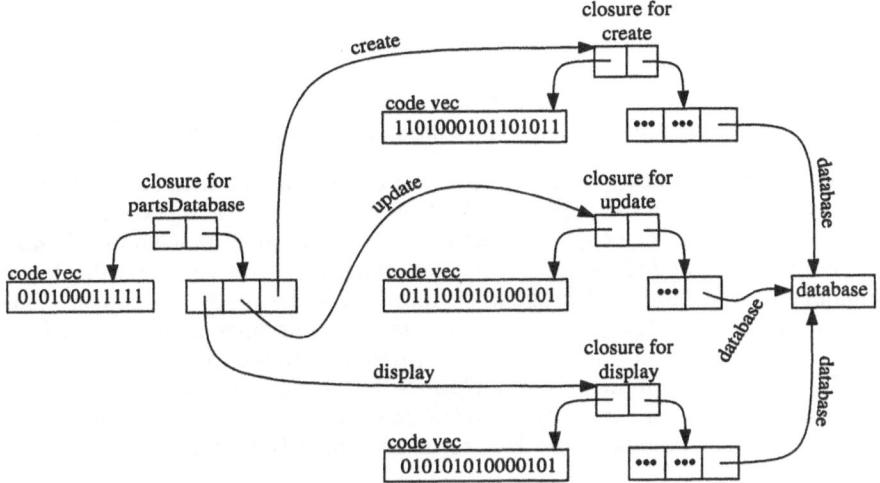

Figure 4: Conceptual view of the *partsDatabase* application.

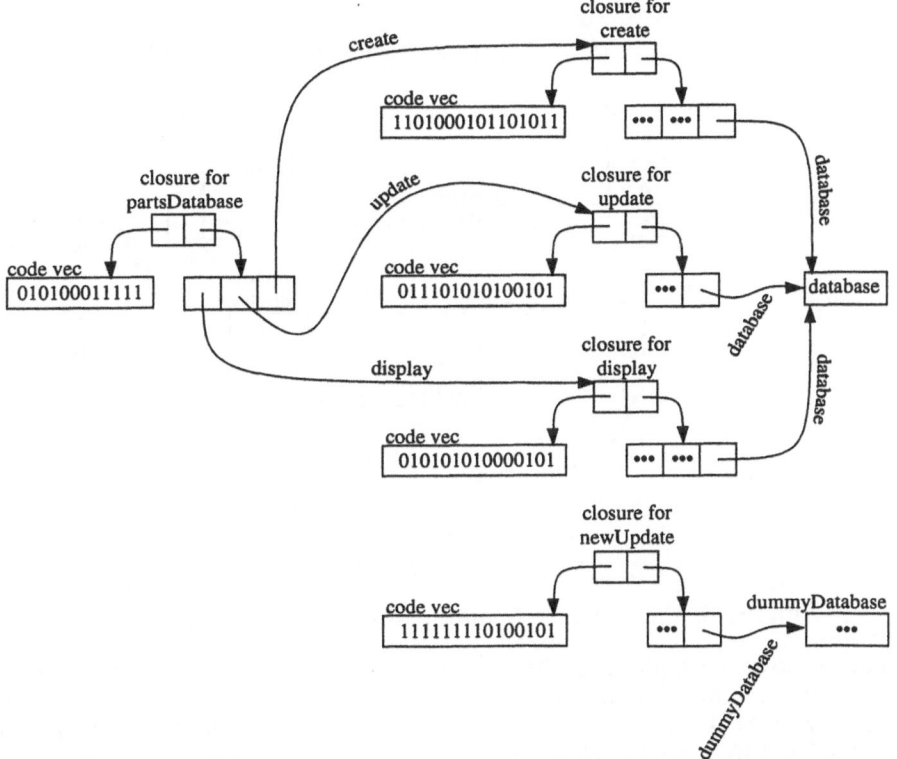

Figure 5: View of *newUpdate*, the replacement procedure for *update*.

Octopus may be used to traverse object graphs, access encapsulated values, and perform rebinding of new values. For example, consider the *update* procedure used

308

by *partsDatabase*, *update* is faulty as it increments the *id* field of a part instead of the *quantity* field, so it needs to be replaced. There are two steps involved in making this change:

1.   The new procedure must be created and bound to *database*, and
2.   the *partsDatabase* application must be bound to the new procedure.

In order to bind the new procedure to *database*, it must be located. This may be achieved by traversing the object graph of the *partsDatabase* application using the Octopus operations. Once located, the new procedure may be bound to *database*. This could be achieved using the Octopus *add* operation or, since the location containing the database used by the new procedure is known, by assignment. Finally the rewired procedure may be bound into the *partsDatabase* application using the Octopus *add* operation. This process is illustrated in Figures 5 and 6.

In Figure 5, a procedure *newUpdate* has been created to be used as the replacement for *update*. Initially, *newUpdate* is bound to a dummy database; this is to be replaced by a binding to the database used in *partsDatabase*.

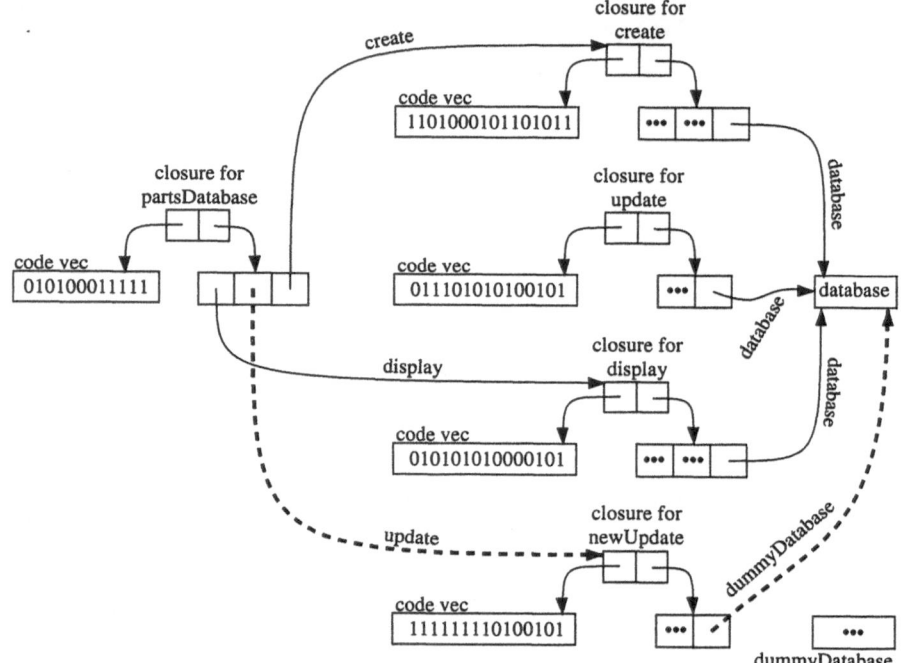

Figure 6: View of *partsDatabase* after wiring in *newUpdate*.

Figure 6 shows the application after *newUpdate* has been bound to the database and *partsDatabase* to *newUpdate*. There are no other bindings to the old *update* procedure or the dummy database and these will be garbage collected by the system. The Napier88-like pseudo code in Figure 7 shows how these steps are achieved.

The first line of the program constructs a dummy instance of a database. Next, a procedure *newUpdate* intended as a replacement for the faulty *update* procedure is declared; this procedure is bound to *dummyDatabase*. Then, *newUpdate* and *partsDatabase* are hoisted into Octopuses using the special function *coerceToOctopus*. The *getBinding* operation of the hoisted database is used to obtain a binding to the original *update* procedure, which is then hoisted. Similarly, the *getBinding* operation of the hoisted original *update* procedure is used to obtain the binding to the old database, which is then assigned to *dummyDatabase*. Finally, the binding to the old *update* procedure is cut and the *newUpdate* procedure wired in.

Octopus allows arbitrary object graphs to be interrogated, but only allows values within the graphs to be manipulated or replaced. No support is given to enable changes in schema to be propagated through the graphs. For example, if the type *Part* in the parts database is extended to include the year in which a part was manufactured, then three activities need to occur. Firstly, the source code for the application needs to be modified to use the new type. Secondly, the programs need to be recompiled and lastly, the values in the database need to be evolved to be consistent with the new type. This may be achieved by traversing the database using Octopus and constructing an isomorphic graph of values which include the new field. The new database may then be wired into the new application.

```
let dummyDatabase := ... !** declare a dummy value.

!** The new version of update
• let newUpdate = proc( partName : string ; amount : int )
begin
        let part = dummyDatabase( lookup )( partName )
        part( quantity ) := part( quantity ) + amount
end

let hoistedDb            =  coerceToOctopus( partsDatabase )
let oldUpdateBinding     =  hoistedDb( getBinding )( "update" )
let oldUpdate            =  oldUpdateBinding( get )()
let hoistedOldUpdate     =  coerceToOctopus( oldUpdate )
let oldDbBinding         =  hoistedOldUpdate( getBinding )( "database" )
dummyDatabase            := oldDbBinding( get )()

let ok    := oldUpdate( cut )()
ok        := oldUpdate( add )( newUpdate )
```

Figure 7: Replacing the *update* procedure using Octopus.

3 Propagating Type Changes

On its own, the Octopus mechanism is not suitable for evolving programs in which changes of type have occurred. This section describes an extension of the Octopus mechanism which allows type dependent information inside programs to be manipulated. The mechanism is an extension of Octopus in that type specific information is extracted from executable code and stored inside the environment vector.

When a type used by a program changes, it is not always necessary to make syntactic changes to the program in order to reflect the new type. For example, if the type of *Part* in the *partsDatabase* example is extended with a new field, the *update* operation does not need to be changed syntactically, but must be recompiled in order to update any type specific information in its executable form.

The *create* and *display* operations must be modified to include the new field. The nature of the resulting changes in executable code depend on how each procedure uses the type information.

In general, programs depend on types in three ways. These are classified as:
1.   signature,
2.   field, and
3.   constructor.

The nature of these dependencies and their effects on the executable forms of programs are described below.

Programs which contain signature dependencies contain code to perform type checking on values dynamically. For example consider the *display* procedure in the parts database example. This procedure attempts to locate procedures called *writeString* and *writeInt* in the persistent store. Locating the procedures requires type checking to be performed dynamically. For this reason, representations of the types of the procedures are kept in the persistent store. In order to locate the procedures, the executable code of *display* contains a representation of the expected types of the procedures and uses them to compare with the representation encountered in the persistent store.

The executable form of a program containing a signature dependency is bound to a representation of the type. In the event that a change occurs in the signature, the source code may or may not require modification. However, the only change required in the executable form is that it should be bound to the new type representation.

Field dependencies arise in programs which dereference or assign to record fields. For example, the *update* procedure makes both a dereference and assignment to a *Part* field. The executable code contains information about the offset of the *quantity* field in the part. If, for example, a new field were added to *Part*, then the source code for *update* would remain the same: the only difference would be that the executable code would require updated information about the offset of the *quantity* field in the *Part* record. In such cases, recompilation could be avoided by updating the offset information bound to the executable code.

A constructor dependency arises when a program constructs an instance of a type. For example, in the case of the *create* procedure, the executable code constructs an instance of the type *Part* using the values passed as parameters to the procedure. If the type *Part* changes, the program *create* would also need to be changed. This involves syntactically changing the source code of *create* and recompiling it.

3.1   Operations for Evolving Types

The dependencies described above indicate that not all programs need to undergo recompilation if the types they use change. More specifically, if programs contain only signature and/or field dependencies, the programs may be evolved without the expense of recompilation if the types they use are evolved. The three operations in Figure 8 provide a way in which the type dependencies of programs may be queried, and the programs updated without recompilation where possible.

The *updateType* operation replaces representations of type *old* with representations of type *new* in the procedure *aProc*. If *aProc* contains field dependencies then the offsets are also updated. If the procedure contains occurrences of structurally equivalent types, then all such instances are updated; it is necessary to recompile the procedure if a subset of all equivalent types requires updating[*]. The *getDepend* operation returns a value indicating the nature of the dependency of *aProc* on the type *theType*. These values are integers combined from the following:

0	no dependency,
1	signature dependency,
2	field dependency,
4	constructor dependency, and
8	semantic dependency of some other kind.

updateType	:	**proc(**	aProc : **any** ; old,new : Type → **bool**)
getDepend	:	**proc(**	aProc : **any** ; theType : Type → **int**)
scanTypes	:	**proc(**	aProc : **any** ;
			user : **proc(** aType : Type ;
			aDep : **int**))

Figure 8: Operations for type evolution and dependency querying.

Combinations are produced by adding the appropriate values; for example, the value 5 indicates a constructor and signature dependency. The final operation, *scanTypes*, allows a user specified procedure to be iteratively applied to each dependent type of the procedure *aProc*. The operations described above may be used to more efficiently evolve an application in which type changes occur. However, the operations do not provide a way of avoiding recompilation in all cases: if a program requires syntactic change, then recompilation is unavoidable.

4   Nodules

The operations provided to support type evolution behave in a similar fashion to the Octopus operations. In Octopus, all bindings are removed from the executable code stream and stored separately in an environment vector. This principle is extended to support type evolution by extracting all type representations and field offsets from the code stream and planting them in the environment vector with the bindings. For example, Figure 9 shows the environment vector of the *update* procedure in the parts database storing the offset of the *quantity* field inside a part.

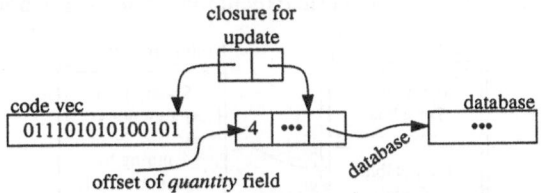

Figure 9: Storing type information in environment vectors.

The result is that all attributes of the executable code which may be modified without recompilation are stored separately. Consequently, the reusability of executable code is considerably extended: the same executable code may be used with a different environment vector to operate on different values with different types.

---

[*]In programming languages which employ name equivalence on types, this would not necessarily be the case.

One method of constructing general purpose code is to use generators [4]. This technique involves parameterising a procedure with all relevant intermediate free variables. For example, the *update* procedure needs to be bound to a database, so a generator may be constructed which takes a database as a parameter and returns an update procedure bound to that database as shown in Figure 4.2.

```
let updateGen = proc( db : Database → proc( string,int ) )
begin
      proc( partName : string ; amount : int )
      begin
        let part = db( lookup )( partName )
        part( quantity ) := part( quantity ) + amount
      end
end
```

Figure 10: A generator for *update* procedures.

The generator in Figure 10 has a single parameter *db* of type *Database*. All the instances of *update* produced by *updateGen* may be potentially bound to different databases which have the same type, namely *Database*. This may be generalised by the construction of a generator which is parameterised by the type of the database, i.e. to use a form of polymorphism. However, it is not possible to construct an unbounded universally quantified polymorphic generator since there are implicit constraints on the type of the database. Each generated procedure requires that the database has a field called *lookup* which is a procedure that takes a string as a parameter and returns a record. Furthermore, the returned record must have an integer field called *quantity*. These constraints require bounded universal quantification.

Constructing bounded universally quantified procedures adds considerable complexity to the applications being constructed. Ideally, such complexity would be hidden by appropriate tools in the programming environment. A new mechanism called a *Nodule* (Napier module) [11] is introduced which provides this ability. Nodules provide a way in which generic code may be specified and reused. They may be highly parameterised by the values and types used by a program, thus forming a template from which specialised instances may be obtained. Each specialised instance of a Nodule is bound to the same generic executable code as illustrated in Figure 11.

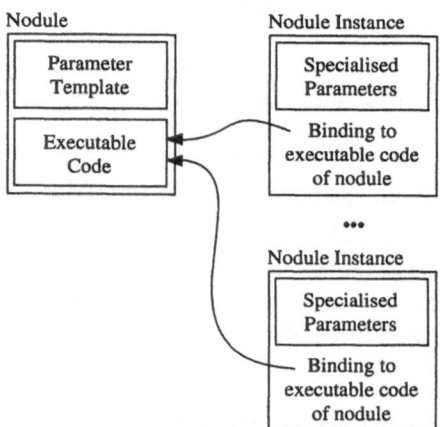

Figure 11: Conceptual view of Nodules and instances.

Nodules consist of five parts: type parameters, value parameters, functional parameters, executable code and an interface description of each Nodule instance. A Nodule is constructed and instantiated independently. Nodule instantiation involves supplying some or all of the necessary parameters to the Nodule in order to produce either a complete specialised instance or a more restricted Nodule. The latter technique is akin to *currying* and results in a new Nodule with fewer unbound parameters.

The Nodule in Figure 12 describes a parameterised version of the *update* procedure used in constructing the *partsDatabase* application.

```
NODULE UpdateNodule
PARAMETERS
    TYPE Database
    VALUE database: Database
INTERFACE
    update: proc( string,int )
```
```
SOURCE
let update= proc( name : string ; amount : int )
begin
    let part= database( lookup )( name )
    part( quantity ) := part( quantity ) + amount
end
```

Figure 12: A Nodule describing a parameterised *update* procedure.

The type *Database* and the database instance are parameters to the Nodule. There are no explicit constraints upon the type of the database; however, implicit constraints do exist: firstly, the Nodule code constrains the type *Database* to be a type which has the appropriate functionality. In this context, the type *Database* must contain the function *lookup*, which takes as its parameter a string, and returns a record which must contain an integer field, *quantity*. When a concrete type *Database* is supplied to the Nodule along with a database, a fully bound executable procedure of type **proc(string,int)** is obtained. The generic code contained in a Nodule represents a form of bounded universal quantification. However, this polymorphism is not provided by the programming language, Nodules are a mechanism used within the programming environment.

5   Environment Support

Nodules are not a feature of the programming language, instead they reside in the programming environment. In addition to tools which provide a graphical user interface to Nodules, the programming environment contains tools which allow the persistent store to be navigated, and for types and values to be located. Using a combination of these tools, users may locate Nodules, use a browser to discover values and types, and instantiate Nodules using the discovered entities. Thus, applications may be constructed without the need to write programs.

314

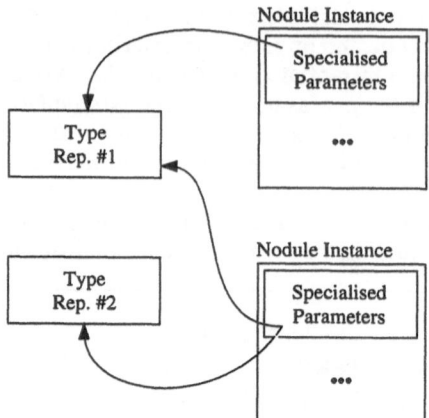

Figure 13: Storing type dependencies in Nodule instances.

Once Nodule instances have been created, they may be used as parts of other applications. The instances are values in the programming language space and therefore, if necessary, they may be manipulated by Octopus and the type evolution operations. Furthermore, Nodule instances contain information about the types on which they depend. By querying an application using Octopus, the Nodule instances dependent on a particular type may be discovered in addition to the types on which any particular Nodule instance depends. Therefore, given a particular application constructed using Nodules, if a change occurs in the schema of the application then all affected nodes may be located. Using the evolutionary mechanisms described earlier, the necessary components may then be evolved. This arrangement is shown in Figure 13.

6   Conclusions

We have presented a number of mechanisms which provide support for evolution and reuse in a persistent programming environment. Octopus permits systems of code and data to be evolved, even if they are encapsulated. This is achieved by separating pure code from bound values and providing meta level operations on all values, regardless of their type. The difficult problem of type evolution is addressed by extending the Octopus architecture to separate type information from the executable code. In many cases type evolution is possible, without the expense of total or partial system recompilation.

Nodules, a programming environment mechanism for specifying reusable components, has also been described. Nodules are complementary to the mechanisms described above and allow parameterised templates to be defined independently of any referencing environment. Nodules may be specialised in order to yield components by binding them to values and types. Since this is supported by the environment, the activity of application construction may be performed without the need to write programs. Nodules also provide added support for evolution by recording the relationship between the schema and bound Nodule instances.

Acknowledgements

We would like to thank John Rosenberg, Karen Wyrwas, Sam Bushell and David Hulse for their comments on this paper. This work was supported by the Defence Science and Technology Organisation of Australia.

References

1. Booch, G. "Object Oriented Design", Benjamin-Cummings, 1991.

2. Connor, R. C. H. "The Napier Type-Checking Module", Universities of Glasgow and St Andrews, Technical Report PPRR-58-88, 1988.

3. Dearle, A. and Brown, A. L. "Safe Browsing in a Strongly Typed Persistent Environment", *The Computer Journal*, vol 31, 6, pp. 540-545, 1988.

4. Dearle, A., Cutts, Q. and Connor, R. "Using Persistence to Support Incremental System Construction", *Microprocessors and Microsystems*, vol 17, 3, pp. 161-171, 1993.

5. Farkas, A. and Dearle, A. "The Octopus Model and its Implementation", in *Proceedings of the 17th Australian Computer Science Conference, Australian Computer Science Communications*, vol 16, pp. 581-590, 1994.

6. Farkas, A. and Dearle, A. "Octopus: A Reflective Language Mechanism for Object Manipulation", in *Proceedings of the Fourth International Workshop on Database Programming Languages*, New-York, Springer-Verlag, 1994.

7. Kirby, G. N. C., Connor, R. C. H., Cutts, Q. I., Dearle, A., Farkas, A. M. and Morrison, R. "Persistent Hyper-Programs", *5th International Workshop on Persistent Object Systems*, San Miniato, *Persistent Object Systems*, Springer-Verlag, Workshops in Computing, pp. 86-106, 1992.

8. Liskov, B. H. and Zilles, S. N. "Programming with Abstract Data Types", *SIGPLAN Notices*, vol 9, 4, 1974.

9. Morrison, R., Brown, A. L., Connor, R. C. H. and Dearle, A. "Polymorphism, Persistence and Software Reuse in a Strongly Typed Object Oriented Environment", Universities of Glasgow and St Andrews, Technical Report PPRR-32-87, 1987.

10. Morrison, R., Brown, A. L., Connor, R. C. H. and Dearle, A. "The Napier88 Reference Manual", University of St Andrews, Technical Report PPRR-77-89, 1989.

11. Farkas, A. and Dearle, A. "Integrated Support for Incremental Software Development and Evolution", University of Adelaide, Technical Report PS-24, May 1994.

Reflection and
New Language Constructs

Ray Welland
Computing Science Department, University of Glasgow
Glasgow, G12 8QQ, Scotland
ray@dcs.gla.ac.uk

In the first paper of this session, presented by Alan Kaplan, it was argued that the **name management** capabilities of current persistent object systems are weak. While some systems have dealt with the problem of uniformity of names for transient and persistent objects, none have adequate mechanisms for controlling the availability of names for use. This paper presented the results of an experiment in providing a general mechanism to support *contexts* - a flexible set of bindings which can be used for manipulating objects. A context controls which names (transient or persistent) are available for use at any point within a program. Applications have explicit control over context specification, and it is possible to query contexts and reason about them.

In the discussion following this paper, the main points raised concerned interoperability, name clashes and type checking. In trying to combine databases there will be naming problems, with the same names sometimes meaning the same thing and sometimes not. The context formation process can assist in resolving these clashes but there is a need for a renaming facility. The question of typing was also raised - when disambiguating names, how can it be ensured that the types are correct? This is a problem which has not yet been tackled in this research.

The other two papers in this session, presented by Richard Cooper and Graham Kirby, both discussed type-safe run-time **linguistic reflection**. Both started from the premise that reflection is a powerful mechanism for developing applications but that it is difficult for programmers to use effectively. Examples of the uses of reflection were configurable (or generic) programs, self-adaptive programs, such as type-safe browsers, and evolution of long-lived programs and data. Both papers discussed mechanisms for generating reflective programs in Napier88.

Richard Cooper described an approach based on the use of *templates* with placeholders for variable parts of the generator definition. He then discussed tools to manage templates and placeholders, together with a more powerful support tool for generating reflective programs. Graham Kirby described an approach based on *hyper-programming*. Instead of placeholders, the variable parts within a generator are presented as hyper-text links; this allows the different parts of a generator definition to be distinguished easily. The use of hyper-programming also provides an additional binding mechanism as the generated code may contain hyper-program links.

Much of the discussion following these two papers concerned the comparison between run-time linguistic reflection and other approaches to the problem, particularly Tim Sheard's work on TRPL and macro facilities in LISP. There was considerable discussion about the distinction (or blurring) between compile-time and run-time when you have a run-time compiler!

Graham Kirby was asked whether it was possible to separate the generated reflective code from the tool, for export to another site for example. At the moment this is not possible but Graham felt it would be possible to dump a representation of the code.

The general discussion returned to the similarity between macros and reflection and eventually it was agreed that this topic was worth a separate session. Later, Jim O'Toole and Paul Wilson gave a tutorial on the macro facilities in LISP systems to provide a comparison with the linguistic reflection techniques described by Cooper and Kirby.

The topics of all three papers came together in a discussion about names and their use with reflection. Alan Kaplan felt that the names generated during the reflection process were meaningless and that it would be better to make bindings explicit. At the other extreme, Graham Kirby took the view that hyper-programming tries to get rid of names; the names attached to buttons are arbitrary although they are of assistance to the programmer. Richard Cooper felt that names were the key to lots of hard problems and that the type system of Napier88 makes reflection easier; it would be even easier if there was a name type in the system.

Run-time reflection was compared with partial evaluation. There is an overlap in the computations that can be conveniently constructed by these two methods. However, it was pointed out that for languages that have static type-checking, run-time reflection allows more type-dependent computations while avoiding extra levels of interpretation.

When this session finished there was still a lively discussion going on about macros versus reflection, the use of names when generating code and whether static type-checking and reflection are compatible. It seems that there are still plenty of problems to be solved and research to be done in this area.

Conch: Experimenting with Enhanced Name Management for Persistent Object Systems*

Alan Kaplan

Department of Computer Science, University of Massachusetts
Amherst, MA USA

Jack C. Wileden

Department of Computer Science, University of Massachusetts
Amherst, MA USA

Abstract

The name management capabilities currently provided by most existing persistent object systems (POSs) are rather limited. In particular, existing POSs tend to lack powerful and general mechanisms for forming, manipulating, controlling and reasoning about contexts. As a result, these POSs offer only weak or awkward support for large-scale data storage, multi-user computing, code reuse, interoperation of independently developed object stores and other similarly important classes of applications. As part of our work on improved name management for convergent computing systems, we have developed a framework for uniform treatment of the context and interface control facets of name management. In this paper we describe a realization of that framework, in the form of a shell-style user interface to a POS, that we are using to experiment both with the framework itself and with enhanced context control capabilities for POSs.

1 Introduction

A *convergent computing system* is any system in which two or more distinct computing domains or paradigms are combined into what is intended to be a synergistic whole. Naturally, various issues and complications arise in constructing such systems.

We are particularly interested in name management for convergent computing systems. By *name management* we mean the way in which a computing system allows names to be established for objects, permits objects to be accessed using names, and controls the availability and meaning of names at any point in time. Problems that arise in convergent computing systems often result from complexities or shortcomings in the name management mechanisms

---

*This material is based upon work sponsored by the Advanced Research Projects Agency under grant MDA972-91-J-1009 and by Texas Instruments under grant SRA-2837024. The content does not necessarily reflect the position or policy of the U S. Government or Texas Instruments and no official endorsement should be inferred.

of their underlying components or from incompatibilities among those mechanisms. An important goal of our research is improved mechanisms for name management in convergent computing systems.

Persistent object systems (POSs) are a particularly interesting class of convergent computing systems. POSs promise to break down barriers between capabilities traditionally found in programming languages, database systems and operating systems and to combine all (or at least most) of the best features of each. In recent years, POS research has led to significant progress at overcoming barriers and synergistically combining capabilities related to various aspects of such systems, including type models (e.g., [1]), persistence mechanisms (e.g., [2]), optimization techniques (e.g., [3]) and concurrency control mechanisms (e.g., [4]).

A notable exception to this trend is the limited attention that has been given to name management for POSs. There have been a few instances of POSs offering some improvements in name management (e.g., [5, 6, 7, 8, 9]). By and large, however, the relatively weak name management mechanisms found in the ancestors of POSs, i.e., programming languages, database systems and operating systems, have tended to endure in POSs, being neither improved nor even effectively integrated. Without better name management, POSs will likely prove cumbersome to use and prone to error, will provide inadequate support for large-scale data storage, multi-user computing, code reuse and interoperation of independently developed object stores, and will therefore fail to realize their potential for beneficial employment in a variety of important application areas.

We believe that our work on name management for convergent computing systems has particular relevance for POSs. In fact, our interest in the general topic of name management grew out of earlier work on PGraphite [2, 10] and R&R [11], two complementary prototype systems that together implemented a rudimentary persistent object capability as an extension to Ada. Experimental use of these systems highlighted a number of name management problems, arising primarily from the need to simultaneously manage names of both transient and persistent objects. Among these, the two most fundamental were the problems of:

Uniformity: the lack of integration between names for transient (programming language-internal) and persistent (programming language-external) data objects, and

Context Control: the incommensurate, and inadequate, mechanisms for controlling exactly which names (of both transient and persistent objects) are available for use (at any given point) within a program.

Having observed these problems while experimenting with PGraphite and R&R, we soon discovered that similar problems existed in most other POSs[1] and, more generally, in most convergent computing systems. Both problems are particularly prevalent in "persistent[X]" POSs, those created by extending some existing programming language with support for persistence (and possibly some additional database and operating systems capabilities), but otherwise leaving the underlying language unchanged. The other major class of POSs, namely the *de novo* POSs, i.e., those that have been created by defining new

---

[1]In fact, in their list of requirements for persistence [12], Atkinson and Buneman appear to refer to both of these problems (requirements (4) and (9)).

languages specifically designed to provide persistence (and possibly some additional database and operating system capabilities), have sometimes avoided the uniformity problem but generally not the context control problem.

Initially, our research on name management for convergent computing systems centered on defining a taxonomy of problems and potential solutions, and on developing and experimenting with some simple, but uniform, naming mechanisms [13], as a basis for addressing the uniformity problem. More recently, we have focused on context control issues. In particular, we have defined a framework, called PICCOLO, for describing context control problems and mechanisms in convergent computing systems [14] and begun to experiment with its use.

In this paper, we describe an ongoing experiment in improving the context control facet of name management in POSs. We begin by sketching some representative context control problems arising in POSs and outlining the PICCOLO framework. We then describe a prototype realization of the framework in the form of CONCH, a shell-style user interface to a persistent[C++] POS, and show how it can be used to address the representative problems. The paper concludes with an assessment of the current status of the experiment, a discussion of related work, and a summary of ongoing and future efforts aimed at further improvements in name management for POSs.

2   Context Control Problems in POSs

As noted in the previous section, POSs tend to provide inadequate approaches to name management, especially with respect to controlling context. While orthogonal persistence should obviate the need for traditional persistence mechanisms, such as file systems and databases (at least from the programmer's perspective), users of POSs are typically still faced with using primitive name management mechanisms, based on those found in operating systems or database management systems, for controlling the meanings of names for persistent objects. As a result, existing POSs tend to lack powerful and general mechanisms for forming, manipulating, controlling and reasoning about contexts.

As an illustration of the shortcomings of context control for POSs, consider the situation facing a hypothetical application developer wishing to build a system that accesses various electronic mail-related objects from a persistent store. Some name management problems that the developer must resolve include:

1. The developer wants to be able to organize objects and their names in the persistent store into logical, meaningful collections.

2. The developer wants to be able to flexibly form contexts giving particular meanings to names used in the application. The resulting contexts may not correspond exactly to any single collection in the set of collections from (1) above. Furthermore, the developer wants to be able to specify different contexts for the application without necessarily having to re-compile (or possibly even re-link) the application.

3. The developer wants to be able to reason about how contexts are formed and used by the application. For example, given an application, the developer should be able to determine what names the application refers to,

whether objects corresponding to those names exist, whether the objects can be accessed and/or modified by others, and whether the names used have unambiguous meanings.

As an example of the first point, our hypothetical developer might wish to impose the conceptual organization depicted in Figure 1 on a relevant subset of objects in the persistent store. In this figure, persistent objects are represented

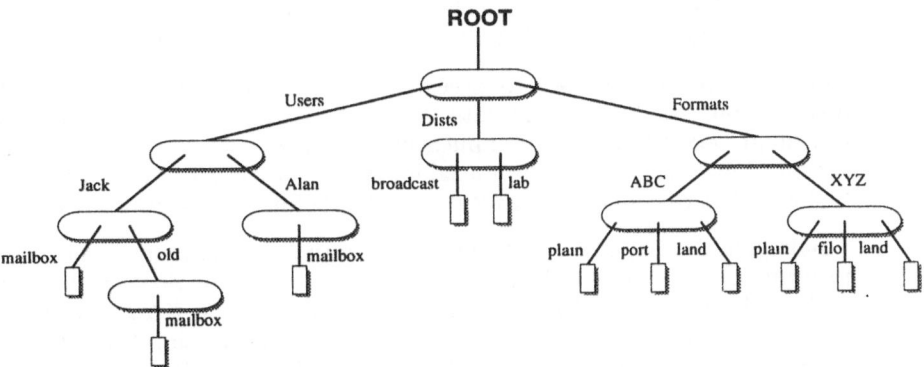

Figure 1: Conceptual Organization of the Persistent Store

by both ellipses and rectangles. Ellipses denote collections of named objects, where names are attached to arcs emanating from an ellipse to a corresponding object, represented by either a rectangle or another ellipse. The only exception to this is the name ROOT, which identifies the root collection of the structure and is not contained in any other collection. For the purposes of this example, assume that the objects named **mailbox** contain electronic mail messages, that the objects named **broadcast** and **lab** represent distribution lists, and that the collections named **ABC** and **XYZ** contain a variety of message-printing formats provided by two different vendors. Note that these collections happen to have common names for some objects, a problematic, though not uncommon, situation in the commercial arena [15]. In addition, assume that multiple users and/or applications may be accessing and modifying the persistent store.

Given this logical organization of the persistent store, our developer's goal is an application that can manipulate a user's mailbox (e.g., compose, send, read, print and archive messages), making use of all the distribution lists and some subset of the message formats. Correct execution of this application will depend upon the availability of an appropriate context, connecting names used by the application with specific objects in the persistent store. Thus the application developer, or user, needs some means of controlling context formation. For example, the developer should be able to specify what names are needed in the desired context, what objects are bound to those names, at what point in the application's lifetime name-object associations are formed, and whether names are associated with existing objects or copies of objects in the persistent store.[2]

---

[2]For example, linkers in traditional programming environments typically create copies of object code modules from libraries and make links to the copies, rather than to the library modules themselves, when constructing an executable program.

For instance, one possible set of context requirements (and clearly not the only set) for this hypothetical application might include the following:

1. It should be possible to use the application with *any* user's mailbox without either having to re-compile (or re-link) the application or having to interactively interrogate the user for the location of the mailbox. This means that the context for the application must include an association between the name **mailbox** and a specific object in the persistent store that is formed at the time when the mailbox object is actually accessed in the application (as opposed to at compile-time, link-time or load-time).

2. The application will need to access both the **broadcast** and the **lab** distribution lists, but the contents of these lists should be constant during any single execution of the application. Hence the context associating specific (and subsequently immutable) objects with those names should be formed at the time the application is loaded into the run-time system.

3. Finally, our developer is satisfied with the current versions of the message-printing formats named **plain** and **port** contained in the **ABC** collection, and the formats named **filo** and **land** contained in the **XYZ** collection. So, it would be appropriate to form a context associating those names with copies of those specific objects at compile-time. This means that, once compiled, the application will be shielded from any changes to the objects through the persistent store (e.g., name changes, message format changes).

One goal, then, for a context control mechanism is to give developers and users explicit control over context specification for persistent objects [16]. Another important goal is to give subsequent developers or maintainers access to this information in a uniform manner. In other words, instead of having the tedious and error-prone task of manually analyzing source code and/or configuration scripts, developers and maintainers should be able to query an object directly for its relevant context formation information. Similarly, both humans and automated tools should be able to reason about this context information, thus facilitating the detection of potential name management-related inconsistencies and errors.

Most existing POSs support few, if any, of these capabilities. In the next two sections, we outline a framework and a prototype realization of that framework with the potential to support all these capabilities and more in a uniform and powerful way.

3   Piccolo

As a step toward enhanced name management for convergent computing systems, and specifically for POSs, we wish to provide powerful and general mechanisms for forming, manipulating, controlling and reasoning about contexts. By the very nature of a convergent computing system, such as a POS, the context mechanism we seek must be uniformly applicable across a broad range of computing paradigms. In the case of POSs, in particular, it should be applicable to context-related aspects of programming languages, databases and operating systems, and should apply to both persistent and transient objects.

We believe that this goal is best achieved by basing the mechanism on an abstract model or framework. We have therefore developed the PICCOLO model, a framework for Precise Interface and Context Control in Object Libraries and Objects. PICCOLO is inspired in part by the PIC framework for precise interface control in programming languages [17]. In the remainder of this section we briefly outline the PICCOLO framework. The next section describes one realization of the framework that we are currently using to experiment both with the framework itself and with enhanced context control capabilities for POSs.

The PICCOLO framework is based on the following set of fundamental name management concepts:

object: An item of interest in a given setting.

name: An identifier used to reference, access or manipulate an object.

binding: In its simplest, most basic form a (name,object) pair. The availability of binding (n, o) makes it possible to use name n to reference, access or manipulate object o. Bindings may also include additional information, such as type and mutability information (as, for example, in Napier [18]).

binding space: A set of bindings that serves as a collection of definitions for names.

context: A set of bindings that is available for use in referencing, accessing or manipulating objects. A context may consist of, or be formed from, one or more binding spaces, or parts of binding spaces, or other contexts. PICCOLO's explicit distinction between binding spaces, which are primarily a means for organizing collections of bindings, typically for user convenience, and contexts, which a system uses in interpreting names during its operation, significantly facilitates modeling of many name management approaches.

closure: In its simplest, most basic form an (object, context) pair. Given the existence of the closure (o, c), it is possible for object o to use context c in referencing, accessing or manipulating other objects.

resolution: The action of returning an object when given a name and a context.

Given these fundamental concepts, the PICCOLO framework defines specific name management approaches and mechanisms using the following two kinds of components:

context formation template (CFT): A collection of directives governing the formation of contexts. In a typical approach to name management we can further distinguish between two kinds of CFTs:

Requestor: A CFT Requestor (or CFTR) describes the context requirements for an object. In particular, it specifies a collection of names referenced by the object. It can additionally include directives indicating such things as preferred sources of definitions (i.e., binding spaces) for the referenced names and preferred times (i.e., epochs) for context formation or modification steps.

Provider: A CFT Provider (or CFTP) describes the context definitions potentially available from an object. Analogously to CFTRs, it can additionally specify such things as preferred targets (i.e., other objects) for these definitions and preferred times for context formation or modification steps.

context formation process (CFP): A procedure that produces a context from an initial context and one or more CFTs.

As suggested by the above definitions of CFTR and CFTP, the PICCOLO framework provides a means for explicitly representing distinct times at which context manipulation activities may occur:

epoch: An epoch denotes a particular time period during which context manipulation activities may take place. The set of all epochs is described by an enumeration such as $E = \{e_1, e_2, \ldots\}$.

Applying the PICCOLO framework involves defining a specific set of epochs appropriate to the host system's context formation and manipulation needs, specific kinds of directives that can appear in CFTs and one or more specific CFPs. It also implies a suitable generalization of the concept of closure, such as the following:

closure $\equiv (o, (C_i, \{CFT*, CFP*\}))$ where C_i represents an initial context, $CFT*$ represents a (possibly empty) set of context formation templates for directing the incremental formation of future contexts, and $CFP*$ represents a corresponding set of context formation processes that will be directed by those CFTs during incremental formation of future contexts.

One example application of the framework is the experimental context control shell, CONCH, which is described in Section 4.

We envision two major categories of use for the PICCOLO framework. First, it can serve as a basis for analyzing context control mechanisms and problems, especially in convergent computing systems but in more traditional settings as well. Careful description of a particular context control mechanism in terms of PICCOLO's CFT and CFP constructs permits rigorous reasoning about and comparison of various existing, proposed or possible approaches to context control.

Second, the PICCOLO framework can serve as a foundation for defining and implementing context control mechanisms. We are, of course, especially interested in applying it to the definition and implementation of such mechanisms for convergent computing systems, such as POSs. By defining a mechanism using the framework, we can avoid *ad hoc* solutions, reason about properties of a mechanism before implementing it, and achieve uniformity in the functioning of the mechanism. This latter feature is particularly important in the setting of convergent computing systems, where the mechanism may well have several different realizations corresponding to different aspects, or ancestral constituents, of the convergent system.

In the next section, we describe an experiment in which we have implemented a context control mechanism based on the PICCOLO framework in the form of a shell-style user interface to a POS. While there are several other forms in which this mechanism might, and probably should, be realized in a

POS, we have found this one convenient for experimentation and also rather easy and natural to use for certain kinds of context control operations. We will provide further assessment of this experiment in the paper's final section.

4   Conch: A Context Control Shell

The idea of a "shell" acting as an intermediary between applications and the underlying persistent store is by no means a new one. In traditional systems, such as UNIX,[3] a variety of shells have been implemented to provide an interface between programs and the UNIX file system. Similarly, relational database systems often provide an interactive SQL that allows users to interact with the database. In recent years, graphical browsers for POSs have begun to emerge [19, 20]. Neither previously existing shells nor graphical browsers, however, provide sufficiently powerful and general context control capabilities for use with convergent computing systems like POSs. In this section, we report on CONCH, a prototype CONtext-Controlling sHell for POSs that we have implemented as a user interface for Open OODB, a persistent[C++] POS [21]. We then illustrate how CONCH can be applied to the scenario presented earlier in Section 2.

CONCH is a realization of the PICCOLO framework. It facilitates experimentation with that framework as well as with enhanced context control capabilities for POSs. More specifically, the present version of the CONCH prototype represents an experiment with a particular method of providing a particular set of name management capabilities and an attempt to unify these capabilities from a "shell" perspective.

In its plain, vanilla form, Open OODB[4] provides relatively limited support for name management for persistent objects. There exists only a single, flat space of names; names for persistent objects must always be resolved at runtime and always return a reference to an object (instead of, perhaps, a copy of that object); and reuse of a name always overrides the existing binding.

The CONCH prototype addresses many of these shortcomings and has resulted in improved support for name management in Open OODB. The current set of commands defined by the CONCH interface is listed in Table 1. (Since Open OODB ordinarily runs under UNIX, the CONCH command names and syntax are intentionally UNIX-like.) First, CONCH directly supports the PICCOLO concepts of *name*, *object*, *binding* and *binding space*, thus, allowing persistent stores to be organized similarly to the one depicted in Figure 1. Furthermore, the commands **lbs**, **abs**, **cbs**, **rtbs**, **rmb**, and **bind** permit developers and users to easily traverse, modify and query the Open OODB persistent store. Similarly to other shell-style approaches, CONCH supports the notion of an *active* (or current) binding space. Note that the only way to create new bindings from the shell is through use of the **bind** command. In addition, CONCH provides a collection of C++ class interfaces that allow applications to interact with the persistent store in a similar manner.

Second, CONCH allows developers to precisely and explicitly express context formation requirements for applications accessing the persistent store by pro-

---

[3]UNIX is a registered trademark in the United States and other countries, licensed exclusively through X/OPEN corporation.
[4]Alpha Release 0.2

326

Command	Description
lbs	List contents of the *active* binding space
abs \<name\>	Binding space with name \<name\> becomes *active* binding space
cbs \<name\>	Create a new binding space
rtbs	ROOT binding space becomes active
rmb \<name\>	Remove binding for name \<name\>
bind \<name1\> \<name2\>	Bind name \<name2\> to object bound to name \<name1\>
cftr \<name\>	Create a CFTR with name \<name\>
cftp \<name\>	Create a CFTP with name \<name\>
cftq \<name\>	Query the CFT with name \<name\>
inclos \<cft-name\> \<obj-name\>	Insert CFT into object's closure
prclos \<name\>	Print contents of object's closure

Table 1: Conch Commands

viding specific kinds of CFTRs, CFTPs, and CFPs. The commands **cftr**, **cftp** and **cftq** allow users to create and query CFTs. More specifically, a CFTR in CONCH consists of one or more *request* clauses, where a request clause consists of the following fields:

Names: the names whose corresponding bindings should be contained in the context.

Bind: an indication of whether the bindings should be to existing objects (REF) or to copies of objects (COPY).

Epoch: when the bindings in the context should be formed. (CONCH supports the epochs {COMPILE, LOAD, RUN}.)

Sources: the source binding spaces for the desired bindings.

Similarly to a CFTR, a CFTP in CONCH consists of one or more *provide* clauses, where a provide clause consists of analogous fields. Finally, CONCH defines a rudimentary CFP for forming contexts. In the current prototype, this CFP is automatically included in the closure for all objects, thus ensuring that all objects utilize the same method for context formation. The pseudo-code for the CFP employed by CONCH is shown in Figure 2. This simple CFP creates a new context by augmenting the contents of a given context with the bindings as directed by a CFTR and the current epoch. It also checks to ensure that the resulting context is valid and provides warning or error information in the event the checking should fail. Note that the CFP is not an explicit command in CONCH. Instead, in the prototype the CFP is invoked by various system-level tools, such as the compiler, linker and run-time system.

To illustrate the use of CONCH, we return to the scenario outlined in Section 2, in which a developer is faced with the problem of specifying and constructing a context that associates appropriate objects in the persistent store with names used in a mail system application. The developer's task is complicated by the fact that the different bindings in the resulting context must satisfy different requirements. With CONCH, one way to solve the problem in

```
Context CFP (Context current,           request plain, port
             CFTR c,                    copy
             Epoch current)             compile
begin                                   sources Root.Formats.ABC;
  Context new = current
  foreach clause in c do                request filo, land
    if current = clause.Epoch then      copy
      foreach name in clause.Names do   compile
        object = find (name) in         sources Root.Formats.XYZ;
               clause.Sources
        if not found then               request broadcast, lab
          raise ContextError            copy
        if clause.Value = copied then   load
          new.Insert (name, object.copy) sources Root.Dists;
        else
          new.Insert (name, object)     request mailbox
                                        ref
  return new                            run
end CFP                                 sources *active*;
```

Figure 2: Default CFP   Figure 3: Example CFTR

the scenario is to use the **cftr** and **inclos** commands to create the CFTR shown in Figure 3 and form a closure associating that CFTR and the application code.

The CFTR directs a context to be created as follows:

- At compile-time, the context must contain the names **plain**, **port**, **filo** and **land**, each bound to a copy of the appropriate persistent object. The preferred source for the objects named **plain** and **port** is the binding space named **ABC**, while the preferred source for the objects named **filo** and **land** is the binding space named **XYZ**.

- When the program is first loaded into the run-time system, the context must additionally contain the names **broadcast** and **lab** bound to copies of the appropriate persistent objects, whose preferred source is the **Dists** binding space.

- Each time the mailbox object is accessed, the context should be updated to contain a binding pairing the name **mailbox** with the then-current object associated with the name **mailbox** in the *active* binding space.

Once this CFTR has been created and inserted into the applications' closure, the next step is to compile, link and run the application. The entire process is depicted in Figure 4, where the arrows denote and identify epoch boundaries. The starting point is a closure consisting of the application source code, an (initially) empty context, the CFP from Figure 2, and the CFTR from Figure 3. Invocation of the compiler initiates the **compile** epoch. The CFP, CFTR and context are retrieved from the source code's closure and a new closure consisting of a binary executable, a (partially formed) context, the CFP and the CFTR is produced. Then, using the **cbs** command, the user sets the

328

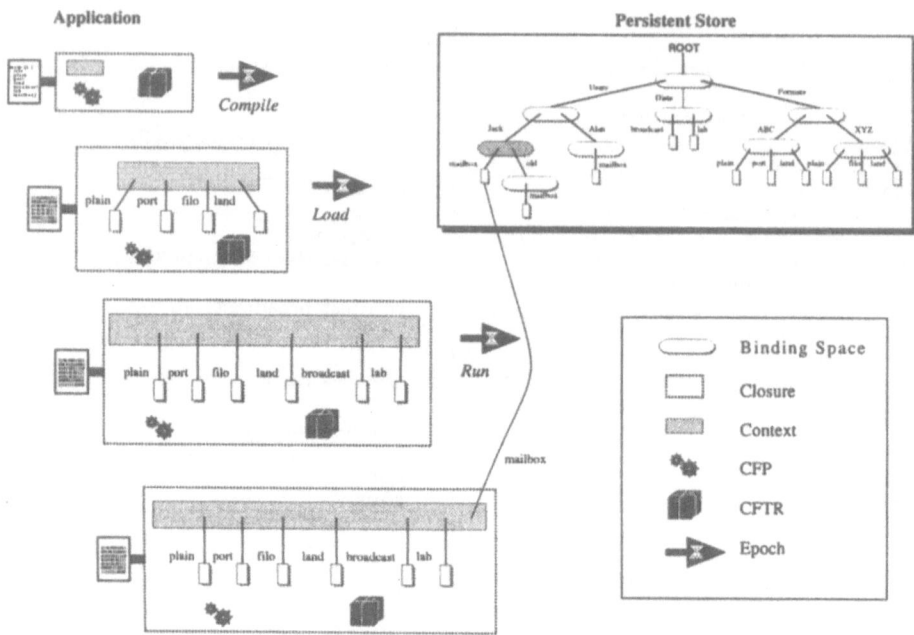

Figure 4: Context Formation Process

active binding space to be **Jack**.[5] In Figure 4, the shaded ellipse denotes the *active* binding space. Next the program is loaded into the run-time system. This signals initiation of the **load** epoch, so the CFTR directs the context to be augmented appropriately and a correspondingly updated closure is formed. Finally, execution of the application begins, initiating the **run** epoch, and the mailbox object is accessed. As directed by the CFTR, the context is now augmented with a binding pairing the name **mailbox** with the object associated with the name **mailbox** in the *active* binding space, i.e., the object named **mailbox** in the binding space named **Jack**.

Note that the closure mechanism in CONCH associates a CFP and a CFTR as well as a context with each object. Although not illustrated in this simple example, maintaining this information allows application developers and maintainers to easily determine the context formation requirements for an application using the **prclos** command.

5 Summary

In this paper we have described CONCH, a prototype context-controlling shell implemented as a user interface to Open OODB, and briefly outlined the PIC-COLO framework on which it is based. Initial experimentation with CONCH appears to confirm our expectation that a context control mechanism based

---

[5]In fact, this step could be taken either earlier or later than this, so long as it has occurred before the beginning of the **run** epoch.

on PICCOLO would provide more general, flexible and powerful context control than that available in existing POSs. In particular, the approach facilitates the sharing of context information among objects, while at the same time permitting individual objects to define their own context formation requirements. Furthermore, since context data is never discarded, application developers and maintainers can access this valuable information in a uniform and efficient manner. We therefore believe that the approach embodied in CONCH and PICCOLO can contribute to making POSs easier to use, less prone to error and better suited for use in a wide range of applications. Experimentation has, however, also pointed up a number of possible improvements and extensions that would make the approach even more beneficial.

We believe that existing approaches to context control in POSs are not as powerful and general as the approach described in this paper. While Napier [22, 18], for example, certainly allows for flexible organizations of persistent stores, developers must describe specific persistent store navigations in each application [23]. Moreover, Napier does not provide adequate means for querying objects regarding their contextual formation information. This can be problematic in Napier programs that create bindings in closures local to a procedure, since there is no means for determining whether other Napier programs may be able to access the objects in those bindings. The approach taken by Farkas et al. [9] ameliorates these problems to some degree, but it is unclear how well a graphical browsing paradigm is suited for managing contexts in large and complex applications. We view our work on the PICCOLO framework and the CONCH shell as an approach that could complement these and other approaches in existing and future POSs. Indeed, in the near future we hope to explore the incorporation of CONCH-like capabilities into a *de novo* POS such as Napier in order to further assess the generality and the efficacy of both the PICCOLO framework and the CONCH constructs.

As noted above, experiments with CONCH have suggested a number of improvements and extensions that could be made. Some of these involve additional capabilities for the shell, such as richer mechanisms for binding specification (e.g., allowing CFTs to specify local renaming of objects), for context specification (e.g., incorporating CFTPs into closure definitions or allowing CFTRs to define sources as combinations of binding spaces [13]) and for creating and querying CFPs. Others would make the approach more user-friendly; the existing, relatively low level and explicit, shell commands are suitable for the fine-grained control needed in experimentation, but much of the effort involved in creating and manipulating CFTs could, and probably should, be automated or hidden to benefit POS users. Still others involve enhancements to the underlying PICCOLO framework. For example, the relationship of context manipulation to such traditional mechanisms as versioning and transactions needs further exploration; either descriptions of such mechanisms in terms of PICCOLO need to be formulated or else the PICCOLO framework should be extended to account for them. We are already pursuing some of these directions, and we expect that continued refinement and further experimentation with both CONCH and PICCOLO will contribute to significant enhancements in name management capabilities for POSs and, more generally, for convergent computing systems.

References

[1] R.C.H. Connor, A.L. Brown, Q.I. Cutts, A. Dearle, R. Morrison, and J. Rosenberg. Type equivalence checking in persistent object systems. In *Proceedings of the Fourth International Workshop on Persistent Object Systems*, pages 154–167, Martha's Vineyard, MA, August 1990.

[2] J.C. Wileden, A.L. Wolf, C.D. Fisher, and P.L. Tarr. PGRAPHITE: An experiment in persistent typed object management. In *Proceedings of the Third Symposium of Software Development Environments*, pages 130–142, September 1988.

[3] V. Benzaken and C. Delobel. Enhancing performance in a persistent object store: Clustering strategies in O_2. In *Proceedings of the Fourth International Workshop on Persistent Object Systems*, pages 403–412, Martha's Vineyard, MA, August 1990.

[4] M.H. Nodine, A.H. Skarra, and S.B. Zdonik. Synchronization and recovery in cooperative transactions. In *Proceedings of the Fourth International Workshop on Persistent Object Systems*, pages 329–344, Martha's Vineyard, MA, August 1990.

[5] M.P. Atkinson and R. Morrison. Types, bindings and parameters in a persistent environment. In *Data Types and Persistence*, pages 3–20. Springer-Verlag, 1988. (*Proceedings of the First International Workshop on Persistent Object Systems*, Appin, Scotland, August, 1985).

[6] M.P. Atkinson and R. Morrison. Polymorphic names, types, constancy and magic in a type secure persistent object store. In *Proceedings of the Second International Workshop on Persistent Object Systems*, pages 1–12, Appin, Scotland, August 1987.

[7] P.A. Buhr and C.R. Zarnke. Persistence in an environment for a statically-typed programming language. In *Proceedings of the Second International Workshop on Persistent Object Systems*, pages 317–336, Appin, Scotland, August 1987.

[8] J.W. Schmidt and F. Matthes. Naming schemes and name space management in the DBPL persistent storage system. In *Proceedings of the Fourth International Workshop on Persisent Object Systems*, pages 39–58, September 1990.

[9] A.M. Farkas, A. Dearle, G.N.C. Kirby, Q.I. Cutts, R. Morrison, and R.C.H. Connor. Persistent program construction through browsing and user gesture with some typing. In *Proceedings of the Fifth International Workshop on Persistent Object Systems*, pages 375–394, San Miniato, Italy, 1992.

[10] P.L. Tarr, J.C. Wileden, and A.L. Wolf. A different tack to providing persistence in a language. In Richard Hull, Ronald Morrison, and David Stemple, editors, *Second International Workshop on Database Programming Languages*, pages 41–60, June 1989.

[11] P.L. Tarr, J.C. Wileden, and L.A. Clarke. Extending and limiting PGRAPHITE-style persistence. In *Proceedings of the Fourth International Workshop on Persistent Object Systems*, pages 74–86, Martha's Vineyard, MA, August 1990.

[12] M.P. Atkinson and P. Buneman. Types and persistence in database programming languages. *ACM Computing Surveys*, 19(2):105–190, June 1987.

[13] A. Kaplan and J.C. Wileden. Name management and object technology for advanced software. In *International Symposium on Object Technologies for Advanced Software*, number 742 in Lecture Notes in Computer Science, pages 371–392, Kanazawa, Japan, November 1993.

[14] A. Kaplan and J.C. Wileden. More precise name management for object-oriented methods, systems and databases. In preparation.

[15] T. Andrews. Designing linguistic interfaces to an object database or what do C++, SQL and Hell have in common? In *Fourth International Workshop on Database Programming Languages*, New York, NY, Aug–Sep 1993. (Invited Talk).

[16] M.P. Atkinson, P. Buneman, and R. Morrison. Binding and type checking in database programming languages. *The Computer Journal*, 31(2):99–109, February 1988.

[17] A.L. Wolf, L.A. Clarke, and J.C. Wileden. The AdaPIC Tool Set: Supporting interface control and analysis throughout the software development process. *IEEE Transactions on Software Engineering*, 15(3):250–263, March 1989.

[18] R. Morrison, F. Brown, R. Connor, Q. Cutts, A. Dearle, G. Kirby, and D. Munro. The Napier88 reference manual (release 2.0). Technical Report CS/93/150, University of St. Andrews, St. Andrews, U.K., 1993.

[19] A. Dearle and A.L. Brown. Safe browsing in a strongly typed persistent environment. *The Computer Journal*, 31(6):540–544, April 1988.

[20] A. Dearle, Q.I. Cutts, and G.N.C. Kirby. Browsing, grazing and nibbling persistent data structures. In John Rosenberg and David Koch, editors, *Proceedings of the Third International Workshop on Persisent Object Systems*, pages 56–69, Newcastle, Australia, January 1989.

[21] D.L. Wells, J.A. Blakely, and C.W. Thompson. Architecture of an open object-oriented database management system. *IEEE Computer*, 25(10):74–82, October 1992.

[22] A. Dearle. Environments: A flexible binding mechanism to support system evolution. In *22nd Hawaii International Conference on System Sciences*, pages 46–55, Hawaii, January 1989.

[23] M.P. Atkinson. Persistent programming practices. In *Proceedings of the Fifth International Workshop on Persistent Object Systems*, pages 352–353, San Miniato, Italy, 1992.

Type-Safe Linguistic Run-time Reflection
A Practical Perspective

Richard Cooper and Graham Kirby*

Dept. of Computing Science, University of Glasgow. Glasgow G12 8QQ, Scotland

*Division of Computer Science, University of St Andrews,
North Haugh, St Andrews, Fife KY16 9SS, Scotland

Abstract

Reflection is a property of application development systems which permits programs to change their own behaviour. Linguistic reflection is a variety in which this is carried out by extending the program with extra modules which are created, compiled and linked in by the program itself. With run-time reflection this happens during the running of the program. Typically this occurs by including commands in the program to create the new module as a string and then call either the compiler or interpreter for the language to create an executable form. When combined with persistence, the executable code can then be stored for re-use. However, writing programs which exploit reflection can be a daunting task, since keeping track of multiple representations of a program can involve copious amounts of intricate string manipulation. This paper sets out to analyse some of the issues which make for difficulty, to outline some support tools which have been created and then to discuss the possibilities of an underlying language-independent theory for reflection.

1   Introduction

The development of programming languages for building persistent applications has been motivated by the need to support the secure description of computation over long-lived values with complex structures [1]. Since the programs and data are both expected to be long lasting and therefore run-time errors may not be detected for some considerable time, it is essential that there is as much checking of the program at compile time as possible. Hence there is a great benefit if database programming languages are strongly typed and, wherever possible, statically typed.

There is, however, an inevitable tension between type security and programming flexibility. In an inflexibly typed language, such as Pascal, there needs to be much repetitive programming and some kinds of computation can only be expressed in cumbersome and inefficient ways. Modern type systems attempt to ameliorate this situation by providing type constructors which allow more general programming.

Parametric types allow the programming of code against values drawn from a range of types which vary only in the type of some component value which the code does not touch [2]. Dynamic types package a range of types so that they appear to be the same type [3]. Using these techniques a great many programs can be written which are general to a range of types – polymorphic programs. However, all such polymorphic programming works either by assuming that detail in the type information can be abstracted over or, in the case of *ad hoc* polymorphism, that the range of types is known at the outset and can thus be catered for.

This leaves a range of applications in which: the program needs to make use of the detail of the type information; this type detail varies between the types that the program has to deal with; and the range of types to be dealt with is not known by the programmer at the time that the program is written. Consider, for instance the creation of a program which is to display the value of a variable which is passed to it. If this program is to cope with values which may be scalars, then it will be possible to write a piece of *ad hoc* polymorphic code, since there are a known and limited set of scalar types in the language. If arrays are also to be included, then it is possible to write generic code as long as the type of an array does not depend on its size. If, however, the values may also include records, simple *ad hoc* polymorphism will not work. Take for instance an attempt to print out the value of a *Person* record where the record has a *name* and an *age* field. Using Pascal notation, there needs to be a line in the code of the form:

```
writeLn( P.name, P.age )
```

In other words, the program has to have type specific detail (the names of the fields) embedded in it.

This is the situation in which reflection becomes a suitable technique. A **reflective language** is one in which it is possible to write programs which can adapt their behaviour to cope with novel data [4]. There are essentially two ways in which a program can adapt its behaviour, either by changing its execution environment or by changing itself. The former case we call **behavioural reflection** and this includes systems in which the program can affect internal structures of the compiler or run-time environment which cause the program to work differently [5]. Some object oriented systems, such as Modulex, provide a form of behavioural reflection by use of meta-classes [6]. Meta-classes are classes whose members are themselves classes. The meta-class to which an object belongs determines a great deal about the form and facilities associated with that object. If an application can change a meta-class in the same way as it can change an ordinary class, then the program can change the behaviour of its classes.

The other form of reflection is **linguistic reflection**, in which the program changes itself directly. Lisp [7] was the first language to provide this with the *eval* function and POP2 [8] was another language in which mini-programs could be constructed and executed at run-time. Both of these languages were untyped and so the problem of matching individually typed incarnations of the code caused no problems. TRPL [9] applied linguistic reflection to a strongly typed language, by making the reflection happen at compile time. TRPL provides macros which are evaluated at compile time and these macros can allow the compiled program to vary depending upon the context in which it is compiled.

The particular form of reflection with which this paper concerns itself is **type-safe run-time linguistic reflection**. That is, the program modifies itself at run-time, but always through the inclusion of code which is type checked. The paper will discuss two systems which provide this facility. Napier88 [10] does so by supplying the compiler as a system function which can be called at any time during the run of a program to transform a string containing source code into a new fragment of the program. O$_2$ [11] provides reflection in the form of a system function which calls the interpreter – again the interpreter is passed a string and the result can be a modification to the application.

The problem with the use of linguistic reflection is that it requires the use of a daunting amount of manipulation of code representations and the careful control of different program representations in the same environment. The program contains fragments which are normal code, pieces which are code representations and pieces which connect the two. To this end a number of proposals have been made to simplify the problem of writing reflective programs [12, 13, 5], but no firm solution is yet in place. In this paper, tools are described which make reflective programming significantly easier. The paper concludes with insights into the interaction between the nature of the type system and the ways in which reflection can be produced. To start with, however, the technique will be described with examples and the uses of reflection will be categorised.

2 Type-Safe Run-Time Linguistic Reflection

A language, *L*, exhibits type-safe run-time linguistic reflection if the run-time environment of the language contains 1) a module, callable at run-time, which is capable of generating code and checking its validity, and 2) a method of linking that code into the running program. For the purposes of this paper, the module will be restricted to being a version of the compiler or interpreter used by the system.

Thus, in general, if there is a module, *M*, which takes source code in the form of a string – either from a file or from the terminal and produces code, i.e:

$$\text{M: string} \rightarrow \text{code}$$

then the kinds of system being dealt with here provide a version of *M* which takes a string within the program and creates code.

2.1 Type-Safe Run-Time Linguistic Reflection in Napier88

In Napier88, this module is a version of the compiler, callable at run-time, which takes in a string containing a block of code and returns a compiled form of the block. A block of code in Napier88 is a sequence of void clauses (i.e. clauses which return no value) possibly ending with a clause which does return a value. Thus:

```
I := 1
J := 2
I+J
```

is a block of type **int** in Napier88. The run-time compiler returns the compiled form of the code, but as this might be of any legal Napier88 type, the return type of the compiler is the dynamic type, **any**, which is the infinite union of all Napier88 types. To derive the actual value out of the dynamic type, Napier88 provides the **project** clause which reveals the actual type. The detail of this is slightly different for void and non-void blocks.

If *source* is a string containing a void block, the following code will cause it to be compiled and executed:

```
object := compile( source)
project object as O onto
    string: writeString( "Errors: " ++ O )        ! If the compilation fails.
    proc(): O()                                    ! Executes the program.
    default: writeString( "Internal compiler error" )   ! Should never happen.
```

The **project** statement projects the compiled form, *object*, either as a string containing error messages or as a parameterless procedure (i.e. a compiled form of the block in *source*) which can then be executed. So if the only visibly effecting part of *source* was the line "writeString("ABC")" then the execution of the above code would result in "ABC" being displayed.

Blocks which return values are handled slightly differently. For instance, if *source* contains just the expression: "1+2", then the following code assigns the sum to the variable *result*:

```
object := compile( source )
project object as O onto
    string: writeString( "Errors: " ++ O )        ! If the compilation fails.
    proc(→ any): project O() as OO onto           ! Evaluates the program.
        int: result := OO
        default: writeString( "Unexpected result" )   ! Should not happen.
    default: writeString( "Internal compiler error" )   ! Should never happen.
```

The result of compiling a block which returns a value is a procedure which when will called will return the value of the expression wrapped up into an **any** value. When this is projected out, the integer appears to be stored in integer variable, *result*..

Using one of the two forms above it is possible to create stand-alone programs, evaluate expressions or to generate procedures with their parameters. The latter is just an instance of the expression evaluation – in this case the type of the expression is a procedure type. Thus if *source* contains the string: "proc(X, Y: int → int); X+Y" which is a procedure which adds two numbers together and returns the result, then the following code:

```
object := compile( source )
project object as O onto
        string: writeString( "Errors: " ++ O )          ! If the compilation fails.
        proc(→ any): project O() as OO onto      ! Evaluates the program.
                proc( int, int → int ): result := OO
                        default: writeString( "Unexpected result" )  ! Should not happen.
                default: writeString( "Internal compiler error" )  ! Should never happen.
```

sets *result* to the compiled form of this procedure.

By using the compiler in this way, the programmer can generate code which is both type-safe and efficient. Once generated and integrated with the program there is no way of distinguishing code which has been generated reflectively from that which has been written in the normal way.

2.2   Type-Safe Run-Time Linguistic Reflection in O_2

O_2 [11] is an object oriented database system built around an object-oriented model which pays more than usual attention to support for orthogonal persistence. Programs in O_2 can manipulate both values (which may be of base type or be sets, bags, lists or records) and objects, where objects are members of classes which are arranged into a multiple inheritance graph. Each class is built on top of a type, usually a record type, and has methods associated with it. Application development is built in terms of a schema and each schema can be associated with a set of databases, a set of persistent roots, a set of application programs and a set of free standing functions, as well as sets of types and classes. Orthogonality is a guiding principal in that equivalent facilities are provided for values of all types and for objects of all classes.

O_2 comes with a distinguished schema called *Meta_schema* and this contains a number of classes whose members are meta-data. Note, first of all, that these are not true meta-classes in the sense mentioned in the introduction, since these classes hold, not classes as instances, but meta-information about classes and types. There is a class, *Meta*, which holds meta-information about schemata, and classes which hold meta-information about types and classes. O_2 also provides a method which makes it reflective. The class *Meta* has a method called *command* which sends an O_2 instruction to the O_2 interpreter. Since the O_2 system provides incremental schema development, this means that the program can change the schema at run-time, adding more code as new values are input.

To illustrate this with a trivial example, the following method can be executed against any object and will then add to the class of the object, a method which returns the value 123. The reflective method is added to the most general class, *Object*, in order to make it available to all objects and is:

```
method body add123Method in class Object
{   o2 Meta_class theClass = Schema→class( self );
    /* Returns class meta-data */

    o2 string className = theClass→Name;
    o2 string source =
            "method public Method123: integer in class " + className + ";" +
            "method body Method123: integer in class " + className + ";" +
            "{ return (123); }"
    o2 integer noErrors = Schema→command( source )
}
```

Since the meta-data can be accessed, the technique shown here can be used to add methods which are tailored to suit particular features of the type of the class. Reflection can also be used to write methods which add new classes or persistent roots automatically and also to write methods for the class *Object* which vary depending upon the type of the object. For instance, it has been found possible to write a method which displays all of the base data which is a component of the object.

3   Uses of Reflection

The examples given in Section 2 have been restricted to trivial examples which compile at run-time programs which could be written statically. Reflection comes into its own when creating code which cannot be written statically, since it depends upon some information which will only be available at run-time. There are two sources of such information, which require rather different handling. Firstly, the extra information may come from input from the user during the run of the program. Secondly, the extra information may come from the meta-information about novel types of data being encountered by the program.

The first is primarily met in those systems which are intended to be user configurable. In such systems, the functionality is programmed in the form of a **template**, which the user may then customise. The template contains **placeholders** which are replaced by user choices. The configurable system is supported by a superstructure which permits multiple versions of the functionality to co-exist.

The second use is for programs which must support an *ad hoc* style of polymorphic programming in the face of a potentially infinite set of types. In such cases, the basic functionality is again provided as a template, but now the placeholders are automatically filled by meta-information derived from the particular type encountered. For instance, the field names from records might be embedded in a placeholder reserved for the purpose. This use of reflection is inherently more difficult to manage than the user-configurable form since there is a possible complicating factor of recursion added to the process.

Examples will now be given of the two kinds of use, in the context of which the nature of the difficulties facing the programmer will be discussed.

338

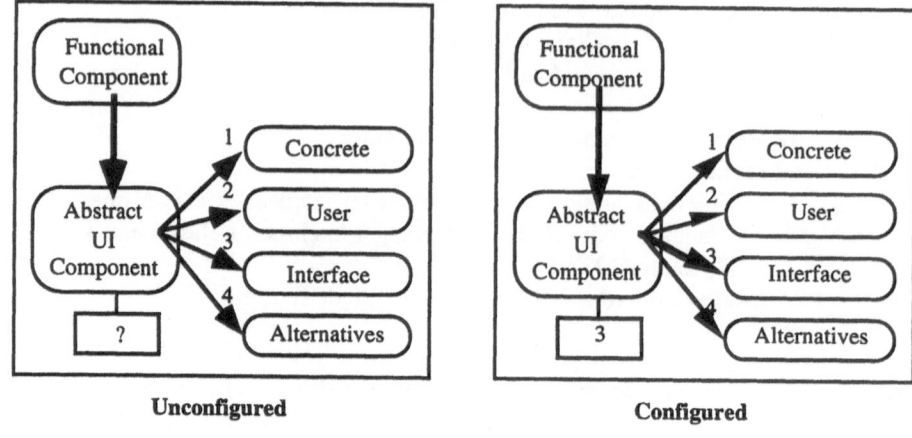

Unconfigured   Configured

Configurability by Indirection

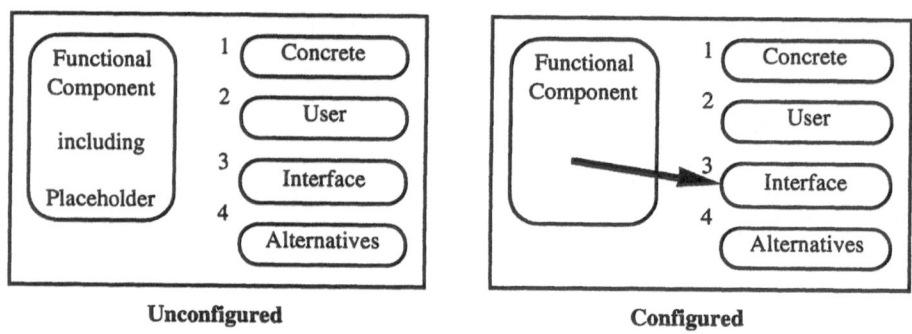

Unconfigured   Configured

Configurability by Reflection

Figure 1 Two Ways of Providing Configurability

3.1 An Example of Using Reflection for Configurable Programs

The first class of uses for reflection comprises those programs which are provided as an extensible set of parallel versions. To take a common example, let us suppose that the user interface to a program is to be made customisable. The process of customising the interface consists of binding together two sets of software – the underlying functionality and a set of concrete interaction primitives. Presuming a system component which allows the person configuring the interface to identify and pair the components, there are two ways in which the configured interface can be built, illustrated respectively by the top and bottom halves of Figure 1:

i)   by **indirection** – the interaction needs of the functional components are met by calls to abstract modules – these modules include a switching command which chooses between the concrete versions of the interface component – the user supplies a choice and the abstract module uses this.

ii)   by **reflection** – the functional components are stored as source templates, which include place-holding slots where calls to the UI components should be – the user selection results in these being replaced by source which directly calls the selected component – the completed template is compiled and stored for future use.

The version resulting from reflection appears to be superior to that resulting from indirection in at least two respects. Firstly, the code is simpler. It is not difficult to imagine that there might be many different user interface components being connected in various ways. In this case the number of interconnections would grow quite quickly into a complex web. More importantly, however, the indirect approach has in-built inefficiency – for every call to an interface components, there must be an extra procedure call and a case statement. The disadvantage of the reflective approach is a loss of flexibility. In the example the interface could no longer be reconfigured simply by updating the switch value.

Another problem with the reflective approach is that the code for the functional component is really being written in a somewhat different language than that for a normal program and suitable support needs to be provided for this. To illustrate the point, a particular usage of reflection for configurability will now be discussed.

The Configurable Data Modelling System (CDMS) has been created as a prototype system in which user interaction facilities (UIFs) can be configured [14]. CDMS tackles the problem that whereas DBMS are designed for a wide range of user, the user interfaces provided are few in number and often poor in quality [15]. CDMS provides a component which allows novel UIFs to be created without recourse to repetitive low level programming. To this end CDMS allows the configuration of UIFs, where each UIF consists of a conceptual model tied to a concrete user interface. The conceptual model is built as an instantiation of a highly abstract generic model and each conceptual model can be associated with many user interfaces. The user interface style may be graphical, form-based or textual and the system is being built to bring all aspects of data management into a common framework. To this end, the generic conceptual model is being enhanced with facilities to manage constraints and active values [16].

One aspect of CDMS is the part which configures textual interfaces – i.e. query languages [17]. The process of configuration takes in the following steps:

i)   The human configurer selects, names and constrains the constructs which make up the conceptual model – the constructs are either some kind of data value (for instance, entity, record or base value) or some relationship between (attribution, part-of or inheritance).

ii) The system builds data structures to hold such values and primitive operations to manage them automatically – the operations allow values to be created, deleted, edited and displayed.

iii) The configurer designs compound operations out of the primitive ones using a menu driven interface – for instance it is simple to create an operation to create an entity together with its attributes, or an operation to update selected values from a relation, or the **select .. from .. where** operation of SQL.

iv) The system automatically builds parameterised procedures to implement the configurer's design. The parameters are derived from the parts of the design that the configurer leaves unspecified.

v) The configurer inputs a syntactic description for each operation which the query language is to support directly. This is entered in a flavour of Backus Naur Form.

vi) The configurer associates the syntaxes with the operations, tying up slots in the syntax with parameters to the operation. There is a direct manipulation interface to achieve this.

vii) A parser/interpreter is built to manage the syntax structures provided.

viii) Finally the system takes all of the configurer's decisions and builds and compiles an interpreter for the query language. This is stored in the set of available interfaces for the data model.

A typical pairing of a compound operation with syntax is the following which creates a relation. The syntax:

create table <rname> (<aname> : <adomain> { , <aname> : <adomain>}*)

is paired with the operation:

createRelation = **proc**(Rname:**string**; Anames:***string**; Atypes:***string**)

The software is built in Napier88 around an interpreter whose template looks as follows:

```
let interpreter = proc()    ! all interpreters are parameterless procedures
begin
        ....hardwired modules for expression management and persistence

        %$DataModelPrimitives%$         ! placeholder filled in at stage (ii)

        %$Compound Operations%$         ! placeholder filled in at stage (iv)

        ...hardwired code to manage user input and provide syntax analysis

        %$PARSER%$                      ! placeholder filled in at stage (vii)

        ... (mostly) hardwired evaluator    ! completed at stage (viii)
end
```

Each of the strings "%$XXXX%$" denotes a placeholder which is replaced by strings derived from configuration decisions. The data modelling primitives are themselves built out of templates. Each kind of value and relationship has a template with placeholders for such information as the name of the construct in the configured conceptual model. The compound operations are built by glueing together pieces of code in accordance with the design. The parser is generated using standard techniques.

So, we see here the interpreter being written in a subtly different language from the normal one. In order to make the coding tractable, an informal extension to the normal Napier88 syntax has been added. Placeholders always appear surrounded in "%$" braces, so that a uniform set of support tools can be provided for instantiating them. Worse is the management of strings within the program. Since the whole program must be held in a string, strings inside the program must have their delimiters escaped, thus changing the syntax of the program. No completely satisfactory answer to this has been found, but perhaps the least inadequate response is to replace the usual string characters (" is the delimiter and ' is the escape character) with different characters which have no particular meaning in Napier88 (for instance, "£" for the delimiter and "\" for the escape character).

3.2   Using Reflection for Self-Adaptive Programs

The second set of uses to which reflection has been put is for program modules which are required to adapt themselves to varying types of input. This mechanism has been used extensively in Napier88 and its predecessor language PS-algol [18]. Among the uses have been the PS-algol browser [19] and a strongly typed relational system [20]. The former allows the user to navigate about values in the PS-algol persistent store, displaying an automatically generated menu for the current value, from which the user can traverse to a related value. The browser works from a template source module for the menu which it fills in with type specific information. By use of reflection, the browser is written entirely in PS-algol, without having to resort to type-unsafe access to the underlying structures in the implementation environment. The relational system produced an abstract data type of algebraic operations for relations which managed relation-specific record structures. For instance, the *select* operation was generated specifically for each kind of relation encountered, thus avoiding the inefficiencies associated with an indirect approach.

To demonstrate how the technique is used, consider a procedure which is to display the value of any type which it is passed. To understand how this is programmed, it is necessary first to describe the subset of the Napier88 type system which the procedure can handle.

Napier88 supports the following types:

- a set of base types including **int**, **real**, **string** and **bool**;

- a constructor for arrays (called **vectors** in Napier88) – for any type *t*, the type **t* is the type of a vector whose values are of type *t*;

- a constructor for records – for instance, the type **structure**(name: **string**; age: **int**) may be the type of a record holding information about a person;

- a constructor for variants – for instance, the type **variant**(number: **int**; text: **string**) might be a general type for identifying "numbers", which are either integers or strings;

- the type **any** is the infinite union of all types. Thus **any**(123) and **any**("ABC") have the same type **any**. For example a value *X* of type **any** could be used as follows:

project X **as** Y **onto**
      int: { writeString("int:") ; writeInt(Y) }
      string: { writeString("string:") ; writeString(Y) }
      default: writeString("not int or string")

The language also supports graphical types, extensible environments, procedures and abstract data types, but these will be ignored in the following discussion. Napier88 also allows the description of parameterised type operators, for instance it is possible to define a type of homogeneous pairs:

      type pair[t] **is structure**(one, two: t)

meaning that any instance of this type is a record of two values with the same type. Type operators must be specialised before use so any reflective procedure does not have to deal explicitly with such values.

The requirement in this example is for a procedure *Print*, which takes a value of type **any** and then prints it out in the following way:

- if the value is an instance of a base type, print it;
- if it is a vector, print out the values of its components;
- if it is a record, print out the names and values of its fields;
- if it is a variant, print out which variant it is and its value.

The following code handles the case if the value injected into the any is an integer:

```
let intPrint = proc( X: any )
      project X as Y onto
            int: writeInt( Y )
            default: writeString( "error: not an int" )
```

To complete the handling of base type values, equivalent procedures are produced for **string, real** and **bool**.

There is now a need for a context in which these alternative procedures are built. To manage this, an associative access mechanism such as the *Map* bulk type [21], is useful. A Map of **string** to **proc(any)** is created and initially populated with the pairings "int" to intPrint, "string" to stringPrint, etc.

The overall strategy for our *Print* procedure can now be described:

i)   obtain a string representation of the underlying type of the value;
ii)   look up the Map to find if a version for this type already exists – if so retrieve and use it;
iii)   if it is not there, build a procedure, similar in structure to *intPrint*, compile it, store it in the Map and then use it.

To support the building of these procedures, templates are created for each of the type constructors for vectors, records and variants. Outlines of these now follow:

vectors   **for** i = lwb[%$TY%$](Y) **to** upb[%$TY%$](Y) **do** Print(**any**(Y(i)))

records   *for each field:* writeString("%$FN%$"); Print(**any**(Y(%$FN%$)))

variants project Y **as** Z **onto**
                %$VN%$: Print(**any**(Z))

In these we see placeholders for the type of the components ("%$TY%$") of the vector, the names of fields ("%$FN%$") in the record template and the variant branches ("%$VN%$") in the variant template. Appendix A shows the full details.

To summarise, the need for reflection of this kind arises in the context of programs which are expected to handle a potentially infinite number of types of values and yet do so in a type secure manner. The technique of reflection resolves the conflict between requiring both generality and type security by supporting the creation of a program which generates the versions which the programmer would have written had he or she been able to anticipate the types which actually arise. However, a glance at Appendix A will demonstrate that the writing of such programs is a complex task – and remember this is only a print procedure, hand picked since it is a simple and useful reflective program. Yet notice, that if another reflective procedure was required, *a very similar program would result*. In essence the only pieces of the code which specify that this is a print routine are the name

("Print"), the signature ("proc(X:any)") and the pieces of code shown in outline font – i.e. one piece of code for each base type and one for each type constructor. This points the way both towards some tools for simplifying the task of writing reflective programs and also towards an underlying theory of what is actually required for reflection in other programming systems.

4   Support Tools for Reflection

This section describes the tools that have been implemented to make writing reflective programs easier. The context will once more be Napier88, but similar tools will be required in any equivalent environment. The first subsection outlines the tools which support both uses of reflection in that they make easier the management of the supporting structures – the set of equivalent versions and the templates. The second subsection describes a more powerful tool which allows programs such as the one shown in Appendix A to be generated from the essential code fragments which distinguish different reflective programs.

4.1   Basic Support Tools

The first important technique which has been introduced is the notion of a template [13]. A template is a string containing mostly Napier88 code with two exceptions:

- the delimiters and escape characters of strings are replaced by different characters, since, as they need to be embedded in strings they would otherwise perturb the normal compilation of the code – "£" and "\" are used for the delimiter and escape character respectively;
- at some points where type specific or user supplied detail is required, the code is replaced with a placeholder – which is identified as being a string surrounded by "%$" delimiters.

The first requirement is for procedures which manage these differences:

stringReplace: **proc**(template: **string** → **string**) is a procedure which takes in a template and replaces all instances of "£" and "\" with appropriately escaped Napier88 versions.

replace: **proc**(this, that, template: **string** → **string**) is a procedure which takes in a template and replaces all instances of "%$"++*this* ++ "%$" by *that*.

The second technique that has been introduced is the Map which holds the versions, and an important aspect of this is the generation of appropriate unique values for the keys. This requirement is met by one of the procedures which are needed to generate and analyse the type description for embedding in the template:

getType: **proc**(X: **any** → typeRep) generates a structured value holding all of the component information of the type of the input value;

describeType: **proc**(T: typeRep → **string**) generates a legal Napier88 type expression for the type – it is essential that it be possible to introduce complete type specifications into the generated code;

componentType: **proc**(T: typeRep → **string**) generates a type description of the component type of a vector;

fieldNames: **proc**(T: typeRep → ***string**) generates a vector of strings being the names of fields of a record type;

variantNames: **proc**(T: typeRep → ***string**) generates a vector of strings being the names of variants of a variant type.

makeDefault: **proc**(typeRep → **string**) generates a string containing a default value for the type – for instance if the type were **real**, this would return "0.0". This is required to handle procedures which return a result – see below.

In fact the output of *describeType*, being a unique description of the type, is used for the key to the Map. The construction of an appropriate structure to hold type representations is discussed at length in [22].

4.2   A Reflective Program Generator

This section tackles the problem of creating a generator for reflective programs. In essence, it employs the technique described in section 3.1 to provide a support tool for generating the kinds of program discussed in section 3.2. The basic component is a procedure, called *makeReflect*, which takes in a number of strings which describe the name and signature of the procedure, and one string each containing the required functionality when each of the base types and one or more strings for each of the type constructors[1] is encountered.

To illustrate this, the following call would be sufficient to generate the program in Appendix A:

```
makeReflect( "Print",              ! the name
             "proc( X: any )",     ! the signature
             "writeInt( Y )",      ! integer functionality
             "writeBool( Y )",     ! boolean functionality
             "writeReal( Y )",     ! real functionality
```

---

[1]There is also one other parameter in which the programmer must provide details of how to retrieve required values (including the system functions) which are used in the code fragments. This is omitted for brevity, but is just a single piece of pure Napier88 code.

```
"writeString( Y )",              ! string functionality
"",                              ! vector functionality before the loop
"Print( any( Y(i) ) )",          ! vector functionality inside the loop
"",                              ! vector functionality after the loop
"",                              ! record functionality before the fields
"writeString( £%$FN%$: £ )       ! functionality for each record field
Print( any( Y( %$FN%$ ) ) )
writeString( £\n£ )",
"",                              ! record functionality after the fields
"writeString( £%$VN%$: £ )       ! functionality for each variant
Print( any(Z) )
writeString( £\n£ )" )
```

Use of the procedure *makeReflect* greatly simplifies the creation of reflective procedures since the programming task has been reduced to its essential core – i.e. what code should be provided for each type of data encountered. In order to use it though, certain conventions must be met when writing the code fragments:

- there is only one reflective variable, which must be called X and be declared to be of type **any**;
- where the underlying type of X is used, it must be called Y; and
- if X is itself a variant, then the projected value must be called Z.

The procedure works by turning the program in Appendix A into a configurable template by replacing all of the functionality (i.e. the pieces of code in outline font), the procedure name, signature, type and parameter lists (i.e. those pieces of code which are underlined) by place holders which are substituted by the arguments of the procedure. The program has also to be modified because now some parts of the code are doubly reflective, since *makeReflect* generates a program which itself generates programs. This means that we have strings inside strings inside strings and this requires careful handling.

This template works only for procedures which do not return a result and a different template is required for those which do – since the syntactic context of these are different. In essence, the difference is that a result value is declared at the top of the procedure (the creation of a default value for any type is a non-trivial piece of code) and each block of functional code is turned into a block whose value is passed to the return variable. Thus the following would be created for a procedure which returns a real value:

```
let result := 0.0                              ! generated by makeDefault
let theMap = m_empty[string, proc( any → real ) ]()       ! create map
...
let intVersion = proc( X: any → real )
        project X as Y onto
            int: result := begin
                            writeInt( Y )      ! sample functionality for an
                            5.3 * float( Y )   ! integer parameter
                       end
          default: writeString( "Will not get here" )
...
etc.
```

5   Conclusions

5.1   Towards a Theory of Reflective Programs

This section attempts to bring together the previous discussion and place it in a more general context. Reviewing the previous sections:

- Applications which manage long-lived data are best programmed in a type secure environment, since a great number of run-time errors, which potentially could occur many years after the program was written, can be eliminated.

- Many polymorphic programs which require type specific information as part of their code are difficult to write efficiently in strongly typed languages.

- Similarly, programs which are intended to be user-configurable, if programmed normally, will tend to become inefficient.

- Linguistic reflection is a technique which attempts to solve these problems by allowing programs to be written which extend themselves. The technique allows type-specific versions of procedures to be generated as new types of data are encountered. It also allows template programs to be configured from user input. In both cases the program generated is that which would have been written had a programmer been on hand to write it.

- The technique involves building new code fragments as strings which merge template versions of the code with type-specific or user-provided input. The strings are then compiled and stored for later re-use.

- Support tools are required to make the creation of such programs tractable. Tools were discussed which manage templates with placeholders, the extraction of type information and the storage of versions of compiled programs.

- Finally, a tool, *makeReflect*, was discussed which enables reflective programs to be built more easily, by providing just the functional code.

The structure of the procedure *makeReflect* was largely determined by the type system of Napier88 (or rather that part of the type system which it can currently manage). Essentially, *makeReflect* can be analysed as comprising the following parts:

- a store of versions, indexed by the type they manage;

- a non-type-specific template which provides an abstract structure for housing any application;

- type-specific templates which are embedded into the general template; and

- a program which takes in one piece of functional code for each construct in the type system and embeds it in its type-specific template.

The possibility therefore exists of using this structure to generate a theory of reflective programs, which may proceed as follows.

Let $\mathcal{T} = \{\ \mathcal{TOP},\ \mathcal{BT}_1,\ \dots\ \mathcal{BT}_m,\ \mathcal{TC}_1,\ \dots\ \mathcal{TC}_n\ \}$ be a type system with m base types and n type constructors and a type, $\mathcal{TOP}$, which is the union of all other types. It then becomes possible to provide reflection by supplying two system functions:

typeDesc: $\mathcal{TOP} \rightarrow$ **string** returns a unique syntactically correct description of the type; and

compile: **string** $\rightarrow \mathcal{TOP}$ returns a compiled form of the string.

It is then possible to use these for the creation of programs of the form:

program: $\mathcal{PROGRAM}$

where type $\mathcal{PROGRAM} = \mathcal{TOP},\ \mathcal{T}_1,\ \dots\ \mathcal{T}_p \rightarrow \mathcal{RT}$

in which the first parameter is a reflective, there are p other parameters of fixed types and one result type, $\mathcal{RT}$. It is also possible to supply support tools which perform as follows:

enter: **string**, $\mathcal{PROGRAM}$ which stores the pairing of a type description and a program version for that type;

baseTypeVersion$_i$: $\mathcal{PROGRAM}$ for i = 1 to m, which instantiates the program for that base type;

*typeConstructorTemplate*ⱼ: **string** for j = 1 to *n*, which contains a generalised template for handling values of each constructed type;

*typeConstructorGenerator*ⱼ: **string** → $\mathcal{PROGRAM}$ for j = 1 to *n*, which takes in a type description and returns a version for the type described by the string;

generator: $\mathcal{PROGRAM}$ which brings the *baseTypeVersion*ᵢ; and *typeConstructorGenerator*ⱼ into a common program which can handle all types;

makeReflect: **string, string** ... **string** which takes in one code fragment for each base type and type constructor and returns a program generator for the supplied functionality.

Keeping this as a general model, it should become possible to provide linguistic reflection for any language which has a most general type, such as **any**, and the ability to manage code fragments as first-class values.

5.2   Research Directions

The discussion so far has centred on linguistic reflection using string representations of program fragments. The advent of hyper-programming [5], which allows programs in a persistent environment to contain direct links to values and types in that environment, raises further possibilities for reflection. The ability of generators to manipulate hyper-program representations rather than strings provides a safe, convenient and efficient mechanism by which generated code may access values and types in the generator evaluation environment. This also removes the need to flatten complex type representations to strings [23].

Another area for research is the incorporation of the structured program representations and pattern matching found in TRPL into a run-time reflective system.

Acknowledgements

The work has been developed in the context of collaborative research between the Persistent Programming Research Groups led at the University of St Andrews by Professor Ron Morrison and at the University of Glasgow by Professor Malcolm Atkinson. Among those whose influence have been vital to the development of these ideas have been Al Dearle, Fred Brown, Richard Connor, Quintin Cutts, Paul Philbrow and Zhenzhou Qin. Miguel Mira da Silva provided very useful comments on an earlier draft of this paper. The work has been supported by ESPRIT Basic Research Activity 6309, FIDE2, and by SERC Research Grants H17671, Configurable Data Modelling, and GR/F 02953.

References

1. Atkinson MP, Bailey PJ, Chisholm KJ, Cockshott WP, Morrison R. An Approach to Persistent Programming. Comp. J. 1983; 26,4:360-365

2. Cardelli L, Wegner P. On Understanding Types, Data Abstraction and Polymorphism. ACM Comp. Surveys 1985; 17,4:471-523

3. Cardelli L. Amber. AT&T Bell Labs, Murray Hill Report AT7T, 1985

4. Stemple D, Stanton RB, Sheard T et al. Type-Safe Linguistic Reflection: A Generator Technology. ESPRIT BRA Project 3070 FIDE Report FIDE/92/49, 1992

5. Kirby GNC. Reflection and Hyper-Programming in Persistent Programming Systems. Ph.D. thesis, University of St Andrews, 1992

6. Wirth N. Programming in Modula-2. Springer-Verlag, 1983

7. McCarthy J, Abrahams PW, Edwards DJ, Hart TP, Levin MI. The Lisp Programmers' Manual. M.I.T. Press, Cambridge, Massachusetts, 1962

8. Burstall RM, Collins JS, Popplestone RJ. Programming in POP-2. Edinburgh University Press, Edinburgh, Scotland, 1971

9. Sheard T. Automatic Generation and Use of Abstract Structure Operators. ACM ToPLaS 1991; 19,4:531-557

10. Morrison R, Brown AL, Connor RCH et al. The Napier88 Reference Manual (Release 2.0). University of St Andrews Report CS/93/15, 1993

11. Bancilhon F, Delobel C, Kanellakis P. The Story of O_2: Building an Object-Oriented Database System. Morgan Kaufmann, 1992

12. Cooper RL. On The Utilisation of Persistent Programming Environments. Ph.D. thesis, University of Glasgow, 1990

13. Kirby GNC. Persistent Programming with Strongly Typed Linguistic Reflection. In: Proc. 25th International Conference on Systems Sciences, Hawaii, 1992, pp 820-831

14. Cooper RL. Configurable Data Modelling Systems. In: Proc. 9th International Conference on the Entity Relationship Approach, Lausanne, Switzerland, 1990, pp 35-52

15. Stonebraker M, Agrawal R, Dayal U, Neuhold EJ, Reuter A. DBMS Research at a Crossroads: The Vienna Update. In: Proc. 19th International Conference on Very Large Databases, Dublin, 1993, pp 688-692

16. Cooper RL, Qin Z. A Generic Data Model for the Support of Multiple User Access Mechanisms. *submitted*

17. Cooper RL. Configuring Database Query Languages. *submitted*

18. PS-algol Reference Manual, 4th edition. Universities of Glasgow and St Andrews Report PPRR-12-88, 1988

19. Dearle A, Brown AL. Safe Browsing in a Strongly Typed Persistent Environment. Comp. J. 1988; 31,6:540-544

20. Cooper RL, Atkinson MP, Dearle A, Abderrahmane D. Constructing Database Systems in a Persistent Environment. In: Proc. 13th International Conference on Very Large Data Bases, 1987, pp 117-125

21. Atkinson MP, Lécluse C, Philbrow P, Richard P. Design Issues in a Map Language. In: P. Kanellakis and J. W. Schmidt (ed) Bulk Types & Persistent Data. Morgan Kaufmann, 1991, pp 20-32

22. Connor RCH. Types and Polymorphism in Persistent Programming Systems. Ph.D. thesis, University of St Andrews, 1990

23. Kirby GNC, Connor RCH, Morrison R. START: A Linguistic Reflection Tool Using Hyper-Program Technology. To Appear: Proc. 6th International Workshop on Persistent Object Systems, 1994

Appendix A - A Reflective Program to Print Any Value

The core of the program is the template, assigned to the variable *source*. This holds two placeholders - one for a description of the type and one for the detailed code which is required for this type. This code is built up by extracting information from the type description. There is a different piece of code for managing each kind of type (chosen by the **case** statement at the top of the second page). Eventually, the variable *source* holds a complete procedure for handling values of the type and this is compiled, stored and used.

```
! Set up the context - the map and the base type versions
    let theMap = m_empty[string, proc( any ) ]( )   ! Create the map
    let enter = proc( S:string; P:proc( any ) )        ! A procedure to add an entry
        m_isu_insert[string, proc( any )]( theMap, S, P )
    let intVersion = proc( X: any )                    ! Create the integer version
        project X as Y onto
        int: writeInt( Y )

        default: writeString( "Will not get here" )
    enter( "int", intVersion )                         ! Enter the integer version
    let boolVersion = proc( X: any )
        project X as Y onto
        bool: writeBool( Y )

        default: writeString( "Will not get here" )
    enter( "bool", boolVersion )                       ! Enter the boolean version
    let realVersion = proc( X: any )
        project X as Y onto
        real: writeReal( Y )

        default: writeString( "Will not get here" )
    enter( "real", realVersion )                       ! Enter the real version
    let stringVersion = proc( X: any )
        project X as Y onto
        string: writeString( Y )

        default: writeString( "Will not get here" )
    enter( "string", stringVersion )                   ! Enter the string version

    let error = proc( S: string)                       ! An error message procedure
        writeString( "'n**** ERROR: " ++ S ++ "'n'n" )

! Templates for the constructed types.
    let vectorTemplate =
        "for i = lwb[%$TY%$]( Y ) to upb[%$TY%$]( Y ) do Print( any( Y(i) ) )"
    let structureTemplate =
```

```
        "writeString( £%$FN%$ £ );
        Print( any(Y(%$FN%$)) );writeString(£\n£)"
    let variantTemplate = "%$VN%$:  begin
                                      writeString(£%$VN%$: £ )
                                      Print( any(Z) )
                                      writeString( £\n£ )
                              end"
! The main procedure.
   let Print = proc( X:any )
     begin
       let T = getType( X )                    ! Get the type of the value
       let S = describeType( T )               ! Get a string description
       if m_contains[string, proc( any )]( theMap, S )
          then begin                           ! If there is a version for this type
             let P = m_find[string,proc( any ) ](theMap,S) ! extract and use it.
             P( X )
          end
          else  begin                          ! Otherwise
             let source := "proc( X: any )      ! Start with a template for the
                          begin     ! procedure
                              rec type t1 is %$TYPEDESC%$
                              project X as Y onto
                              t1: begin
                                      %$DETAIL%$
                                  end
                                  default: writeString( £Will not get here£ )
                          end"
             source := replace( "TYPEDESC", S, source )   ! put in actual type

             case kind(T) of
                 "base": begin
                          error( "Unknown Base Type" )
                          source := ""
                        end
                 "vector": begin   ! insert the template and component type
                          source := replace( "DETAIL", vectorTemplate, source )
                          source := replace( "TY", componentType( T ), source )
                        end
                 "structure": begin
                          let heart := ""          ! build a string containing
                          let FNS = fieldNames( T )    ! one line for each field
                          for i = lwb[string](FNS) to upb[string](FNS) do
                              heart := heart ++
                                  replace( "FN", FNS(i), structureTemplate )
                          ! put this in the source
```

```
                source := replace( "DETAIL", heart, source )
            end
        "variant": begin
                ! build a string containing
                ! one line for each variant
                let heart := "project Y as Z onto'n"
                let VNS = variantNames( T )
                for i = lwb[string](VNS) to upb[string](Ftypes) do
                    heart := heart ++
                            replace( "VN", VNS(i), variantTemplate)
                heart := heart ++ "default: writeString( £Bad Variant£ )"
                ! put this in the source
                source := replace( "DETAIL", heart, source )
            end
        default: begin
                error( "Sorry - cannot deal with this type" )
                source := ""
            end

    if source ~= "" do
    begin
        let object = compile( source )            ! compile the source
        project object as O onto
            string: writeString( "COMPILE FAILED'n" ++ O ++
                                source )          ! error
            proc( → any ):                        ! success
                project O() as P onto
                    proc( any ):                  ! extract the procedure
                        begin
                            enter( S, P )         ! store it
                            P( X )                ! and use it
                        end
                    default: writeString( "Will not get here'n" )
            default: writeString( "Will not get here'n" )
    end
  end
end
```

START: A Linguistic Reflection Tool Using Hyper-Program Technology

G.N.C. Kirby, R.C.H. Connor and R. Morrison

Division of Computer Science, University of St Andrews,
North Haugh, St Andrews, Fife KY16 9SS, Scotland

Abstract

The mechanism of linguistic reflection allows a programming system to generate new program fragments and incorporate them into the system. Although this ability has important applications in persistent systems, its use has been limited by the difficulty of writing reflective programs. This paper analyses the reasons for this difficulty and describes *START*, a hyper-text based tool for reflection which has been implemented in the Napier88 hyper-programming environment.

START supports the definition of structured program generators which may contain embedded direct links to other generators and to values, locations and types extant in the persistent environment. The benefits are greater ease of understanding through a clean separation of generator components, and a safer and more efficient mechanism for communication between generator and generated code.

1   Introduction

Linguistic reflection gives a programming system the ability to generate new pro-gram fragments and incorporate them into the ongoing computation. This has sev-eral applications in a persistent environment including supporting safe evolution of long-lived programs and data, and specifying highly generic programs that may be reused in many contexts. In strongly typed systems the linguistic reflection process includes checking of the generated program fragments to ensure type safety.

The details of linguistic reflection have been described by a number of authors [1-11]. A short overview of the technique and its applications in persistent systems will be given in order to motivate the main part of the paper, which analyses the problems involved in writing reflective generator programs and describes *START* (St Andrews Reflection Tool), a tool which aids in this process. One feature of START is its hyper-text user interface which allows conceptually different parts of a generator definition to be distinguished easily. The other main feature is the use of hyper-program representations [8, 12] to provide an additional binding mecha-nism. This gives increased safety and efficiency, and avoids the need to flatten type representations to textual form.

Forms of linguistic reflection are provided in Lisp [13], Scheme [14] and POP-2 [15]. This paper, however, will consider only strongly typed languages, relevant examples of which include PS-algol [16], Napier88 [17] and TRPL [18]. Linguistic reflection in these languages involves the execution of generator procedures which produce as their results representations of program fragments in the corresponding language. These program fragments are incorporated into the application after the appropriate validity checks.

Two varieties of type-safe linguistic reflection can be identified; these vary as to the time at which generator execution takes place. With compile time linguistic reflection, supported in TRPL, the generators are evaluated during the course of program compilation and the new code produced is incorporated into the program being compiled. This technique could be viewed as a sophisticated form of macro expansion, where the language used to evaluate the macro is the same as the programming language itself. With run time linguistic reflection, supported in PS-algol and Napier88, the generators are evaluated during program execution and the new code produced is compiled and executed in the same context. Both forms of linguistic reflection have the effect of blurring the distinction between compile time and run time.

One application of linguistic reflection is in supporting evolution in strongly typed persistent systems. The inevitable changes to meta-data in long-lived systems give rise to the problem of consistently changing all the affected programs and data. Given some mechanism for locating the relevant programs and data, linguistic reflection can be used to introduce transformed versions in a controlled manner. One approach to limited automation of this process is described in [19].

Another application is in providing highly generic programs. The reuse of existing software reduces development and maintenance costs; the more generic, or widely applicable, a software component is, the more likely it will be reused. Polymorphism [20, 21] is one powerful mechanism for genericity. There exist, however, some generic computations which are hard or impossible to express using parametric or inclusion polymorphism. The difficulty lies in the fact that the course of such a computation depends on details of the types of the input parameters, while parametric and inclusion polymorphism by their nature abstract such details away. A well used example is that of a strongly typed natural join function [22, 23], where the algorithm and the type of the result relation depend on the types of the input relations. This can be implemented using linguistic reflection, by defining a generator procedure which accepts representations of the types of the relations to be joined and generates the representation of a procedure to perform the join for those types.

Thus linguistic reflection provides a rich form of ad-hoc polymorphism [24, 25], with which generic yet type-dependent operators can be defined over wide ranges of types [1, 3, 23]. This mechanism has some similarities with that of 4GL systems, where generic application descriptions are automatically tailored to specific instances. In this case the structure of the type system and the language defines the primitives over which the generators are written.. It is somewhat ironic that the type system itself, which is often seen as restricting the expressibility of the language, can be used as the basis of very flexible and high level generation mechanisms. The technique is particularly suited to persistent systems since the persistent environment may be used as a cache to store executable versions of generated procedures.

This means that the generator need not be executed more than once for given parameters.

The next section discusses the problems encountered in writing reflective generator procedures for uses such as those outlined above. The remainder of the paper then introduces START, a generator editing tool which combines a hyper-text interface with hyper-program technology in an effort to tackle some of these problems.

2 Reflective Generators

This section examines the structure and role of the generator in the reflection process.

2.1 The Reflection Process

The process of linguistic reflection has been characterised in [10] as follows:

Programs in a language L manipulate a domain of values Val. This domain differs between languages. Examples of Val include numbers, character strings, final machine states, the state of a persistent object store, and the set of bindings of variables produced by the end of a program's execution.

For linguistic reflection to occur, there must be a subset of Val, called Val_L, that can be mapped into L. Since Val_L is a subset of Val that may be translated into the language L it may be thought of as a representation of L. In the known implementations of linguistic reflection Val_L is the set of character strings containing syntactically correct expressions in the cases of PS-algol and Napier88, and the set of valid parse trees in the case of TRPL.

A subset of L consisting of those language constructs that cause reflective computation is denoted by L_R. L_R is called the reflective sub-language. An evaluation of an expression in L_R invokes a generator, a program that produces another program. Generators are written in a subset of the language L denoted by L_{Gen}. L_{Gen} may include all of L but the programs written in L_{Gen} must produce results in Val_L. Linguistic reflection thus involves the following steps during evaluation of a program in L:

- a construct in L_R is encountered;
- this causes a generator, written in L_{Gen}, to be evaluated;
- the result, a value in Val_L, represents a new construct in L;
- the new construct is checked and, if valid, executed.

Note that this description does not specify whether the generator evaluation takes place during compilation or execution, and is valid for either case.

2.2 Generator Structure

Each generator contains a result expression that when evaluated produces the generated program fragment. The code in this expression itself represents code, thus it belongs to the subset of L containing sentences that, when evaluated, produce values in Val_L. This subset will be denoted by L_L. The set L_L can be partitioned into two subsets, $L_{L_{Const}}$ and $L_{L_{Var}}$. The former, $L_{L_{Const}}$, contains those sentences that produce the same values in Val_L for all executions, while the latter, $L_{L_{Var}}$, contains sentences that may evaluate to different values on different executions. This is illustrated in Figure 1:

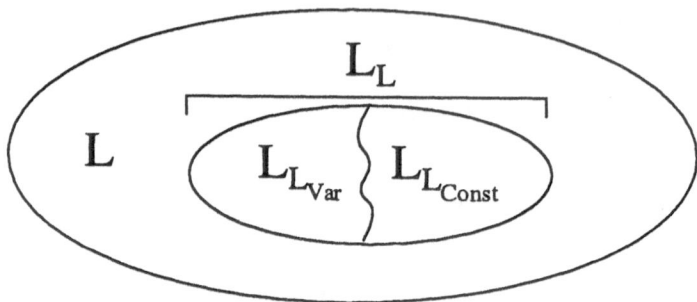

Figure 1: Subset relationships between code categories

Some examples of sentences in these sets are shown below for a language in which members of Val_L are strings, *makeCode()* denotes a call to a generator *makeCode*, and ++ denotes concatenation:

```
a := a + 1                    ∈         L
"a := a + 1"                  ∈         L_{L_Const}
makeCode()                    ∈         L_{L_Var}
"a := " ++ makeCode()         ∈         L_{L_Var}
```

Note that the last example is itself a composition of two code fragments, one a member of $L_{L_{Const}}$ and the other a member of $L_{L_{Var}}$. In general a generator body contains a section of code in L, here termed the *prelude*, followed by a section of code in $L_{L_{Var}}$ that defines the resulting generated fragment, here termed the *result definition*. This is illustrated in Figure 2. The purpose of the prelude is to set up an environment in which the result definition is evaluated.

In simple cases the generator body may contain only the result definition, and that code may lie in $L_{L_{Const}}$ rather than $L_{L_{Var}}$. In the general case the execution of a generator involves the evaluation of the prelude and those parts of the result definition that lie in $L_{L_{Var}}$, i.e., the variable parts. The parts in $L_{L_{Const}}$ do not need to be evaluated as they are constant over all executions of the generator. Typically the evaluation of the prelude affects the program fragments produced in the result defi-

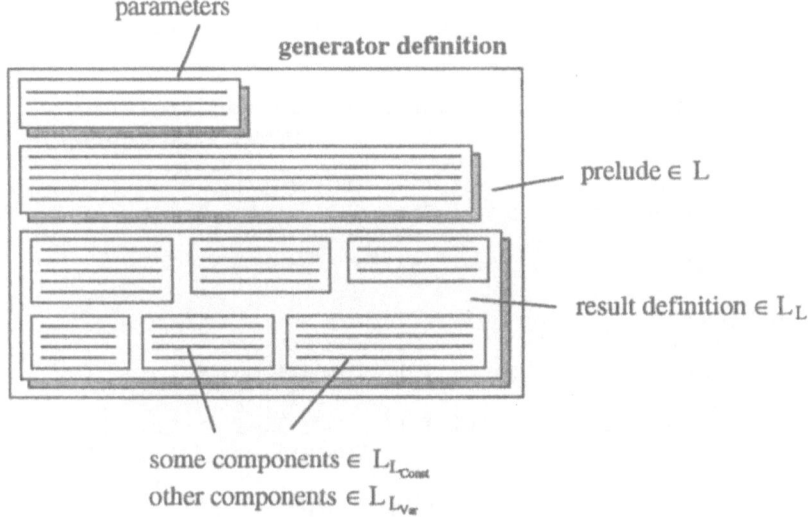

parameters

generator definition

prelude $\in$ L

result definition $\in$ L$_L$

some components $\in$ L$_{L_{Const}}$
other components $\in$ L$_{L_{Var}}$

Figure 2: Structure of a generator

nition. The result of the generator is obtained by composing the newly created fragments with the constant parts of the result definition.

2.3   An Example of a Generator

The next section will identify some of the problems involved in programming generators. This section concentrates on an example written in Napier88. Lack of space prevents comparison with other languages and notations. Rather than use a complete but trivial example, the main part of a generator for the (non-trivial) natural join problem is shown in Figure 3. To save space, various auxiliary procedure definitions are omitted. The form of the generator is a procedure which takes as parameters the representations of two structure types. These define the types of the relations to be joined: each relation is modelled as a set of structures. The output of the generator is the representation of a procedure to perform natural join over pairs of relations of these types.

The generator procedure, *defineJoin*, takes as parameters the type representations *type1* and *type2*, and returns a code representation as a string. First two strings are defined. *defineTypes* represents the definition of the type constructors *Comparison* and *Set* used within the generated code. *getPredefined* represents code to bind to the existing procedures *mkEmptySet* and *mkComparison* in the persistent environment.

Next, a representation of the type of the join result, *resultType*, is computed from the input type representations by an auxiliary procedure *joinResultType*. Details of error reporting at this and other stages have been omitted for simplicity—for example the input types might not have compatible common fields on which to join, in which case the execution of the generator would fail. The generated code is then obtained by concatenating the type definitions and binding code with the definition

```
let defineJoin = proc( type1, type2 : TypeRep -> string )
begin
    let defineTypes =
    "type Comparison[ T ] is structure( equal, lessThan :
                                        proc( T, T -> bool )
    rec type Set[ T ] is structure(
        insert :        proc( T -> Set[ T ] );
        difference :    proc( Set[ T ] -> Set[ T ] ) );
        ...
        size :          proc( -> int ) )"

    let getPredefined =
    "use PS() with
        mkEmptySet :    proc[ T ]( Comparison[ T ] ->
                                    Set[ T ] );
        mkComparison : proc[ T ]( proc( T, T -> bool ) ->
                                    Comparison[ T ] ) in"

    let resultType = joinResultType( type1, type2 )

    defineTypes ++ "'n" ++ getPredefined ++ "'n" ++

    "begin
        rec let join = proc(
            rel1 : Set[ " ++ writeType( type1 ) ++" } ;
            rel2 : Set[ " ++ writeType( type2 ) ++ " ] ->
            Set[ " ++ writeType( resultType ) ++ " ] )

        project rel1 as first onto
        populated :
        begin
            let joinOne = " ++
                defineOneJoin( type1, type2, resultType ) ++
                "( first( choose )(), rel2 )
            let joinOthers = join( first( rest )(), rel2 )

            project joinOne as firstJoined onto
            populated : firstJoined( union )( joinOthers )
            default :   joinOthers
        end
        default : mkEmptySet[ " ++ writeType( resultType ) ++
                    " ]( " ++
                    defineCompareResult( resultType ) ++ " )
        join
    end"
end
```

Figure 3: Example generator definition in Napier88

of the join procedure itself. The general form of the join procedure is fixed by the string literals which are concatenated with the type dependent code fragments obtained by computing over the type representations.

The definitions of the auxiliary procedures *writeType*, *defineOneJoin* and *defineCompareResult* are omitted, as are the definitions of the types against which the generator itself is compiled and parts of the type definition string *defineTypes*. Details of how an executable version of the generated code is obtained are also not shown.

2.4 Why Programming Generators is Hard

Programmers writing generators in various languages have reported that generators are considerably more difficult to write and understand than conventional programs [3, 5, 7]. Some possible reasons for this are:

- A generator may describe a large class of programs rather than a single one. Although a conventional program may have many different possible execution paths, its structure is fixed. The structure of different programs produced by a single generator may differ widely. To understand a generator the reader must determine the features common to all programs produced by it, and understand how the parts that vary among the resulting programs relate to the input parameters to the generator. In the example the overall structure of the *join* procedure is constant while the details of the result type and the *joinOne* procedure are dependent on the input types.

- The programmer must perform a mental mapping between sentences in L and their representations in L_L. This is trivial for the example of "rec let join = ..." but less so for writeType(type1).

- The constant and variable parts of the result definition appear different even though they both represent parts of the resulting program fragment. By the end of the generator execution they are integrated seamlessly but this is not apparent from inspection of the generator source code. This is seen in the same line as the previous example: ...Set[" ++ writeType(type1) ++ "] ...

- Code in different parts of the generator is evaluated at different times. During the execution of the generator, the prelude and those parts of the result definition in $L_{L_{Var}}$ are evaluated. Later during the reflection process the new code produced by the generator, comprising the $L_{L_{Const}}$ parts of the result definition composed with the fragments produced by the evaluation of the $L_{L_{Var}}$ parts, is evaluated. Thus adjacent parts of the result definition may be evaluated at different times and in different environments. In the example, execution of the generator involves evaluation of joinResultType(type1,type2) in the prelude and writeType(type1) in $L_{L_{Var}}$. Later the code rel1 : Set[, composed with the result of writeType(type1), is evaluated.

- Communication of data between evaluation environments is unwieldy. It may be that a value computed during the execution of a generator prelude is required in the generated code. This involves either generating code to create a copy of the value, or placing a reference to the value in some storage accessible from both evaluation environments and then generating code to retrieve it. The first option involves an execution overhead and precludes communication of the identity of the value. The latter option also involves an execution overhead, and in addition there may be a risk of the value being removed from the environment before the generated code is executed. This second mechanism is used in the example: the generator produces code to retrieve the procedures *mkEmptySet* and *mkComparison* from the persistent store.

- There may be a lot of syntactic noise in the code of a generator, particularly where constant and variable parts of the result definition are composed together. The example contains many concatenation and quote symbols.

- In languages where Val_L comprises string expressions, manipulation of program representations is unwieldy. One example of such a manipulation is determining the result type of a procedure from its representation. This is non-trivial when the representation is a string, since it involves parsing the string. A parse tree representation presents less of a problem, since the representation of the result type may be a component which can be accessed directly. This problem does not arise in the example since the generator is parameterised only by type representations.

These factors suggest several desirable features for any generator notation:

- Syntactic noise should be cut to a minimum.

- It should be easy to identify which parts of the result definition are constant, in $L_{L_{Const}}$, and which parts are variable, in $L_{L_{Var}}$.

- It should be possible to use different code representation forms in the constant and variable parts of the result definition. A textual form, such as strings, is easy to read in the constant parts since it gives a simple mapping between $L_{L_{Const}}$ and L. An abstract syntax form may be more suitable for the variable parts as it facilitates the expression of code representation manipulations.

- There should be a simple mechanism enabling the generated code to refer to values in scope in the generator prelude.

- Supplementary tools to aid understanding of generators should be provided. For example, a tool could display the resulting code produced by a generator for given inputs. This could help in understanding the relationships between generator parameters and the code fragments produced by $L_{L_{Var}}$ code.

3 START: The Generator Tool

3.1 Design Criteria

This section describes START, a tool designed to aid writing generators in Napier88. It is implemented within the Napier88 hyper-programming environment [26]. The principal ideas are:

1) to display the variable parts within a generator result definition as hyper-text links; and

2) to allow generated code to contain hyper-program links.

The first point addresses the problems of excessive syntactic noise within result definitions and distinguishing between constant and variable parts, by presenting a clean user interface. The second addresses the problem of communicating between the separate evaluation environments of generator and generated code, by allowing generators to produce *hyper-program* representations. A hyper-program is a program which contains both text and embedded direct links to existing values in the persistent environment [27, 8, 12]. A generated hyper-program may thus contain a direct link to a value in scope within the generator.

A window-based generator editor is used to allow the programmer to view a generator at various degrees of detail. At the most abstract level the programmer sees only the prelude code and the fixed parts of the result definition. The positions of the variable parts are indicated by light-buttons embedded in the code. This level of detail shows the programmer the main structure of the generated result, while abstracting over the variations that depend on the particular specialisation. To examine the details of the variations the programmer may press a button and view the corresponding code in a separate window. This use of windows allows much of the noisy syntax involved in combining parts of the result definition to be omitted, making it easier to read.

The usefulness of this ability to separate constant and variable parts of the result definition depends on the style in which generators are written. It is always possible to write generators in such a way that the entire result definition is variable; however the assumption is made that programmers will choose to write constant definitions for the generated code fragments that are common to all inputs.

Two additional design criteria were to give uniformity between generators and the variable $L_{L_{Var}}$ parts of result definitions—which may themselves be regarded as generators—and to allow arbitrary nesting of generators.

3.2 Generator Model Details

START supports a model in which each generator has two separate components: a *prelude* and a *result definition*. The prelude is a procedure that processes the parameters input to the generator, while the result definition is a variant that may be either a fragment of hyper-program source code or a procedure that produces such a fragment. These source code fragments may contain place-holders corresponding to further generators. Thus each $L_{L_{Var}}$ part of the result definition is itself represented by another generator.

To evaluate a generator its prelude is executed with the generator parameters passed to it. If the result definition is a procedure then it is executed in turn, with the results produced by the prelude passed to it. The result of this procedure, or the result definition itself in the other case, is a source code fragment which may contain place-holders for other generators. If so these generators are themselves evaluated and the resulting code fragments incorporated into the result. This process is continued until a source code representation without generator place-holders is obtained. A generator could be recursive, containing a place-holder to itself within its result definition, although the practical usefulness of this capability is questionable.

The ability of a generator to produce hyper-program source code containing links to data items means that generated code can refer directly to values constructed by the generator, or to values in the persistent store at the time of generator execution.

Figure 4 shows some of the Napier88 type definitions describing this model. Type *HyperText*, omitted to save space, represents fragments of hyper-text and is parameterised by the type of the embedded links. An instance of *HyperText* contains a text string and a list of *<link value, text position>* pairs. The definition of *Binding* is also omitted: this is used to denote hyper-program values, and instances may represent values, locations or types.

Generators are represented by instances of the structure type *Generator*. The first component is a procedure, *prelude*, that takes a Napier88 environment as its parameter and returns another environment. These environments contain the generator parameters and prelude results respectively.

The second component of a generator, the result definition, is an instance of the variant type *GeneratorResult*. Its value may be either an instance of type *GeneratorSource* or a procedure that takes an environment and produces a *GeneratorSource*. In the first case the result definition is a literal code fragment while in the second case it is a procedure that must be executed to produce a code fragment. In both cases the code fragment may contain hyper-program links and links to sub-generators, both represented by instances of the variant type *BindingOrGenerator*.

Note that the *literal* branch of *GeneratorResult* is redundant so far as expressiveness is concerned: a literal result definition could be expressed as a procedure which ignored its parameters and always produced the same result. However, the presence of this branch enables the generator editor to display a meaningful representation of the result definition.

The generator construction system provides a number of pre-defined types and procedures that may be linked into generators and generated code. The procedures provide set operations and analysis and synthesis of both type representations and

```
! Hyper-text with embedded references to instances of type Link
type HyperText[ Link ] is …

! Value, location or type
type Binding is …

! Generator containing a prelude and a result definition
rec type Generator is structure( prelude : proc( env -> env ) ;
                                  resultDefn : GeneratorResult )

! Result definition can be fixed or dependent on inputs
& GeneratorResult is variant(
          literal : GeneratorSource ;
          expression : proc( env -> GeneratorSource ) )

! Generated code is text with links to Bindings and
! other Generators
& GeneratorSource is HyperText[ BindingOrGenerator ]

& BindingOrGenerator is variant( binding : Binding ;
                                 generator : Generator )
```

Figure 4: Napier88 description of generator model

source representations. Procedures and types may be linked directly into generator definitions using hyper-program construction tools [8].

3.3   The START Generator Editor

3.3.1   User Interface

The generator editor provides a form window with a number of fields corresponding to the various components of a generator. When a particular component is not present, or empty, the field is not displayed. To create a generator the programmer fills in the fields as appropriate. All fields may contain hyper-program links to values, locations and types identified using an external browsing tool [26]. These are distinguished by the prefixes *V:*, *L:* and *T:* respectively shown on the link labels.

The first set of fields contains the prelude definition. One field contains the names and types of the prelude parameters. As a short cut for the programmer a separate field is provided for type representation parameters, since these are expected to be particularly common. Here the programmer need only specify the names of the parameters, since they are assumed to be of type *TypeRep*.

Other fields contain the body of the prelude code and the outputs from the prelude which will be passed on to the variable parts of the result definition. The result definition itself may be an expression, in which case the result varies between evaluations, or a literal, in which case the result is always the same. For an expression the editor provides fields for both general parameters and type representations, as for the prelude parameters. The result body then contains code which when executed will generate a code representation.

For a literal a single field contains the result code. In addition to the normal hyper-program links, a literal result definition may also contain links to sub-generators, corresponding to embedded variable parts of the result. These links are distinguished by the prefix *G:* on their labels. The programmer creates a sub-generator at the current insertion point by pressing the **sub-generator** button. This inserts a link and invokes a new generator editing window. The nesting of generators may be continued to any depth. If the insertion point lies within an expression definition when the sub-generator button is pressed a new generator is created but the link to it is a hyper-program link and has a *V:* prefix. Thus a result definition is represented as a form of hyper-text comprising a graph of linked generators and sub-generators.

Figure 5 shows an example of a generator which prompts the user for a string, converts it to a source representation, and incorporates it into the generated representation of a procedure mapping reals to reals. The names on the buttons denoting the links are present to aid understanding but do not affect the semantics of the code fragments: the programmer could change the button names if desired. The initial names are supplied by the browsing tool with which the links are created.

When all details have been filled in the programmer can create an instance of type *Generator* by pressing the **compose** button. The generator is passed to the browsing system where it may be evaluated for particular parameters, stored or manipulated in any other manner.

3.3.2 Example

Figure 6 shows a generator editor used for the natural join example. The large window contains the generator for *join* itself, while the others contain sub-generators *type1* and *type2* and an auxiliary procedure *joinResultType*.

The prelude takes two type representation parameters of type *TypeRep*, representing the tuple types of the input relations. For brevity the checks to ensure that they represent structure types are not shown. The prelude enriches the input environment with three new values: *resultType*, which represents the tuple type of the result relation, and *type1Fields* and *type2Fields* which are sets containing the field information for the two input types. The value *resultType* is obtained by calling a procedure *joinResultType*, a direct link to which is contained in the prelude code. The structure field information is obtained using the pre-defined procedure *getStructureFields* which returns a set of *<name, type representation>* pairs.

The result definition is a literal and contains the definition of the generated *join* procedure. The code contains a number of links to sub-generators. These are used to define, in order of appearance, the first input type, the second input type, the result type (twice), a procedure to perform a join between a single tuple and a relation, and a procedure to compare instances of the result type.

The result definition also contains a direct link to the pre-defined procedure *mkEmptySet*. This contrasts with the Napier88 solution in which the result definition contains code to link to the procedure in the persistent store. The direct link notation is both more concise and more secure, as there is no danger of access to the

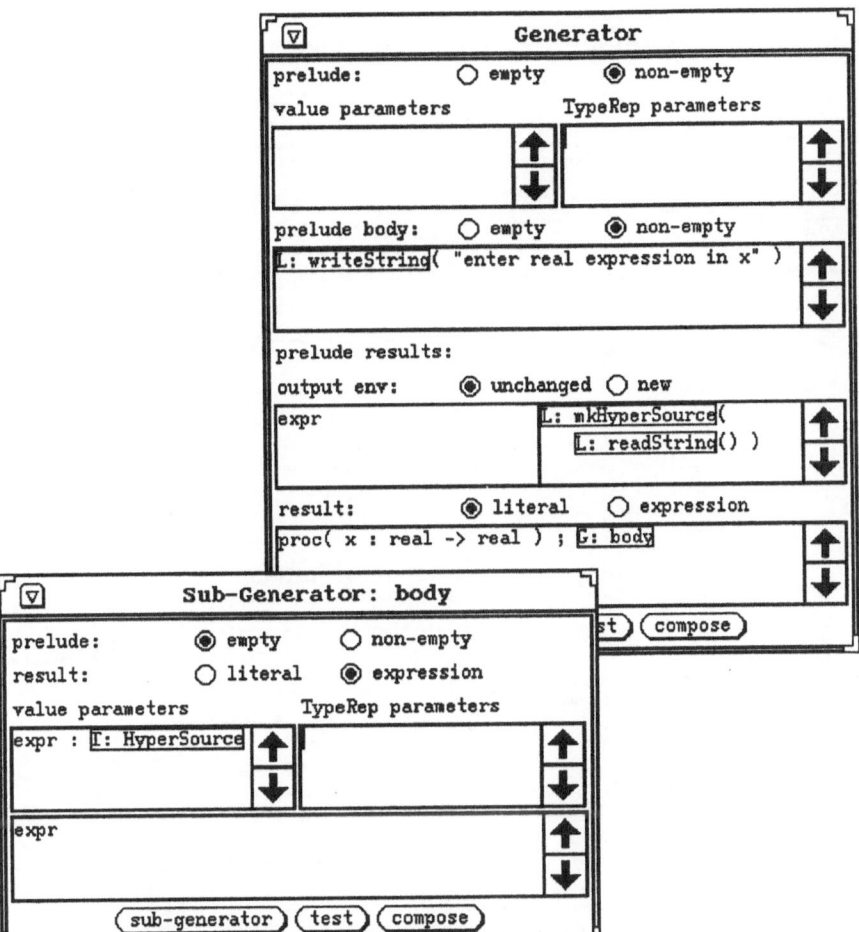

Figure 5: A simple generator

procedure being removed between the times of evaluation of the generator and execution of the generated result.

Figure 6 also shows the definition of the procedure *joinResultType* which computes a representation of the result type. This is achieved by constructing the union of the two sets containing the names and types of the fields of the input types and using the pre-defined procedure *mkStructureType* to create a type representation. The other windows show the sub-generators *type1* and *type2*. These generators use the pre-defined procedure *mkTypeLink* to obtain links to the types represented by the input type representations.

The point of having a distinguished literal branch in the result definition type, rather than representing all result definitions as procedures, should now be apparent. It means that the fixed parts of the result definition can be displayed in the generator editor without having to evaluate the generator against any particular parameters.

368

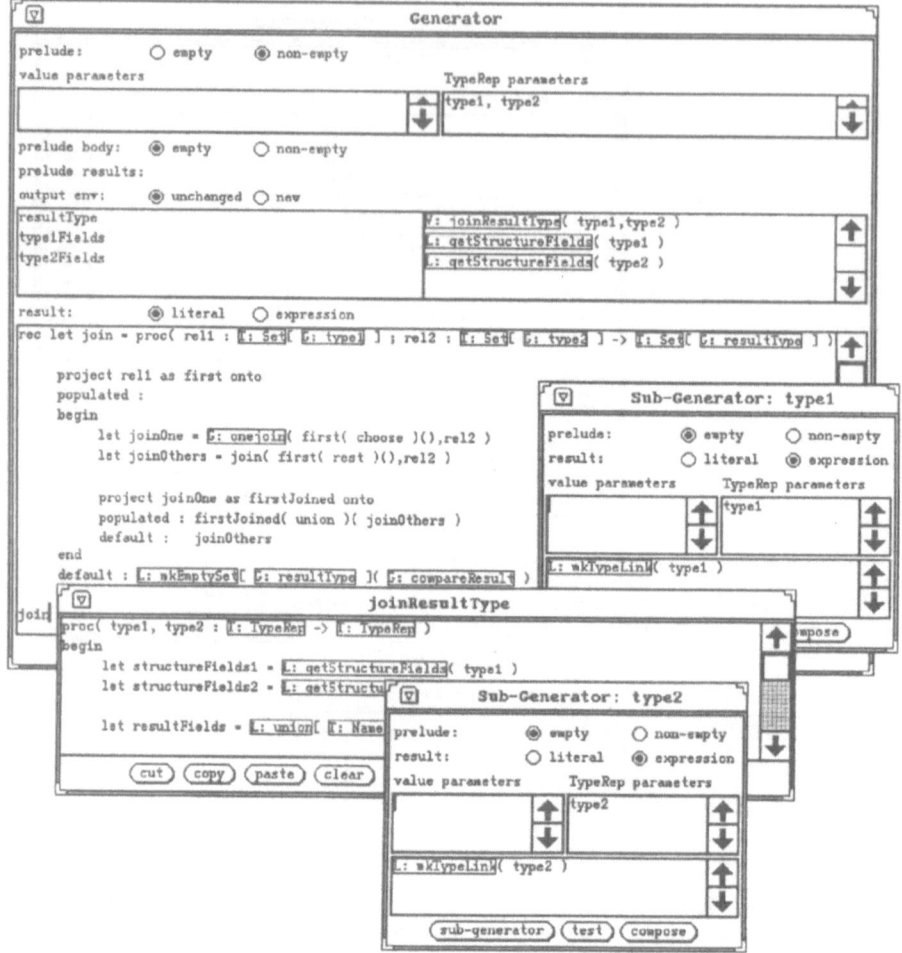

Figure 6: Generators *join*, *type1* **and** *type2*

The combination of the START tool with the hyper-programming environment gives the following advantages over the pure Napier88 solution of Figure 3:

- It may be easier to understand the general form of the generated code, that of a procedure which takes two sets as parameters and returns a third.
- Less code is generated since type definitions and specifications of how to access values in the persistent environment are replaced by hyper-program links.
- There is no need to flatten a structured type representation to a textual form for inclusion in the generated code, as performed by the procedure *writeType* in Figure 3.

3.4 Testing Generators

The testing facility allows the programmer to test a generator with various inputs. When the **test** button is pressed a new window is displayed, containing a sub-window in which values for the generator parameters may be entered. The programmer can then press the **generate code** button to evaluate the generator with those parameters. If the generator executes successfully the resulting code representation is displayed in the lower sub-window. One possible reason for failure of the generator is that the parameters supplied are not compatible with those expected by the generator: in this case a message to that effect is displayed. When generated successfully, the code may itself be evaluated by pressing the **evaluate** button. If the generated code is well formed it is executed and any resulting value displayed by the browsing system; otherwise messages indicating the errors are displayed.

Figure 7 shows a test window for a generator which takes no parameters. The **generate code** button has been pressed and a procedure definition has been generated. The generated code contains hyper-program links to the existing procedure locations *sin* and *f*. The programmer could now create an instance of the new procedure by pressing **evaluate**.

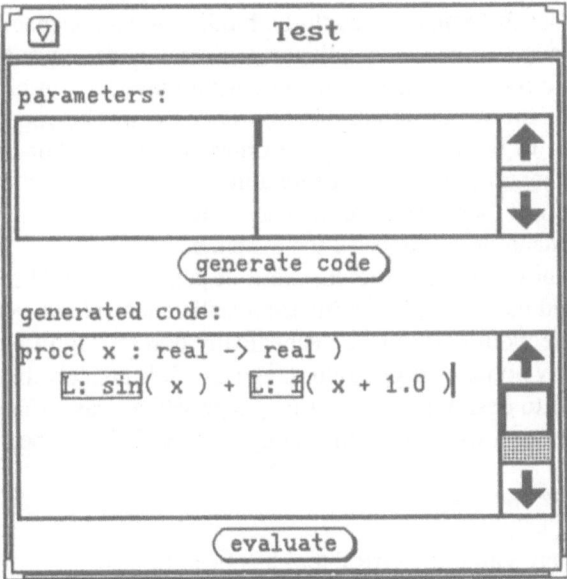

Figure 7: Generator test window

4 Open Problems and Future Work

4.1 Errors

Many problems with this technique remain. One of the principal problems is dealing with errors, which may arise at any of the following points:

- during the execution of a generator;
- during compilation of the generated code produced by a generator; or
- during execution of the generated code.

An exception mechanism supported by the underlying language could be used to handle errors occurring during the execution phases. In the absence of such a mechanism the generator model could be refined to allow a generator to return errors instead of a code fragment. For example, a natural join generator could return a *join not defined* error when the input types had no common fields.

Errors during compilation and execution of the generated code are more problematic for the user, who is unlikely to know or care about the details of the generator. In the absence of such errors the user may even be unaware of the existence of the generated code: the generator could be hidden by an encapsulating procedure which calls the generator and then calls the generated code to produce the required result. However, errors in the generator code itself may result in invalid code being generated. While the resulting compilation errors could be reported to the user these are unlikely to be useful to anyone other than the author of the generator. Similarly errors may arise during the execution of the generated code; the challenge is to be able to report these errors to the user in terms of the user problem domain rather than the domain of execution of the generated code.

It is not clear how far the static checking of generators can be developed. An ideal system would be able to determine from static analysis of a generator whether the generated code would always be syntactically correct. Intuitively this appears undecidable for any non-trivial generator language. It is conceivable however that it would be possible to design a generator language which was sufficiently restricted to allow static checking while retaining enough expressibility to be useful.

4.2 Language Issues

The approach taken with the START tool has been to design a generator model as an add-on to the unchanged Napier88 language. Alternatively, *generator* could be provided as a construct within a language. This would be a more elegant solution but it is not clear what other benefits, if any, would result. Two other possibilities for future work are to allow pattern matching on the structure of type and program representations within generators, and to allow more highly structured program representations to be used in conjunction with string representations. These features are both found in TRPL [18], and in the persistent context might allow manipulation of program representations to be expressed more clearly and succinctly.

4.3 User Interface

Plans for further development in the user interface area include provision of enhanced tools for testing generators, and the use of colour in the generator editor to distinguish the varieties of embedded links.

5 Conclusions

Linguistic reflection has a number of applications in persistent systems, but the difficulty of writing and understanding generators has limited its use. This paper has identified some of the reasons for this and described START, a hyper-text based generator editor tool designed to ease the process. The tool relies heavily on the existing Napier88 hyper-programming environment [26].

One feature of START is its hyper-text user interface which allows conceptually different parts of a generator definition to be distinguished easily. It enables the programmer to concentrate either on the form of the generated code common to all uses or details of type dependent parts as required. The other main feature is the use of hyper-program representations to provide an additional binding mechanism. Where appropriate the code generated may contain embedded direct hyper-program links to values, locations and types in the persistent environment. This results in shorter generated code and increased safety and efficiency. It also avoids the need to flatten type representations to textual form.

The generator editor has been implemented in the Napier88 hyper-programming environment. Although the current editor only supports the development of Napier88 generators, it is believed that the concepts could be applied to any self-supporting persistent programming system.

6 Acknowledgements

We thank Dave Stemple for many stimulating discussions on the topics discussed here. This work was supported by ESPRIT III Basic Research Action 6309 FIDE$_2$ and SERC grant GR/F 02953.

References

1.*   Dearle A, Brown AL. Safe Browsing in a Strongly Typed Persistent Environment. Comp. J. 1988; 31,6:540-544

2.   Alagic S. Persistent Metaobjects. In: A. Dearle, G. M. Shaw and S. B. Zdonik (ed) Implementing Persistent Object Bases, Proc. 4th International Workshop on Persistent Object Systems, Martha's Vineyard, USA. Morgan Kaufmann, 1990, pp 27-38

3.   Cooper RL. On The Utilisation of Persistent Programming Environments. Ph.D. thesis, University of Glasgow, 1990

4.   Philbrow PC. Indexing Strongly Typed Heterogeneous Collections Using Reflection and Persistence. In: Proc. ECOOP/OOPSLA Workshop on Reflection and Metalevel Architectures in Object-Oriented Programming, Ottawa, Canada, 1990

5. Sheard T. Automatic Generation and Use of Abstract Structure Operators. ACM ToPLaS 1991; 19,4:531-557

6. Hook J, Kieburtz RB, Sheard T. Generating Programs by Reflection. Oregon Graduate Institute of Science & Technology Report CS/E 92-015, 1992

7.* Kirby GNC. Persistent Programming with Strongly Typed Linguistic Reflection. In: Proc. 25th International Conference on Systems Sciences, Hawaii, 1992, pp 820-831

8.* Kirby GNC. Reflection and Hyper-Programming in Persistent Programming Systems. Ph.D. thesis, University of St Andrews, 1992

9. Stemple D, Sheard T, Fegaras L. Linguistic Reflection: A Bridge from Programming to Database Languages. In: Proc. 25th International Conference on Systems Sciences, Hawaii, 1992, pp 844-855

10.* Stemple D, Stanton RB, Sheard T et al. Type-Safe Linguistic Reflection: A Generator Technology. ESPRIT BRA Project 3070 FIDE Report FIDE/92/49, 1992

11.* Stemple D, Morrison R, Kirby GNC, Connor RCH. Integrating Reflection, Strong Typing and Static Checking. In: Proc. 16th Australian Computer Science Conference, Brisbane, Australia, 1993, pp 83-92

12.* Kirby GNC, Connor RCH, Cutts QI, Dearle A, Farkas AM, Morrison R. Persistent Hyper-Programs. In: A. Albano and R. Morrison (ed) Persistent Object Systems, Proc. 5th International Workshop on Persistent Object Systems, San Miniato, Italy. Springer-Verlag, 1992, pp 86-106

13. McCarthy J, Abrahams PW, Edwards DJ, Hart TP, Levin MI. The Lisp Programmers' Manual. M.I.T. Press, Cambridge, Massachusetts, 1962

14. Rees J, Clinger W. Revised Report on the Algorithmic Language Scheme. ACM SIGPLAN Notices 1986; 21,12:37-43

15. Burstall RM, Collins JS, Popplestone RJ. Programming in POP-2. Edinburgh University Press, Edinburgh, Scotland, 1971

16. PS-algol Reference Manual, 4th edition. Universities of Glasgow and St Andrews Report PPRR-12-88, 1988

17.* Morrison R, Brown AL, Connor RCH et al. The Napier88 Reference Manual (Release 2.0). University of St Andrews Report CS/94/8, 1994

18. Sheard T. A user's Guide to TRPL: A Compile-time Reflective Programming Language. COINS, University of Massachusetts Report 90-109, 1990

19.* Connor RCH, Cutts QI, Kirby GNC, Morrison R. Using Persistence Technology to Control Schema Evolution. In: Proc. 9th ACM Symposium on Applied Computing, Phoenix, Arizona, 1994, pp 441-446

20. Strachey C. Fundamental Concepts in Programming Languages. Oxford University Press, Oxford, 1967

21. Milner R. A Theory of Type Polymorphism in Programming. Journal of Computer and System Sciences 1978; 17,3:348-375

22. Codd EF. Extending the relational model to capture more meaning. ACM ToDS 1979; 4,4:397-434

23. Stemple D, Fegaras L, Sheard T, Socorro A. Exceeding the Limits of Polymorphism in Database Programming Languages. In: F. Bancilhon, C. Thanos and D. Tsichritzis (ed) Lecture Notes in Computer Science 416. Springer-Verlag, 1990, pp 269-285

24. Kaes S. Parametric Overloading in Polymorphic Programming languages. In: Lecture Notes in Computer Science 300. Springer-Verlag, 1988, pp 131-144

25. Wadler P, Blott S. How to Make ad-hoc Polymorphism Less ad-hoc. In: Proc. 16th ACM Symposium on Principles of Programming Languages, Austin, Texas, 1989

26.* Kirby GNC, Brown AL, Connor RCH et al. The Napier88 Standard Library Reference Manual Version 2.2. University of St Andrews Report CS/94/7, 1994

27.* Farkas AM, Dearle A, Kirby GNC, Cutts QI, Morrison R, Connor RCH. Persistent Program Construction through Browsing and User Gesture with some Typing. In: A. Albano and R. Morrison (ed) Persistent Object Systems, Proc. 5th International Workshop on Persistent Object Systems, San Miniato, Italy. Springer-Verlag, 1992, pp 376-393

*Available via anonymous *ftp* from
`ftp-fide.dcs.st-andrews.ac.uk/pub/persistence.papers`

or via *http* from
`http://www-fide.dcs.st-andrews.ac.uk/Publications.html`

DAIS: An Object-Addressed Processor Cache

Gordon Russell   Paul Shaw
Paul Cockshott
Department of Computer Science, University of Strathclyde
Glasgow, Scotland

Abstract

DAIS is a proposed processor incorporating hardware-based object addressing. By providing only the very minimum of support for objects, it allows efficient access via a novel caching scheme. Object addressing is supported at the instruction level, with virtually the same performance as a processor using virtual addressing. This paper begins with a justification of the method by which objects are accessed in the DAIS design, and then goes on to describe the hardware caching mechanisms to efficiently support it. Finally, some analysis of benchmarks is given, and dynamic program traces are used to show the performance of the caching scheme.

1   Introduction

DAIS is a design study of an architecture which supports object addressing at the instruction level. The addressing model is designed to allow a large collection of machines each with a large number of objects. The virtual memory architecture allows both position and media independence of data.

The motivation for moving the object addressing into hardware is to provide both security and speed. There have of course been many previous attempts to do this. In all of these, the addition of object addressing has involved considerable complexity in the memory access mechanism that has translated into a reduction in performance. Our objective has been to come up with mechanisms that will allow the greater logical complexity of object-based architectures to be short circuited during execution of progams by a judicious use of caches.

In specifying this hardware support, lessons in traditional processor design have been borne in mind; the proponents of RISC taught us that simplicity and provision of the minimum general support result in flexibility and speed. For this reason, we have examined the simplest methods of object access first, and moved only to more complex ones when we deemed it necessary: The dictionary definition of *dais* is a low platform, and we believe that the DAIS architecture is the lowest (simplest) hardware platform which supports object addressing, identifier validation, and bounds checking.

DAIS makes use of a cache structure based directly on object descriptors and offsets, rather than the more common physically or virtually addressed cache. This cache structure has been designed to allow access to fields within an object after a single clock cycle.

To explain how this is achieved we will first present the logical model of our object addressing scheme, then look at the time penalties that it would incur in the absence of suitable caches before showing how our object cache works.

Currently DAIS is only a proposed architecture, and that no hardware version of the processor exists. This paper deals only with the caching strategy, although details of other aspects (*i.e.* the register file and pipeline) of the processor's design are available from the authors.

2 Addressing models

In RISC processors all memory accesses occur in load and store instructions. An example of such a load might be

```
LOAD r1,[r2]
```

The effect of which would be to perform the operation $r_1 \leftarrow memory[r_2]$. On a simple RISC microcontroler equipped with fast memory, this can be performed in a single clock cycle since the contents of r_2 can be simply placed on the address bus with the data returning on the next cycle, giving the sequence.

$$abus \leftarrow r_2, r_1 \leftarrow dbus \tag{1}$$

where operations on one line are assumed to take place in a single cycle. As memory sizes go up, the speed tends to go down as slower cheaper components are used, but RISC designers try to maintain single cycle load operation by the use of caches.

2.1 Cached RAM access

The sequence of operations involved in a load from address r_2 into r_1 now is:

1. if r_2 in cache then $r_1 \leftarrow dcache$ else

   (a) $abus \leftarrow r_2$
   (b) *wait 2 cycles*
   (c) $r_1 \leftarrow dbus$

2.2 Virtual memory access

When virtual memory is introduced the logical sequence of operations becomes longer. In principle we have to do the following:

1. Use the top 20 bits of r_2 to index the page table.

2. If page not present cause an interrupt, else $t \leftarrow PageTab[r_2(31:12)]$

3. $r_1 \leftarrow Memory[t + r_2(11:0)]$

This now involves two memory accesses where we had one before, each of which could take several clock cycles. Virtual memory only becomes viable to the extent that caches could be used to short circuit this process. First, address translation caches were used to allow the virtual to physical address translation to be done in one cycle. Then processor designers introduced caches indexed by virtual rather than physical addresses. The end result is that for perhaps 95% of loads, the **Virtual memory access** is reduced to a **Cached RAM access** that runs in one cycle. Virtually-addressed caches are not frequently used in data caches, due to context-switch overheads (changing virtual to physical mappings usually means that a virtually-addressed cache must be flushed).

Let us now look at the logical sequence of operations involved in object addressing.

2.3 Object Mapping

In DAIS, object IDs are used for all user-based memory references, including stack accesses. This makes memory referencing uniform over the whole instruction set. All object references are specified in the form *object ID* plus *offset*, where a legal offset must lie between zero and the length of the object minus one inclusive.

Load instructions now take the form:

```
LOAD r1,r2[r3]
```

As before, r_1 is the destination register. The address is now provided by two registers; r_2 specifies an object-ID and r_3 an offset into the object.

To access main memory, the object-ID/offset pair must be translated into a physical RAM address. RISC philosophy suggests that all aspects of a processor should be kept as simple as possible, and the simplest possible translation between object IDs (OIDs) and physical addresses is for the OID to be its object's **physical RAM** address. This approach, which we shall term case 1, incurs no translation overhead in accessing objects, but is not without its difficulties.

Additional instructions have to be planted on each object access to test if the OID currently refers to disk or RAM. When an object is returned to disk, any pointer fields must be checked to ensure that they point at disk addresses. This is undesirable because it implies that the swapper must know about the data structures used by higher level software.

In traditionally-addressed processors, virtual memory is often used to enable main memory to act as a direct-mapped window onto an I/O mapped backing store. This approach unifies backing store and main memory addressing. If our object processor used the virtual address of the object data as the OID, then the address renaming required to support the backing store in case 1 is no longer required. We shall term this approach case 2.

This has its own difficulties. In particular it makes it difficult to compact the virtual address space as objects are deleted. This leads to a fragmented virtual address space in which excessive paging can occur during object allocation or traversal. Although algorithms do exist to allow heap compaction on a single processor, their use on a distributed shared virtual memory is much more problematic.

Other disadvantages of using virtual addresses as OIDs are;

• Since *every* object access should be bounds checked against the length of the object, as well as other checks which may be required (*e.g.* read/write bits), direct use of virtual addresses provides no protection of this sort.

• It becomes hard to provide access control at a granularity of less than a page.

We propose that an OID be the virtual address of the object descriptor, which in turn contains (amongst other things) the virtual address of the object's data part. The virtual memory itself is split up into a number of partitions, each handled by independent memory management software. The object descriptors lie in their own partition, while object data lie within another. Object addressing is now a level of abstraction on top of virtual addressing.

The logical sequence of steps to access an object

```
LOAD r1,r2[r3]
```

now are:

1. The OID is used as the virtual address of the object descriptor as in section 2.2.

2. From this, the virtual address of the object data is obtained.

   $oa \leftarrow VMem[r_2 + \text{addrfield}]$

3. The object offset is then added to the object data address,

   $fa \leftarrow oa + r_3$

   to obtain a field address.

4. The bounds of the object are now found from the descriptor.

   $br \leftarrow VMem[r_2 + \text{boundsfield}]$

5. The bounds are compared with the field offset for access validity.

   Interrupt if $r_3 > br$

6. The field address is used as the virtual address of the object data to be accessed.

   $r_1 \leftarrow VMem[\text{fa}]$

   This is again a virtual memory access.

This process is clearly more costly than a simple memory access. It involves three memory accesses and four arithmetic operations. Even assuming that the full paraphanelia of virtual addressed caches is available, this is still at least a five cycle operation. One of our key aims has been to show that this can be achieved in a single cycle.

2.4 Comparison to other Systems

The proposal given above is not the only possible method for successfully implementing object-based addressing. Other object systems have approached the problem in different manners. For comparison purposes, let us consider five other architectures; the Rekursiv,MUTABOR, MONADS, the iAPX-432, and System/38.

The Rekursiv [1] holds the object descriptor and data together in a single unit. No virtual memory management is used, and instead OID to physical address translation is performed in a64 K-entry direct-mapped hashing table. When an object is needed, this table is checked. If the OID is not present in the table, then the OID which is currently held there is removed, and its corresponding object descriptor and data copied in its entirety onto the backing store.The desired object is then copied from the store, and the table updated with the new OID. The direct-mapped strategy used in the table could cause object thrashing between main memory and the store, and the lack of virtual memory makes supporting large objects less efficient than smaller ones.

MUTABOR [2, 3]uses a *two-space* model, as opposed to a flat object space. The processor accesses objects within the *active space*, where short object names are used as the virtual address of their respective objects. When an object is needed but not present in the active space, it is copied from the *passive space*. The passive object IDs are larger than those used in the active space, and are based on backing-store (rather than virtual) addresses. Transfers between active and passive space require that all OIDs be converted to the appropriate ID type. This conversion is similar to that discussed for case 1 above. The need to perform conversion is fundamental in this two-space approach. For simplicity, a single object naming scheme for all objects in the heap would have been preferable.Each object in MUTABOR must be contained within a single 4 KByte page. Up to 16 objects can share a single page. Objects larger than a page are not supported. Capabilities(*i.e.* methods) for an object are also stored within the same page. Inheritance of methods requires that the methods from one page be copied to the new method's page. This is not as flexible as a true single-level store, where only a pointer to the old methods would have to be duplicated.

MONADS [4, 5] uses a hierarchical construction of modules and objects. A module contains executable code and objects, and generally represents a source-code module. Object data contained within a module can not be read outwith the module, and instead has to be passed via procedure called with the executable parts of the module. This layered approach is similar to that used in MUTABOR. OIDs are formed from the virtual address of the module, plus type, offset from the start of the module,and length information for the desired object. These OIDs are called capabilities. Since the capabilities carry their own length information, changing the length of an object would require that all capabilities for that object be tracked down and changed, so this action is not supported by MONADS.

The iAPX-432 [6, 7]holds object permissions, data, and other object information in a number of separate objects. Yet more details on objects are held in type managers (*i.e.* methods). This allows support for flexible inheritance and object length modification, at the expense of being overly complex. The 432's OID translation mechanism passes through many levels of indirection, before pinpointing the required object data. This makes OID translation a costly process. In a similar approach to MUTABOR, the 432 makes use of a two-space memory model, except that transfers between the spaces is under control of the type managers (unlike the automatic scheme of MUTABOR). When necessary, the type managers ask for an object to be transferred into the active space. There, the manager will make all necessary changes to the object, before finally asking the system to return the object into the passive space.

Finally, SYSTEM/38 [8, 9] uses an OID structure which contains the virtual address of the object, a checkcode, and type information (access rights, length, *etc.*). The checksum is required to avoid using an OID to reference a previously deleted object, which is possible in SYSTEM/38 since it uses explicit object deletion and *not* automatic garbage collection. Holding the type information in the OID complicates object size changes (not done in SYSTEM/38). This system could only supported a maximum of 2^{24} objects, although it was possible to have OIDs to select areas within objects (although the need for this is questionable).

3   DAIS

DAIS is a processor design in the RISC philosophy targeted towards general-purpose programming. Its load and store instructions are based on objects and offsets. It can efficiently execute applications written in both object-based and traditional languages. This is achieved by the use of caches within the processor to store frequently used object data, removing the need for object address translation for the vast majority of object accesses.

OID to physical translation in DAIS is based on the object-descriptor/object-data model proposed earlier. In this approach, memory addressing is performed using OID/offset pairs. We call the object-based view of memory *object space*. Each OID is the virtual address of the respective object descriptor. The descriptor contains the virtual address, object status, and the overall length (in bytes) of the object data (see figure 1). We say that all virtual memory accesses lie in *virtual space*. Using virtual-to-physical translation, virtual addresses are converted to physical ones, which all lie in *physical space*. In object space, each unit of offset from an OID is equivalent to 8 bits.

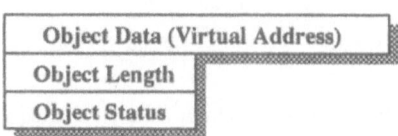

Figure 1: DAIS Object Descriptor

The OID size used in the DAIS proposal is largely independent of the underlying design of DAIS. It is however assumed that an OID can be communicated between the processor and the external memory interface in a single transfer. Without this assumption all transfer rates concerning internal cache spills and refills will need to be adjusted with respect to the time to load OIDs and their relative frequency of occurrence in cache activity.

4 Primary Processor Cache

RISC designs frequently make use of on-chip caches to hold instructions and data. To reduce the complexity of the initial DAIS design, we use separate direct mapped data and instruction caches. Together, these caches are collectively named the primary processor caches. Other cache organizations could be investigated in the future.

The caches are mapped using a hash of the OID and offset. This allows different parts of one object to be spread over several cache lines. The use of OIDs and offsets to cache object data is not a technique found in other object-based processors, where caching of the conversion from OID to virtual address (with caching of object data occurring as a second step using the resulting virtual address) is generally accepted as the norm. This allows us to bypass the OID to virtual address translation step of object accesses when the relevant object data is in the primary caches. The structure of the D-cache (data cache) is shown in figure 2. The I-cache (instruction cache) is similar to the D-cache, except that the cache access - write block, along with the dirty and RO parts of the cache, are not implemented (the I-cache is read-only).

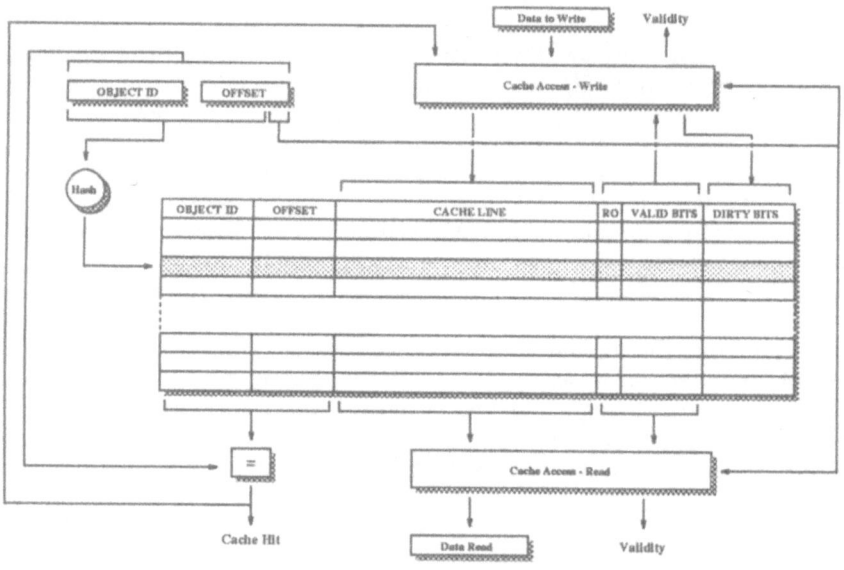

Figure 2: Structure of Data and Instruction Caches.

In the D-cache, a write to any word of the cache line sets the dirty bit for that word. This is used when the cache is being flushed (*e.g.* if the line is being replaced by another object entry). Only words in the cache marked as dirty need to be written back to memory. In this way, the D-cache acts as a *write-back* cache. If the D-cache contains information which is read-only, the RO bit of that cache line is set, and any attempt to write to that line is trapped by the processor.

Using hardware logic to perform the boundary check on object accesses would reduce the performance of the caches. To remove the need for an arithmetic-based bounds-check on each object access, valid bits are used instead. Each valid bit corresponds to a single byte (the smallest element which can be accessed using a load/store instruction) of the cache line. If the bit is clear, then that byte of the cache is unaccessible. The valid bits are set for bytes within the bounds of an object, and cleared for all other data. Attempting to access data whose valid bit is clear is interpreted as accessing the object beyond its actual size, and is trapped.

If objects were close enough together, then a cache line could contain data from more than one object. Even so, only the object hashed to that line is accessible, with data from the others being unaccessible (their corresponding valid bits would be clear).

The use of the primary caches frequently eliminate the need to convert OIDs to virtual addresses. Range checking of object accesses is also eliminated in the traditional sense, requiring only a bit test involving the valid bits of the relevant cache line. These two features give DAIS a similar memory access rate as those obtainable from traditional (*i.e.* virtual-addressed) processors.

5   Primary-Cache Misses

On a primary cache miss, the desired object's descriptor must be accessed. This contains the virtual address of the object data, along with the object's length and status information. The data can then be transferred from main memory to the cache. Once the transfer has completed, all the dirty bits (for the D-cache) are cleared, and the valid bits are initialized. The valid bits are set only for the data bytes which lie within the object's boundaries. This is calculated from the object's length, and the offset (from the start of the object data) used in loading the cache line. Cache line data is aligned to line-length boundaries, which simplifies the cache-load hardware.

For the D-cache, before a cache line can be loaded the current contents of the line must be checked. If the line contains dirty words, then these words must first be flushed to memory. This requires that the line's relevant object descriptor be loaded, allowing the virtual address of the dirty words to be calculated.

The RO (read-only) bit of the D-cache is calculated from the virtual memory protection present on the object data being loaded. If the protection is read-write, then the RO bit is cleared, otherwise it is set. There is also a FRO (force read-only) bit in the status information held in each object descriptor. If that bit is set, then so is the RO bit for that object in the primary cache. This access protection could be used in an operating system to implement object locking.

With the need to access an object descriptor at least once on each primary cache refill, the idea of caching the object descriptors themselves appears attractive, and therefore this descriptor cache has been included in the DAIS proposal. We have termed this cache the *secondary* or *O-cache*. The benefits of using an O-cache are investigated in the analysis section.

Although we have only described the CPU operating with object-based addressing, it can also use physical addressing. Physical addressing is restricted to supervisor mode, and allows the object management routines to bypass both the fault- and virtual memory-manager.

With so little information held within each cache entry, cache access rates should be similar to standard data caches. Additionally, since an object's virtual address and overall length changes infrequently, the primary caches are rarely flushed.

Consider a DAIS implementation whose data and instruction cache both hold 256 lines of information. From the analysis presented later in this paper, which assumes an OID size of 64 bits[1], it is suggested that an instruction cache size of 8 KBytes is used, and this corresponds to a line length of 256 bits. Again from the analysis, the data cache line length suggested is 128 bits (4 KBytes of storage). This equates to a data cache consisting of 7584 bytes of storage, and the instruction cache to 12032 bytes. The object cache contains 128 entries, requiring 2464 bytes of storage. The total space for all three caches is approximately 22 KBytes, which is similar in size to many modern processor designs.

6 Benefits of the Object Cache

The layered approach to DAIS' caching structure has been put forward as a benefit over other object-oriented architectures. However, what exact benefit does the secondary (*i.e.* object) cache give? Here, a short theoretical analysis of the object cache performance is presented. Space considerations force this analysis to be summary; the authors can give more detailed analysis on request. The following symbols are used here:

$$
\begin{aligned}
M_I, M_D, M_O &= \text{I-, D- and O-cache miss rates} \\
P_I, P_D, P_O &= \text{I-, D- and O-cache miss penalty} \\
T_I &= \text{Time to read one I-cache line} \\
T_D &= \text{Time to read/write one D-cache line} \\
m &= \text{Fraction of instructions referencing D-cache} \\
d &= \text{Probability that a memory word in D-cache is dirty} \\
n &= \text{Number of memory words per D-cache line}
\end{aligned}
$$

First, as with RISC designs, we assume DAIS can execute one instruction per cycle (ignoring pipeline stalls). The overhead per instruction for I-cache misses is $M_I P_I$ cycles. Similarly, the overhead per instruction owing to D-cache misses is $m M_D P_D$. The total CPI is thus:

$$ CPI = 1 + M_I P_I + m M_D P_D $$

Here, both miss penalties include the time taken to fetch the object descriptor and then fetch the cache line of object data. To discover performance with and without O-cache, it is necessary to derive formulae for P_I and P_D under both conditions. Without proof, we state that without an O-cache,

$$ P_I = P_O + T_I $$

$$ P_D = (2 - (1-d)^n)P_O + (1+d)T_D $$

---

[1] As OID size increases, then the effective size of the data cache will be reduced, since a larger proportion of each data cache line is needed to hold OIDs (in comparison to holding non-OIDs whose size does not change with different OID-size implementations).

Table 1: Data Cache Miss Rates (Per Instruction)

Benchmark	4K cache		8K cache	
	16 byte lines	32 byte lines	16 byte lines	32 byte lines
TEX	1.79%	1.88%	1.24%	1.23%
DeTEX	1.15%	1.93%	0.56%	1.32%
Zoo	2.46%	2.26%	1.84%	1.53%
Fig2dev	1.04%	0.99%	0.53%	0.47%
Average	1.61%	1.76%	1.04%	1.14%
Weighted Av	1.76%	1.86%	1.21%	1.22%

and with an O-cache,

$$P_I = 1 + M_O P_O + T_I$$

$$P_D = 2 + M_O P_O \left[2 - (1-d)^n\right] - (1-d)^n + (1+d)T_D$$

7 Some Example Figures

Here, some well known programs have been simulated using the above I- and D-cache miss penalties to give the reader some idea of the increase in efficiency the O-cache gives.

TEX, DeTEX, Zoo, and Fig2dev were simulated. These programs were choosen for their general availability, coupled with their cpu-bound and non-interactive nature. If we consider all heap and stack accesses in these applications would be converted to object accesses in DAIS, then the analysis performed should not be unreasonable. The miss rates for direct mapped caches of 4K and 8K bytes with line lengths of 16 and 32 bytes are shown in tables 1 and 2. These were derived using SHADOW[10] (a tool to trace binaries) on a SPARC. For the case of the D-cache, the miss rates given are *per instruction*, and not per D-cache access. The averages shown in these tables are both 'straight', and weighted on the number of instructions executed by each of the simulations. Other results from these simulations (pertaining to write-backs of cache lines) where used to estimate d at 0.2.

The size of OIDs was assumed to be 64 bits. In the applications examined, the proportion of address pointers to non-address information was small, and so the effect of increasing address size of 32 bits (as used in the SPARC) to 64 bit OIDs was ignored. In other applications whose data consists of a larger proportion of OIDs to data, then the effect of using 64 bit addressing could become significant.

Unfortunately, the miss rate of the O-cache cannot be predicted from such a cache trace (since the programs traced are not object based). However, analysis shows that over half of the object descriptor accesses are caused by I-cache misses. Since temporal locality of instruction objects is high, it is anticipated that nearly all O-cache misses will result from D-cache misses. For analysis purposes, the O-cache miss rate was assumed to be a pessimistic 10%. Interestingly, doubling this value only has a small effect on the performance.

Table 2: Instruction Cache Miss Rates

Benchmark	4K cache		8K cache	
	16 byte lines	32 byte lines	16 byte lines	32 byte lines
TEX	5.99%	3.74%	3.74%	2.35%
DeTEX	7.31%	5.08%	3.73%	2.72%
Zoo	1.12%	0.78%	0.35%	0.23%
Fig2dev	9.95%	6.70%	5.74%	3.98%
Average	6.09%	4.08%	3.39%	2.32%
Weighted Av	5.94%	3.81%	3.74%	2.37%

In a system without an external cache, the performance degradation is under 4%. With external cache, the degradation is only 2%.

Four scenarios have been staged; all combinations of processors either with or without O-cache and an external cache. When the processor has no O-cache, each object descriptor must be fetched from main store. The assumption is made that without external cache each main store access requires 5 processor cycles. For a system with this external cache, access is assumed to require an average of 2 cycles. The miss rates used for the I- and D-caches where the *weighted averages* shown in tables 1 and 2. For all four cases, the resultant CPI (disregarding other processor stalls such as branching stalls) is shown for different combinations of I- and D-cache sizes (4 and 8 KBytes) and line lengths (16 and 32 bytes) in figures 3–6. The minimum CPI from each cache size combination is highlighted.

From these four tables, the trade-offs in choosing I- and D-cache sizes and line lengths can be investigated. The benefits of including an object or external cache are also part of these tables. In all cases adding an O-cache resulted in better performance than doubling the size of a 4 KByte D-cache. For the cache setup detailed in section 4, the CPI are:

O-cache	External Cache	CPI
No	No	2.16
No	Yes	1.46
Yes	No	1.78
Yes	Yes	1.34

Hence, the O-cache gives a 21% speed improvement when there is no external cache present, and a 9% improvement if there is.

8   Conclusions

The caching structure of the DAIS architecture incorporates features allowing the architecture to run at around the same speed as non object-based processors. DAIS achieves efficiency by providing only the minimum of object-access instructions. On a RISC architecture, only load and store instructions need be concerned with objects, which greatly simplifies processor design.

Table 3: CPI with no O- or E-cache

		Instruction Cache			
		4K/16	4K/32	8K/16	8K/32
	4K/16	2.64	**2.59**	2.20	**2.16**
Data	4K/32	2.93	2.89	2.49	2.45
Cache	8K/16	2.50	**2.45**	2.06	**2.02**
	8K/32	2.67	2.63	2.23	2.20

Table 4: CPI with O- but no E-cache

		Instruction Cache			
		4K/16	4K/32	8K/16	8K/32
	4K/16	**1.97**	2.10	**1.71**	1.78
Data	4K/32	2.22	2.34	1.95	2.03
Cache	8K/16	**1.89**	2.02	**1.63**	1.70
	8K/32	2.04	2.17	1.78	1.85

Table 5: CPI with E- but no O-cache

		Instruction Cache			
		4K/16	4K/32	8K/16	8K/32
	4K/16	1.66	**1.64**	1.48	**1.46**
Data	4K/32	1.75	1.74	1.58	1.56
Cache	8K/16	1.60	**1.58**	1.42	**1.41**
	8K/32	1.66	1.64	1.48	1.47

Table 6: CPI with both O- and E-cache

		Instruction Cache			
		4K/16	4K/32	8K/16	8K/32
	4K/16	**1.44**	1.48	**1.32**	1.34
Data	4K/32	1.54	1.58	1.42	1.44
Cache	8K/16	**1.40**	1.44	**1.28**	1.30
	8K/32	1.47	1.51	1.35	1.37

A cache structure based on objects and offsets rather than on virtual addresses allows object data to be accessed without the need for an address translation. This scheme allows object bounds to be checked by examination of validity bits; no arithmetic is necessary.

The results of simulation of some standard programs show that a non-superscaler version of DAIS using 64 bit OIDs with external cache takes 1.34 cycles to execute each instruction (ignoring other pipeline stalls). This result is for a system with 8K of instruction cache, 4K of data cache and 2K of object cache. In this analysis we have made the single conservative assumption that the O-cache has a 10% miss rate. The object cache justifies its existence since a system with 8K of both instruction and data cache but no object cache has poorer performance.

DAIS is part of a proposed object-oriented persistent environment. We use 256 bit OIDs, as the proposed system utilizes secure world-wide object addressing. More information on DAIS and the object-oriented environment can be found in [11].

References

[1] David M. Harland. *REKURSIV, Object Oriented Computer Architecture*. Ellis Horwood Limited, 1988.

[2] Jörg Kaiser. An object-oriented architecture to support system reliability and security. In *Computer Architecture to Support Security and Persistence of Information*, pages (9–1)–(9–15). University of Bremen, May 1990.

[3] Jörg Kaiser and Karol Czaja. An architecture to support persistence in object-oriented systems. Available from the authors at kaiser@gmdzi.gmd.de or czaja@gmdzi.gbx.de, 1990.

[4] J[ames] Leslie Keedy. An implementation of capabilities without a central mapping table. In *Proceedings of the Seventeenth Annual Hawaii International Conference on System Sciences*, pages 180–185, 1984.

[5] John Rosenberg and David Abramson. MONADS-PC - a capability-based workstation to support software engineering. In *Proceedings of the Eighteenth Annual Hawaii International Conference on System Sciences*, pages 222–231, 1985.

[6] Colin Hunter, Erin Farquhar, and James Ready. *Introduction to the Intel iAPX432 Architecture*. Reston Publishing Company inc., 1985.

[7] M. van Rumste. The iAPX432, a next generation microprocessor. *Microprocessing and Microprogramming*, 12(2):69–106, February 1983.

[8] G. Soltis. Design of a small business data processing system. *IEEE Computer*, pages 77–93, September 1977.

[9] Frank G. Soltis and Roy L. Hoffman. Design considerations for the IBM SYSTEM/38. In Gerald E. Peterson, editor, *Tutorial: Object-Oriented Computing*, volume 2. IEEE Computer Society, 1987.

[10] SUN Microsystems. *Introduction to SHADOW*, April 1992.

[11] Gordon Russell. DOLPHIN: *Persistent, Object-oriented, and Networked*. PhD thesis, University of Strathclyde, 1994. Submitted. A draft copy is available by email from the author (gor@cs.strath.ac.uk).

Hardware Support for Stability in a Persistent Architecture

*F. A. Henskens, †D. M. Koch, *R. Jalili & *J. Rosenberg

*Department of Computer Science
University of Sydney
N.S.W., 2006, Australia
{fransr,rasool,john}@cs.su.oz.au

†Department of Computer Science
University of Newcastle
N.S.W., 2308, Australia
dmk@cs.newcastle.edu.au

Abstract

Persistent stores support uniform management of data objects regardless of their lifetimes and locations. Such stores typically maintain a self-consistent state even after failure of the host computer system. This property is termed stability, and may be achieved using operations called checkpoints. When objects in the store are modified, or modified objects are accessed, dependencies are created between the modifying processes and the objects. Directed graphs may be used to describe such dependencies. For the persistent store to maintain a consistent state, all dependent entities must be checkpointed together. In this paper we show that hardware support can assist in the construction of stable stores for which stability is based on dependency graphs. We then describe an implementation of such support in the Monads-MM computer.

1 Introduction

Persistent systems support mechanisms which allow programs to create and manipulate arbitrary data structures which outlive the execution of the program which created them [2]. This has many advantages from both a software engineering and an efficiency viewpoint. In particular it removes the necessity for the programmer to flatten data structures in order to store them permanently. In this sense a persistent system provides an alternative to a conventional file system for the storage of permanent data. This alternative is far more flexible in that both the data and its interrelationships can be stored in their original form. In order to achieve this a uniform storage abstraction is required. Such an abstraction is often called a *persistent store*. A persistent store supports mechanisms for the storage and retrieval of objects and their interrelationships in a uniform manner regardless of their lifetime.

Persistent stores thus abstract over the distinction between primary and secondary storage. The state of the store at any instant is a combination of the contents of the volatile data held in main memory (RAM) and the more stable data held in secondary memory (disk). When a system unexpectedly shuts down, for instance as a result of hardware failure or loss of power, the contents of main memory are typically lost. As a result of such failures the data stored in secondary memory may be inconsistent or unreachable. Cockshott [5] and later Brown [3] proposed that the abstraction over storage should include transparent recovery from such store failures so that the store contents are guaranteed to be consistent even after unexpected store failure. Such stores are said to be stable, and move between stable states through a sequence of operations called checkpoints.

In section 2 of this paper we examine techniques used in the implementation of stable stores and introduce the concept of object level checkpoints. In section 3 we show that such checkpoints must consider logical relationships between objects or associations [11], and describe a scheme for expressing associations based on directed graphs. We then show in section 4 how appropriate hardware support facilitates the implementation of stable stores based on this scheme and introduce issues related to multiprocessor architectures. Finally in section 5 we describe the implementation of such hardware support in the latest generation of the Monads architecture.

2 Implementation of stability

A persistent store is said to be stable if it automatically recovers to a consistent state after a failure which has prevented orderly system shutdown. Techniques which achieve stability are typically based on the use of operations called checkpoints which commit all recent modifications to stable secondary storage. The act of checkpointing a store in effect flushes all modified data currently held in main memory to disk, and creates a snapshot of the store at that moment. Processing usually ceases on the store during such a checkpoint operation.

Between checkpoint operations on a store, the state of the store is represented by the contents of disk plus the contents of modified data held in main memory. If it could be guaranteed that the contents of disk were never modified between checkpoints, and that the checkpoint operation itself was atomic, then the contents of disk would always represent a stable state of the store. In fact, virtual memory management requires that from time to time main memory pages are re-assigned. Pages containing unmodified data may be safely re-used without disk access. Modified data, however, must firstly be saved before the page(s) containing the data can be re-used. This is typically achieved by flushing the entire page contents to disk. Writing such a page back to its original location on disk potentially leads to the disk representation of the store being inconsistent and therefore unstable. Shadow paging [12] is a technique that allows modified page discard without causing an inconsistent disk version of the store. The atomicity of checkpoint operations may be guaranteed using Challis' algorithm [4]. In the following discussion the term *object* is used to describe an arbitrarily large unit of logically related data.

2.1 Shadow paging

This technique maintains two forms of data which has been modified between checkpoint operations; the stable data as it existed at the last checkpoint (shadow data) and the latest version of the data (current version data). The scheme may be implemented for individual objects, but is more typically applied at the virtual page level. In the usual paged store, implementation of shadowing at the virtual page level minimises fragmentation by allowing more than one object to reside in the same page, and improves the efficiency of shadowing for objects that span multiple pages.

Shadow paging may be implemented using either before-look or after-look strategies. The before-look strategy takes an on-disk shadow copy of a page prior to its modification and allows discard of the current version page to the original page disk location. A checkpoint operation flushes modified main memory pages to their original locations on disk and causes the return of disk pages containing shadow copies to the pool of free disk space. Recovery from store failure involves copying shadow versions of pages onto their original disk locations. This strategy has the advantage that it maintains the physical location of data on disk, and was implemented in Brown's stable store [3].

The after-look strategy allocates a new disk page for storage of the current version, and retains the previous unmodified version in its original location as a shadow copy. In effect the disk pages existing immediately after a checkpoint form shadow pages until the next checkpoint. A checkpoint operation flushes modified main memory pages to the current version disk locations and returns the disk space occupied by shadow copies to the pool of free disk pages. Since the data structures describing the disk are also stabilised at a checkpoint, recovery from store failure is automatic. This strategy has the advantage that it requires one less write operation for modified pages between each checkpoint but results in the random distribution of data on disk. It has been implemented for Monads [14] and Casper [17].

Both strategies require atomicity of checkpoint operations. Since writing to disk is a sequential operation, such atomicity can only be an abstraction. This is achieved by viewing the store as a structure accessible from a single point or root, and changing that root according to Challis' algorithm as the last step in a checkpoint operation.

2.2 Challis' algorithm

Challis proposed that atomicity could be achieved by starting and ending a root page with a timestamp. Such timestamps are never the same for consecutive versions of a root page. If a root-page write operation is successful, the disk version of the page will have identical timestamps; if it fails then the first timestamp will differ from the last, which will remain at the value prior to the failed write operation.

By maintaining two root pages in well known locations on disk, ensuring that there is always one valid root block and using a system of timestamps which allow determination of the most recent correct root page, it becomes possible to atomically commit a checkpoint operation. Further, because the root page either contains or points to structures which describe the store, it is possible after failure to determine which root points to the most recent stable state and to access that state.

The problem with the stability scheme as described is that the entire store must be checkpointed at the same time. Since user processing must either cease or be severely restricted during such an operation, a checkpoint involves 'stopping the world'. In a multi-user store involving multiple nodes this would result in unacceptable degradation of performance. Accordingly, systems have been developed which checkpoint parts of the store independently [8, 17]. The stable state of such a store is the collection of these stable parts.

While checkpointing parts of the store independently has a positive effect on performance, it creates the possibility of logical inconsistencies between data. Modified data from one object may influence the way a process modifies data in some other object. As a result the two objects have a dependency relationship which must be considered when checkpointing either of them. Such dependencies have been described using sets of pages in Casper, and more recently using directed graphs of entities [9]. Other work based on message-passing research is currently investigating the maintenance of causality relationships to allow reconstruction of consistent states (which are not necessarily recreations of previous states) following failure [16].

In the following section we refer to data as being modified if it has been changed or created since the last time the object containing the data was checkpointed. The term *entity* in this discussion refers to an object (as defined for the system) or a process.

3 Inter-relationships between system entities

As processes access data objects in a store, these accesses may result in dependencies being created between the processes and the objects. Such dependencies are established as a result of write operations which modify data, and subsequent read operations on such modified data. It is important to note that data objects cannot become inter-dependent without processes, and that processes cannot become inter-dependent without data objects. It should also be noted that read operations on unmodified data do not create dependencies.

By way of example of the creation of a dependency between objects, consider a motor car registration system in which a vehicle cannot have its registration renewed unless it has current insurance. Assume a system consisting of an insurance object, a registration object and a number of user-level processes. If one process updates the insurance object to indicate that the insurance on a particular vehicle has been renewed, and another process subsequently queries the insurance status of the vehicle and allows and records the vehicle's re-registration, this activity results in a dependency between the involved entities. If the registration object were checkpointed independently of the insurance object, a failure could result in the store recording that the vehicle was registered without being insured.

Ideally dependencies should be established based on knowledge of access to data at the basic unit of data reference (eg. byte, word). In a typical paged store, however, it is overly expensive to monitor access behaviour at this level. The basic unit of transfer of data between secondary and primary storage and of virtual to physical address mapping is the virtual page. Accordingly a virtual memory system is required to maintain access behaviour knowledge at, and hardware support is optimised to, the virtual page level. It is prudent to use the same granularity in determining inter-object dependencies. Such dependencies, while detected at the virtual page level, result in checkpoint dependencies at the large object level. Thus dependency information is maintained at the large object level for the purpose of controlling checkpoint operations. The dependency between such objects may be represented using a set called an *association* [11].

3.1 Describing dependencies using associations

As defined for Casper, associations are sets of dependent entities [11]. After it has been checkpointed, an entity belongs to an association of which it is the only member. Over time entities interact with other entities causing their respective associations to merge. To ensure logical consistency it is necessary to checkpoint all members of an association together in an atomic operation.

If such a checkpoint operation fails, or a system failure occurs, all members of an association roll-back by reverting to their last stable states. The use of associations guarantees that such reversion results in entities with no inconsistent inter-relationships. It is apparent, however, that the use of a single structure to describe both the checkpoint and the roll-back relationships between entities often results in unnecessarily large checkpoint and roll-back operations. Moreover checkpoint operations are expensive and roll-back operations may result in unnecessary loss of data modifications. In the motor car registration example, for instance, it is not really necessary to checkpoint the registration object when the insurance object is checkpointed, but it is necessary to checkpoint the insurance object with the registration object. Accordingly it should not be necessary to roll-back the insurance object because of a failure resulting in the roll-back of the registration object. Such a situation may occur if the insurance and registration objects were stored on different nodes in a distributed store.

The use of directed graphs has been shown to minimise the extent of checkpoint and roll-back operations.

3.2 Describing dependencies using directed graphs

Using directed graphs it is possible to separately represent the checkpoint and roll-back dependencies between entities [9]. Graphs are created in a similar way to associations, however different graphs are traversed depending on the operation being performed. The → edge is used to specify the dependency between two entities. E1 → E2 means that E1 depends on E2. → is transitive, but not symmetric ie. if E1 depends on E2 (E1 → E2) then E2 does not necessarily have the same relationship with E1 (¬ E2 → E1). The relationship E1 → E2 is established if E1 reads modified data from E2. Write operations lead to a pair of dependencies; instead of indicating two unilateral arrows (E1 → E2 and E2 → E1), the notation E1 ↔ E2 is used. Note also that the expression E1 → E2 is congruent to the expression E2 ← E1.

While a single graph can be used to describe both checkpoint and roll-back dependencies, the edges have different meanings for each purpose. Thus, in effect, a single dependency directed graph represents separate checkpoint and roll-back graphs. The relationship between the edges forming a dependency graph and their meanings in checkpoint and roll-back graphs are shown in figure 1.

Dependency Graph	Stabilising Graph	Roll-back Graph
→	$\overset{S}{\rightarrow}$	$\overset{R}{\leftarrow}$
←	$\overset{S}{\leftarrow}$	$\overset{R}{\rightarrow}$
↔	$\overset{S}{\leftarrow}$ and $\overset{S}{\rightarrow}$	$\overset{R}{\rightarrow}$ and $\overset{R}{\leftarrow}$

Figure 1. The relationship between Dependency Graph, Stabilising Graph, and Roll-back Graph.

As described in section 2, a typical checkpoint operation in a paged persistent store results in the flushing to disk of main memory pages containing unstable modified data. Similarly dependencies between entities should only be established through accesses involving modified data. In the following section we show how explicit hardware support improves the efficiency of such stability-related operations.

4 Hardware support for stability

We have earlier argued the benefits of support for dual object sizes [7] providing both small objects corresponding to the logical units of data manipulated by programs (structures, etc) and paged large objects comprising collections of logically related small objects.

In this discussion we assume that either:

- the object store supports both small and large objects as described above, with stability being implemented at the large object level, or

- the object store supports a single paged object type.

To enable implementation of the checkpoint operation for such a store it is necessary to be able to detect:

(1) which main memory pages have been modified by some process,

(2) which main memory pages have been accessed in this time-slice by the currently executing process, and

(3) which main memory pages have been modified in this time-slice by the currently executing process.

The need for these abilities, and features which provide support for them are discussed in the following sections.

4.1 Identification of modified main memory pages

This requirement should not be confused with the ability to identify dirty pages which is essential to virtual memory management. Conventional architectures typically provide that ability through the implementation of a *dirty* bit in their address translation unit (ATU). On page discard the dirty bit is queried and accordingly the page-frame is immediately re-allocated if clean, or is flushed prior to re-allocation. Such dirty bits are used in exactly the same way for management of the proposed store.

The proposed *modified* ATU bit is used to indicate that the contents of this page frame have been modified by some process since the object containing the page was last checkpointed. As described in section 3, subsequent access by another process to such a page creates a dependency situation involving the object containing the page, and the modifying and accessing processes. The modified bits for the pages of an object are, of course, cleared when the object is checkpointed.

Implementation of stability without this bit involves using the dirty bit for two purposes:

(1) for virtual memory page discard decisions, and

(2) to detect subsequent accesses to modified pages.

This is inefficient because a dirty page which is discarded as part of virtual memory management and later retrieved for read access would need to be loaded with the dirty bit set. As a result the page would be flushed again on its next discard or when its object was checkpointed. It is recognised that the modified bit duplicates information available from the shadow paging data structures; however these data structures are typically stored in main memory, and speed is of the essence given that the modified bit is checked on every memory access. It is thus necessary that separate dirty and modified bits are implemented in the ATU.

The implementation of the modified bit requires that the virtual memory page table(s) used to locate pages for loading into main memory must be extended to indicate whether non-resident pages have been modified since the last checkpoint. The page table is used to retrieve pages, and this extra information is used to appropriately set the modified bit when the page is mapped in to the ATU. The ATU dirty bit for the page is not set, ensuring that the page may be later discarded without being flushed to disk (unless of course it is subsequently further modified). Subject to the same caveat the page will not be flushed when its object is next checkpointed.

The features described in the next section serve to improve the efficiency of construction of dependency graphs by allowing them to be updated once per process time-slice.

4.2 Lazy dependency graph construction

The building of a dependency graph requires detection of process access to modified data and of process modification of object data. Such events may be detected and if necessary recorded either eagerly (i.e. after every access to an object) or lazily. Identification of critical accesses at the time of those accesses would cause an unacceptable deterioration in system performance.

The collection of appropriate data during a process' time-slice is proposed, thus allowing dependency graphs to be updated at the time of a process switch. Accordingly it is necessary to record the accesses and modifications performed by a process during its latest activation.

4.2.1 Identification of accessed main memory pages

Pages may remain in main memory for a period encompassing many process activations. The *m_accessed* bit maintained by the ATU allows detection of process access to modified object data during the current time-slice. This bit is set for a page if the page is accessed while the modified bit for the page is set. Dependencies between a process and the objects containing pages with the m_accessed bit set are represented by the addition of appropriate → edges to the dependency graph at the conclusion of the process' period of activation. All m_accessed bits must be clear at the commencement of a process time-slice; this may be achieved in a single operation using appropriate hardware.

4.2.2 Identification of written main memory pages

The inclusion of a *written* bit maintained by the ATU allows detection of object data modifications made by the current process. This bit is distinct from the modified bit described in section 4.1 because it describes the modification behaviour of the current process only rather than the status of the virtual page itself.

The written bit is set together with the modified and dirty bits, but is cleared as part of the dependency graph update at the conclusion of the process time-slice. In contrast the modified bit is cleared at the next object checkpoint and the dirty bit is cleared when the page is flushed to disk. Pages with the written bit set cause the inclusion of an appropriate ↔ dependency graph edge. The operation of the ATU with respect to the described status bits is shown in figure 2.

OPERATION	DIRTY	MODIFIED	M_ACCESSED	WRITTEN
Unmodified page retrieved	Cleared	Cleared	Cleared	Cleared
Modified page retrieved	Cleared	Set	Cleared	Cleared
Process reads data from page	Unchanged	Unchanged	Copy *modified*	Unchanged
Process writes to page	Set	Set	Set	Set
End of process time-slice	Unchanged	Unchanged	Cleared	Cleared
Page flushed	Cleared	Unchanged	Unchanged	Unchanged
Object checkpoint	Cleared	Cleared	Unchanged	Unchanged

Figure 2. Effect of operations on page status bits.

In the following section we discuss the implications of m_accessed and written bits when used in multiprocessor machines.

4.3 Multiprocessor architectures

In a multiprocessor machine multiple processes are able to execute in parallel. It is thus necessary to maintain m_accessed and written bits for a page frame on a *per process* (and thus per processor) basis. Thus for any page frame there is an array of m_accessed bits and an array of written bits. One element of each of these arrays represents each attached processor.

Multiprocessor computers increase the complexity of the described operations because they introduce the aspect of causal ordering of events. Such ordering is important because of:

(1)   its impact on the discard of pages during virtual memory operation and

(2)   the impact of a checkpoint involving one process on other executing processes.

4.3.1 Parallel page discard

Lazy dependency graph construction, as described, is dependent on the important condition that no page is discarded while its m_accessed or written bits are set. For a single processor machine this is not an issue because page discard occurs synchronously with process activation. A multi-processor computer allows several processes to execute simultaneously, and thus page discard may occur in parallel with process activation.

When a page is selected for discard, the arrays of m_accessed and written bits for the page are scanned, and the process executing on any processor for which either bit is set is forced to end its current time-slice (i.e. there is a re-schedule on the processor). This results in merging of the dependency graphs containing the processes. To minimise this imposition on executing processes, the discard algorithm attempts to select pages for which neither bit is set. The number of such pages is minimised by ensuring that processes checkpoint regularly; the effect of this is similar to that of the Unix *sync* operation [13].

4.3.2 Parallel checkpoint and process execution

In a multiprocessor a checkpoint on an object may occur in parallel with execution of other processes. This raises the possibility of an object being checkpointed whilst it is being accessed by a process active on another processor. Such a process must be forced to suspend, causing its dependency graph to be updated. This may result in the process being checkpointed.

The authors are currently investigating multiprocessor and distribution aspects of support for stability and will report their findings in a later paper.

5 An implementation example

This section describes the addition of the above-mentioned hardware support to the Monads-MM architecture [15]. The Monads-MM supports a network of nodes each of which may comprise multiple processors. Each processor generates 128 bit virtual addresses which reference a persistent global distributed shared memory (DSM).

Each node has a single ATU which translates virtual addresses to physical addresses for all of the processors attached to that node. The global address space is structured to assist in determining the physical location of data stored in it [6]. The store provides explicit support for small and large objects called *segments* and *modules* respectively, with segments being positioned orthogonally to page boundaries and logically related segments being collected to form paged modules [7]. Thus many segments may exist within a single virtual page or a segment may span several virtual pages. Modules are self-describing; each module contains internal data describing its own location on disk. As a result there is no need for a central DSM page table.

A two level capability-based protection scheme controls access to the interface procedures of modules and addressing of the data stored in segments [10]. A set of capability registers is provided for the purpose of addressing segments. All addressing is of the form <capabilityregister>+<offset>, providing dynamic bounds and access-rights checked access. Segment capabilities define the identity of the encompassing module; as a result the module is identified with every data access, facilitating collection of dependency information.

The ATU itself is organised as an inverted hash table [1]. To provide the support described above each cell of this table must be extended to provide modified, m_accessed and written bits for the appropriate page frame in addition to the dirty bit already provided. In the Monads-MM implementation we have taken advantage of the machine's architecture by maintaining m_accessed and written information with each processor rather than at the ATU. Moreover such information is maintained at the module level and is thus of the granularity required by the dependency graph.

5.1 Maintenance of access status

Examination of the information content of the proposed modified, m_accessed and written bits reveals that the former conveys page-level information on a between checkpoints basis and the latter two are used to construct module-level information for the current time-slice. Accordingly, and since the appropriate module is identified by every access, it is possible to maintain a cache of module status information with each processor. This is called the *Process Active Object Cache* (PAOC). Data is collected in the PAOC during processing using information provided by the ATU.

A key field attached to each capability register is loaded the first time that register is used in a time-slice. This field points to the appropriate PAOC cell and is used for subsequent accesses to the cache during this process activation. Since capability registers are used to address segments, multiple PAOC key fields may point to any single cache cell. A comparator is used when the PAOC key is invalid to detect whether the required cache entry already exists. If the appropriate entry does exist the PAOC key is set to point to it; if it does not exist a cache entry is created and the key is set.

The contents of the PAOC are used at the completion of a process time-slice to appropriately update dependency information. Finally the cache cells are cleared and capability register key fields are marked invalid in preparation for the next process. This structure is shown in figure 3.

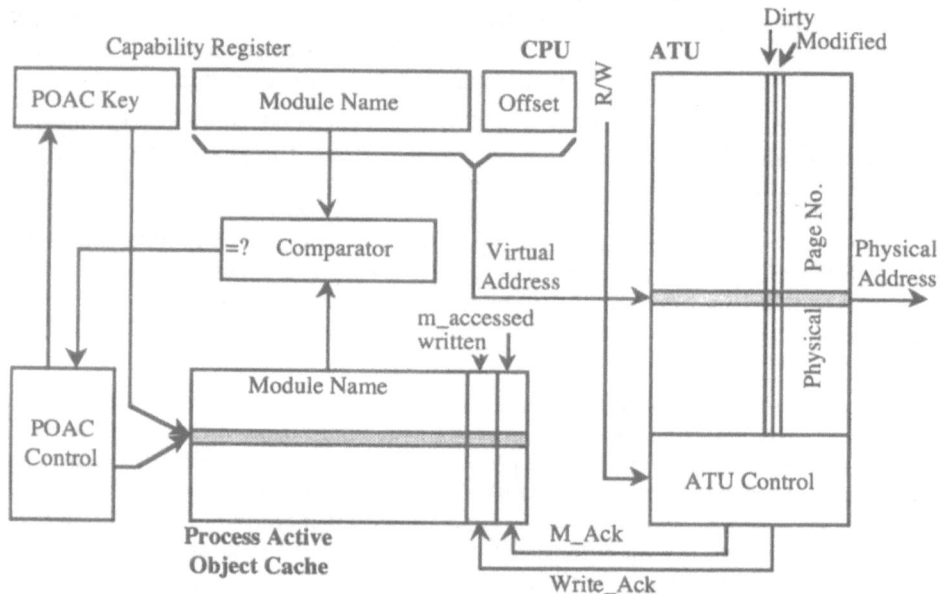

Figure 3. Cache of process related status correlated with module name.

Maintenance of the per-processor module access information separately from the ATU has the advantages that:

- m_accessed and written information is automatically collated at the required module-level granularity during system operation, reducing the cost of the dependency graph update performed at the conclusion of a process' time-slice,

- less hardware is required because m_accessed and written information for each attached processor is not maintained for every main memory page frame and

- it facilitates clearing of the status information at each process switch (compared with selectively clearing ATU bits in a multiprocessor machine).

5.2 Maintenance of page modification status

The provision of a modified bit for each ATU cell allows identification of virtual pages containing data modified since the last checkpoint operation. Information stored by the ATU is ordinarily lost when the page is discarded during virtual memory operation. As described in section 4.1, this situation requires the extension of the virtual memory page table to include modified information. When the object containing a page is checkpointed, the modified bit for the page must be cleared, involving a scan of all page table entries for the object.

Monads modules are self-defining, with each module storing its own page table. We propose that, rather than extending the existing page table entries, an extra bit list is added to the internal data maintained by every module. Each bit would logically form part of a page table entry and would store that page's modified status. The bit list would be checked every time a page from the module was loaded into main memory, and would be updated with every page discard. Segregation of the modified bits in this way facilitates clearing after a checkpoint operation on the module.

6 Conclusion

Stability of persistent object stores may be achieved by checkpointing dependent entities together. Dependencies between entities are created during processing of the data held in the store, and may be recorded using directed graphs. It has been shown that different dependencies are created by read and write access to data. Separately recording these dependencies allows a reduction in the extent of checkpoint and rollback operations.

Maintaining dependency information of read/write granularity appears to require a dependency graph update immediately after every store access. Such expensive updates may be avoided if the ATU maintains extra status information about main memory accesses, allowing a single dependency graph update at the conclusion of each process activation.

Structuring the store to support large objects comprising collections of logically related small objects, and then appropriately naming such large objects, allows the maintenance of process access history at the large object level. This has two significant advantages. Firstly it reduces the quantity of access history data stored and thus the hardware required for such storage. Secondly it removes the necessity to scan the page-related data maintained in the ATU by dynamically collecting an object-level history during process execution for use when updating dependency graphs.

Acknowledgments

Part of this work was supported by a University of Sydney research grant. The authors would also like to acknowledge the contributions of R. M. Wilkinson and L. D. Bacardi to discussions related to this work.

References

1.   Abramson, D. A. "Hardware Management of a Large Virtual Memory", *Proc. 4th Australian Computer Science Conference*, pp. 1-13, 1981.

2.   Atkinson, M. P., Bailey, P., Chisholm, K. J., Cockshott, W. P. and Morrison, R. "An Approach to Persistent Programming", *The Computer Journal*, 26(4), pp. 360-365, 1983.

3.   Brown, A. L. "Persistent Object Stores", Universities of St. Andrews and Glasgow, Persistent Programming Report 71, 1989.

4.   Challis, M. F. "Database Consistency and Integrity in a Multi-user Environment", *Databases: Improving Useability and Responsiveness*, pp. 245-270, 1978.

5.   Cockshott, W. P. "Orthogonal Persistence", Ph.D Thesis, University of Edingurgh, 1983.

6.   Henskens, F. A. "Addressing Moved Modules in a Capability-based Distributed Shared Memory", *Proceedings of the 25th Hawaii International Conference on System Sciences*, vol 1, ed V. Milutinovic and B. D. Shriver, IEEE Computer Society Press, Hawaii, U. S. A., pp. 769-778, 1992.

7.   Henskens, F. A., Brössler, P., Keedy, J. L. and Rosenberg, J. "Coarse and Fine Grain Objects in a Distributed Persistent Store", *Proceedings, Third International Workshop on Object Orientation in Operating Systems*, Ashville, North Carolina, pp. 116-123, 1993.

8.   Henskens, F. A., Rosenberg, J. and Hannaford, M. R. "Stability in a Network of MONADS-PC Computers", *Proceedings of the International Workshop on Computer Architectures to support Security and Persistence of Information*, ed J. Rosenberg and J. L. Keedy, Springer-Verlag and British Computer Society, pp. 246-256, 1990.

9.   Jalili, R. and Henskens, F. A. "Minimising the Extent of Cascadable Operations in Stable Distributed Stores", *Submitted for Publication*, 1994.

10.   Keedy, J. L. and Rosenberg, J. "Support for Objects in the MONADS Architecture", *Proceedings of the International Workshop on Persistent Object Systems*, ed J. Rosenberg and D. M. Koch, Springer-Verlag, 1989.

11.   Koch, B., Schunke, T., Dearle, A., Vaughan, F., Marlin, C., Fazakerley, R. and Barter, C. "Cache Coherence and Storage Management in a Persistent Object System", *Proceedings, The Fourth International Workshop on Persistent Object Systems*, pp. 99-109, 1990.

12.   Lorie, R. A. "Physical Integrity in a Large Segmented Database", *ACM Transactions on Database Systems*, 2(1) pp. 91-104, 1977.

13.   Ritchie, D. M. and Thompson, K. "The UNIX Time-Sharing System", *The Bell System Technical Journal*, 63(6), pp. 1905-1930, 1978.

14.   Rosenberg, J., Henskens, F. A., Brown, A. L., Morrison, R. and Munro, D. "Stability in a Persistent Store Based on a Large Virtual Memory", *Proceedings of the International Workshop on Architectural Support for Security and Persistence of Information*, ed J. Rosenberg and J. L. Keedy, Springer-Verlag and British Computer Society, pp. 229-245, 1990.

15.   Rosenberg, J., Koch, D. M. and Keedy, J. L. "A Massive Memory Supercomputer", *Proc. 22nd Hawaii International Conference on System Sciences*, vol 1, pp. 338-345, 1989.

16.   Vaughan, F., Dearle, A., Cao, J., di Bona, R., Farrow, J. M., Henskens, F. A., Lindström, A. and Rosenberg, J. "Causality Considerations in Distributed Persistent Operating Systems", *Proceedings, 17th Australian Computer Science Conference*, Australian Computer Society, Christchurch, New Zealand, pp. 409-420, 1994.

17.   Vaughan, F., Schunke, T., Koch, B., Dearle, A., Marlin, C. and Barter, C. "A Persistent Distributed Architecture Supported by the Mach Operating System", *Proceedings of the 1st USENIX Conference on the Mach Operating System*, pp. 123-140, 1990.

Optimisation

Sonia Berman
Computing Science Department
University of Cape Town
Cape Town South Africa

The Papers

This session contained two papers which looked at different ways of optimising persistent systems. The first paper, presented by Pedro Sousa, was "Object Clustering in Persistent and Distributed Systems". The second, "Query Processing in PIOS", was presented by Fausto Rabitti.

Object clustering is generally used to physically group objects on a persistent store in such a way as to reduce page faults. The first paper shows how clustering can be used to tackle an altogether different problem: that of managing a very large number of objects in a persistent, distributed environment. Objects are grouped into clusters based on their relationships at storage time. These clusters are analogous to independent name spaces, and the store is managed as a collection of clusters which are manipulated like single objects.

Clustering reduces the number of object identifiers in the system. This simplifies naming, migration, protection and garbage collection, since each is now applied to a cluster at a time, rather than individual objects. The scheme also ensures that widely known objects are mapped to applications independently of each other, which helps to reduce cross-application accesses. Tests showed that on average there is 1 cluster per 200 objects, although some applications produce too many small clusters.

Another way of improving the performance of a persistent object system is to optimise the execution plan (access steps) generated when a bulk data collection is queried. The second paper in this session describes query processing in PIOS and in particular compares the relative improvements of algebraic and physical optimisation.

PIOS has a simple query language which is designed to be the target into which a variety of query languages can be translated. Algebraic optimisation standardises queries after eliminating redundancies and contradictions. Objects can be physically partitioned according to some condition on their values; and this information is also used to prune queries.

During physical optimisation alternative query plans are generated by annotating the operators with different roles. An optimum execution plan is chosen based on a cost model that estimates the number of disk accesses associated with these candidate plans. A technique was developed that limits the search space to ensure that a reasonable amount of resources are used by this process. Performance tests showed that physical optimisation is two orders of magnitude more effective than algebraic optimisation in reducing disk accesses.

The Discussion

The questions following on Pedro Sousa's talk concerned two main issues, namely the effect of reclustering and the separation of logical from physical clustering. In the first instance, Pedro said that new clusters can arise only when data is flushed to the persistent store or when a "child" is sent as parameter in a remote procedure invocation. One of two major applications of the system was a shared multi-user graphical editor, and applications had not changed much over the course of the experiment. Mostly they involved one person working on a single cluster representing a drawing; when drawings were shared global identifiers became necessary and so clustering was reduced. Physical clustering had not been considered in their scheme because they focused on reducing the number of object identifiers. Eliot Moss observed that this should go hand in hand with their logical clustering scheme to give real benefit, and that mapping tables could be used to cater for pointers that escape clusters.

Following on the talk on the PIOS query processor, it was suggested that physical optimisation start from multiple alternatives rather than the single "best" formulation arrived at after algebraic simplification. Fausto replied that experience showed that this was not worthwhile in the context of their specific query language. Malcolm Atkinson wondered to what extent their results could be regarded as typical, or whether they were influenced by the St Andrews POS that underlies PIOS. Fausto replied that the only costs taken into account in their measurements was that of disk accesses. Regarding data placement, the physical clustering of objects by "class" was arranged by grouping them into a single (POS) object in the mapping from logical to physical schema. Steve Rozen was interested in data set and cache sizes. The experiment had been based on a store of approximately 200 megabytes. This had been considered fairly large; but it appears that we need to redefine a "large" store in the light of earlier talks at the workshop! The measurements had been made on top of the cache; Steve pointed out that cache size can affect the importance of query optimisations.

The session ended with a discussion on good benchmarks. Neither speaker had used standard benchmarks in evaluating his system. Pedro had used fairly large applications involving a few hundred classes. He thought a good means of evaluating his scheme would be to measure the average size of the routing tables which keep track of object location. Paulo Ferreira asked what his tests had shown about the size of cycles of garbage that were not reclaimed. These had been small cycles; Paulo wondered whether this was possibly an artefact of their applications.
Malcolm suggested a good benchmark would be one that took you by surprise; and Eliot Moss added that it should be broad enough.

Object Clustering in Persistent and Distributed Systems

Pedro Sousa and José Alves Marques

Inesc, I.S.T.

R. Alves Redol n°9, 1000 Lisboa, Portugal

email: {pms,jam}@inesc.pt

Abstract

This paper presents a simple approach for clustering objects in persistent systems. The proposed mechanism groups objects based on their current relations in such way that only a single object is known outside the cluster. It is particularly suited to support orthogonal persistence. Although the basic ideas behind our work are not new, they have not been used in persistent object systems.

The paper discusses the benefits of the proposed strategy based on the experience implementing and using the IK system. IK supports distribution and orthogonal persistence of fine grained objects. Object references can be freely passed during remote invocations or stored persistently.

The proposed strategy reduces the assignment of OIDs to the actual applications needs, with major benefits on object location, garbage collection and overall system scalability. In our applications, we found that only one object identifier was used for each 200 persistent objects saved in the persistent store. It also allows most persistent objects to be garbage collected autonomously, without involving a system wide collection.

1 Introduction

A major difficulty when supporting fine-grained objects in a persistent and distributed environment is the management of a potentially very large population of objects. Object clustering is an usual mechanism to increase locality of reference and reduce the number of page faults and disk I/O [1, 2, 3, 4, 5]. Clustering techniques address fundamentally the problem of packing and moving object data in large units. The problem of naming individual objects is normally considered orthogonal to the clustering mechanism. We think clustering can be used also as an encapsulation mechanism to convert a large population of objects into a small population of clusters which are the only identifiable entities in the persistent store, simplifying the constraints of the addressing mechanism.

We explore a dynamic clustering strategy based on object relations at the moment of their storage, in such a way that only a single object is referenced outside the cluster. This allows the cluster to assume the identity of that object. This strategy allows clusters to be handled as a single entity (an object), without the need to further discriminate internal objects and without limiting the capacity objects have to refer or being referenced.

The encapsulation provided by our strategy yields important optimizations in the support of fine-grained objects in a uniform model, where each object is able to refer any other within the persistent and distributed space. It reduces the assignment of object identifiers[1] (OIDs) to a minimum, with major benefits on object location, garbage collection and overall system scalability.

The paper presents the general idea of cluster encapsulation and discusses its impact in the IK [6, 7, 8] platform. IK was developed in the framework of the Comandos ESPRIT project [9, 10]. In IK, all objects are created and accessed in a single and uniform manner, regardless of their relative location. Persistence is a dynamic attribute of all objects and orthogonal to their types. All objects are maintained by the system while reachable from an Eternal Root. A set of storage servers implement the persistent store, each holding a fraction of the distributed population of persistent objects. Storage servers store and retrieve objects given an OID and have no knowledge of the object internals. Clustering is done by the application's run-time support before transferring objects to storage servers. Thus, storage servers ignore the concept of clustering.

Applications map objects from different storage servers transparently. Mapping an object means migrating the object from the storage server holding the object to the application address space. Even though a copy remains at the server side, if a second application requests the object, it will not see the server's copy but instead the one migrated to the first application. Both application must agree on how the object should be shared.

Objects are allowed to migrate between storage servers. So, the system must deal with a potentially large number of cross references among storage servers. This reduces the effectiveness of server's local garbage collection, and the object location within the system. Our clustering approach minimize the dependencies between storage servers, thus improving overall system scalability.

IK is mainly targeted to cooperative applications executing in a local network. Applications are structured based on fine-grained objects and are written in EC++ [11, 7], a language similar to C++ with some semantic extensions and restrictions. The programming environment is based on a version of the ET++[12] library ported to our platform, providing a framework for application development.

The paper is organized as follows: next section presents the related work; section 3 describes the clustering mechanism and discusses its major advantages and disadvantages; section 4 overviews the implementation of the algorithm. Finally, in section 5, we evaluate the proposed approach and draw some conclusions based on our applications.

2 Related Work

The idea of grouping object graphs into black box units has been used in many different areas. Although with different objectives, our clusters are similar to

---

[1] We are not concerned with the actual scope or structure of OIDs. In this paper, OIDs are simply the names used to identify objects in the distributed persistent store.

object islands proposed by Hogg [13]. Both strategies provide encapsulation on a graph of objects. Hogg uses islands as a mechanism to prevent aliasing and side effects in object oriented languages. We use encapsulation as the rule to assign objects to clusters. To our knowledge, it hasn't been used as a clustering mechanism in persistent object systems.

Object Data Management Systems (ODMS) use many different strategies to determine which cluster an object should be placed in: the object's type [2, 14], allocation regions [5], placement trees [4], statistical information from training traces [15] or various forms of graph traversal [16, 2]. None of these systems ensure cluster encapsulation, allowing objects within a cluster to be referenced from other clusters. Therefore, clusters do not hide the identification of enclosed objects, and each persistent object must have an OID. We assign OIDs to objects according to the objects' visibility, and allow the use of local and transient values as references among closely related objects in the persistent store.

Object composition techniques used in ODMS also define and manipulate a set of objects as a single logical entity [14]. However, object composition is a static specification aimed for semantic integrity and restricts the visibility of encapsulated objects. Our clustering is dynamic and imposes no restrictions on objects' visibility.

A number of object oriented languages and libraries offer support for dynamically storing and retrieving an object graph in a single unit with a single name assigned by the programmer [17, 18, 19]. These mechanisms do not allow cross references between different units, making each a closed and independent world. In our strategy, encapsulated objects can refer other clusters. Thus, clusters are not independent worlds.

Our work is also related with the issue of using a flat address space versus a set of local addresses. In [20], Moss presents the advantages of small contextual OIDs against a flat space of OIDs. The encapsulation provided by our clusters allows the use of small and contextual OIDs for clustered objects, even though, conceptually, they are uniquely and globally identified. Thus, we can benefit from a flat OID space and avoid most of the reported disadvantages.

3 Object Clustering

Our clustering mechanism converts a population of objects into a population of clusters based on some initial roots. The roots are the objects considered to be widely referenced, and thus already having an OID.

A cluster is composed of a head object and a body containing the objects belonging to its private sub-graph. An object A belongs to the private sub-graph of another object B if all paths from the roots to A include B. Thus, the head object is the only object in a cluster referenced outside the cluster, and all objects in the cluster are reachable from its head object.

Clustering starts by considering initial roots as heads of initial clusters. The graph of each head object is traversed recursively, and objects reachable from more than one head object are promoted to heads of new clusters. The process stops when all objects reachable from the roots have been grouped.

As an example, processing the graph of figure 1 with objects $O1$ and $O5$ as initial roots produces three clusters. These clusters can be handled as normal objects in the persistent store: they can be identified with the OIDs of corresponding head objects ($O1$, $O5$ and $O10$), and have an instance data composed by the private sub-graphs of these objects. The dark arrows represent the references that are full OIDs, and the thin ones the contextual references. Notice that object $O11$ was not clustered because it was not reachable from the initial roots.

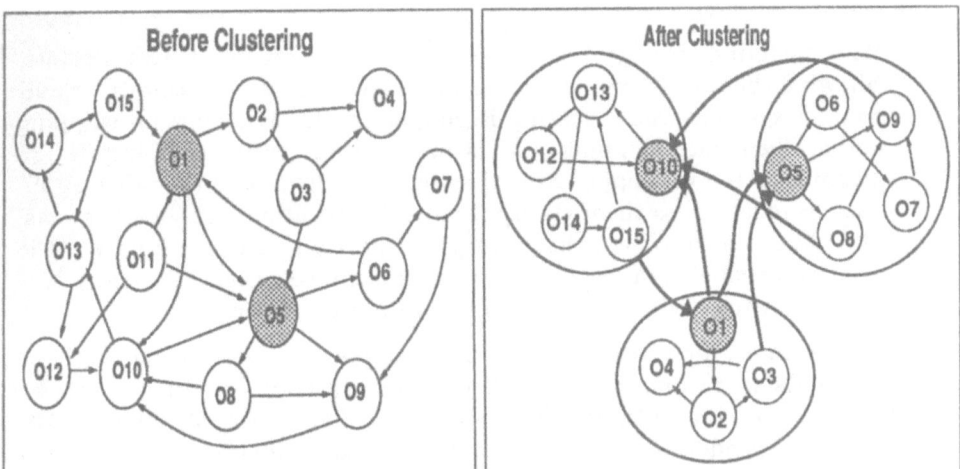

Figure 1: Object Clustering

The output of the algorithm depends mostly on the initial roots. In the limit, if a single object is given as root, then a single cluster will be created with all objects accessible from that root. Conversely, if all objects are presented as roots, then every object becomes a cluster.

3.1 Advantages of Cluster Encapsulation

The encapsulation provided by this clustering strategy has immediate benefits in object location, sharing, migration, protection, garbage collection and overall system management:

- *Object Location*

  A price one pays by grouping objects is a further step in the process of locating an object given its OID: one must (i) find in which cluster the object is stored, (ii) determine the location of that cluster (i.e. the storage sterver where the cluster is) and finally, (iii) find the location of the object within the cluster.

This chain can be shortened by encoding location information directly in the object's OIDs, with the well known disadvantages, namely those regarding object and cluster mobility. Cluster encapsulation automatically eliminates the need for steps (i) and (iii), without any disadvantages. Step (i) is immediate because the OID of the object is the OID of the cluster. Step (iii) is also immediate because OIDs always refers to the head object, that can have a fixed location in the cluster.

Following the example of figure 1, locating object $O1$ means locate cluster $O1$ and get its head object.

- *Object Sharing.*

The clustering strategy keeps widely known objects in different clusters, allowing them to be mapped independently. This is particularly important in systems where sharing is supported through function shipping rather then data shipping. IK is one of these systems. Clusters are mapped in the first application that requests them, and the other applications must access them via cross-context invocations. In these systems, the placement of objects has a major impact on performance given the relative cost between cross-context and local invocations. Therefore it is important to be able to map well known objects independently.

For example, if clusters $O1$ and $O5$ are mapped in different applications, the decision to map cluster $O10$ together with $O1$ or with $O5$ can be delayed until one of them refers object $O10$. This is possible because $O10$ is an independent cluster, and is not clustered with either $O1$ or $O5$.

- *Object Migration.*

Clusters are also suited to be the unit of object migration because the system only has to handle the migration of the head object. Enclosed objects are mere instance data of the head object.

Consider that objects in figure 1 are mapped in one application, and object $O10$ is sent to another application. By sending instead the cluster $O10$, the receiving application also gets objects $O12$, $O13$, $O14$ and $O15$, without the need for extra OIDs, other than $O10$. This provides an immediate performance advantage and also a long term benefit, since it scales down the number of OIDs in the system[2].

- *Garbage Collection.*

Encapsulation enables important optimizations in garbage collection. Since the path to reach any object in the cluster goes through the head object, the whole cluster can be recycled once the head object is found to be

---

[2]Notice that, even though migrating the cluster is an optimal solution from a naming point of view it does not attempt to minimize remote communications. For example, if objects $O15$ and $O1$ interact intensively, leaving $O15$ behind would generate fewer cross-context invocations.

garbage. This reduces the cost of global garbage collection in the persistent store because clusters are the only entities known, and there will be much less clusters than objects.

The usage of contextual references to identify enclosed objects favors autonomy of application's garbage collection. For example, if cluster $O1$ is mapped in an application, the local garbage collector is able to decide if the objects $O2$, $O3$ and $O4$ are garbage by processing only the local roots. If these object had OIDs, the local garbage collector would have to cooperate with a global one before reclaiming them.

- *Object Protection.*

  Protection is an important issue in the clustering policy. If objects with different protection levels are considered as initial roots, the resulting clusters are particularly suited to support protection, because they are also the only entities to protect in the persistent store. Since head objects act as fire-walls to encapsulated objects, protection of encapsulated objects can be defined solely in the universe of the cluster.

  In the figure 1, if objects $O1$ and $O5$ have different protections levels, than objects they share ($O10$, $O12$, $O13$, $O14$ and $O15$) may need to be protected differently, and therefore are grouped together in cluster $O10$. Only three entities ($O1$, $O5$ and $O10$) need system wide protection.

3.2 Disadvantages of Encapsulation

Unfortunately, our clustering approach also has its share of disadvantages. Since clusters are defined according to object relations, objects must be reclustered when object graphs change. In our architecture, this means applications must recluster objects before storing them in the storage servers. In general, this implies traversing the object graphs and copying object's data. However, these tasks are already necessary to support orthogonal persistence and heterogeneity. Object graphs are traversed to detect which objects must be stored. Object's data is copied when it is converted to a machine independent format. As presented in section 5, the performance results of our implementation showed that our clustering strategy has only a small contribution in the overhead of object storage.

Another potential problem is that there is no control over the granularity of clusters; they can be very large or very small. Large clusters have no major disadvantages if they can be mapped page by page. On the other hand, small clusters can be a major disadvantage when they appear in large number. The granularity and cardinality of the cluster population is related with the actual objects relationship and, fundamentally, with the number of initial roots chosen. It is expected that the amount of roots grows with the level of concurrent object sharing between applications, since more OIDs are needed.

4 Implementing Object Clustering in IK

In IK all objects reachable from an eternal root are maintained by the system[3]. The eternal root holds the associations between user level names and global names. Therefore, programmers do not need to know *which* objects are actually persistent, nor *when* they are stored/retrieved or simply discarded, nor *how* object data is actually stored. Programmers control object persistence simply by assigning and de-assigning user level names to the roots of the object graphs.

The support of this object model requires, at least at the architectural level, a global and persistent object space, where objects are identified with unique and long lived OIDs. We assign OIDs to objects whose references were sent as parameters in remote invocations. Since we do not want to keep track of OIDs in remote nodes, we must take a conservative approach and consider that all objects with OIDs are reachable from the eternal root. They are recycled when the global garbage collector concludes they are garbage. The run-time of applications keeps track of all OIDs known by the application, in a table called Known Object Table (KOT). Objects with OIDs are the initial roots upon which clusters are created.

Object Clustering

Objects are clustered when they leave the application address space, either to be saved in the persistent store or migrated to other applications. In a first phase we consider each object in the KOT as the head of a new cluster. The graph of each head object is traversed and visited objects are tagged with the mark of the head object. The traversal does not propagate to objects in the KOT, because they will be the starting point of new traversals. If an object is tagged with different marks, meaning that it is reachable from different cluster heads, it is promoted to a new cluster head: an OID is assigned to it and inserted in the KOT, to be traversed next. The entries in the KOT that refer to objects already unmapped or mapped remotely are ignored.

After marking all objects reachable from the KOT with a cluster head mark, objects with the same mark are grouped together. The head object is inserted first, and the others are appended to the cluster. There are two tables in a cluster: one holding outgoing references (OIDs) and another holding offsets of objects within the cluster. Within the cluster object references are indexes of these tables. Objects are folded as they are being inserted into the cluster: references are swizzled to indexes in the corresponding cluster table and their data is translated into a machine independent format (we use XDR).

Applying the algorithm to the example of figure 2 would result in four clusters. Initially objects A and B are considered globally known and are registered in the KOT. Objects C and D cannot be hidden in A or B private subgraphs

---

[3]This does not mean that all objects reachable from the eternal root have a representation on the persistent store. Reachability from the eternal root is only computed at some point in time, normally at application termination or when explicitly demanded. In fact, all objects are temporarily reachable from the eternal root when they are created. See [8] for more details.

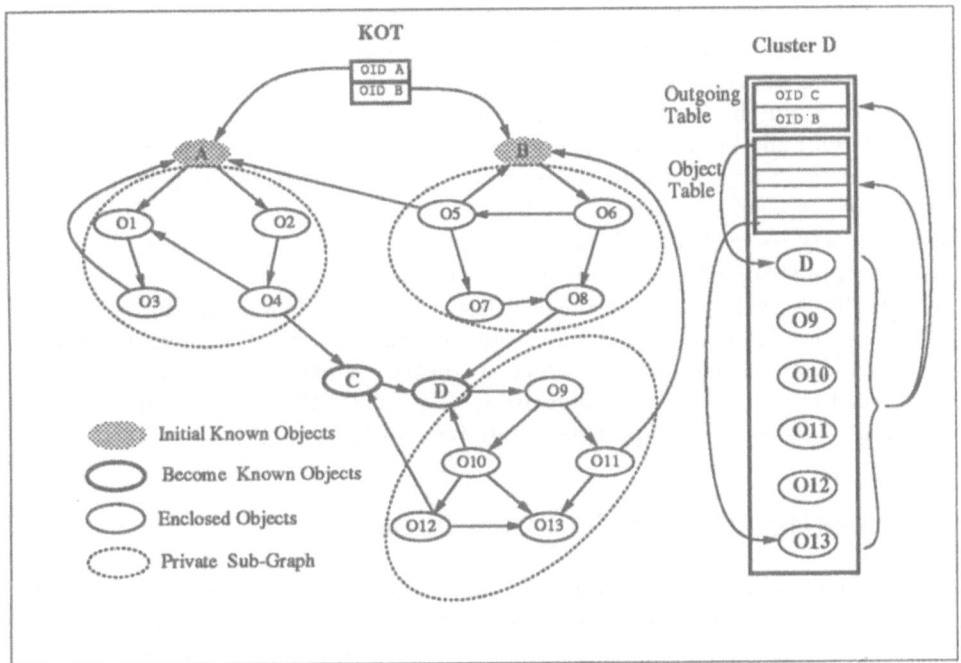

Figure 2: Definition of clusters from object graphs.

and are promoted to cluster heads, receiving an OID each. The figure also illustrates the cluster created to store object D and its private subgraph.

Once a cluster is created and sent to the persistent store, there is no way an enclosed object becomes referenced outside the cluster, because all references to it were also encapsulated in the same cluster. When the cluster is mapped again in some application, encapsulated objects are no longer different from newly created objects, in the sence that none have and OID, and reclustering is necessary to reflect the updates in the object graph.

Garbage Collection

The encapsulation provided by our cluster strategy, allows us to divide the problem of distributed garbage collection in three independent steps: one garbage collection to recycle objects within an application address space, a second one to recycle objects within a cluster, and a third one to eliminate clusters that are no longer reachable from the eternal root.

Objects without an OID (either volatile or persistent) are recycled using a generation scavenging algorithm [21] within each application. For local collections to proceed autonomously, it is necessary to consider the entries in the KOT as local roots. When a cluster is mapped, clustered objects are considered to belong to the oldest generation.

According to the cluster definition given in section 3, all objects within a cluster are reachable form its head object. This is true when the cluster is built from scratch. However, for optimization purposes, clusters can be partly rebuilt from previous images (see [8]), which may contain objects no longer reachable from the head object, and thus garbage. Since the cluster head is the only globally known object in the cluster, clusters can be garbage collected autonomously: any object in the cluster not reachable from the head object is certainly garbage. Clusters are garbage collected off-line, by a process running continuously on each storage node. Clusters are locked while being recycled, forcing applications to wait until the cluster is saved back.

Finally, a system-wide garbage collector deletes clusters in the persistent store that are no longer reachable from the eternal root. We haven't invested much effort in this component, which currently is a straightforward implementation of the mark-and-sweep algorithm. It provides the minimal functionality to allow us to have a comprehensive analyses of the system.

5 Evaluation and Conclusions

The evaluation of our clustering approach is difficult given the multiple issues addressed and applications dependencies. Some of the applications we experimented are a cooperative calendar manager that allows several users to schedule and negotiate meetings, a cooperative graphical editor that supports multiple users working concurrently, a browser and an inspector for application development and a tool for the analysis, design and implementation of distributed applications. The applications and the ET++ library all together comprise about 500 classes, a number we consider sufficient for a initial evaluation.

Since clusters are the only entities in the persistent store, the cluster population reflects the effectiveness of encapsulation as a grouping algorithm. In figure 3 we present the distribution of cluster population in the persistent store according to their size. Bars represent the percentage of clusters whose size is between two consecutive powers of two. Dark bars refer to clusters reachable from the Eternal Root. White ones refer to dead cluster and we will refer to them later. The average size of objects in clusters is approximately 42 bytes.

Approximately 70% of alive clusters are larger than 4K bytes, most of them containing between 500 and 1000 of objects. They result from applications that handle information in a hierarchical fashion, where nodes are not exported outside the graph. The remaining 30% consist of very small graphs containing only a few objects. Such clusters are generated when graphs are traversed remotely. In fact, some of our applications do tend to fragment clusters, because they scan lists mapped remotely, forcing the system to assign an OID to each visited element, and making them heads of new clusters. In such cases, objects are actually being referenced across the network and there is nothing one can do to hide them.

For most cases, the proposed clustering approach is able to encapsulate fine-grained objects into units suitable to be stored as files in traditional file systems. However, some applications produce too small and too many clusters,

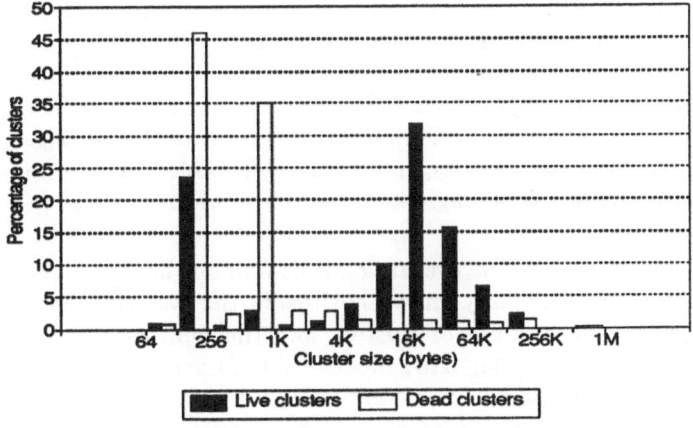

Figure 3: Granularity of Cluster Population.

making files no longer suited to support cluster storage directly. In these cases, a simple key/value database is more adequate to provide persistent support for clusters.

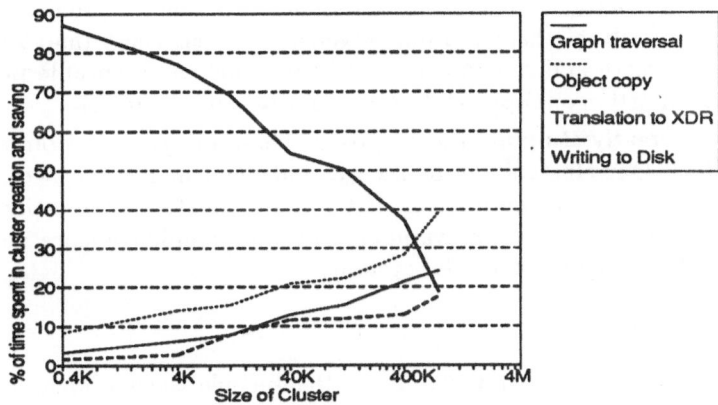

Figure 4: Costs of Cluster Creation

The analysis of the population of garbage clusters is important to better understand and improve the system performance. We found significant differences between garbage and non-garbage cluster populations, as shown by the white bars of figure 3. About 80% of garbage clusters are smaller than 1K bytes. They contain mainly transient information used in communication between the various components of distributed applications. In most cases, such objects become globally known when references to them are sent as parameters in remote

412

invocations. Our conservative approach, in considering that all references sent to other contexts are reachable from the eternal root, promotes these objects to cluster heads and saves them when the application finishes. We implemented a simple termination protocol between the various components to detect and ignore such garbage. However, we found out that most of the garbage generated this way forms distributed cycles, not easily collectible. We are now planing to migrate such clusters to a single node, which would be able to recycle them more easily.

An important aspect of the evaluation is to find out how clustering actually reduces the number of globally known entities in the system. This is given by the ratio between the number of clusters and the number of objects stored, which is approximately 0.005. This means that, in average only 1 object out of 200 that were stored in the persistent store becomes globally known. Such reduction of OIDs surely has major impact on the system by keeping OID tables small, and thus improving overall system performance.

A complete evaluation of the cost to cluster objects would require an exhaustive trace in a representative set of applications. We measured the costs of object clustering only as a function of the cluster size. We traced the clustering of object graphs during the execution of our applications, rather than using a single well known graph. Figure 4 presents the relative cost of each phase of cluster creation. The costs are dominated by the cluster I/O, followed by the in memory copy of objects to the cluster's body. For clusters smaller than 40K bytes (the majority of them), graph traversal represents less than 13% of the total time to create and save a cluster, which seems an acceptable price given the benefits of orthogonal persistence and cluster encapsulation.

We are currently studying the proposed clustering strategy from a naming point of view. Our clusters can be seen as independent name spaces, and the clustering strategy as a mechanism that build contextual name spaces based on object relations. This seems valuable to promote independence and decentralization of names in distributed systems.

Acknowledgments. We would like to thank Paulo Guedes, Manuel Sequeira, André Zúquete, Paulo Ferreira, Cristina Lopes, José Pereira, João Pereira, David Matos, Helena Oliveira, Pedro Trancoso, Miguel Castro and António Rito for their work on the IK system. Special thanks to Nuno Neves for implementing most of the clustering layer in IK.

References

[1] M. P. Atkinson, P. J. Bailey, P. J. Cockshott, K. J. Chisholm, and R. Morrison. An Approach to Persistent Programming. *The Computer Journal*, 26(4):360–365, November/December 1983.

413

[2] Mark F. Hornick and Stanley B. Zdonik. A Shared, Segmented Memory System for an Object-Oriented Database. *ACM transactions on Office Information Systems*, 5(1):70–97, January 1987.

[3] Joel E. Richardson and Michael J. Carey. Persistence in the E language: Issues and Implementation. *Software - Practice and Experience*, 19(12):1115–1150, December 1989.

[4] Verónique Benzanken and Claude Delobel. Enhancing Performance in a Persistent Object Store: Clustering Strategies in O_2. In *Proc. of Workshop on Persistent Object Systems*, pages 375–384, Martha Vineyard, France, 1990.

[5] C. Lamb, G. Landis, J. Orenstein, and D. Weinreb. The ObjectStore database system. *Communications of the ACM*, 34(10), October 1991.

[6] José Alves Marques and Paulo Guedes. Extending the Operating System to Support and Object-Oriented Environment. In *Proc. of the OOPSLA 89*, New Orleans, USA, 2-6th Octer 1989.

[7] Pedro Sousa, Manuel Sequeira, André Zúquete, Paulo Ferreira, Cristina Lopes, José Pereira, Paulo Guedes, and José Alves Marques. Distribution and Persistence in the ik Platform: Overview and Evaluation. *Usenix Computing Systems*, 6(4):391–424, Fall 1993.

[8] Pedro Sousa, André Zúquete, Nuno Neves, and José Alves Marques. Persistence in a Heterogeneous Distributed Oriented Environment. *The Computer Journal*, 37(4), 1994. To appear.

[9] José Alves Marques, Roland Balter, Vinny Cahill, Paulo Guedes, Neville Harris, Chris Horn, Sacha Krakoviak, Andre Kramer, John Slattery, and Gerard Vandôme. Implementing the COMANDOS Architecture. In *Proc. of Esprit Technical Week*, Brussels, Belgium, November 1988. North-Holland.

[10] V. Cahill, R. Balter, N.R. Harris, and X. Rousset de Pina (Eds.). *The Comandos Distributed Application Platform*. Springer-Verlag, 1993.

[11] Manuel Sequeira and José Alves Marques. Can C++ be Used for Programming Distributed and Persistent Objects? In *Proc. of the Int. Workshop on Object Orientation in Operating Systems - IEEE*, Palo Alto, USA, October 1991.

[12] Erich Gamma, André Weinand, and Rudolf Marty. ET++ - An Object-Oriented Application Framework in C++. In *EUUG*, Cascais, Portugal, October 1988.

[13] John Hogg. Islands: Aliasing Protection In Object Oriented Languages. In *OOPSLA '91 Proceedings*, pages 271–285, Phoenix, Arizona, October 1991.

[14] Won Kim, Jay Banerjee, Hong-Tai Chou, Jorge F. Garza, and Darrel Woelk. Composite object support in an object-oriented database system. In *Proceedings of OOPSLA 87*, 4-8th October 1987.

[15] Manolis M. Tsangaris and Jeffrey F. Naughton. A stochastic approach for clustering in object stores. In *Proc. of the SIGMOD Int. Conf. on Management of Data*, Denver, Colorado, May 1991.

[16] James W. Stamos. Static Grouping Objects to Enhance Performance of a Paged Virtual System. *ACM Transactions on Comp. Systems*, pages 155–180, May 1984.

[17] Bertrand Meyer. *Object-Oriented Software Construction*. Prentice Hall, 1988.

[18] Brad Cox. *Object-Oriented Programming: An Evolutionary Approach*. Addison-Wesley, 1986.

[19] Andr Weinand, Erich Gamma, and Rudolf Marty. ET++ – An Object-Oriented Application Framework in C++. In *OOPSLA'88 Proceedings*, pages 46–57, San Diego, California, November 1988. ACM/SIGPLAN.

[20] J. Eliot B. Moss. Addressing Large Distributed Collections of Persistent Objects: The Mneme Project's Approach. In *Proc. of the 2nd Int. Workshop on Datadase Programming Languages*, Gleneden Beach, Oregon, USA, June 1989.

[21] Paulo Ferreira. Reclaiming Storage in an Object Oriented Platform Supporting Extended C++ and Objective-C Applications. In *Proc. of the Int. Workshop on Object Orientation in Operating Systems - IEEE*, Palo Alto, USA, October 1991.

Query Processing in PIOS

Fausto RABITTI, Leonardo BENEDETTI, Federico DEMI

IEI-CNR
Via S.Maria, 46
56126 Pisa, Italy

Abstract

An approach to query processing in object-oriented stores supporting physical data independence is proposed in this paper. In particular, the problem of query optimization (i.e. finding efficient execution plans for declarative queries) has been investigated. A set of rewrite rules has been defined in order to allow an algebraic optimization phase. A local search procedure, based on a cost model of the store, has been tailored to the task of physical optimization. To support the physical data independence in the store, a translation algorithm, dealing with the actual storage organization of the database, has been studied. A comprehensive example illustrates these mechanisms. Finally, performance results are presented.

1 Introduction

Object-oriented database management systems (OODBMSs) are the result of new technologies which aim at tackling the data management problem of engineering applications like CASE and CAD systems. In the last few years, a number of prototypes (e.g. IRIS, Gemstone, Object Store, ORION, and O2) have been developed.

If we consider the performance of such systems, a key problem to solve is the optimization of queries formulated with the declarative query languages supported. Several techniques that have been designed for other environments (e.g. query optimizers for relational DBMSs, code optimization strategies for object-oriented programming languages) may turn out to be useful in this context.

This paper presents the study, description, and evaluation of query processing and query optimization strategies implemented in PIOS [1], an object server which supports physical data independence (i.e. it allows the definition of a *canonical schema*, that describes logical aspects of the database and against which operations are requested, and a *storage schema* which defines how objects are actually stored). This implies that queries (and all canonical operations offered by PIOS) have to be translated by the system against the storage schema.

Query processing is essentially the mapping of a declarative query expression into a procedural sequence of access plan primitives (i.e. execution plan). Query optimization is the selection of an efficient execution plan belonging to the set of all the equivalent plans for a given query (i.e. search space). For non-trivial queries, this process can become quite expensive, therefore the search strategy has to be carefully tuned, possibly taking into account results gathered over a sequence of queries being optimized. Moreover, as new query evaluation techniques prove to be useful, the optimizer has to be extensible enough to allow their integration.

All the above aspects have been studied for the design of the PIOS query processor (a more comprehensive description can be found in [2]). A set-oriented, non-procedural query language has been defined in order to be easily manageable and efficiently optimizable. Its expressions are checked for type consistency and submitted to a two-step optimization process: (*i*) *algebraic optimization*, performed by means of a set of rewrite rules using heuristics for ameliorating the expression and schema information for pruning it, (*ii*) *physical optimization*, a randomized search based on a cost model exploiting data distribution statistics, in addition to heuristics for reducing the search space.

The search space is modeled annotating with *roles* the operators of the physical expression resulting from the algebraic optimization phase. It includes the choice of traversal order for path navigations starting everywhere in the path expression (i.e. join reordering) and the selection of existing indices. Adapting rules for annotating the expression should guarantee the optimizer extensibility and improvability.

The cost-driven physical optimization is usually not implemented in existing OODBMSs (e.g. O_2, Object Store), or it is oversimplified (e.g. ORION). Without a cost model, it is not obvious which query transformation rules have to be applied in order to reach an optimized plan. Therefore, the PIOS query processor performs a rather simple algebraic optimization, using rewrite rules that in the vast majority of cases are able to improve the expression. Instead, PIOS query processor emphasizes the cost-driven physical optimization, which is the main focus of this paper.

An important contribution of the paper is that, within the PIOS context, we are able to compare, in order of magnitude, the relative improvement of algebraic optimization and cost-driven physical optimization.

The rest of the paper is organized as follows. In the next section the PIOS system is briefly described. In section 3, an overview of related research on query processing and query optimization is presented: this serves as introduction for our specific work which covers section 4 and section 5. In particular, in section 4 the algebraic optimization phase and the translation algorithm between canonical and physical level are described, while the physical optimization phase is presented in section 5. Conclusions are in section 6.

2 The PIOS System

PIOS (*Physically Independent Object Server*) [1] is the server component of a client–server architecture and it manages the shared persistent database on behalf of several clients. It supports an object–oriented data model as defined in [3]. Each object of the database is associated with a unique *identifier* CID and belongs to a *class*. Classes are organized in a multiple inheritance hierarchy (through the *is a* relationship).

One of the most important features of PIOS is the support of *physical data independence* [4]. For this purpose two data models are provided: a *canonical data model* and a *storage data model*. They respectively allow the definition of the *canonical schema* and of the *storage schema* of the database. The former, that represents the logical organization of the database, is exported to each client, which in turn may offer a special view of it (i.e. a certain *conceptual schema*) to its users. The latter is not visible to the clients, in fact it represents the physical organization of the database (i.e. how canonical objects are actually transformed into physical objects, identified by *physical identifiers* (PID) and grouped in collections in order to be stored in secondary memory). Hence, the database designer can choose among different storage organizations for a specific canonical schema in order to fulfil application performance requirements.

PIOS supports two different strategies for storing class hierarchies (*ODS* and *SDS*), *grouping* and *partitioning* of canonical objects. Grouping allows several canonical objects to be stored by means of a single physical object. Partitioning is the fragmentation of canonical objects into several

418

physical objects (*vertical partitioning*) and the choice of their storage bucket according to a predicate (*horizontal partitioning*). Moreover, in order to speed-up retrieval operations, PIOS allows the definition of value and navigation indices [5]. All these designing operations are submitted to the system using a specific language: the *Object Store Definition Language* [4]. The current version of PIOS does not support schema evolution (neither at the canonical level nor at the storage level).

An example canonical schema that will be used for formulating queries and the definition of a physical schema with value and navigation indices is presented in Appendix A.

3 Related Work

Almost all existing query optimizers for OODBMSs can be partitioned into two different classes: those based on a system of rewrite rules (e.g. [6, 7, 8]) and those exploiting the concept of class extent (e.g. [9, 10, 11]).

An optimizer belonging to the first class is the one designed for the O$_2$ system [8]. Its main features are the algebraic optimization of the queries, exploiting the semantic properties of the language, and the factorization of constant and/or duplicated subexpressions. To somehow complete the approach, a set of heuristics for reducing the rewriting phase and for the selection of suitable indices is defined. The important thing to note here is that the entire process is carried out without the support of a comprehensive cost model.

The other approach has been experimented in the design of the query optimizer for the ORION system [9]. Several techniques for the query optimizers of relational DBMSs have turned out to be useful and easily employable in this project. In particular: the enumeration of all valid permutations of the classes involved in a query, the choice of the best join algorithm and the exploitation of a cost model based on data distribution statistics. A graphical representation of queries and tree traversal algorithms are proposed. There are three methods for evaluating a (sub)query (i.e. for traversing its tree representation). The *forward traversal* starts at the root node and consists of: (*i*) a projection on the children attributes, (*ii*) an evaluation of the qualified children that allows the qualification of their parents. The *backward traversal* starts at the leaves: the qualified attributes are evaluated through a selection, then a semi-join returns the qualified parents. The *mixed traversal* combines the two previous methods.

As stated in the introduction, complex queries give rise to many alternative execution plans that have to be examined in order to produce an *optimized plan*. Query optimizers deal with non-trivial queries, possibly executed only once: therefore, they have to take into account the combinatorial nature of the search space. For common queries of OODBMSs, the latter is usually even wider than the analogous of relational DBMSs. This is due to the fact that path expressions can be viewed as *implicit joins*. Hence, the search strategy may result in a quite time consuming search process (i.e. there is a trade-off between optimization cost and quality of the solution obtained), therefore it needs to be carefully designed and tuned. Two approaches have been proposed [12]: *enumerative* (or *deterministic*) search and *randomized* search.

Enumerative search inspects for optimality several solutions by *depth-first* order (e.g. greedy strategy with augmentation heuristic [13]) or *breadth-first* order (e.g. branch-and-bound algorithm [14] with heuristics for early pruning of inefficient plans). The latter algorithm, combined with restrictions on the search space, has been chosen for the design of the optimizer of the relational DBMS System R [15].

Randomized search aims at improving start solutions until obtaining a *local* optimum. Two algorithms have been proposed: *iterative improvement* (or *local search*) [13] and *simulated annealing* [16]. Comparisons between enumerative and randomized strategies can be found in [17] where, in the context of parallel execution, access plans are modelled as processing trees.

4 Query Processing in PIOS: Algebraic Optimization and Translation

Queries are submitted to PIOS using a specifically defined non-procedural query language: a brief overview of it and of the three-step algebraic optimization phase (see figure 1) is presented in this section (see [2] for details). As far as the latter is concerned, the input is a type-consistent expression of the query language (*initial canonical expression*) to which a set of schema-independent rewrite rules is applied. The resulting expression (*simplified canonical expression*) is then translated into an equivalent one formulated against the storage schema (*initial physical expression*). This expression is finally pruned by means of schema-dependent rewrite rules in order to obtain a *simplified physical expression*.

420

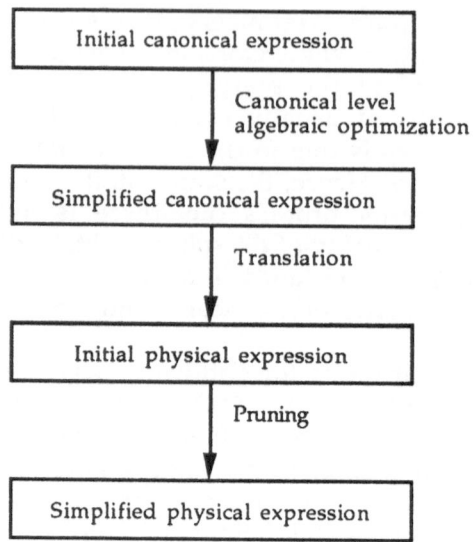

Figure 1 - Algebraic optimization phase

4.1 Query Language

Queries are expressed in PIOS through a *formal, object-preserving,* efficiently optimizable query language. Formal languages provide a sound foundation for equivalence-preserving transformation rules. Object-preserving languages return as query results objects that already exist in the database (they cannot create new objects as side-effects of query executions).

In the following the query language operators are presented. Operands and results are sets of CIDs, thus the language maintains the *closure property*. A query expressed against the canonical schema (i.e. *canonical query*) is an expression *e* compliant with the following grammar rules:

e ::=

	UN(*e* , *elist*)	Union
|	**IN**(*e* , *elist*)	Intersection
|	**DF**(*e* , *elist*)	Difference
|	**F**(*class, expression*)	Selection (Filter)
|	**MB**(*quantifier, attribute, class, e*)	Map Backward
|	**MF**(*quantifier, attribute, class, e*)	Map Forward

elist ::=
   e
  | *e , elist*

expression ::=
   simplePredicate
  | *simplePredicate* **and** *expression*
  | *simplePredicate* **or** *expression*
  | *(expression)*

simplePredicate ::=
   attribute relOp const
  | **TRUE**
  | **FALSE**

attribute ::=
   class_field

relOp ::= < | <= | = | <> | >= | > | **has**

quantifier ::=
   A   Universal Quantifier
  | **E**   Existential Quantifier

Semantics of the query language operators is straightforward. Only map operators need an explanation: MB(E, *A_ref*, *A'*, *S*) is the subset of CIDs of class *A'* that reference, via *A_ref*, at least one object in *S*; meanwhile MB(A, *A_ref*, *A'*, *S*) is the subset of CIDs of class *A'* that reference, via *A_ref*, objects in *S* only. Semantics of Map Forward operators is defined similarly.

The query language presented above is rather simple. This is due to the fact that it has to be general enough in order to be the target language for the compilation of several, different *conceptual languages*; moreover it must have a simple structure in order to be highly optimizable. It can also be used for defining *envelopes* (i.e. portions of database which are sufficient for executing a transaction) as result of queries executed at the server level, and which can be then transmitted to the client for further processing.

In subsequent examples, simple queries formulated using the query language are presented. Of course, they are expressed against the canonical schema defined in Appendix A.

422

Examples

1. Find all Italian libraries

MB(E, Library_Addr, Library,
F(Address, Address_Country = 'Italy'))

2. Find all Italian university libraries

MB(E, Library_Addr, UnivLibrary,
F(Address, Address_Country = 'Italy'))

3. Find all technical books written in English by John Smith, having at least a topic different from Object Store.

IN(IN(F(TechBook, Book_Language='English'),
F(TechBook, Book_Author='John Smith')),
MB(E, TechBook_Topics, TechBook,
F(Topic, Topic_Description<>'Object Store'))
)

This query will be used throughout this paper in order to describe the various phases of query processing.

♦

4.2 Canonical Level Algebraic Optimization

After that the canonical query is checked for type consistency, a set of rewrite rules is applied. These query transformation rules are based on pattern matching and textual substitution and create equivalent expressions (see [2] for details). The overall canonical level algebraic optimization process aims at:
1. eliminating the redundancy possibly contained in the expression;
2. easily checking for contradiction the conditions specified in each selection operator, in order to simplify the entire expression;
3. standardizing the expression structure, in order to make it easier its translation into an equivalent query formulated against the storage schema.

This phase is particularly useful when queries are the result of an automatic process of translation. Next, a very simple transformation (i.e. filter aggregation) performed on the example query is presented.

Example

Initial canonical expression:

IN(IN(F(TechBook, Book_Language='English'),
      F(TechBook, Book_Author='John Smith')),
   MB(E, TechBook_Topics, TechBook,
         F(Topic, Topic_Description<>'Object Store'))
)

Simplified canonical expression (after canonical level algebraic optimization):

IN(F(TechBook, Book_Language='English' $\wedge$
              Book_Author='John Smith'),
   MB(E, TechBook_Topics, TechBook,
         F(Topic, Topic_Description<>'Object Store'))
)

♦

4.3 Translation

Since PIOS supports physical data independence, the simplified canonical expression has to be translated into an equivalent query formulated against the storage schema (*initial physical expression*). The target language for this translation (*physical query language*) is similar to the canonical query language presented in subsection 4.1 and is still declarative enough in order to enable the subsequent phase of physical optimization. Its operands and intermediate results are sets of PIDs. In general, the final result of a physical query is a multi-set of PIDs, which eventually is retransformed by the system into a set of CIDs.

In order to allow an easy factorization of common subexpressions, the working structure for the representation of physical queries is a DAG (*Directed Acyclic Graph*) instead of a tree. Due to space constraints, translation algorithms are not presented here, instead the resulting physical expression for the example query is shown.

Example

Initial physical expression (after translation against storage schema):

424

IN(F(TechBook*, TechBook*_Book.Language='English'
                    ∧ TechBook*_Book.Author='John Smith'),
    MB(E, TechBook*_TechBook.Topics,
            F(Topic*, Topic*_Topic.Description<>'Object Store')))
IN(F(ItalTechBook, ItalTechBook_Book.Language='English'
                    ∧ ItalTechBook_Book.Author='John Smith'),
    MB(E, ItalTechBook_TechBook.Topics, ⸴))

This expression reflects the fact that *TechBook* class has been
horizontally partitioned into two collections: *ItalTechBook* that contains
technical books written in Italian and *TechBook** that contains technical
books not written in Italian. The arrow is the result of the common
subexpression detection mechanism performed at translation time (i.e.
Topic* collection can be accessed only once).

♦

4.4 Pruning

This phase is performed by means of a set of schema-dependent rewrite
rules. In particular, every predicate contained in a selection operator of
the initial physical query is checked for contradiction against the
condition verified by the collection on which it is defined (these
conditions stem from partitionings). Contradictory selection operators are
replaced with the expression F(*collection*, **FALSE**). The effects of such
replacements are then propagated through the entire expression. This
process avoids accessing a collection when its objects have primitive
values not compliant with those requested by the query.

Example

Simplified physical expression (after pruning phase):

IN(F(TechBook*, TechBook*_Book.Language='English'
                    ∧ TechBook*_Book.Author='John Smith'),
    MB(E, TechBook*_TechBook.Topics,
            F(Topic*, Topic*_Topic.Description<>'Object Store')))

It is obtained after that selection operator on *ItalTechBook* collection has
been replaced with F(ItalTechBook, **FALSE**) and the intersection
operator has been subsequently pruned.

♦

The result of all the entire algebraic optimization is a *simplified physical expression* that becomes the feasible starting point for the subsequent physical optimization phase.

5 Query Processing in PIOS: Physical Optimization

Physical optimization is the kernel of the entire query optimization process in PIOS. In fact the *simplified physical expression*, obtained from the previous algebraic optimization phase, can be mapped into several (typically many) equivalent access plans, each exploiting different strategies for accessing data. In order to speed up the evaluation of queries, the physical optimization phase must take into account the low level features of PIOS storage system. In particular: the direct access to physical objects via PIDs, navigations among objects performed through forward and backward references stored in the object's states and the exploitation of value and navigation indices.

The task of choosing an efficient plan is a computationally intractable problem as discussed in section 3. In PIOS, it has been attacked using a local search procedure [14] in addition to a cost model. The latter is able to estimate the cardinalities of each temporary set involved in an access plan and the number of accesses to secondary storage needed for the plan execution. In order to reduce the search space, a set of heuristics and a set of tuning parameters have been defined.

5.1 Physical Level Access Primitives

A PIOS access plan is a sequence of physical level access primitives (*primitives* for short). Each of them takes either one or two sets of PIDs as parameters and produces one set of PIDs as result. There are *set primitives, navigation primitives* (possibly performed through a navigation index) and *selection primitives* (possibly performed using a value index). In the following a survey of all primitives is presented. Meta identifiers such as $T, T1, T2$ etc. stand for temporary sets of PIDs.

These are the *set primitives* supported:

T = T1 **UN** T2	Union
T = T1 + T2	Disjoint union
T = T1 **INT** T2	Intersection
T = T1 \ T2	Difference

T = **sort** T1

426

T = **pids** *collectionName*
It stores in T all the PIDs of the objects belonging to *collectionName* collection.

These are the *navigation primitives*:

T = **MF** [*attributeName*] T1 **by link**
T = **MF** [*attributeName$_1$* ... *attributeName$_n$*] T1 **by** *navigationIndexId*
T = **MB** [*attributeName*] T1 **by link**
T = **MB** [*attributeName$_1$* ... *attributeName$_n$*] T1 **by** *navigationIndexId*

Each navigation primitive specifies the reference(s) to be navigated and the physical access method to be used. The latter can be: (*i*) **by link** if physical pointers are to be used; (*ii*) **by** *navigationIndexId* if a navigation index is to be accessed without materializing the physical objects stored in the collections.

Finally, these are the *selection primitives*:

T = **F** [*conjunct*] T1
The objects of T1 are accessed and the PIDs of those verifying *conjunct* are stored in T.

T = **F** [*conjunct*] *collectionName* **by** *valueIndexId*
The value index *valueIndexId* is accessed to select the subset of the objects stored in *collectionName* which satisfy *conjunct*.

5.2 Cost Model

For assuring high quality results, the task of choosing an efficient plan must be guided by the minimization of the expected time needed for its execution. For that purpose the definition of a *cost model* is needed. In particular, it has to exploit a mathematical model able to estimate the cardinalities of each temporary set of PIDs involved in an access plan. In PIOS, such a model is based on statistics on (*i*) *primitive attributes*: uniform distribution and independence among values of distinct attributes is supposed; (*ii*) *references*: statistics on referenced and referencing objects are collected; (*iii*) *collections*: the number of objects belonging to collections is maintained; (*iv*) *indices*: the number of levels and leaves of the B-trees implementing the indices is maintained as well. In order to avoid an unjustified overhead, the above statistics are only periodically updated (e.g. when the system is shut down).

The approximation adopted for the execution time of an access plan is the estimated *number of pages* accessed by the underlying persistent object store, thus ignoring the delay caused by the CPU for internal processing. Moreover, the interleaving of transactions and the presence of a cache memory are not taken into account by the cost model.

In PIOS, all physical objects belonging to a certain collection are stored in a set of pages that they use exclusively (i.e. it cannot exist a page containing objects belonging to two different collections). A PID contains information about the physical placement on the storage device of the object it refers to. This enables the direct access to an object via its PID. As far as the cost model is concerned, a physical object is always considered to be accessed as a whole (this is rather sensible in a system supporting physical data independence, and simplifies the overall estimation process).

5.3 Search Space

In this subsection it is described the technique implemented in the PIOS query processor for obtaining different, but equivalent, plans for a given physical expression. Plans differ in the exploitation of existing indices (value and navigation indices) and in the ordering of navigation executions.

The general idea is to annotate every operator of the simplified physical expression with a *role* and to provide an algorithm for translating an annotated physical expression into an access plan. Not all the annotations can be mapped into a correct access plan, in subsection 5.4 will be described how the local search procedure can generate legal annotations only (i.e. annotations that give rise to correct access plans).

Definitions

Given a physical expression:
- the *result set* attached to an operator O is the temporary set of PIDs representing the result of the subquery rooted in O.
- the *advance set* attached to an operator O is a temporary set of PIDs that is a superset of the result set of O.

Every physical operator is annotated with one of the following *roles*: *generator* (gen), *propagator* (pro), and *bottom-up* (bup).

An operator annotated with *generator* role creates an advance set for its operands. Operators eligible to be generators are intersections and navigation operators.

An operator annotated with *propagator* role has an advance set attached to itself, and uses it for speeding up its execution and/or for providing an advance set for its operands. Any operator is eligible to be propagator.

An operator that is neither generator nor propagator is said to be annotated with *bottom-up* role.

♦

Subsequent examples are intended to show how different annotations of the same simplified physical expression yield different but equivalent plans.

Example

```
<bup> IN(
<bup>        F(TechBook*, TechBook*_Book.Language='English'
                            ∧ TechBook*_Book.Author='John Smith'),
<bup>        MB(E, TechBook*_TechBook.Topics,
<bup>            F(Topic*, Topic*_Topic.Description<>'Object Store')))
```

Annotating every operator with *bottom-up* role, the resulting plan is obtained translating the physical expression in a bottom-up way.

```
10000#    314$    T0  = pids Topic*
 9999#  20314$    T1  = F[Topic*_Topic.Description<>Object Store] T0
10000#  25569$    T2  = MB[TechBook*_TechBook.Topics] T1 by link
10000#   1303$   *T3  = sort T2
10000#    314$    T4  = pids TechBook*
    1#  20158$    T5  = F[TechBook*_Book.Author=John Smith ^
                         TechBook*_Book.Language=English] T4
    1#      1$   *T6  = sort T5
    1#    159$  !*T7  = T3 INT T6
Execution cost:  68132$.
```

Each primitive has two numbers preceding it: the first one (i.e. it is followed by #) represents the estimated cardinality of the resulting temporary set of PIDs, while the second one (i.e. it is followed by $) is the estimated number of accesses to the secondary storage needed for its computation. Moreover, the * character means that the temporary set is sorted, while the ! character marks the final result sets. In this case, the plan entails the scan of two collections: *Topic** and *TechBook** (the result set is *T7*). In our sample database, objects are usually supposed to span over two physical pages, and a single-page buffer of the same dimension of a physical page is assumed (i.e. reading data of two different pages always implies two accesses to the secondary storage).

Performing a naive selection of indices on the above plan, the following one is obtained (navigation indices are not exploitable for this query):

```
10000#     314$   T0   = pids Topic*
 9999#   20314$   T1   = F[Topic*_Topic.Description<>Object Store] T0
10000#   25569$   T2   = MB[TechBook*_TechBook.Topics] T1 by link
10000#    1303$  *T3   = sort T2
    4#     161$   T4   = F[TechBook*_Book.Author=John Smith] TechBook*
by Vix# 2
    1#      10$   T5   = F[TechBook*_Book.Language=English] T4
    1#       1$  *T6   = sort T5
    1#     159$ !*T7   = T3 INT T6
Execution cost:   47831$.
```

Vix# 2 value index is used for solving the condition on author attribute, therefore *TechBook** collection is not scanned (only a few objects of its are accessed). On the contrary, *Vix# 1* value index (defined on *Topic*_Topic.Description*) is ignored because the condition on topic is not selective enough (i.e. all topics but one are different from Object Store). Changing the physical expression annotation as follows,

```
<gen>  IN(
<pro>       F(TechBook*, TechBook*_Book.Language='English'
                          ∧ TechBook*_Book.Author='John Smith'),
<bup>       MB(E, TechBook*_TechBook.Topics,
<bup>            F(Topic*, Topic*_Topic.Description<>'Object Store')))
```

a plan that entails accessing only those technical books having at least a topic different from Object Store is obtained:

```
10000#     314$   T0   = pids Topic*
 9999#   20314$   T1   = F[Topic*_Topic.Description<>Object Store] T0
10000#   25569$   T2   = MB[TechBook*_TechBook.Topics] T1 by link
    1#   20158$ !  T7   = F[TechBook*_Book.Author=John Smith ^
                            TechBook*_Book.Language=English] T2
Execution cost:   66355$.
```

Advance set *T2* is generated by the intersection operator (through its navigation operand) and then propagated to the selection operator on *TechBook** collection.

If the annotation is the following,

```
<bup>  IN(
<bup>       F(TechBook*, TechBook*_Book.Language='English'
                          ∧ TechBook*_Book.Author='John Smith'),
<gen>       MB(E, TechBook*_TechBook.Topics,
<pro>            F(Topic*, Topic*_Topic.Description<>'Object Store')))
```

a plan that avoids the scan of collections is obtained. Only those topics referenced by at least a technical book stored in *TechBook** collection (i.e. technical books not written in Italian) are accessed:

```
10000#     314$   T0   = pids TechBook*
```

```
  9504#    25563$    T1  = MF[TechBook*_TechBook.Topics] T0 by link
  9504#    19306$    T6  = F[Topic*_Topic.Description<>Object Store] T1
 10000#    24281$    T7  = MB[TechBook*_TechBook.Topics] T6 by link
 10000#     1303$   *T8  = sort T7
     4#      161$    T9  = F[TechBook*_Book.Author=John Smith] TechBook*
by Vix# 2
     1#       10$    T10 = F[TechBook*_Book.Language=English] T9
     1#        1$   *T11 = sort T10
     1#      159$  !*T12 = T8 INT T11
Execution cost:   71098$.
```

In this case, the advance set *T1* is created by the map operator and propagated to the selection operator on *Topic** collection. Next, the annotation that gives rise to the optimized plan is presented: it performs a join reordering, only those topics referenced by technical books written in English by John Smith are accessed.

<gen> IN(
<bup>   F(TechBook*, TechBook*_Book.Language='English'
                         ∧ TechBook*_Book.Author='John Smith'),
<pro>   MB(E, TechBook*_TechBook.Topics,
<pro>   F(Topic*, Topic*Topic.Description<>'Object Store')))

```
     4#      161$    T0  = F[TechBook*_Book.Author=John Smith] TechBook*
by Vix# 2
     1#       10$    T1  = F[TechBook*_Book.Language=English] T0
     4#        7$    T2  = MF[TechBook*_TechBook.Topics] T1 by link
     4#       10$    T7  = F[Topic*_Topic.Description<>Object Store] T2
    12#       13$    T8  = MB[TechBook*_TechBook.Topics] T7 by link
    12#        1$   *T9  = sort T8
     1#        1$   *T10 = sort T1
     1#        3$  !*T11 = T9 INT T10
Execution cost:    206$.
```

Next subsection will present an effective method for changing the physical expression annotation, so that various plans exploiting different access strategies can be evaluated and compared.

5.4 Local Search

The physical optimization problem (i.e. the selection of the optimum access plan for a given physical query) is a hard combinatorial problem. Various general techniques have been developed for tackling this kind of problems. In particular, randomized search strategies do not enumerate the entire search space (in our case the set of equivalent plans associated with the simplified physical expression), but attain a *local optimum* possibly different from the global optimum: *local search* [14] is the one chosen for the design of the physical optimization phase in PIOS.
Two concepts are very important for the local search technique:

Move: a perturbation applied to a state belonging to the search space to get another state;

Neighbourhood of a state P: the set of states reachable from *P* with a single move.

The procedure (see figure 2) begins with an *initial state*; a move is accepted if the adjacent state being moved to is of lower cost than the current state. This is done repeatedly until the algorithm attains a state whose cost is lower than that of all neighbouring states (i.e. *local optimum*). After that, a *new starting state* is obtained by making a fixed number of moves from the local optimum; this time each move is accepted irrespective of whether it increases or decreases the cost. When a certain stopping condition is satisfied the entire process is halted and the best local optimum encountered is returned. This general technique has been tailored to the specific problem of query optimization by defining the following aspects:

1. *Selection of the initial state*: all operators of the physical expression are tagged with *bottom-up* role. Navigation indices to be used are selected through heuristics based on the length of the navigation [5]. The problem of choosing the best value index for the execution of a certain selection condition has already been widely studied, therefore standard criteria are used. For each new plan inspected by the search, the choice of value indices is repeated.

2. *Move set*: moves are functions that take as input the annotated physical expression and a particular operator belonging to it and change the annotation according to a certain rule. Three moves have been defined for the local optimum search phase:

   New: a filter operator, annotated with *bottom-up* role and deemed particularly slow to perform, is selected, and an attempt to provide an advance set for it is made. For that purpose an operator with advance set propagation capabilities (i.e. an operator with an already attached advance set or an operator that can generate such a set) is selected among the filter's ancestor operators.

   Stretch: an operator annotated with *generator* role is selected and, in a fashion similar to that devised for the *New* move, an attempt to provide an advance set for it is made.

   Swap: an intersection operator with either *generator* or *propagator* role is selected, and the order of propagation of the advance sets towards two of its operand expressions is reversed.

3. *Local optimum detection*: it would be impractical to exhaustively enumerate all the neighbours of the current state to verify its local optimality. Instead, an approximation based on random sampling is used.

4. *New starting state selection*: it is obtained by making a fixed number of moves from the local optimum without evaluating the cost of the associated plans. Another type of move is added to the move set for this phase only:

   Del: an operator annotated with *generator* role is selected and the advance set it creates is deleted. Of course, the annotation of the entire subexpression may be affected.

5. *Stopping criterion*: the process is stopped either by a timeout or when the cost of the current plan is less than a previously estimated lower bound on the cost of global minimum.

6. *Move selection criterion*: moves are chosen from the move set at random. The probability associated with selecting any particular move is specified along with the move set. Every time an unfeasible move is attempted its selection probability is diminished, and those of the other moves are increased accordingly.

The latter mechanism leads to a twofold adaptability aspect in the random selection of a move: (*i*) *topological adaptability*: probabilities tend to adjust in a way that reflects the shape of the physical query DAG (e.g. a shallow DAGs will force the Stretch move probability to a low value); (*ii*) *temporal adaptability*: certain moves are more needed at an early stage of the local search, others at a later stage. As the former start failing, the latter start being selected more and more often (e.g. *New* move is generally needed at the beginning of the search, in order to create several advance sets, while *Stretch* move and *Swap* move start being useful later for circulating the previously created advance sets).

Local optimum detection, new starting state selection, stopping criterion, and move selection probabilities allow the definition of several parameters that can be used for the fine tuning of the local search procedure. Moreover, modifying the moves guarantee the optimizer adaptability and extensibility.

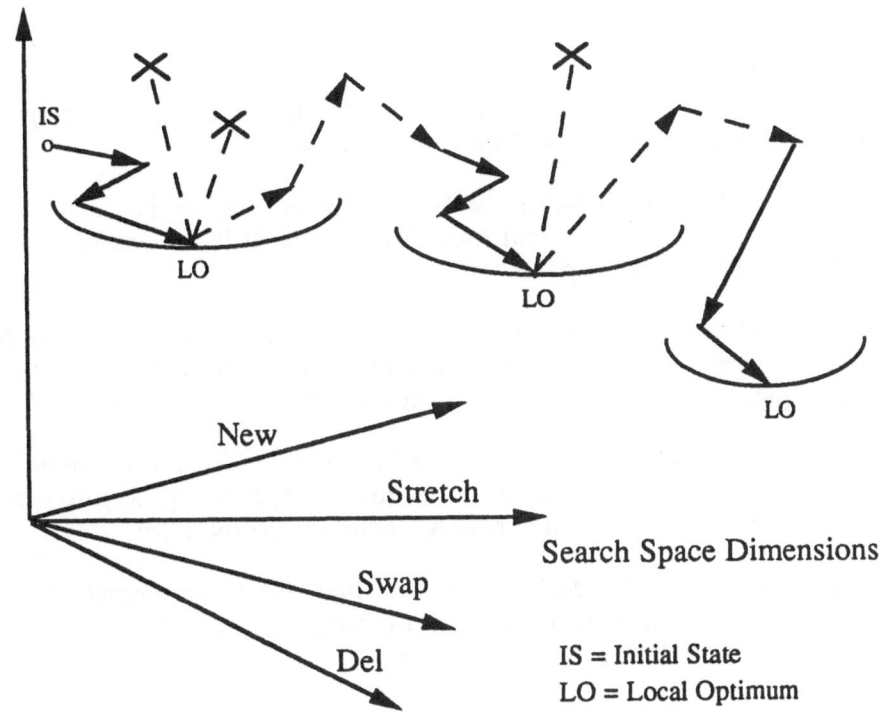

Figure 2 - Local Search algorithm

Example

Let's examine how the local search procedure can change the bottom-up annotation in order to obtain the one that gives rise to the optimized plan. Bottom-up annotation is a local optimum: changing the annotation of whatever selection operator increases the estimated execution cost. Therefore a new starting state must be reached. Let's suppose that *New* move is performed on selection operator on *Topic** collection: the latter is annotated with *propagator* role, while map operator is tagged with *generator* role.

Our goal is eventually attained if *Stretch* move is then performed on map operator: the latter is annotated with *propagator* role, while intersection operator is annotated with *generator* role. This is feasible because intersection operator creates an advance set using the result computed by the filter operator on *TechBook** collection.

5.5 Performance Results

In this subsection we present some meaningful examples of performance gains resulting from algebraic and physical optimization, considering four sample queries. Selected queries are the following:

Query a: *Find all technical books written in English by John Smith, having at least a topic different from Object Store.* It is the example query used throughout this paper.

Query b: *Find all technical books written in English by an author different from John Smith, having Object Store as topic.* It similar to the preceding, except that conditions on author and topic are inverted.

Query c: *Find all technical books written in English by John Smith that do not have History as topic.* It is formulated using a universally quantified map operator (i.e. **MB(A**, TechBook_Topics, ...)).

Query d: *Find all Italian libraries that have Skyscraper plan.* It involves *Plan* collection which contains very large objects, therefore the optimizer has to try to avoid its scan.

For each of the above queries, the following four plans are estimated (results are presented in figure 3):

1. *Plan without optimization*: the initial canonical expression is plainly translated into a physical expression. Therefore both algebraic and physical optimization are ignored.

2. *Initial plan*: it is obtained performing algebraic optimization only (i.e canonical level algebraic optimization and pruning).

3. *Initial plan with naive indices*: it is obtained performing a naive selection of value and navigation indices on the preceding plan. Selection of existing indices is based on heuristics.

4. *Optimized plan*: it is the standard result of the process of query optimization as described in section 4 and section 5.

Comparing the values of *Plan without optimization* with those of *Initial plan with naive indices*, we can observe how algebraic optimization, combined with an index selection guided by heuristics, is generally able to reduce of an order of magnitude the expected execution time. This gain is particularly notable for queries that can be pruned according to the actual storage organization and when predicates involving primitive attributes on which value indices are maintained are rather selective.

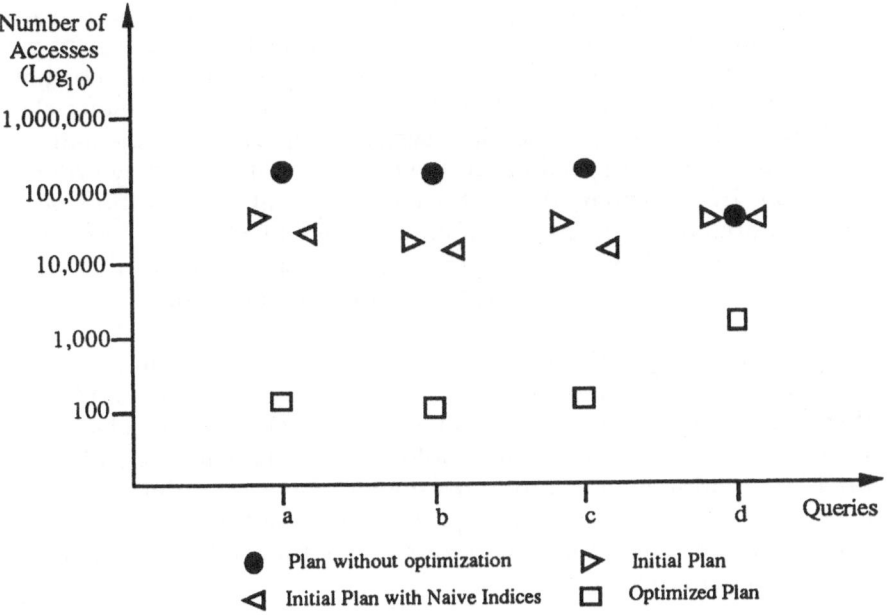

Figure 3 - Performance results (accesses to secondary storage)

However, the cost-driven process of physical optimization (i.e. notice the values of *Optimized plan*) can further reduce of two orders of magnitude the expected execution time. Considering that the local search procedure has to make only a few attempts for obtaining the annotation giving rise to the optimized plan of the above queries, the physical optimization process proves its effectiveness.

6 Conclusion

In this paper, we have presented the entire process of query processing in PIOS, an object server which supports physical data independence. In particular, the declarative, set-oriented query language and the various phases which allow a sound and complete algebraic optimization have been described. The result of this phase is a physical expression that becomes the feasible starting point for the critical process of physical optimization: a local search procedure, which exploits a specific cost model based on statics on stored data, has been designed in order to obtain an optimized access plan within a reasonable amount of resources (i.e. CPU time and central memory).

The search space is modelled annotating with *roles* the physical expression operators. It includes the selection of the best ordering for path navigations (starting everywhere in the path expression) and the choice of available value and navigation indices: experimental results show that these techniques, combined in a system supporting fragmentation of objects, are capable of speeding up the execution of queries by orders of magnitude. In particular, the cost-driven physical optimization phase, usually ignored by existing query optimizers of OODBMSs, has proved its effectiveness. In fact, it is able to generate and estimate plans that would be discarded by systems based on rewrite rules and heuristics.

The overall physical optimization phase has been designed in order to be easily extensible to new advanced query processing techniques and/or new index structures: adding new local search moves able to change the physical expression annotation should be sufficient for extending the search space. Moreover, various parameters have been defined for the local search procedure, so that its progressive fine tuning can tackle the traditional trade-off between the resources used for optimization and the quality of the produced results.

References

1.   F. Rabitti, G. Mainetto, P. Zezula, S. Barneva, N. Aloia, L. Benedetti, S. Biscari, P. Carcaci, E. Criscuoli, F. Demi, F. Giannasio, and U. Pasquali. Design and Implementation of PIOS: a Physically Independent Object Server. In *Technical Report FIDE/93/70, ESPRIT BRA Project No. 6309, FIDE-2 (Formally Integrated Data Environment)*, 1993

2.   F. Rabitti, L. Benedetti, and F. Demi. Query Processing in PIOS. In *Technical Report FIDE/94/83, ESPRIT BRA Project No. 6309, FIDE-2 (Formally Integrated Data Environment)*, 1994

3.   M. Atkinson, F. Bancilhon, D. DeWitt, K. Dittrich, D. Maier, and S. Zdonik. The Object-Oriented Database System Manifesto. In *Proceedings of DOOD-89, Kyoto, Japan*, 1989

4.   N. Aloia, S. Barneva, and F. Rabitti. Supporting Physical Independence in an Object Database Server. In *Proceedings of ECOOP-92*, 1992

5.   P. Zezula and F. Rabitti. Object Store with Navigation Accelerator. In *Information Systems Vol. 18, No. 7, Springer-Verlag*, 1993

6.   G. Shaw and S. Zdonik. An Object-Oriented Query Algebra. In *Proceedings of DBPL-89, Salishan Lodge, Oregon*, 1989

7.   D. D. Straube and M. T. Özsu. Queries and Query Processing in Object-Oriented Database Systems. In *ACM Transactions on Information Systems Vol. 8, No. 4*, 1990

8.   S. Cluet. *Langages et Optimisation de Requêtes pour Systèmes de Gestion de Base de Données Orientés-Objet*. Thèse de doctorat présentée à l'Université de Paris-Sud - Centre d'Orsay, 1991

9.   P. Jenq, D. Woelk, W. Kim, and W. Lee. Query Processing in Distributed ORION. In *Proceedings of EDBT, Venice, Italy*, 1990

10.   A. Kemper and G. Moerkotte. Advanced Query Processing in Object Bases Using Access Support Relations. In *Proceeedings of VLDB-90, Brisbane, Australia*, 1990

11.   R. Lanzelotte, P. Valduriez, M. Ziane, and J. Cheiney. Optimization of Nonrecursive Queries in OODBs. In *Proceedings of DOOD-91*, 1991

12.   R. Lanzelotte and P. Valduriez. Extending the Search Strategy in a Query Optimizer. In *Proceedings of VLDB-91, Barcelona, Spain*, 1991

13. A. Swami. Optimization of Large Join Queries: Combining Heuristics and Combinatorial Techniques. In *Proceedings of ACM-SIGMOD-89*, 1989

14. C. H. Papadimitriou and K. Steiglitz. *Combinatorial Optimization: Algorithms and Complexity*. Prentice Hall, 1982

15. P. Selinger, M. Astrahan, D. Chamberlin, R. Lorie, and T. Price. Access Path Selection in a Relational Database Management System. In *Proceedings of ACM-SIGMOD-79*, 1979

16. Y. Ioannidis and Y. Cha Kang. Left-Deep vs. Bushy Trees: an Analysis of Strategy Spaces and its Implications for Query Optimization. In *Proceedings of ACM-SIGMOD-91*, 1991

17. R. Lanzelotte, P. Valduriez, and M. Ziane. On the Effectiveness of Optimization Search Strategies for Parallel Execution Spaces. In *Proceedings of VLDB-93, Dublin, Ireland*, 1993

Appendix A   Example Database

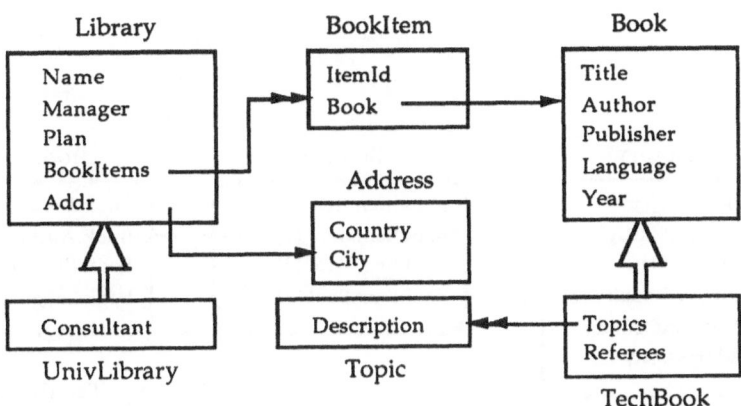

Figure A.1 - Canonical schema

An example of a *canonical schema* is presented in figure A.1. The main entities represented in it are libraries and books. Libraries contain book items referring books. Moreover, there exist university libraries characterized by a consultant and technical books characterized by a set of topics. In figure A.2 is depicted an example of a *storage schema* obtained as result of a process of storage level design. In particular,

- the class hierarchy involving *Library* and *UnivLibrary* classes is stored with SDS strategy, while the other is stored with ODS strategy;

- *Plan* attribute (a long data field) is stored separately from its library object;

- technical books written in Italian are stored in a different collection (*ItalTechBook*);

- libraries are stored together with their address;

- three value indices (attributes on which they are defined are underlined) and a navigation index (references involved have a circle) are maintained.

440

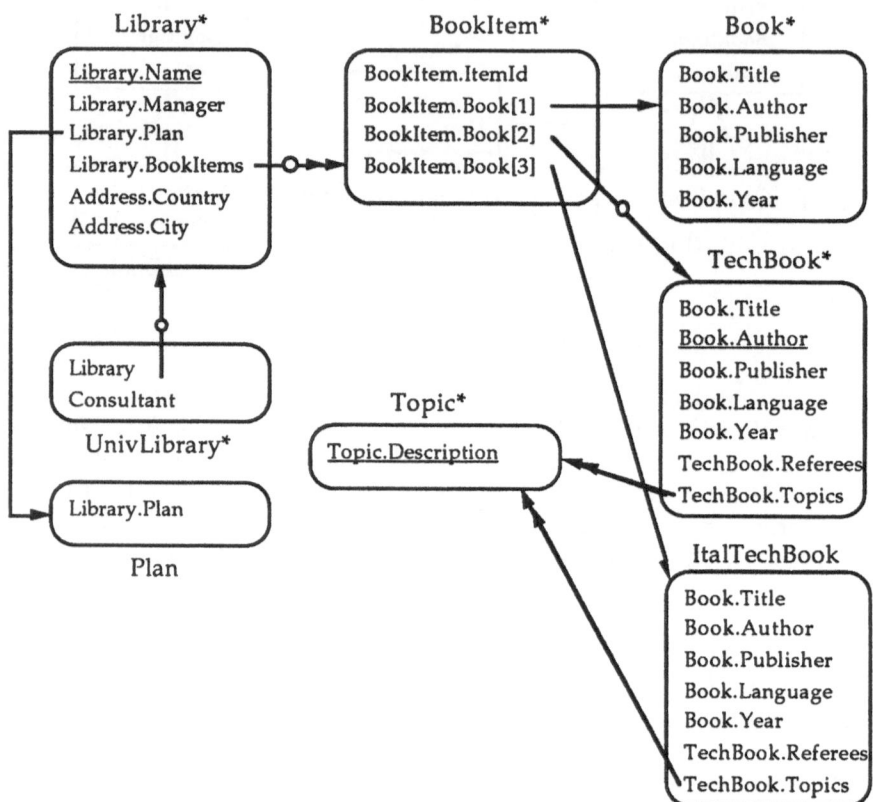

Figure A.2 - Storage schema

Application of Persistent Object Systems 2

Liuba Shrira
Laboratory of Computer Science
Massachusetts Institue of Technology
545 Technology Square
Cambridge MA02139 USA

The last session on Thursday dealt with heterogeneity issues in building large persistent object system applications. Two papers were presented, one by David Blakeman on the inter-application communication mechanism in the Feinman system, the other by Jean-Claude Franchitti on the Amalgalme interoperability toolkit.

The first paper described a type-safe communication mechanism for interconnecting applications that need to share and communicate objects without sharing a common object type system. This addresses a common problem that arises in long lived industrial strength systems. The Feinman communication mechanism is based on the interconnecting applications establishing an identity based type equivalence relation for the shared message types, and type checking at runtime that only messages of the expected type or its subtype are received. When the relationship between the message types can not be captured by simple subtype relationship, the Feinman system provides a mechanism called user-guided transformer, supported by tools, that allow the application integrator to introduce more complex mappings between the message types.

The second paper presented the Amalgame interoperability toolkit that supports integration mechanisms for combining and evolving existing persistent object systems. A designer interacts with the toolkit by submitting scripts written in Amalgame specification language. The two main toolkit components are the Amalgame framework, providing a repository of software components and application schemas, and the Amalgame toolset, providing an extensible set of services that operate on the framework by interpreting the Amalgame scripts. The toolkit was used in a concrete experiment to extend the Chimera hypertext link manager application from originally accessing a single persistent object base to accessing multiple persistent object bases.

Lively discussions followed both presentations and a joint discussion session went into gear when a discrete note from Malcolm was forwarded to Liuba pointing out that there was no joint discussion time planned in the program...

The discussion following David's presentation started out by Malcolm asking to clarify David's statement about large applications being boring, contrary to Malcolm's experience that large applications are the most interesting. Turns out, what David considers as boring is writing the large Cobol applications that he used to handle in the past. Instead of rewriting these Cobol applications anew to accommodate changes in other parts of the system, David prefers to build an infrastructure that allows him to reuse the old code by gluing together old and new application pieces. This is in fact the main motivation for his current work.

Peter Dickman asked what experiments could be used to evaluate the Feinman approach. David suggested that migrating an existing application to a new system and looking at the required modifications would be a good potential stress test for the Feinman framework.

Richard Cooper expressed a doubt, shared also by Malcolm, whether identity based type equivalence is at all practical in a very large system. David suggested that in real world applications shared types are "semantically co-ordinated" so even though there is no common type system, the interconnecting applications have a common model which is used to establish the type equivalence.

Peter Dickman wondered how the unique type names actually be achieved. David answered that uniqueness is obtained by a combination of a context and a unique identity within a context.

Malcolm wondered whether an application composition without a common type system is possible at all. David agreed that indeed it is a very hard problem and therefore the glue (transformers) is necessary.

Liuba questioned the scalability of the Feinman approach that requires pairwise connections and so n square mappings. David answered that in real applications only few types are widely used and shared while the rest are not. Moreover, in practice, one does not interconnect all application to each other which further reduces the total number of required pairwise mappings.

The discussion following the second presentation started out with David Grossman asking Jean-Claude how the Amalgame approach relates to the CORBA effort. Jean-Claude explained that Amalgame supports CORBA OMG object service as one of the communication mechanism. The main focus of Amalgame is to address and explore complex interoperability issues that arise in providing additional OMG-compliant services like persistence, language translation, and activeness modules. Amalgame provides extensions to IDL and programming language bindings for supporting these various services.

Malcolm wanted to know what are the guidelines that an engineer could use in putting components together with the Amalgame toolkit. Jean-Claude explained that Amalgame uses active database technology to guide selection of the candidate components, infer about validity of their interconnections, and supply the partial mappings. This partially automates the process and therefore the engineer would need to resolve the limited amount of heterogeneity issues that cannot be resolved by the underlying rule base.

Peter Dickman was confused and asked for clarification of what is done where is this system. Jean-Claude explained that the main part of the work is done in the Amalgame services within the toolset.

Eliot wondered if the main complexity of the Amalgame approach resides in writing the wrappers. Jean-Claude answered that it all depends on how much of the required wrapper functionality is available initially.

Stephen Blott commented that hiding complexity in the wrappers is a practical approach but it can easily get out of hands and become too complicated. Jean-Claude replied that some of the services allow to generate wrappers automatically instead of writing everything by hand.

At this point, the above mentioned discrete message from Malcolm arrived..

Type-safe Inter-application Communication in the Feynman Persistent Environment

P.D. Blakeman & M.S. Powell
University of Manchester Institute of Science and Technology,
Software Engineering Tools Group,
Sackville Street,
Manchester M60 1QD
United Kingdom

email: db@sna.co.umist.ac.uk

Abstract

An important area of research into industrial strength persistent systems is the need for applications which interact with data produced by other applications in a secure, type-safe way. Traditional solutions to this problem have centred around several approaches including the use of 'standard' formats, 'copy and paste' and file-format conversion. However, these mechanisms are inappropriate for persistent applications which require communication between instances of complex types across applications.

The authors propose an alternative approach based on the use of many small application components (mini-applications), which may be integrated in a type-safe manner. These applications communicate by use of generic message passing, and the use of subtype discrimination on instances of message types to extract details of the message. In addition, the use of first class types and first class messages allows a third party to enhance the information content of default messages by describing the relationships between related message types using transformers.

1 Introduction

From our previous experience of implementing persistent object systems for use in industrial environments, with the Abstract Data Store (ADS) [1, 2, 3, 4, 5, 6], we have identified a number of areas which require solutions in order to make such systems widely useful. One of these is the development of a mechanism to allow applications which operate on intersecting data structures to interact with each other in a secure, type-safe way.

Our experience has shown that the use of persistent programming to construct complex applications has resulted in very large gains in the reliability of application software and also in drastically reduced development times - over an 18 month period just three failures of the ADS persistent environment have been reported on a large multi-user CASE tool which is in full-time concurrent use by approximately 15 analysts, and currently manages in excess of three million objects.

However, along with these benefits come the responsibilities of maintaining and expanding such applications. The success of the work to date has been such that rather than simply demanding small extensions to the existing CASE tool, users are now requesting entirely new tools to interact with it. The existing application is already large, with over 900 object types, each of which has approximately 50-100 methods, and extending it in a conventional fashion will eventually result in an intractable mass of congealed software, mirroring most large, non-persistent systems.

As a consequence, we have evaluated means of enabling an existing persistent application to interact with other persistent applications, without either application needing detailed knowledge of the type structure or internal organisation of the other. Persistent technology enables such interaction, as will become apparent later in the paper. In particular, the authors argue that much of the benefit of a persistent system results from the ability to specify the interaction between general-purpose software components without regard to storage representation or store architecture.

2   Existing Solutions

Traditional (non-persistent) solutions to this problem have centred around several approaches. The first is to provide a number of 'standard' formats (such as text and graphics), and encourage developers to provide facilities to import and export information in these formats. Examples of this approach include copy and paste on windowing systems [7, 8], and UNIX pipes [9]. These approaches have the disadvantage that data is typically only communicated in an unstructured form, and must be parsed by the receiving application to reconstitute its structure. In addition, *copies* of the data are made, resulting in potential integrity problems.

Another approach is to provide 'file format converters' - an application provides converters for file formats of other related applications. Such converters operate only at the file level (making it difficult to import smaller units of data), and again produce *copies* of the data, resulting in problems in maintaining the integrity of that data. In addition, such mechanisms must be regularly upgraded to cope with new versions of the original application, and this requires access to low-level details of the internal representation of the original application's data.

Thirdly, at least one system [10], supports publish and subscribe, allowing data elements created by one application to be shared by others. However, the medium for this sharing is the filing system, and it is not difficult for a user to accidentally corrupt that sharing simply by moving, deleting or renaming files. In addition, this mechanism is very slow, and is not suited to the number and complexity of interactions which we require.

Finally, some recent systems have started to support object messaging. Such approaches typically rely upon a complex message topology (the Apple Event Suite [11] now numbers some 700 events). In conventional systems, types are regarded as a static language issue, and are discarded as soon as an application is compiled. The message topology just described performs the role of a surrogate typing system.

None of the mechanisms described above are appropriate for persistent applications requiring communication between instances of diverse types across applications. The problem appears to be that the *type* of the information to be communicated is not available to both applications, even where some description of type is available, it is unlikely to be able to represent the complexity of data

446

interchange in which we are interested. In a persistent system, however, it can be arranged for types to be available to the execution abstraction of an application.

3 The Feynman System

The aim of the Feynman project at UMIST [12, 13] has been to explore the development of a commercial application support environment based on the use of persistent object technology. The authors believe that persistence both makes available and requires the use of new computing techniques, and that the these are not best exploited simply by grafting persistence into existing computing environments. At the outset of the project it was decided to abandon any dependence on existing operating systems and languages, whilst bearing in mind the important pragmatic necessity of providing a bridge between any new system and its predecessors.

The project has therefore advanced on a broad front considering programming language issues and type domains, the design of the core runtime support facilities, application development and maintenance strategies, and the problems of information storage and distribution. It has been important to ensure at each stage that decisions made about one aspect of the project are consistent with all others. It might seem that the consideration of so many factors at the same time requires vast resources if a useful end result is to be achieved. However, the experience of the relatively small team involved is consistent with the view described by Polya as the "Inventor's Paradox" [14], i.e. that the more ambitious plan may have more chance of success.

A key goal of the Feynman project has been the need to make all components scalable, from small single-user systems through to distributed, multinational systems with potentially many thousands of concurrent users in hundreds of locations. A direct consequence of this goal is that all relationships between types are explicit, and that all type equivalence is through identity equivalence.

The reasons for this decision are important. Consider a simple example: the following two types exist in an application, and *coincidentally* have the same structure:

```
TYPE person    = RECORD
                    name: string;
                    age : integer
                 END;

TYPE wine      = RECORD
                    name: string:
                    age : integer
                 END;
```

Using structural equivalence [15], these two types are treated as equivalent. Thus a potentially dangerous insecurity exists: a wine may be used in any context where a person is expected. A criticism of this argument is that this is unlikely, but in a complex application (such as the CASE tool described above) with nearly 1000 types, the risk of two semantically different types having the same structure is high, and the consequences of a user or developer accidentally updating an object with an inappropriate value (which would not be trapped by a compiler using structural equivalence checking) may be significant. When we consider the number of types required to describe the entire operation of a large organisation (tens of thousands), such unsafe behaviour is an unacceptable risk in the opinion of the authors.

4   Mini-Applications

Within the Feynman system, application assembly is based on the use of many small application components (<u>mini-applications</u>), which may be integrated in a type-safe manner. Each mini application provides a means of directly manipulating instances of a data structure, and provides a user interface to such a data structure. A mini-application may consist of and use many types, but can be regarded as independent, standalone software component. Each mini-application resides in the persistent store, and its communication interface (but not its internal structure) is available to other mini-applications, as shown below:

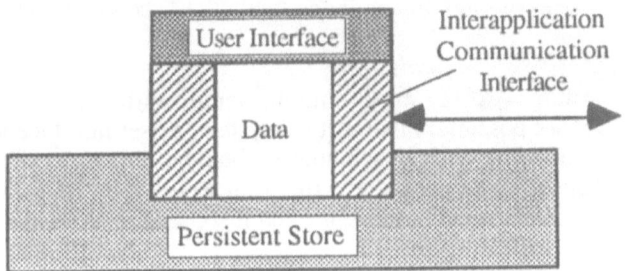

We can partially describe the interface to a mini-application as shown below[1]:

```
TYPE mini_application;
   PROCEDURE message(msg: any_message);
   FUNCTION   understands(msg: any_message): boolean;
   PROCEDURE connect(sink: mini_application);
   ....
END;

TYPE any_message;
END;
```

The `msg` parameter of the `message` and `understands` methods specify the message to be communicated. A `mini_application` for a drawing application and one for a writing application are partially described below:

```
TYPE drawing_application;
   SUPERTYPES mini_application;
   ....
END;

TYPE writing_application;
   SUPERTYPES mini_application;
   ....
END;
```

Notice that both `drawing_application` and `writing_application` inherit the properties of a `mini_application`, including the ability to exchange messages.

---

[1]The syntax used is that of the Feynman Programming Language - specific features of the language will be described as they are encountered.

448

We can now describe a slightly more interesting message used to pass text from one mini_application to another:

```
TYPE text_message(text: string)²;
   SUPERTYPES any_message;
   FUNCTION text_of: string = text;
END;
```

This message has a text string as its parameter. When an instance of the message is created, it must be given a text_string, e.g.

```
VAR m: text_message;
    m:=text_message('Hello Dave')³;
```

As text_message is a subtype of any_message, it can be passed to the message method⁴ of any mini_application.

Every mini_application provides a means of connecting to other mini_applications through the connect method, as shown below:

```
app_1.connect(app_2);
```

This states that app_1 may communicate with app_2, but inverse communication is not possible. In a practical system, a user interface would provide a means of interactively creating such connections, but this is outside of the scope of this paper⁵. Having connected app_1 (the source) to app_2 (the sink), app_1 can determine if app_2 understands a message, and if so, send it, as shown below:

```
IF sink.understands(text_message(s)) THEN
   sink.message(text_message(s));
```

However, this still leaves us the problem of how app_2 is to detect the fact that the message is a text_message rather than simply an any_message. This we do using the subtype discrimination facility of the Feynman Programming Language. The understands and message methods of mini_application are redefined for app_2 as shown below:

```
FUNCTION understands(msg: any_message): boolean;
USE msg AS the_msg IN
  <= text_message: result:=true
END
ELSE result:=false;

PROCEDURE message(msg: any_message);
USE msg AS the_msg IN
  <= text_message: self.paste_text(the_msg.text_of)
END
ELSE self.beep;
```

---

²In the Feynman Programming Language, attributes are not visible outside of the types which own them, hence the need for a function 'text_of' to export the value of the attribute 'text'.

³Instance creation in the Feynman Programming Language is through the use of a type name as a generator, together with values for the type's arguments. Types may also have internal attributes, although none are illustrated here.

⁴'Method' refers to both procedures and functions.

⁵This paper assumes that only one other mini-application may be connected at any time. In practice this restriction does not exist.

These methods both perform a runtime check to see if the type of `msg` is either a `text_message` or a subtype of it. If this is the case, `the_msg` takes the value of `msg`, but takes its type as `text_message`. This means that `the_msg` can have all of the operations provided by `text_message` applied to it. In this case, the method `text_of` does not exist on `any_message`, but does exist on `text_msg`, thus it would be a compile-time error to write `msg.text_of`.

The use of '<=' means that not only can a `text_message` be received, but also any subtype of `text_message`. For example, consider the type `signed_text_message` below:

```
TYPE signed_text_message(author: string) 6;
   SUPERTYPES text_message;
   FUNCTION author_of: string = author;
END;
```

This type could still be passed to the `writing_application`, where it would be treated exactly as a `text_message` (its `author` attribute would be ignored). Thus an application can selectively control the detail it extracts from a message.

5   Resolving Message Incompatibilities

The above approach works well when two applications share message descriptions, and maximises the amount of interaction which can occur between two discrete applications. However, it is frequently necessary to connect apparently diverse applications. For example, it would be of great benefit to a production engineer to connect a design tool, a project planning tool and a spreadsheet in such a way that changes to data in any tool are reflected automatically in each of the others.

As was mentioned above, we expect every `mini_application` to support a number of its own message types. However, we do not wish to impose the constraint that any application must support all message types - this is incompatible with our goal of developing scaleable systems. However, we wish to allow messages to be transformed from one format to another. We can illustrate this as shown below, where M1 and M2 are of different message types, and M1 is transformed into M2, using a *transformer*.

However, M1 and M2 are of different types, and we need a means to convert between these types. The authors take the view that any attempt at automatic type coercion is inherently dangerous and should be avoided at all costs. However, it is not unreasonable to describe a type *transformation* explicitly. Consider that M1 and M2 have the following definitions:

6In the Feynman Programming Language, attributes of subtypes are appended to the attributes of their supertypes. Thus in this case, signed_text_message has two attributes, 'text' and 'author'.

```
TYPE m1(name: string; salary_in_pence: integer);
   SUPERTYPES any_message;
   FUNCTION name_of: string = name;
   FUNCTION salary_of: integer = salary_in_pence;
END;

TYPE m2(name: string; salary_in_pounds: integer; married: boolean);
   SUPERTYPES any_message;
   FUNCTION name_of: string = name;
   FUNCTION salary_of: integer = salary_in_pounds;
   FUNCTION is_married: boolean = married;
END;
```

These types are incompatible, but a coercion seems reasonable. We can now manually construct a type-safe conversion, as shown below:

```
FUNCTION transform_m1_to_m2(input: m1): m2 =
   m2(m1.name_of, m1.salary_of DIV 100, false) 7;
```

Although this mechanism achieves the desired effect, it is extremely tedious when specifying conversions between large numbers of messages, especially when they have large number of components. To alleviate this problem, we can take advantage of the fact that in the Feynman environment, types are first class objects, and they persist with the application's environment, as is described in the next section.

6   User-Guided Transformers

The Feynman type system is based around a type lattice, with the type any as the supertype of all types (including itself), and the type nil as a subtype of all types [16], as shown below:

The type any provides several operations which are applicable to all instances, a partial definition of which is shown below:

7This creates a new instance of m2 with its attributes initialised to the specified arguments.

```
TYPE any;

  FUNCTION type_of: type = ...;

END;
```

The `type_of` function returns the abstract type of the current instance. Having obtained this type, it may then be examined to discover the number and types of each of the attributes of the current instance. This enables the production of simple but powerful tools, such as generic store browsers. However, for our purposes, we can use this information for a tool to assist an application integrator in the creation of a transformer between two message types.

The user commences the creation of a transformer by selecting the source message, and the sink message to which it should be transformed. The transformer then checks that the messages are incompatible (otherwise no work need be performed). Assuming the messages are incompatible, the following dialog is displayed:

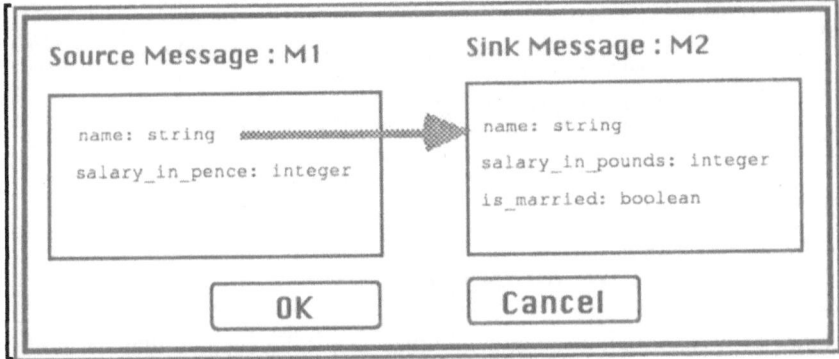

The names and types of each field of both messages are displayed. In addition, when the names and types of two fields in different messages are identical, a default mapping is suggested, as shown by the greyed arrow above. The user is now required to complete the mapping by dragging fields from source to destination. In addition, more complex transformations can be specified by adding Feynman Programming Language expressions to the mapping. For example, the mapping from `salary_in_pence` to `salary_in_pounds` would be specified as shown below:

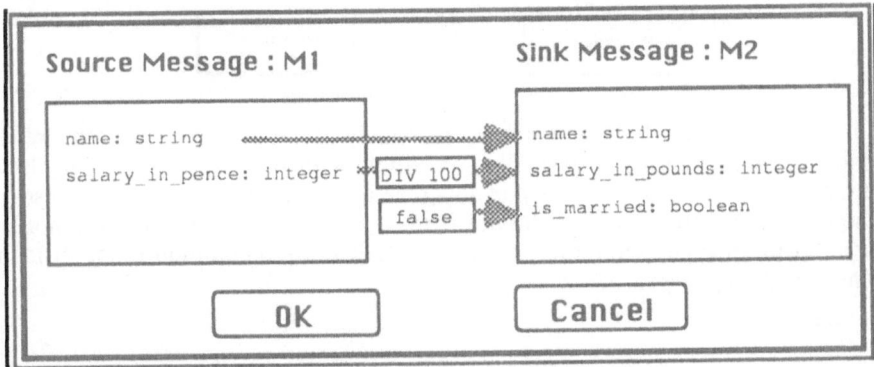

452

This diagram also demonstrates how default initialisation is specified. The `married` field is assigned the constant false. Note that the expressions can be of arbitrary complexity, and may include references to other methods and attributes. When the user clicks 'OK', the dialog is converted into a method `'transform_m1_to_m2'`, and compiled.

The transformer must now be introduced between the two applications which wish to interact. To enable this, we generate a new mini-application, `app1_app2_transformer`, which includes each of the message transformers required. At the same time, we now introduce two new parameters of the `message` method, as shown below:

```
PROCEDURE message(msg: any; source, sink: mini_application);
```

We can now make use of the `source` and `sink` attributes of the `message` method to create a two-way transformer mini-application, as shown below:

```
TYPE app_1_app_2_transformer;

  SUPERTYPES mini_application;

  PROCEDURE message(msg: any; source, sink: mini_application);
  USE source AS source_kind IN
    app_1: ...;
    app_2: USE msg AS the_msg IN
            <= m1: sink.message(self.transform_m1_to_m2(the_msg))
          END;
  END;

END;
```

8   Lowest Common Supertype

In a more complex situation, a message type hierarchy such as that shown below may occur:

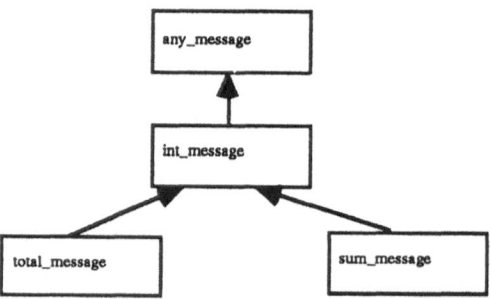

In this case, rather than generating a completely new transformer, we can already deduce that total_message is partially compatible with sum_message, as they have common supertypes, int_message and any_message. The most compatible message is the lowest common supertype (in this case int_message), and this is an important characteristic of type hierarchies in general. Therefore a common function lcs is defined on the type *type*:

```
TYPE type;
```

```
FUNCTION lcs(other_type: type): type = ...;
....
END;
```

When using User-Guided Transformers such as those described above, we can firstly determine the lowest common supertype of two messages by the following:

```
common:=m1.type_of.lcs(m2.type_of)
```

This information can then be used to produce an automatic translation for the common parts of the two messages, allowing the user to concentrate on specifying mappings for the non-common parts of those messages.

9 Current Status and Future Work

The Feynman project has been developed using a rapid-prototyping approach. The language, runtime environment and store have evolved over the last two years, and have continually been enhanced in response to ongoing use both by students and professionals. A wide variety of applications have been written including: structure editors, compilers, CASE tools, graphics applications and telematics applications. The interapplication communication work described in this paper exists in a prototype state, and has been used to construct simple interacting applications, such as spreadsheets and project management tools.

It is envisaged that as software components become more specialised, the task of integrating them will become more complex, hence the need for User-Guided Transformers. In addition, it is likely that a mechanism similar to this will be of use in general data migration, and for specifying type coercions in general.

We believe that this approach to inter-application communication has emerged as a consequence of the fact that we have control over the entire Feynman Environment, including its language, store and runtime environment.

10 Acknowledgements

The authors wish to acknowledge the support of AT&T ISTEL and particularly the feedback on ADS use from John Alexander and Jon Twigge. Thanks are also due to the intrepid band of Feynman users who have put up with having to rewrite their applications every time the authors decided to change the language. In particular, we would like to thank Pete Ross and Jon Twigge for their patience while we endeavoured to implement their suggestions.

454

11 References

1. Hughes J.W. and Powell M.S., A Strongly-Typed Distributed Virtual Memory. In: Proceedings of the SERC Distributed Systems Conference, ed. Duce, D.A. Peter Perigrinus, 1984.
2. Powell, M.S., Adding Programming Facilities to an Abstract Data Store. In: Proceedings of the First International Conference on Persistent Object Systems, Appin, Scotland, 1985.
3. Powell, M.S., Strongly Typed User Interfaces in an Abstract Data Store, Software Practice and Experience, Vol 17, pp 241-266, April 1987.
4. Powell M.S., A Modular Persistent Store. In: Implementing Persistent Object Bases, ed. Dearle, A, Shaw, G., Zdonik, S. Morgan Kaufmann, 1990.
5. Blakeman, P.D., Version and Variant Control for a Commercial Application of Persistence. In: Implementing Persistent Object Bases, ed. Dearle, A, Shaw, G., Zdonik, S.Morgan Kaufmann 1990.
6. Alexander, J. and Hicks, K., ISTEL Applications Architecture. In: CASE: Current Practice, Future Prospects, John Wiley, 1992.
7. Apple Computer, Inside Macintosh, Volume 1, Addison Wesley, 1985.
8. Microsoft Corp., Windows Application Development Guidelines, Microsoft Press, 1989.
9. Haviland and B. Salama, UNIX System Programming ,1987, Addison Wesley.
10. Apple Computer, Inside Macintosh Volume VI, 1992, Addison Wesley.
11. Apple Computer, The Apple Event Suite, Apple Developer's Documentation, 1992.
12. Blakeman P.D. and Powell, M.S., The Feynman Persistent Application Support Environment. Submitted for publication in Sixth Persistent Object Systems Conference, May 1994.
13. Blakeman P.D. and Powell. M.S., The Feynman Language Manual, UMIST Software Engineering Tools Group Internal Report, January 1994.
14. Polya, G. 'How to Solve It', Second Edition, Princeton University Press, 1971.
15. Connor, R., Brown, A., Cutts, Q., Dearle A., Morrison R and Rosenberg J., Type Equivalence Checking in Persistent Object Systems. In: Implementing Persistent Object Bases, ed. Dearle, A, Shaw, G., Zdonik, S.Morgan Kaufmann 1990.
15. Albano, A., Bergamini, R., Ghelli, G., Rosini, R. An Introduction to the Database Programming Language Fibonacci. FIDE Technical Report FIDE/93/94 of Esprit BRA Project 6309, 1993

A Toolkit to Support Scalable Persistent Object Base Infrastructures[*]

Jean-Claude Franchitti, Roger King, and Omar Boucelma[†]

Department of Computer Science

University of Colorado at Boulder

Campus Box 430

Boulder, Colorado 80309-430

e-mail:{franchit,roger,omar}@cs.colorado.edu

Abstract

Supporting a wide range of persistent applications imposes challenging requirements on the implementation of Persistent Object Bases (POBs). This explains the recent proliferation of POBs, each of them focusing on particular application domains. To fulfill the needs of a variety of persistent applications while leveraging off existing POBs, we are using an extensible interoperability toolkit. Our toolkit supports integration mechanisms for enriching and evolving combinations of pre-existing POBs. In this paper, we explain our approach, describe our toolkit, and illustrate how it is used to support scalable POBs.

---

[*]This material is based on work sponsored by the Advanced Research Projects Agency under Grant Numbers MDA972-91-J-1012 and N00014-92-J-1862, and by the Office of Naval Research under Grant Number N00014-92-J-1917. The content of the information does not necessarily reflect the position or the policy of the U.S. Government, and no official endorsement should be inferred.

[†]On leave from Université de Provence, France

1 Introduction

An increasing variety of application domains impose new requirements on POB technology. As an example, CAD systems, CASE tools, Software Development Environments, etc., require special data structures such as graphs [TC93]. This explains the recent proliferation of POBs which attempt to support a variety of application domains. Some POB systems and projects focus on specific domains. Some other projects investigate "scalable" architectures to encompass various domains. For instance, the TI Open OODB system [WTB92] suggests an *open, seamlessly* extensible POB architecture. The Brown Object Store System [ZL92] targets distributed POB issues. The SHORE project [CWF+94] focuses on high-performance and scalable POBs. Some other researchers are also exploring new foundations for scalable POBs architectures [ASM93, Atk92].

We believe that the needs of a variety of persistent applications can sometimes be satisfied by extending or combining existing POBs. It is clear that this proposed methodology introduces serious interoperability problems at various levels and granularities of semantics. However, with the emergence of new interoperability standards [Cat93, OMG91], it is opportune to perform experiments to validate this methodology.

To support our proposed approach, we are using a general purpose interoperability toolkit called *Amalgame*[1] [FK93]. We have been using Amalgame in the context of several large experiments involving tools developed by ARPA POB [Wie92] and Arcadia[2] [TBC+92] researchers. In these experiments, we explored the incremental integration of heterogeneous database applications. These applications are software systems which are pieced together from existing database application components. The Amalgame toolkit provides extensible support modules to assist the integration of various database systems. In particular, communication, programming language integration, persistence, and transaction support modules are built into the Amalgame extensible library.

In this paper, we first describe the Amalgame toolkit. We then show, in a concrete experiment, how Amalgame's integration mechanisms are used for enriching and evolving combinations of pre-existing POBs. The experiment illustrates the construction of a multidatabase layer for the Chimera[3] hypertext link manager [AT93]. Chimera was originally implemented on top of a single POB, and did not support the storage of objects manipulated by Chimera client applications. These applications usually have their own separate POBs. To limit our current research scope, we adopted the multidatabase paradigm for combining multiple POBs. The goal of our multidatabase layer is to reconcile the various POBs involved in a Chimera application.

The remainder of this paper is organized as follows. In the next section we give an overview of Amalgame. Section 3 describes the Chimera experiment in two steps. The first step instantiates the multidatabase platform core component. The second step extends the core component to accommodate new requirements. Section 4 gives concluding remarks.

---

[1] We are using the French spelling for the equivalent English word "amalgam"

[2] Arcadia is a collaborative software engineering research programs encompassing groups at several universities

[3] This system was developed by Arcadia researchers at University of California at Irvine.

2 An Overview of Amalgame

In this section, we give a brief overview of the Amalgame toolkit. We describe the toolkit from a designer's point of view, and outline its internal architecture.

2.1 The Designer's View

Amalgame provides a toolkit to assist the construction of heterogeneous database or multidatabase applications. These applications are built from software components which are pieced together from (all or parts of) one or many pre-existing application programs. The toolkit consists of two main components, the Amalgame framework, and the Amalgame toolset. The toolset provides an extensible set of services to operate on the framework. The Amalgame designer interacts with the toolkit by submitting scripts written in the Amalgame Specification Language (ASL). The ASL is an extension of the Eiffel language. Some of the ASL constructs are used to define, refine, test, and assemble framework components. Other ASL constructs help manipulate the Amalgame basic and extended functionality. In section 3, we illustrate the use of the ASL in building a multidatabase layer.

Figure 1 illustrates the various components of the Amalgame toolkit. In this figure, the Amalgame framework acts as a "repository" for various software components and application schemas managed by Amalgame. To manipulate software components, Amalgame uses surrogates encapsulated into classes of the Eiffel object-oriented programming environment [Mey90]. The relationships among components of new or pre-existing programs are captured into Amalgame application schemas. Amalgame currently supports the encapsulation of components written in C, C++, Ada, and Eiffel. The Amalgame toolset provides an extended set of tools to operate on the Amalgame framework.

The basic toolset functionality includes an ASL processor, a browser, a run-time generator, and an execution driver. The toolset language processor performs lexical analysis and parsing of ASL scripts. The browser allows designers to peruse, edit and query existing framework objects. The run-time generator packages framework components specified in heterogeneous application schemas. The execution driver is used to spawn, control and terminate the execution of resulting heterogeneous programs.

The Amalgame extended toolset provides surrogates to interact with various integration toolkits such as *Findit* [BKZ91], *Panorama* [ZKB91], and *A la carte* [DKB90]. *Findit* documents, organizes, and helps users locate underlying application components on wide area networks. *Panorama* supports the evaluation of reusable object queries. *A la carte* supports heterogeneous transaction protocols. The Amalgame extended toolset also provides the following services: a user interface design subsystem, programmatic and menu-based interfaces to the Amalgame language processor, and a set of modules to support data translation, communication, persistence, and transaction management.

2.2 The Internal Architecture

To use our toolkit, a designer must be aware of the Amalgame concept of *environment*. He must also understand how to efficiently use and define Amalgame

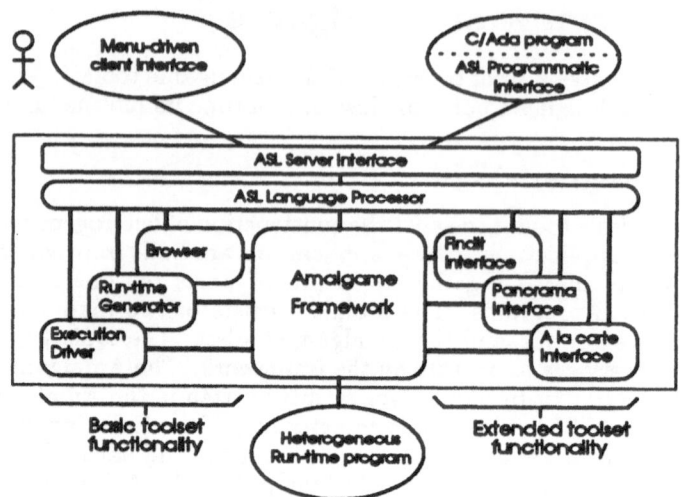

Figure 1: The Various Components of the Amalgame Toolkit

services. In this section, we define the various types of Amalgame environments and services. We also explain how they are manipulated by the Amalgame engine to support interoperability.

The Various Types of Amalgame Environments

Amalgame environments are (object-oriented) classes which act as containers for application components and services. Amalgame environments are either homogeneous, or heterogeneous.

Homogeneous environments are defined at encapsulation time. These environments are populated with an initial set of surrogates which encapsulates selected semantics of pre-existing applications. As described in the previous section, Amalgame supports the encapsulation of software components written in various programming languages. In Amalgame terminology, the various programming languages involved are referred to as Underlying Specification Languages (USLs). Services supported in the extensible toolset are usually required to properly encapsulate software components in the Amalgame framework. Features provided by these services are used to specify mapping components which link surrogates to pre-existing applications. Amalgame designers may specify mapping components in any USL supported by Amalgame, as long as a binding to the required services is provided for that particular USL.

An Amalgame heterogeneous environment groups components supplied by at least two different homogeneous or heterogeneous environments. It also contains the specification of an application schema, and necessary information to build a corresponding run-time heterogeneous program. To build heterogeneous environments, designers can reuse existing components. They may decide to adapt these components so that they can be used in different contexts, each context corresponding to a particular heterogeneous environment. These component mutations are implemented as context-based wrappers, also called modifier components in Amalgame terminology.

The Various Types of Amalgame Services

Services are another class of software objects which can be created or manipulated by Amalgame designers. Service components can be either passive or programmable. Passive services are directly accessible from USLs through associated Amalgame components (referred to as passive extension connectors). To illustrate the use of passive services, let us consider the object translation and communication mechanisms supplied by Q [May90], one of the interoperability tool supported by Amalgame. Using specific communication and translation extensions, Q features can be accessed directly from Amalgame components specified in the Eiffel, C or Ada USLs. In order to use Q within an Amalgame component written in an unsupported USL, a mapping from that USL to one of the above mentioned languages would need to be specified and encapsulated within Amalgame. This mapping would be implemented as an additional passive extension component which would be required by the unsupported USL to properly access Q.

Programmable services are created and manipulated in a different way. When adding a programmable service module, designers are required to register an associated Amalgame component (referred to as an active extension connector) which is used to process any Amalgame component based on this service. Examples of programmable services are USLs such as C, Ada or MIF languages [BPP+91]. If a component has been encapsulated using C as a USL, Amalgame will compile it at packaging time according to the process defined in the associated active extension component.

The Amalgame Runtime Support for Interoperability

In a nutshell, Amalgame users can validate, store, and enact heterogeneous programs by assembling components from various environments. To support seamless integration, the Amalgame runtime system is built on top of an active database engine. The active database engine supports rules, hypothetical states, selectable execution models, and conventional database amenities such as transaction management and concurrency control. Application components are stored and managed by the active database engine. Each state of the underlying database models an homogeneous or heterogeneous environment. Modifier components are defined and stored as (transformation) rules in the underlying active database framework. When a component is accessed, rules are triggered to adapt its structure and/or behavior to the corresponding environment context.

The above described architecture helps define, and keep track of valid heterogeneous components interconnections. Using hypothetical states, modifier search and pruning techniques implemented on top of various rule execution models, it is also possible to imply, derive, and reason about new heterogeneous environments on top of an existing application component database.

To illustrate how the Amalgame active database framework handles semantic heterogeneity, let us consider a simple example of type inference. Let us assume that transformation rules tr1, and tr2 are (triggered and) applied to the signature of method ma(a1:t1, a2:t2) of component A when ma is invoked by component B in an heterogeneous environment H. In other words, parameters a1 (of type t1), and a2 (of type t2) are respectively "transformed" via tr1, and tr2 before they are passed to ma. For example, it may be that B is passing an array of integers as parameter a1, while the type of a1 expected by ma is a linked list. In this case, tr1 would implement a mapping between the array and the linked list. Let us now assume that an Amalgame user is exploring the feasibility of semantic interoperability between component B and component D in an "hypothetical" heterogeneous environment H'. In H', component B invokes method md(a2:t2, a3:t3, a1:t1) of component D (in the place of method ma of component A). Using its rule base the Amalgame engine infers that tr1, and tr2 are a viable subset of transformation rules. Amalgame also suggests an order for executing these rules which matches the order of md's parameters. In this particular example, unless further information can be derived from the rule base, the user is prompted (to prevent a type mismatch) for an additional transformation rule to handle the remaining parameter a3.

We are currently investigating the use of the H2O active database system to support component activeness in Amalgame. H2O is being developed at University of Colorado at Boulder as part of the I3 ARPA research project. Part of the modifications to the existing Amalgame prototype will consist in rehosting the ASL on top of the Active Object Query Language (AOQL) being developed for H2O.

3 An Amalgame Generated Multidatabase Layer for Chimera

In this section, we illustrate the use of Amalgame as a multidatabase system generator. Our goal is twofold: show a practical use of the Amalgame features which can assist multidatabase application designers, and illustrate the flexibility of Amalgame generated multidatabase layers. In particular, we show how Amalgame generated multidatabase systems can accommodate changes to underlying databases, such as the addition of new features, without affecting the interoperation of the various underlying systems.

To illustrate the multidatabase support features of the Amalgame system, we show how Amalgame can be used to quickly prototype a tailorable multidatabase layer for the Chimera hypertext link manager.

3.1 Building the Core Component of the Chimera Multidatabase Layer

As described in the introduction, Chimera imposes challenging requirements on its underlying multidatabase support. Indeed, from a software engineering standpoint, the ideal database support system should be extensible. It cannot be a black box which offers no control over complex underlying database functionality. Basically, software engineers would like to extend and program underlying facilities and still expect high performance in their resulting systems.

To achieve this goal in the scope of our Chimera experiment, we tailor a database support layer to replace the persistence solution initially used by Chimera. To build this support layer, we use the Amalgame persistence module to generate Persistent Abstract Machines (PAMs) with encapsulated interfaces. This technology provides a flexible tool for implementing persistence solutions tailored to various existing applications.

The Amalgame persistence module currently supports interfaces to the Exodus storage manager [CDF+86], the TI Open OODB, the Mneme storage manager [MH89], and the Unix filesystem. The module can be extended to support additional persistent stores. In particular, the module is language independent and is not biased toward any particular persistence model. As shown in the example described in section 2.2, the Amalgame rule base can be used to (semi-) automate the addition of other persistent stores in the Amalgame module. We could also extend the module to include such active capabilities in its runtime. To this extent, Amalgame helps support seamless heterogeneous database federations.

The selection of one or more underlying database system(s) can be performed directly from the application component source code using generic language constructs provided by Amalgame to control the persistence module. The persistence module can also be controlled directly using the set_pob_name and set_pob_type methods of the Amalgame class ENVIRONMENT as illustrated in Figure 5. As a result multiple underlying databases can coexist in one Amalgame generated system. In our current implementation, it is possible for various underlying databases to have redundant data across them. Amalgame does select a default database system if none have been selected by application designers. In its current implementation, the persistence module does not keep multiple databases up to date with respect to each other. We are currently investigating extensions which will enable heterogeneous constraints support across various underlying databases. This functionality will rely on support provided by the Heraclitus active database system [GHJ92].

In the current implementation of the Amalgame persistence module, we rely on the user for selecting the underlying target database(s). However, additional semantics could be added to the module to automate the choice of underlying stores based, for example, on rules associated to the type of data being stored. Our implementation choice is clearly a compromise between supporting full seamless heterogeneous federations and providing the multidatabase module user with some control of the underlying functionality.

PAMs generated by Amalgame support *persistence independence* and *persistence orthogonality*, and overall management of persistence in terms of duration and sharing alternatives of persistent entities. The heterogeneous global transaction model currently supported uses a two-phase commit protocol, and allows references to multiple stores within a single transaction. The homogeneous local transaction protocols rely on the mechanisms provided by the various underlying stores. We are currently investigating extensions to support heterogeneous nested transactions. Other possible future enhancements include support for distributed heterogeneous transactions, and coordinated crash recovery.

Since Chimera already supports persistence via an interface to the Mneme storage manager, our intent is to generate a flexible replacement to the existing solution. In particular, our layer provides the added benefit of supporting a selectable set of underlying POBs. Figure 2 below illustrates the proposed modifications to the existing Chimera Mneme-based persistence layer. In this figure, we use dashes to outline the suggested interface components. To implement the proposed solution, we use Amalgame and its persistence module to generate a PAM and an Amalgame generated server which emulates the interface of the existing Mneme-based interface. It is clear from the proposed architecture that the Amalgame generated persistence layer provides powerful multidatabase capabilities.

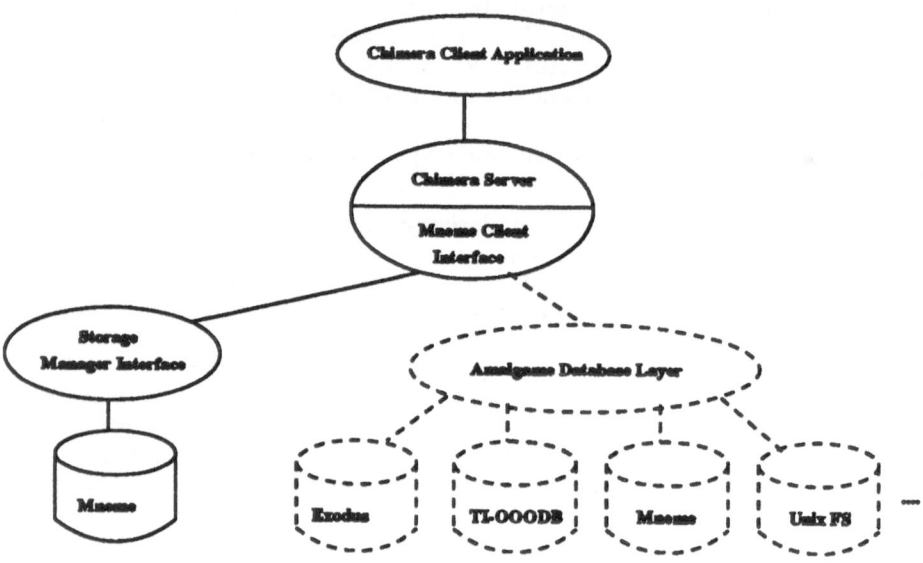

Figure 2: Towards a Scalable Persistence Layer for Chimera

Specifying the proposed PAM interface using Amalgame is straightforward. Indeed, we simply use the Chimera low-level persistence interface to Mneme and create a corresponding Amalgame component which encapsulates the existing interface. The PAM interface is specified using the ASL. We first define an Amalgame environment which acts as a container for the PAM encapsulated component. The corresponding ASL script portion is shown in Figure 3.

The next step is to specify an Amalgame component which contains the PAM encapsulated interface. The corresponding ASL script portion is illustrated in Figure 4.

Figure 5 illustrates the encapsulation of the read_value_object function defined in the original Chimera interface. We use Eiffel to code the PAM interface encapsulation.

Low-levels Eiffel libraries are provided by Amalgame to interface the various passive services required to support our application. Figure 5 illustrates the use of Amalgame services in the context of our Chimera experiment. In particular, we use the Amalgame Q service to generate a serverized component. Also,

```
-- Create a new Amalgame environment for the Chimera components
-- Specify remote environment name
   Attach Environment   CHIMERA_ENVIRONMENT
-- Specify remote environment specifics
   With                 "UNAME:SunOS-4.1.2","USL:Eiffel"
-- Specify Amalgame environment name
   To                   A_CHIMERA
```

Figure 3: Creating an Amalgame Environment

```
-- Specify an encapsulated Amalgame component which will communicate
-- with the remote Chimera application to support read object requests
-- given the persistent id of an object and the persistent id of
-- the persistent collection where it is stored.  The Amalgame
-- interface implements the Mneme interface to Chimera using Amalgame
-- persistent collections of objects stored in TIOOODB.
   Encapsulate From   CHIMERA_ENVIRONMENT
-- Specify as Amalgame sub-component type
   Type Is            "SUBCOMPONENT"
-- Specify Amalgame environment name
   In                 · A_CHIMERA
-- Specify Amalgame component name
   As                 LIBRARY.READ_VALUE_OBJECT
```

Figure 4: Defining an Amalgame Encapsulated Component

in our example we use TI Open OODB for physical storage and concurrency control.

Finally, Figure 5 illustrates various support methods for implementing the server component instantiation (create method) and the server main processing loop (execute method). To use our Amalgame generated persistence server, Chimera storage manager requests are sent to the PAM server instead of the Mneme interface server. Storage requests are interpreted by our encapsulated PAM interface and directed to TI Open OODB.

```
-- Specify PAM interface component using Eiffel as a USL
   With Specification |->
-- USL specification for encapsulated component starts
         inherit
-- We use the Amalgame Q module to implement this server
         APC_Q_SERVER, ADR_Q
         define
-- Since the inherited APC_RPC_SERVER class defers the implementation of
-- the execute method, execute needs to be tailored to the requirements
-- of our server
         execute
           feature
-- The Amalgame ENVIRONMENT class provides a seamless interface to
-- multiple POBs.
             env:  POB_ENV;  -- Underlying POB interface object
         Create is
         do
-- Setup underlying POB and initialize Q server
             env.set_pob_name("TIOOODB"); -- Name store
             server.initialize;
         end; (...)
-- The read_value_object function requests an object value given the
-- persistent object id and the persistent id of the collection where
-- it is stored
    read_value_object(Process_Id:  INTEGER,
                       Transaction_Id:  TRANSACTION_ID_TYPE,
                       PCollection_Id:  COLLECTION_ID_TYPE,
                       PValue_Id:  VALUE_ID_TYPE,
                       result_buffer:  STRING) is
         do
             env.set_pob_type(pob);   -- Select proper store
             env.open(PCollection_Id);   (...)
             result_buffer:= env.retrieve(Pvalue_Id); (...)
             env.close;
         end; -- read_value_object (...)
-- The execute method is called from the generic low-level server
-- component generated by Amalgame.The execute method decodes the
-- result_buffer and returns either an error, or an array of bytes
-- corresponding to the requested object value and an integer
-- corresponding to the value length.
         execute is
         local(...)
             result_buffer:  STRING;
         do  (...)
         end;      -- execute
<-|       -- end of USL specification for Encapsulate construct
```

Figure 5: Specifying an Amalgame Encapsulation

The approach suggested in this experiment has various benefits. First, the use of the Amalgame persistence module reduces implementation costs. Second, the approach provides a seamless interface to a selectable set of underlying POBs. Finally, the approach allows other languages or applications to reuse and possibly customize the Amalgame generated persistence layer. Note that our experiment does not illustrate the control of persistence from within the application language itself. This issue is covered in [FKB94]. It became clear from this experiment that our persistence module should provide active capabilities in its runtime. With such support, new persistent stores could be added seamlessly, and full module tunability could be achieved without having to regenerate the applications built on top of our persistent module.

In the next section, we show the Amalgame generated multidatabase layer can accommodate changes to its underlying databases resulting from the addition of new features. In particular, we show how such modifications can be performed without affecting the interoperation of the various underlying POBs.

3.2   Extending the Chimera Multidatabase Layer

In the previous section, we described the various steps required to generate a multidatabase layer for Chimera. The proposed layer was targeted initially to a single Chimera server. However, for scalability and performance reasons, it may become necessary to run multiple concurrent Chimera server instances. For example, in a distributed architecture where large numbers of clients are located on different physical machines, it may be more efficient to have one Chimera server per site. In this case, our Amalgame generated multidatabase layer will be exposed to concurrent requests from the various Chimera servers. Unfortunately, in our initial design, we relied on an implementation of Mneme which does not support transaction management or concurrency control. Also, the Chimera server itself does not use transactions.

To address the above mentioned problems, we show how Amalgame can be used to extend the previously generated multidatabase layer. In particular, we show how the independently developed underlying object stores which compose our multidatabase may inter-operate while continuing to evolve independently. To illustrate this claim, we use Amalgame services to add concurrency control and transaction management support to the underlying Mneme storage manager. We also modify our multidatabase layer to support heterogeneous and local transaction management so that multiple Chimera servers can operate concurrently on top of our multidatabase. The various modifications provide a solution to our problem, without requiring any changes to the Chimera server application code.

As mentioned in earlier sections, Amalgame provides a transaction module which can be used in combination with the Amalgame persistence module to specify heterogeneous global and autonomous local transaction models. The Amalgame transaction module provides a programmable interface to the A la carte toolkit. This interface allows the specification of various assemblies of A la carte encapsulated components implementing concurrency control, transaction, and recovery management algorithms. A la carte is used to detect incompatibilities between the various classes of algorithms involved in a suggested configuration. A la carte also generates autonomous and heterogeneous managers for the suggested (valid) configurations. The homogeneous and heterogeneous runtime managers which are produced by A la carte correspond to Abstract Transaction Machines (ATMs). These ATMs can be combined with the various components of the persistence module to generate multidatabase layers which support global management of transaction over a set of local databases.

In its current state, our programmable interface to A la carte allows incremental support of global and local transaction models as new autonomous database systems are added to our layer. To add the necessary support to our Chimera multidatabase layer, we modify the Amalgame scripts which specify the various components included in our multidatabase layer. As part of the modified script, we request that the A la carte service generates a local transaction manager to operate on top of the Mneme storage manager. We also specify the use of a heterogeneous transaction manager to control concurrent transactions directed to the Mneme storage manager (augmented with local transaction support), and TI Open OODB. Since TI Open OODB already supports transaction management, we simply connect our heterogeneous transaction manager component to use TI Open OODB's existing programmatic interface. The various modifications for adding transaction support to our Chimera multidatabase layer are illustrated in Figure 6.

```
-- The A la carte service generates autonomous/heterogeneous managers
    inherit A_LA_CARTE_TAM_GENERATOR
    Create is
    do
-- We instantiate an A la carte (default) autonomous manager for Mneme
        Mneme_Tam := Autonomous_Manager.Create;
-- An A la carte (default) heterogeneous manager is used for our layer
        Chimera_Tam := Heterogeneous_Manager.Create;
    end;
-- We redefine the various methods of our Chimera heterogeneous manager
    env:  POB_ENV;
    Begin is
    do
        if env.is_pob_name("MNEME") then
-- We access the Mneme autonomous TAM generated by A la carte
            Mneme_Tam.Begin
        elseif env.is_pob_name("TI_OOODB") then
-- Our Chimera layer provides a surrogate component "Ti_ooodb"
-- to access the features of the underlying TI system.
            Ti_ooodb.Begin (...)
    end
    end;
```

Figure 6: Adding Transaction Support to the Chimera Persistence Layer

As another important modification, we convert our original single threaded multidatabase server to a multi-threaded server which can handle requests from multiple Chimera servers. This modification is handled very simply by modifying the ASL script which controls the Amalgame communication module in the original specification of the Chimera multidatabase layer. The corresponding changes are illustrated in Figure 7.

```
-- The following line is commented out in the script shown in Figure 5
   -- APC_Q_SERVER, ADR_Q
-- We now use the Q communication module multi-threaded server component
   APC_Q_MULTI_SERVER, ADR_Q
```

Figure 7: Multi-threaded Server Support for the Chimera Layer

Finally, since we do not want to modify the Chimera server source code, we use the various input sockets of our modified multidatabase to identify requests incoming from the various Chimera servers. We wrap each request with Begin and End transaction statements, and add the necessary support for transaction management in our multidatabase layer.

As a result, we can see that moving from the original version of our Amalgame multidatabase layer to the new version, requires modifications to the Amalgame scripts specifying the layer. Once regenerated, the layer behaves as expected. Our experiment does require a shutdown of the multidatabase layer while moving from one version to another. However, we are currently looking into automating the regeneration process. Our automated regeneration scheme will monitor confirmed changes to the Amalgame scripts implementing the layer. It will then complete any ongoing transactions, save the current multidatabase layer state and regenerate the layer automatically. Proper support of this scheme may require minimal changes in the clients to support a standby mode in order to avoid client timeouts resulting from extended communication delays while the multidatabase layer is in its unactive "regeneration" mode.

An alternative to this "regeneration" scheme would be to include Amalgame-like active database capabilities in our multidatabase module runtime. In this approach, the module could use a rule base in most cases to (semi-automatically) tune itself at runtime without requiring regeneration. However, generated applications based on such an active module would have a higher footprint and may not be as efficient. For this reason, we will certainly end up using an active version of our multidatabase module to help prototype persistent applications. We will then use the automated "regeneration" process to create a final (optimized) version based on a non-active multidatabase module.

4   Conclusion

As part of the experiment described in this paper, promising results were obtained while experimenting with Amalgame for composing multidatabase applications. However, open problems still remain in the areas of semantic hetero-geneity, type systems, and execution model interoperability. In addition, the emergence of interoperability (candidates) standards requires more experimen-tation. Consequently, the support of a scalable POB infrastructure needs fur-ther improvement. For instance, change propagation and heterogeneous nested transaction models are topics that deserve more attention. Our future research will focus on these topics.

References

[ASM93] M. P. Atkinson, D. I. K Sjoberg, and R. Morrison. Managing change in persistent object systems. In *Proceedings of the First JSSST In-ternational Symposium on Object Technologies for Advanced Soft-ware, LNCS 742*, pages 315–338, Kanazawa, Japan, November, 4–6 1993. Springer-Verlag.

[AT93] K. Anderson and R. N. Taylor. Hypertext for Software Environ-ments: Heterogeneous Databases, Presentation-Specific Anchors, and Composable Links. Technical report, Department of Com-puter Science, University of California, California, Irvine, 92717-3425, 1993.

[Atk92] M. P. Atkinson. Persistent foundations for scalable multi-paradigmal systems. In *Proceedings of the International Workshop on DOM*, Edmonton, Canada, 1992. Morgan Kaufmann Publishers, Inc.

[BKZ91] A. Bouguettaya, R. King, and K. Zhao. FINDIT: A Server Based Approach to Finding Information in Large Scale Heterogeneous Databases. In *First International Workshop on Interoperability in Multidatabase Systems, Kyoto, Japan*, pages 191–194, April 7–9 1991.

[BPP+91] R. Balzer, D. E. Perry, J. Purtilo, R. T. Snodgrass, A. L. Wolf, and J. Ward. Technical notes 1–9, September 1990–November 1991. Technical report, DARPA Module Interconnection Formalism Working Group, 1991.

[Cat93] R.G.G. Cattell. *The Object Database Standard: ODMG-93*. Morgan Kaufmann, 1993.

[CDF+86] M. J. Carey, D. J. DeWitt, D. Frank, G. Graefe, M. Muralikr-ishna, J. E. Richardson, and E. J. Shekita. The Architecture of the EXODUS Extensible DBMS. In *International Workshop on Object-Oriented Database Systems*, pages 52–65, 1986.

[CWF+94] M. Carey, D. J. De Witt, M. Franklin, N. Hall, M. McAuliffe J. F. Naughton, and al. Shoring Up Persistent Applications. In *Proceed-ings of the ACM SIGMOD Conference*, Minneapolis, May, 24–27 1994. ACM.

[DKB90]   P. Drew, R. King, and J. Bein.   A la carte: An Extensible Framework for the Tailorable Construction of Heterogeneous Object Stores. In *Implementing Persistent Object Bases: Principles and Practice, The Fourth International Workshop on Persistent Object Systems*. Morgan Kaufmann Publishers, Inc., 1990.

[FK93]   J. C. Franchitti and R. King. A Language for Composing Heterogeneous, Persistent Applications. In *Proceedings of the Workshop on Interoperability of Database Systems and Database Applications*, Fribourg, Switzerland, October 13-14 1993. Springer-Verlag, LNCS.

[FKB94]   J. C. Franchitti, R. King, and O. Boucelma. An Extensible Toolkit for Composing Multidatabase Applications. Research report, University of Colorado, Boulder, Department of Computer Science, Campus Box 430, Boulder, CO 80309, 1994. Submitted to publication.

[GHJ92]   S. Ghandeharizadeh, R. Hull, and D. Jacobs. Implementation of Delayed Updates in Heraclitus. In *Proc. of Intl. Conf. on Extending Data Base Technology*, 1992.

[May90]   M. Maybee. Q: A Multi-lingual Interprocess Communications System. Reference Manual. Technical report, University of Colorado, Department of Computer Science, Campus Box 430, University of Colorado, Boulder, CO 80309–0430, 1990.

[Mey90]   B. Meyer. An Eiffel Collection. Technical Report TR–EI–20/EC, ISE, 270 Storke Road, Suite 7, Goleta CA 93117, U.S.A, November 1990.

[MH89]   J. Eliot B. Moss and Tony Hosking. *Managing Persistent Data With Mneme: User's Guide to the Client Interface*. University of Massachusetts, Object Oriented Systems Laboratory, Department of Computer and Information Science, University of Massachusetts, Amherst, MA 01003, 1989.

[OMG91]   OMG. The Common Object Request Broker: Architecture and Specification. Technical Report 91.12.1, Revision 1.1, OMG, December 1991.

[TBC⁺92] R. N. Taylor, F. C. Belz, L. A. Clarke, L. Osterweil, R. W. Selby, J. C. Wileden, A. L. Wolf, and M. Young. Issues Encountered in Building a Flexible Software Development Environment: Lessons Learned from the Arcadia Project. In *Proceedings SDE5*, pages 169–180, December 1992.

[TC93]   P. L. Tarr and L. A. Clarke. PLEIADES:An Object Management System for Software Development Environment. In *In Proceedings of ACM SIGSOFT '93: Symposium on Foundations of Software Engineering*, December 1993.

[Wie92]   G. Wiederhold. Objectives of the Persistent Object Base Program. In *DARPA Software Technology Conference*, pages 256–258, Los Angeles, CA, April, 28–30 1992. DARPA.

470

[WTB92]   D. L. Wells, Craig W. Thompson, and Jose A. Blakeley. DARPA
           Open Object-Oriented Database System. Technical report, Texas
           Instrument Incorporated, P.O. Box 655474, MS 238, Dallas, Texas
           75265, U.S.A., 1992.

[ZKB91]   K. Zhao, R. King, and A. Bouguettaya. Incremental Specification of
           Views Across Databases. In *First International Workshop on Inter-
           operability in Multidatabase Systems, Kyoto, Japan*, pages 187–190,
           April 7–9 1991.

[ZL92]   S. B. Zdonik and D. E. Langworthy. The Brown Object Storage
           System. In *DARPA Software Technology Conference*, pages 275–
           276, Los Angeles, CA, April, 28–30 1992. DARPA.

Keynote Discussion on Evolution in Persistent Systems

Richard Connor, Alex Farkas[†] & Dave Maier[‡]

Department of Mathematical and Computational Science,
University of St Andrews, St Andrews, Fife, Scotland KY16 9SS

[†]Department of Computer Science, University of Adelaide,
Adelaide 5005, South Australia

[‡]Oregon Graduate Institute, PO Box 91000,
Portland 97291 - 1000, Oregon, USA

richard@dcs.st-andrews.ac.uk
alex@cs.adelaide.edu.au
maier@cse.ogi.edu

Abstract

Evolution is without doubt one of the hardest problems to address with respect to programming systems. When the systems under consideration handle large amounts of long-lived data, the ability to handle evolution becomes not only essential, but also even harder to provide. When some of the intrinsic restrictions of traditional databases are removed, as is the case with persistent programming systems, the problems become harder still.

Very little work has been done on system evolution in persistent systems, probably for the reason that it is simply too hard. A major result of this keynote discussion, however, was to show that the current state of thinking about evolution is at least sufficiently advanced for a reasonable level of technical discussion to emerge amongst the workshop participants. Persistent systems research seems to have advanced at least to the stage where problems as hard as these may start to be addressed.

1.   Introduction

"Everything is required of us, and everything will be given." Thus the villagers of Titlipur were informed of their task to cross the Arabian Sea on foot. The same description could equally be used to inform the designers of persistent systems of their task: to provide applications builders with the ability for their applications to evolve in sympathy with the changing needs of their users.

To explain this perhaps fanciful notion, the overall feeling of the workshop participants during the discussion session could be summarised in two main points:

•   allowing for evolution in persistent systems poses a set of problems which are very much harder to solve than those in traditional database systems

•   persistence technology, however, provides us with a much more powerful set of paradigms with which to tackle these problems than is available in a more traditional context

It is undoubtedly too early to judge whether, given both of these points, the capacity for evolution provision in persistent systems will be better or worse overall than in traditional systems; however, there seemed to be a general optimistic consensus that, as a community, research has at least arrived at the state of maturity when the problems may start to be addressed.

It is very difficult to retrospectively assign views and statements to individuals during a lively debate. An attempt has been made to distill most of the essence of the proceedings into this report; the caveat should be made that some of the points presented here may not be agreed upon by all, or indeed any, of the authors!

2.   What is needed?

A requirement of any large system is that the evolution of data and programs should be controllable. Since the uses of data and programs cannot be predicted, it is necessary to support the construction of new software systems which make use of existing data and programs, even when they have been defined independently from current program and data. For large scale, widely used or continuously used systems any alteration to the system should not necessarily require total rebuilding. There is therefore a fundamental requirement to support the following in persistent programming systems:

•   the creation and binding of new objects
•   the reuse of existing objects (program and data) by new objects
•   new combinations of existing and/or new objects
•   incremental construction of objects
•   alteration of existing objects (including value and type)

Even although this set of requirements may be difficult to support coherently in persistent systems, the state of the art in the more traditional database context is arguably advanced to the stage where supporting modifications to a single instance of a database or application is no longer considered to be an interesting research challenge. In the relational world more sophisticated challenges already have some solutions; for example the database restructuring operations themselves may planned and robustly executed in their own right. The planned change to the database may be configured as a batch of operations, which is applied to a system or a number of dependent systems in a single pass. In cases of contention the execution of the planned change may be restarted or resumed as appropriate, thus bringing the process of schema evolution nearer to the normal transactional computation model.

Another problem occurs when systems are derived from others; in these cases, it is often desirable for changes made to the original system also to be propagated to its derivations. The possibility of conflict, as illustrated in Figure 1, then arises when installed systems may derive from a number of different development systems. Once again, this is not only a real problem, but one for which at least partial solutions exist in the relational database community. This gives another example of a complex problem area which must eventually be addressed in persistent systems if they are to successfully rival relational ones.

Development System   Installed Systems

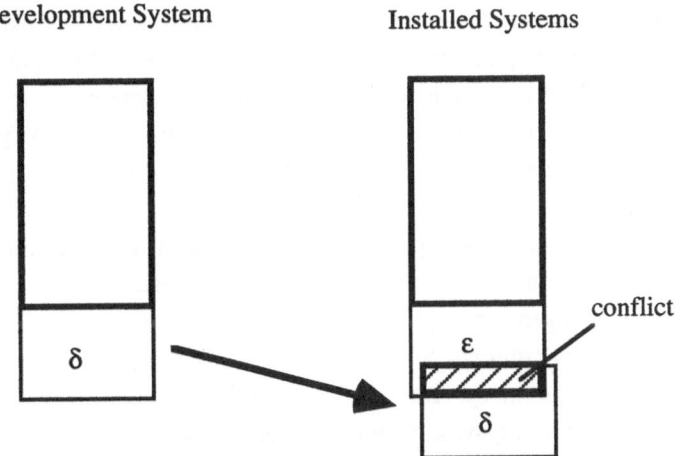

Figure 1 : Conflict detection after independent change

A further problem related to evolution in persistent systems is that of evolving application code. This problem is not normally addressed in traditional database systems, as the code is resident in a different domain beyond the jurisdiction of the database. In persistent systems however the code and data reside in the same conceptual space, and so it must be addressed. With respect to the evolution of application code, the following desiderata have been identified:

• Ideally, we would like to maintain as much static type checking as possible: in particular, we would like to retain the programming language in its original form, changing only the implementation where necessary rather than the language.

• Evolving an application should take place with minimal effort, depending on the nature of the required changes. In particular, we would like to minimise the need to recompile and/or rebind application components and data.

- It is desirable to maintain the optimisability of the code: we do not wish to compromise the performance of an application for the sake of evolvability, when the level of evolution eventually required is not known.

3.   Why are the problems harder?

The problems of controlling evolutionary change in persistent systems appear to be exacerbated by the very flexibility that it is the purpose of persistence to provide. A recurring theme of the discussion was the tradeoff between flexibility and control, and it was suggested that sufficient control may in some circumstances be attainable only by the judicious removal of some of the flexibility.

A very clear example of this was the problem of schema control in persistent systems. A view held by at least some of the participants, although vigorously argued by others, is that a necessary consequence of orthogonal persistence is that there can be no central schema definition. The schema is generally regarded to mean the set of types which is sufficient to describe the persistent data; as this set can vary unpredictably during the execution of a program especially in systems with dynamic binding or reflection, any kind of central schema management is difficult to achieve.

The use of structural type equivalence in a pure form actually precludes many of the activities normally associated with schema management, for example centralised type management, explicit type changes, and the management of extents even when limited by context. Structural equivalence is commonly regarded as a requirement of persistent systems, to allow activities such as the merging of independently prepared sub-systems; however there was much debate about whether it is a more general requirement or not. This certainly seemed like an area where the controlled removal of flexibility may greatly enhance management potential without having particularly damaging effects on usability.

4.   How can persistence help?

Some of the paradigms which have been developed in, and as a result of, persistent systems seem to be of significant help in addressing the hard problems of evolution. Some of those identified during the discussion are as follows:

- The mechanism of type-safe linguistic reflection allows systems to evolve without reference to any outside authority, thus allowing the evolution and the normal computation to occur within a single coherent programming model.
- Flexible binding mechanisms, which may occur at any time between composition and execution, allow the explicit coding of whether subsequent changes

should be visible to a application component. Composition time bindings in particular give the ability to re-compile a program without losing the integrity of the reference. Mechanisms for unbinding, and programming models which operate over bindings, such as the Nodule mechanism described in this volume, give a way for parts of applications to be manipulated.

- First class programs mean that the binding mechanisms to code and data are identical within an address space. Advantage may be taken of these bindings by keeping reverse bindings between data and code, thus giving the potential to locate any code which depends on particular data.
- Separate name and value spaces mean that names in persistent systems may be flexibly allocated. This means that, rather than changing the meaning of a name, a new name may be introduced which will eventually take over the meaning of an old name, at which point it may be reassigned.
- Persistent systems can support much more sophisticated models of type than traditional databases; sufficiently general models of polymorphism should obviate the requirement for unnecessary change to programs whose semantics is unaltered in evolving systems.

5. What else can help?

From the relational experience a number of tools and methodologies have been shown to help with problems of evolution. Many of these are well suited to a persistent environment.

- A bulk loader / bulk dumper facility has been found useful during system development and for virtual image transport during application delivery. This kind of application is particularly well-suited to the use of reflection, and in fact a number of such applications already exist for other reasons in persistent systems.
- An explicit distinction between internal and external names in a system has been discovered important for the treatment of evolution; this ties in well with the separation of name and value spaces often advocated for persistent systems.
- Keeping separate the concepts of subtype and implementation hierarchies is important for smooth evolution; this must be regarded as a challenge for the ultimate persistent type system as alluded to in the previous section!
- The use of extents in a programming language (that is, collections of all values belonging to a particular type) has found to be harmful for evolution. In the database world, limiting extents to contexts has been found to help; this ties in strongly, but from the opposite viewpoint, with the discussion about possible limitations of structural type equivalence.

- Dependency tracking is clearly vitally important. Persistent systems have potential leverage here in the use of composition-time bindings, which may be used to keep direct and reversible mappings between code and data, thus making many dependencies more explicit and amenable to such tools.

6. Conclusions

Research in evolution in persistent systems is just beginning; thus it is by no means surprising that the discussion generated no real solutions to any of the hard problems. However, the lively discussion both indicated that most participants have been starting to think of the issues, and also generated a number of interesting questions. (It should be admitted that at some point during the debate an interesting question was defined as one which had no good solution.) We look forward to seeing some real solutions at the next POS workshop!

Persistent Systems Engineering

Anne Doucet

LRI- University of Orsay
91405 Orsay Cedex, France

This session contained three papers, only loosely related to each other, but addressing important aspects of persistent systems engineering. The first paper, written by Erik Odberg, deals with schema modification management. The second paper was presented by Luca Vinciotti and addresses the problem of distribution in Galileo, the persistent programming language developed at the University of Pisa. Finally, the third paper, presented by Steve Rozen, describes the construction of a domain-specific DBMS, LabBase, on top of an existing persistent object system,

Object Store.

The paper presented by Erik Odberg proposes an interesting way of managing schema modifications in the context of object oriented databases. The presented approach adopts a schema versioning approach to schema modification management. A Change Specification Language, allowing the definition of new schema versions, is defined, and the problem of achieving schema versions compatibility is addressed, considering three dimensions of concerns (classification, interface and representation compatibility).

The proposed approach presents many advantages : while most existing approaches only consider changes which involve a single class, the use of versions allows to consider modifications involving multiple classes; as opposed the approach taken by Gemstone and Orion, which regards all schema modifications as corrective, the schema versioning approach does not obsolete former specifications, allowing existing applications not to be affected by change; finally, this approach promotes a global perspective of change, over all specifications of the database, considering semantic dependencies applying between non-consecutive versions of the schema.

The second paper, presented by L. Vinciotti, discusses the problems of concurrency in the context of a distributed database system. In this system, end-users can access a shared value environment and a shared type environment stored in a remote server. The users can use their own private persistent environments that are transparently integrated with the shared ones. The notion of transaction in this context is defined. It can operates transparently on shared and private persistent values. The idea of a transaction is implicit in the language, and a transaction is a top-level expression. Implicit transactions allow functionalities to be designed which operate on databases without specifying any particular transaction operation construct. Then the global architecture of the distributed Galileo is described, as well as its main system aspects (persistence management, concurrency control, recovery).

478

The third paper, presented by S. Rozen, deals with the problem of using an existing Persistent Object System to construct a domain-specific DMBS, LabBase. The domain considered in this experience is the domain of laboratory information systems. Such systems record the experimental steps performed and experimental results obtained during the operation of a laboratory production line. Among their characteristics, it is important to point out that these systems require multilingual access to the database, need to accommodate constant re-engineering of the experimental production line, and need to view experimental results both historically and statically.

Instead of modelling the information directly as C++ classes, the authors choose to build a layer of abstraction in C++. C++ classes are used to model the generic attributes of the application domain. These attributes can be specialised for specific applications within the domain, using a data definition facility. The design and implementation of LabBase are described, and the advantages and disadvantages of this approach are fully discussed.

In the first part of the discussion, questions mainly concerned the first two papers. Several questions were related to performance problems. The Change Specification Language supports a lot of changes, but is it efficient ? The performance measures done for Galileo show a gap with OODBs. In fact, cold start performance is comparable with other systems. The problems are for the warm ones. Other questions concerned the utility of versions for schema modification management. Is it useful to see all versions of objects ? Would it not be better to have just a schema and work with different views ? Views and versions are related, but they are not the same : it is possible to hide information, but it is not possible to add new ones. Furthermore views do not deal with dependencies.

The second part of the discussion concerned the last paper. Problems of recovery were largely discussed. Why LabBase does not use the recovery system provided by ObjectStore? The recovery system of ObjectStore is used for the store itself, but another log is necessary for LabBase specific problems. Considering that the size of applications is huge, performance problems were also discussed. Finally questions about the configuration of the system were asked. The users of these applications are mainly biologists. They are used to work on small machines (Macintosh for instance) and to program with simple languages. It is crucial to let them work in the environment they are used to.

A Global Perspective of Schema Modification Management for Object-Oriented Databases

Erik Odberg*
Department of Computer Science
Norwegian Institute of Technology

Abstract

Schema Modification Management (SMM) is concerned about how schema changes should affect the object base in order to make database objects be compatible with specifications after change. However, a particular problem with existing SMM approaches is the lack of concern for *schema-level* changes (which may involve *multiple* classes), or semantic dependencies which applies between *non-consecutive* versions of the schema.

The presented approach adopts a schema *versioning* approach to SMM (allowing multiple schema versions to coexist), and promotes a *global perspective* of change management: A powerful means is provided for specifying the presence and maintenance of *arbitrary* semantic relationships between classes and properties as defined for *any* schema version in the derivation hierarchy. The fundamental assumption is that semantic dependencies between schema versions do not only follows the *derivation* relationship, but may go in any directions. To ensure the database behaves consistently as regarded within any schema version context, it is essential that all semantic dependencies are maintained.

The approach is able to handle schema version derivations in arbitrary directions, including complex modifications to the class hierarchy, and in accordance with the inherently unpredictable nature of change.

1 Introduction and Motivation

A database schema is a model of some domain of discourse, reflecting a particular need to store and manipulate information about the domain. Over time, the domain itself may evolve, new needs for information storage and manipulation may arise, and there may be a need for different clients to regard the same domain in *different* ways, possibly in terms of *different* abstractions over the real world and which may be *organized* in different ways.

---

*Detailed address: Department of Computer Science, Norwegian Institute of Technology (NTH), N-7034 Trondheim-NTH, Norway. Phone: +47 73 594484. Fax: +47 73 594466. Email: eriko@idt.unit.no

In order to have the database reflect an evolving domain or nformation requirements, the *schema* will have to change in accordance. In particular, for large, long-lived databases it is unreasonable that the initial schema specification may continue to satisfy all needs for data storage and manipulation. Moreover, over time it is reasonable to believe that for different communities the needs for database support will grow in *different* directions, and so that it may not be sufficient with a *single* database schema specification. While some changes are inherently *corrective*, clearly reflecting a change to the domain itself, other changes may reflect the introduction of a new world perception partially in overlap with other perceptions. This may be compared to the way a software system evolves by defining *revisions* and *variants*. Change is inherently unpredictable, and cannot be planned for. Change may take any direction and not necessarily according to a structured path of evolution. This mean that, over time it may be expected that *multiple* chains of evolution, reflecting different (but overlapping) specifications of the same database, must be maintained.

In fact, these issues are *particularly* profound for object-oriented databases (OODBs), which typically find application in environments characterized by exploratory work, experimental activity and iterative design, and for which there are frequently different needs for database provisions. While traditional databases are typically *data intensive*, involving a large number of instances of a relatively small number of classes (types), OODBs are generally *computation intensive*, with a smaller number of instances of a larger number of classes. This means that classes (i.e. the schema contents) are even *more* likely to change. In conclusion, there is a particularly important need to address the problem of schema modifications for OODBs.

1.1   Schema Modification Management

The fundamental problem about schema modifications is that different specifications are generally *incompatible*. An object is always *created* as an instance of a class in accordance with a particular schema specification, and which will define how it classifies as well as association with properties. Objects are *referenced* by clients which may assume *another* specification of the same database, and which will define a particular expectation of object behavior which need *not* necessarily comply with object provisions decided upon creation. Compliance with different specifications is an inherent source for provision/expectation conflicts.

Schema Modification Management (SMM) is concerned about how schema change should affect the object base in order to make database objects be compatible with specifications after change. The *schema evolution* approach (e.g. GemStone [1] and Orion [2]), regards all schema modifications as *corrective*, and is concerned about how objects may be converted to comply with the most recent specification of its class. All application programs must be modified and recompiled in accordance with the most recent specifications. In contrast, the *schema versioning* approach (e.g. Avance [3], Encore [4], CLOSQL [5], Clamen's work [6] and Bratsberg's work [7]) does *not* obsolete former specifications. Existing applications are unaffected by change, and may regard the database in the same way as before the modification was performed. In this way the schema versioning approach promotes *change transparency*, there is no need for change and recompilation. The primary concern of a schema versioning approach is how objects may behave in compliance with *multiple* different specifications.

The common approach to SMM is to, when a class is modified, define *coercion functions* between the former and the new version of this class. These functions describe the relationship between properties defined for the two versions of the class, i.e. how an object created as an instance of one class version may be "coerced" to behave in accordance with other versions of the same class. Under the evolution approach, coercion functions are defined in *one* direction, describing how existing objects must be (eagerly or lazily) converted to comply with the most recent version of its class. Under the versioning approach, coercion functions must be defined in *both* directions upon class change. By transitive application of coercion functions, objects may behave consistently as an instance of *any* version of its class, irrespective of the version of creation[1].

Problems with existing work

An important problem about existing work is the lack of concern for *schema level* modifications, i.e. modifications which involve *multiple* classes. Most existing approaches only consider changes which involve a *single* class, emphasizing the importance of *class versions*. However, a schema describes a consistent and complete world perception, and so that changes to *one* class frequently must be regarded in conjunction with changes to *other* classes as well. For instance, properties may be *moved* between classes, or the class hierarchy *reorganized*, which will have significant impacts to the management of change.

A related issue is the lack of concern for the *classification* dimension of object modeling. Existing SMM work is mostly concerned about the *property* dimension of modeling, and how objects may have a different (but overlapping) collection of properties when regarded as an instance of different versions of its class. However, a class hierarchy does not only describe an organization of properties, but more importantly a particular *conceptual model* of a particular domain. Associated with each class a particular *classification semantics* is implicitly assumed, saying which objects may be regarded members of the class. Different schema specifications may reflect a *different* perception of the domain in terms of which abstractions are relevant, how they are organized and what is the perceived semantics of classification. As a consequence, objects may be perceived to *classify* differently in different contexts, i.e. be perceived to be a a member of *different* classes. Existing SMM work disregards this aspects of schema modifications, which is particularly important to consider in the case of class hierarchical changes.

Finally, a problem with existing SMM work is that dependencies between schema spec-

---

[1] For [6, 7] coercion functions are more like *triggers* invoked upon object mutation to ensure the effect is consistently propagated to other class version perspectives of the object. [4] adopts a different scheme, for which coercion functions are defined between each class version and the *totality* of properties (interface) defined for *some* version of the class.

482

ifications may only be expressed in terms of coercion functions between *consecutive* class versions. However, in many cases we find there are semantic connections which apply between *non-consecutive* schema specifications as well. For instance, a property may *reappear* in the new specification without being included in the previous, or the same property may be *independently defined* in different derivation branches. Furthermore, there are often also dependencies between *classifications* as of non-consecutive schema specifications, for instance if one class is first removed, but reintroduced in a later specification. In order to ensure that *all* semantic dependencies between schema specifications are properly maintained it may often be necessary to assume a *global* perspective over *all* specifications of the database, establishing semantic connections in *arbitrary* directions, without being constrained by the class (or schema) version derivation relationship. This is not possible under existing SMM approaches. It must be noted that there is a *particular* problem about schema *evolution* approaches as the introduction of a new schema specification may imply that some information is *lost* for existing database objects. This means it may be *impossible* to maintain dependencies between non-consecutive specifications.

2   Schema Versioning and Schema Version Definition

A fundamental assumption behind our work is that different users may frequently have a *different* perception of the same domain in terms of relevant abstractions, how they are organized and what is the perception of individual abstractions. For this reason, the schema *versioning* approach, which promotes a *multi-perspectived* world view, is adopted.

The basic object model is "traditional" in that it is based on C++ with persistence. *Classes* are templates for object creation, and contain *attributes* and *methods* (commonly denoted *properties*). Each property may be *public* (externally visible) or *private* (accessible to class method implementations only), as for C++ (*public* is default, however). The collection of public properties is also referred to as the *interface* of the class[2]. Each class may have one or more *superclasses*, which describes property *inheritance* as well as *is-a* links between classes. A *schema* is a collection of class definitions, and is defined in the Data Definition Language (DDL). On the basis of the schema definition, C++ *persistent classes* are generated to correspond to the schema classes, and which are used to manipulate persistent objects within C++ application programs. Additional aspects of the object model not relevant for the discussions in this paper are discussed in [8, 9, 10].

The following illustrates the DDL definition of a class Employee which is a subclass of a class Person not shown here[3]:

```
CLASS Employee : Person {
    string dept;
```

---

[2]The class interface may contain both methods and attributes; Attributes are *abstractly* accessible (i.e. through generated *access functions*).

[3]string is a specially provided attribute domain, and methods are implemented separately.

```
int salary;
string phone;};
```

2.1 Schema versions

A *schema version* is one consistent and complete specification of a particular domain of concern, and has a unique identifier - the Schema Version Identifier (SVId). The granularity of change is the complete *schema* level: Changes to one part of the schema may often have to be considered in conjunction with changes to *other* parts, and so that several primitive changes are committed together to form a new version of the schema as a whole. Clients (application programs) statically associate with a schema version to define its view of the object base. This association defines the context of observation, manipulation and creation of objects for the application program, and is also denoted the *schema version context*. The schema version context decides the expectation of object appearance as well as how new objects will appear. Schema version association may *change* over time, which generally requires that the application is modified accordingly, and recompiled.

The definition of a new schema version generally involves the addition of new classes along with the removal of and modifications to existing ones. A new *class version* (CV) is defined when (1) The collection or definition of properties of the class itself is modified, *or* (2) The collection of superclass links is modified, *or* (3) A new version of a *superclass* (possibly transitively) is defined. Consequently, a new class version will always imply new versions of subclasses as well. Class versions are interesting as objects will always be *created* as an instance of a particular class version, the version of the class defined in the creation schema version context. Object creation defines how the object *classifies* (which classes it is a member of) and association with properties. However, the object must be transparently accessible as an instance of *other* class versions, in other schema version contexts, as well.

2.2 Schema version definition

A new schema version is defined *relatively* to a *base* schema version, specifying how the new version is *different* from the base version. *Any* schema version may constitute the base for the derivation of a new schema version. This means that schema version derivation will construct a *hierarchy* rather than a linear chain. In this respect there is no strict notion of a "most recent" schema version; there may be *multiple* leaves in the schema version derivation hierarchy. All schema versions, both internal and leaf nodes in the derivation hierarchy, reflect different (but overlapping) specifications of the same domain of interest, and are valid for client association. For now, the schema version derivation relationship is most important as a *reuse* relationship, i.e. it describes from which schema version specifications are "inherited", although arbitrary modifications may be performed as part of the new schema version. The selection of a base schema version is based on which existing schema version has the closest *"affinity"* to the intentions of the new schema version, in this way reusing specifications most efficiently.

A relative specification formalism is preferable to an absolute specification of the new schema version (e.g. through a *copy-edit-commit* process) as the latter frequently cannot precisely formulate the intended *semantics* of the schema change, i.e. *how* the new schema version differs from the base schema version. While a copy-edit-commit paradigm may be convenient for defining the *contents* of the new schema version, we must also be concerned about *how* schema versions are different (or similar). Unless all semantic dependencies between schema versions are properly established, a database behaving consistently in all contexts may not be expected. Special abilities are needed to specify the presence and maintenance of these dependencies.

2.3   The Change Specification Language – CSL

A new schema version is defined in the *Change Specification Language* (CSL). The CSL provides facilities to identify a base schema version, as well as defining how properties and classes are added, removed, changed and moved in the new schema version as related to the base. There are many similarities between the DDL and the CSL. Below we will see how the CSL is used to describe changes to class association with properties, as well as changes to the class hierarchy itself. Sections 3 and 5 will discuss how the CSL may be used to establish arbitrary semantic connections between schema versions.

Changing class association with properties

Addition and removal of properties for an existing class **Employee** may be described in the following way:

```
CLASS Employee {
   ADD string office;
   REM salary;
   ADD int employed_since
   ADD int Salary();};
```

For the addition of *methods*, the implementation is given separately. For the *removal* of properties, it is normally *not* necessary to indicate the domain. Only non-inherited properties may be removed from a class. An attribute domain modification is defined as a combination of removal and addition, along with the specification of a special *relationship* between the old and new manifestation to indicate the semantic connection (cfr. Section 5).

Properties may also be *moved* within (i.e. a *rename*) or between classes using the MOV operator. A MOV statement is associated with the *target* class, identifying which property (and possibly which *source* class) is to be moved to the target class (possibly with a new name). Simultaneously, the property is *"removed"* from the source class, or more precisely: The source property will not be "inherited" into the new schema version. The new (target) property will have the *same* definition as the source. Semantically, *attributes* will be recorded as being the *same* in the different schema versions, and so that these will be maintained in *synchronization* for objects which contain both (regarded within the different schema version contexts). The following illustrates a property *rename* defined by a MOV statement:

```
CLASS Employee {
  MOV employed_since starting_date;};
```

Properties may be moved *between* classes to change organization of information, and may be particularly common in conjunction with changes to the class hierarchy. The following MOV statement establishes that that only *clerks*, and not all *employees*, actually have an office:

```
CLASS Clerk : Employee {
  MOV Employee.office office;};
```

An important characteristic of the approach is the ability to specify a property move not only from the base schema version of derivation, but from *any* existing schema version: This means that attributes defined in non-consecutive schema versions may still be maintained in synchronization, e.g. to manage the *reappearance* of an attribute defined in *some* former schema version, or to be able to specify that attributes *independently* defined in different schema version derivation branches are really to be regarded the same. This is achieved by *explicitly* denoting the schema version (and possibly class) which is to constitute the source of the MOV:

```
CLASS Employee {
  MOV SV0::Employee.salary wage;};
```

For this example, it is assumed that SV0 identifies the initial schema version, i.e. before the **salary** attribute was removed. The implication is that **salary** and **wage**, as defined for the different schema versions, are maintained in synchronization. It must be noted that, in order to be able to establish such dependencies between schema versions, the schema designer must assume a *global perspective* over all versions of the schema, in this way being able to detect the presence of all semantic dependencies which exist. In fact, this is *particularly* important when there are many versions of the schema, as may be reasonable to expect for a long-lived database with multiple evolution branches.

Changing class hierarchy

The CSL also includes abilities to add or remove *classes* in the new schema version as related to the base, or to change the superclass binding of existing classes. A class **FacultyMember** may be added as a new internal class in the class hierarchy (assuming **Prof**, **AssocProf** and **AssistProf** were formerly subclasses of **Employee**) in the following way:

```
ADD CLASS FacultyMember : Employee {
  <properties>};

CLASS Prof : FacultyMember {};
CLASS AssocProf : FacultyMember {};
CLASS AssistProf : FacultyMember {};
```

As seen from the example, **Prof**, **AssocProf** and **AssistProf** must be explicitly *re-connected* to the new superclass. If no explicit reconnection is performed, classes will retain the same superclass connection as within the base schema version. Classes are removed using the **REM CLASS** operator, and which also may have the implication that former (direct) subclasses must be reconnected appropriately.

A special characteristic of the approach is the notion of a *class equality relationship*. A class equality relationship says that a new class, within the schema version to be defined, should be regarded as the *same* as some class as defined in some other (not necessarily the base) schema version. In this way the new class will "inherit" the properties and superclass connection of the other class, but may change these in the same way as described above. Furthermore, the classes will be regarded as the "same", and thus fundamentally to have the same members as well. This issue is elaborated upon in Section 3.

```
ADD CLASS FacMember = FacultyMember{           (1)
  <change properties> };

ADD CLASS Worker = <SVId>::Employee {          (2)
  <change properties> };
```

(1) describes how a base schema version class may be *renamed* in the new schema version. In this case the former manifestation of the class (**FacultyMember**) will *implicitly* be removed from the new schema version, and possible subclasses reconnected accordingly to **FacMember**. (2) describes how a class **Worker** is specified to be the samne as a class **Employee** in an explicitly denoted schema version. This may express the *reappearance* of a formerly defined (but non-existent in the base schema version) class, or a class which is *independently defined* in different schema version derivation branches. The system will maintain the semantics that these reflect the same abstraction, i.e. the members are fundamentally the same.

The notion of class equality relationships provides a primitive means for naturally "*incorporating*" individual classes from any schema versions, even if the schema version derivation hierarchy does not allow for merging schema versions. Furthermore, the striking similarity with the intentions and semantics of the **MOV** operator, which have application for properties, must be noted.

Schema version compatibility

Above CSL primitives have been introduced which are used to define the *contents* of the new schema version relatively to a base version. However, an important aspect of a schema versioning approach is to promote a database which consistently and simultaneously may comply with *any* of the versions of the schema. Special corrective actions are required in order to:

- Ensure that the database *structures* are enhanced to comply with any version of the schema, and so that a shared database may be provided even if there is not a single specification of its contents.

- For any kind of overlaps and dependencies between specifications in different versions of the schema, it must be ensured that these are in some way *expressed* and so that they may be properly *maintained* within the shared database.

Some schema version dependencies inherently arise on the basis of CSL specifications as introduced above. The "inheritance" of a class from a base schema version, or the establishment of equality relationships between classes, also implies that *membership* in these classes in different contexts naturally should be regarded the same. Furthermore, *properties* (most interestingly attributes) "inherited" from the base schema version, or defined through MOV operations, are also semantically equivalent and thus must be maintained in synchronization. However, there are always *other* dependencies which arise between schema versions as well, and which must be explicitly expressed by some other means.

Ensuring that database structure are provided and consistently maintained for all schema versions will be referred to as achieving *schema version compatibility*. Schema version compatibility is concerned about *overcoming* the inherent incompatibilities and differences between schema versions, ensuring consistent coexistence. In the sections to come we will see how three different dimensions of concerns are addressed to achieve schema version compatibility. Section 3 discusses how objects are ensured to *classify* consistently within each context of access, and how special *classification relationships* may be established to more precisely express dependencies between classes within different schema versions. Section 4 is concerned about how objects may *behave* consistently as an instance of a class for which it is a member in each schema version, i.e. ensuring that all requests may be answered. Section 5 is concerned about how objects are able to *hold* and *maintain* consistently all information as an instance of each class it is an instance in some schema version. These aspects of schema version compatibility are referred to as *Classification*, *Interface* and *Representation* compatibility, respectively.

3   Classification Compatibility

A class abstracts over *two* different aspects of the real world. First, a class reflects an abstraction over a collection of *properties*, and so that every object which is an instance of the class will contain these properties. We will refer to this as the *property dimension* of modeling. Second, a class reflects an abstraction over a *collection* of objects (the *extent*) perceived to have some characteristic in common. We say that objects *classify* as a member of the same class according to some conception of sameness. This aspect of the class construct is denoted the *classification dimension* of modeling, and will talk about the particular *classification semantics* as associated with a class to reflect the client perception of classification "criteria".

The classification dimension of modeling refer to what an object "*is*" as a *member-of* a class. Object creation "*says*" something about the object in terms of how it classifies, assuming a particular real-world perception as given by the context of creation. In contrast, the property dimension reflects what an object may *do* as an *instance-of* a particular class. While the class construct reflects both property and classification dimension of modeling, the clear distinction between them forms an important foundation for the presented approach. In this section we will be concerned about the classification dimension of modeling, i.e. how objects are regarded members of classes (how they *classify*) rather than property association. Moreover, we will be concerned about how different schema versions may assume *different* semantics of classifications, typically due to changes to the structure of the class hierarchy. As a consequence, objects need *not* classify in the same way in different contexts. *Classification compatibility* is concerned about how objects consistently classify in different contexts, according to implicit and explicit semantic connections between classes in different schema versions.

3.1 Implicit classification semantics

Any object is created as an instance of a class within a particular context, and which will make the object be a member of this class as well as all superclasses of the class as defined in this particular schema version[4]. These classes are denoted *explicit* classes of the object, emphasizing the importance of classes some client has *explicitly* requested the object to be a member of in some context. *Fundamentally*, an object may only be regarded a member of its explicit classes within the creation context, as a different semantics of classification may be associated with a class as appearing in different schema versions. However, membership in explicit classes (in the creation context) will transitively *propagate* over schema version boundaries, following schema version derivation relationships (in the direction of *both* base and derived schema versions) and class equality relationships. In this way an objects will be a member of its explicit classes in *any* schema version context where defined. In addition, in order to ensure that *inclusion semantics* is properly maintained for each schema version class hierarchy, the object will also be a member of all *superclasses* of its explicit classes within individual schema versions. These are denoted *implied* class memberships, always assumed on a schema version individual basis.

An important consequence of these implicit rules for object classification is that the creation of an object as an instance of the same class in different contexts may have *different* impacts with respect to how objects classify in different contexts, as the collection of explicit classes need not be the same. That is, the context of creation may

---

[4] [8, 10] also discuss how class memberships may be added and removed *dynamically*, in this way allowing objects to evolve. This is beyond the scope of this paper.

be significant. In general, objects may classify *differently* in different schema version contexts.

The following example illustrates the application of the implicit rules for the addition of a new internal class TechnAdm, which generalizes two existing classes Technician and AdmPerson formerly subclasses of Employee:

```
ADD CLASS TechnAdm : Employee {...};
CLASS Technician : TechnAdm {...};
CLASS AdmPerson : TechnAdm {...};
```

When an object is created as an instance of Technician or AdmPerson in the context of the former schema version this class will be *explicit*, and thus TechnAdm will be *implied* in the new schema version. This means that TechnAdm is most likely populated upon introduction; all existing instances of subclasses are also members of TechnAdm. On the other hand, creating an instance of TechnAdm in the new schema version implies the object may only be regarded as an instance of Employee (which is an explicit class) in the former context.

Figure 1 illustrates another example in which a superclass link is removed.

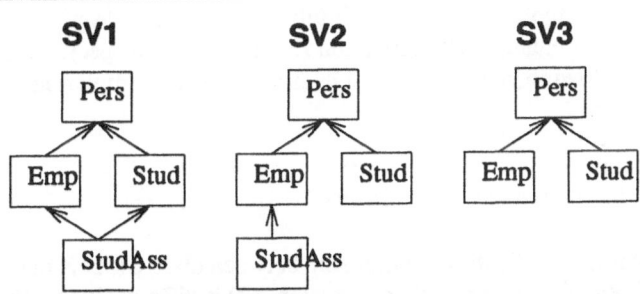

Figure 1: Different organization of StudAss hierarchy

Schema versions SV1 and SV2 reflect different perceptions of a StudAss. Within SV1 it is a requirement that all StudAss objects are simultaneously also Students, while there is no such requirement in SV2. Schema version SV3 reflects a more restricted world perspective in which there is no interest in regarding StudAss objects. A StudAss object created in SV1 may be regarded a member of Employee and Student in SV1, SV2 and SV3, as well as a StudAss in both SV1 and SV2: All these classes are explicit classes of the object. An important consequence is that the object in SV2 and SV3 may be regarded as a member of *multiple* most-specific classes StudAss and Stud. This is a significant characteristic of the approach, but is beyond the scope of this paper. It is referred to [8, 10] for an in-depth discussion of these issues. Creating a StudAss object in SV2 rather than SV1, Stud would *not* be an explicit class of the object (and thus the object would not be a Stud in SV2 or SV3), however it would be *implied* in SV1. That is, creation of a **StudAss** in SV1 or SV2 "says" different things about the semantics of the object.

3.2   Classification relationships

The assumption behind the implicit rules for object classification is that the classification semantics for a class is fundamentally the same in each schema version where the class is included. For this reason membership in explicit classes in some context will unconditionally propagate to all other contexts. However, frequently there are other semantic connections between classes in different schema versions. New schema versions may define other ways of partitioning the world into abstractions (classes), typically by adding and removing classes or reorganizing the class hierarchy. In this way more complex dependencies between classes in different schema versions, and how objects classify, will arise. There is a need for more precisely expressing these dependencies to ensure consistent classification of objects in different contexts. For this reason a notion of a *classification relationship* is introduced.

A *classification relationship* describes an arbitrary semantic connection between classes in different schema versions, generalizing and refining implicit propagation relationships, and more precisely expressing how classes are related. Classification relationships are established when the implicit rules do *not* properly express the particular intention of change. Classification relationships are specified in the CSL, and may take the following general forms. **OP** is some classification relationship operator described below:

```
ClassX          OP ClassY        (1)
<SVId>::ClassX  OP ClassY        (2)
```

(1) says there is a classification relationship between class **ClassX** in the *base* schema version and **ClassY** in the *new* schema version. **(2)** is different in that the classification relationship applies between a class as defined in an *explicitly* indicated schema version (generally different from the base), and the new schema version. An important aspect of the approach is the ability to express arbitrary relationships between classes which do *not* only follow the direction of schema version derivation. That is, two classes may perfectly well be related qith respect to classification semantics even if not defined in consecutive schema versions.

Propagation relationships

A classification relationship may be a *propagation relationship*, which defines how membership in a class in one schema version may *propagate* to another class in some other schema version. Propagation relationships may be necessary when implicit propagations do not reflect all semantics of change. **ClassX -> ClassY** says that an object membership in **ClassX** in the previous schema version will *propagate* to make the object also be a member of **ClassY** (and implicitly all superclasses) in the new schema version. The operator <- establish a propagation in the other direction, while <-> establish a *bidirectional* propagation. <SVId>::ClassX -> ClassY says that membership in ClassX in an explicitly indicated schema version is to propagate into ClassY in the new schema version.

Propagation relationships typically find application in change situations where one or more classes in the new schema version *substitute* one or more classes in some other (often the base) schema version, which may not be handled properly by the implicit classification rules. For instance, in the following example a class Student is *split* into GradStudent and UnderGrad:

```
REM CLASS Student;
ADD CLASS GradStudent : Person {...};
ADD CLASS UnderGrad : Person {...};

Student <- GradStudent;
Student <- UnderGrad;
```

This specification of propagation relationships adds the knowledge that any GradStudent or UnderGrad in the new schema version context necessarily should be regarded as a Student in the former context. However, it is still a problem that a Student object created in the former schema version context may only be regarded a Person within the new context, as it is for now *not* possible to deduce what kind of student the Person is in the new context. This problem will be discussed again below.

Inhibition relationships

According to the implicit classification rules, membership in explicit classes of an object will propagate (transitively) over schema version boundaries, and so that the object will also be a member of the same classes in other contexts than that of creation. An *inhibition relationship* is established in order to *inhibit* an implicit propagation of class membership over a particular schema version boundary, in this way restricting object assumption of class memberships. ClassX -% ClassX says that an object membership in ClassX in the previous schema version will *not* propagate into ClassX in the new schema version. Operators %- and %-% are used to define an inhibition of propagation in the *other* direction, or in *both* directions, respectively. <SVId>::ClassX -% ClassY says that membership in ClassX in an explicitly indicated schema version will *not* propagate into ClassY in the new schema version. Naturally, such a specification is only reasonable in the case there is an equality relationship between these two classes, otherwise there is no implicit propagation between them.

The application of inhibition relationships is commonly motivated by change situations where the semantic affinity between versions of the same class is *not* so close that it is reasonable to automatically propagate membership between them (in some direction). That is, for different class versions which are non-equivalent with respect to classification semantics, a conservative approach may be taken by deciding *not* to propagate membership. Expressing a restricted compatibility between class versions in this way is traditionally a *non-goal* of SMM, which is primarily concerned about the *sharing* of extents. However, in many cases it may still be a reasonable alternative. For instance, consider the schema versions as shown in Figure 2.

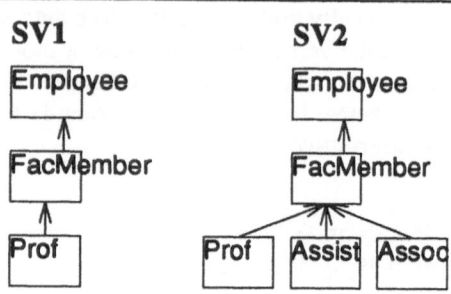

Figure 2: "Detaching" classes

For schema version SV1, the class Prof will include *any* kind of professor, while schema version SV2 more precisely reflects the different kinds of professors which may be. This change may be regarded as "detaching" two new classes AssocProf and AssistProf from the former class Prof: Any Prof object in schema version SV1, reflecting any kind of professor, will in schema version SV2 be a Prof (reflecting a *full* professor), an AssocProf or an AssistProf. The new schema version is defined in the following way:

```
ADD CLASS AssocProf : FacultyMember {};
ADD CLASS AssistProf : FacultyMember {};

Prof -% Prof;
Prof <- AssistProf;
Prof <- AssocProf;
```

The important characteristic about this example is that the classification semantics of the Prof class is *changed* as part of the new schema version. In the former schema version a Prof object is *any* professor, while in the new schema version only *full* professors qualify as members of this class. This means that members of Prof, AssistProf and AssocProf in the new schema version will *all* be members of Prof in the former schema version, while members of Prof in the former schema version may only be regarded a member of FacultyMember in the new schema version. That is, it is (for now) *not* possible to know what kind of professor a general Prof from the former schema version will be in the new schema version. As a *consequence*, membership in Prof in SV1 may *not* propagate to Prof in SV2, and an inhibition relationship is defined for the *right* direction. In contrast, note that it *is* known that an SV2 Prof (or any other SV2 professor) is necessarily a Prof in SV1.

Conditional classification relationships

One problem about classification relationships as introduced above is that only *complete* propagation or inhibition of propagation may be expressed. In many cases it is more realistic that classes are *partially* overlapping, and so that propagation/inhibition applies only for *some* objects. For this reason, a notion of a *conditional* classification relationship is introduced. A conditional classification relationship is characterized by the association with a *predicate* in each direction for which a propagation or inhibition is defined. In this paper we will only consider predicates which are C++ boolean expressions over the *attributes* of the source class of the classification relationship. Other capabilities are discussed in [8, 9]. The predicate is defined over objects as instances of the class on the source side of classification relationship, expressing *which* of the source side objects should propagate (over a propagation relationship) or *not* propagate (due to an inhibition relationship) onto to the target side. In this way the *nature* of the classification relationship may be more precisely described, defining *how* classes in different schema versions may be semantically related. Predicates are evaluated *dynamically*, and so that membership propagation may implicitly change over time.

Conditional propagation relationships typically find application in change situations where it is possible to define a semantic connection between different classes intentionally, possibly on the basis of a "type attribute". For instance, consider the split of the **Student** class above, and how it may be possible to refine the specifications provided a **status** attribute was defined for the **Student** class:

```
REM CLASS Student;
ADD CLASS GradStudent : Person {...};
ADD CLASS UnderGrad : Person {...};

Student [ status == grad ] <-> GradStudent;
Student [ status == ugrad ] <-> UnderGrad;
```

Note that the propagation relationships are *bidirectional* in this case, however conditional only in one direction. Without the conditional propagation relationships in the right direction, objects created as instances of **Student** in the context of the former schema version would only be possible to regard as members of **Person** in the context. We see how there is a clear semantic connection between object state (in the former context) and classification in the new context. [9] also discusses how to manage dependencies in the *other* direction, i.e. how state may be dependent on classification.

A conditional inhibition relationship may be established in a similar way, typically applicable in situations where versions of a class are non-equivalent with respect to classification, but related. Often it may be possible to establish the dependency intentionally, and so that the complete inhibition of propagation may be relaxed. Only *some* of the members of the source class will not propagate.

494

3.3 Concluding remarks

The ability to establish classification relationships between any schema versions[5] provides a powerful means for expressing any semantic dependency in the classification dimension, and which is maintained by propagation of membership between schema version contexts. The presence of classification relationships may have significant effects to the way objects classify in different contexts. Object membership in explicit classes will transitively propagate from the schema version of creation, across schema version boundaries for *implicit* and *explicit* propagation relationships, possibly *inhibited* by inhibition relationships, and possibly changing over time depending on the satisfaction of predicates. Accordingly, an object may be regarded a member of a class in some schema version context if a *propagation path* may be found to some explicit class and creation context. [10, 9] elaborates on these issues, also considering how objects may *evolve* over time by explicitly adding and removing membership in classes.

4 Interface Compatibility

While classification compatibility is concerned about how objects *classify* in different contexts, *interface compatibility* is concerned about how an object may provide the properties as an instance of classes for which it is a member in all schema version contexts. Interface compatibility is concerned about type safety, and how objects properly behave in each context.

Within each schema version context, objects will be a member of one or more *most-specific* classes, i.e. a class which is so that the object is not a member of any *subclasses* of the class in the same context. For each *class version* which corresponds to a most-specific class of an object in some schema version context (i.e. the version of the class defined in the particular schema version), a *class version role* (CV role) is (logically) instantiated for the object[6]. A CV role contains properties as defined for the particular version of the class, including properties inherited from superclasses (in the same schema version). In this way objects are implicitly *enhanced* with additional abilities to behave in different contexts. Each CV role provides a *client perspective* of the object, making it able to properly behave according to expectation as an instance of classes for which it is a member (the class itself and superclasses) in one or more schema version contexts.

The collection of CV roles resulting from the multi-instantiation of class versions provides all possible perspectives of the object, being visible within some context(s). Any object reference will implicitly bind to one particular CV role, decided by the

---

[5]The examples have for simplicity only illustrated the establishment of classification relationships between *consecutive* schema versions, but may just as well be defined between *any* schema versions in the derivation hierarchy.

[6]In [8, 10] an *object role* is defined as a perspective of an object regarded as an instance of a class for which it is a member. Object roles and CV roles are concerned about what must be supported *locally* (in one schema version) and *globally*, respectively.

schema version association of the client. In this way references to the object as an instance of the same class in different contexts will generally bind to *different* CV roles.

A significant characteristic of the CV role notion is that objects are represented by multiple *independent* contexts which reflect all valid perspectives of the object. This allows for properties of different class versions to have the same domain/signature, but still allow them to be *semantically* different, and thus behave differently in different schema version contexts. For instance, the *scale* of an attribute or the *implementation* of a method may be changed, but still exhibiting properly in the different contexts of reference. In contrast, Encore [4] defines a *single* access context to apply for *all* versions of the class[7]. A multi-context approach more precisely reflects semantic differences between class versions and their interfaces.

5 Representation Compatibility

The *representation* of an object is the collection of attributes contained. Representation is important as it reflects the fundamental information-bearing elements of objects, maintaining the *state*. *Representation compatibility* is concerned about the *consistent availability* of all object representation, as a member of classes in different schema versions. In Section 4 it was assumed that CV roles instantiate representation in the same way as other properties of the class version are instantiated. However, for representation associated with different versions of the same class there are generally significant *overlaps* and *dependencies*: Versions of the same class reflect different manifestations of the same real-world abstraction, and it is a reasonable assumption that the *information contents* is very similar. Ensuring that objects behave consistently according to any class version for which it is an instance thus means that modifications to *one* CV role (in one schema version context) usually must also be reflected by the state as of *other* CV roles as well. For this reason, we do *not* want to multi-instantiate representation associated with class versions. Rather, a *sharing approach* is adopted for the management of object representation, and so that the *disjoint union* of all object CV role representation is maintained separately.

For efficiency reasons, and to achieve some regularity in representation structures, representation sharing will be defined at the level of *class* rather than for individual objects. In this way sharing patterns may be defined *statically*, upon schema version definition. For *each* class which is defined in some version of the schema, a *shared representation* (SR) is maintained as a container for *all* representation which is directly defined (i.e. non-inherited) for *some* version of the class[8]. This means that an SR will always be monotonically *increasing*, no attribute is ever removed from a class SR. To ensure representation compatibility, objects will allocate (persistently) SRs

---

[7] Evolution approaches also define a single context of access, which is always the *most recent* version.

[8] As an object need not necessarily be an instance of *all* versions of classes for which it is an instance of *some*, this means that the SR model of sharing implies that *redundant* representation (i.e. representation not contained by the object in any schema version context) may be allocated for some objects. However, this is acceptable in order to retain a class-based and statically determinable shared representation.

corresponding to each class it is a member of in *some* schema version context. In this way there will always be a direct correspondence between any CV role assumed attribute onto an attribute defined for the SR corresponding to the class for which the attribute was defined. Finally, existing database objects may also be affected when a class SR is *extended* due to the definition of a new version of the class. Each objects which in some context is a member of the class corresponding to the extended SR must be extended accordingly to be able to appear as an instance of the class version in the new schema version context. [9] discusses how certain *initializers* may be associated with representation which may be implicitly allocated for objects.

5.1   Representation relationships

The model of sharing is concerned about representation availability, ensuring attributes which are *identical* in multiple class versions are instantiated only once. In addition there are frequently *other* dependencies between attributes defined within different schema versions, both internal to and between classes. To ensure a consistently operating database there is a need to *establish* all these dependencies. For this reason a notion of *representation relationships* is introduced.

A *representation relationship* describes a semantic connection between one or more attributes (associated with a particular class "expanded" over inheritance) in the new schema version, and one or more attributes (associated with a possibly different class) in some former (most often the base) schema version. A representation relationship is always *bidirectional*, saying that that two groups of attributes are mutually dependent on each other. Special abilities are provided to say *how* the two groups of attributes are related (how the relationship is maintained).

A representation relationship is defined by the <-> operator, and may take different forms:

```
<class> {<AG> <-> <AG>}                              (1)
<class1> {<AG>} <-> <class2> {<AG>                   (2)
<SVId>::<class1> {<AG>} <-> <class2> {<AG>}          (3)
```

AG is an *attribute group*, i.e. some comma-separated list (often singular) of attributes defined for the particular class and schema version (i.e. class version). One attribute may be participate in multiple AGs. AGs are important as they define the unit for consistency maintenance: Any AG attribute generally depends on *all* attributes on the other side of the representation relationship. (1) applies for representation defined for the *same* class for the base (left side) and new (right side) schema version, for instance applicable for an attribute *domain modification* (for which the AGs are singular). For (2) the representation is associated with *different* classes in the two schema versions, for instance to reflect representation which is moved and simultaneously taking another form. Finally, for (3) the representation relationship applies between representation defined for a class in an *explicitly* indicated schema version, and for the new one. This is an important property of the approach, and in accordance with former discussions of this paper: Semantic dependencies need *not* necessarily follow the direction of schema version derivation relationships. In this way formerly defined representation may *reappear* in another form, or may be defined to have a different form in schema versions of different schema version derivation branches. Naturally, it may be a hard task for the schema designer to *detect* all such dependencies between schema versions, however it is important in order to ensure that the database behaves consistently as within any schema version context. Special *tools* should be provided in order to ease this task for the schema designer.

With each AG attribute a *mutation propagation function* (MPF) is associated which says *how* a new value for the attribute is computed when some attribute on the other side of the representation relationship is mutated. An MPF is a *"coercion"* function implemented in C++ which is executed in the context of the other side AG, and may reference *all* attributes in that AG (and no others). It is invoked when *some* attribute in the AG on the other side is mutated, and will implicitly bind to the new value for the modified attribute while reading other attributes from the database[9]. The result of the computation is assigned to (propagates to) the attribute to which it associates. MPFs define how representation relationships are to be *maintained*, and in this way may be said to define the *semantics* of the particular relationship. A MOV operation may be regarded as a representation relationship for which AGs are singular and both MPFs assignment operations.

The notion of MPFs may be compared with a notion of database *triggers*: When some attributes is modified, this may trigger a modification of other attributes (for the same object) to ensure that declared semantic relationships are consistently maintained for this object. Triggering may be performed over *multiple* representation relationships (in different directions), as well as *transitively*. However, no transitive representation relationships to representation visible within the *same* schema version (i.e. cycles in the dependency graph) are legal. It must be noted that representation relationships between non-consecutive schema versions need *only* be specified in the case there is no *transitive* representation relationship which express the same semantics.

An example representation relationship specification is given for a class GeomPoint, originally represented using polar coordinates, but in the new schema version modified to be represented using rectangular coordinates:

```
CLASS GeomPoint {
  REM theta;
  REM rho;
  ADD int x;
  ADD int y;

  rho [ sqrt(x*x + y*y) ],
  theta [ if (x==0) signum(y*pi/2.0)
          else arctan(y/x) ]
    <->
  x [ rho*cos(theta) ], y [ rho*sin(theta) ]};
```

---

[9] That is, all attribute references uniquely map to a corresponding SR attribute.

In some cases we may also have that we know there *is* a semantic dependency between attributes as of different schema versions, however *without* being able to express this dependency completely in terms of an MPF. In this case *Nil*-assignment may be applied, indicating that the particular attribute value may *not* be consistently derived over object modifications. We say that the attribute is *non-derivable* over the representation relationship, or possibly *partially* derivable in the case it is non-derivable only for *some* values of attributes in the other side AG. Partially derivable attributes are typically common for attribute generalizations or specializations.

Representation Implementation

One problem about the propagation scheme for maintenance of representation relationships is that all relationships are maintained in an *eagerly* manner between separate chunks of storage. Frequently, *redundant* storage will be maintained in this way. Moreover, in many cases it may be possible to *implement* an attribute in terms of other attributes, for the same or different SR for the same object. An attribute is *implementable* (in terms of other attributes), provided that any *write-request* may be consistently reflected by the other attributes and that any *read-request* may be answered by deriving the value from the other attributes. Attributes may typically be implementable over representation relationships, in the case that consistent MPFs are defined in each direction. For instance, attributes on both sides of the representation relationship in the GeomPoint example are implementable over the representation relationship. In this case it is *not* necessary with a separate persistent slot for attributes. Attribute implementation promotes *"late derivation"* as a substitute for eager propagation, and will ensure that representation relationships are *implicitly* maintained. Storage requirements are reduced, and often efficiency is improved.

5.2 Concluding remarks

Representation relationships may be regarded as a generalization of a MOV operation, with possibly multiple attributes participating in the relationship and with an ability to specify arbitrary semantic connections between representation. In the same way as for MOV, representation relationships may be established between attributes associated with arbitrary classes in arbitrary schema versions.

While representation relationships are defined between two schema versions, they will have global applicability in that *any* mutation of an attribute (irrespective of context of mutation) which participate in a representation relationship will invoke MPFs. An important characteristic of the approach is the adoption of a global perspective of representation management. Rather than having coercion function between individual versions of a class, the approach maintains a mapping between individual versions and a *totality* of representation for the object. Ensuring the totality is consistently maintained, any client perspective is consistently maintained as well. CSL specifications are applied to define the totality as well as how it is to be consistently maintained.

Finally, the similarity between classification and representation relationships must be noted. Both express semantic dependencies between any classes in any schema version, and which are maintained by propagation (of membership or mutation, respectively). Additional aspects of representation management and relationships are beyond the scope of this paper. It is referred to [9] for an elaborated discussion of these issues.

6 Comparison

Most existing SMM work is solely concerned about how objects may behave in accordance with other versions of its creation class, by (transitive) application of coercion functions. For the evolution approach only the most recent class version is interesting. Most frequently (e.g. ORION [2], GemStone [1] and O_2 [11]), a restricted taxonomy of change is assumed along with predefined rules for how the object base is to be affected by the particular change. OTGen [12] allows for the specification of *schema-level* modifications as well, but still upgrades the database to make all objects comply with the most recent specification only. Similar to us, OTGen provides a *relative* specification formalism: A tabular specification of schema version differences is generated on the basis of a syntactical "diff", with an ability to modify the default interpretation of change to define a particular intention of change. [13] also discusses some aspects of the necessity of class hierarchical changes.

Under the versioning approach, objects must be able to behave according to *any* version of its class. AVANCE [3] allows for defining *substitute read and write functions* for individual attributes, "*coercing*" between representation as of different versions of a class. Substitute functions may be defined between consecutive and non-consecutive class versions, and the approach provides some abilities to *restrict* the complete compatibility between versions of a class if desired. CLOSQL [5, 14] is similar, having update/backdate functions to define "coercion" procedures (in both directions) between consecutive versions (in a linear chain) of the same class. Dynamically, objects are coerced along the chain from the creation version to the referenced class version. Encore [4] defines a notion of a *version set interface* as the disjoint union of all interface defined for *some* version of the class. All objects must support this interface, and special *error handlers* must be defined (and implemented in terms of individual class version provisions) to handle all requests which may not be responded to by *all* versions of the class. A particular problem is that objects may *not* be enhanced with new representation to support new versions of the class. Furthermore, the presence of a *single* access context means that differences in the *semantics* of the interface (not also reflected by the syntactical definition), cannot be managed. Clamen [6] have objects maintain a "*facet*" for each version of the the object's class, somewhat similar to our notion of CV roles. Attributes of a class version may be characterized as *independent*, *shared, dependent* or *derived* as related to attributes of other class versions, however it is unclear whether these relationships may be defined between attributes in *arbitrary* versions of the class. The paper discusses how these relationships may be maintained in an eager or lazy manner, however the approach is not very concrete with respect to object management. Bratsberg [7, 15] defines a general framework for *any* evolution of classes, and constitutes an important source for inspiration for some mechanisms part of the presented approach. In the framework there is no notion of a schema involved, only a collection of classes. A new class may be added at any time, and may be related to existing classes by the introduction of *extent propagation links* (EPL), defining how membership in either or both of the classes may *propagate* into the other. In order to have objects appear consistently as a member of classes over propagation, special *consistency relationships* may be associated with EPLs. These have some similarities to our notion of representation relationships, but provides more elaborated mechanisms for consistency maintenance. The major problem with the approach is the lack of any notion of *schema* or *schema version*, there is only a non-partitioned collection of classes. As a consequence, there is no ability for *schema-level* modifications. Class versioning may only be *simulated* by bidirectional EPLs between classes, but all "versions" will be globally visible. Furthermore, consistency relationships may only be described over EPLs, i.e. in the direction of "derivation". The approach is fundamentally a *framework* for evolution and integration of classes, rather than directly addressing all problems of SMM.

7   Conclusions, Contributions and Further Work

The paper has presented a *versioning* approach to SMM which promotes a multi-perspectived view of the database. New schema versions are defined relatively to some existing schema version in the Change Specification Language (CSL), and so that a schema version derivation *hierarchy* is constructed. The approach adopts the *schema level* as the granularity of change, and so that a collection of primitive changes define a new version of the schema as a whole. In this way a change may involve *multiple* classes, for instance to *restructure* the hierarchical organization of classes or class association with properties. A CSL specification defines the *contents* of the new schema version in terms of how it differs from the base version. The CSL also allows for the specification of arbitrary *semantic relationships* (as well as how these are *maintained*) between classes and properties as defined in *any* schema version.

The most important contribution of the approach is the concern for the *global perspective* of SMM: Changes to *one* class frequently cannot be seen in isolation from changes to *other* classes, and the specification of *one* schema version cannot be regarded in isolation from other schema versions. As schema versions reflect different but overlapping specifications of the *same* database, it is necessary to express and maintain *all* semantic dependencies which exist between schema versions. Otherwise, it may *not* be guaranteed that the database may behave in a consistent manner, for all schema version perspectives, and over database modifications as performed within any schema version context. The awareness of these issues has resulted in the particular concern for specification and management of the deeper *semantics* of schema change. The notions of classification and representation relationships constitute powerful mechanisms for specifying and maintaining semantic dependencies for object classification and state between *arbitrary* schema versions, and *not* necessarily only in the direction of schema version derivation. In this way the approach permits the derivation of new schema versions in arbitrary and unpredictable directions, *particularly* important for long-lived databases for which a number of database specification may frequently be expected, and *without* compromising database consistency. Schema Modification Management, and in particular schema *versioning*, is a hard, but important, problem to address. It is our belief that the approach reflects a deeper understanding of the complexity of change, providing appropriate mechanisms for its specification and management.

A limited functionality prototype is under implementation. In this way we hope to to demonstrate the implementational feasibility, and to gain more insight about the applicability of the ideas. We would also like to investigate the applicability of the ideas within the context of *existing* OODBs.

References

[1] D. Jason Penney and Jacob Stein. Class Modification in the GemStone Object-Oriented DBMS. In *Proceedings of the Conference on Object-Oriented Systems, Languages and Applications (OOPSLA), Orlando, Florida, USA*, pages 111–117, October 1987.

[2] Jay Banerjee, Won Kim, Hyoung-Joo Kim, and Henry F. Korth. Semantics and Implementation of Schema Evolution in Object-Oriented Databases. In *Proceedings of ACM/SIGMOD (Management of Data), Chicago, Illinois, USA, 1987*, pages 311–322, May 1987.

[3] M. Ahlsén, A. Björnerstedt, S. Britts, C. Hultén, and L. Söderlund. Making Type Changes Transparent. In *Proceedings of IEEE Workshop on Languages for Automation, Chicago*, pages 110–117. IEEE Computer Society Press, November 1983.

[4] Andrea H. Skarra and Stanley B. Zdonik. Type Evolution in an Object-Oriented Database. In *Bruce Shriver and Peter Wegner (Eds.): Research Directions in Object-Oriented Programming*, pages 393–415. MIT Press, 1987.

[5] S.R. Monk and I. Sommerville. A Model for Versioning of Classes in Object-Oriented Databases. In *10th British National Conference on Databases (BNCOD '92), Aberdeen, Scotland July 1992*, pages 42–58, July 1992.

[6] Stewart M. Clamen. Type Evolution and Instance Adaptation. Technical Report CMU-CS-92-133, School of Computer Science, Carnegie Mellon University, Pittsburgh, PA 15213-3890, USA, June 1992. 27 pages.

[7] Svein Erik Bratsberg. *Evolution and Integration of Classes in Object-Oriented Databases*. PhD thesis, Department of Computer Systems and Telematics, Norwegian Institute of Technology, June 1993.

[8] Erik Odberg. Category Classes: Flexible Classification and Evolution in Object-Oriented Databases. In Gerhard Wijers, Sjaak Brinkkemper, and Tony Wasserman, editors, *Proceedings of the 6th Conference on Advanced Information*

Systems Engineering (CAISE '94), Utrecht, The Netherlands, pages 406–420. Springer-Verlag, June 1994. Lecture Notes in Computer Science no. 811.

[9] Erik Odberg. *MultiPerspectives: Object Evolution and Schema Modification Management in Object-Oriented Databases*. PhD thesis, Department of Computer Systems and Telematics, Norwegian Institute of Technology, 1994. In preparation.

[10] Erik Odberg. MultiPerspectives: The Classification Dimension of Schema Modification Management for Object-Oriented Databases. In *TOOLS USA '94 (Technology of Object-Oriented Languages and Systems), Santa Barbara, California, USA*, August 1994.

[11] Gilles Barbedette. Schema Modifications in the $LISPO_2$ Persistent Object-Oriented Language. In *ECOOP '91. European Conference on Object-Oriented Programming, Geneva, Switzerland*, pages 77–96. Springer-Verlag, 1991.

[12] Barbare Staudt Lerner and A. Nico Habermann. Beyond Schema Evolution to Database Reorganization. In *Proceedings of the Joint Conference on Object-Oriented Systems, Languages and Applications (OOPSLA) and ECOOP, Ottawa, Canada*, pages 67–76, October 1990.

[13] Barbare Staudt Lerner. Extending the Notion of Type Conformance to Interfaces and Type Systems, September 1993. Presented at OOPSLA '93 Workshop on *"Supporting the Evolution of Class Definitions"*.

[14] Simon Monk and Ian Sommerville. Schema Evolution in OODBs using Class Versioning. *SIGMOD Record*, 22(3):16–22, September 1993.

[15] Svein Erik Bratsberg. Unified Class Evolution by Object-Oriented Views. In *Proceedings of the 11th International Conference on the Entity-Relationship Approach, 7–9 October 1992, Karlsruhe, Germany*, pages 423–439, October 1992.

Distributed Galileo: a Persistent Programming Language with Transactions[1]

G. Mainetto
M. Di Giacomo
CNUCE, Institute of CNR
Pisa Italy

L. Vinciotti
ENGINEERING SpA
Pisa Italy

Abstract

Several research projects aim to integrate the functionalities of a database management system with those of a programming language. This is the main goal of Persistent Programming Languages. An open issue in these systems is to define and develop the important functionality that allows several end–users to concurrently access shared persistent data. This paper presents the problems we encountered and the techniques we used to provide the persistent programming language Galileo with the support for concurrent transactions that access a shared remote database. In our system, end–users can access a shared value environment and a shared type environment stored in a remote server. Every user can also use his own private persistent environments that are transparently integrated with the shared ones. Private environments are not directly visible to the other end–users, but there may be some subtle interactions on persistent private data due to inheritance. This system uses a strict two–phase locking technique to ensure serializability of concurrent transactions. Furthermore, it guarantees the recovery of persistent data in case of system and transaction failures.

1   Introduction

The recent development of both Persistent Programming Languages (PPLs) and Object–Oriented Data Bases (OODBs) technologies has meant that their technical solutions could be adapted to a Distributed Galileo system. Distributed Galileo is a system in which a limited number of users can develop and run database applications that use structurally complex data. The language used for the definition and manipulation of persistent data is Galileo [1]. Galileo is a PPL because it satisfies the following properties [2]:
- *orthogonal persistence*
- *persistence independence*

The first property concerns how persistent values are declared. It establishes that a value of any type expressible in the language has the right to persist, i.e. it can last

---

[1] This work has been partly supported by the EU under contracts No ERB-CIPA-CT-93-1616 and ESPRIT BRA No 6309 FIDE2 (Formally Integrated Data Environment).

after the end of the execution of the program that generated it. The second property relates to the run–time support of a PPL. It says that the code of a fragment of a program can be applied to both persistent and temporary values with unchanged semantics. For example, the code of the body of a function must operate on both persistent and temporary actual parameters[2].

PPL programs that access a database are called *transactions*, i.e. concurrent processes that execute sequences of actions dealing with temporary and shared persistent values. Actions performed on shared persistent values during a transaction execution are reading, updating, creation and deletion. From a PPL point of view, transactions are sequences of complex statements that can activate functions and procedures. Therefore PPL transactions must satisfy two properties: persistence independence and *atomicity*. A transaction executes atomically if [3]:

- it accesses shared persistent values without interfering with other transactions;
- when it commits, all its changes become persistent; otherwise it has no effect on the database.

The first aspect of a transaction's atomicity regards the *concurrency control* mechanism supplied by a PPL system. The second aspect relates to *recovery*: if a *transaction* failure, or a *system* failure or a *media* failure occurs during the execution of a transaction, then the PPL system must preserve the consistency of the database.

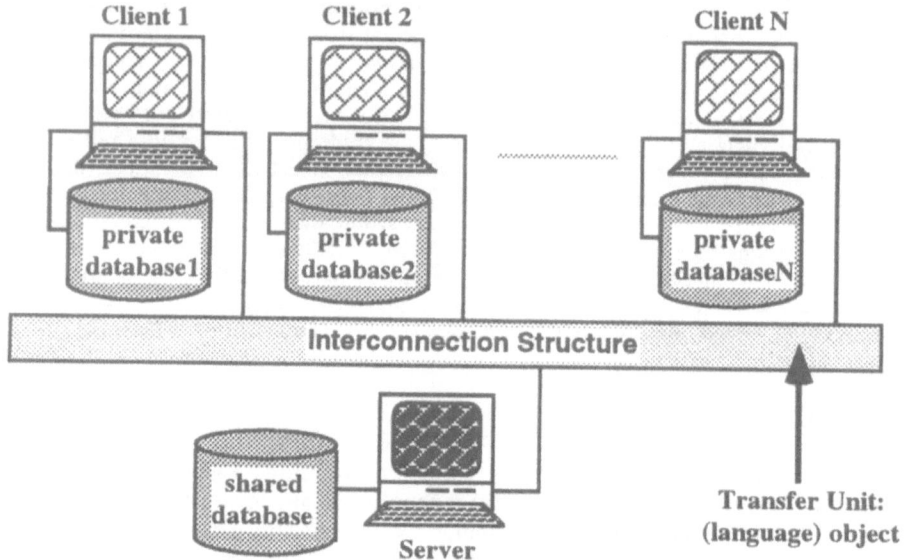

Figure 1. General architecture of Distributed Galileo

This paper shows the main technical solutions adopted to render Galileo a PPL system with transaction management. We designed Distributed Galileo so that several system components can exploit semantic information about managed entities. To this aim, we have only modified the architecture of the run–time support, without

---

[2] We use the term "temporary value" for a value stored in temporary (volatile) storage. In Distributed Galileo, temporary storage is the virtual memory of a process. A temporary value ceases to exist when its process ends.

changing the syntax and the semantics of the language. The resulting architecture is a *distributed client–server architecture* where each client has a private database integrated with the shared database of the server (**Figure 1**). The unit of transfer between the clients and the server is a single object[3]. Besides object identity and relationship, the server can also understand part of the information on the type of an object, and in particular, whether it is modifiable or not. Distributed Galileo supports *implicit serializable short* transactions, whose duration is for seconds.

This paper is organised as follows. Section 2 introduces the notions of persistence and transaction provided by Galileo; Section 3 outlines the main features of the client-server architecture and the technical solutions adopted for developing this architecture; Section 4 describes persistence management; Section 5 deals with concurrency control and Section 6 with recovery; Section 7 gives some performance figures of the Distributed Galileo system; in Section 8 some conclusions related to this experiment are drawn.

2 Persistence, Distribution and Transactions in Galileo

2.1 Main Features

Galileo is a strongly and statically typed language that supports the abstraction mechanisms of both modern programming languages and semantic data models (classification, aggregation and generalisation). Galileo has the most important features required by OODB languages [4]. As far as this paper is concerned, the following are relevant Galileo features:

1) Type orthogonality.
   All data types have the same rights. A value of any type can be a component of any data structure, dynamically created, passed as a parameter, returned as the result of a function, etc.

2) Rich type system.
   Along with basic types (such as integer, boolean, string, real, etc.), Galileo also provides the following type constructors: tuple, record, sequence of homogeneous values, union, reference (updatable value of any type), table, vector, and function. Moreover, a mechanism for the definition of semi–abstract record types with name equivalence exists. A subtyping relationship is defined on types. This relationship allows the language to support *inclusion polymorphism* [5] [6].

3) Class and subclass.
   A class is a structured value that consists of a modifiable sequence of semi–abstract records. The modifiable sequence represents the *extension* of a class, while the semi–abstract records are the *instances*[4]. The programmer explicitly populates a class. A class can be a subclass of a superclass. In this case there exists simultaneously a subset relationship between the subclass extension and

---

[3] By "objects" we mean data objects of variable sizes (sometimes called cells), i.e. memory elements that are (parts of) the representation of a (structured) value of the language.

[4] We use the term "instance" to avoid excessive overloading of the word "object". "Instances" are the "objects" of OODBs.

superclass extension, and a subtype relationship between the type of the subclass instances and the type of the superclass instances. This mechanism allows the programmer to work on the extension of a superclass by inspecting all the instances, including those which are members of its subclasses, but only using the properties specified in the superclass. Inheritance is *single*. Late binding is used.

4) Side–effects on a limited number of types.
Side–effects can only occur on values of the following types: class, when either the programmer adds or removes an instance from the extension or he specialises an instance from a superclass into a subclass; semi–abstract record, when an instance is specialised; and reference, when an assignment statement is performed.

5) Functionality.
Functions are values and so they have the property (1). Functionality allows OODB objects with methods to be modelled through instances with functional components.

6) Transparency of pointers.
The language hides all pointers. Values are automatically shared because the semantics of parameter passing is by reference. The need to pass a parameter by reference derives from inclusion polymorphism and persistence independence.

7) Exceptions handling.
Constructs of the language allow us to raise an exception and to catch the exception raised during the evaluation of an expression.

8) Interactivity.
An interaction with the system consists of typing Galileo sentences at the terminal. A sentence can either be an expression or a declaration. If it is a declaration, the system extends the *global* environment with the bindings specified in the declaration. If it is an expression, the system evaluates the expression in the current environment and shows the outcome.

2.2 Persistence

The Galileo model of persistence derives from the interactivity of the system and from the *scoping* rules of identifiers. Every top-level declaration automatically extends the global environment with new bindings. The extended global environment is visible to declarations and expressions typed in later on. The persistence rule derives from the scoping rule: *every top-level declared value is implicitly persistent and will continue to persist until there is an access path to it*. This model of persistence is called *general* persistence. In practice, values and types defined in the global environment are automatically persistent, and they persist after the end of their declaration evaluation.

The combination of a persistence rule with type orthogonality means that Galileo can be classified as a language with orthogonal persistence. Consequently, a Galileo database consists of top–level declared values, i.e. basic values and arbitrarily constructed ones, including classes that play the most important role in modelling the database.

2.3 Distribution

The new applications supported by PPLs naturally fit decentralised organisational structures. Thus, we designed Distributed Galileo, a system that supports local distribution of persistent data. In the context of local distribution, the client–server architecture is emerging as the standard of the 1990s. Advantages of this architecture are good performance, scalability and possibility of using specialised hardware in client and server machines. Distributed Galileo system has a client–server architecture. In designing Distributed Galileo we have taken into account the inalterability of Galileo syntax and semantics, and the issue of *location transparency*.

The persistence model of Galileo has been adapted to deal with client–server distribution. The global environment has been split into two parts:

- A single *global shared* environment.
  Its definition is the result of the development phases of the shared database. The shared environment is frozen as far as the names of persistent values are concerned.
- One *global private* environment for every client.
  Each global private environment can be extended with new bindings. Only the user that created a global private environment can access it. This environment represents local persistent values of the specific user. It is placed in an intermediate position between the global shared environment and the last expression introduced at the terminal.

An interesting situation arises from the combination of this model of distribution and late binding of class methods. For example, if a programmer redefines a method of a subclass of his global private environment, then a user of a different client that operates on the shared superclass extension could automatically activate that private method because of subset relationship between subclass /superclass extensions and late binding.

2.4 Transactions

In Distributed Galileo the notion of transaction comes from the interactivity of the system, like for persistence. When a Galileo user introduces an expression into the system, its evaluation can cause the access to persistent values: *a transaction is a top-level expression*. The idea of transaction is implicit in the language.

A Distributed Galileo transaction operates transparently on shared and private persistent values. A transaction can consist of an initial set of declarations of temporary values followed by a sequence of expressions, whose evaluation can access values of any longevity. Persistence independence allows a temporary function to be declared which operates on both persistent and temporary values.

The approach used in the definition of persistence, distribution and transaction is particularly advantageous for Distributed Galileo programmers. The implicit orthogonal persistence of the declarations allows the programmer to create database schemas without any constraints on the use of type constructors. Persistence independence means that temporary and persistent functions can be designed without thinking about the different longevity of the actual parameters. Implicit transactions allow functionalities to be designed which operate on databases without specifying any particular transaction operation construct. Location transparency and inheritance permit to safely use persistent data of private and shared environments. Programmers thus only need to know Galileo.

508

2.5 An example

We consider a medium sized dealer of a car producer. This dealer is organised into several divisions such as Sales, Purchases, Repairs, Administration, etc. Each division operates on persistent values, either shared with other divisions or solely belonging to its own division. For example, the Purchases division must make orders to the car producer and update the set of unsold cars when ordered cars are delivered to the dealer. The Sales division obviously sells cars, giving priority to unsold ones. Thus the management of the unsold car warehouse must be shared between the Sales and Purchases divisions.

The automation of a car producer dealer is an example of an application distributed on a local network, where private and shared persistent data need to be integrated, and with a few end–users.

2.5.1 The Shared Database

Initially the application designer defines the global shared environment. In this phase a single–user version of the Galileo system is used, which provides support for type and value persistence and which guarantees single-user transaction recovery [7].

```
use type liras <-> int assert this>0 ;

use Car_Models class
    carmodel <-> (|
        CarProducer: string and
        Model: string and
        Price: var liras
    |);

use Unsold_Cars class
    unsoldcar <-> (|
        Carmodel: carmodel and
        Code: int and
        Colourcode: int and
        ...
        |);
```

Figure 2. Shared environment definition

Figure 2 shows a part of the definition of the shared global environment for our example. In the first line there is a semi–abstract data type definition with an assertion; two class definitions follow. Car_Models class represents all the models that the dealer can sell; Unsold_Cars class represents unsold cars in the warehouse. Each unsold car is univocally associated with a model (Carmodel component of the instances of Unsold_Cars class).

Note the presence in class declarations of a name for the extension (Car_Models, Unsold_Cars) and a name for the instance type (carmodel, unsoldcar). The type of an instance is a semi–abstract record type, on which components are selected through the same operator defined for standard record selection (overloaded operator of). An instance component whose value can change is declared by way of the reference constructor var.

The figure does not illustrate the answers of the single–user Galileo system when declarations are successfully evaluated. In particular, the system signals the presence of an instance constructor for every declared class. An instance constructor is a system generated function that has a record value as its only parameter, and whose effect is the creation of an instance which is then inserted into the extension of the class (and into all superclass extensions).

2.5.2 Private Databases

Once the global shared environment has been completely defined, single–user Galileo permanent storage becomes the shared database of the Distributed Galileo, without any modifications.

In our example, the application designer will develop the private environment of the Sales division. **Figure 3** shows a part of it: a clients class that represents those people that have ordered a model; Buyers subclass representing those who have been assigned an unsold car; and Sold_Cars class representing sold cars assigned to a buyer. The last class is a subclass of the shared class Unsold_Cars.

```
use Clients class
    client <-> (|
          Name: string and
          Address:(| City: string and Street: string |) and
          Model: carmodel and
          ...
          |);

use rec Buyers subset of Clients class
    buyer <-> (|
          is client and
          Car:= derived
                  get c in Sold_Cars with Buyer of c = this
          |)

    and Sold_Cars subset of Unsold_Cars class
    soldcar <-> (|
          is unsoldcar and
          Buyer: buyer
          |);

use AssignCar:= fun (Aclient: client) is
    use Acar :=
          (get c in Unsold_Cars
              with Model of c = Model of Aclient
              And Not (c alsoin Sold_Cars)
          iffails failwith ("Not available yet!") )
    in insoldcar (Acar, (|Buyer:= inbuyer (Aclient)|)))
```

Figure 3. Private environment definition

Note that buyers and their assigned cars are defined in a mutually recursive manner; instance components have arbitrarily constructed types (functional component Car of the instance of Buyers class, record component Address of Clients class).

The functional persistent value AssignCar verifies whether there is an unsold car of a model required by a client in the warehouse, and if this unsold car has not yet been assigned. If this is the case, it specialises the client into a buyer and the unsold car into a sold one; otherwise it fails.

510

To understand the meaning of function's last statement, the reader needs to know that when a class is defined, the system automatically generates a function that allows an instance of its superclass to be specialised into an instance of the subclass (`insoldcar` for class `Sold_Cars` and `inbuyer` for class `Buyers`). The parameters of a specialisation function are the identity of a superclass instance and a record, which defines the components to add to the instance for generating the specialisation. The return value of the specialisation function is the identity of the new subclass instance, which is the same of the superclass instance. Moreover, it is possible to verify whether an instance is a member of a class (`alsoin` predicate).

The construct **iffails** traps all the exceptions generated during the evaluation of the preceding expression (**get**...), and it gives the control to expression that follows (**failwith**...). In the example, if an exception raises when the functional persistent value `AssignCar` is looking for an unsold car, then the exception will be propagated (**failwith**...).

Note that the application programmer uses types and values of the shared environment in the definition of the private environment: `Sold_Cars` private class instances are subtypes of `Unsold_Cars` shared class instances; the private functional value `AssignCar` uses the shared value representing the extension of `Unsold_Cars` class.

2.5.3 Transactions

When private databases have been defined, the user can issue transactions that transparently access temporary, shared persistent and private persistent values. The following expressions are transactions (system answers are in bold italics):

```
E: mkclient                     % Tran1: client constructor call%
>      (|Name:= "Bosses' boss" and
>      Address:=(|City:="Rome"and Street:="c/o H.Raphael"|)and
>      Model:= get c in Car_Models           % shared class %
>                 with Model of c = "Prison-van" and
>      ...|);

E: AssignCar (get c in Clients       %Tran2: AssignCar call %
>                 with Name of c = "Bosses' boss");
Failure: Not available yet!
```

Both transactions may fail for several reasons. The transaction programmer has decided that if an exception arises, for example because the `Prison-van` model ordered by the `Bosses' boss` client has not arrived yet, this exception will propagate up to the top-level.

3 Architecture of Distributed Galileo

3.1 Object Server

[8] analysed three alternative client–server architectures for the Distributed Galileo system, considering concurrency control, recovery, cache management and clustering issues. The three architectures analysed, described in detail in [9], are those usually used for OODBs, because of the analogies with PPLs. The classification of the

architectures is based on the unit of transfer between a client and the server, and they are named *Object Server*, *Page Server* and *File Server*.

We decided to use the Object Server because the remaining architectures are only meaningful when the system supports clustering. The current Galileo system provides neither a language for defining the physical organisation of persistent values nor a component that automatically performs this task during the operational activity of the system. Some shortages derived from the absence of clustering, such as access time to persistent values, can be mitigated by the copying compacting atomic garbage collector supplied by the system. In fact, this functionality automatically reorganises persistent object placements into permanent storage according to the physical relationships among them. In addition, we were interested in testing the use of the Persistent Object Store (POS) [10], which provides an object interface, and semantic information about objects in Distributed Galileo.

Sections 7 and 8 summarise the results of our experiment.

3.2 Incremental Persistent Compiler

The Distributed Galileo system uses an incremental persistent compiler to interface application programmers and end–users. In each client, a declaration and a transaction are firstly compiled. Because of portability requirements, the code generated by the compiler does not belong to a particular host machine, but to an intermediate machine, the *Client Functional Abstract Machine* (CFAM). The Galileo compiler generates the intermediate code and stores it in CFAM memory. Then an interpreter executes it, and finally the result of the interpretation is displayed on the screen **(Figure 4)**.

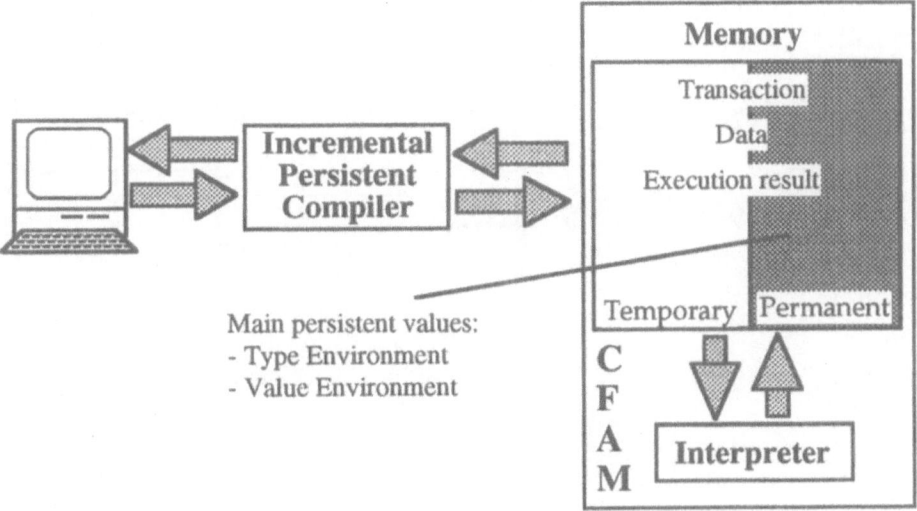

Figure 4. Distributed Galileo compiler and interpreter

The system manages declarations like transactions because a declaration may introduce a new binding between an identifier and a value that may be the result of a function application, and the called function might access shared and private persistent values.

512

Data structures needed by the compiler, *type* and *value environments*, are also persistent. To make them persistent, the two data structures are stored in the memory of the intermediate machine and are managed as if they were persistent values. They are accessed by the compiler through the functions implemented in the intermediate machine for persistent value access. [11] reports on technical details about the implementation of type and value environment persistence.

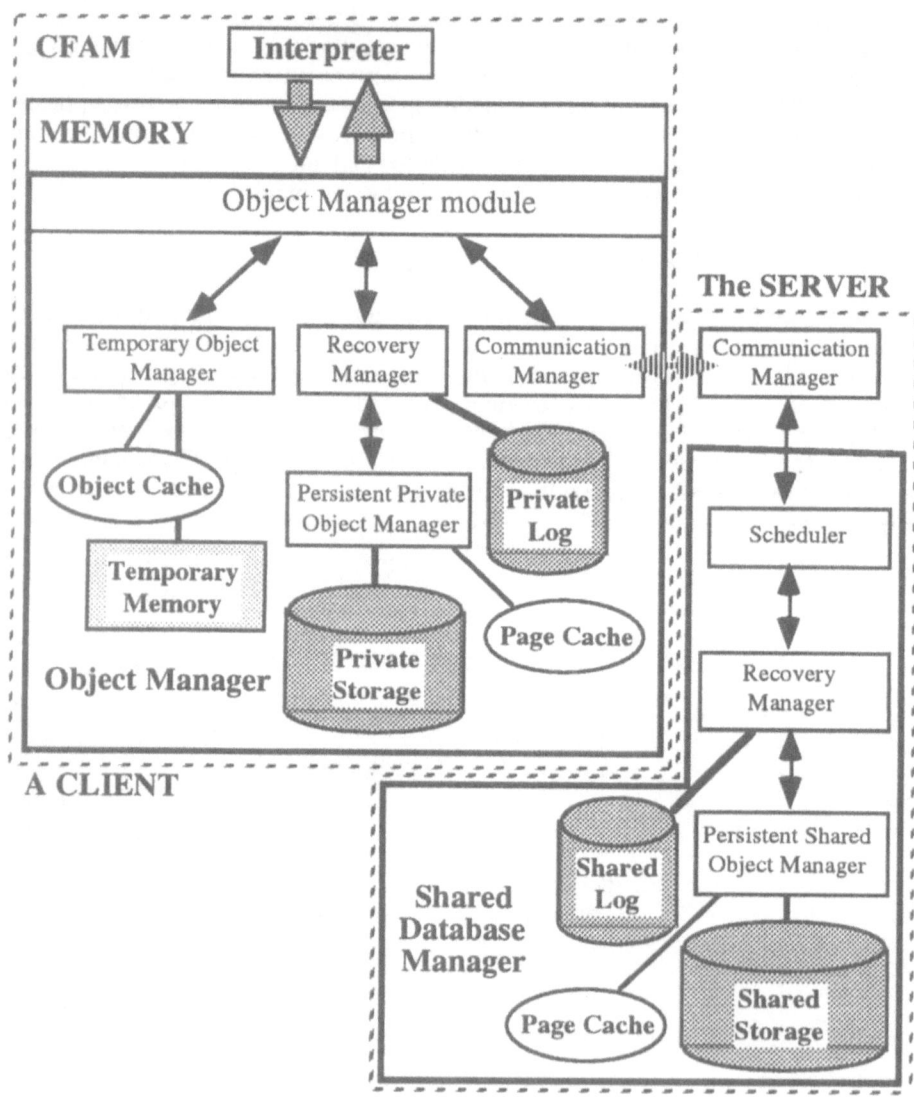

Figure 5. CFAM and Server architectures

513

3.3 Client Functional Abstract Machine and the Server

Figure 5 shows the organisation of the CFAM intermediate machine and of the server, including component modules (rectangles), subsystems (bold rectangles), caches (ellipses), and temporary and permanent storages. For the purposes of this paper, Object Manager subsystem and the Shared Database Manager are the most important components.

CFAM is a C program that represents the main part of Distributed Galileo run–time support. It is an extension of the *Functional Abstract Machine* [12], modified to support classes, persistence and atomicity of transactions for the Galileo system. CFAM is a stack machine, designed to optimise the execution of the functional languages, where function application is the most frequent operation.

3.3.1 Interpreter

CFAM interpreter consists of a set of procedures that implement specific operations of every intermediate machine data type. The most important operations supplied are:
(1) Management of a wide set of data structure operations, including allocation, selection and control flow primitives. Along with the traditional data type operations, operations to create and manage reference values, extensible instances, lists and closures are also provided.
(2) Control operations to apply a closure, to return from a closure application, and to execute conditional and non conditional jumps.
(3) Exception handling operations that can be nested.
(4) Transaction operations, and particularly begin transaction and successful transaction completion operations. The other transaction operations are implicitly carried out according to accessed/created values and to the flow of control during transaction interpretation.
The interpreter uses the functionalities supplied by the Structured Data Manager to access the values stored in the three memories. This module, not shown in the figure, supplies primitives to allocate a data structure representing a value of a specific type and to access a data structure component. The CFAM interpreter expresses selection and modification of a data structure component as the *selection of a record field*. Therefore, the main task of the Structured Data Manager module is to map associative access, through a label, into accesses through a base address and a displacement. The base address relates to the identity of an object.

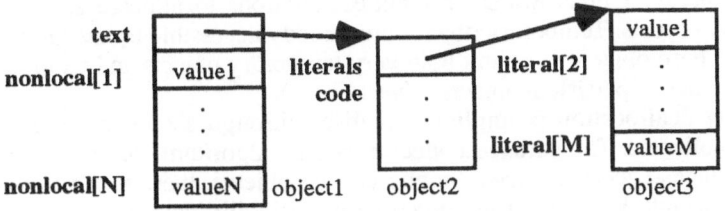

Figure 6. Closure data structure

Figure 6 shows how the interpreter sees a closure data structure, and the representation of a closure in terms of objects. A closure data structure consists of three objects:
 – nonlocal environment object (*object1*);

- closure text object (*object2*), the text is the intermediate machine code;
- literals (*object3*), i.e. constant values found in the text of the closure.

The interpreter selects the components of the closure using the name of the label (in bold).

3.3.2 Object Manager

The Object Manager is the *subsystem* that provides transaction and persistence supports. It shows the interpreter a 'potentially unbounded' addressable storage containing persistent and temporary objects. This manager does not know the object type but only whether an object is modifiable. The Object Manager supplies functions operating on a single object (allocation, selection and updating of a component), and functions representing transaction operations (transaction begin, transaction commit, transaction abort). This subsystem implicitly deals with object deallocation during garbage collections.

The Object Manager simultaneously manipulates temporary and permanent storages, which are each organised as an object heap. One object is a *vector of words* where every word is 32 bit long. Objects are identified by their addresses. The format of an object distinguishes between references and data. A reference can be either the address of an object (its identity) or an immediate value (short integer, boolean, etc.), i.e. a value that occupies the same amount of memory as a reference. In **Figure 6** the closure value is composed of three objects: *object1* is composed of N+1 references; *object2* consists of a reference and a data part (the code); and *object3* has M references that may be immediate.

The terminology used for dealing with objects is the same as in the graph theory. The directed graph representing a set of objects consists of associating a node with each object and an edge with each object identity stored in the object.

The Object Manager *module* controls the flow of objects among memories, interacting with the underlying modules. During its activity, the Object Manager module ensures the uniqueness of an object. To this end, it holds a *Correspondence Table* that associates the identity of an object stored in temporary memory (TID) with the identity of the same object in permanent storage (PID). A TID is associated with a temporary memory address, a PID is associated with a permanent storage one. TIDs and PIDs are unique, but indirectly associated with addresses.

3.3.3 Temporary Object Manager

The Temporary Object Manager supplies functions to allocate and to deallocate temporary objects. Temporary objects are directly accessible by the Object Manager module. These objects represent both very temporary objects and temporary objects that are copies of persistent objects (*object cache*).

Object deallocation is implicitly realised through a copying and compacting garbage collector. The garbage collector uses an algorithm, described in Section 4, that privileges cached objects. Among cached objects, there is a different level of privilege which depends on the potential modifiability and effective update of an object.

Figure 7 shows the format of temporary objects. Using the tag field the system can determine the total size of the object and the number of references in it. The PID field is only meaningful if the temporary object is in the cache.

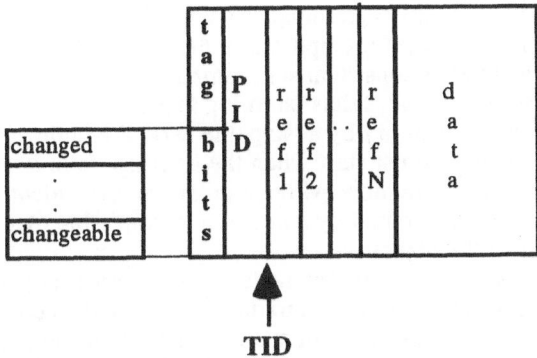

Figure 7. Temporary object format

3.3.4 Communication Managers

The system uses a local area network with a synchronous protocol to access shared persistent objects. Each client communicates with a dedicated process which sends requests to the Shared Database Manager. The answers follow the inverse route.

The communication always begins from a client. A client sends its request and then stops its execution to wait for the answer. The communication schema allows the server to block a transaction by delaying the sending of the answer message.

3.3.5 Scheduler

This server module grants the serializability of the execution of concurrent transactions. It uses algorithms that exploit the knowledge of the static semantics of objects. The Strict Two Phase Locking (S2PL) is the policy used, with an object as its lock unit. The protocol used for committing a distributed transaction is a simplified version of the Two Phase Commit protocol (2PC).

3.3.6 Recovery Managers

Client and server Recovery Managers in this version of the system allow a client and the server to be correctly resynchronized when a system failure occurs during the 2PC. Private and Shared Logs are *temporary logs* [13].

3.3.7 Shared and Private Persistent Object Managers

The Persistent Object Manager used is POS, a library expressly designed to be used as the persistent object store of a PPL. This library is currently used in the implementation of several languages with different paradigms such as Galileo, Napier88, PS-Algol, STAPLE, and Quest [14].

POS does not support transactions. It supplies a persistent object heap with objects of different sizes. To operate independently of the supported languages, POS does not manage object formats which specifically belong to a particular language, but it supplies a generic format for persistent objects like the one described above. It provides primitives to:
1) access a persistent object through its identity;

2) allocate a persistent identity and initialise a new object;
3) render atomically persistent the updates to the state of the database thus leading
the database into another consistent state (*stabilise*);
4) remove database state updates thus returning to a previous consistent state;
5) collect the permanent memory by a 'stop–the–world' atomic garbage collector.
Atomic garbage collection must start when the database is in a consistent state. To
move objects in permanent memory while maintaining their identities, the persistent
identity of an object is represented by a key in a lookup table that maps the key into
the physical address of the object.

The system and the database are interacted by input/output operations of physical
pages. These pages, which are moved into the database and vice versa, automatically
become virtual memory pages of client shared database manager processes because
POS uses a memory mapped file technique [15]. The supporting operating system
manages page cache on demand of POS.

POS uses a shadow paging technique to ensure the atomicity of database updates
[16]. The first time a persistent object placed on a physical page is updated or the
first time a persistent object is created, leads to the creation of a shadow version of
that physical page. *stabilise* is the primitive that replaces original physical pages
with shadow ones by atomically updating the page table.

4 Persistence Management

In the Distributed Galileo system any transaction can simultaneously operate on
three different memories, each one organised as a heap of objects with an identity
associated with its physical address. Each heap has a statically defined size. The
Object Manager has to deal with the following problems connected with persistence:
(1) how to distinguish persistent object identities from temporary ones;
(2) when to load an object into temporary memory and how many objects to load at
a time;
(3) which objects to keep in temporary memory during garbage collection;
(4) which objects to store in permanent memories.

Temporary and Persistent Identities. Persistence independence imposes the constraint
that persistent and temporary identities have the same sizes. For example the same
closure code must operate on persistent and temporary actual parameters: because in
Galileo the actual parameters are passed by reference, the system needs to reserve the
same space for storing the identities. A temporary identity has to be distinguished
from an immediate value. To distinguish between persistent and temporary identities,
the system places them in separate address spaces. In Distributed Galileo the
persistent address space must be further divided into private persistent and shared
persistent. A memory address in Distributed Galileo occupies a word of 32 bits; so
the system can address 2^{30} temporary objects, 2^{29} private persistent objects and 2^{29}
shared persistent objects. This is sufficient for our experimentation.

Persistent Object Loading. Distributed Galileo only loads one object at a time on
demand of the computation. The first time the system executes the dereferencing of a
persistent object identity, the Object Manager finds this persistent object in
permanent memory, copies the object state into the temporary memory, inserts the
pair <PID, TID> in the Correspondence Table, and finally rewrites the persistent

identity that gave rise to the dereferencing with the new temporary identity. The table allows any further dereferencing of the same PID in the same TID. The Object Manager supplies the interpreter with a dereferencing function that the interpreter calls every time it has to navigate in the heap.

Garbage Collection and Cache Management. Heap management is based on the principle that all objects reachable from an identifier existing in the current scope cannot be collected. This principle allows us to solve the remaining problems, if we include the Correspondence Table into the notion of current scope used by a Galileo transaction. Garbage collection of the temporary heap is one critical point in the system. Our solution uses a self–adapting policy based on computation needs, aimed at always non reducing the overall throughput of the system. The first time that the garbage collector operates during a transaction execution, it collects only temporary objects unreachable from the local environment and from the Correspondence Table. The object cache remains unchanged. In the next phase, if the system underestimates the percentage of previously collected memory, the garbage collector also collects non–modifiable objects in the cache. Finally, modifiable non updated objects in the cache are collected as well. This differentiated policy allows a transaction to continue its execution, with the hope that an object removed from the cache will not be accessed again in the immediate future. These objects may then be reloaded if necessary. This may generate an overhead in the computation, but it does not limit concurrency among transactions. The cache of persistent non–modifiable objects is maintained among successive executions of transactions in the same session. This does not prevent the correctness criterion of serializability used by Distributed Galileo from taking place.

Persistent Object Storing. The system uses the Correspondence Table to determine which objects it must store. Firstly, the client sends the server all the objects belonging to the transitive closure that are rooted in an updated shared persistent object; then it stores transitive closures of updated private objects. If a transaction corresponds to a declaration, it will modify the private environment and objects will be stored in the private database. The order that the visit of the object graph is made is important. The system begins with the shared persistent objects because they might have been updated in order to refer private persistent objects. In this case, the system must move the persistent private objects in the shared persistent store and replace the old private versions with dummy objects. These objects indicate shared objects where the current up–to–date version can be found (in Gemstone, an object of this kind is called a *proxy* [17]). The use of dummy private objects modifies the dereferencing algorithm of persistent private identities.

5 Concurrency Control

The S2PL protocol grants the serializability of concurrent transactions. A transaction begins in the client when the CFAM interpreter executes the first statement of the intermediate code. Before the first shared object is requested, a client communicates transaction starting with the server; then the client begins to ask the server to read and send shared persistent object states. When the CFAM interpreter executes the last statement of the intermediate code representing a transaction, the client will send the server all the updated shared objects and the newly created ones. Finally, the

518

distributed 2PC takes place. Note that only changeable objects can be updated and that a shared persistent object will be updated when a copy of it is available in the client. As a consequence, the scheduler will first be asked to read an object and then to write it. The scheduler has to support lock escalation.

Distributed Galileo concurrency control has the following features:

1) The scheduler uses the information connected with the modifiability of every object to minimise the cost of managing the Lock Table. Information about shared and exclusive locks is only held for the modifiable objects accessed by a transaction.

2) In the growing phase, firstly a transaction T acquires all shared locks, one at a time, and then requests simultaneously all the exclusive locks needed (**Figure 8**). Exclusive locks requested by T relate to a subset of the objects on which T has already obtained shared locks. The scheduler tries to grant all the exclusive locks requested. If it is not successful, because an object to be updated has been read from another transaction, then it only grants the exclusive locks that do not generate conflicts, and the scheduler records which other transactions T depends on. If this dependency generates a cycle, because another transaction has requested an exclusive lock on an object that T wishes to update too, then T is ordered to fail. When another transaction is successful or fails, it releases all its locks which are then assigned to T in exclusive mode. If another transaction generates a cycle in the Wait For Graph, requiring an exclusive lock on an object T is waiting for, then it is forced to abort and the exclusive lock is granted to T. To summarise, either T immediately fails because of lock escalation, or is granted access to exclusive resources.

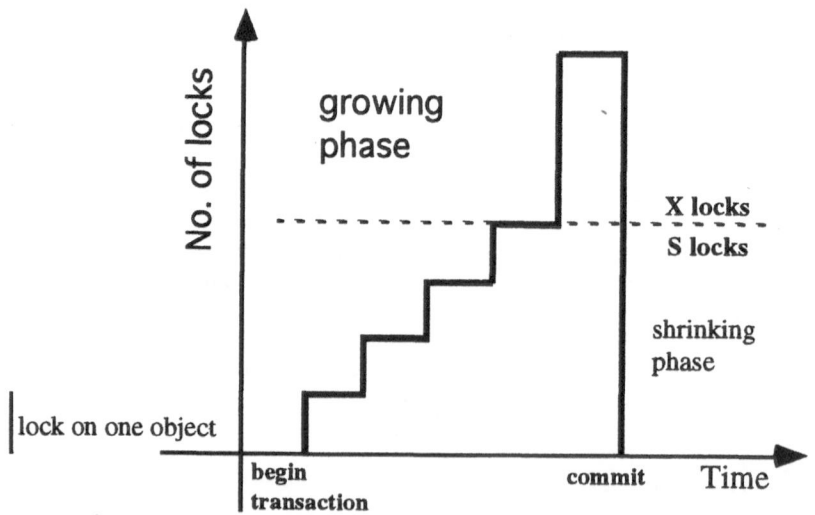

Figure 8. Phases of a Distributed Galileo transaction

3) The commit protocol used is a simplified version of 2PC, because only two processes are involved. The starting hypothesis is that if a system failure generates during the *uncertainty period*, then it will always be possible that a client and the server will resynchronize again and they will be able to solve the uncertainty. This hypothesis is realistic because the architecture of the system is

locally distributed and there is not a large number of clients. After obtaining exclusive locks, the client, which acts as the *coordinator*, requests all shared persistent identities to assign them to the new shared objects. The client then copies new and updated private objects into the shadow pages of the private POS and it writes the correspondent records in the private log. Subsequently, the coordinator sends all the new versions of shared persistent objects to the server in a single group. The server stores these objects in the buffer of the shared log. The coordinator writes the record $start2PC$ in the private log, beginning the uncertainty period, and it sends the server the request to commit. The server stores the objects in the shadow pages of shared POS and flushes the shared log buffer. If the total size of the shadow pages is sufficient, it stores the record commit–transaction in the log, sends an affirmative answer back to the client, and makes the new state permanent. The client executes the same operations.

In Distributed Galileo the problem of reporting the logical lock (on the object) to the physical level (on pages) does not exist. The smaller granularity of objects compared to that of pages should grant, in theory, a greater real concurrency among transactions. The policy chosen for the commit in the server is a form of anticipated commit that makes permanent updates after the commit record has been flushed in shared log. Writing in the database is deferred. The performance of the system very much depends on the buffer management of the shared log.

6 Recovery

There are three types of failures: media, system and transaction. For each failure the system must provide an ad–hoc recovery mechanism.

6.1 Media Failures

Media failures can damage the permanent storage where databases are stored. To protect a database against a crash, database management systems usually replicate information on persistent data in a log file. The log is duplicated to prevent the loss of its contents from a media failure. The operator periodically makes a dump of the database and empties the log at the same time.

This version of Distributed Galileo system is not reliable against crashes, but this system already has the most important component needed, i.e. temporary log. The system lacks duplication of the log information and procedures for restoring the state of databases. Clearly, a complete Galileo system dealing with media failures should be based on a *logical logging* technique. This technique should use a *redo* algorithm for restoring database states generated from committed transactions.

Logical logging has the following advantages compared other logging techniques that store physical pages in the log: the size of log file is small, the expense for physical I/O operations during normal processing is very low, and the expense for recovery is medium.

6.2 System Failures

System failures cause the loss of the contents in temporary memory, but they do not affect the permanent storage. If a system failure generates in the server, then all the active transactions will be involved. In designing Distributed Galileo we took into account two system failures: power failure and communication failure over local networks.

Shadow paging technique ensures database consistency against power failures, both in the server and in clients.

We did not consider specific problems caused by the communication protocol because the communication is synchronous and uses very reliable standard network protocols. When either a client or the server generates a communication failure, the system automatically detects the failure, and the peer process involved in the communication that is still active considers the transaction aborted.

An exception to this general framework is the uncertainty period of 2PC, which starts when a client stores the start2PC record and finishes when the commit record is in the private log. During this period there is no automatic abort of the transaction: a client and the server have to reconnect and to resynchronize their actions. Our 2PC protocol is protected against system failures. For example, if the communication fails just after the beginning of the uncertainty period, the server will consider the transaction aborted, and at resynchronization it communicates the abort decision to the client. If there is a power failure in the server after that the commit record has been stored in the shared log and before that shared database updates have been made permanent, the recovery procedure firstly redoes updates and then the server communicates the commit decision to the client when they resynchronize.

6.3 Transaction Failures

Transaction failures do not cause the loss of the content of temporary and permanent storages.

In Distributed Galileo a transaction failure is a situation not foreseen by a program or a situation that a program cannot foresee. Examples of failures that a program can foresee are: user generated exception, division by zero, bad input, etc. We call them *logical errors*. Situations that a program cannot foresee are: deadlock, exhaustion of free space in a temporary heap, exhaustion of the space reserved for the shadow pages in private and shared databases, exhaustion of space in the private and shared databases, communication failure, etc. We call these failures *system errors*.

Galileo integrates the mechanisms of exception handling with transaction management, providing the programmer with a unique vision similar to nested transactions [18].

Section **2.4** showed how the Galileo system provides constructs to raise and to catch exceptions. An *exception handler* is the construct that catches an exception raised by an *action*. An exception handler can catch either a generic exception corresponding to all logical errors or a specific exception, such as the one that arises when there is a division by zero[5]. Exception handlers can be arbitrarily nested (**h** nodes in **Figure 9**).

The flow of the control in a Galileo transaction as follows: if the evaluation of an expression does not raise exceptions, then Galileo executes the 'next' expression (; nodes); whereas, if the evaluation of an expression raises an exception, then Galileo executes the first expression after the 'father' exception handler. In the first case, the execution of the transaction in **Figure 9** transfers the control from Exp1 to Exp2; from Exp2 to Exp3; from Exp3 or Exp4 or Exp5 to Exp6. If an exception

---

[5] There is also a construct for the selective catching of an exception based on the string raised as an exception.

arises, the sample transaction transfers the control from Exp2 or Exp3 to Exp4; and from Exp4 to Exp5.

Galileo Transaction:
(Exp1; (Exp2; Exp3) **iffails** (Exp4 **iffails** Exp5); Exp6);

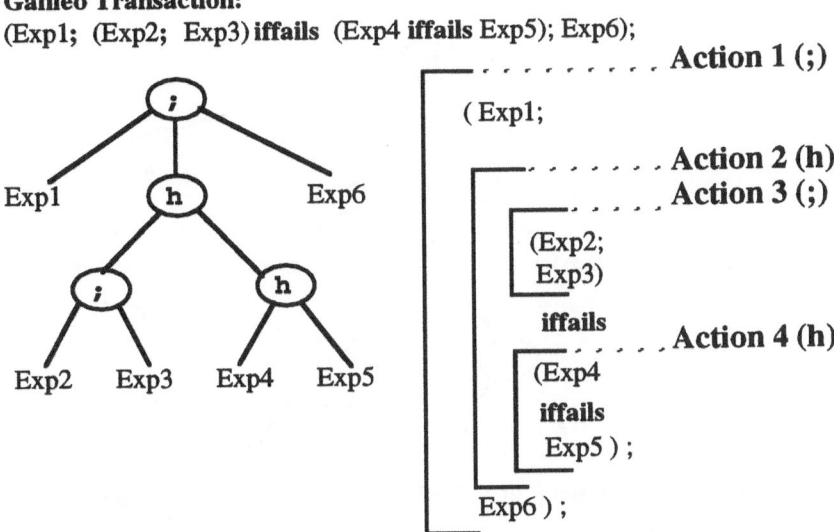

Figure 9. Galileo transaction with exception handlers

This behaviour, used in the original FAM for flow control purpose, has been extended by associating the functionality of the object state recovery to the exception handlers. A *recoverable action* is a top–level expression or an expression representing the left argument of an exception handler construct (**Figure 9**). The semantics of nested recoverable actions obeys to the following rules:

1) When an action creates a new modifiable object, it is automatically *the owner of the object*.
2) When an action updates an object that is not owned for the first time, before updating the object and becoming the object owner, it saves the previous object state and the name of its previous owner in a copy.
3) Every newly created object, owned by an action that successfully finishes, becomes the property of the father action.
4) Every updated object, owned by an action that successfully finishes, is (anti)inherited from the father action. If the father is the owner of a copy of the object, the copy is discarded.
5) Every newly created object, owned by an action that finishes by raising an exception, is automatically lost.
6) Every updated object, owned by an action that finishes by raising an exception, is automatically recovered to its original state and to its original owner.

Garbage collection automatically accomplishes rule (5); to realise rule (6) the system uses the copies of the updated objects to recover the original values and then discards the copies.

This mechanism of exception handling has been inserted into the transaction mechanism, giving it the following meaning: if an exception reaches the top–level, then the transaction is aborted, otherwise it ends successfully (**Figure 10**). Exceptions generated when a system error occurs cannot be caught by user

522

programmed exception handlers (**h** node), but are only intercepted by a system provided exception handler (**H** node). This system provided exception handler intercepts all the exceptions that reach the top–level and it causes the abort of the transaction.

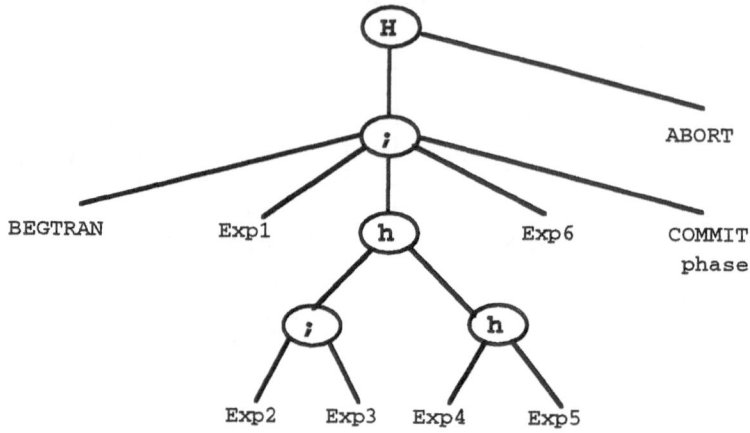

Figure 10. Meaning of a Galileo transaction with exceptions

7 Performance

PPLs are a new approach to the management of persistent data. At present universally accepted benchmarks to measure their performances do not exist. To measure the performance we have compared Distributed Galileo with OODB systems, where some commercial products already exist and where the OO1 benchmark is a standard [19].

OO1 measures the performance of the new generation of applications that use persistent data (CAD/CAM, CASE systems, etc.). These types of applications differ from the traditional data management applications where the structural complexity of data is irrelevant and the complexity of the applications derives only from the large number of concurrent users. The targets of OO1 are the same applications that should be supported by a PPL.

OO1 uses a database independent of any data model. The database is populated in a pseudo–casual way. The benchmark uses three types of transactions. The first type of transaction (*Lookup*) measures the ability of the system to visit a single class by searching all the instances that have some properties. The second type (*Traversal*) carries out the same operation as the first one but visiting many classes simultaneously. The third type (*Insert*) measures the performance when the system creates a given number of class instances. These transactions are executed a number of times proportional to their frequencies of appearance in new generation applications: the number of reading operations is ten times greater than the number of writes. The sum of the three measures is the final measure of the benchmark.

OO1 can be used with small, medium or large databases, and the databases may also be remote. **Figure 11** illustrates the measures of Distributed Galileo, with a small database on a remote server. Its measures are compared with an average relational DBS, with an average OODBs and with a very simple package that arranges only for a B-tree to access persistent data[6]. [19] is the source for these last three measures.

Measure	Cache	INDEX	RDBMS	OODBM	GALILEO
DB Size		3.3 Mb	4.5 Mb	3.7 Mb	9.0 Mb
Lookup	cold	7.6	29.0	20.0	19.9
	warm	2.4	19.0	1.0	5.7
Traversal	cold	17.0	94.0	17.0	20.5
	warm	8.4	84.0	1.2	11.1
Insert	cold	8.2	20.0	3.6	7.3
	warm	7.5	20.0	2.9	5.5
Total	cold	32.8	143.0	40.6	47.7
	warm	18.3	123.0	5.1	21.3

Figure 11. OO1 for Distributed Galileo

The total measure of our system demonstrates that Distributed Galileo has a performance comparable with OODBs when they are both executed for the first time, exploiting to a limited extent the presence of the cache (cold start). After the cold start, Distributed Galileo performances are better but they do not improve to the extent that OODBs do. The reason is that caching pages performs better than caching objects in the absence of concurrency. The OO1 benchmark does not allow for comparison of the performances of systems that execute concurrent transactions. We expect to reduce the gap with OODBs when we will be able to compare our results through a benchmark that measures performance of the concurrency control component. In our system the locking unit is smaller and we use static semantic information on the locking unit.

The figure shows that Galileo requires a relatively large amount of storage for the database. This does not depend on the physical data structures used but on the fact that the Galileo shared persistent store includes all compiler data structures and all the system libraries (written in Galileo).

The real bottleneck in our system is the loading phase of persistent objects, because Galileo loads one object at a time. A viable solution to overcome this is *prefetching*, which is the ability to simultaneously load a set of persistent objects with a single access to the shared database. In the next section we will comment on this problem.

8 Conclusions

This paper has presented a survey of the architecture and the technical solutions adopted in Distributed Galileo. Distributed Galileo has been mainly developed to test a PPL architecture that exploits the knowledge of the static information on objects in cache and concurrency control management. We have already outlined the advantages

---

[6] We used the Distributed Galileo system version running on a network of Sun Sparc 2 workstations. The operating system was Sun UNIX OS 4.0.3.

and the disadvantages of the solutions provided by Distributed Galileo. This section summarises the results of the experiment and makes some final comments on the language and its supporting architecture.

1) Languages that support inclusion polymorphism can easily be extended to deal with persistence independence because the management of inclusion polymorphism implies the support of pointers and hence these languages implement the concept of object identity which is essential for persistence independence.

2) The model of interaction provided by interactive functional programming languages can fit nicely into the *general* model of orthogonal persistence, into the model of implicit transactions, and into the kind of client–server database distribution we have presented.

3) The intermediate machine has been adapted to integrate transaction failures with exception handling and to let information on object modifiability flow through the layers of the architecture. This means that the intermediate machine was originally well designed and organised, so that its architecture can be a reference point for this class of persistent languages.

4) The most controversial issue is *page* versus *object* server. We chose in favour of the object server for two reasons: smaller granularity implies greater concurrency and a more efficient logical logging. We have shown that our object server approach results in poor performance compared to page server. This mainly depends on the persistent object loading phase, because during the storing phase, a set of object states can be transmitted from a client to the server in a single packet. We believe that prefetching persistent objects is the solution that can improve Distributed Galileo, rendering its performance closer to page servers, without removing all the advantages deriving from the knowledge of objects. Furthermore, the issue of prefetching should be kept separate from clustering. In fact, clustering relates to an improvement of performance in accessing persistent objects stored in the shared database. It is thus a server problem that deals with *all* the transactions in the system. On the other hand, in our architecture prefetching is the problem of packaging sets of persistent objects to improve network performance which involves one client executing a *single* transaction. Of course, the two problems are related, but if we keep them separate then we can isolate problems and reach better solutions. Research into finding an optimal prefetching for Galileo is in progress (see [20] for some general ideas) and is based on the static analysis of a Galileo transaction to annotate points in the program with approximate information representing the "future" needs of computation in terms of persistent object accesses.

5) POS, the Persistent Object Store used in this experiment, should be extended with an explicit notion of transaction ([21] has already recognised this need). A further improvement could be the support of a bulk data type for mapping Galileo classes onto persistent data structures. Finally, POS is the component in the architecture that is supposed to deal with the physical placement of persistent objects and clustering.

Acknowledgements. We would like to thank Antonio Albano, Renzo Orsini and Giorgio Ghelli for initial discussions about the work presented in this paper and the anonymous referees for their comments.

9 References

1. Albano A., L. Cardelli and R. Orsini, "Galileo: A strongly typed interactive conceptual language", *ACM Trans. on Database Systems, Vol. 10, No. 2*, pp. 230-260, 1985.
2. Atkinson M. P. and O. P. Buneman, "Types and Persistence in Database Programming Languages", *ACM Computer Surveys, Vol 19, No. 2*, pp. 105–190, 1987.
3. Bernstein P., V. Hadzilacos and N. Goodman, *Concurrency Control and Recovery in Database System*, Addison - Wesley, Reading, MA, 1987.
4. Atkinson M.P., Bancilhon F., DeWitt D., Dittrich K., Maier D. and Zdonik S., "The Object–Oriented Database System Manifesto", *Proc. Int. Conf. DOOD* , Kyoto, Japan, pp. 40–57, 1989.
5. Cardelli L., "A Semantics of Multiple Inheritance", in *Semantics of Data Types, LNCS, Vol. 173*, G. Kahn, D. B. MacQueen and G. Plotkin (eds.), Springer Verlag, NY, pp. 51–67, 1984.
6. Cardelli L. and P. Wegner, "On Understanding Types, Data Abstraction and Polymorphism", *ACM Computing Surveys, Vol. 17, No. 4*, pp. 471–522, 1985.
7. Mainetto G., "Funzionalità del gestore della memoria del Galileo Stabile", *Tech. Rep. 5/60*, Progetto Finalizzato "Sistemi Informatici e Calcolo Parallelo", CNR (in italian), 1991.
8. Di Giacomo M., G. Mainetto and L. Vinciotti, "Architettura e Realizzazione del Sistema Galileo Distribuito", *Tech. Rep. 5/111*, Progetto Finalizzato "Sistemi Informatici e Calcolo Parallelo", CNR (in italian), 1992.
9. D. J. DeWitt, P. Futtersack, D. Maier and F. Velez, "A Study of Three Alternative Workstation-Server Architectures for Object–Oriented Database Systems", *Proc. 16th Int. Conf. on VLDB*, Brisbane, Australia, pp. 107–121, 1990.
10. Brown A. L., "Persistent Object Stores", *Persistent Programming Res. Rep. 71-89*, Dep. of Computing Science, Univ. of Glasgow and St. Andrews, Scotland, UK, 1989.
11. Diotiallevi M., "Una Proposta per la Realizzazione del Compilatore del Galileo Persistente", *Tech. Rep. 5/35*, Progetto Finalizzato "Sistemi Informatici e Calcolo Parallelo", CNR (in italian), 1990.
12. Cardelli L., "The Functional Abstract Machine", *AT&T Bell Laboratories, Tech. Rep. TR-107*, Murray Hill, NJ, 1983.
13. Haerder T. and A. Reuter, "Principles of Transaction–Oriented Database Recovery",*ACM Computing Surveys, Vol. 15, No. 4*, pp. 287–317, 1983.
14. Brown A.L., G. Mainetto, F. Matthes, R. Mueller and D.J. McNally, "An Open System Architecture for a Persistent Object Store", *Proc. 25th Hawaii Int. Conf. on System Sciences*, Hawaii, USA, pp. 766–776, 1992.
15. Bensoussan A., C. Clingen and R. Daley, "The Multics Virtual Memory", *Proc. 2nd Symp. on Operating Systems Principles*, Princeton University, NY, 1969.
16. Lorie R. A., "Physical Integrity in a Large Segmented Database", *ACM Transactions on Database Systems, Vol. 2, No. 1*, pp. 91–104, 1977.
17. Purdy A., B. Schuchardt and D. Maier, "Integrating an Object Server with Other Worlds", *ACM Transactions on Office Information Systems, Vol. 5, No. 1*, pp. 27–47, 1987.
18. Moss J. E. B., *Nested Transactions: An Approach to Reliable Distributed Computing*, The MIT Press, Cambridge, MA, 1985.
19. Cattel R. G. G. and J. Skeen, "Object Operations Benchmark", *ACM Transactions on Database Systems, Vol. 17, No. 1*, pp. 1–31, 1992.
20. Amato G., F. Giannotti and G. Mainetto, "Data Sharing Analysis for a Database Programming Language via Abstract Interpretation", *Proc. 19th Int. Conf. on VLDB*, Dublin, Ireland, pp. 405–415, 1993.
21. Munro D. S., "On the Integration of Concurrency, Distribution and Persistence", *Computational Science Res. Rep. CS/94/1*, Dep. of Mathematical and Computational Sciences, Univ. St. Andrews, Scotland, UK, 1994.

Constructing a Domain-Specific DBMS using a Persistent Object System *

Steve Rozen   Lincoln Stein

Nathan Goodman

{steve,lstein,nat}@genome.wi.mit.edu

Whitehead Institute for Biomedical Research

One Kendall Square

Cambridge MA 02139

Constructing a light-weight domain-specific database management system (DBMS) is one way "...to design applications that effectively exploit...persistent technology". We have implemented a domain-specific DBMS, LabBase, on top of the ObjectStore persistent object system (which is basically a persistent C++). LabBase is tailored to the application domain of laboratory information systems: it is designed to record experimental steps and results in a high-throughput laboratory production line—for example, one of those operated as part of the Whitehead/MIT Genome Center's genome-mapping projects.

Given the task of representing the materials and experimental steps of a laboratory production line in C++, one could take two approaches:

1. Model each laboratory material and experimental step directly as a C++ class. A system constructed in this way can record the operations of a single laboratory production line.

2. Build a layer of abstraction in C++ in the form of a data definition facility based on *general* notions of laboratory materials and experimental steps. A system constructed in this way can be adapted to various laboratory production lines by supplying appropriate data definitions for the laboratory materials and experimental steps particular to specific production lines.

For LabBase we chose the second approach—that of creating a domain-specific DBMS—in light of our previous experiences working with a system based on the first approach.

We detail the considerations that led to this choice, and we describe LabBase's design and our experiences implementing it. We use our experiences with LabBase to illuminate the advantages and disadvantages of this approach to exploiting persistent technology. We also analyze how ObjectStore's particular characteristics shaped LabBase's design.

1 Introduction

LabBase is a light-weight domain-specific DBMS implemented on top of the ObjectStore persistent object system [1, 2, 3]. The implementation of LabBase is

---

*This work was supported by funds from the U.S. National Institutes of Health, National Center for Human Genome Research, grant number P50 HG00098.

evidence that constructing a domain-specific DBMS is one workable solution to the problem of "[h]ow to design applications that effectively exploit...persistent technology".

Constructing a laboratory information system using a persistent C++ to provide database facilities presents a number of challenges. The most salient of these are:

- The need to provide multilingual access—an essential requirement of laboratory information systems—to a monolingual persistent object store.

- The need to accommodate constant re-engineering of the experimental production line as the laboratory seeks to lower costs and increase throughput.

- The need to view experimental results both historically—in the context of the sequence of experiments that produced the results—and statically—in terms of the current "final" result, even when experimental steps are repeated.

In addition, the solution of creating a domain-specific DBMS is important because it allows us, to some extent, to sidestep the problem of "[h]ow to build, maintain and operate large persistent applications". Creating a domain-specific DBMS allows us to build a relatively small persistent application (around 10,000 lines of C++ code) and lots of loosely coupled non-persistent applications. C++ classes are used to model the *generic* attributes of the application domain, while a data definition facility is used to specialize these attributes for specific applications within the domain. The additional layer of abstraction offered by a domain-specific DBMS also allows us to adapt more easily to re-engineering of the experimental production line.

The approach of creating a domain-specific DBMS offers some distinct advantages over the alternative of modeling the application classes directly in C++. We have, of course, also found disadvantages to using a domain-specific DBMS. We discuss both the advantages and disadvantages below in section 4, after having first described the application domain of laboratory information systems and how LabBase implements a domain-specific DBMS in ObjectStore.

1.1 Laboratory Information Systems

LabBase is designed to store data for laboratory information systems. A laboratory information system records the experimental steps performed and experimental results obtained during the operation of a laboratory production line. Examples of laboratory information systems are described in [4, 5, 6]. Laboratory information systems share much in common with classical information systems: in particular, the database component must provide a central repository of carefully administered, mission-critical data, and must integrate the operations of diverse software and human agents. A term commonly used in conjunction with the database component of laboratory information systems is "automated laboratory notebook". The database is notebook-like because all experimental results are recorded in it, along with information about the experimental step itself, such as when it was performed and by whom. LabBase can be thought of as a generic automated laboratory notebook.

We emphasize that many genomic applications are not laboratory information systems, but rather are charged with integrating and publishing results from numerous independent laboratories. For example, both the worldwide sequence databases (e.g. GenBank [7]) and the various integrated organism-specific databases (e.g. the *Caenorhabditis elegans* database [8]) have very different requirements from laboratory information systems.

Laboratory information systems such as those used at the Whitehead/MIT Genome Center (Genome Center) typically involve several components in addition to a database component:

- External compute servers, for example servers to look for possible genes in DNA sequences.

- External data sources, such as the worldwide DNA sequence databases.

- Data analysis programs, such as programs to construct genetic maps from raw data on co-inheritance of particular DNA sequences. Often these programs are written at another laboratory or as part of a separate project in the same laboratory, and consequently they cannot be closely tied to the data representation in the database.

- Human data entry programs, often consisting of customized standard software. For example, at the Genome Center, much data entry is done on Excel spreadsheets, sometimes connected to a digitizing tablet.

- Interfaces to laboratory machinery, such as pipetting robots.

- Periodic progress reports and status reports that allow scientists to monitor production-line activity and detect possible problems with it.

- Interfaces—such as e-mail and WorldWide Web [9] servers—that publish released data over the internet.

It is the heterogeneity of these components that gives rise to the requirement of multilingual access to the database. For example, at the Genome Center, many of the status report programs are written in perl [10], as are many small "glue" programs that connect various independently developed components (e.g. customized Excel spreadsheets and external compute servers) to the database.

1.2 Why ObjectStore?

Our design of LabBase was heavily influenced by our experience developing and operating a previous laboratory database, MapBase [11, 12]. Like LabBase, MapBase is constructed in ObjectStore. However, unlike LabBase, MapBase models each experimental step as a separate C++ class. Because of the requirement for multilingual access, MapBase (like LabBase) offers a query language. However, the LabBase query language (a non-recursive datalog) is much more general than MapBase's.[1]

---

[1] The ObjectStore query language described in [2] and referred to as ObjectStore DML in [3] is a preprocessor extension to C++. Because queries have to be compiled into the ObjectStore client, this query language is not workable as a multilingual application program interface.

We expect LabBase to replace MapBase as the database component of the Genome Center's mouse genetic-mapping and human physical-mapping production lines. A LabBase database is currently "shadowing" the MapBase database for the human physical-mapping project as a first step toward putting LabBase into production.

We chose to use ObjectStore for MapBase's successor for the following reasons:

- We have almost three year's experience operating ObjectStore applications and have confidence in its robustness.

- We have garnered considerable expertise in ObjectStore development and operation.

- We know the limitations of the current release of ObjectStore with respect to our applications, and we have techniques (developed for MapBase) for working around them.

- We know, based on our experience with MapBase, that we can obtain the necessary performance from ObjectStore.

We originally used a persistent object system for MapBase because we believed that that would be the best way to get the modeling expressiveness we would require. Among the object systems that were available in early 1991, we focused on the C++-based systems because it seemed that C++ was becoming the ascendant object-oriented language, and that consequently at least some of the C++-based systems would survive in the marketplace. Furthermore, there were at least three commercial C++-based systems available: ONTOS [13], VERSANT [14], and ObjectStore. Therefore we felt that if necessary we could port from one C++-based system to another with relatively little difficulty should one system fail in the marketplace or prove technically unsuitable. (We have ported a subset of MapBase to VERSANT with relatively little difficulty, which supports this rationale for choosing a C++-based system.)

Among ONTOS, VERSANT, ObjectStore, we chose ObjectStore as the most robust in early 1991.

2   Design and Rationale

Figure 1 represents the architecture of LabBase and its clients. The two processes labeled lbserv and lbback, together with the ObjectStore database, constitute LabBase, and the various clients are to the left. We first briefly describe LabBase's major components and their roles, and then discuss the rational for this design below.

The lbserv process is written in perl, and manages connections from multiple clients. It can buffer partial queries from several clients. Once a complete query is available, lbserv forwards it to lbback, which executes it. lbserv also logs all transactions to a logical archive log. (By "logical" we mean that the log contains statements in the LabBase query language rather than page images, and by "archive" we mean that the log can be used to reconstruct the state of the database in the event of a disk-media failure or a dirty software failure that corrupts the database.)

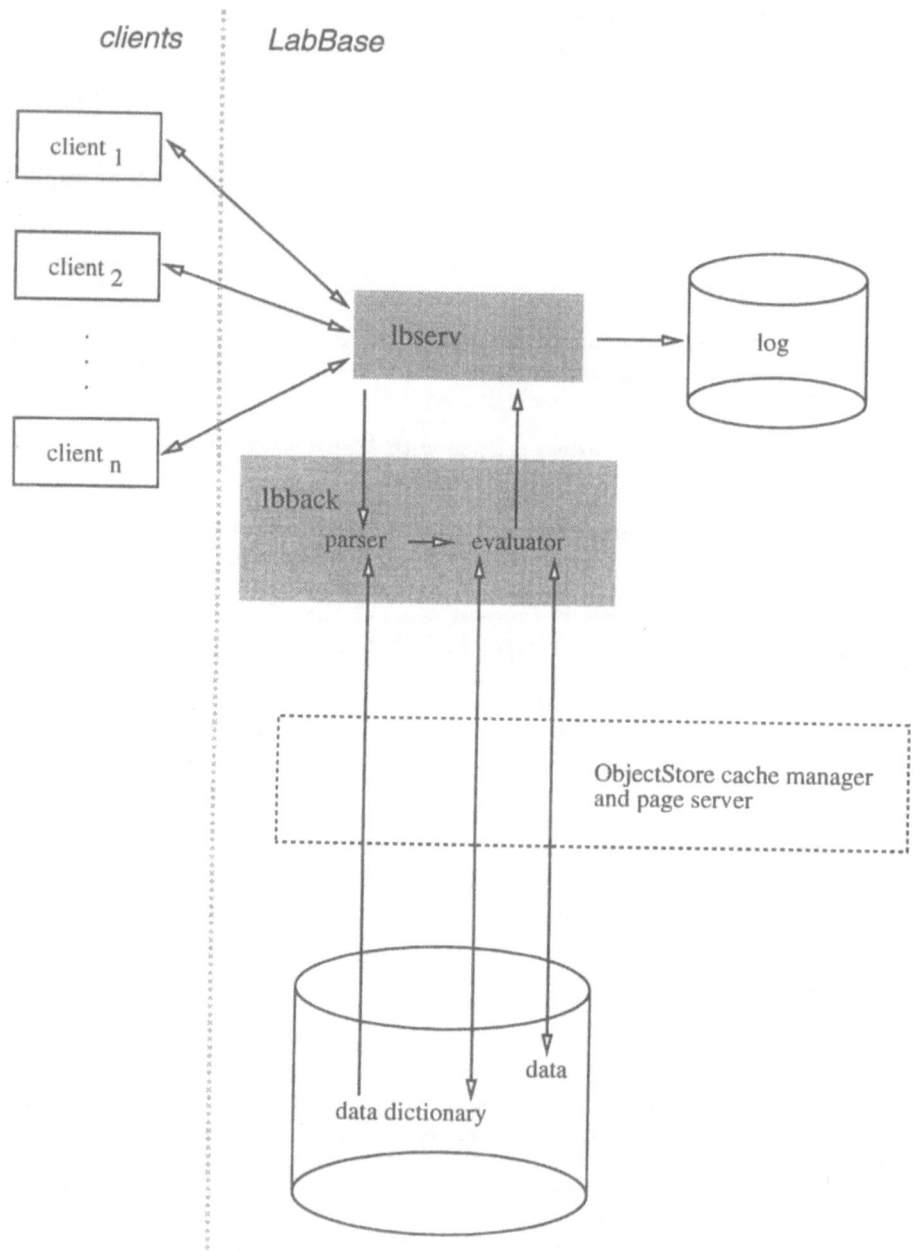

Figure 1: LabBase Architecture.

The lbback process executes as an ObjectStore client written in C++ that implements the LabBase data definition facility and query language (discussed in more detail in section 2.1). Queries received from lbserv are first parsed (with the help of schema information stored in the data dictionary), and then executed by the evaluator. The evaluator (which requires information from the data dictionary) stores and retrieves database data, and can also update the data dictionary.

The parser and evaluator retrieve database objects from 3 persistent roots, which constitute the persistent part of the data dictionary. (The data dictionary also has a transient part, not shown in figure 1, which records the addresses of functions that implement built-in predicates.)

2.1 Query Language and Data Model

Recall that an important requirement for the database component of a laboratory information system is access from programs written in many languages (and running on diverse platforms—all of the laboratory information systems discussed in [4, 5, 6] use both Macintoshes and Unix machines).

In the absence of interlingual object standards, a straightforward way to provide multilingual access is to offer a query language, and this is the approach that we took in both LabBase and its predecessor, MapBase. The MapBase query language was an ad hoc construction, in which the "from" clause was always the set of all markers—short DNA sequences used for genome mapping—in the database, or certain extensionally defined subsets of these.

The MapBase query language was satisfactory as long as we only wanted to store information about markers, but it broke down rapidly when we had to record information about additional laboratory materials (other than markers) used in the Genome Center's human physical-mapping production line.

In order for LabBase to provide a more general query language than MapBase's we chose a non-recursive datalog. We selected a logic programming language for LabBase for the following reasons:

- The language is intended for use as an application program interface and for occasional data-dredging queries [15] posed by programmers. End-user queries are rare or non-existent, so we do not require the language to be end-user-friendly.

- We are not primarily language designers. Adapting a well-understood, flexible, and general language seemed preferable to expending effort inventing some new language.

- Datalog is syntactically and semantically simpler than other standard database languages that we might have selected, especially given LabBase's need to store historical data.

- An easy-to-implement, bottom-up evaluation of datalog queries seemed adequate to our needs for the near future.

- We hope to enhance the LabBase query language with rules and recursion, or replace it with a full-scale logic-programming implementation such as CORAL [16] or LDL [17].

- Even if, in the future, we use a language-independent object system, we would nevertheless still want associative queries.

Besides providing multilingual access, a query language such as LabBase's provides two interrelated advantages:

1. One can often express all or part of ad hoc data-dredging queries in an associative language that is closer to the application domain than C++. Furthermore, errors in ad hoc queries are trapped by the query language parser and evaluator, thereby increasing the robustness of the lbback process. Even though C++'s static type checking makes new C++ code more likely to be correct than the corresponding "traditional" C code, it is still difficult to avoid errors in new C++ code, especially in the management of heap-allocated storage.

2. The presence of a query language promotes a division of labor between the few developers that work on the implementation of lbback, and the relatively many that work on applications. The data definition facilities and query language present a more tractable interface than numerous C++ classes, and less chance for an application programmer to do harm—an important consideration when many applications are written by students.

These latter two considerations also convinced us to create our own modeling facilities and data dictionary as a source of meta data for parsing and evaluating queries. Thus LabBase provides a domain-specific data model.

LabBase's data model is based on the notions of *materials* and *steps*. All data about a material is entered in the context of a series of experimental steps, the material's *step history*. Each step is a mapping from *tags* (which are essentially attribute names) to *values*. Each tag is associated with a unique type. Only values that conform to the type of a tag can be associated with it in the database. (The query language itself performs only dynamic type checking.)

In the current implementation the atomic types are BOOLEAN, INTEGER, DATE, FLOAT, STRING, and DNA_SEQUENCE. For any types, $\alpha_1, \ldots, \alpha_n$, $n \geq 1$ whether atomic or complex, LIST$(\alpha_1, \ldots, \alpha_n)$ and SET$(\alpha_1, \ldots, \alpha_n)$ are complex types. These types characterize lists or sets (respectively) of tuples whose ith element has type α_i, $1 \leq i \leq n$. Elements of a LIST or SET can be retrieved with the element predicate. The constituent tuples have integer attribute labels, and tuples are decomposed with the subscripting predicate ith. For example, the query

```
element({[a,1],[b,2]},E),ith(E,1,I).
```

causes I to be bound successively to 1 and 2—though not necessarily in that order. (Curved braces enclose sets, and square braces enclose lists and tuples.) The following table shows some values and the types that describe them.

value	type
3.4	FLOAT
'D1Mit44'	STRING
1994:09:02:00:00:00	DATE
[1, 2, 5]	LIST(INTEGER)
{[1.0, 6] [3.4, 9]}	SET(FLOAT,INTEGER)
[[3],[],[5,7,9]]	LIST(LIST(INTEGER))

The DATE type is really a date-and-time type.

In addition to the atomic types and the type constructors (**LIST** and **SET**) already enumerated, there is also a type that describes materials, which can be used like an atomic type. Materials are not denotable in the query language, but they can be retrieved by their id. For example,

```
marker_id(M,'D1118').
```

is true if there is a marker with id **D1118**, in which case **M** is bound to that marker.

Data can be viewed as a static attribute of the material by requesting the value associated with the most recent instance of a particular tag in the history of a material. Data can also be viewed in the historical context of previous and subsequent experimental steps by requesting all the steps associated with one or more materials. Queries about step histories are useful in refining experimental protocols. For example, one could pose a query to find out how often some expensive operation is being performed on erroneous data (by detecting a correction step after the expensive operation in the step history). Queries to the system can freely intermingle both static and historical aspects.

Materials and steps have *kinds*, and these kinds, together with tags, can be used as predicates when querying LabBase. Additional built-in predicates provide negation, disjunction, some aggregates, boolean comparison operators, and so forth.

An example of a query that focuses on the most recent results relating to materials is the following, which finds the most recent DNA sequence associated with each marker:

```
marker(M),dna_sequence(M,S).
```

In evaluating this query, **M** is bound to each marker in the database, and, for each marker, m, **S** is bound to m's most recently entered sequence. (More than one DNA sequence could be associated with m if its DNA sequence is re-read because experimental results suggest that the initial DNA sequence is incorrect.) The predicate **marker** is, in addition, a material kind, and the predicate **dna_sequence** is a tag. For any material kind, κ, $\kappa(X)$ is true of all materials, X, of kind κ. Similarly, for a tag, τ, and a material, μ, the predicate $\tau(\mu, V)$ is true for that value, V, that is the most recent value associated with τ in μ's step history.

An example of a query that focuses on the history of steps associated with a material is the following, which finds all the DNA sequence steps (the steps that read the marker's DNA sequence) associated with marker **D1118**:

```
marker_id(M,'D1118'),all_steps(M,S),
dna_sequence_step(S).
```

In this query, **M** becomes bound to the marker with id **D1118**, **S** is successively bound to each step in **D1118**'s step history, and **dna_sequence_step** restricts the results of the query to steps that are of kind **dna_sequence_step**.

Our guiding philosophy in implementing the LabBase query language has been to keep it, as much as *reasonably* possible, a subset of Prolog. In particular, negation is provided by a **not** predicate, which, as in Prolog, succeeds exactly when its argument (a term) fails.

534

Updates are carried out by predicates with side effects, much like Prolog's `assertz`. To insert a new material or a new experimental step one uses the predicate `insert`. The query

```
insert(marker(marker_id='D1118',
              who=steve,
              when=1994:04:01:16:45:11)).
```

creates a new marker with id D1118. Even the creating of a material must be annotated with

- the user (**steve**) responsible for the creation and

- a timestamp (**1994:04:01:16:45:11**) representing the valid time for the creation—the time at which the material should be considered in reality to have been created.

The query

```
marker_id(M,'D1118'),
insert(dna_sequence_step(material=M,
                         dna_sequence='CTGACCTG···GGTTA',
                         who=steve,
                         when=1994:04:01:16:48:23)).
```

inserts a **dna_sequence_step** onto the history of marker D1118. LabBase currently does not support deletes or updates of materials or steps.

A notable area in which LabBase is not a subset of Prolog is provision for aggregates. Our approach here is exemplified by the predicate `gather_in_set`:

$$\text{gather\_in\_set}(term_1 \ldots term_n, V, Set)$$

is true if **Set** contains exactly those bindings of **V** that are among the bindings that make the query $term_1 \ldots term_n$ true.

As discussed in section 4, LabBase does not currently support rules, but the addition of rules would probably be the most beneficial enhancement we could make to LabBase, since it would increase the readability of long queries (some of which have more than 20 lines). More details on LabBase's data model and more example queries are provided in [18].

2.2 System Architecture and Implementation

The system architecture represented in figure 1 is partly dictated by the technical characteristics of ObjectStore. In particular, the choice of single process (lbback) mediating all access to the ObjectStore database is independent of the idea of creating a domain-specific DBMS. We previously used this design in MapBase to work around the concurrency characteristics of ObjectStore Release 1. A notable deficiency of this design is that one client's long-running query excludes other queries for the entire duration of its execution. This exclusion results from the fact that lbback executes each query completely until it is done, and from the fact that there is a single lbback server for each database. ObjectStore's developers claim improvements in the area of concurrent performance for Release 3 [19], which we are now testing. Therefore we intend to reexamine the possibility of using multiple lbback servers interleaving their query executions by relying on ObjectStore's concurrency-control mechanism.

The roll-forward log (shown at the right in figure 1) to which lbserv logs all queries is another work-around, which is also independent of the idea of a domain-specific DBMS. ObjectStore offers no mechanism by which a periodic snapshot can be brought up-to-date by reading a log of transactions that followed the backup. ObjectStore's developers plan to provide this database amenity in its next major release [19], calling it "archive logging". At that time we might revise LabBase's implementation to rely ObjectStore-provided archive logging.

The implementation of lbserv in perl seems to impose some performance burden. But this choice of implementation language seems justified for the time being by the fact that we hope to replace much of lbserv with improved ObjectStore facilities in the future. The implementation of lbserv requires fewer than 1000 lines of code.

The implementation of lbback requires around 9,000 lines of C++ code, with about 50 classes. The parser and lexer are implemented in 500 lines of lex and yacc code [20].

We have taken some care to make it relatively easy to add new built-in predicates to lbback, and it should also be possible to add new types that can be associated with tags. We have not yet attempted any extensive performance tuning on LabBase, but its performance seems similar to MapBase's when they are both managing the same amount of data (around 60 Megabytes for MapBase and 80 Megabytes for LabBase). Our strategy with ObjectStore so far has been to make sure that the ObjectStore cache file (i.e., a paging file for lbback that contains database pages mapped into lbback's address space) is large enough to store the entire database. Making the cache file large is important because inserting database pages into the cache file seems to be a slow operation relative to paging by lbback against the cache file. It is also desirable to avoid paging out of the cache file, so we plan to buy additional physical memory as the database size grows. We expect eventually to have databases containing around 400 Megabytes of data.

We have also arranged for clustering of data in a few main segments: one for materials and their identifiers, one for step histories and steps exclusive of their associated values, and one for the values associated with steps.

Many of the clients communicate with LabBase using a perl library developed for the purpose. The library presents a set-at-a-time interface to perl clients, with all rows being stored in a single perl array. Each row can be transformed into an associative array (i.e. a hash table) implementing a partial map from variable identifier to binding.

3 Related Work

The idea of creating a domain-specific DBMS for the Genome Center's laboratory information systems came from two sources.

One source is the description of the target applications for ObjectStore. These are referred to as *CAx applications* in [2]. Example CAx applications include CAD (computer-aided design), CASE (computer-aided software engineering), CAP (computer-added publishing), and GIS (geographic information systems). It seemed that, just as one would not require the user of a CAD system to code a C++ class in order to model, say, a new kind of screw, perhaps one should not require the user of a laboratory information system database to code a C++ class in order to model a new kind of laboratory step. In other words, a CAD system provides an abstraction that is closer to the user's view of the world than C++, and it makes sense for our laboratory database to do the same.

The second source of the idea of a domain-specific DBMS is the extensive literature on extensible databases and database tool kits. Extensible databases (e.g. Starburst [21], Montage [22], GENESIS [23, 24]) are predicated on the notion of customizability for particular application domains, though the customizations are conceived primarily in terms of providing new storage structures, new query execution strategies, and new types and operations, rather than in terms of fundamental changes to the data model. For example [25] discusses using GENESIS to create "special-purpose database management systems" for applications such as CAD and textual databases, but the GENESIS data definition language is fixed.

The implementation of LabBase is in broad outline extremely similar to the implementation of a DAPLEX [26] DBMS in PS-Algol [27] described in [28]. In this implementation, as in LabBase, an interpreted query language and data model were implemented in a persistent programming language.

VODAK [29] is a full-featured object-oriented DBMS, which uses ObjectStore as a storage manager [30]. VODAK provides its own concurrency control, and previous releases were built on a different storage manager. Besides providing its own concurrency control, VODAK provides many other capabilities not provided in LabBase, including a highly developed data-modeling language with methods and query optimization. Although both LabBase and VODAK use ObjectStore as a storage manager, their design objectives are different: LabBase is designed as a light-weight, domain-specific DBMS, whereas VODAK is designed as a full-featured, generic DBMS (although it has many features designed to support multi-media applications). These differing objectives are reflected in the fact that VODAK's implementation requires over 10 times as much code as LabBase's.

4 Evaluation and Conclusion

Our experience with LabBase demonstrates some strengths of using a persistent C++ to create a domain-specific DBMS:

- A domain-specific DBMS can provide a query language. Having a query language seems to be a inevitable requirement for some application domains, including that of laboratory information systems. We did not find implementing a simple query language burdensome, though we hope in the future to replace the LabBase query language with a more general one. In particular, it would be useful to be able to define new predicates within the query language, rather than having to add new built-in predicates in the C++ code.

  Because we use perl so heavily, we do not suffer from impedance mismatch due to a set-at-a-time versus a tuple-at-a-time view: we retrieve entire query results into single perl arrays. We do lose type information (see below), though perl is so weakly typed that this loss is not an *added* disadvantage.

- As compared to using a generic DBMS, one can tune the data modeling facilities to the target application domain. For example, LabBase provides special support for storing histories of experimental steps, and for retrieving the most recent result of a particular sort.

  As compared to modeling an application directly in C++, the additional layer of abstraction presented by a domain-specific DBMS factors out commonality among applications in that domain, simplifying the data modeling task. This factoring can also reduce code size. LabBase offers more functionality than MapBase, with fewer than 1/3 as many lines of code (including lbserv). The factoring out of commonality among applications in a domain is challenging, but apparently well worth the effort.

- The interpreted query language and data model insulate the C++ implementation of LabBase from most schema changes required by LabBase users. Only the addition of a new built-in type necessitates a database reload.

- Application programs do not have access to the address space of the database, as they would if they were coded in C++ using ObjectStore's persistence mechanisms directly. This simplifies their view of the database contents, and excludes the possibility of database corruption due to low-level errors such as including dangling pointers in a database object.

- Because the domain-specific DBMS is coded in C++, one can extend its types and representations by adding new C++ classes. For example, since DNA sequences can be represented using 3 bits per base, one could design a representation that uses less memory than if one were to store them as strings of characters.

- One can also add new built-in predicates. For example, LabBase provides *reverse complementation*, a common operation on DNA sequences. (To take the reverse complement of a DNA sequence it is reversed, and the bases are substituted by the Watson-Crick paring rules: G↔C, A↔T. E.g., the reverse complement of CCATG is CATGG.)

Our experience with LabBase also reveals some weaknesses of using a persistent C++ to create a domain-specific DBMS:

- There can be a loss of type information at the interface between the query language and the application program. In particular, it is not clear how to move objects or object references from the DBMS to an application program.

- To the extent that the data model is less expressive than that of C++, there will be a loss of modeling ability. This loss is mitigated by the fact that a DBMS extender could add new types to the domain-specific DBMS.

- Even though it is possible to tune representations (such as those of DNA sequences), it is not easy to figure out how to provide tuning *options* for different uses of the domain specific DBMS. For example, we have not been able to decide what clustering options LabBase should provide.

- Even though it is not burdensome to implement a simple query language like LabBase's non-recursive datalog, implementing a full-scale query language, with recursion, unification, and optimization, is a different matter.

- There is a danger of devising idiosyncratic data models and query languages.

In addition, a domain-specific DBMS implemented in a persistent C++ derives many of its operational characteristics from the underlying persistent object system. For LabBase this has meant good performance provided we keep the entire database in lbback's virtual memory, but it has also meant that we had to give up native ObjectStore concurrency and implement our own roll-forward archive logging. Presumably using another persistent object systems would provide a different constellation of characteristics, dictating a system architecture different from LabBase's.

Persistent object systems are much more diverse than relational DBMSs in terms of data modeling approach, query language, and operational characteristics. Therefore we can only speculate about how we would construct a system like LabBase using a language-independent persistent object system such as O_2 [31], Gemstone [32], or Thor [33, 34]. We are currently attempting a prototype reimplementation of LabBase in Thor, partly with the goal of answering this question. We speculate that if we were to re-implement LabBase in a persistent language, such as Napier88 [35], that provides linguistic reflection, we would make the language's type system visible to the LabBase user, and perhaps dynamically compile predicate implementations (such as those for tag predicates) that depend on the LabBase data dictionary.

We think that creating generic abstractions for materials, histories of experimental steps, and for retrieving the most recent experimental result of a particular sort would still be valuable. In the most extreme case, one could do away with the LabBase query language in favor of the query language of the object system (if it provides one). In this case, LabBase would resemble so-called "third-party" packages (e.g. accounting packages) that are sometimes built on top of a relational DBMS. Of course, unlike the case with third-party packages built on top of today's relational DBMSs, considerable customization or extension of the object system would be feasible, and one could use this to create the generic abstractions discussed above.

Another possibility would be to keep the LabBase query language, but to take advantage of an object system's ability to create new classes from running applications and use the object system's run-time type data ("metadata") as the data dictionary. Thus, for example, each LabBase material kind could be represented as a subclass of a `Material` class.

There are a number of enhancements we would like to see for LabBase:

- Support for constraints on the tags that can appear on a particular kind of step, and for constraints on step orders to flag unusual orders as possible errors,

- A full-fledged logic programming language, with rules, as a query language, which would reduce the need to code new built-in predicates in C++, allow some applications to be coded entirely in the query language, and allow us to assemble complex queries from component predicates.

- An ObjectStore-free version of LabBase to remove obstacles to its free distribution to other laboratories.

LabBase is a success within the Whitehead/MIT Center for Genome Research. Our hope is that it will also be useful to other laboratories.

Acknowledgments Barbara Levy provided editorial assistance. Andre Marquis has helped in the implementation of LabBase. Mary-Pat Reeve, the first non-developer user, offered useful suggestions that will be incorporated into LabBase. Tony Bonner provided valuable input on the design of the LabBase query language. We have incorporated numerous useful suggestions offered by the anonymous referees.

References

[1] C. Lamb, G. Landis, J. Orenstein, and D. Weinreb, "The ObjectStore database system," *Communications of the ACM*, vol. 34, pp. 50–63, Oct. 1991.

[2] J. Orenstein, S. Haradhvala, B. Margulies, and D. Sakahara, "Query processing in the ObjectStore database system," in *Proceedings of the 1992 ACM SIGMOD International Conference on Management of Data* (M. Stonebraker, ed.), pp. 403–412, June 1992.

[3] Object Design, Inc., 25 Burlington Mall Rd., Burlington MA 01803-4194, USA, Manual set for ObjectStore Release 3.0 for UNIX Systems, Dec. 1993.

[4] A. R. Kerlavage, M. D. Adams, J. C. Kelly, *et al.*, "Analysis and management of data from high-throughput expressed sequence tag projects," in *Proceedings of the 26th Annual Hawaii International Conference on System Sciences* (T. N.Mudge, V. Milutinovic, and L. Hunter, eds.), vol. 1, pp. 585–594, IEEE Computer Society Press, Jan. 1993.

[5] S. P. Clark, G. A. Evans, and H. R. Garner, "Informatics and automation used in physical mapping of the genome," in *Biocomputing Informatics and Genome Projects* (D. W. Smith, ed.), pp. 13–49, Academic Press, Inc., 1994.

[6] L. Stein, A. Marquis, E. Dredge, *et al.*, "Splicing UNIX into a genome mapping laboratory," in *USENIX Summer 1994 Technical Conference*, pp. 221–229, June 1994.

[7] C. Burks, M. Cassidy, M. J. Cinkosky, *et al.*, "GenBank," *Nucleic Acids Research*, pp. 2221–2225, 1991.

540

[8] R. Durbin and J. Thierry-Mieg, "A *C. elegans* database," 1991. Documentation, code and data available from anonymous `ftp` servers at `lirmm.lirmm.fr`, `cele.mrc-lmb.cam.ac.uk` and `ncbi.nlm.nih.gov`.

[9] T. Berners-Lee, R. Cailliau, J.-F. Groff, and B. Pollermann, "World-Wide Web: The information universe," *Electronic Networking: Research, Applications and Policy*, vol. 2, no. 1, pp. 52–58, 1992. Also available at `http://info.cern.ch/hypertext/WWW/Bibliography/Papers.html`.

[10] L. Wall and R. L. Schwartz, *Programming perl.* O'Reilly & Associates, Inc., 1990.

[11] N. Goodman, "An object oriented DBMS war story: Developing a genome mapping database in C++," in *Modern Database Management: Object-Oriented and Multidatabase Technologies* (W. Kim, ed.), ACM Press, 1994.

[12] N. Goodman, S. Rozen, and L. Stein, "Requirements for a deductive query language in the MapBase genome-mapping database," in *Applications of Deductive Databases (tentative)* (R. Ramakrishnan, ed.), Kluwer, 1994. In press. Available at `ftp://genome.wi.mit.edu/pub/papers/Y1994/requirements.ps`.

[13] ONTOS, Inc., Three Burlington Woods, Burlington MA 01803, USA, *ONTOS DB 2.2 Developer's Guide*, Feb. 1992.

[14] Versant Object Technology Corporation, 4500 Bohannon Drive, Menlo Park CA 94025, USA, *VERSANT Object Database Management System Release 2 System Manual*, July 1993. Part Number 1003-0793.

[15] S. Tsur, "Data dredging," *Data Engineering*, vol. 13, Dec. 1990.

[16] R. Ramakrishnan, D. Srivastava, and S. Sudarshan, "CORAL–control, relations and logic," in *Proceedings of the 18th International Conference on Very Large Data Bases* (L.-Y. Yuan, ed.), pp. 238–250, Aug. 1992. A longer version is available from the authors.

[17] S. Tsur and C. Zaniolo, "LDL: a logic-based data language," in *Proceedings of the 12th International Conference on Very Large Data Bases*, pp. 33–41, Aug. 1986.

[18] S. Rozen, L. Stein, and N. Goodman, *LabBase User Manual.* Available at `ftp://genome.wi.mit.edu/pub/papers/Y1994/labbase-manual.ps`.

[19] P. O'Brien, "R3 & R4 product directions overview," Mar. 1994. Talk presented at ObjectStore Northeast users group meeting.

[20] T. Mason and D. Brown, *lex & yac.* O'Reilly & Associates, 1991.

[21] L. Haas *et al.*, "Starburst mid-flight: As the dust clears," *IEEE Trans. on Knowledge and Data Eng.*, vol. 2, Mar. 1990.

[22] M. Stonebraker, "Object-relational data base systems," 1993. Distributed with Montage (now called Illustra) sales literature.

541

[23] D. S. Batory, J. R. Barnett, J. F. Garza, *et al.*, "GENESIS: An extensible database management system," *IEEE Trans. on Software Eng.*, vol. 14, pp. 1711–1730, Nov. 1988.

[24] D. Batory and S. O'Malley, "The design and implementation of hierarchical software systems with reusable components," *ACM Trans. on Software Engineering*, vol. 1, Oct. 1992.

[25] D. S. Batory, T. Y. Leung, and T. E. Wise, "Implementation concepts for an extensible data model and data language," *ACM Trans. on Database Syst.*, vol. 13, pp. 231–262, Sept. 1988.

[26] D. W. Shipman, "The functional data model and the data language DAPLEX," *ACM Trans. on Database Syst.*, vol. 6, no. 1, pp. 140–173, 1981.

[27] M. P. Atkinson, P. J. Bailey, K. J. Chisholm, W. P. Cockshott, and R. Morrison, "An approach to persistent programming," *The Computer Journal*, vol. 26, no. 4, pp. 360–365, 1983.

[28] K. G. Kulkarni and M. P. Atkinson, "Implementing an extended functional data model using PS-algol," *Software—Practice and Experience*, vol. 17, pp. 171–183, Mar. 1987.

[29] W. Klas, K. Aberer, and E. Neuhold, "Object-oriented modeling for hypermedia systems using the VODAK Modelling Language (VML)," in *Object-Oriented Database Management Systems, NATO ASI Series*, Springer Verlag, Aug. 1993.

[30] E. Neuhold. Personal communication, Sept. 15, 1994. Additional information, including VODAK source code, is available at http:// este.darmstadt.gmd.de:5000/dimsys/home.html.

[31] O. Deux *et al.*, "The O₂ system," *Communications of the ACM*, vol. 34, pp. 34–48, Oct. 1991.

[32] P. Butterworth, A. Otis, and J. Stein, "The GemStone object database management system," *Communications of the ACM*, vol. 34, pp. 65–77, Oct. 1991.

[33] B. Liskov, M. Day, and L. Shrira, "Distributed object management in Thor," in *Distributed Object Management* (T. Ozsu, U. Dayal, and P. Valduriez, eds.), Morgan Kaufmann, 1994.

[34] M. Day, R. Gruber, B. Liskov, and A. C. Myers, "Abstraction mechanisms in Theta," 1994. Submitted for publication.

[35] R. Morrison, A. L. Brown, R. C. H. Connor, *et al.*, "The Napier88 reference manual (release 2.0)," Tech. Rep. CS/93/15, University of St. Andrews, 1993.

Concluding Remarks

Fred Brown, Peter Buneman, Fausto Rabitti

The sixth persistent object systems workshop brought together researchers from a wide variety of areas covered by the persistence umbrella. As with the previous 5 workshops [1,2,3,4,5], a major theme was the engineering of persistent object systems addressing issues such as buffer management, recovery techniques, caching, pointer swizzling, garbage collection and code generation. At higher levels, the problems of managing change within type secure persistent stores, optimisation techniques, name management and the consequences of distribution were discussed. Finally, experience with a range of emerging applications of persistent systems was presented.

Although there were excellent papers and discussions on implementation and optimisation techniques most implementation work is still performed in the context of persistent language X or persistent object store Y, typically on top of UNIX. A major problem that must be addressed is understanding what effect technology transfer between systems would have. For example, to what extent are implementations operating system independent?

Metrics for persistent object systems are becoming more and more important: we know how to build object stores but not why to use particular techniques. Similarly, it is also very difficult to make credible comparisons of alternate systems.

One approach may be to construct a series of experiments with minimal variations, for example, take programming language X and implement it on both stores Y and Z. Subsequently measure the two systems and highlight the differences between stores Y and Z in the context of programming language X. Repeat the process for different levels of architecture and for different programming languages.

The end result of the experiments wont be any definitive answers as to which store technology is best, the very nature of computer science is a continual changing of the engineering tradeoffs presented by our favourite toys. However, it should be possible to define some characteristic benchmarks that can be used to guide our design decisions. Remember benchmarks do not tell us very much but can be useful for establishing suitability for particular patterns of use. Ideally we will get non-UNIX metrics but, whatever we end up with we must be up-front about our assumptions.

The challenges facing us at the higher levels of our technology are no less demanding. Keynote discussions were devoted to the topics of managing system evolution and employing persistence in a distributed system. Present system design techniques have clear limitations when it comes to managing change in very large and/or complex systems. The effect of these problems can be limited by very careful initial design of systems with built in mechanisms to support change. Further benefits can be achieved through the use of persistence which is intended to abstract over the significant fraction of a system dedicated to storage management. However, it is not yet clear whether persistent systems designed to support evolution can solve the problems of managing truly massive systems or just make them a little less painful to build. Future work on evolution and persistence will give us a better understanding of the complexities involved and whether or not the problems we face are tractable.

Attempts to integrate persistence with distribution give rise to some interesting pragmatic problems. Our first concern is what do we mean by distribution, a system potentially linking the entire universe, a small group of tightly coupled computers giving the illusion of a single system, a multi-processor workstation, or something else? Discussion on this topic is akin to the "what is an object?" discussions at early conferences on object-orientation. The key point is that the physical storage in a distributed system may exhibit some failure modes relating to the locality of data which a programmer needs to know about. However, the major benefits of persistence are derived from the fact that physical properties of storage are abstracted over including its failure modes and locality of data. Thus, the hard problem in integrating distribution and persistence is how to reintroduce the concept of data locality without reintroducing all the complexity that persistence abstracts over.

Applications of persistence to real problems were presented in the context of manipulating scientific data. A disturbing characteristic of current experience is the reliance on existing file systems as *redo* logs for persistent stores. It would seem that existing persistent object store technology is either not yet mature enough or more likely not yet trusted enough to fully replace filesystems in a programmer's mind-set. Hopefully future workshops will find a change of emphasis and be able to report on substantial persistent systems that are truly robust and trustworthy. The future success of persistence based technologies depends on this.

As we look forward to the next POS workshop it is clear that there is still a wide number of interesting persistence related problems being addressed that will form the basis of another enjoyable weeks' work. We trust that the next organisers, who ever and where ever, will be able to find us another beautiful setting, with more excellent food and challenging excursions.

References

1. "Databases and Persistence", *Proceedings of Data Types and Persistence Workshop,* August 1985, Appin, Scotland (ed M.P. Atkinson, P. Buneman and R. Morrison), Springer-Verlag, 1988.
2. *Proceedings of the 2nd International Workshop on Persistent Object Systems*, Appin, August 1987, (ed. M.P. Atkinson and R. Morrison), Universities of Glasgow and St.Andrews, PPRR-44, 1987.
3. "Persistent Object Systems", *Proceedings of the 3rd International Workshop on Persistent Object Systems*, Newcastle, Australia (ed J. Rosenberg and D.M. Koch), Springer-Verlag, 1989.

4. "Implementing Persistent Object Bases: Principles and Practice", *Proceedings of the 4th International Workshop on Persistent Object Systems*, Marthas Vineyard, USA (ed A.Dearle, G.M. Shaw and S.B. Zdonik), Morgan-Kaufmann, 1990.
5. "Persistent Object Systems, San Miniato 1992", *Proceedings of the 5th International Workshop on Persistent Object Systems*, San Miniato (Pisa), Italy, (ed A. Albano and R. Morrison), Springer-Verlag, 1992.

Author Index

Published in 1990–92

AI and Cognitive Science '89, Dublin City University, Eire, 14–15 September 1989
Alan F. Smeaton and Gabriel McDermott (Eds.)

Specification and Verification of Concurrent Systems, University of Stirling, Scotland, 6–8 July 1988
C. Rattray (Ed.)

Semantics for Concurrency, Proceedings of the International BCS-FACS Workshop, Sponsored by Logic for IT (S.E.R.C.), University of Leicester, UK, 23–25 July 1990
M. Z. Kwiatkowska, M. W. Shields and R. M. Thomas (Eds.)

Functional Programming, Glasgow 1989
Proceedings of the 1989 Glasgow Workshop, Fraserburgh, Scotland, 21–23 August 1989
Kei Davis and John Hughes (Eds.)

Persistent Object Systems, Proceedings of the Third International Workshop, Newcastle, Australia, 10–13 January 1989
John Rosenberg and David Koch (Eds.)

Z User Workshop, Oxford 1989, Proceedings of the Fourth Annual Z User Meeting, Oxford, 15 December 1989
J. E. Nicholls (Ed.)

Formal Methods for Trustworthy Computer Systems (FM89), Halifax, Canada, 23–27 July 1989
Dan Craigen (Editor) and Karen Summerskill (Assistant Editor)

Security and Persistence, Proceedings of the International Workshop on Computer Architectures to Support Security and Persistence of Information, Bremen, West Germany, 8–11 May 1990
John Rosenberg and J. Leslie Keedy (Eds.)

Women into Computing: Selected Papers 1988–1990
Gillian Lovegrove and Barbara Segal (Eds.)

3rd Refinement Workshop (organised by BCS-FACS, and sponsored by IBM UK Laboratories, Hursley Park and the Programming Research Group, University of Oxford), Hursley Park, 9–11 January 1990
Carroll Morgan and J. C. P. Woodcock (Eds.)

Designing Correct Circuits, Workshop jointly organised by the Universities of Oxford and Glasgow, Oxford, 26–28 September 1990
Geraint Jones and Mary Sheeran (Eds.)

Functional Programming, Glasgow 1990
Proceedings of the 1990 Glasgow Workshop on Functional Programming, Ullapool, Scotland, 13–15 August 1990
Simon L. Peyton Jones, Graham Hutton and Carsten Kehler Holst (Eds.)

4th Refinement Workshop, Proceedings of the 4th Refinement Workshop, organised by BCS-FACS, Cambridge, 9–11 January 1991
Joseph M. Morris and Roger C. Shaw (Eds.)

AI and Cognitive Science '90, University of Ulster at Jordanstown, 20–21 September 1990
Michael F. McTear and Norman Creaney (Eds.)

Software Re-use, Utrecht 1989, Proceedings of the Software Re-use Workshop, Utrecht, The Netherlands, 23–24 November 1989
Liesbeth Dusink and Patrick Hall (Eds.)

Z User Workshop, 1990, Proceedings of the Fifth Annual Z User Meeting, Oxford, 17–18 December 1990
J.E. Nicholls (Ed.)

IV Higher Order Workshop, Banff 1990
Proceedings of the IV Higher Order Workshop, Banff, Alberta, Canada, 10–14 September 1990
Graham Birtwistle (Ed.)

ALPUK91, Proceedings of the 3rd UK Annual Conference on Logic Programming, Edinburgh, 10–12 April 1991
Geraint A. Wiggins, Chris Mellish and Tim Duncan (Eds.)

Specifications of Database Systems
International Workshop on Specifications of Database Systems, Glasgow, 3–5 July 1991
David J. Harper and Moira C. Norrie (Eds.)

7th UK Computer and Telecommunications Performance Engineering Workshop
Edinburgh, 22–23 July 1991
J. Hillston, P.J.B. King and R.J. Pooley (Eds.)

Logic Program Synthesis and Transformation
Proceedings of LOPSTR 91, International Workshop on Logic Program Synthesis and Transformation, University of Manchester, 4–5 July 1991
T.P. Clement and K.-K. Lau (Eds.)

Declarative Programming, Sasbachwalden 1991
PHOENIX Seminar and Workshop on Declarative Programming, Sasbachwalden, Black Forest, Germany, 18–22 November 1991
John Darlington and Roland Dietrich (Eds.)